937
V 8

# THE DECLINE AND FALL OF THE

## ROMAN EMPIRE

### VOL. VI.

THE DECLINE AND FALL OF THE

ROMAN EMPIRE

VOL. VI.

# THE HISTORY

#### OF THE

## DECLINE AND FALL OF THE ROMAN EMPIRE

BY

## EDWARD GIBBON

EDITED IN SEVEN VOLUMES

WITH INTRODUCTION, NOTES, APPENDICES, AND INDEX

BY

## J. B. BURY, M.A.

HON. LITT.D. OF DURHAM ; HON. LL.D. OF EDINBURGH

CORRESPONDING MEMBER OF THE IMPERIAL ACADEMY OF SCIENCES, ST. PETERSBURG

FELLOW OF TRINITY COLLEGE, AND REGIUS PROFESSOR OF GREEK

IN THE UNIVERSITY OF DUBLIN

### VOL. VI.

## METHUEN & CO.

36 ESSEX STREET, W.C.

LONDON

1902

*Second Edition*

# CORRIGENDA AND ADDENDA

## VOLUME VI.

P. 6, l. 4, *for* prompted *read* promoted

P. 46, to footnote [112]. By the kindness of M. A. Vasil 'ev I have received his revised Greek text of the Martyrium of the forty-two Amorian Martyrs, published in 1898 (Grecheski tekst zhitiia soroka dvuch amoriiskich muchenikov; in the Mémoires of the St. Petersburg Academy, Cl. Hist.-Phil.).

P. 57, marginal note, *for* Reductien *read* Reduction

P. 343. [The marginal notes should be corrected in two points : Baldwin III. was succeeded by Amalric in 1163, and Amalric by Baldwin IV. in 1174. See Mr. Archer's paper, fixing the true chronology, in Eng. Hist. Review, Jan. 1889, 89 *sqq.*]

P. 459, note 10. [Since this note was written, an edition of the Correspondence of Theodore Lascaris was published by N. Festa]

P. 528. [To works on the Fourth Crusade may now be added W. Norden's Der vierte Kreuzzug im Rahmen der Beziehungen des Abendlandes zu Byzanz, 1898.]

P. 533, l. 16, *for* κλεισοίρα *read* κλεισούρα

P. 549, l. 28, *for* Atelkuzn *read* Atelkuzu

P. 549, l. 28, *for* next note *read* note [13], p. 551

P. 554, l. 29, *for* Oproisch- *read* O proisch-

P. 560, l. 12 from foot, *for* 1309-1521 *read* 1309-1522

# CONTENTS OF THE SIXTH VOLUME.

## CHAPTER LII

*The Two Sieges of Constantinople by the Arabs—Their Invasion of France, and Defeat by Charles Martel—Civil War of the Ommiades and Abbassides—Learning of the Arabs—Luxury of the Caliphs—Naval Enterprises on Crete, Sicily, and Rome—Decay and Division of the Empire of the Caliphs—Defeats and Victories of the Greek Emperors*

## CHAPTER LIII

*State of the Eastern Empire in the Tenth Century—Extent and Division—
Wealth and Revenue—Palace of Constantinople—Titles and Offices—
Pride and Power of the Emperors—Tactics of the Greeks, Arabs, and
Franks—Loss of the Latin Tongue—Studies and Solitude of the Greeks*

# CONTENTS

## CHAPTER LIV

*Origin and Doctrine of the Paulicians—Their Persecution by the Greek Emperors—Revolt in Armenia, &c.—Transplantation into Thrace—Propagation in the West—The Seeds, Character, and Consequences of the Reformation*

## CHAPTER LV

*The Bulgarians—Origin, Migrations and Settlement of the Hungarians—Their Inroads in the East and West—The Monarchy of Russia—Geography and Trade—Wars of the Russians against the Greek Empire—Conversion of the Barbarians*

# CONTENTS

## CHAPTER LVI

*The Saracens, Franks, and Greeks, in Italy—First Adventures and Settlement of the Normans—Character and Conquest of Robert Guiscard, Duke of Apulia—Deliverance of Sicily by his Brother Roger—Victories of Robert over the Emperors of the East and West—Roger, King of Sicily, Invades Africa and Greece—The Emperor Manuel Comnenus—Wars of the Greeks and Normans—Extinction of the Normans*

# CONTENTS

## CHAPTER LVII

*The Turks of the House of Seljuk—Their Revolt against Mahmud, Conqueror of Hindostan—Togrul subdues Persia, and protects the Caliphs—Defeat and Captivity of the Emperor Romanus Diogenes by Alp Arslan—Power and Magnificence of Malek Shah—Conquest of Asia Minor and Syria—State and Oppression of Jerusalem—Pilgrimages to the Holy Sepulchre*

## CHAPTER LVIII

*Origin and Numbers of the First Crusade—Characters of the Latin Princes—
Their March to Constantinople—Policy of the Greek Emperor Alexius—
Conquest of Nice, Antioch, and Jerusalem, by the Franks—Deliverance of
the Holy Sepulchre—Godfrey of Bouillon, first King of Jerusalem—
Institutions of the French or Latin Kingdom*

# CONTENTS

## CHAPTER LIX

*Preservation of the Greek Empire—Numbers, Passage, and Event, of the Second and Third Crusades—St. Bernard—Reign of Saladin in Egypt and Syria—His Conquest of Jerusalem—Naval Crusades Richard the First of England Pope Innocent the Third; and Fourth and Fifth Crusades—The Emperor Frederic the Second—Louis the Ninth of France; and the two last Crusades—Expulsion of the Latins or Franks by the Mamalukes*

## CHAPTER LX

*Schism of the Greeks and Latins—State of Constantinople—Revolt of the Bulgarians—Isaac Angelus dethroned by his Brother Alexius—Origin of the Fourth Crusade—Alliance of the French and Venetians with the Son of Isaac—Their Naval Expedition to Constantinople—The Two Sieges and final Conquest of the City by the Latins*

# CONTENTS

xiii

## CHAPTER LXI

*Partition of the Empire by the French and Venetians—Five Latin Emperors of the Houses of Flanders and Courtenay—Their Wars against the Bulgarians and Greeks—Weakness and Poverty of the Latin Empire—Recovery of Constantinople by the Greeks—General Consequences of the Crusades*

## CHAPTER LXII

*The Greek Emperors of Nice and Constantinople—Elevation and Reign of Michael Palæologus—His false Union with the Pope and the Latin Church—Hostile Designs of Charles of Anjou—Revolt of Sicily—War of the Catalans in Asia and Greece—Revolutions and Present State of Athens*

## CHAPTER LXIII

*Civil Wars, and Ruin of the Greek Empire—Reigns of Andronicus, the Elder and Younger, and John Palæologus—Regency, Revolt, Reign, and Abdication of John Cantacuzene—Establishment of a Genoese Colony at Pera or Galata—Their Wars with the Empire and City of Constantinople*

# CONTENTS

# LIST OF MAPS

# NOTE

I AM fortunate enough to have again received generous help from my friend Mr. Stanley Lane-Poole in the revision of four chapters in this volume which deal with oriental history.

J. B. B.

# THE HISTORY

### OF THE

# DECLINE AND FALL OF THE ROMAN EMPIRE

## CHAPTER LII

*The two Sieges of Constantinople by the Arabs—Their Invasion of France, and Defeat by Charles Martel—Civil War of the Ommiades and Abbassides—Learning of the Arabs—Luxury of the Caliphs—Naval Enterprises on Crete, Sicily, and Rome—Decay and Division of the Empire of the Caliphs—Defeats and Victories of the Greek Emperors*

WHEN the Arabs first issued from the desert, they must have been surprised at the ease and rapidity of their own success. But, when they advanced in the career of victory to the banks of the Indus and the summit of the Pyrenees, when they had repeatedly tried the edge of their scymetars and the energy of their faith, they might be equally astonished that any nation could resist their invincible arms, that any boundary should confine the dominion of the successor of the prophet. The confidence of soldiers and fanatics may indeed be excused, since the calm historian of the present hour, who strives to follow the rapid course of the Saracens, must study to explain by what means the church and state were saved from this impending and, as it should seem, from this inevitable danger. The deserts of Scythia and Sarmatia might be guarded by their extent, their climate, their poverty, and the courage of the northern shepherds; China was remote and inaccessible; but the greatest part of the temperate zone was subject to the Mahometan conquerors, the Greeks were exhausted by the calamities of war and the loss of their fairest provinces, and the barbarians of Europe might justly tremble at the precipitate fall of the Gothic monarchy. In this inquiry I shall unfold the events that rescued our ancestors of Britain, and our neighbours of Gaul, from the civil and

religious yoke of the Koran; that protected the majesty of
Rome, and delayed the servitude of Constantinople; that invigorated the defence of the Christians, and scattered among
their enemies the seeds of division and decay.

First siege of
Constantino-
ple by the
Arabs.
A.D. 668-675
Forty-six years after the flight of Mahomet from Mecca, his
disciples appeared in arms under the walls of Constantinople.[1]
They were animated by a genuine or fictitious saying of the
prophet, that, to the first army which besieged the city of the
Cæsars, their sins were forgiven; the long series of Roman
triumphs would be meritoriously transferred to the conquerors
of New Rome; and the wealth of nations was deposited in this
well-chosen seat of royalty and commerce. No sooner had the
caliph Moawiyah suppressed his rivals and established his throne
than he aspired to expiate the guilt of civil blood by the success
and glory of his holy expedition;[2] his preparations by sea and
land were adequate to the importance of the object; his standard
was entrusted to Sophian,[3] a veteran warrior, but the troops were
encouraged by the example and presence of Yezid, the son and
presumptive heir of the commander of the faithful. The Greeks
had little to hope, nor had their enemies any reasons of fear,
[Constantine
IV.]
from the courage and vigilance of the reigning emperor, who
disgraced the name of Constantine, and imitated only the in-

[1] Theophanes places the *seven* years of the siege of Constantinople in the year of
*our* Christian æra 673 (of the Alexandrian 665, September 1), and the peace of the
Saracens, *four* years afterwards: a glaring inconsistency! which Petavius, Goar,
and Pagi (Critica, tom. iv. p. 63, 64) have struggled to remove. Of the Arabians,
the Hegira 52 (A.D. 672, January 8) is assigned by Elmacin, the year 48 (A.D. 668,
February 20) by Abulfeda, whose testimony I esteem the most convenient and
creditable. [Theophanes gives 672-3 as the year of Moāwiya's preparation of the
expedition, 673-4 as that of his investment of Constantinople. It seems safest to
follow Theophanes here; the Arabic authors say little or nothing of an event which
was disgraceful in Mohammadan history. But we cannot accept his statement that
the siege lasted seven years; in fact he contradicts it himself, since he places the peace
in the fifth year after the beginning of the siege. We have no means of determining
with certainty the true duration. Nicephorus (p. 32, ed. de Boor) states that the
*war* lasted seven years, and, though he evidently identifies the war with the siege,
we may perhaps find here the clue to the solution. The war seems to have begun
soon after the accession of Constantine (εὐθύς, Niceph. *ib.*); and perhaps its
beginning was dated from the occupation of Cyzicus by Phadalas in 670-1 (Theoph.
A.M. 6162), and peace was made in 677-8. Thus we get *seven* years for the duration
of the war (671-7), and perhaps three for the siege (674-6).]

[2] For this first siege of Constantinople, see Nicephorus (Breviar. p. 21, 22 [p. 32,
ed. de Boor]), Theophanes (Chronograph. p. 294 [A.M. 6165]), Cedrenus (Compend.
p. 437 [i. 764, ed. Bonn]), Zonaras (Hist. tom. ii. l. xiv. p. 89 [c. 20]), Elmacin
(Hist. Saracen. p. 56, 57), Abulfeda (Annal. Moslem. p. 107, 108, vers. Reiske),
d'Herbelot (Bibliot. Orient. Constantin.), Ockley's Hist. of the Saracens, vol. ii. p.
127, 128.

[3] [The expedition was first entrusted to Abd ar-Rahmān, but he was killed, and
was succeeded by Sofyān.]

glorious years of his grandfather Heraclius. Without delay or opposition, the naval forces of the Saracens passed through the unguarded channel of the Hellespont, which even now, under the feeble and disorderly government of the Turks, is maintained as the natural bulwark of the capital.[4] The Arabian fleet cast anchor, and the troops were disembarked near the palace of Hebdomon, seven miles from the city. During many days, from the dawn of light to the evening, the line of assault was extended from the golden gate to the eastern promontory, and the foremost warriors were impelled by the weight and effort of the succeeding columns. But the besiegers had formed an insufficient estimate of the strength and resources of Constantinople. The solid and lofty walls were guarded by numbers and discipline ; the spirit of the Romans was rekindled by the last danger of their religion and empire ; the fugitives from the conquered provinces more successfully renewed the defence of Damascus and Alexandria ; and the Saracens were dismayed by the strange and prodigious effects of artificial fire. This firm and effectual resistance diverted their arms to the more easy attempts of plundering the European and Asiatic coasts of the Propontis ; and, after keeping the sea from the month of April to that of September, on the approach of winter they retreated fourscore miles from the capital, to the isle of Cyzicus, in which they had established their magazine of spoil and provisions. So patient was their perseverance, or so languid were their operations, that they repeated in the six following summers the same attack and retreat, with a gradual abatement of hope and vigour, till the mischances of shipwreck and disease, of the sword and of fire, compelled them to relinquish the fruitless enterprise. They might bewail the loss or commemorate the martyrdom of thirty thousand Moslems, who fell in the siege of Constantinople ; and the solemn funeral of Abu Ayub, or Job, excited the curiosity of the Christians themselves. That venerable Arab, one of the last of the companions of Mahomet, was numbered among the *ansars*, or auxiliaries, of Medina, who sheltered the head of the flying prophet. In his youth he fought, at Bedar and Ohud, under the holy standard ; in his mature age he was

[4] The state and defence of the Dardanelles is exposed in the Mémoires of the Baron de Tott (tom. iii. p. 39-97), who was sent to fortify them against the Russians. From a principal actor, I should have expected more accurate details ; but he seems to write for the amusement, rather than the instruction, of his reader. Perhaps, on the approach of the enemy, the minister of Constantine was occupied, like that of Mustapha, in finding two Canary birds who should sing precisely the same note.

the friend and follower of Ali; and the last remnant of his strength and life was consumed in a distant and dangerous war against the enemies of the Koran. His memory was revered; but the place of his burial was neglected and unknown, during a period of seven hundred and eighty years, till the conquest of Constantinople by Mahomet the Second. A seasonable vision (for such are the manufacture of every religion) revealed the holy spot at the foot of the walls and the bottom of the harbour; and the mosque of Ayub has been deservedly chosen for the simple and martial inauguration of the Turkish sultans.[5]

Peace and tribute, A.D. 677

The event of the siege revived, both in the East and West, the reputation of the Roman arms, and cast a momentary shade over the glories of the Saracens. The Greek ambassador was favourably received at Damascus, in a general council of the emirs or Koreish; a peace, or truce, of thirty years was ratified between the two empires; and the stipulation of an annual tribute, fifty horses of a noble breed, fifty slaves, and three thousand pieces of gold, degraded the majesty of the commander of the faithful.[6] The aged caliph was desirous of possessing his dominions, and ending his days, in tranquillity and repose; while the Moors and Indians trembled at his name, his palace and city of Damascus was insulted by the Mardaites, or Maronites, of mount Libanus, the firmest barrier of the empire, till they were disarmed and transplanted by the suspicious policy of the Greeks.[7] After the revolt of Arabia and Persia, the house of Ommiyah[8] was reduced to the kingdoms of Syria and Egypt; their distress and fear enforced their compliance with the pressing demands of the Christians; and the tribute was increased to a slave, an horse, and a thousand pieces of gold, for each of the three hundred and sixty-five days of the solar year. But as soon as the

[5] Demetrius Cantemir's Hist. of the Othman Empire, p. 105, 106. Rycaut's State of the Ottoman Empire, p. 10, 11. Voyages de Thévenot, part i. 189. The Christians, who suppose that the martyr Abu Ayub is vulgarly confounded with the patriarch Job, betray their own ignorance rather than that of the Turks.

[6] Theophanes, though a Greek, deserved credit for these tributes (Chronograph. p. 295, 296, 300, 301 [A.M. 6169, 6176]), which are confirmed, with some variation, by the Arabic history of Abulpharagius (Dynast. p. 128, vers. Pocock).

[7] The censure of Theophanes is just and pointed, τὴν Ῥωμαικὴν δυναστειαν ἀκρωτηριασας . . . πάνδεινα κακὰ πέπονθεν ἡ Ῥωμανια ὑπὸ τῶν Ἀράβων μέχρι τοῦ νῦν (Chronograph. p. 302, 303 [A.M. 6178]). The series of these events may be traced in the Annals of Theophanes, and in the Abridgment of the Patriarch Nicephorus, p. 22, 24.

[8] These domestic revolutions are related in a clear and natural style, in the second volume of Ockley's history of the Saracens, p. 253-370. Besides our printed authors, he draws his materials from the Arabic Mss. of Oxford, which he would have more deeply searched, had he been confined to the Bodleian library instead of the [Cambridge] city jail: a fate how unworthy of the man and of his country!

empire was again united by the arms and policy of Abdalmalek, he disclaimed a badge of servitude not less injurious to his conscience than to his pride ; he discontinued the payment of the tribute ; and the resentment of the Greeks was disabled from action by the mad tyranny of the second Justinian, the just rebellion of his subjects, and the frequent change of his antagonists and successors. Till the reign of Abdalmalek, the Saracens had been content with the free possession of the Persian and Roman treasures, in the coin of Chosroes and Cæsar. By the command of that caliph, a national mint was established, both of silver and gold, and the inscription of the Dinar, though it might be censured by some timorous casuists, proclaimed the unity of the God of Mahomet.[9] Under the reign of the caliph Waled, the Greek language and characters were excluded from the accounts of the public revenue.[10] If this change was productive of the invention or familiar use of our present numerals, the Arabic or Indian *cyphers*, as they are commonly styled, a regulation of office has promoted the most important discoveries of arithmetic, algebra, and the mathematical sciences.[11]

Whilst the caliph Waled sat idle on the throne of Damascus, while his lieutenants achieved the conquest of Transoxiana and Spain, a third army of Saracens overspread the provinces of Asia Minor, and approached the borders of the Byzantine capital. But the attempt and disgrace of the second siege was reserved for his brother Soliman, whose ambition appears to have been

*[marginal notes:]* [Abd al-Malik. A.D. 685-705] [Walid I. A.D. 705-715] [Second siege of Constantinople. A.D. 716-718] [Soliman. A.D. 715-7]

[9] Elmacin, who dates the first coinage A.H. 76, A.D. 695, five or six years later than the Greek historians, has compared the weight of the best or common gold dinar, to the drachm or dirhem of Egypt (p. 77), which may be equal to two pennies (48 grains) of our Troy weight (Hooper's Enquiry into Ancient Measures, p. 24-36) and equivalent to *eight shillings* of our sterling money. From the same Elmacin and the Arabian physicians, some dinars as high as two dirhems, as low as half a dirhem, may be deduced. The piece of silver was the dirhem, both in value and weight ; but an old though fair coin, struck at Waset, A.H. 88, and preserved in the Bodleian library, wants four grains of the Cairo standard (see the Modern Universal History, tom i. p. 548 of the French translation). [But see Appendix 2.]

[10] Καὶ ἐκώλυσε γράφεσθαι ἑλληνιστὶ τοὺς δημοσίους τῶν λογοθεσιων κωδικας αλλ᾽ [ἐν] Ἀραβιοις αὐτὰ παρασημαινεσθαι χωρὶς τῶν ψηφων, ἐπειδη ἀδυναστον τῇ εκεινων γλωσσῃ μοναδα, ἢ δυάδα, ἢ τριαδα, ἢ οκτὼ ἡμισυ ἢ τρια γραφεσθαι. Theophan. Chronograph. p. 314 [A.M. 6199]. This defect, if it really existed, must have stimulated the ingenuity of the Arabs to invent or borrow.

[11] According to a new though probable notion, maintained by M. de Villoison (Anecdota Græca, tom. ii. p. 152-157), our cyphers are not of Indian or Arabic invention. They were used by the Greek and Latin arithmeticians long before the age of Boethius. After the extinction of science in the West, they were adopted by the Arabic versions from the original Mss. and *restored* to the Latins about the eleventh century. [There is no doubt that our numerals are of Indian origin (5th or 6th cent. ?); adopted by the Arabians about 9th cent. The circumstances of their first introduction to the West are uncertain, but we find them used in Italy in 13th cent.]

quickened by a more active and martial spirit. In the revolutions of the Greek empire, after the tyrant Justinian had been punished and avenged, an humble secretary, Anastasius or Artemius, was promoted by chance or merit to the vacant purple. He was alarmed by the sound of war ; and his ambassador returned from Damascus with the tremendous news that the Saracens were preparing an armament by sea and land, such as would transcend the experience of the past, or the belief of the present, age. The precautions of Anastasius were not unworthy of his station or of the impending danger. He issued a peremptory mandate that all persons who were not provided with the means of subsistence for a three years' siege should evacuate the city ; the public granaries and arsenals were abundantly replenished ; the walls were restored and strengthened ; and the engines for casting stones, or darts, or fire, were stationed along the ramparts, or in the brigantines of war, of which an additional number was hastily constructed. To prevent is safer, as well as more honourable, than to repel an attack ; and a design was meditated, above the usual spirit of the Greeks, of burning the naval stores of the enemy, the cypress timber that had been hewn in mount Libanus, and was piled along the sea-shore of Phœnicia, for the service of the Egyptian fleet. This generous enterprise was defeated by the cowardice or treachery of the troops who, in the new language of the empire, were styled of the *Obsequian Theme*.[12] They murdered their chief, deserted their standard in the isle of Rhodes, dispersed themselves over the adjacent continent, and deserved pardon or reward by investing with the purple a simple officer of the revenue. The name of Theodosius might recommend him to the senate and people ; but, after some months, he sunk into a cloister, and resigned, to the firmer hand of Leo the Isaurian, the urgent defence of the capital and empire. [Maslama] The most formidable of the Saracens, Moslemah the brother of the caliph, was advancing at the head of one hundred and twenty thousand Arabs and Persians, the greater part mounted on horses

[12] In the division of the *Themes*, or provinces described by Constantine Porphyrogenitus (de Thematibus, l. i. p. 9, 10 [p. 24-26, ed. Bonn]), the *Obsequium*, a Latin appellation of the army and palace, was the fourth in the public order. Nice was the metropolis, and its jurisdiction extended from the Hellespont over the adjacent parts of Bithynia and Phrygia (see the two maps prefixed by Delisle to the Imperium Orientale of Banduri). [Gibbon omits to mention the most remarkable incident in this episode. The Opsician troops proceeded to Constantinople and besieged Anastasius. The fleet and the engines, which had been prepared by the Emperor to defend the city against the Saracens, had to be used against the rebels. When Theodosius ultimately effected his entry, the Opsicians pillaged the city. For the Themes see Appendix 3.]

or camels; and the successful sieges of Tyana, Amorium, and Pergamus were of sufficient duration to exercise their skill and to elevate their hopes. At the well-known passage of Abydus, on the Hellespont, the Mahometan arms were transported, for the first time,[13] from Asia to Europe. From thence, wheeling round the Thracian cities of the Propontis, Moslemah invested Constantinople on the land side, surrounded his camp with a ditch and rampart, prepared and planted his engines of assault, and declared, by words and actions, a patient resolution of expecting the return of seed-time and harvest, should the obstinacy of the besieged prove equal to his own. The Greeks would gladly have ransomed their religion and empire, by a fine or assessment of a piece of gold on the head of each inhabitant of the city; but the liberal offer was rejected with disdain, and the presumption of Moslemah was exalted by the speedy approach and invincible force of the navies of Egypt and Syria. They are said to have amounted to eighteen hundred ships; the number betrays their inconsiderable size; and of the twenty stout and capacious vessels, whose magnitude impeded their progress, each was manned with no more than one hundred heavy armed soldiers. This huge armada proceeded on a smooth sea and with a gentle gale, towards the mouth of the Bosphorus; the surface of the strait was overshadowed, in the language of the Greeks, with a moving forest, and the same fatal night had been fixed by the Saracen chief for a general assault by sea and land. To allure the confidence of the enemy, the emperor had thrown aside the chain that usually guarded the entrance of the harbour; but, while they hesitated whether they should seize the opportunity or apprehend the snare, the ministers of destruction were at hand. The fireships of the Greeks were launched against them; the Arabs, their arms, and vessels, were involved in the same flames, the disorderly fugitives were dashed against each other or overwhelmed in the waves; and I no longer find a vestige of the fleet that had threatened to extirpate the Roman name. A still more fatal and irreparable loss was that of the caliph Soliman, who died of an indigestion [14] in his camp

---

[13] [At the previous siege, Saracens had also landed on European soil; see above, p. 3.]

[14] The caliph had emptied two baskets of eggs and of figs, which he swallowed alternately, and the repast was concluded with marrow and sugar. In one of his pilgrimages to Mecca, Soliman ate, at a single meal, seventy pomegranates, a kid, six fowls, and a huge quantity of the grapes of Tayef If the bill of fare be correct, we must admire the appetite rather than the luxury of the sovereign of Asia (Abul-

near Kinnisrin, or Chalcis in Syria, as he was preparing to lead
against Constantinople the remaining forces of the East. The
brother of Moslemah was succeeded by a kinsman and an enemy;
and the throne of an active and able prince was degraded by the
useless and pernicious virtues of a bigot. While he started and
satisfied the scruples of a blind conscience, the siege was continued through the winter by the neglect rather than by the
resolution of the caliph Omar.[15] The winter proved uncom-
monly rigorous; above an hundred days the ground was covered
with deep snow, and the natives of the sultry climes of Egypt
and Arabia lay torpid and almost lifeless in their frozen camp.
They revived on the return of spring; a second effort had been
made in their favour; and their distress was relieved by the
arrival of two numerous fleets, laden with corn, and arms, and
soldiers; the first from Alexandria, of four hundred transports
and galleys; the second of three hundred and sixty vessels from
the ports of Africa. But the Greek fires were again kindled,
and, if the destruction was less complete, it was owing to the
experience which had taught the Moslems to remain at a safe
distance, or to the perfidy of the Egyptian mariners, who deserted with their ships to the emperor of the Christians. The
trade and navigation of the capital were restored; and the produce of the fisheries supplied the wants, and even the luxury, of
the inhabitants. But the calamities of famine and disease were
soon felt by the troops of Moslemah, and, as the former was
miserably assuaged, so the latter was dreadfully propagated, by
the pernicious nutriment which hunger compelled them to
extract from the most unclean or unnatural food. The spirit of
conquest, and even of enthusiasm, was extinct: the Saracens
could no longer straggle beyond their lines, either single or in
small parties, without exposing themselves to the merciless

[Omar II.
A.D. 717-20]

feda, Annal. Moslem. p. 126). [Though the manner of Sulaiman's death is uncertain,
it is agreed that he was a voluptuary. Tabari says that cooking and gallantry were
the only subjects of conversation at his court.]

[15] See the article of Omar Ben Abdalaziz [ibn Abd al Azīz], in the Bibliothèque
Orientale (p. 689, 690), præterens, says Eimacin (p. 91), religionem suam rebus suis
mundanis. He was so desirous of being with God that he would not have anointed
his ear (his own saying) to obtain a perfect cure of his last malady. The caliph had
only one shirt, and in an age of luxury his annual expense was no more than two
drachms (Abulpharagius, p. 131). Haud diu gavisus eo principe suit orbis Moslemus
(Abulfeda, p. 127). [Weil takes another view of the virtues of the bigot, and writes:
"The pious Omar was greater than all his predecessors, not excepting Omar I.,
in one respect; he sought less to increase or enrich Islam at the cost of the unbeliever than to augment the number of Musulmans without making forced conversions." Gesch. der Chalifen, i. p. 582.]

retaliation of the Thracian peasants. An army of Bulgarians was attracted from the Danube by the gifts and promises of Leo; and these savage auxiliaries made some atonement for the evils which they had inflicted on the empire, by the defeat and slaughter of twenty-two thousand Asiatics. A report was dexterously scattered that the Franks, the unknown nations of the Latin world, were arming by sea and land in the defence of the Christian cause, and their formidable aid was expected with far different sensations in the camp and city. At length, after a siege of thirteen months,[16] the hopeless Moslemah received from the caliph the welcome permission to retreat. The march of the Arabian cavalry over the Hellespont and through the provinces of Asia was executed without delay or molestation; but an army of their brethren had been cut to pieces on the side of Bithynia, and the remains of the fleet was so repeatedly damaged by tempest and fire that only five galleys entered the port of Alexandria to relate the tale of their various and almost incredible disasters.[17]

*Failure and retreat of the Saracens*

In the two sieges, the deliverance of Constantinople may be chiefly ascribed to the novelty, the terrors, and the real efficacy of the *Greek fire*.[18] The important secret of compounding and directing this artificial flame was imparted by Callinicus, a native of Heliopolis in Syria, who deserted from the service of the caliph to that of the emperor.[19] The skill of a chymist and engineer was equivalent to the succour of fleets and armies; and this discovery or improvement of the military art was fortunately

*Invention and use of the Greek fire*

[16] Both Nicephorus and Theophanes agree that the siege of Constantinople was raised the 15th of August (A.D. 718); but, as the former, our best witness, affirms that it continued thirteen months, the latter must be mistaken in supposing that it began on the same day of the preceding year. I do not find that Pagi has remarked this inconsistency. [Tabari places the beginning of the siege in A.H. 98 = A.D. 716-17, but does not mention the month; and he makes Omar II. recall Maslama in A.H. 99 (Aug. 25, 717--Aug. 2, 718). See Tabari, ed. de Goeje, ii. 1342.]

[17] In the second siege of Constantinople, I have followed Nicephorus (Brev. p. 33-36 [pp. 53-4, ed. de Boor]), Theophanes (Chronograph. p. 324-334 [A.M. 6209, 6210]), Cedrenus (Compend. p. 449-452 [i. 787, ed. Bonn]), Zonaras (tom. ii. p. 98-102 [xv. c. l.]), Elmacin (Hist. Saracen. p. 88), Abulfeda (Annal. Moslem. p. 126), and Abulpharagius (Dynast. p. 130), the most satisfactory of the Arabs.

[18] Our sure and indefatigable guide in the middle ages and Byzantine history, Charles du Fresne du Cange, has treated in several places of the Greek fire, and his collections leave few gleanings behind. See particularly Glossar. Med. et Infim. Græcitat. p. 1275, sub voce Πῦρ θαλάσσιον ὑγρόν. Glossar. Med. et Infim. Latinitat. *Ignis Græcus*. Observations sur Villehardouin, p. 305, 306. Observations sur Joinville, p. 71, 72. [See below, note 22.]

[19] Theophanes styles him ἀρχιτέκτων (p. 295 [A.M. 6165]). Cedrenus (p. 437 [i. p. 765]) brings this artist from (the ruins of) Heliopolis in Egypt; and chemistry was indeed the peculiar science of the Egyptians.

reserved for the distressful period, when the degenerate Romans
of the East were incapable of contending with the warlike
enthusiasm and youthful vigour of the Saracens.  The historian
who presumes to analyse this extraordinary composition should
suspect his own ignorance and that of his Byzantine guides, so
prone to the marvellous, so careless, and in this instance so
jealous, of the truth.  From their obscure and perhaps fallacious
hints, it should seem that the principal ingredient of the Greek
fire was the *naptha*,[20] or liquid bitumen, a light, tenacious, and
inflammable oil,[21] which springs from the earth and catches fire
as soon as it comes in contact with the air.  The naptha was
mingled, I know not by what methods or in what proportions,
with sulphur and with the pitch that is extracted from ever-
green firs.[22]  From this mixture, which produced a thick smoke
and a loud explosion, proceeded a fierce and obstinate flame,
which not only rose in perpendicular ascent, but likewise burnt
with equal vehemence in descent or lateral progress ; instead of
being extinguished, it was nourished and quickened, by the
element of water ; and sand, urine, or vinegar were the only
remedies that could damp the fury of this powerful agent, which
was justly denominated by the Greeks the *liquid* or the *maritime*

---

[20] The naptha, the oleum incendiarium of the history of Jerusalem (Gest. Dei per
Francos, p. 1167), the Oriental fountain of James de Vitry (l. iii. c. 84), is introduced
on slight evidence and strong probability.  Cinnamus (l. vi. p. 165 [c. 10]) calls
the Greek fire πῦρ Μηδικόν; and the naptha is known to abound between the Tigris
and the Caspian Sea.  According to Pliny (Hist. Natur. ii. 109) it was subservient
to the revenge of Medea, and in either etymology the ἔλαιον Μηδίας or Μηδείας
(Procop. de Bell. Gothic. l. iv. c. 11) may fairly signify this liquid bitumen.

[21] On the different sorts of oils and bitumens, see Dr. Watson's (the present bishop
of Llandaff's) Chemical Essays, vol. iii. essay i., a classic book, the best adapted to
infuse the taste and knowledge of chemistry.  The less perfect ideas of the ancients
may be found in Strabo (Geograph. l. xvi. p. 1078 [1315]), and Pliny (Hist. Natur.
ii. 108, 109): Huic (*Napthae*) magna cognatio est ignium, transiliuntque protinus
in eam undecunque visam.  Of our travellers I am best pleased with Otter (tom.
i. p. 153, 158).

[22] Anna Comnena has partly drawn aside the curtain.  Ἀπὸ τῆς πεύκης καὶ
ἄλλων τινῶν τοιούτων δένδρων ἀειθαλῶν συνάγεται δάκρυον εὔκαυστον.  Τοῦτο μετὰ θείου
τριβόμενον ἐμβάλλεται εἰς αὐλίσκους καλάμων καὶ ἐμφυσᾶται παρὰ τοῦ παίζοντος λάβρῳ
καὶ συνεχεῖ πνεύματι (Alexiad. l. xiii. p. 383 [c. 3]).  Elsewhere (l. xi. p. 336 [c. 4])
she mentions the property of burning, κατὰ τὸ πρανὲς καὶ ἐφ' ἑκάτερα.  Leo, in the
nineteenth chapter [§ 51, p. 1008, ed. Migne] of his Tactics (Opera Meursii, tom.
vi. p. 843, edit. Lami, Florent. 1745), speaks of the new invention of πῦρ μετὰ βροντῆς
καὶ καπνοῦ.  These are genuine and *Imperial* testimonies.  [It is certain that one
kind of "Greek" or "marine" fire was gunpowder.  The receipt is preserved in
a treatise of the ninth century, entitled Liber ignium ad comburendos hostes, by
Marcus Graecus, preserved only in a Latin translation (edited by F. Höfer in Histoire de la chimie, vol. 1, 1842).  But other inflammable compounds, containing
pitch, naphtha, &c., must be distinguished.  See further Appendix 5.]

fire. For the annoyance of the enemy it was employed with equal effect, by sea and land, in battles or in sieges. It was either poured from the rampart in large boilers, or launched in red-hot balls of stone and iron, or darted in arrows and javelins, twisted round with flax and tow, which had deeply imbibed the inflammable oil: sometimes it was deposited in fire-ships, the victims and instruments of a more ample revenge, and was most commonly blown through long tubes of copper, which were planted on the prow of a galley, and fancifully shaped into the mouths of savage monsters, that seemed to vomit a stream of liquid and consuming fire. This important art was preserved at Constantinople, as the palladium of the state; the galleys and *artillery* might occasionally be lent to the allies of Rome; but the composition of the Greek fire was concealed with the most jealous scruple, and the terror of the enemies was increased and prolonged by their ignorance and surprise. In the treatise of the Administration of the Empire the royal author [23] suggests the answers and excuses that might best elude the indiscreet curiosity and importunate demands of the barbarians. They should be told that the mystery of the Greek fire had been revealed by an angel to the first and greatest of the Constantines, with a sacred injunction that this gift of heaven, this peculiar blessing of the Romans, should never be communicated to any foreign nation; that the prince and subject were alike bound to religious silence under the temporal and spiritual penalties of treason and sacrilege; and that the impious attempt would provoke the sudden and supernatural vengeance of the God of the Christians. By these precautions, the secret was confined, above four hundred years, to the Romans of the East; and, at the end of the eleventh century, the Pisans, to whom every sea and every art were familiar, suffered the effects, without understanding the composition, of the Greek fire. It was at length either discovered or stolen by the Mahometans; and, in the holy wars of Syria and Egypt, they retorted an invention, contrived against themselves, on the heads of the Christians. A knight, who despised the swords and lances of the Saracens, relates, with heartfelt sincerity, his own fears, and those of his companions, at the sight and sound of the mischievous engine that discharged a torrent of the Greek fire, the *feu Gregeois*, as it is styled by the more early of the French

---

[23] Constantin. Porphyrogenit. de Administrat. Imperii, c. xiii. p. 64, 65 [vol. iii. p. 84-5, ed. Bonn].

writers.   It came flying through the air, says Joinville,[24] like a
winged long-tailed dragon, about the thickness of an hogshead,
with the report of thunder and the velocity of lightning ; and
the darkness of the night was dispelled by this deadly illumina-
tion.   The use of the Greek or, as it might now be called, of
the Saracen fire was continued to the middle of the fourteenth
century,[25] when the scientific or casual compound of nitre, sulphur, and charcoal effected a new revolution in the art of war
and the history of mankind.[26]

Invasion
of France
by the
Arabs.
A.D. 721,
&c.

Constantinople and the Greek fire might exclude the Arabs
from the Eastern entrance of Europe ; but in the West, on the
side of the Pyrenees, the provinces of Gaul were threatened
and invaded by the conquerors of Spain.[27]   The decline of the
French monarchy invited the attack of these insatiate fanatics.
The descendants of Clovis had lost the inheritance of his
martial and ferocious spirit ; and their misfortune or demerit
has affixed the epithet of *lazy* to the last kings of the Mero-

[24] Histoire de St. Louis, p. 39, Paris, 1668 ; p. 44, Paris, de l'imprimerie Royale,
1761 [xliñ., § 203 *sqq.* in the text of N. de Wailly].   The former of these editions
is precious for the observations of Ducange ; the latter, for the pure and original
text of Joinville.   We must have recourse to the text to discover that the
feu Gregeois was shot with a pile or javelin, from an engine that acted like a
sling.

[25] The vanity, or envy, of shaking the established property of Fame has tempted
some moderns to carry gunpowder above the fourteenth (see Sir William Temple,
Dutens, &c.), and the Greek fire above the |seventh, century (see the Saluste du
Président des Brosses, tom. ii. p. 381); but their evidence, which precedes the
vulgar æra of the invention, is seldom clear or satisfactory, and subsequent writers
may be suspected of fraud or credulity.   In the earliest sieges some combustibles
of oil and sulphur have been used, and the Greek fire has *some* affinities with gun-
powder both in nature and effects : for the antiquity of the first, a passage of
Procopius (de Bell. Goth. l. iv. c. 11), for that of the second, some facts in the
Arabic history of Spain (A.D. 1249, 1312, 1332, Bibliot. Arab. Hisp. tom. ii. p. 6,
7, 8), are the most difficult to elude.

[26] That extraordinary man, Friar Bacon, reveals two of the ingredients, saltpetre
and sulphur, and conceals the third in a sentence of mysterious gibberish, as if he
dreaded the consequences of his own discovery (Biographia Britannica, vol. i. p.
430, new edition).

[27] For the invasion of France, and the defeat of the Arabs by Charles Martel,
see the Historia Arabum (c. 11, 12, 13, 14) of Roderic *Ximenes*, archbishop of
Toledo, who had before him the Christian chronicle of Isidore Pacensis, and
the Mahometan history of *Novairi*.   [And Chron. Moissiac. ad. ann. 732 (in
Pertz, Mon. vol. i.).]   The Moslems are silent or concise in the account of their
losses ; but M. Cardonne (tom. i. p. 129, 130, 131) has given a *pure* and simple
account of all that he could collect from Ibn Halikan, Hidjasi, and an anonymous
writer.   The texts of the chronicles of France, and lives of saints, are inserted in
the Collection of Bouquet (tom. iii.) and the Annals of Pagi, who (tom. iii. under the
proper years) has restored the chronology, which is anticipated six years in the
Annals of Baronius.   The Dictionary of Bayle (*Abderame* and *Munuza*) has more
merit for lively reflection than original research.

vingian race.[28] They ascended the throne without power, and
sunk into the grave without a name. A country palace, in the
neighbourhood of Compiègne,[29] was allotted for their residence
or prison; but each year, in the month of March or May, they
were conducted in a waggon drawn by oxen to the assembly
of the Franks, to give audience to foreign ambassadors, and to
ratify the acts of the mayor of the palace. That domestic
officer was become the minister of the nation, and the master
of the prince. A public employment was converted into the
patrimony of a private family; the elder Pepin left a king of
mature years under the guardianship of his own widow and her
child; and these feeble regents were forcibly dispossessed by
the most active of his bastards. A government, half savage and
half corrupt, was almost dissolved; and the tributary dukes, the
provincial counts, and the territorial lords were tempted to
despise the weakness of the monarch and to imitate the ambition of the mayor. Among these independent chiefs, one of the
boldest and most successful was Eudes, duke of Aquitain, who,
in the southern provinces of Gaul, usurped the authority and
even the title of king. The Goths, the Gascons, and the
Franks assembled under the standard of this Christian hero; he
repelled the first invasion of the Saracens; and Zama, lieutenant [A.D. 721,
of the caliph, lost his army and his life under the walls of [June 9]
Toulouse.[30] The ambition of his successors was stimulated by
revenge; they repassed the Pyrenees with the means and the
resolution of conquest. The advantageous situation which had
recommended Narbonne [31] as the first Roman colony was again

[90] Eginhart. de Vitâ Caroli Magni, c. ii. p. 13-18, edit. Schmink, Utrecht, 1711.
Some modern critics accuse the minister of Charlemagne of exaggerating the
weakness of the Merovingians; but the general outline is just, and the French
reader will for ever repeat the beautiful lines of Boileau's Lutrin.

[29] *Mamaccae* on the Oise, between Compiègne and Noyon, which Eginhart calls
perparvi reditus villam (see the notes, and the map of ancient France for Dom.
Bouquet's Collection). Compendium, or Compiègne, was a palace of more dignity
(Hadrian, Valesii Notitia Galliarum, p. 152), and that laughing philosopher, the
Abbé Galliani (Dialogues sur le Commerce des Bleds), may truly affirm that it
was the residence of the rois très Chrétiens et très chevelus.

[30] [The first invasion of Gaul was probably that of Al-Hurr in A.D. 718, but it is
not quite clear whether the invasion had any abiding results. It is a question
whether the capture of Narbonne was the work of Al-Hurr (as Arabic authors state),
or of Al-Samā (as Weil inclines to think: Gesch. der Chal. i. p. 610, note). The
governor Anbasa crossed the Pyrenees in 725 to avenge the defeat of Toulouse, and
captured Carcassonne and reduced Nemausus. Gibbon's "successors" refers to
him and Abd ar-Rahmān.]

[31] Even before that colony, A.U.C. 630 (Velleius Patercul. i. 15), in the time of
Polybius (Hist. l. iii. p. 265, edit. Gronov. [B. 34, c. 6, § 3]), Narbonne was a Celtic
town of the first eminence, and one of the most northern places of the known world
(d'Anville, Notice de l'Ancienne Gaule, p. 473).

chosen by the Moslems : they claimed the province of Septimania, or Languedoc, as a just dependence of the Spanish
monarchy : the vineyards of Gascony and the city of Bordeaux
were possessed by the sovereign of Damascus and Samarcand ;
and the south of France, from the mouth of the Garonne to
that of the Rhone, assumed the manners and religion of Arabia.

Expedi-
tion and
victories
of Abde-
rame.
A.D. 731

But these narrow limits were scorned by the spirit of
Abdalrahman, or Abderame, who had been restored by the
caliph Hashem [32] to the wishes of the soldiers and people of
Spain. That veteran and daring commander adjudged to the
obedience of the prophet whatever yet remained of France or
of Europe ; and prepared to execute the sentence, at the head
of a formidable host, in the full confidence of surmounting all
opposition, either of nature or of man. His first care was to
suppress a domestic rebel, who commanded the most important

[Abu-Nesa]

passes of the Pyrenees : Munuza, a Moorish chief, had accepted
the alliance of the duke of Aquitain ; and Eudes, from a motive
of private or public interest, devoted his beauteous daughter to
the embraces of the African misbeliever. But the strongest
fortresses of Cerdagne were invested by a superior force ; the
rebel was overtaken and slain in the mountains ; and his widow
was sent a captive to Damascus, to gratify the desires, or more
probably the vanity, of the commander of the faithful. From
the Pyrenees Abderame proceeded without delay to the
passage of the Rhone and the siege of Arles. An army of
Christians attempted the relief of the city ; the tombs of their
leaders were yet visible in the thirteenth century ; and many
thousands of their dead bodies were carried down the rapid
stream into the Mediterranean sea. The arms of Abderame
were not less successful on the side of the ocean. He passed
without opposition the Garonne and Dordogne, which unite their
waters in the gulf of Bordeaux ; but he found, beyond those
rivers, the camp of the intrepid Eudes, who had formed a
second army, and sustained a second defeat, so fatal to the
Christians that, according to their sad confession, God alone
could reckon the number of the slain. The victorious Saracen
overran the provinces of Aquitain, whose Gallic names are disguised, rather than lost, in the modern appellations of Périgord,
Saintonge, and Poitou : his standards were planted on the walls,
or at least before the gates, of Tours and of Sens ; and his
detachments overspread the kingdom of Burgundy, as far as

[32] [Hishām, A.D. 724, Jan.—743, Feb.]

the well-known cities of Lyons and Besançon. The memory of these devastations, for Abderame did not spare the country or the people, was long preserved by tradition; and the invasion of France by the Moors or Mahometans affords the ground-work of those fables which have been so wildly disfigured in the romances of chivalry and so elegantly adorned by the Italian muse. In the decline of society and art, the deserted cities could supply a slender booty to the Saracens; their richest spoil was found in the churches and monasteries, which they stripped of their ornaments and delivered to the flames; and the tutelar saints, both Hilary of Poitiers and Martin of Tours, forgot their miraculous powers in the defence of their own sepulchres.[33] A victorious line of march had been prolonged above a thousand miles from the rock of Gibraltar to the banks of the Loire; the repetition of an equal space would have carried the Saracens to the confines of Poland and the High-lands of Scotland: the Rhine is not more impassable than the Nile or Euphrates, and the Arabian fleet might have sailed without a naval combat into the mouth of the Thames. Perhaps the interpretation of the Koran would now be taught in the schools of Oxford, and her pulpits might demonstrate to a circumcised people the sanctity and truth of the revelation of Mahomet.[34]

From such calamities was Christendom delivered by the genius and fortune of one man. Charles, the illegitimate son of the elder Pepin, was content with the titles of mayor or duke of the Franks, but he deserved to become the father of a line of kings.[35] In a laborious administration of twenty-four years, he restored and supported the dignity of the throne, and the rebels of Germany and Gaul were successively crushed by the activity of a warrior, who, in the same campaign, could display his

*Defeat of the Saracens by Charles Martel. A.D 732*

---

[33] With regard to the sanctuary of St. Martin of Tours, Roderic Ximenes accuses the Saracens of the *deed*. Turonis civitatem, ecclesiam et palatia vastatione et incendio simili diruit et consumpsit The continuator of Fredegarius imputes to them no more than the *intention*. Ad domum beatissimi Martini evertendam destinant. At Carolus, &c. The French annalist was more jealous of the honour of the saint.

[34] Yet I sincerely doubt whether the Oxford mosque would have produced a volume of controversy so elegant and ingenious as the sermons lately preached by Mr. White, the Arabic professor, at Mr. Bampton's lecture. His observations on the character and religion of Mahomet are always adapted to his argument, and generally founded in truth and reason. He sustains the part of a lively and eloquent advocate; and sometimes rises to the merit of an historian and philosopher.

[35] [For the life and acts of Charles see T. Breysig's monograph, Karl Martell, in the series of the Jahrbücher der deutschen Geschichte.]

banner on the Elbe, the Rhone, and the shores of the ocean. In the public danger, he was summoned by the voice of his country; and his rival, the duke of Aquitain, was reduced to appear among the fugitives and suppliants. "Alas!" exclaimed the Franks, "what a misfortune! what an indignity! We have long heard of the name and conquests of the Arabs: we were apprehensive of their attack from the East; they have now conquered Spain, and invade our country on the side of the West. Yet their numbers, and (since they have no buckler) their arms, are inferior to our own." "If you follow my advice," replied the prudent mayor of the palace, "you will not interrupt their march, nor precipitate your attack. They are like a torrent, which it is dangerous to stem in its career. The thirst of riches, and the consciousness of success, redouble their valour, and valour is of more avail than arms or numbers. Be patient till they have loaded themselves with the encumbrance of wealth. The possession of wealth will divide their counsels and assure your victory." This subtle policy is perhaps a refinement of the Arabian writers; and the situation of Charles will suggest a more narrow and selfish motive of procrastination: the secret desire of humbling the pride, and wasting the provinces, of the rebel duke of Aquitain. It is yet more probable that the delays of Charles were inevitable and reluctant. A standing army was unknown under the first and second race; more than half the kingdom was now in the hands of the Saracens; according to their respective situation, the Franks of Neustria and Austrasia were too conscious or too careless of the impending danger; and the voluntary aids of the Gepidæ and Germans were separated by a long interval from the standard of the Christian general. No sooner had he collected his forces than he sought and found the enemy in the centre of France, between Tours and Poitiers. His well-conducted march was covered by a range of hills, and Abderame appears to have been surprised by his unexpected [October] presence. The nations of Asia, Africa, and Europe advanced with equal ardour to an encounter which would change the history of the whole world. In the six first days of desultory combat, the horsemen and archers of the East maintained their advantage; but in the closer onset of the seventh day the Orientals were oppressed by the strength and stature of the Germans, who, with stout hearts and *iron* hands,[36] asserted the

---

[36] Gens Austriæ membrorum pre-eminentiâ valida, et gens Germana corde et corpore præstantissima, quasi in ictu occuli manu ferreâ et pectore arduo Arabes extinxerunt (Roderic. Toletan. c. xiv.).

civil and religious freedom of their posterity. The epithet of *Martel*, the *Hammer*, which has been added to the name of Charles, is expressive of his weighty and irresistible strokes: the valour of Eudes was excited by resentment and emulation; and their companions, in the eye of history, are the true Peers and Paladins of French chivalry. After a bloody field, in which Abderame was slain, the Saracens, in the close of the evening, retired to their camp. In the disorder and despair of the night, the various tribes of Yemen and Damascus, of Africa and Spain, were provoked to turn their arms against each other: the remains of their host was suddenly dissolved, and each *emir* consulted his safety by an hasty and separate retreat. At the dawn of day, the stillness of an hostile camp was suspected by the victorious Christians: on the report of their spies, they ventured to explore the riches of the vacant tents; but, if we except some celebrated relics, a small portion of the spoil was restored to the innocent and lawful owners. The joyful tidings were soon diffused over the Catholic world, and the monks of Italy could affirm and believe that three hundred and fifty, or three hundred and seventy-five, thousand of the Mahometans had been crushed by the hammer of Charles;[37] while no more than fifteen hundred Christians were slain in the field of Tours. But this incredible tale is sufficiently disproved by the caution of the French general, who apprehended the snares and accidents of a pursuit, and dismissed his German allies to their native forests. The inactivity of a conqueror betrays the loss of strength and blood, and the most cruel execution is inflicted, not in the ranks of battle, but on the backs of a flying enemy. Yet the victory of the Franks was complete and final; Aquitain was recovered by the arms of Eudes; the Arabs never resumed the conquest of Gaul,[38] and they were soon driven beyond the Pyrenees by Charles Martel

*They retreat before the Franks*

---

[37] These numbers are stated by Paul Warnefrid, the deacon of Aquileia (de Gestis Langobard. l. vi. p. 921, edit. Grot. [c. 46]), and Anastasius, the librarian of the Roman church (in Vit. Gregorii II.), who tells a miraculous story of three consecrated spunges, which rendered invulnerable the French soldiers among whom they had been shared. It should seem that in his letters to the pope Eudes usurped the honour of the victory, for which he is chastised by the French annalists, who, with equal falsehood, accuse him of inviting the Saracens.

[38] [This is not quite accurate. Maurontius, the duke of Marseilles, preferred the alliance of the misbelievers to that of the Frank warrior, and handed over Arles, Avignon, and other towns to the lords of Narbonne, who also obtained possession of Lyons and Valence. They were smitten back to Narbonne by Charles the Hammer in A.D. 737, and yet again in 739. Cp. Weil, *op. cit.* p. 647. Okba was at this time governor of Spain. For the expedition of Charles in 737, see Contin. Fredegar., 109.]

and his valiant race.[39]  It might have been expected that the
saviour of Christendom would have been canonized, or at least
applauded, by the gratitude of the clergy, who are indebted
to his sword for their present existence.  But in the public
distress the mayor of the palace had been compelled to apply
the riches, or at least the revenues, of the bishops and abbots to
the relief of the state and the reward of the soldiers.  His
merits were forgotten, his sacrilege alone was remembered,
and, in an epistle to a Carlovingian prince, a Gallic synod presumes to declare that his ancestor was damned; that on the
opening of his tomb the spectators were affrighted by a smell of
fire and the aspect of a horrid dragon; and that a saint of
the times was indulged with a pleasant vision of the soul and
body of Charles Martel burning, to all eternity, in the abyss
of hell.[40]

The loss of an army, or a province, in the Western world was
less painful to the court of Damascus than the rise and progress
of a domestic competitor.  Except among the Syrians, the caliphs
of the house of Ommiyah had never been the objects of the
public favour.  The life of Mahomet recorded their perseverance
in idolatry and rebellion; their conversion had been reluctant,
their elevation irregular and factious, and their throne was
cemented with the most holy and noble blood of Arabia.  The
best of their race, the pious Omar, was dissatisfied with his own
title; their personal virtues were insufficient to justify a departure from the order of succession; and the eyes and wishes of
the faithful were turned towards the line of Hashem and the
kindred of the apostle of God.  Of these the Fatimites were
either rash or pusillanimous; but the descendants of Abbas
cherished, with courage and discretion, the hopes of their rising
fortunes.  From an obscure residence in Syria, they secretly
dispatched their agents and missionaries, who preached in the
Eastern provinces their hereditary indefeasible right; and Mo-

[39] Narbonne, and the rest of Septimania, was recovered by Pepin, the son of
Charles Martel, A.D. 755 (Pagi, Critica, tom. iii. p. 300).   Thirty-seven years
afterwards it was pillaged by a sudden inroad of the Arabs, who employed the
captives in the construction of the mosque of Cordova (de Guignes, Hist. des Huns,
tom. i. p. 354).

[40] This pastoral letter, addressed to Lewis the Germanic, the grandson of
Charlemagne, and most probably composed by the pen of the artful Hincmar, is
dated in the year 858, and signed by the bishops of the provinces of Rheims and
Rouen (Baronius, Annal. Eccles. A.D. 741; Fleury, Hist. Ecclés. tom. x. p. 514-
516).   Yet Baronius himself, and the French critics, reject with contempt this
episcopal fiction.

hammed, the son of Ali, the son of Abdallah, the son of Abbas, the uncle of the prophet, gave audience to the deputies of Chorasan, and accepted their free gift of four hundred thousand pieces of gold. After the death of Mohammed, the oath of allegiance was administered in the name of his son Ibrahim to a numerous band of votaries, who expected only a signal and a leader; and the governor of Chorasan continued to deplore his fruitless admonitions and the deadly slumber of the caliphs of Damascus, till he himself, with all his adherents, was driven from the city and palace of Meru, by the rebellious arms of Abu Moslem.[41] That maker of kings, the author, as he is named, of the *call* of the Abbassides, was at length rewarded for his presumption of merit with the usual gratitude of courts. A mean, perhaps a foreign, extraction could not repress the aspiring energy of Abu Moslem. Jealous of his wives, liberal of his wealth, prodigal of his own blood, and of that of others, he could boast with pleasure, and possibly with truth, that he had destroyed six hundred thousand of his enemies; and such was the intrepid gravity of his mind and countenance that he was never seen to smile except on a day of battle. In the visible separation of parties, the *green* was consecrated to the Fatimites; the Ommiades were distinguished by the *white;* and the *black*, as the most adverse, was naturally adopted by the Abbassides. Their turbans and garments were stained with that gloomy colour; two black standards, on pike-staves nine cubits long, were borne aloft in the van of Abu Moslem; and their allegorical names of the *night* and the *shadow* obscurely represented the indissoluble union and perpetual succession of the line of Hashem. From the Indus to the Euphrates, the East was convulsed by the quarrel of the white and the black factions; the Abbassides were most frequently victorious; but their public success was clouded by the personal misfortune of their chief. The court of Damascus, awakening from a long slumber, resolved to prevent the pilgrimage of Mecca, which Ibrahim had undertaken with a splendid retinue, to recommend himself at once to the favour of the prophet and of the people. A detachment of cavalry intercepted his march and arrested his person; and the [A.D. 744] unhappy Ibrahim, snatched away from the promise of untasted

---

[41] The steed and the saddle which had carried any of his wives were instantly killed or burnt, lest they should be afterwards mounted by a male. Twelve hundred mules or camels were required for his kitchen furniture; and the daily consumption amounted to three thousand cakes, an hundred sheep, besides oxen, poultry, &c. (Abulpharagius, Hist. Dynast. p. 140).

royalty, expired in iron fetters in the dungeons of Haran. His two younger brothers, Saffah [42] and Almansor, [43] eluded the search of the tyrant, and lay concealed at Cufa, till the zeal of the people and the approach of his eastern friends allowed them to expose their persons to the impatient public. On Friday, in the dress of a caliph, in the colours of the sect, Saffah proceeded with religious and military pomp to the mosque ; ascending the pulpit, he prayed and preached as the lawful successor of Mahomet ; and, after his departure, his kinsmen bound a willing people by an oath of fidelity. But it was on the banks of the Zab, and not in the mosque of Cufa, that this important controversy was determined. Every advantage appeared to be on the side of the white faction : the authority of established government ; an army of an hundred and twenty thousand soldiers,

[Marwan II.  against a sixth part of that number ; [43a] and the presence and merit
A.D. 744-50]  of the caliph Mervan, the fourteenth and last of the house of Ommiyah. Before his accession to the throne, he had deserved, by his Georgian warfare, the honourable epithet of the ass of Mesopotamia ; [44] and he might have been ranked among the greatest princes, had not, says Abulfeda, the eternal order decreed that moment for the ruin of his family : a decree against which all human prudence and fortitude must struggle in vain. The orders of Mervan were mistaken or disobeyed ; the return of his horse, from which he had dismounted on a necessary occasion, [45] impressed the belief of his death ; and the enthusiasm of the black squadrons was ably conducted by Abdallah, the uncle of his competitor. After an irretrieveable defeat, the caliph escaped to Mosul ; but the colours of the Abbassides were displayed from the rampart ; he suddenly repassed the Tigris, cast a melancholy look on his palace of Haran, crossed the Euphrates, abandoned the fortifications of Damascus, and, without halting in Palestine, pitched his last and fatal camp at Busir on the banks

42 [Abd Allāh Abū-l-Abbās al-Saffāh (the bloody), caliph 750-754.]

43 [Abū-Jafar Mansūr, caliph 754-775.]

43a [So Tabari, ed. de Goeje, iii. 45.]

44 *Al Hamar.* He had been governor of Mesopotamia, and the Arabic proverb praises the courage of that warlike breed of asses who never fly from an enemy. The surname of Mervan may justify the comparison of Homer (Iliad v. 557, &c.), and both will silence the moderns, who consider the ass as a stupid and ignoble emblem (d'Herbelot, Bibliot. Orient. p. 558).

45 [This motive seems to have been drawn from Persian sources—Gibbon took it from Herbelot. We must rather follow Tabari's account. Marwān sent his son with some troops back to the camp to rescue his money. This back movement was taken by the rest of the army as a retreat and they all took to flight. See Weil, *op. cit.* i. p. 701 ; Tabari, ed. de Goeje, iii. 38 *sqq.*]

of the Nile.[46]  His speed was urged by the incessant diligence Fall of the Ommiades. A.D. 750, Feb. 10 of Abdallah, who in every step of the pursuit acquired strength and reputation; the remains of the white faction were finally vanquished in Egypt; and the lance, which terminated the life and anxiety of Mervan, was not less welcome perhaps to the unfortunate than to the victorious chief.  The merciless inquisition of the conqueror eradicated the most distant branches of the hostile race : their bones were scattered, their memory was accursed, and the martyrdom of Hossein was abundantly revenged on the posterity of his tyrants.  Fourscore of the Ommiades, who had yielded to the faith or clemency of their foes, were invited to a banquet at Damascus.  The laws of hospitality were violated by a promiscuous massacre ; the board was spread over their fallen bodies; and the festivity of the guests was enlivened by the music of their dying groans.  By the event of the civil war the dynasty of the Abbassides was firmly established ; but the Christians only could triumph in the mutual hatred and common loss of the disciples of Mahomet.[47]

Yet the thousands who were swept away by the sword of war Revolt of Spain. A.D. 755 might have been speedily retrieved in the succeeding generation, if the consequences of the revolution had not tended to dissolve the power and unity of the empire of the Saracens.  In the proscription of the Ommiades, a royal youth of the name of Abdalrahman alone escaped the rage of his enemies, who hunted the wandering exile from the banks of the Euphrates to the valleys of mount Atlas.  His presence in the neighbourhood of Spain revived the zeal of the white faction.  The name and cause of the Abbassides had been first vindicated by the Persians ; the

---

[46] Four several places, all in Egypt, bore the name of Busir, or Busiris, so famous in Greek fable.  The first, where Mervan was slain, was to the west of the Nile, in the province of Fium, or Arsinoe ; the second in the Delta, in the Sebennytic nome ; the third, near the pyramids ; the fourth, which was destroyed by Diocletian (see above, vol. i. p. 439), in the Thebais.  I shall here transcribe a note of the learned and orthodox Michaelis : Videntur in pluribus Ægypti superioris urbibus Busiri Coptoque arma sumpsisse Christiani, libertatemque de religione sentiendi defendisse, sed succubuisse quo in bello Coptos et Busuris diruta, et circa Esnam magna strages edita.  Bellum narrant sed causam belli ignorant scriptores Byzantini, alioqui Coptum et Busirim non rebellasse dicturi, sed causam Christianorum suscepturi (Not. 211, p. 100).  For the geography of the four Busirs, see Abulfeda (Descript. Ægypt. p. 9, vers. Michaelis.  Gottingæ, 1776, in 4to), Michaelis (Not. 122-127, p. 58-63), and d'Anville (Mémoire sur l'Egypte, p. 85, 147, 205).

[47] See Abulfeda (Annal. Moslem. p. 136-145), Eutychius (Annal. tom. ii. p. 392, vers. Pocock), Elmacin (Hist. Saracen. p. 109-121), Abulpharagius (Hist. Dynast. p. 134-140), Roderic of Toledo (Hist. Arabum, c. 18, p. 33), Theophanes (Chronograph. p. 356, 357 [A.M. 6240, 6241], who speaks of the Abbassides under the n a es of Χωρασανῖται and Μαυροφόροι), and the Bibliothèque of d'Herbelot, in the articles of *Ommiades*, *Abbassides*, *Marvan*, *Ibrahim*, *Saffah*, *Abou Moslem*, [Tabari, vol. iii. 44-51.]

West had been pure from civil arms ; and the servants of the abdicated family still held, by a precarious tenure, the inheritance of their lands and the offices of government. Strongly prompted by gratitude, indignation, and fear, they invited the grandson of the caliph Hashem to ascend the throne of his ancestors ; and, in his desperate condition, the extremes of rashness and prudence were almost the same. The acclamations of the people saluted his landing on the coast of Andalusia ; and, [A.D. 756] after a successful struggle, Abdalrahman established the throne of Cordova, and was the father of the Ommiades of Spain, who reigned above two hundred and fifty years from the Atlantic to the Pyrenees.[48] He slew in battle a lieutenant of the Abbassides, who had invaded his dominions with a fleet and army : [A.D. 763] the head of Ala, in salt and camphire, was suspended by a daring messenger before the palace of Mecca ;[49] and the caliph Almansor rejoiced in his safety, that he was removed by seas and lands from such a formidable adversary. Their mutual designs or declarations of offensive war evaporated without effect; but, instead of opening a door to the conquest of Europe, Spain was dissevered from the trunk of the monarchy, engaged in perpetual hostility with the East, and inclined to peace and friendship with the Christian sovereigns of Constantinople and Triple division of the caliphate France. The example of the Ommiades was imitated by the real or fictitious progeny of Ali, the Edrissites of Mauritania, and the more powerful Fatimites of Africa and Egypt. In the tenth century, the chair of Mahomet was disputed by three caliphs or commanders of the faithful, who reigned at Bagdad, Cairoan, and Cordova, excommunicated each other, and agreed only in a principle of discord, that a sectary is more odious and criminal than an unbeliever.[50]

Magnificence of the caliphs. A.D. 750-960          Mecca was the patrimony of the line of Hashem, yet the

[48] For the revolution of Spain, consult Roderic of Toledo (c. xviii. p. 34, &c.), the Bibliotheca Arabico-Hispana (tom. ii. p. 30, 198), and Cardonne (Hist. de l'Afrique et de l'Espagne, tom. i. p. 180-197, 205, 272, 323, &c.).

[49] [Others say the head was exposed at Kairawān ; Dozy, Hist. des Musulm. d'Espagne, i. 367.]

[50] I shall not stop to refute the strange errors and fancies of Sir William Temple (his works, vol. iii. p. 371-374, octavo edition) and Voltaire (Histoire Générale, c. xxviii. tom. ii. p. 124, 125, édition de Lausanne), concerning the division of the Saracen empire. The mistakes of Voltaire proceeded from the want of knowledge or reflection ; but Sir William was deceived by a Spanish impostor, who has framed an apocryphal history of the conquest of Spain by the Arabs. [The Omayyad rulers of Spain called themselves emirs (Amīr) for a century and three-quarters. Abd ar-Rahmān III. (912-961) first assumed the higher title of caliph in 929. Thus it is incorrect to speak of two Caliphates, or a western Caliphate, until 929 ; the Emirate of Cordova is the correct designation.]

Abbassides were never tempted to reside either in the birth-place or the city of the prophet. Damascus was disgraced by the choice, and polluted with the blood, of the Ommiades; and, after some hesitation, Almansor, the brother and successor of Saffah, laid the foundations of Bagdad,[51] the Imperial seat of his posterity during a reign of five hundred years.[52] The chosen spot is on the eastern bank of the Tigris, about fifteen miles above the ruins of Modain ; the double wall was of a circular form ; and such was the rapid increase of a capital, now dwindled to a provincial town, that the funeral of a popular saint might be attended by eight hundred thousand men and sixty thousand women of Bagdad and the adjacent villages. In this *city of peace*,[53] amidst the riches of the East, the Abbassides soon disdained the abstinence and frugality of the first caliphs, and aspired to emulate the magnificence of the Persian kings. After

[51] The geographer d'Anville (l'Euphrate et le Tigre, p. 121-123), and the Orientalist d'Herbelot (Bibliothèque, p. 167, 168), may suffice for the knowledge of Bagdad. Our travellers, Pietro della Valle (tom. i. p. 688-698), Tavernier (tom. i. p. 230-238), Thévenot (part ii. p. 209-212), Otter (tom. i. p. 162-168), and Niebuhr (Voyage en Arabie, tom. ii. p. 239-271), have seen only its decay; and the Nubian geographer (p. 204), and the travelling Jew, Benjamin of Tudela (Itinerarium, p. 112-123, à Const. l'Empereur, apud Elzevir, 1633), are the only writers of my acquaintance, who have known Bagdad under the reign of the Abbassides. [See Ibn Serapion's description of the canals of Baghdād, translated and annotated by Mr. Le Strange, in the Journal of the Asiatic Society, N. S. vol. 27 (1895), p. 285 *sqq.*, and Mr. Le Strange's sketch plan of the city (*ib.*, opposite p. 33).]

[52] The foundations of Bagdad were laid A.H. 145, A.D. 762 ; Mostasem [Mustasim, 1242-1258], the last of the Abbassides, was taken and put to death by the Tartars, A.H. 656, A.D. 1258, the 20th of February.

[53] Medinat al Salem, Dar al Salem [Dār al-Salām]. Urbs pacis, or, as is more neatly compounded by the Byzantine writers, Εἰρηνόπολις (Irenopolis). There is some dispute concerning the etymology of Bagdad, but the first syllable is allowed to signify a garden, in the Persian tongue ; the garden of Dad, a Christian hermit, whose cell had been the only habitation on the spot. ["The original city as founded by the Caliph Al-Mansūr was circular, being surrounded by a double wall and ditch, with four equidistant gates. From gate to gate measured an Arab mile (about one English mile and a quarter). This circular city stood on the western side of the Tigris, immediately above the point where the Sarāt Canal, coming from the Nahr 'Isā, joined the Tigris, and the Sarāt flowed round the southern side of the city." "In the century and a half which had elapsed, counting from the date of the foundation of the city down to the epoch at which Ibn Serapion wrote, Baghdād had undergone many changes. It had never recovered the destructive effects of the great siege, when Al-Amin had defended himself, to the death, against the troops of his brother Al-Mamūn ; and again it had suffered semi-depopulation by the removal of the seat of government to Samarrā (A.D. 836-892). The original round city of Al-Mansūr had long ago been absorbed into the great capital, which covered ground measuring about five miles across in every direction, and the circular walls must, at an early date, have been levelled. The four gates, however, had remained, and had given their names to the first suburbs which in time had been absorbed into the Western town and become one half of the great City of Peace." Mr. Guy Le Strange, *loc. cit.*, pp. 288, 289-90.]

his wars and buildings, Almansor left behind him in gold and silver about thirty millions sterling; [54] and this treasure was exhausted in a few years by the vices or virtues of his children.

[Al-Mahdi]

His son Mahadi, in a single pilgrimage to Mecca, expended six millions of dinars of gold.  A pious and charitable motive may sanctify the foundation of cisterns and caravanseras, which he distributed along a measured road of seven hundred miles ; but his train of camels, laden with snow, could serve only to astonish the natives of Arabia, and to refresh the fruits and liquors of the royal banquet.[55]  The courtiers would surely praise the liberality of his grandson Almamon, who gave away four-fifths of the income of a province, a sum of two millions four hundred thousand gold dinars, before he drew his foot from the stirrup.  At the nuptials of the same prince, a thousand pearls of the largest size were showered on the head of the bride,[56] and a lottery of lands and houses displayed the capricious bounty of fortune.  The glories of the court were brightened rather than impaired in the decline of the empire ; and a Greek ambassador might admire

[Al-Muktadir]

or pity the magnificence of the feeble Moctader.  " The caliph's whole army," says the historian Abulfeda, " both horse and foot, was under arms, which together made a body of one hundred and sixty thousand men.  His state-officers, the favourite slaves, stood near him in splendid apparel, their belts glittering with gold and gems.  Near them were seven thousand eunuchs, four thousand of them white, the remainder black.  The porters or door-keepers were in number seven hundred.  Barges and boats, with the most superb decorations, were seen swimming upon the Tigris.  Nor was the palace itself less splendid, in which were hung up thirty-eight thousand pieces of tapestry, twelve thousand five hundred of which were of silk embroidered with gold.  The carpets on the floor were twenty-two thousand.  An hun-

[54] Reliquit in ærario sexcenties millies mille stateres, et quater et vicies millies mille aureos aureos. Elmacin, Hist. Saracen. p. 126.  I have reckoned the gold pieces at eight shillings, and the proportion to the silver as twelve to one.  [But see Appendix 2.]  But I will never answer for the numbers of Erpenius ; and the Latins are scarcely above the savages in the language of arithmetic.

[55] D'Herbelot, p. 530.  Abulfeda, p. 154.  Nivem Meccam apportavit, rem ibi aut nunquam aut rarissime visam.

[56] Abulfeda, p. 184, 189, describes the splendour and liberality of Almamon. Milton has alluded to this Oriental custom :—

　　　　—Or where the gorgeous East, with richest hand,
　　　　　Showers on her kings Barbaric pearls and gold.

I have used the modern word *lottery* to express the *Missilia* of the Roman emperors, which entitled to some prize the person who caught them, as they were thrown among the crowd.

dred lions were brought out, with a keeper to each lion.[57]
Among the other spectacles of rare and stupendous luxury, was
a tree of gold and silver spreading into eighteen large branches,
on which, and on the lesser boughs, sat a variety of birds made
of the same precious metals, as well as the leaves of the tree.
While the machinery affected spontaneous motions, the several
birds warbled their natural harmony. Through this scene of
magnificence, the Greek ambassador was led by the visir to the
foot of the caliph's throne." [58] In the West, the Ommiades
of Spain supported, with equal pomp, the title of commander
of the faithful. Three miles from Cordova, in honour of his
favourite sultana, the third and greatest of the Abdalrahmans
constructed the city, palace, and gardens of Zehra. Twenty-five
years, and above three millions sterling, were employed by the
founder : his liberal taste invited the artists of Constantinople,
the most skilful sculptors and architects of the age ; and the
buildings were sustained or adorned by twelve hundred columns
of Spanish and African, of Greek and Italian marble. The hall
of audience was encrusted with gold and pearls, and a great
bason in the centre was surrounded with the curious and
costly figures of birds and quadrupeds. In a lofty pavillion of
the gardens, one of these basons and fountains, so delightful in
a sultry climate, was replenished not with water, but with the
purest quicksilver. The seraglio of Abdalrahman, his wives,
concubines, and black eunuchs, amounted to six thousand three
hundred persons ; and he was attended to the field by a guard
of twelve thousand horse, whose belts and scymetars were studded
with gold.[59]

In a private condition, our desires are perpetually repressed
by poverty and subordination ; but the lives and labours of

*Its consequences on private and public happiness*

[57] When Bell of Antermony (Travels, vol. i. p. 99) accompanied the Russian
ambassador to the audience of the unfortunate Shah Hussein of Persia, *two* lions
were introduced, to denote the power of the king over the fiercest animals.

[58] Abulfeda, p. 237 ; d'Herbelot, p. 590. This embassy was received at Bagdad A.H. 305, A.D. 917. In the passage of Abulfeda, I have used, with some
variations, the English translation of the learned and amiable Mr. Harris of Salisbury (Philological Enquiries, p. 363, 364).

[59] Cardonne, Histoire de l'Afrique et de l'Espagne, tom. i. p. 330-336. A just
idea of the taste and architecture of the Arabians of Spain may be conceived from
the description and plates of the Alhambra of Grenada (Swinburne's Travels, p.
171-188). [Owen Jones, Plans, elevations, sections and details of the Alhambra,
2 vols., 1842-5. On Saracen architecture and art in general, see E. S. Poole's
Appendix to 5th ed. of Lane's Modern Egyptians, 1860. Architecture in Spain
may be studied in the colossal Monumentos Architectonicos de España (in double
elephant folio). For a brief account of Saracenic architecture in Spain, see Burke's
History of Spain, vol. ii. p. 15 *sqq.*]

millions are devoted to the service of a despotic prince, whose laws are blindly obeyed, and whose wishes are instantly gratified. Our imagination is dazzled by the splendid picture; and, whatever may be the cool dictates of reason, there are few among us who would obstinately refuse a trial of the comforts and the cares of royalty. It may therefore be of some use to borrow the experience of the same Abdalrahman, whose magnificence has perhaps excited our admiration and envy, and to transcribe an authentic memorial which was found in the closet of the deceased caliph. "I have now reigned above fifty years in victory or peace; beloved by my subjects, dreaded by my enemies, and respected by my allies. Riches and honours, power and pleasure, have waited on my call, nor does any earthly blessing appear to have been wanting to my felicity. In this situation I have diligently numbered the days of pure and genuine happiness which have fallen to my lot: they amount to Fourteen :—O man! place not thy confidence in this present world!" [60] The luxury of the caliphs, so useless to their private happiness, relaxed the nerves, and terminated the progress, of the Arabian empire. Temporal and spiritual conquest had been the sole occupation of the first successors of Mahomet; and, after supplying themselves with the necessaries of life, the whole revenue was scrupulously devoted to that salutary work. The Abbassides were impoverished by the multitude of their wants and their contempt of œconomy. Instead of pursuing the great object of ambition, their leisure, their affections, the powers of their mind, were diverted by pomp and pleasure; the rewards of valour were embezzled by women and eunuchs, and the royal camp was encumbered by the luxury of the palace. A similar temper was diffused among the subjects of the caliph. Their stern enthusiasm was softened by time and prosperity: they sought riches in the occupations of industry, fame in the pursuits of literature, and happiness in the tranquillity of domestic life. War was no longer the passion of the Saracens; and the increase of pay, the repetition of donatives, were insufficient to allure the posterity

[60] Cardonne, tom. i. p. 329, 330. This confession, the complaints of Solomon of the vanity of this world (read Prior's verbose but eloquent poem), and the happy ten days of the emperor Seghed (Rambler, No. 204, 205), will be triumphantly quoted by the detractors of human life. Their expectations are commonly immoderate, their estimates are seldom impartial. If I may speak of myself (the only person of whom I can speak with certainty), *my* happy hours have far exceeded, and far exceed, the scanty numbers of the caliph of Spain; and I shall not scruple to add that many of them are due to the pleasing labour of the present composition.

of those voluntary champions who had crowded to the standard of Abubeker and Omar for the hopes of spoil and of paradise.

Under the reign of the Ommiades, the studies of the Moslems were confined to the interpretation of the Koran, and the eloquence and poetry of their native tongue. A people continually exposed to the dangers of the field must esteem the healing powers of medicine or rather of surgery ; but the starving physicians of Arabia murmured a complaint that exercise and temperance deprived them of the greatest part of their practice.[61] After their civil and domestic wars, the subjects of the Abbassides, awakening from this mental lethargy, found leisure and felt curiosity for the acquisition of profane science. This spirit was first encouraged by the caliph Almansor, who, besides his knowledge of the Mahometan law, had applied himself with success to the study of astronomy. But, when the sceptre devolved to Almamon, the seventh of the Abbassides, he completed the designs of his grandfather, and invited the muses from their ancient seats. His ambassadors at Constantinople, his agents in Armenia, Syria, and Egypt, collected the volumes of Grecian science ; at his command they were translated by the most skilful interpreters into the Arabic language ; his subjects were exhorted assiduously to peruse these instructive writings ; and the successor of Mahomet assisted with pleasure and modesty at the assemblies and disputations of the learned. " He was not ignorant," says Abulpharagius, " that *they* are the elect of God, his best and most useful servants, whose lives are devoted to the improvement of their rational faculties. The mean ambition of the Chinese or the Turks may glory in the industry of their hands or the indulgence of their brutal appetites. Yet these dexterous artists must view, with hopeless emulation, the hexagons and pyramids of the cells of a bee-hive :[62] these fortitudinous

Introduction
of learning
among the
Arabians.
A.D. 754, &c.
813, &c.

---

[61] The Gulistan (p. 239) relates the conversation of Mahomet and a physician (Epistol. Renaudot. in Fabricius, Bibliot. Græc. tom. i. p. 814). The prophet himself was skilled in the art of medicine ; and Gagnier (Vie de Mahomet, tom. iii. p. 394-405) has given an extract of the aphorisms which are extant under his name.

[62] See their curious architecture in Réaumur (Hist. des Insectes, tom. v. Mémoire viii.). These hexagons are closed by a pyramid ; the angles of the three sides of a similar pyramid, such as would accomplish the given end with the smallest quantity possible of materials, were determined by a mathematician, at 109 degrees 26 minutes for the larger, 70 degrees 34 minutes for the smaller. The actual measure is 109 degrees 28 minutes, 70 degrees 32 minutes. Yet this perfect harmony raises the work at the expense of the artist : the bees are not masters of transcendent geometry. [An attempt has recently been made to show that there is no discrepancy between the actual dimensions of the cells and the measures which would require the minimum of material.]

heroes are awed by the superior fierceness of the lions and tigers; and in their amorous enjoyments they are much inferior to the vigour of the grossest and most sordid quadrupeds. The teachers of wisdom are the true luminaries and legislators of a world which, without their aid, would again sink in ignorance and barbarism." [63] The zeal and curiosity of Almamon were imitated by succeeding princes of the line of Abbas; their rivals, the Fatimites of Africa and the Ommiades of Spain, were the patrons of the learned, as well as the commanders of the faithful; the same royal prerogative was claimed by their independent emirs of the provinces; and their emulation diffused the taste and the rewards of science from Samarcand and Bochara to Fez and Cordova. The visir of a sultan consecrated a sum of two hundred thousand pieces of gold to the foundation of a college at Bagdad, which he endowed with an annual revenue of fifteen thousand dinars. The fruits of instruction were communicated, perhaps at different times, to six thousand disciples of every degree, from the son of the noble to that of the mechanic; a sufficient allowance was provided for the indigent scholars; and the merit or industry of the professors was repaid with adequate stipends. In every city the productions of Arabic literature were copied and collected by the curiosity of the studious and the vanity of the rich. A private doctor refused the invitation of the sultan of Bochara, because the carriage of his books would have required four hundred camels. The royal library of the Fatimites consisted of one hundred thousand manuscripts, elegantly transcribed and splendidly bound, which were lent, with jealousy or avarice, to the students of Cairo. Yet this collection must appear moderate, if we can believe that the Ommiades of Spain had formed a library of six hundred thousand volumes, forty-four of which were employed in the mere catalogue. Their capital, Cordova, with the adjacent towns of Malaga, Almeria, and Murcia, had given birth to more than three hundred writers, and above seventy public libraries were opened in the cities of the Andalusian kingdom. The age of Arabian learning continued about five hundred years, till the great irruption of the Moguls, and was coeval with the darkest and most slothful period of European annals; but, since the sun of science has arisen in the

---

[63] Said Ebn Ahmed, cadhi of Toledo, who died A.H. 462, A.D. 1069, has furnished Abulpharagius (Dynast. p. 160) with this curious passage as well as with the text of Pocock's Specimen Historiæ Arabum. A number of literary anecdotes of philosophers, physicians, &c., who have flourished under each caliph, form the principal merit of the Dynasties of Abulpharagius,

West, it should seem that the Oriental studies have languished and declined.[64]

In the libraries of the Arabians, as in those of Europe, the far greater part of the innumerable volumes were possessed only of local value or imaginary merit.[65] The shelves were crowded with orators and poets, whose style was adapted to the taste and manners of their countrymen; with general and partial histories, which each revolving generation supplied with a new harvest of persons and events; with codes and commentaries of jurisprudence, which derived their authority from the law of the prophet; with the interpreters of the Koran and ortho-dox tradition; and with the whole theological tribe, polemics, mystics, scholastics, and moralists, the first or the last of writers, according to the different estimate of sceptics or believers. The works of speculation or science may be reduced to the four classes of philosophy, mathematics, astronomy, and physic. The sages of Greece were translated and illustrated in the Arabic language, and some treatises, now lost in the original, have been recovered in the versions of the East,[66] which possessed and studied the writings of Aristotle and Plato, of Euclid and Apol-lonius, of Ptolemy, Hippocrates, and Galen.[67] Among the ideal

*Their real progress in the sciences*

[64] These literary anecdotes are borrowed from the Bibliotheca Arabico-Hispana (tom. ii. p. 38, 71, 201, 202), Leo Africanus (de Arab. Medicis et Philosophis, in Fabric. Bibliot. Græc. tom. xiii. p. 259-298, particularly p. 274), and Renaudot (Hist. Patriarch. Alex. p. 274, 275, 536, 537), besides the chronological remarks of Abulpharagius.

[65] The Arabic catalogue of the Escurial will give a just idea of the proportion of the classes. In the library of Cairo, the Mss. of astronomy and medicine amounted to 6500, with two fair globes, the one of brass, the other of silver (Bibliot. Arab. Hisp. tom. i. p. 417).

[66] As for instance, the fifth, sixth, and seventh books (the eighth is still wanting) of the Conic Sections of Apollonius Pergæus [flor. circa, 200 B.C.], which were printed from the Florence Ms. 1661 (Fabric. Bibliot. Græc. tom. ii. p. 559). Yet the fifth book had been previously restored by the mathematical divination of Viviani (see his Eloge in Fontenelle, tom. v. p. 59, &c.). [The first 4 books of the κωνικὰ στοιχεῖα are preserved in Greek. Editions by Halley, 1710; Heiberg, 1888.]

[67] The merit of these Arabic versions is freely discussed by Renaudot (Fabric. Bibliot. Græc. tom. i. p. 812-816), and piously defended by Gasira (Bibliot. Arab. Hispana, tom. i. p. 238-240). Most of the versions of Plato, Aristotle, Hippocrates, Galen, &c., are ascribed to Honain [Ibn Ishak, a native of Hira], a physician of the Nestorian sect, who flourished at Bagdad in the court of the caliphs, and died A.D. 876 [874]. He was at the head of a school or manufacture of translations, and the works of his sons and disciples were published under his name. See Abulpharagius, (Dynast. p. 88, 115, 171-174, and apud Asseman, Bibliot. Orient. tom. ii. p. 438), d'Herbelot (Bibliot. Orientale, p. 456), Asseman (Bibliot. Orient. tom. iii. p. 164), and Casiri, Bibliot. Arab. Hispana, tom. i. p. 238, &c., 251, 286-290, 302, 304, &c. [See also Wenrich, de auctorum Græcorum versionibus et commentariis Syriacis, 1842; J. Lippert, Studien auf dem Gebiete der griechisch-arabischen Uebersetzungs-Litteratur, pt. 1, 1894. On Arabic versions from Latin, see Wüstenfeld, Die Uebersetzungen arab. Werke in das Lat. seit dem xi. Jahrh., in Abh. d. k. Ges. d. Wiss. zu Göttingen, vol. 22, 1877.]

systems, which have varied with the fashion of the times, the
Arabians adopted the philosophy of the Stagirite, alike intelli-
gible or alike obscure for the readers of every age.   Plato wrote
for the Athenians, and his allegorical genius is too closely
blended with the language and religion of Greece.   After the
fall of that religion, the Peripatetics, emerging from their
obscurity, prevailed in the controversies of the Oriental sects,
and their founder was long afterwards restored by the Mahometans of Spain to the Latin schools.[68]   The physics both of the
Academy and the Lyceum, as they are built, not on observation,
but on argument, have retarded the progress of real knowledge.
The metaphysics of infinite or finite spirit have too often been
enlisted in the service of superstition.   But the human faculties
are fortified by the art and practice of dialectics; the ten predicaments of Aristotle collect and methodize our ideas,[69] and his
syllogism is the keenest weapon of dispute.   It was dexterously
wielded in the schools of the Saracens, but, as it is more effectual
for the detection of error than for the investigation of truth, it
is not surprising that new generations of masters and disciples
should still revolve in the same circle of logical argument.   The
mathematics are distinguished by a peculiar privilege that, in
the course of ages, they may always advance and can never
recede.   But the ancient geometry, if I am not misinformed,
was resumed in the same state by the Italians of the fifteenth
century; and, whatever may be the origin of the name, the
science of algebra is ascribed to the Grecian Diophantus by the
modest testimony of the Arabs themselves.[70]   They cultivated
with more success the sublime science of astronomy, which
elevates the mind of man to disdain his diminutive planet and
momentary existence.   The costly instruments of observation
were supplied by the caliph Almamon, and the land of the
Chaldeans still afforded the same spacious level, the same un-

[68] See Mosheim, Institut. Hist. Eccles. p. 181, 214, 236, 257, 315, 338, 396, 438
&c.

[69] The most elegant commentary on the Categories or Predicaments of Aristotle
may be found in the Philosophical Arrangements of Mr. James Harris (London,
1775, in octavo), who laboured to revive the studies of Grecian literature and philosophy.

[70] Abulpharagius, Dynast. p. 81, 222.   Bibliot. Arab. Hist. tom. i. p. 370, 371.
In quem (says the primate of the Jacobites) si immiserit se lector, oceanum hoc in
genere (*algebrae*) inveniet.   The time of Diophantus of Alexandria is unknown
[probably 4th century A.D.], but his six books are still extant, and have been illustrated by the Greek Planudes and the Frenchman Meziriac (Fabric. Bibliot. Græc.
tom. iv. p. 12-15).   [His work entitled Αριθμητικά originally consisted of 13 books;
only 6 are extant.   Meziriac's ed. appeared in 1621, and Fermat's text in 1670;
but these have been superseded by P. Tannery's recent edition.]

clouded horizon. In the plains of Sinaar, and a second time in [Sinjar] those of Cufa, his mathematicians accurately measured a degree of the great circle of the earth, and determined at twenty-four thousand miles the entire circumference of our globe.[71] From the reign of the Abbassides to that of the grandchildren of Tamerlane, the stars, without the aid of glasses, were diligently observed; and the astronomical tables of Bagdad, Spain, and Samarcand,[72] correct some minute errors, without daring to renounce the hypothesis of Ptolemy, without advancing a step towards the discovery of the solar system. In the eastern courts, the truths of science could be recommended only by ignorance and folly, and the astronomer would have been disregarded, had he not debased his wisdom or honesty by the vain predictions of astrology.[73] But in the science of medicine, the Arabians have been deservedly applauded.[74] The names of Mesua and Geber, of Razis and Avicenna, are ranked with the Grecian masters; in the city of Bagdad, eight hundred and sixty physicians were licensed to exercise their lucrative profession;[75] in Spain, the life of the Catholic princes was entrusted to the skill of the Saracens,[76] and the school of Salerno, their legitimate offspring, revived in Italy and Europe the precepts of the healing art.[77] The success of each professor must have been influenced by personal and accidental causes; but we may form a

[71] Abulfeda (Annal. Moslem. p. 210, 211. vers. Reiske) describes this operation according to Ibn Challecan and the best historians. This degree most accurately contains 200,000 royal or Hashemite cubits, which Arabia had derived from the sacred and legal practice both of Palestine and Egypt. This ancient cubit is repeated 400 times in each basis of the great pyramid, and seems to indicate the primitive and universal measures of the East. See the Métrologie of the laborious M. Paucton, p. 101-195. [See Al-Masûdî, Prairies d'or, i. 182-3; and cp. Sedillot, Hist. Générale des Arabes, ii. Appendice 256-7. There seems to be no mention of the degree in Tabari. There is a mistake in Gibbon's reference to Abulfeda, which the editor is unable to correct.]

[72] See the Astronomical Tables of Ulegh Begh, with the preface of Dr. Hyde, in the first volume of his Syntagma Dissertationum, Oxon., 1767.

[73] The truth of astrology was allowed by Albumazar, and the best of the Arabian astronomers, who drew their most certain predictions, not from Venus and Mercury, but from Jupiter and the sun (Abulpharag. Dynast. p. 161-163). For the state and science of the Persian astronomers, see Chardin (Voyages en Perse, tom. iii. p. 162-203).

[74] [Wüstenfeld, Geschichte der arabischen Aerzte.]

[75] Bibliot. Arabico-Hispana, tom. i. p. 438. The original relates a pleasant tale, of an ignorant but harmless practitioner.

[76] In the year 956, Sancho the fat, king of Leon, was cured by the physicians of Cordova (Mariana, l. viii. c. 7, tom. i. p. 318).

[77] The school of Salerno, and the introduction of the Arabian sciences into Italy, are discussed with learning and judgment by Muratori (Antiquitat. Italiæ Medii Ævi, tom. iii. p. 932-940) and Giannone (Istoria Civile de Napoli, tom. ii. p. 119-127). [The school of Salerno was *not* under the influence of Arabic medicine. See below, p. 189.]

less fanciful estimate of their general knowledge of anatomy,[78] botany,[79] and chemistry,[80] the threefold basis of their theory and practice. A superstitious reverence for the dead confined both the Greeks and the Arabians to the dissection of apes and quadrupeds; the more solid and visible parts were known in the time of Galen, and the finer scrutiny of the human frame was reserved for the microscope and the injections of modern artists. Botany is an active science, and the discoveries of the torrid zone might enrich the herbal of Dioscorides with two thousand plants. Some traditionary knowledge might be secreted in the temples and monasteries of Egypt; much useful experience had been acquired in the practice of arts and manufactures; but the *science* of chemistry owes its origin and improvement to the industry of the Saracens. They first invented and named the alembic for the purpose of distillation, analysed the substances of the three kingdoms of nature, tried the distinction and affinities of alcalis and acids, and converted the poisonous minerals into soft and salutary medicines. But the most eager search of Arabian chemistry was the transmutation of metals and the elixir of immortal health; the reason and the fortunes of thousands were evaporated in the crucibles of alchymy, and the consummation of the great work was promoted by the worthy aid of mystery, fable, and superstition.

Want of erudition, taste, and freedom

But the Moslems deprived themselves of the principal benefits of a familiar intercourse with Greece and Rome, the knowledge of antiquity, the purity of taste, and the freedom of thought. Confident in the riches of their native tongue, the Arabians disdained the study of any foreign idiom. The Greek interpreters were chosen among their Christian subjects; they formed their translations, sometimes on the original text, more frequently perhaps on a Syriac version; and in the crowd of astronomers

---

[78] See a good view of the progress of anatomy in Wotton (Reflections on ancient and modern Learning, p. 208-256). His reputation has been unworthily depreciated by the wits in the controversy of Boyle and Bentley.

[79] Bibliot. Arab. Hispana, tom. i. p. 275. Al Beithar [Abd Allāh al-Baitar] of Malaga, their greatest botanist, had travelled into Africa, Persia, and India.

[80] Dr. Watson (Elements of Chemistry, vol. i. p. 17, &c.) allows the *original* merit of the Arabians. Yet he quotes the modest confession of the famous Geber of the ninth century (d'Herbelot, p. 387), that he had drawn most of his science, perhaps of the transmutation of metals, from the ancient sages. Whatever might be the origin or extent of their knowledge, the arts of chemistry and alchymy appear to have been known in Egypt at least three hundred years before Mahomet (Wotton's Reflections, p. 121-133. Pauw, Recherches sur les Egyptiens et les Chinois, tom. i. p. 376-429). [The names alcali, alcohol, alembic, *al*chymy, &c., show the influence of the Arabians on the study of chemistry in the West.]

and physicians there is no example of a poet, an orator, or even an historian being taught to speak the language of the Saracens.[81] The mythology of Homer would have provoked the abhorrence of those stern fanatics ; they possessed in lazy ignorance the colonies of the Macedonians, and the provinces of Carthage and Rome : the heroes of Plutarch and Livy were buried in oblivion ; and the history of the world before Mahomet was reduced to a short legend of the patriarchs, the prophets, and the Persian kings.  Our education in the Greek and Latin schools may have fixed in our minds a standard of exclusive taste ; and I am not forward to condemn the literature and judgment of nations of whose language I am ignorant.  Yet I *know* that the classics have much to teach, and I *believe* that the Orientals have much to learn ; the temperate dignity of style, the graceful proportions of art, the forms of visible and intellectual beauty, the just delineation of character and passion, the rhetoric of narrative and argument, the regular fabric of epic and dramatic poetry.[82]  The influence of truth and reason is of a less ambiguous complexion. The philosophers of Athens and Rome enjoyed the blessings, and asserted the rights, of civil and religious freedom.  Their moral and political writings might have gradually unlocked the fetters of Eastern despotism, diffused a liberal spirit of enquiry and toleration, and encouraged the Arabian sages to suspect that their caliph was a tyrant and their prophet an impostor.[83]  The instinct of superstition was alarmed by the introduction even of the abstract sciences ; and the more rigid doctors of the law condemned the rash and pernicious curiosity of Almamon.[84]  To the thirst of martyrdom, the vision of paradise, and the belief of predestination, we must ascribe the invincible enthusiasm of the

---

[81] Abulpharagius (Dynast. p. 26, 148) mentions a *Syriac* version of Homer's two poems, by Theophilus, a Christian Maronite of Mount Libanus, who professed astronomy at Roha or Edessa towards the end of the eighth century.  His work would be a literary curiosity.  I have read somewhere, but I do not believe, that Plutarch's Lives were translated into Turkish for the use of Mahomet the Second.

[82] I have perused with much pleasure Sir William Jones's Latin Commentary on Asiatic Poetry (London, 1774, in octavo), which was composed in the youth of that wonderful linguist.  At present, in the maturity of his taste and judgment, he would perhaps abate of the fervent, and even partial, praise which he has bestowed on the Orientals.

[83] Among the Arabian philosophers, Averroes has been accused of despising the religion of the Jews, the Christians, and the Mahometans (see his article in Bayle's Dictionary).  Each of these sects would agree that in two instances out of three his contempt was reasonable.

[84] D'Herbelot, Bibliothèque Orientale, p. 546.  [Abd Allāh al-Mamūn (813-833 A.D.).]

prince and people.   And the sword of the Saracens became less formidable, when their youth was drawn away from the camp to the college, when the armies of the faithful presumed to read and to reflect.   Yet the foolish vanity of the Greeks was jealous of their studies, and reluctantly imparted the sacred fire to the barbarians of the East.[85]

In the bloody conflict of the Ommiades and Abbassides, the Greeks had stolen the opportunity of avenging their wrongs and enlarging their limits.   But a severe retribution was exacted by Mohadi,[86] the third caliph of the new dynasty, who seized in his turn the favourable opportunity, while a woman and a child, Irene and Constantine, were seated on the Byzantine throne.   An army of ninety-five thousand Persians and Arabs was sent from the Tigris to the Thracian Bosphorus, under the command of Harun,[87] or Aaron, the second son of the commander of the faithful.   His encampment on the opposite heights of Chrysopolis, or Scutari, informed Irene, in her palace of Constantinople, of the loss of her troops and provinces.   With the consent or connivance of their sovereign, her ministers subscribed an ignominious peace ; and the exchange of some royal gifts could not disguise the annual tribute of seventy thousand dinars of gold, which was imposed on the Roman empire.   The Saracens had too rashly advanced into the midst of a distant and hostile land ; their retreat was solicited by the promise of faithful guides and plentiful markets ; and not a Greek had courage to whisper that their weary forces might be surrounded and destroyed in their necessary passage between a slippery mountain and the river Sangarius.   Five years after this expedition, Harun ascended the throne of his father and his elder brother ;[88] the most powerful and vigorous monarch of his race, illustrious in the West as the ally of Charlemagne, and familiar to the most childish readers as the perpetual hero of the Arabian tales.   His title to the

---

[85] Θεόφιλος ἄτοπον κρίνας εἰ τὴν τῶν ὄντων γνῶσιν, δι' ἣν τὸ Ῥωμαίων γένος θαυμάζεται, ἔκδοτον ποιήσει τοῖς ἔθνεσι, &c. ; Cedrenus, p. 548 [ii. p. 169, ed. Bonn], who relates how manfully the emperor refused a mathematician to the instances and offers of the caliph Almamon.   This absurd scruple is expressed almost in the same words by the continuator of Theophanes (Scriptores post Theophanem, p. 118 [p. 190, ed. Bonn]).   [The continuation of Theophanes is the source of Scylitzes, who was the source of Cedrenus.]

[86] [Al-Mahdī Mohammad ibn Mansūr, A.D. 775-785.]

[87] See the reign and character of Harun al Rashid [Hārūn ar-Rashīd, caliph 786-809 A.D.], in the Bibliothèque Orientale, p. 431-433, under his proper title ; and in the relative articles to which M. d'Herbelot refers.   That learned collector has shewn much taste in stripping the Oriental chronicles of their instructive and amusing anecdotes.

[88] [Abū Mohammad Mūsā Al-Hādī, A.D. 785-6.]

name of *Al Rashid* (the *Just*) is sullied by the extirpation of the generous, perhaps the innocent, Barmecides ; yet he could listen to the complaint of a poor widow who had been pillaged by his troops, and who dared, in a passage of the Koran, to threaten the inattentive despot with the judgment of God and posterity. His court was adorned with luxury and science ; but, in a reign [A.D. 786-807] of three-and-twenty years, Harun repeatedly visited his provinces from Chorasan to Egypt ; nine times he performed the pilgrimage of Mecca ; eight times he invaded the territories of the Romans ; and, as often as they declined the payment of the tribute, they were taught to feel that a month of depredation was more costly than a year of submission. But, when the un- [A.D. 802] natural mother of Constantine was deposed and banished, her successor Nicephorus resolved to obliterate this badge of servitude and disgrace. The epistle of the emperor to the caliph was pointed with an allusion to the game of chess, which had already spread from Persia to Greece. " The queen (he spoke of Irene) considered you as a rook and herself as a pawn. That pusillanimous female submitted to pay a tribute, the double of which she ought to have exacted from the barbarians. Restore therefore the fruits of your injustice, or abide the determination of the sword " At these words the ambassadors cast a bundle of swords before the foot of the throne. The caliph smiled at the menace, and drawing his scymetar, *samsamah,* a weapon of historic or fabulous renown,[88a] he cut asunder the feeble arms of the Greeks, without turning the edge or endangering the temper of his blade. He then dictated an epistle of tremendous brevity : " In the name of the most merciful God, Harun al Rashid, commander of the faithful, to Nicephorus, the Roman dog. I have read thy letter, O thou son of an unbelieving mother. Thou shalt not hear, thou shalt behold, my reply." It was written in characters of blood and fire on the plains of Phrygia ; and the warlike celerity of the Arabs could only be checked by the arts of deceit and the show of repentance. The triumphant caliph retired, after the fatigues of the campaign, to his favourite palace of Racca, on the Euphrates ; [89] but the distance of five hundred

---

[88a] [Samsāma,= " inflexible sword," was particularly the name of the sword of the Arab hero Amr ibn Madi Kerib.]

[89] For the situation of Racca, the old Nicephorium, consult d'Anville (l'Euphrate et le Tigre, p. 24-27). The Arabian Nights represent Harun al Rashid as almost stationary in Bagdad. He respected the royal seat of the Abbassides, but the vices of the inhabitants had driven him from the city (Abulfed. Annal. p. 167). [" The extirpation of the Barmecides made such a bad impression in Bagdad, where the family was held in high respect, that Harun was probably induced thereby to transfer his residence to Rakka." Weil, *op. cit.*, vol. ii. p. 144.]

[A.D. 808]

miles, and the inclemency of the season, encouraged his adversary
to violate the peace.   Nicephorus was astonished by the bold and
rapid march of the commander of the faithful, who repassed, in
the depth of winter, the snows of mount Taurus : his stratagems
of policy and war were exhausted ; and the perfidious Greek
escaped with three wounds from a field of battle overspread with
forty thousand of his subjects.[90]   Yet the emperor was ashamed
of submission, and the caliph was resolved on victory.   One hundred and thirty-five thousand regular soldiers received pay, and
were inscribed in the military roll ; and above three hundred
thousand persons of every denomination marched under the
black standard of the Abbassides.   They swept the surface of
Asia Minor far beyond Tyana and Ancyra, and invested the
Pontic Heraclea,[91] once a flourishing state, now a paltry town ;
at that time capable of sustaining in her antique walls a month's

[A.D. 806]

siege against the forces of the East.   The ruin was complete, the
spoil was ample ; but, if Harun had been conversant with Grecian
story, he would have regretted the statue of Hercules, whose
attributes, the club, the bow, the quiver, and the lion's hide,
were sculptured in massy gold.   The progress of desolation by
sea and land, from the Euxine to the isle of Cyprus, compelled
the emperor Nicephorus to retract his haughty defiance.   In the
new treaty, the ruins of Heraclea were left for ever as a lesson
and a trophy ; and the coin of the tribute was marked with the
image and superscription of Harun and his three sons.[92]   Yet
this plurality of lords might contribute to remove the dishonour
of the Roman name.   After the death of their father, the heirs
of the caliph were involved in civil discord, and the conqueror,

[90] [Acc. to Arabic authorities Hārūn himself invaded Asia Minor twice in A.D.
803.   The first time he appeared before Heraclea and the promise of tribute induced him to retreat ; but the tribute was not paid and he repassed the Taurus at
the end of the year to exact it.   The battle in which 40,000 Greeks are said to have
fallen was fought in the following year, A.D. 804, but Hārūn's general, Jabril, led
the invaders.   Heraclea was not taken till a subsequent campaign, A.D. 806.   Cp.
Weil, op. cit., ii. p. 159-60.   Tabāri, ed. de Goeje, iii. 695-8.]

[91] M. de Tournefort, in his coasting voyage from Constantinople to Trebizond,
passed a night at Heraclea or Eregri.   His eye surveyed the present state, his
reading collected the antiquities of the city (Voyage du Levant, tom. iii. lettre xvi.
p. 23-35).   We have a separate history of Heraclea in the fragments of Memnon,
which are preserved by Photius.

[92] The wars of Harun al Rashid against the Roman empire are related by
Theophanes (p. 384, 385, 391, 396, 407, 408 [sub A.M. 6274, 6281, 6287, 6298, 6300]),
Zonaras (tom. ii. l. xv. p. 115, 124 [c. 10 and c. 15]), Cedrenus (p. 477, 478 [ii. p.
34, ed. Bonn]), Eutychius (Annal. tom. ii. p. 407), Elmacin (Hist. Saracen. p.
136, 151, 152), Abulpharagius (Dynast. p. 147, 151), and Abulfeda (p. 156, 166-
168).   [Add Tabari, ed. cit., 701, 708-10 (A.H. 187-190).   See Weil, op. cit., ii. p.
155 sqq.]

the liberal Almamon, was sufficiently engaged in the restoration of domestic peace and the introduction of foreign science.

Under the reign of Almamon at Bagdad, of Michael the Stammerer at Constantinople, the islands of Crete[93] and Sicily were subdued by the Arabs. The former of these conquests is disdained by their own writers, who were ignorant of the fame of Jupiter and Minos, but it has not been overlooked by the Byzantine historians, who now begin to cast a clearer light on the affairs of their own times.[94]  A band of Andalusian volunteers, discontented with the climate or government of Spain, explored the adventures of the sea; but, as they sailed in no more than ten or twenty galleys, their warfare must be branded with the name of piracy.  As the subjects and sectaries of the *white* party, they might lawfully invade the dominions of the *black* caliphs.  A rebellious faction introduced them into Alexandria;[95] they cut in pieces both friends and foes, pillaged the churches and the mosques, sold above six thousand Christian captives, and maintained their station in the capital of Egypt, till they were oppressed by the forces and the presence of Almamon himself. From the mouth of the Nile to the Hellespont, the islands and sea-coasts, both of the Greeks and Moslems, were exposed to their depredations; they saw, they envied, they tasted the fertility of Crete, and soon returned with forty galleys to a more serious attack. The Andalusians wandered over the land fearless and unmolested;

The Arabs subdue the isle of Crete, A.D. 823

[93] The authors from whom I have learned the most of the ancient and modern state of Crete are Belon (Observations, &c., c. 3-20, Paris, 1555), Tournefort (Voyage du Levant, tom. i. lettre ii. et iii.), and Meursius (CRETA, in his works, tom. iii. p. 343-544). Although Crete is styled by Homer πίειρα, by Dionysius λιπαρή τε καὶ εὔβοτος, I cannot conceive that mountainous island to surpass, or even to equal, in fertility the greater part of Spain.

[94] The most authentic and circumstantial intelligence is obtained from the four books of the Continuation of Theophanes, compiled by the pen or the command of Constantine Porphyrogenitus, with the Life of his father Basil the Macedonian (Scriptores post Theophanem, p. 1-162, a Francis. Combefis., Paris, 1685). The loss of Crete and Sicily is related, l. ii. p. 46-52.  To these we may add the secondary evidence of Joseph Genesius (l. ii. p. 21, Venet. 1733 [p. 46-49, ed. Bonn]), George Cedrenus (Compend. p. 506-508 [ii. p. 92 *sqq.* ed. Bonn]), and John Scylitzes Curopalata (apud Baron. Annal. Eccles. A.D. 827, No. 24, &c.).  But the modern Greeks are such notorious plagiaries that I should only quote a plurality of names. [These historiographical implications are not quite correct. Genesius is not a "secondary" authority in relation to the Scriptores post Theophanem; on the contrary, he is a source of the Continuation of Theophanes. See above, Appendix 1 to vol. 5, p. 504; for the sources of Genesius himself, *ib.* p. 503. The order of "plagiarism" is (1) Genesius, (2) Continuation of Theophanes, (3) Scylitzes, (4) Cedrenus.]

[95] Renaudot (Hist. Patriarch. Alex. p. 251-256, 268-270) has described the ravages of the Andalusian Arabs in Egypt, but has forgot to connect them with the conquest of Crete.  [Tabari places the conquest of Crete in A.H. 210.]

but, when they descended with their plunder to the sea-shore,
[Abu Hafs] their vessels were in flames, and their chief, Abu Caab, confessed
himself the author of the mischief. Their clamours accused his
madness or treachery. "Of what do you complain?" replied
the crafty emir. "I have brought you to a land flowing with milk
and honey. Here is your true country; repose from your toils,
and forget the barren place of your nativity." "And our wives
and children?" "Your beauteous captives will supply the place
of your wives, and in their embraces you will soon become the
fathers of a new progeny." The first habitation was their camp,
with a ditch and rampart, in the bay of Suda; but an apostate
monk led them to a more desirable position in the eastern parts;
[Khandak] and the name of Candax, their fortress and colony, had been extended to the whole island, under the corrupt and modern appellation of *Candia*. The hundred cities of the age of Minos
were diminished to thirty; and of these, only one, most probably
Cydonia, had courage to retain the substance of freedom and
the profession of Christianity. The Saracens of Crete soon repaired the loss of their navy; and the timbers of mount Ida were
launched into the main. During an hostile period, of one hundred and thirty-eight years, the princes of Constantinople attacked
these licentious corsairs with fruitless curses and ineffectual arms.

and of Sicily, The loss of Sicily [96] was occasioned by an act of superstitious
A.D. 827-878
rigour. An amorous youth, who had stolen a nun from her
cloister, was sentenced by the emperor to the amputation of his
[A.D. 826] tongue. Euphemius [97] appealed to the reason and policy of the
Saracens of Africa; and soon returned with the Imperial purple,
a fleet of one hundred ships, and an army of seven hundred horse

[96] Δηλοῖ (says the continuator of Theophanes, l. ii. p. 51 [p. 32, ed. Bonn]) δὲ
ταῦτα σαφέστατα καὶ πλατικώτερον ἡ τότε γραφεῖσα Θεογνώστῳ καὶ εἰς χεῖρας ἐλθοῦσα ἡμῶν.
This [contemporary] history of the loss of Sicily is no longer extant. Muratori
(Annali d'Italia, tom. vii. p. 7, 19, 21, &c.) has added some circumstances from the
Italian chronicles. [For the Saracens in Sicily the chief modern work is M. Amari's
Storia dei Musulmani di Sicilia, in 3 vols. (1854-68). The same scholar published
a collection of Arabic texts relating to the history of Sicily (1857) and an Italian
translation thereof (Bibloteca arabo-sicula, 2 vols., 1880, 1889). There had been
several previous Saracen descents on Sicily: in A.D. 652 (the island was defended
by the Exarch Olympius); in A.D. 669 Syracuse was plundered. Both these invasions were from Syria. Then in A.D. 704 the descents from Africa began under
Mūsā with the destruction of an unnamed town on the west coast, which Amari
has identified with Lilybæum. The new town of Marsa-Ali (Marsala) took its
place. In 705 Syracuse was plundered again; and the island was repeatedly invaded
in the eighth century. A. Holm has summarised these invasions in vol. 3 of his
Geschichte Siciliens im Alterthum (1898), p. 316 *sqq.*]

[97] [Euphemius revolted and declared himself Emperor in A.D. 826. See Amari,
Storia d. Mus., i. 239 *sqq.* He was soon thrust aside by the Saracens. His name
survives in the name of the town Calatafimi.]

and ten thousand foot.   They landed at Mazara near the ruins [June 13, A.D. 827] of the ancient Selinus ; but, after some partial victories, Syracuse [98] was delivered by the Greeks, the apostate was slain before her walls, and his African friends were reduced to the necessity of feeding on the flesh of their own horses.   In their turn they were relieved by a powerful [99] reinforcement of their brethren of Andalusia ; the largest and western part of the island was gradually reduced, and the commodious harbour of Palermo was chosen [A.D. 831] for the seat of the naval and military power of the Saracens. Syracuse preserved about fifty years the faith which she had sworn to Christ and to Cæsar.   In the last and fatal siege, her citizens displayed some remnant of the spirit which had formerly [Siege of Syracuse. A.D. 877-8] resisted the powers of Athens and Carthage.   They stood about twenty days against the battering-rams and *catapultae*, the mines and tortoises of the besiegers ; and the place might have been relieved, if the mariners of the Imperial fleet had not been detained at Constantinople in building a church to the Virgin Mary.   The deacon Theodosius, with the bishop and clergy, was dragged in chains from the altar to Palermo, cast into a subterraneous dungeon, and exposed to the hourly peril of death or apostacy. His pathetic, and not inelegant, complaint may be read as the epitaph of his country.[100]   From the Roman conquest to this [May 21, A.D. 878] final calamity, Syracuse, now dwindled to the primitive isle of Ortygia, had insensibly declined.   Yet the relics were still precious ; the plate of the cathedral weighed five thousand pounds of silver ; the entire spoil was computed at one million of pieces of gold (about four hundred thousand pounds sterling) ; and the captives [Capture of Taormina. A.D. 902, Aug. 1] must out-number the seventeen thousand Christians who were transported from the sack of Tauromenium into African servitude. In Sicily the religion and language of the Greeks were eradi-

[98] The splendid and interesting tragedy of *Tancrede* would adapt itself much better to this epoch than to the date (A.D. 1005) which Voltaire himself has chosen. But I must gently reproach the poet for infusing into the Greek subjects the spirit of modern knights and ancient republicans.

[99] [Hardly powerful ; the important help which led to the capture of Palermo came from Africa in A.D. 830.   The invaders tried hard to take the fortress of Henna, but did not succeed till 859.]

[100] The narrative or lamentation of Theodosius is transcribed and illustrated by Pagi (Critica, tom. iii. p. 719, &c.).   Constantine Porphyrogenitus (in Vit. Basil. c. 69, 70, p. 190-192) mentions the loss of Syracuse and the triumph of the demons. [The letter of Theodosius to his friend Leo on the capture of Syracuse is published in Hase's ed. of Leo Diaconus (Paris, 1819), p. 177 *sqq.*—It may be well to summarise the progress of the Saracen conquest of Sicily chronologically : Mazara captured 827 ;   Mineo 828 ;   Palermo 831 ;   c. 840, Caltabellotta and other places ; 847 Leontini ;   848 Ragusa ;   853 Camarina ;   858 Gagliano and Cefalù ;   859 Henna ; 868-70 Malta ;   878 Syracuse ;   902 Taormina, Rametta, Catania.]

cated; and such was the docility of the rising generation that fifteen thousand boys were circumcised and clothed on the same day with the son of the Fatimite caliph. The Arabian squadrons issued from the harbours of Palermo, Biserta, and Tunis; an hundred and fifty towns of Calabria and Campania were attacked and pillaged; nor could the suburbs of Rome be defended by the name of the Cæsars and Apostles. Had the Mahometans been united, Italy must have fallen an easy and glorious accession to the empire of the prophet. But the caliphs of Bagdad had lost their authority in the West; the Aglabites and Fatimites usurped the provinces of Africa; their emirs of Sicily aspired to independence; and the design of conquest and dominion was degraded to a repetition of predatory inroads.[101]

Invasion of<br>Rome by the<br>Saracens.<br>A.D. 846
In the sufferings of prostrate Italy, the name of Rome awakens a solemn and mournful recollection. A fleet of Saracens from the African coast presumed to enter the mouth of the Tiber, and to approach a city which even yet, in her fallen state, was revered as the metropolis of the Christian world. The gates and ramparts were guarded by a trembling people; but the tombs and temples of St. Peter and St. Paul were left exposed in the suburbs of the Vatican and of the Ostian way. Their invisible sanctity had protected them against the Goths, the Vandals, and the Lombards; but the Arabs disdained both the gospel and the legend; and their rapacious spirit was approved and animated by the precepts of the Koran. The Christian *idols* were stripped of their costly offerings; a silver altar was torn away from the shrine of St. Peter; and, if the bodies or the buildings were left entire, their deliverance must be imputed to the haste, rather than the scruples, of the Saracens.[102] In their course along the Appian way, they pillaged Fundi and besieged Gayeta; but they had turned aside from the walls of Rome, and, by their divisions, the Capitol was saved from the yoke of the prophet of Mecca. The same danger still impended on the heads of the Roman people; and their domestic force was unequal to the assault of an African emir. They claimed the protection of their Latin sovereign;

[101] The extracts from the Arabic histories of Sicily are given in Abulfeda (Annal. Moslem. p. 271-273) and in the first volume of Muratori's Scriptores Rerum Italicarum. M. de Guignes (Hist. des Huns, tom. i. p. 363, 364) has added some important facts.

[102] [See the account in Gregorovius, Rome in the Middle Ages (E. T.), vol. 3, p. 87 *sqq*. Gregorovius describes the wealth of St. Peter's treasures at this time. Gibbon omits to mention that Guy of Spoleto relieved Rome.]

but the Carlovingian standard was overthrown by a detachment of the barbarians ; they meditated the restoration of the Greek emperors ; but the attempt was treasonable, and the succour remote and precarious.[103] Their distress appeared to receive some aggravation from the death of their spiritual and temporal chiefs ; but the pressing emergency superseded the forms and intrigues of an election ; and the unanimous choice of pope [A.D. 947] Leo the Fourth [104] was the safety of the church and city. This pontiff was born a Roman ; the courage of the first ages of the republic glowed in his breast ; and, amidst the ruins of his country, he stood erect, like one of the firm and lofty columns that rear their heads above the fragments of the Roman forum. The first days of his reign were consecrated to the purification and removal of relics, to prayers and processions, and to all the solemn offices of religion, which served at least to heal the imagination, and restore the hopes, of the multitude. The public defence had been long neglected, not from the presumption of peace, but from the distress and poverty of the times. As far as the scantiness of his means and the shortness of his leisure would allow, the ancient walls were repaired by the command of Leo ; fifteen towers, in the most accessible stations, were built or renewed ; two of these commanded on either side the Tiber ; and an iron chain was drawn across the stream, to impede the ascent of an hostile navy. The Romans were assured of a short respite by the welcome news that the siege of Gayeta had been raised and that a part of the enemy, with their sacrilegious plunder, had perished in the waves.

But the storm which had been delayed, soon burst upon them with redoubled violence. The Aglabite,[105] who reigned in Africa, and had inherited from his father a treasure and an [Victory and reign of Leo IV. A.D. 849]

[103] One of the most eminent Romans (Gratianus, magister militum et Romani palatii superista) was accused of declaring, Quia Franci nihil nobis boni faciunt, neque adjutorium præbent, sed magis quæ nostra sunt violenter tollunt. Quare non advocamus Græcos, et cum eis fœdus pacis componentes, Francorum regem et gentem de nostro regno et dominatione expellimus ? Anastasius in Leone IV. p. 199.

[104] Voltaire (Hist. Générale, tom. ii. c. 38, p. 124) appears to be remarkably struck with the character of pope Leo IV. I have borrowed his general expression ; but the sight of the forum has furnished me with a more distinct and lively image.

[105] De Guignes, Hist. Générale des Huns, tom. i. p. 363, 364. Cardonne, Hist. de l'Afrique et de l'Espagne, sous la Domination des Arabes, tom. ii. p. 24, 25. I observe, and cannot reconcile, the difference of these writers in the succession of the Aglabites. [The Aghlabid who reigned at this time was Mohammad I. (840-856). For the succession see S. Lane-Poole, Mohammadan Dynasties, p. 37.]

army : a fleet of Arabs and Moors, after a short refreshment in
the harbours of Sardinia, cast anchor before the mouth of the
Tiber, sixteen miles from the city ; and their discipline and
numbers appeared to threaten, not a transient inroad, but a
serious design of conquest and dominion. But the vigilance of
Leo had formed an alliance with the vassals of the Greek
empire, the free and maritime states of Gayeta, Naples, and
Amalfi ; and in the hour of danger their galleys appeared in the
port of Ostia, under the command of Cæsarius, the son of the
Neapolitan duke, a noble and valiant youth, who had already
vanquished the fleets of the Saracens. With his principal companions, Cæsarius was invited to the Lateran palace, and the
dexterous pontiff affected to inquire their errand, and to accept,
with joy and surprise, their providential succour. The city
bands, in arms, attended their father at Ostia, where he reviewed and blessed his generous deliverers. They kissed his
feet, received the communion with martial devotion, and listened to the prayer of Leo, that the same God who had supported St. Peter and St. Paul on the waves of the sea would
strengthen the hands of his champions against the adversaries
of his holy name. After a similar prayer, and with equal resolution, the Moslems advanced to the attack of the Christian
galleys, which preserved their advantageous station along the
coast. The victory inclined to the side of the allies, when it
was less gloriously decided in their favour by a sudden tempest,
which confounded the skill and courage of the stoutest mariners. The Christians were sheltered in a friendly harbour,
while the Africans were scattered and dashed in pieces among
the rocks and islands of an hostile shore. Those who escaped
from shipwreck and hunger neither found nor deserved mercy
at the hands of their implacable pursuers.[106] The sword and
the gibbet reduced the dangerous multitude of captives ; and
the remainder was more usefully employed, to restore the
sacred edifices which they had attempted to subvert. The
pontiff, at the head of the citizens and allies, paid his grateful
devotion at the shrines of the apostles ; and, among the spoils
of this naval victory, thirteen Arabian bows of pure and massy
silver were suspended round the altar of the fishermen of
Galilee. The reign of Leo the Fourth was employed in the
defence and ornament of the Roman state : the churches were
renewed and embellished ; near four thousand pounds of silver

[106] [The battle of Ostia is the subject of a fresco of Raffaelle in the Vatican.]

were consecrated to repair the losses of St. Peter; and his sanctuary was decorated with a plate of gold the weight of two hundred and sixteen pounds; embossed with the portraits of the pope and emperor, and encircled with a string of pearls. Yet this vain magnificence reflects less glory on the character of Leo than the paternal care with which he rebuilt the walls of Horta and Ameria; and transported the wandering inhabitants of Centumcellæ to his new foundation of Leopolis, twelve miles from the seashore.[107]   By his liberality a colony of Corsicans, with their wives and children, was planted in the station of Porto at the mouth of the Tiber; the falling city was [Rebuilding of Portus] restored for their use, the fields and vineyards were divided among the new settlers; their first efforts were assisted by a gift of horses and cattle; and the hardy exiles, who breathed revenge against the Saracens, swore to live and die under the standard of St. Peter.   The nations of the West and North, who visited the threshold of the apostles, had gradually formed the large and populous suburb of the Vatican, and their various habitations were distinguished, in the language of the times, as the *schools* of the Greeks and Goths, of the Lombards and Saxons.   But this venerable spot was still open to sacrilegious insult; the design of inclosing it with walls and towers exhausted all that authority could command or charity would supply; and the pious labour of four years was animated in every season, and at every hour, by the presence of the indefatigable pontiff.   The love of fame, a generous but worldly passion, may be detected in the name of the *Leonine city*, which Foundation of the Leonine he bestowed on the Vatican; yet the pride of the dedication city. A.D. was tempered with Christian penance and humility.   The 852 boundary was trod by the bishop and his clergy, barefoot, in sackcloth and ashes; the songs of triumph were modulated to psalms and litanies; the walls were besprinkled with holy water; and the ceremony was concluded with a prayer that, under the guardian care of the apostles and the angelic host,

---

[107] Beretti (Chorographia Italiæ Medii Ævi, p. 106, 108) has illustrated Centumcellæ, Leopolis, Civitas Leonina, and the other places of the Roman duchy. [Leopolis never flourished.   For the walls of the Leonine city see Gregorovius, *op. cit.*, p. 97 *sqq.*   The fortification of the Vatican had been already designed and begun by Pope Leo III.   "The line of Leo the Fourth's walls, built almost in the form of a horseshoe, is still in part preserved, and may be traced in the Borgo near the passage of Alexander the Sixth, near the Mint or the papal garden as far as the thick corner tower, also in the line of the Porta Pertusa, and at the point where the walls form a bend between another corner tower and the Porta Fabrica."   Gregorovius, *ib.*, p. 98.]

both the old and the new Rome might ever be preserved pure, prosperous, and impregnable.[108]

The emperor Theophilus, son of Michael the Stammerer, was one of the most active and high-spirited princes who reigned at Constantinople during the middle age. In offensive or defensive war, he marched in person five times against the Saracens, formidable in his attack, esteemed by the enemy in his losses and defeats. In the last of these expeditions he penetrated into Syria, and besieged the obscure town of Sozopetra : the casual [Mutasim] birth-place of the caliph Motassem, whose father Harun was attended in peace or war by the most favourite of his wives and concubines. The revolt of a Persian impostor employed at that moment the arms of the Saracen, and he could only intercede in favour of a place for which he felt and acknowledged some degree of filial affection. These solicitations determined the emperor to wound his pride in so sensible a part. Sozopetra was levelled with the ground, the Syrian prisoners were marked or mutilated with ignominious cruelty, and a thousand female captives were forced away from the adjacent territory. Among these a matron of the house of Abbas invoked, in an agony of despair, the name of Motassem ; and the insults of the Greeks engaged the honour of her kinsman to avenge his indignity and to answer her appeal. Under the reign of the two elder brothers, the inheritance of the youngest had been confined to Anatolia, Armenia, Georgia, and Circassia ; this frontier station had exercised his military talents ; and, among his accidental claims to the name of *Octonary*,[109] the most meritorious are the *eight* battles which he gained or fought against the enemies of the Koran. In this personal quarrel, the troops of Irak, Syria, and Egypt, were recruited from the tribes of Arabia and the Turkish hordes : his cavalry might be numerous, though we should deduct some myriads from the hundred and thirty thousand horses of the royal stables ; and the expense of the

---

[108] The Arabs and the Greeks are alike silent concerning the invasion of Rome by the Africans. The Latin chronicles do not afford much instruction (see the Annals of Baronius and Pagi). Our authentic and contemporary guide for the Popes of the ixth century is Anastasius, librarian of the Roman church. His Life of Leo IV. contains twenty-four pages (p. 175-199, edit. Paris) ; and, if a great part consists of superstitious trifles, we must blame or commend his hero, who was much oftener in a church than in a camp.

[109] The same number was applied to the following circumstance in the life of Motassem : he was the *eighth* of the Abbassides ; he reigned *eight* years, *eight* months, and *eight* days ; left *eight* sons, *eight* daughters, *eight* thousand slaves, *eight* millions of gold.

armament was computed at four millions sterling, or one hundred thousand pounds of gold. From Tarsus, the place of assembly, the Saracens advanced in three divisions along the high road of Constantinople : Motassem himself commanded the centre, and the vanguard was given to his son Abbas, who, in the trial of the first adventures, might succeed with the more glory, or fail with the least reproach. In the revenge of his injury, the caliph prepared to retaliate a similar affront. The father of Theophilus was a native of Amorium [110] in Phrygia ; the original seat of the imperial house had been adorned with privileges and monuments ; and, whatever might be the indifference of the people, Constantinople itself was scarcely of more value in the eyes of the sovereign and his court. The name of AMORIUM was inscribed on the shields of the Saracens ; and their three armies were again united under the walls of the devoted city. It had been proposed by the wisest counsellors to evacuate Amorium, to remove the inhabitants, and to abandon the empty structures to the vain resentment of the barbarians. The emperor embraced the more generous resolution of defending, in a siege and battle, the country of his ancestors. When the armies drew near, the front of the Mahometan line appeared to a Roman eye more closely planted with spears and javelins ; but the event of the action was not glorious on either side to the national troops. The Arabs were broken, but it was by the swords of thirty thousand Persians, who had obtained service and settlement in the Byzantine empire. The Greeks were repulsed and vanquished, but it was by the arrows of the Turkish cavalry ; and, had not their bow-strings been damped and relaxed by the evening rain, very few of the Christians could have escaped with the emperor from the field of battle. They breathed at Dorylæum, at the distance of three days ; and Theophilus, reviewing his trembling squadrons, forgave the common flight both of the prince and people. After this discovery of his weakness, he vainly hoped to deprecate the fate of Amorium : the inexorable caliph rejected with contempt his prayers and promises ; and detained the Roman ambassadors to be the witnesses of his great revenge. They had nearly been the witnesses of his shame.

[110] Amorium is seldom mentioned by the old geographers, and totally forgotten in the Roman Itineraries. After the vith century it became an episcopal see, and at length the metropolis of the new Galatia [formed by Theodosius the Great] (Carol. Sancto Paulo, Geograph. Sacra, p. 234). The city rose again from its ruins, if we should read *Ammuria* not *Anguria*, in the text of the Nubian geographer, p. 236. [The site is near Hanza Hadji. See Hamilton, Researches in Asia Minor, i. p. 451 ; Ramsay, Asia Minor, p. 230-1.]

The vigorous assaults of fifty-five days were encountered by a
faithful governor, a veteran garrison, and a desperate people ;
and the Saracens must have raised the siege if a domestic traitor
had not pointed to the weakest part of the wall, a place which
was decorated with the statues of a lion and a bull. The vow
of Motassem was accomplished with unrelenting rigour ; tired,
rather than satiated, with destruction, he returned to his new
palace of Samara, in the neighbourhood of Bagdad, while the
*unfortunate* [111] Theophilus implored the tardy and doubtful aid of
his Western rival, the emperor of the Franks. Yet in the siege
of Amorium above seventy thousand Moslems had perished ;
their loss had been revenged by the slaughter of thirty thousand
Christians, and the sufferings of an equal number of captives,
who were treated as the most atrocious criminals. Mutual
necessity could sometimes extort the exchange or ransom of
prisoners ; [112] but in the national religious conflict of the two
empires peace was without confidence, and war without mercy.
Quarter was seldom given in the field ; those who escaped the
edge of the sword were condemned to hopeless servitude or
exquisite torture ; and a Catholic emperor relates, with visible
satisfaction, the execution of the Saracens of Crete, who were
flayed alive, or plunged into caldrons of boiling oil.[113] To a
point of honour Motassem had sacrificed a flourishing city, two
hundred thousand lives, and the property of millions. The
same caliph descended from his horse and dirtied his robe to
relieve the distress of a decrepit old man, who with his laden
ass had tumbled into a ditch. On which of these actions did

[Samarra supersedes Bagdad for 55 years. A.D. 836-892]

[111] In the East he was styled Δυστυχής (Continuator Theophan. l. iii. p. 84 [p. 135, l. 10, ed. Bonn]) ; but such was the ignorance of the West that his ambassadors, in public discourse, might boldly narrate, de victoriis, quas adversus exteras bellando gentes cœlitus fuerat assecutus (Annalist. Bertinian. apud Pagi, tom. iii. p. 720 [Pertz, Mon. i. 434]). [For Samarrā cp. Le Strange in Journal As. Soc. vol. 27, p. 36.]

[112] Abulpharagius (Dynast. p. 167, 168) relates one of these singular transactions on the bridge of the river Lamus [Lamas Su] in Cilicia, the limit of the two empires, and one day's journey westward of Tarsus (d'Anville, Géographie Ancienne, tom. ii. p. 91). Four thousand four hundred and sixty Moslems, eight hundred women and children, one hundred confederates, were exchanged for an equal number of Greeks. They passed each other in the middle of the bridge, and, when they reached their respective friends, they shouted *Allah Acbar*, and *Kyrie Eleison*. Many of the prisoners of Amorium were probably among them, but in the same year (A.H. 231) the most illustrious of them, the forty-two martyrs, were beheaded by the caliph's order. [For exchanges of prisoners on the Lamos see also Theoph. Contin. p. 443, ed. Bonn.] By the kindness of M. A. Vasil 'ev I have received his revised Greek text of the Martyrium of the forty-two Amorian Martyrs, published in 1898 (Grecheski tekst zhitiia soroka dvuch amoriiskich muchenikov ; in the Mémoires of the St. Petersburg Academy, Cl. Hist.-Phil.).

[113] Constantin. Porphyrogenitus, in Vit. Basil. c. 61, p. 186. These Saracens were indeed treated with peculiar severity as pirates and renegadoes.

he reflect with the most pleasure, when he was summoned by the angel of death ?[114]

With Motassem, the eighth of the Abbassides, the glory of his family and nation expired.   When the Arabian conquerors had spread themselves over the East, and were mingled with the servile crowds of Persia, Syria, and Egypt, they insensibly lost the freeborn and martial virtues of the desert.   The courage of the South is the artificial fruit of discipline and prejudice ; the active power of enthusiasm had decayed, and the mercenary forces of the caliphs were recruited in those climates of the North, of which valour is the hardy and spontaneous production. Of the Turks [115] who dwelt upon the Oxus and Jaxartes, the robust youths, either taken in war or purchased in trade, were educated in the exercises of the field and the profession of the Mahometan faith.   The Turkish guards stood in arms round the throne of their benefactor, and their chiefs usurped the dominion of the palace and the provinces.   Motassem, the first author of this dangerous example, introduced into the capital above fifty thousand Turks: their licentious conduct provoked the public indignation, and the quarrels of the soldiers and people induced the caliph to retire from Bagdad, and establish his own residence and the camp of his barbarian favourites at Samara on the Tigris, about twelve leagues above the city of Peace.[116]   His son Motawakkel was a jealous and cruel tyrant ; odious to his subjects, he cast himself on the fidelity of the strangers, and these strangers, ambitious and apprehensive, were tempted by the rich promise of a revolution.   At the instigation, or at least in the cause, of his son, they burst into his apartment at the hour of supper, and the caliph was cut into seven pieces by the same swords which he had recently distributed among the guards of his life and throne.   To this throne, yet streaming with a father's blood, Montasser was triumphantly led ; but in a

*Disorders of the Turkish guards.  A.D. 841-870, &c.*

*[Mutawakkil. A.D. 847-861]*

*[Muntasir. A.D. 861-2]*

[114] For Theophilus, Motassem, and the Amorian war, see the Continuator of Theophanes (l. iii. p. 77-84 [p. 124 *sqq.* ed. Bonn]), Genesius (l. iii. p. 24-34 [p. 51 *sqq.*]), Cedrenus (528-532 [li. 129 *sqq.* ed. Bonn]), Elmacin (Hist. Saracen. p. 180), Abulpharagius (Dynast. p. 165, 166), Abulfeda (Annal. Moslem. p. 191), d'Herbelot (Bibliot. Orientale, p. 639, 640).

[115] M. de Guignes, who sometimes leaps, and sometimes stumbles, in the gulf between Chinese and Mahometan story, thinks he can see that these Turks are the *Hoei-ke*, alias the *Kao-tche*, or *high-waggons ;* that they were divided into fifteen hordes, from China and Siberia to the dominions of the caliphs and Samanides, &c. (Hist. des Huns, tom. iii. p. 1-33, 124-131).

[116] He changed the old name of Sumere, or Samara, into the fanciful title of *Ser-men-rai*, that which gives pleasure at first (d'Herbelot, Bibliothèque Orientale, p. 808 ; d'Anville, l'Euphrate et le Tigre, p. 97, 98).   [*Surra men raä =* " who so saw, rejoiced ".]

reign of six months he found only the pangs of a guilty conscience.   If he wept at the sight of an old tapestry which represented the crime and punishment of the son of Chosroes ; if his days were abridged by grief and remorse, we may allow some pity to a parricide, who exclaimed, in the bitterness of death, that he had lost both this world and the world to come.   After this act of treason, the ensigns of royalty, the garment and walking staff of Mahomet, were given and torn away by the foreign mercenaries, who in four years created, deposed, and murdered three commanders of the faithful.   As often as the Turks were inflamed by fear, or rage, or avarice, these caliphs were dragged by the feet, exposed naked to the scorching sun, beaten with iron clubs, and compelled to purchase, by the abdication of their dignity, a short reprieve of inevitable fate.[117] At length, however, the fury of the tempest was spent or diverted ; the Abbassides returned to the less turbulent residence of Bagdad ; the insolence of the Turks was curbed with a firmer and more skilful hand, and their numbers were divided and destroyed in foreign warfare.   But the nations of the East had been taught to trample on the successors of the prophet ; and the blessings of domestic peace were obtained by the relaxation of strength and discipline.   So uniform are the mischiefs of military despotism that I seem to repeat the story of the prætorians of Rome.[118]

Rise and progress of the Carmathians A.D. 890-951   While the flame of enthusiasm was damped by the business, the pleasure, and the knowledge, of the age, it burned with concentrated heat in the breasts of the chosen few, the congenial spirits, who were ambitious of reigning either in this world or in the next.   How carefully soever the book of prophecy had been sealed by the apostle of Mecca, the wishes, and (if we may profane the word) even the reason, of fanaticism might believe that, after the successive missions of Adam, Noah, Abraham, Moses, Jesus, and Mahomet, the same God,

[117] Take a specimen, the death of the caliph Motaz : Correptum pedibus retrahunt, et sudibus probe permulcant, et spoliatum laceris vestibus in sole collocant, præ cujus acerrimo æstu pedes alternis attollebat et demittebat.   Adstantium aliquis misero colaphos continuo ingerebat, quos ille objectis manibus avertere studebat. . . . Quo facto traditus tortori fuit totoque triduo cibo potuque prohibitus. . . . Suffocatus, &c. (Abulfeda, p. 206).   Of the caliph Mohtadi, he says, cervices ipsi perpetuis ictibus contundebant, testiculosque pedibus conculcabant (p. 208).

[118] See under the reigns of Motassem, Motawakkel, Montasser, Mostain, Motaz, Mohtadi, and Motamed, in the Bibliothèque of d'Herbelot, and the now familiar annals of Elmacin, Abulpharagius, and Abulfeda.   [Mustāin, A.D. 862-6 ; Mutazz, A.D. 866-9 ; Muhtadi, A.D. 869-70 ; Mutamid, A.D. 870-92.]

in the fulness of time, would reveal a still more perfect and
permanent law.   In the two hundred and seventy-seventh year
of the Hegira, and in the neighbourhood of Cufa, an Arabian
preacher, of the name of Carmath,[119] assumed the lofty and [Hamdān ibn Ashath]
incomprehensible style of the Guide, the Director, the De-
monstration, the Word, the Holy Ghost, the Camel, the Herald
of the Messiah, who had conversed with him in a human shape,
and the representative of Mohammed the son of Ali, of St.
John the Baptist, and of the angel Gabriel.   In his mystic
volume, the precepts of the Koran were refined to a more
spiritual sense; he relaxed the duties of ablution, fasting, and
pilgrimage; allowed the indiscriminate use of wine and forbidden food; and nourished the fervour of his disciples by the
daily repetition of fifty prayers.   The idleness and ferment of
the rustic crowd awakened the attention of the magistrates of
Cufa; a timid persecution assisted the progress of the new
sect; and the name of the prophet became more revered after
his person had been withdrawn from the world.   His twelve
apostles dispersed themselves among the Bedoweens, "a race
of men," says Abulfeda, "equally devoid of reason and of
religion;" and the success of their preaching seemed to
threaten Arabia with a new revolution.   The Carmathians were
ripe for rebellion, since they disclaimed the title of the house
of Abbas and abhorred the worldly pomp of the caliphs of
Bagdad.   They were susceptible of discipline, since they vowed
a blind and absolute submission to their imam, who was called
to the prophetic office by the voice of God and the people.
Instead of the legal tithes, he claimed the fifth of their substance and spoil; the most flagitious sins were no more than
the type of disobedience; and the brethren were united and
concealed by an oath of secrecy.   After a bloody conflict, they [Their military ex-
ploits. A.D.
900, &c.]

[119] [The "Carmathian" movement has received its name, not from its origina-
tors, but from the man who placed himself at its head and organized it at Kūfa—
Hamdān ibn Ashath, called Carmath.   The true founder of the Carmathian movement was Abd Allāh ibn Maimun al-Kaddah, the active missionary of the Ismail-
ite doctrine.   This doctrine was that Ismail son of Jafar al-Sadik was the seventh
imam from Ali; and that Ismail's son Mohammad was the seventh prophet of the
world (of the other six, Adam, &c., are mentioned above, in the text)—the Mahdi
(or Messiah).   Mohammad had lived in the second half of the eighth century, but
he would come again.   Abd Allāh and his missionaries propagated their doctrines
far and wide; they sought to convert Sunnites as well as Shiites, and even Jews
and Christians.   To the Jews they represented the Mahdi as Messias; to the
Christians as the Paraclete.   Abd Allāh's son Ahmad continued his work, and it
was one of his missionaries who converted Carmath.   The new interpretations of
the Koran mentioned in the text were due not to Carmath, but to Abd Allāh.   See
Weil's account, op. cit., ii. p. 498 sqq.]

prevailed in the province of Bahrein, along the Persian Gulf; far and wide, the tribes of the desert were subject to the sceptre, or rather to the sword, of Abu Said and his son Abu Taher; and these rebellious imams could muster in the field an hundred and seven thousand fanatics. The mercenaries of the caliph were dismayed at the approach of an enemy who neither asked nor accepted quarter; and the difference between them in fortitude and patience is expressive of the change which three centuries of prosperity had effected in the character of the Arabians. Such troops were discomfited in every action; the cities of Racca and Baalbec, of Cufa and Bassora, were taken and pillaged; Bagdad was filled with consternation; and the caliph trembled behind the veils of his palace. In a daring inroad beyond the Tigris, Abu Taher advanced to the gates of the capital with no more than five hundred horse. By the special order of Moctader, the bridges had been broken down, and the person or head of the rebel was expected every hour by the commander of the faithful. His lieutenant, from a motive of fear or pity, apprised Abu Taher of his danger, and recommended a speedy escape. "Your master," said the intrepid Carmathian to the messenger, "is at the head of thirty thousand soldiers: three such men as these are wanting in his host:" at the same instant, turning to three of his companions, he commanded the first to plunge a dagger into his breast, the second to leap into the Tigris, and the third to cast himself headlong down a precipice. They obeyed without a murmur. "Relate," continued the imam, "what you have seen: before the evening your general shall be chained among my dogs." Before the evening, the camp was surprised and the menace was executed. The rapine of the Carmathians was sanctified by their aversion to the worship of Mecca: they robbed a caravan of pilgrims, and twenty thousand devout Moslems were abandoned on the burning sands to a death of hunger and thirst.[120]  Another year they suffered the pilgrims to proceed without interruption; but, in the festival of devotion, Abu Taher stormed the holy city and trampled on the most venerable relics of the Mahometan faith. Thirty thousand citizens and strangers were put to the sword; the sacred precincts were polluted by the burial of three thousand dead bodies; the well of Zemzem overflowed with blood; the golden spout was forced from its place; the veil of the Caaba was

[Abū Tahir Sulaiman]

[A.D. 923-924]

[A.D. 926]

[A.D. 906]

They pillage Mecca. A.D. 929

---

[120] [Abū Tahir also plundered pilgrim caravans in A.D. 924.]

divided among these impious sectaries; and the black stone, the first monument of the nation, was borne away in triumph to their capital. After this deed of sacrilege and cruelty, they continued to infest the confines of Irak, Syria, and Egypt; but the vital principle of enthusiasm had withered at the root. Their scruples or their avarice again opened the pilgrimage of Mecca and restored the black stone of the Caaba; and it is needless to inquire into what factions they were broken, or by whose swords they were finally extirpated. The sect of the Carmathians may be considered as the second visible cause of the decline and fall of the empire of the caliphs.[121]

The third and most obvious cause was the weight and magnitude of the empire itself. The caliph Almamon might proudly assert that it was easier for him to rule the East and the West than to manage a chess-board of two feet square; [122] yet I suspect that in both those games he was guilty of many fatal mistakes; and I perceive that in the distant provinces the authority of the first and most powerful of the Abbassides was already impaired. The analogy of despotism invests the representative with the full majesty of the prince; the division and balance of powers might relax the habits of obedience, might encourage the passive subject to inquire into the origin and administration of civil government. He who is born in the purple is seldom worthy to reign; but the elevation of a private man, of a peasant perhaps, or a slave, affords a strong presumption of his courage and capacity. The viceroy of a remote kingdom aspires to secure the property and inheritance of his precarious trust; the nations must rejoice in the presence of their sovereign; and the command of armies and treasures are at once the object and the instrument of his ambition. A change was scarcely visible as long as the lieutenants of the caliph were content with their vicarious title; while they solicited for themselves or their sons a renewal of the Imperial grant, and still maintained on the coin, and in the public prayers, the name and prerogative of the commander of the faithful. But in the long and hereditary exercise of power,

*Revolt of the provinces. A.D. 800-936*

---

[121] For the sect of the Carmathians, consult Elmacin (Hist. Saracen. p. 219, 224, 229, 231, 238, 241, 243), Abulpharagius (Dynast. p. 179-182), Abulfeda (Annal. Moslem. p. 218, 219, &c., 245, 265, 274), and d'Herbelot (Bibliothèque Orientale, p. 256-258, 635). I find some inconsistencies of theology and chronology, which it would not be easy nor of much importance to reconcile. [De Goeje, Mémoire sur les Carmathes du Bahraïn (1886).]

[122] Hyde, Syntagma Dissertat. tom. ii. p. 57, in Hist. Shahiludii. [Also: Al Nuwairi, in de Sacy, Exposé de la religion des Druzes, vol. i.]

they assumed the pride and attributes of royalty ; the alternative of peace or war, of reward or punishment, depended solely on their will ; and the revenues of their government were reserved for local services or private magnificence. Instead of a regular supply of men and money, the successors of the prophet were flattered with the ostentatious gift of an elephant, or a cask of hawks, a suit of silk hangings, or some pounds of musk and amber.[123]

The independent dynasties

After the revolt of Spain from the temporal and spiritual supremacy of the Abbassides, the first symptoms of disobedience broke forth in the province of Africa. Ibrahim, the son of Aglab, the lieutenant of the vigilant and rigid Harun, bequeathed to the dynasty of the *Aglabites* the inheritance of his name and power. The indolence or policy of the caliphs dissembled the injury and loss, and pursued only with poison the founder of the *Edrisites*,[124] who erected the kingdom and city of Fez on the shores of the western ocean.[125] In the East, the first dynasty was that of the *Taherites*,[126] the posterity of the valiant Taher, who, in the civil wars of the sons of Harun, had served with too much zeal and success the cause of Almamon

The Aglabites. A.D. 800-941 [909]

The Edrisites. A.D. 829-907

The Taherites. A.D. 813-872

---

[123] The dynasties of the Arabian empire may be studied in the Annals of Elmacin, Abulpharagius, and Abulfeda, under the *proper* years, in the dictionary of d'Herbelot, under the *proper* names. The tables of M. de Guignes (Hist. des Huns, tom. i.) exhibit a general chronology of the East, interspersed with some historical anecdotes; but his attachment to national blood has sometimes confounded the order of time and place.

[124] The Aglabites and Edrisites are the professed subject of M. de Cardonne (Hist. de l'Afrique et de l'Espagne sous la Domination des Arabes, tom. ii. p. 1-63). [The Aghlabid dynasty lasted from A.D. 800 to 909, when it gave way to the Fátimids. Its chief achievement was the conquest of Sicily. These princes also annexed Sardinia and Malta, and harried the Christian coasts of the Western Mediterranean.]

[125] To escape the reproach of error, I must criticize the inaccuracies of M. de Guignes (tom. i. p. 359) concerning the Edrisites.  1. The dynasty and city of Fez could not be founded in the year of the Hegira 173, since the founder was a *posthumous* child of a descendant of Ali, who fled from Mecca in the year 168.  2. This founder, Edris the son of Edris, instead of living to the improbable age of 120 years, A.H. 313, died A.H. 214, in the prime of manhood.  3. The dynasty ended A.H. 307, twenty-three years sooner than it is fixed by the historian of the Huns. See the accurate Annals of Abulfeda, p. 158, 159, 185, 238.  [Idrīs, who founded the dynasty of the Idrīsids, was great-great-grandson of Alī.  He revolted in Medīna against the caliph Mahdī in A.D. 785, and then he fled to Morocco, where he founded his dynasty (in A.D 788), which expired in A.D. 985.  For the succession cp. S. Lane-Poole, Mohammadan Dynasties, p. 35.]

[126] The dynasties of the Taherites and Soffarides, with the rise of that of the Samanides, are described in the original history and Latin version of Mirchond ; yet the most interesting facts had already been drained by the diligence of M. d'Herbelot.  [Tāhir was appointed governor of Khurāsān in A.D. 820 ; he and his successors professed to be vassals of the Caliphs.]

the younger brother.  He was sent into honourable exile, to
command on the banks of the Oxus ; and the independence of
his successors, who reigned in Chorasan till the fourth generation, was palliated by their modest and respectful demeanour,
the happiness of their subjects, and the security of their frontier.
They were supplanted by one of those adventurers so frequent
in the annals of the East, who left his trade of a brazier (from
whence the name of *Soffarides*) for the profession of a robber. The Soffarides. A.D
In a nocturnal visit to the treasure of the prince of Sistan, 872-902
Jacob, the son of Leith,[127] stumbled over a lump of salt, which
he unwarily tasted with his tongue.  Salt, among the Orientals,
is the symbol of hospitality, and the pious robber immediately
retired without spoil or damage.  The discovery of this honourable behaviour recommended Jacob to pardon and trust ; he led
an army at first for his benefactor, at last for himself, subdued
Persia, and threatened the residence of the Abbassides.  On
his march towards Bagdad, the conqueror was arrested by a
fever.  He gave audience in bed to the ambassador of the
caliph ; and beside him on a table were exposed a naked
scymetar, a crust of brown bread, and a bunch of onions.  " If
I die," said he, " your master is delivered from his fears.  If I
live, this must determine between us.  If I am vanquished, I
can return without reluctance to the homely fare of my youth."
From the height where he stood, the descent would not have
been so soft or harmless : a timely death secured his own re- [A.D. 878]
pose and that of the caliph, who paid with the most lavish
concessions the retreat of his brother Amrou to the palaces of
Shiraz and Ispahan.  The Abbassides were too feeble to con-
tend, too proud to forgive : they invited the powerful dynasty
of the *Samanides*,[128] who passed the Oxus with ten thousand The Samanides. A.D.
horse, so poor, that their stirrups were of wood ; so brave, that 874-999
they vanquished the Soffarian army, eight times more numerous
than their own.  The captive Amrou was sent in chains, a [A.D. 900]
grateful offering to the court of Bagdad ; and, as the victor was
content with the inheritance of Transoxiana and Chorasan, the
realms of Persia returned for a while to the allegiance of the

---

[127] [Yakūb, son of al-Layth, a coppersmith (saffār), conquered successively Fārs,
Balkh, and Khurāsān.  The Saffārid dynasty numbered only three princes :
Yakūb, his brother Amr, and Amr's son Tāhir, whose power was confined to Sīstān,
which he lost in A.D. 903.  Cp. S. Lane-Poole, *op. cit.*, p. 129, 130.]

[128] [The Sāmānid dynasty, which held sway in Transoxiana and Persia, was
founded by Nasr ben-Ahmad, great-grandson of Sāmān (a nobleman of Balkh).
This dynasty lost Persia before the end of the 10th century and expired in A.D.
999.  Cp. S. Lane-Poole, *op. cit.*, p. 131-3.]

caliphs. The provinces of Syria and Egypt were twice dis-
membered by their Turkish slaves, of the race of *Toulun* and
*Ikshid.*[129] These barbarians, in religion and manners the countrymen of Mahomet, emerged from the bloody factions of the
palace to a provincial command and an independent throne :
their names became famous and formidable in their time ; but
the founders of these two potent dynasties confessed, either in
words or actions, the vanity of ambition. The first on his death-
bed implored the mercy of God to a sinner, ignorant of the
limits of his own power : the second, in the midst of four
hundred thousand soldiers and eight thousand slaves, concealed
from every human eye the chamber where he attempted to
sleep. Their sons were educated in the vices of kings ; and
both Egypt and Syria were recovered and possessed by the
Abbassides during an interval of thirty years. In the decline
of their empire, Mesopotamia, with the important cities of
Mosul and Aleppo, was occupied by the Arabian princes of the
tribe of *Hamadan.* The poets of their court could repeat without a blush, that nature had formed their countenances for
beauty, their tongues for eloquence, and their hands for
liberality and valour ; but the genuine tale of the elevation and
reign of the *Hamadanites* exhibits a scene of treachery, murder
and parricide. At the same fatal period, the Persian kingdom
was again usurped by the dynasty of the *Bowides*, by the sword
of three brothers, who, under various names, were styled the
support and columns of the state, and who, from the Caspian
sea to the ocean, would suffer no tyrants but themselves.
Under their reign, the language and genius of Persia revived,
and the Arabs, three hundred and four years after the death of
Mahomet, were deprived of the sceptre of the East.[130]

The Tou-
lonides. A.D.
868-905

The Ikshid-
ites. A.D.
934 [935]-968
[969]

The Hama-
danites. A.D.
892-1001

The Bowides.
A.D. 933 [932]-
1055

[129] M. de Guignes (Hist. des Huns, tom. iii. p. 124-154) has exhausted the Tou-
lonides and Ikshidites of Egypt, and thrown some light on the Carmathians and
Hamadanites. [The Tūlūnid dynasty was founded by Ahmad, son of Tūlūn (a
Turkish slave), who established his capital at the suburb of al-Katāi between Fustāt
and the later Cairo. Syria was joined to Egypt under the government of Ahmad in
A.D. 877.—Mohammad al-Ikhshīd, founder of the Ikhshīdid dynasty, was son of
Tughj, a native of Farghānā. His government of Egypt began in A.D. 935 ; Syria
was added in 941, and Mecca and Medīna in 942. Cp. S. Lane-Poole, *op. cit.*, p. 69.
The Fātimids succeeded the Ikhshīdids in 969.—The influence of the Hamdānids
in Mosul (Mōsil) may be dated from c. A.D. 873, but their independent rule there
begins with Hasan (Nāsir ad-dawla) A.D. 929 and lasts till 991, when they gave
way to the Buwayhids. In Aleppo, the Hamdānid dynasty lasted from A.D. 944 to
1003, and then gave way to the Fātimids. See S. Lane-Poole, *op. cit.*, p. 111-113.]

[130] [The three brothers, sons of Buwayh (a highland chief, who served the Ziyārid
lord of Jurjān), formed three principalities in the same year (932) : 1. Imād ad-
dawla, in Fārs ; 2. Muizz ad-dawla in Irāk and Kirmān ; 3. Rukn ad-dawla in

Rahdi, the twentieth of the Abbassides, and the thirty-ninth of the successors of Mahomet, was the last who deserved the title of commander of the faithful:[131] the last (says Abulfeda) who spoke to the people, or conversed with the learned ; the last who, in the expense of his household, represented the wealth and magnificence of the ancient caliphs.  After him, the lords of the eastern world were reduced to the most abject misery, and exposed to the blows and insults of a servile condition.  The revolt of the provinces circumscribed their dominions within the walls of Bagdad ; but that capital still contained an innumerable multitude, vain of their past fortune, discontented with their present state, and oppressed by the demands of a treasury which had formerly been replenished by the spoil and tribute of nations. Their idleness was exercised by faction and controversy.  Under the mask of piety, the rigid followers of Hanbal[132] invaded the pleasures of domestic life, burst into the houses of plebeians and princes, spilt the wine, broke the instruments, beat the musicians, and dishonoured, with infamous suspicions, the associates of every handsome youth.  In each profession, which allowed room for two persons, the one was a votary, the other an antagonist, of Ali ; and the Abbassides were awakened by the clamorous grief of the sectaries, who denied their title and cursed their progenitors.  A turbulent people could only be repressed by a military force ; but who could satisfy the avarice or assert the discipline of the mercenaries themselves ?  The African and the Turkish guards drew their swords against each other, and

Rayy, Hamadhān, and Ispahan.  The third division of the Buwayhids lasted till 1023, when they were ousted by the Kākwayhids.  The dominions of the second passed under the lords of Fārs in 977 and again permanently in 1012 ; and the dynasty of Fārs survived until the conquest of the Seljūks.  See the table of the geographical distribution of the Buwayhids in S. Lane-Poole, *op. cit.*, p. 142.]

[131] Hic est ultimus chalifah qui multum atque sæpius pro concione perorarit. . . . Fuit etiam ultimus qui otium cum eruditis et facetis hominibus fallere hilariterque agere soleret.  Ultimus tandem chalifarum cui sumtus, stipendia, reditus, et thesauri, culinæ, cæteraque omnis aulica pompa priorum chalifarum ad instar comparata fuerint.  Videbimus enim paullo post quam indignis et servilibus ludibriis exagitati, quam ad humilem fortunam ultimumque contemptum abjecti fuerint hi quondam potentissimi totius terrarum Orientalium orbis domini.  Abulfed. Annal. Moslem. p. 261.  I have given this passage as the manner and tone of Abulfeda, but the cast of Latin eloquence belongs more properly to Reiske.  The Arabian historian (p. 255, 257, 261-269, 283, &c.) has supplied me with the most interesting facts of this paragraph.  [Rādī, A.D. 934-940.]

[132] Their master, on a similar occasion, shewed himself of a more indulgent and tolerating spirit.  Ahmed Ebn Hanbal, the head of one of the four orthodox sects, was born at Bagdad A.H. 164, and died there A.H. 241.  He fought and suffered in the dispute concerning the creation of the Koran.

the chief commanders, the emirs al Omra,[133] imprisoned or deposed their sovereigns, and violated the sanctuary of the mosque and harem.   If the caliphs escaped to the camp or court of any neighbouring prince, their deliverance was a change of servitude, till they were prompted by despair to invite the Bowides, the sultans of Persia, who silenced the factions of Bagdad by their irresistible arms.   The civil and military powers were assumed by Moezaldowlat, the second of the three brothers, and a stipend of sixty thousand pounds sterling was assigned by his generosity for the private expense of the commander of the faithful.   But on the fortieth day, at the audience of the ambassadors of Chorasan, and in the presence of a trembling multitude, the caliph was dragged from his throne to a dungeon, by the command of the stranger, and the rude hands of his Dilemites.   His palace was pillaged, his eyes were put out, and the mean ambition of the Abbassides aspired to the vacant station of danger and disgrace.   In the school of adversity, the luxurious caliphs resumed the grave and abstemious virtues of the primitive times. Despoiled of their armour and silken robes, they fasted, they prayed, they studied the Koran and the tradition of the Sonnites ; they performed with zeal and knowledge the functions of their ecclesiastical character.   The respect of nations still waited on the successors of the apostle, the oracles of the law and conscience of the faithful ; and the weakness or division of their tyrants sometimes restored the Abbassides to the sovereignty of Bagdad.   But their misfortunes had been embittered by the triumph of the Fatimites, the real or spurious progeny of Ali. Arising from the extremity of Africa, these successful rivals extinguished in Egypt and Syria both the spiritual and temporal authority of the Abbassides ; and the monarch of the Nile insulted the humble pontiff on the banks of the Tigris.

In the declining age of the caliphs, in the century which elapsed after the war of Theophilus and Motassem, the hostile transactions of the two nations were confined to some inroads by sea and land, the fruits of their close vicinity and indelible hatred. But, when the Eastern world was convulsed and broken, the Greeks were roused from their lethargy by the hopes of conquest

[Muizz al-dawla]

[Fatimids. A.D. 909-1171]

Enterprises of the Greeks. A.D. 960

[133] The office of vizir was superseded by the emir al Omra [amīr al-umarā] Imperator Imperatorum, a title first instituted by Rahdi [Weil quotes an instance of its use under al-Muktadir, Rādī's father, *op. cit.*, ii. p. 559] and which merged at length in the Bowides and Seljukides ; vectigalibus, et tributis et curiis per omnes regiones præfecit, jussitque in omnibus suggestis nominis ejus in concionibus mentionem fieri (Abulpharagius, Dynast. p. 199).   It is likewise mentioned by Elmacin (p. 254, 255).

and revenge. The Byzantine empire, since the accession of the
Basilian race, had reposed in peace and dignity ; and they might
encounter with their entire strength the front of some petty
emir, whose rear was assaulted and threatened by his national
foes of the Mahometan faith. The lofty titles of the morning
star, and the death of the Saracens,[134] were applied in the public
acclamations to Nicephorus Phocas, a prince as renowned in the
camp as he was unpopular in the city. In the subordinate station
of great domestic, or general of the East, he reduced the island
of Crete, and extirpated the nest of pirates who had so long
defied, with impunity, the majesty of the empire.[135] His military genius was displayed in the conduct and success of the
enterprise, which had so often failed with loss and dishonour.
The Saracens were confounded by the landing of his troops on
safe and level bridges, which he cast from the vessels to the
shore. Seven months were consumed in the siege of Candia ;
the despair of the native Cretans was stimulated by the frequent
aid of their brethren of Africa and Spain ; and, after the massy
wall and double ditch had been stormed by the Greeks, an hopeless conflict was still maintained in the streets and houses of the
city. The whole island was subdued in the capital, and a submissive people accepted, without resistance, the baptism of the
conqueror.[136] Constantinople applauded the long-forgotten pomp

Reduction of Crete. [A.D. 960]

---

[134] Liutprand, whose choleric temper was embittered by his uneasy situation,
suggests the names of reproach and contempt more applicable to Nicephorus than
the vain titles of the Greeks : Ecce venit stella matutina, surgit Eous, reverberat
obtutû solis radios, pallida Saracenorum mors, Nicephorus μέδων. [Legatio, c. 10.]

[135] Notwithstanding the insinuations of Zonaras, καὶ εἰ μή, &c. (tom. ii. l. xvi. p.
197 [c. 23]) it is an undoubted fact that Crete was completely and finally subdued by
Nicephorus Phocas (Pagi, Critica, tom. iii. p. 873-875. Meursius, Creta, l. iii. c.
7, tom. iii. p. 464, 465). [The best account of the recovery of Crete will be found
in Schlumberger's Nicéphore Phocas, chap. 2. There had been two ineffectual
expeditions against Crete in the same century ; in 902 (general Himerius), and in
949 (general Gongylus). We are fortunate enough to possess full details of the
organisation of these expeditions in official accounts which are included in the so-
called Second Book of the de Caerimoniis (chap. 44 and 45 ; p. 651 sqq. ed. Bonn) ;
and these have been utilised by M. Schlumberger for his constructive description of
the expedition of 960. The conquest of Crete was celebrated in an iambic poem
of 5 cantos by the Deacon Theodosius, a contemporary (publ. by F. Cornelius in
Creta Sacra (Venice, 1755); printed in the Bonn ed. of Leo Diaconus, p. 263 sqq.) ;
but it gives us little historical information. Cp. Schlumberger, p. 84.]

[136] A Greek life of St. Nicon [Metanoites], the Armenian, was found in the
Sforza library, and translated into Latin by the Jesuit Sirmond for the use of
cardinal Baronius. This contemporary legend cast a ray of light on Crete and
Peloponnesus in the tenth century. He found the newly recovered island, fœdis
detestandæ Agarenorum superstitionis vestigiis adhuc plenam ac refertam . . .
but the victorious missionary, perhaps with some carnal aid, ad baptismum omnes
veræque fidei disciplinam pepulit. Ecclesiis per totam insulam ædificatis, &c.
(Annal. Eccles. A.D. 961). [The Latin version in Migne, P. G. vol. 113, p. 975 sqq.
Also in the Vet. Scr. ampl. Coll. of Martêne and Durand, 6, 837 sqq.]

of a triumph ; but the imperial diadem was the sole reward that could repay the services, or satisfy the ambition, of Nicephorus.

The Eastern conquests of Nicephorus Phocas, and John Zimisces. A.D. 963-975

After the death of the younger Romanus, the fourth in lineal descent of the Basilian race, his widow Theophania[136a] successively married Phocas and his assassin John Zimisces, the two heroes of the age. They reigned as the guardians and colleagues of her infant sons ; and the twelve years of their military command form the most splendid period of the Byzantine annals. The subjects and confederates, whom they led to war, appeared, at least in the eyes of an enemy, two hundred thousand strong ; and of these about thirty thousand were armed with cuirasses.[137] A train of four thousand mules attended their march ; and their evening camp was regularly fortified with an enclosure of iron spikes. A series of bloody and undecisive combats is nothing more than an anticipation of what would have been effected in a few years by the course of nature ; but I shall briefly prosecute the conquests of the two emperors from the hills of Cappadocia to the desert of Bagdad.[138] The sieges of Mopsuestia and Tarsus in Cilicia first expressed the skill and perseverance of their troops, on whom, at this moment, I shall not hesitate to bestow the name of Romans. In the double city of Mopsuestia, which is divided by the river Sarus, two hundred thousand Moslems were predestined to death or slavery,[139] a surprising degree of population, which must at least include the inhabitants of the dependent districts. They were surrounded and taken by assault ; but Tarsus was reduced by the slow progress of famine ; and no sooner had the Saracens yielded on honourable terms than they were mortified by the distant and unprofitable view of the naval succours of Egypt. They were dismissed with a safe-conduct to the confines of Syria ; a part of the Christians had quietly lived under their dominion ; and the vacant habitations were replenished by a new colony. But the mosque was converted into

Conquest of Cilicia

[Mopsuestia taken. A.D. 964]

[Tarsus. A.D. 965]

---

136a [Leg. Theophano.]

137 Elmacin, Hist. Saracen. p. 278, 279. Liutprand was disposed to depreciate the Greek power, yet he owns that Nicephorus led against Assyria an army of eighty thousand men.

138 [For the Asiatic campaign of Nicephorus and Tzimisces, see Schlumberger, op. cit., and L'épopée byzantine ; and K. Leonhardt, Kaiser Nicephorus II. Phokas und die Hamdaniden, 960-969.]

139 Ducenta fere millia hominum numerabat urbs (Abulfeda, Annal. Moslem. p. 231) of Mopsuestia, or Mafifa, Mampsysta, Mansista, Mamista, as it is corruptly, or perhaps more correctly, styled in the middle ages (Wesseling, Itinerar. p. 580). Yet I cannot credit this extreme populousness a few years after the testimony of the emperor Leo, οὐ γὰρ πολυπληθία στρατοῦ τοῖς Κίλιξι βαρβάροις ἐστίν (Tactica, c. xviii. in Meursii Oper. tom. vi. p. 817 [p. 980, ap. Migne, Patr. Gr. vol. 107]).

a stable; the pulpit was delivered to the flames; many rich crosses of gold and gems, the spoils of Asiatic churches, were made a grateful offering to the piety or avarice of the emperor; and he transported the gates of Mopsuestia and Tarsus, which were fixed in the wall of Constantinople, an eternal monument of his victory. After they had forced and secured the narrow passes of mount Amanus, the two Roman princes repeatedly carried their arms into the heart of Syria. Yet, instead of assaulting the walls of Antioch, the humanity or superstition of Nicephorus appeared to respect the ancient metropolis of the East: he contented himself with drawing round the city a line of circumvallation; left a stationary army; and instructed his lieutenant to expect, without impatience, the return of spring. But in the depth of winter, in a dark and rainy night, an adventurous subaltern, with three hundred soldiers, approached the rampart, applied his scaling-ladders, occupied two adjacent towers, stood firm against the pressure of multitudes, and bravely maintained his post till he was relieved by the tardy, though effectual, support of his reluctant chief. The first tumult of slaughter and rapine subsided; the reign of Cæsar and of Christ was restored; and the efforts of an hundred thousand Saracens, of the armies of Syria and the fleets of Afric, were consumed without effect before the walls of Antioch. The royal city of Aleppo was subject to Seifeddowlat, of the dynasty of Hamadan, who clouded his past glory by the precipitate retreat which abandoned his kingdom and capital to the Roman invaders. In his stately palace, that stood without the walls of Aleppo, they joyfully seized a well-furnished magazine of arms, a stable of fourteen hundred mules, and three hundred bags of silver and gold. But the walls of the city withstood the strokes of their battering-rams; and the besiegers pitched their tents on the neighbouring mountain of Jaushan. Their retreat exasperated the quarrel of the townsmen and mercenaries; the guard of the gates and ramparts was deserted; and, while they furiously charged each other in the market-place, they were surprised and destroyed by the sword of a common enemy. The male sex was exterminated by the sword; ten thousand youths were led into captivity; the weight of the precious spoil exceeded the strength and number of the beasts of burthen; the superfluous remainder was burnt; and, after a licentious possession of ten days, the Romans marched away from the naked and bleeding city. In their Syrian inroads they commanded the husbandmen to cultivate their lands, that they themselves, in the ensuing season, might reap the benefit:

*Invasion of Syria*

[A.D. 968]

*Recovery of Antioch.* [A.D. 969]

[Sayf ad-dawla. A.D. 944-07]

more than an hundred cities were reduced to obedience; and
eighteen pulpits of the principal mosques were committed to the
flames, to expiate the sacrilege of the disciples of Mahomet.
The classic names of Hierapolis, Apamea, and Emesa, revive for
a moment in the list of conquest: the emperor Zimisces encamped in the Paradise of Damascus, and accepted the ransom
of a submissive people; and the torrent was only stopped by the
impregnable fortress of Tripoli, on the sea-coast of Phœnicia.

Passage of<br>the Euph-<br>rates. [A.D.<br>974]Since the days of Heraclius, the Euphrates, below the passage
of mount Taurus, had been impervious, and almost invisible, to
the Greeks.    The river yielded a free passage to the victorious
Zimisces; and the historian may imitate the speed with which
he overran the once famous cities of Samosata, Edessa, Martyropolis, Amida,[140] and Nisibis, the ancient limit of the empire
in the neighbourhood of the Tigris.    His ardour was quickened
by the desire of grasping the virgin treasures of Ecbatana,[141]
a well-known name, under which the Byzantine writer has
concealed the capital of the Abbassides.    The consternation
of the fugitives had already diffused the terror of his name; but
the fancied riches of Bagdad had already been dissipated by the
Danger of<br>Bagdadavarice and prodigality of domestic tyrants.    The prayers of the
people, and the stern demands of the lieutenant of the Bowides,
required the caliph to provide for the defence of the city.    The
helpless Mothi replied that his arms, his revenues, and his provinces had been torn from his hands, and that he was ready to
abdicate a dignity which he was unable to support.    The emir
was inexorable; the furniture of the palace was sold; and the
paltry price of forty thousand pieces of gold was instantly consumed in private luxury.    But the apprehensions of Bagdad
were relieved by the retreat of the Greeks; thirst and hunger
guarded the desert of Mesopotamia; and the emperor, satiated

[140] The text of Leo the deacon, in the corrupt names of Emeta [ˇEμετ, p. 161, l.
19, ed. Bonn] and Myctarsim, reveals the cities of Amida and Martyropolis (Mia-
farekin [Μιεφαρκὶμ, ib. l. 21].    See Abulfeda, Geograph. p. 245, vers. Reiske).
Of the former, Leo observes, urbs munita et illustris; of the latter, clara atque
conspicua opibusque et pecore, reliquis ejus provinciis [leg. provinciæ] urbibus atque
oppidis longe præstans.

[141] Ut et Ecbatana pergeret Agarenorumque regiam everteret . . . aiunt enim
urbium quæ usquam sunt ac toto orbe existunt felicissimam esse auroque ditissi-
mam (Leo Diacon. apud Pagium, tom. iv. p. 34 [p. 162, ed. Bonn]).    This
splendid description suits only with Bagdad, and cannot possibly apply either to
Hamada, the true Ecbatana (d'Anville, Geog. Ancienne, tom. ii. p. 237), or Tauris,
which has been commonly mistaken for that city.    The name of Ecbatana, in the
same indefinite sense, is transferred by a more classic authority (Cicero pro Lege
Maniliâ, c. 4) to the royal seat of Mithridates, king of Pontus.

with glory, and laden with Oriental spoils, returned to Constantinople, and displayed, in his triumph, the silk, the aromatics, and three hundred myriads of gold and silver. Yet the powers of the East had been bent, not broken, by this transient hurricane. After the departure of the Greeks, the fugitive princes returned to their capitals; the subjects disclaimed their involuntary oaths of allegiance; the Moslems again purified their temples, and overturned the idols of the saints and martyrs; the Nestorians and Jacobites preferred a Saracen to an orthodox master; and the numbers and spirit of the Melchites were inadequate to the support of the church and state. Of these extensive conquests, Antioch, with the cities of Cilicia and the isle of Cyprus, was alone restored, a permanent and useful accession to the Roman empire.[142]

[Cyprus recovered. A.D. 965]

[142] See the annals of Elmacin, Abulpharagius, and Abulfeda, from A.H. 351 to A.H. 361; and the reigns of Nicephorus Phocas and John Zimisces, in the Chronicles of Zonaras (tom. ii. l. xvi. p. 199 [c. 24], l. xvii. 215 [c. 4]) and Cedrenus (Compend. p. 649-684 [ii. p. 351 *sqq.* ed. Bonn]). Their manifold defects are partly supplied by the Ms. history of Leo the deacon, which Pagi obtained from the Benedictines, and has inserted almost entire in a Latin version (Critica, tom. iii. p. 873, tom. iv. p. 37). [For Leo the deacon and the Greek text of his work, since published, see above, vol. 5, Appendix, p. 504.]

## CHAPTER LIII

*State of the Eastern Empire in the Tenth Century—Extent and Division—Wealth and Revenue—Palace of Constantinople—Titles and Offices—Pride and Power of the Emperors—Tactics of the Greeks, Arabs, and Franks—Loss of the Latin Tongue—Studies and Solitude of the Greeks*

Memorials of the Greek empire

A RAY of historic light seems to beam from the darkness of the tenth century. We open with curiosity and respect the royal volumes of Constantine Porphyrogenitus,[1] which he composed, at a mature age, for the instruction of his son, and which promise to unfold the state of the Eastern empire, both in peace and war, both at home and abroad. In the first of these works

Works of Constantine Porphyrogenitus. [The Ceremonies]

he minutely describes the pompous ceremonies of the church and palace of Constantinople, according to his own practice and that of his predecessors.[2] In the second he attempts an accurate survey of the provinces, the *themes*, as they were then denomin-

[The Themes]

ated, both of Europe and Asia.[3] The system of Roman tactics,

---

[1] The epithet of Πορφυρογέννητος, Porphyrogenitus, born in the purple, is elegantly defined by Claudian :—

> Ardua privatos nescit fortuna Penates ;
> Et regnum cum luce dedit.   Cognata potestas
> Excepit Tyrio venerabile pignus in ostro.

And Ducange, in his Greek and Latin Glossaries, produces many passages expressive of the same idea. [In connexion with the following account of the work of Constantine, the reader might have been reminded that the Continuation of Theophanes (and also the work of Genesius) were composed at the instigation of this Emperor, and that he himself wrote the Life of his grandfather Basil—a remarkable work whose tendency, credibility, and value have been fully discussed in A. Rambaud's L'empire grec au dixième siècle, p. 137-164.]

[2] A splendid Ms. of Constantine, de Ceremoniis Aulæ et Ecclesiæ Byzantinæ, wandered from Constantinople to Buda, Frankfort, and Leipsic, where it was published in a splendid edition by Leich and Reiske (A.D. 1751[-1754] in folio), with such slavish praise as editors never fail to bestow on the worthy or worthless object of their toil.   [See Appendix 1.]

[3] See, in the first volume of Banduri's Imperium Orientale, Constantinus de Thematibus, p. 1-24, de Administrando Imperio, p. 45-127, edit. Venet.   The text of the old edition of Meursius is corrected from a Ms. of the royal library of Paris, which Isaac Causabon had formerly seen (Epist. ad Polybium, p. 10), and the sense is illustrated by two maps of William Deslisle, the prince of geographers till the appearance of the greater d'Anville.   [On the Themes, see Appendix 3 ; on the treatise on the Administration, see Appendix 4.]

the discipline and order of troops, and the military operations by land and sea, are explained in the third of these didactic collections, which may be ascribed to Constantine or his father Leo.[4] In the fourth, of the administration of the empire, he reveals the secrets of the Byzantine policy, in friendly or hostile intercourse with the nations of the earth. The literary labours of the age, the practical systems of law, agriculture, and history, might redound to the benefit of the subject and the honour of the Macedonian princes. The sixty books of the *Basilics*,[5] the code and pandects of civil jurisprudence, were gradually framed in the three first reigns of that prosperous dynasty. The art of agriculture had amused the leisure, and exercised the pens, of the best and wisest of the ancients ; and their chosen precepts are comprised in the twenty books of the *Geoponics*[6] of Constantine. At his command, the historical examples of vice and virtue were methodized in fifty-three books,[7] and every citizen

*[The Administration of the Empire]*

*[Augmentation of the Basilica]*

*[Edition of the Geoponics]*

*[Historical Encyclopaedia]*

[4] The Tactics of Leo and Constantine are published with the aid of some new Mss. in the great edition of the works of Meursius, by the learned John Lami (tom. vi. p. 531-920, 1211-1417 ; Florent. 1745), yet the text is still corrupt and mutilated, the version is still obscure and faulty. [The Tactics of Constantine is little more than a copy of the Tactics of Leo, and was compiled by Constantine VIII., not by Constantine VII.] The Imperial library of Vienna would afford some valuable materials to a new editor (Fabric. Bibliot. Græc. tom. vi. p. 369, 370). [See Appendix 1.]

[5] On the subject of the *Basilics*, Fabricius (Bibliot. Græc. tom. xii. p. 425-514), and Heineccius (Hist. Juris Romani, p. 396-399), and Giannone (Istoria civile di Napoli, tom. i. p. 450-458), as historical civilians, may be usefully consulted. Forty one books of this Greek code have been published, with a Latin version, by Charles Annibal Fabrottus (Paris, 1647) in seven volumes in folio ; four other books have since been discovered, and are inserted in Gerard Meerman's Novus Thesaurus Juris Civ. et Canon. tom. v. Of the whole work, the sixty books, John Leunclavius has printed (Basil, 1575) an *eclogue* or synopsis. The cxlii novels, or new laws, of Leo, may be found in the Corpus Juris Civilis. [See above, vol. 5, Appendix 11.]

[6] I have used the last and best edition of the Geoponics (by Nicolas Niclas, Leipsic, 1781, 2 vols. in octavo). [Recent edition by H. Beckh, 1895.] I read in the preface that the same emperor restored the long forgotten systems of rhetoric and philosophy ; and his two books of *Hippiatrica*, or Horse-physic, were published at Paris, 1530, in folio (Fabric. Bibliot. Græc. tom. vi. p. 493-500). [All that Constantine did for agriculture was to cause an unknown person to make a very bad copy of the *Geoponica* of Cassianus Bassus (a compilation of the 6th century). See Krumbacher (Gesch. der byz. Litt. p. 262), who observes that the edition produced at the instance of Constantine was so bad that the old copies must have risen in price.]

[7] Of these liii books, or titles, only two have been preserved and printed, de Legationibus (by Fulvius Ursinus, Antwerp, 1582, and Daniel Hœschelius, August. Vindel. 1603) and de Virtutibus et Vitiis (by Henry Valesius, or de Valois, Paris, 1634). [We have also fragments of the titles περὶ γνωμῶν (De Sententiis), ed. by A. Mai, Scr. Vet. Nov. Collect. vol. 2 ; and περὶ ἐπιβουλῶν κατὰ βασιλέων γεγονυιῶν (De Insidiis), ed. C. A. Feder (1848-55). The collection was intended to be an Encyclopædia of historical literature.]

might apply, to his contemporaries or himself, the lesson or the warning of past times. From the august character of a legislator, the sovereign of the East descends to the more humble office of a teacher and a scribe ; and, if his successors and subjects were regardless of his paternal cares, *we* may inherit and enjoy the everlasting legacy.

Their imperfections

A closer survey will indeed reduce the value of the gift, and the gratitude of posterity : in the possession of these Imperial treasures, we may still deplore our poverty and ignorance ; and the fading glories of their authors will be obliterated by indifference or contempt. The Basilics will sink to a broken copy, a partial and mutilated version in the Greek language, of the laws of Justinian ; but the sense of the old civilians is often superseded by the influence of bigotry ; and the absolute prohibition of divorce, concubinage, and interest for money, enslaves the freedom of trade and the happiness of private life. In the historical book, a subject of Constantine might admire the inimitable virtues of Greece and Rome ; he might learn to what a pitch of energy and elevation the human character had

[Lives of the Saints and Acts of the Martyrs]

formerly aspired. But a contrary effect must have been produced by a new edition of the lives of the saints, which the great logothete, or chancellor of the empire, was directed to prepare ; and the dark fund of superstition was enriched by

[Symeon]

the fabulous and florid legends of Simon the *Metaphrast*.[8] The

---

[8] The life and writings of Simon Metaphrastes are described by Hankius (de Scriptoribus Byzant. p. 410-460). This biographer of the saints indulged himself in a loose paraphrase of the sense or nonsense of more ancient acts. His Greek rhetoric is again paraphrased in the Latin version of Surius, and scarcely a thread can be now visible of the original texture. [The most recent investigations of Vasilievski and Ehrhard as to the date of Symeon Metaphrastes confirm the notice in the text. He flourished about the middle and second half of the 10th century ; his hagiographical work was suggested by Constantine Porphyrogennetos and was probably composed during the reign of Nicephorus Phocas. Symeon is doubtless to be identified with Symeon Magister, the chronicler ; see above, vol. 5, App. p. 502. (Cp. Krumbacher, Gesch. der byz. Litt. p. 200.) Symeon's work was not original composition ; he collected and edited older works, lives of saints and acts of martyrs ; he paraphrased them, improved their style, and adapted them to the taste of his contemporaries, but he did not invent new stories. His Life of Abercius has been strikingly confirmed by the discovery of the original inscription quoted in that life. The collection of Symeon was freely interpolated and augmented by new lives after his death, and the edition of Migne, P. G. 114, 115, 116, does not represent the original work. To determine the compass of that original work is of the highest importance, and this can only be done by a comparative study of numerous Mss. which contain portions of it. This problem has been solved in the main by A. Ehrhard, who found a clue in a Moscow Ms. of the 11th century. He has published his results in a paper entitled Die Legendensammlung des Symeon Metaphrastes und ihr ursprünglicher Bestand, in the Festschrift zum elfhundertjährigen Jubiläum des deutschen Campo Santo in Rom, 1897.]

merits and miracles of the whole calendar are of less account in the eyes of a sage than the toil of a single husbandman, who multiplies the gifts of the Creator and supplies the food of his brethren. Yet the royal authors of the *Geoponics* were more seriously employed in expounding the precepts of the destroying art, which has been taught since the days of Xenophon [9] as the art of heroes and kings. But the *Tactics* of Leo and Constantine are mingled with the baser alloy of the age in which they lived. It was destitute of original genius; they implicitly transcribe the rules and maxims which had been confirmed by victories. It was unskilled in the propriety of style and method; they blindly confound the most distant and discordant institutions, the phalanx of Sparta and that of Macedon, the legions of Cato and Trajan, of Augustus and Theodosius. Even the use, or at least the importance, of these military rudiments, may be fairly questioned : their general theory is dictated by reason ; but the merit, as well as difficulty, consists in the application. The discipline of a soldier is formed by exercise rather than by study ; the talents of a commander are appropriated to those calm though rapid minds, which nature produces to decide the fate of armies and nations: the former is the habit of a life, the latter the glance of a moment; and the battles won by lessons of tactics may be numbered with the epic poems created from the rules of criticism. The book of ceremonies is a recital, tedious yet imperfect, of the despicable pageantry which had infected the church and state since the gradual decay of the purity of the one and the power of the other. A review of the themes or provinces might promise such authentic and useful information as the curiosity of government only can obtain, instead of traditionary fables on the origin of the cities, and malicious epigrams on the vices of their inhabitants.[10] Such information the historian would have been

---

[9] According to the first book of the Cyropædia, professors of tactics, a small part of the science of war, were already instituted in Persia, by which Greece must be understood. A good edition of all the Scriptores Tactici would be a task not unworthy of a scholar. His industry might discover some new Mss. and his learning might illustrate the military history of the ancients. But this scholar should be likewise a soldier ; and, alas ! Quintus Icilius is no more. [Köchly and Rüstow have edited some of the Tactici in Greek and German (1853-5); but a complete *corpus* is looked for from Herr K. K. Müller of Jena.]

[10] After observing that the demerit of the Cappadocians rose in proportion to their rank and riches, he inserts a more pointed epigram, which is ascribed to Demodocus :

Καππαδόκην ποτ' ἔχιδνα κακὴ δάκεν, ἀλλὰ καὶ αὐτή
Κάτθανε, γευσαμένη αἵματος ἰοβόλου.

pleased to record; nor should his silence be condemned if the most interesting objects, the population of the capital and provinces, the amount of the taxes and revenues, the numbers of subjects and strangers who served under the Imperial standard, have been unnoticed by Leo the Philosopher and his son Constantine. His treatise of the public administration is stained with the same blemishes; yet it is discriminated by peculiar merit; the antiquities of the nations may be doubtful or fabulous; but the geography and manners of the barbaric world are delineated with curious accuracy. Of these nations, the Franks alone were qualified to observe in their turn, and to describe, the metropolis of the East. The ambassador of the great Otho, a bishop of Cremona, has painted the state of Constantinople about the middle of the tenth century; his style is glowing, his narrative lively, his observation keen; and even the prejudices and passions of Liutprand are stamped with an original character of freedom and genius.[11] From this scanty fund of foreign and domestic materials I shall investigate the form and substance of the Byzantine empire: the provinces and wealth, the civil government and military force, the character and literature, of the Greeks, in a period of six hundred years, from the reign of Heraclius to the successful invasion of the Franks or Latins.

*Embassy of Liutprand. [A.D. 968-9]*

*The themes, or provinces of the empire, and its limits in every age*

After the final division between the sons of Theodosius, the swarms of barbarians from Scythia and Germany overspread the provinces, and extinguished the empire, of ancient Rome. The weakness of Constantinople was concealed by extent of dominion; her limits were inviolate, or at least entire; and the kingdom of Justinian was enlarged by the splendid acquisition of Africa and Italy. But the possession of these new conquests was transient and precarious; and almost a moiety of the Eastern empire was torn away by the arms of the Saracens. Syria and Egypt were oppressed by the Arabian caliphs; and, after the

---

The sting is precisely the same with the French epigram against Fréron; Un serpent mordit Jean Fréron—Eh bien? Le serpent en mourut. But, as the Paris wits are seldom read in the Anthology, I should be curious to learn through what channel it was conveyed for their imitation (Constantin. Porphyrogen. de Themat. c. ii. Brunk, Analect. Græc. tom. ii. p. 56 [p. 21, ed. Bonn]; Brodæi. Anthologia, l. ii. p. 244 [Anthol. Pal., xi. 237]). [Of Constantine's Book on the Themes, M. Rambaud observes: "C'est l'empire au vi^e siècle, et non pas au x^e siècle, que nous trouvons dans son livre" (*op. cit.*, p. 166).]

[11] The Legatio Liutprandi Episcopi Cremonensis ad Nicephorum Phocam is inserted in Muratori, Scriptores Rerum Italicarum, tom. ii. pars i. [In Pertz, Monum. vol. 3. There is a convenient ed. of Liutprand's works by E. Dümmler in the Scr. rer. Germ. 1877.]

reduction of Africa, their lieutenants invaded and subdued the Roman province which had been changed into the Gothic monarchy of Spain. The islands of the Mediterranean were not inaccessible to their naval powers ; and it was from their extreme stations, the harbours of Crete and the fortresses of Cilicia, that the faithful or rebel emirs insulted the majesty of the throne and capital. The remaining provinces, under the obedience of the emperors, were cast into a new mould ; and the jurisdiction of the presidents, the consulars, and the counts was superseded by the institution of the *themes*,[12] or military governments, which prevailed under the successors of Heraclius, and are described by the pen of the royal author. Of the twenty-nine themes, twelve in Europe and seventeen in Asia, the origin is obscure, the etymology doubtful or capricious, the limits were arbitrary and fluctuating ; but some particular names that sound the most strangely to our ear were derived from the character and attributes of the troops that were maintained at the expense, and for the guard, of the respective divisions. The vanity of the Greek princes most eagerly grasped the shadow of conquest and the memory of lost dominion. A new Mesopotamia was created on the Western side of the Euphrates ; the appellation and prætor of Sicily were transferred to a narrow slip of Calabria ; and a fragment of the duchy of Beneventum was promoted to the style and title of the theme of Lombardy. In the decline of the Arabian empire, the successors of Constantine might indulge their pride in more solid advantages. The victories of Nicephorus, John Zimisces, and Basil the Second, revived the fame and enlarged the boundaries of the Roman name ; the province of Cilicia, the metropolis of Antioch, the islands of Crete and Cyprus, were restored to the allegiance of Christ and Cæsar ; one third of Italy was annexed to the throne of Constantinople ; the kingdom of Bulgaria was destroyed ; and the last sovereigns of the Macedonian dynasty extended their sway from the sources of the Tigris to the neighbourhood of Rome. In the eleventh century, the prospect was again clouded by new enemies and new misfortunes ; the relics of Italy were swept away by the Norman adventurers ; and almost all the Asiatic branches were

---

[12] See Constantine de Thematibus, in Banduri, tom. i. p. 1-30, who owns that the word is οὐκ παλαιά. Θέμα is used by Maurice (Stratagem. l. ii. c. 2) for a legion, from whence the name was easily transferred to its post or province (Ducange, Gloss. Græc. tom. i. p. 487, 488). Some Etymologies are attempted for the Opsician, Optimatian, Thracesian, themes. [For the history of the Themes, and Constantine's treatise, see Appendix 3.]

dissevered from the Roman trunk by the Turkish conquerors.
After these losses, the emperors of the Comnenian family con-
tinued to reign from the Danube to Peloponnesus, and from
Belgrade to Nice, Trebizond, and the winding stream of the
Meander. The spacious provinces of Thrace, Macedonia, and
Greece, were obedient to their sceptre ; the possession of Cyprus,
Rhodes, and Crete was accompanied by the fifty islands of the
Ægean or Holy Sea ; [13] and the remnant of their empire trans-
cends the measure of the largest of the European kingdoms.

The same princes might assert with dignity and truth that of
all the monarchs of Christendom they possessed the greatest

General
wealth and
populousness

city,[14] the most ample revenue, the most flourishing and populous
state. With the decline and fall of the empire, the cities of the
West had decayed and fallen ; nor could the ruins of Rome, or
the mud walls, wooden hovels, and narrow precincts of Paris
and London, prepare the Latin stranger to contemplate the
situation and extent of Constantinople, her stately palaces and
churches, and the arts and luxury of an innumerable people.
Her treasures might attract, but her virgin strength had repelled,
and still promised to repel, the audacious invasion of the Persian
and Bulgarian, the Arab and the Russian. The provinces were
less fortunate and impregnable ; and few districts, few cities,
could be discovered which had not been violated by some fierce
barbarian, impatient to despoil, because he was hopeless to possess. From the age of Justinian the Eastern empire was sinking
below its former level ; the powers of destruction were more
active than those of improvement ; and the calamities of war
were embittered by the more permanent evils of civil and ecclesiastical tyranny. The captive who had escaped from the barbarians was often stripped and imprisoned by the ministers of
his sovereign : the Greek superstition relaxed the mind by

[13] Ἅγιος [leg. ἅγιον] πέλαγος, as it is styled by the modern Greeks, from which
the corrupt names of Archipelago, l'Archipel, and the Arches, have been transformed by geographers and seamen (d'Anville, Géographie Ancienne, tom. i. p.
281 ; Analyse de la Carte de la Grece, p. 60). The numbers of monks or caloyers
in all the islands and the adjacent mountain of Athos (Observations de Belon, fol.
32, verso), Monte Santo, might justify the epithet of holy, ἅγιος, a slight alteration
from the original αἰγαῖος, imposed by the Dorians, who, in their dialect, gave the
figurative name of αἶγες, or goats, to the bounding waves (Vossius, apud Cellarium,
Geograph. Antiq. tom. i. p. 829). [αἶγες, waves, has, of course, nothing to do with
αἴξ, a goat. The derivations suggested of Archipelago and ἅγιον πέλογος are not
acceptable.]

[14] According to the Jewish traveller who had visited Europe and Asia, Constantinople was equalled only by Bagdad, the great city of the Ismaelites (Voyage
de Benjamin de Tudèle, par Baratier, tom. i. c. 5, p. 36).

prayer and emaciated the body by fasting; and the multitude of convents and festivals diverted many hands and many days from the temporal service of mankind. Yet the subjects of the Byzantine empire were still the more dexterous and diligent of nations; their country was blessed by nature with every advantage of soil, climate, and situation; and, in the support and restoration of the arts, their patient and peaceful temper was more useful than the warlike spirit and feudal anarchy of Europe. The provinces that still adhered to the empire were repeopled and enriched by the misfortunes of those which were irrecoverably lost. From the yoke of the caliphs, the Catholics of Syria, Egypt, and Africa, retired to the allegiance of their prince, to the society of their brethren : the moveable wealth, which eludes the search of oppression, accompanied and alleviated their exile; and Constantinople received into her bosom the fugitive trade of Alexandria and Tyre. The chiefs of Armenia and Scythia, who fled from hostile or religious persecution, were hospitably entertained; their followers were encouraged to build new cities and to cultivate waste lands; and many spots, both in Europe and Asia, preserved the name, the manners, or at least the memory, of these national colonies. Even the tribes of barbarians, who had seated themselves in arms on the territory of the empire, were gradually reclaimed to the laws of the church and state; and, as long as they were separated from the Greeks, their posterity supplied a race of faithful and obedient soldiers. Did we possess sufficient materials to survey the twenty-nine themes of the Byzantine monarchy, our curiosity might be satisfied with a chosen example : it is fortunate enough that the clearest light should be thrown on the most interesting province, and the name of PELOPONNESUS will awaken the attention of the classic reader.

As early as the eighth century, in the troubled reign of the Iconoclasts, Greece, and even Peloponnesus,[15] were overrun by some Sclavonian bands, who outstripped the royal standard of Bulgaria. The strangers of old, Cadmus, and Danaus, and Pelops, had planted in that fruitful soil the seeds of policy and learning; State of Peloponnesus: Sclavonians

---

[15] Ἐσθλαβώθη δὲ πᾶσα ἡ χώρα καὶ γέγονε βάρβαρος, says Constantine (Thematibus, l. ii. c. 6, p. 25 [p. 53, ed. Bonn]) in a style as barbarous as the idea, which he confirms, as usual, by a foolish epigram. The epitomizer of Strabo likewise observes, καὶ νῦν δὲ πᾶσαν Ἤπειρον καὶ Ἑλλάδα σχεδὸν καὶ Μακεδονίαν, καὶ Πελοπόννησον Σκύθαι Σκλάβοι νέμονται (l. vii. p. 98, edit. Hudson): a passage which leads Dodwell a weary dance (Geograph. Minor. tom. ii. dissert. vi. p. 170-191) to enumerate the inroads of the Sclavi, and to fix the date (A.D. 980) of this petty geographer. [On the Slavonic element in Greece, see Appendix 7.]

but the savages of the north eradicated what yet remained of their sickly and withered roots. In this irruption, the country and the inhabitants were transformed; the Grecian blood was contaminated; and the proudest nobles of Peloponnesus were branded with the names of foreigners and *slaves*. By the diligence of succeeding princes, the land was in some measure purified from the barbarians; and the humble remnant was bound by an oath of obedience, tribute, and military service, which they often renewed and often violated. The siege of Patras was formed by a singular concurrence of the Sclavonians of Peloponnesus and the Saracens of Africa. In their last distress, a pious fiction of the approach of the prætor of Corinth revived the courage of the citizens. Their sally was bold and successful; the strangers embarked, the rebels submitted, and the glory of the day was ascribed to a phantom or a stranger, who fought in the foremost ranks under the character of St. Andrew the Apostle. The shrine which contained his relics was decorated with the trophies of victory, and the captive race was for ever devoted to the service and vassalage of the metropolitan church of Patras. By the revolt of two Sclavonian tribes in the neighbourhood of Helos and Lacedæmon, the peace of the peninsula was often disturbed. They sometimes insulted the weakness, and sometimes resisted the oppression, of the Byzantine government, till at length the approach of their hostile brethren extorted a golden bull to define the rights and obligations of the Ezzerites and Milengi, whose annual tribute was defined at twelve hundred pieces of gold. From these strangers the Imperial geographer has accurately distinguished a domestic and perhaps original race, who, in some degree, might derive their blood from the much-injured Helots. The liberality of the Romans, and especially of Augustus, had enfranchised the maritime cities from the dominion of Sparta; and the continuance of the same benefit ennobled them with the title of *Eleuthero*-or Free-Laconians.[16] In the time of Constantine Porphyrogenitus they had acquired the name of *Mainotes*, under which they dishonour the claim of liberty by the inhuman pillage of all that is shipwrecked on their rocky shores. Their territory, barren of corn, but fruitful of olives, extended to the Cape of Malea; they accepted a chief or prince from the Byzantine prætor, and a light tribute of four hundred pieces of gold was the badge of their immunity rather

*Freemen of Laconia*

[16] Strabon. Geograph. l. viii. p. 562 [5, § 5]. Pausanias, Græc. Descriptio, l. iii. c. 21, p. 264, 265. Plin. Hist. Natur. l. iv. c. 8.

than of their dependence. The freemen of Laconia assumed the character of Romans, and long adhered to the religion of the Greeks. By the zeal of the emperor Basil, they were baptized in the faith of Christ; but the altars of Venus and Neptune had been crowned by these rustic votaries five hundred years after they were proscribed in the Roman world. In the theme of Peloponnesus [17] forty cities were still numbered, and the declining state of Sparta, Argos, and Corinth may be suspended in the tenth century, at an equal distance, perhaps, between their antique splendour and their present desolation. The duty of military service, either in person or by substitute, was imposed on the lands or benefices of the province; a sum of five pieces of gold was assessed on each of the substantial tenants; and the same capitation was shared among several heads of inferior value. On the proclamation of an Italian war, the Peloponnesians excused themselves by a voluntary oblation of one hundred pounds of gold (four thousand pounds sterling) and a thousand horses with their arms and trappings. The churches and monasteries furnished their contingent; a sacrilegious profit was extorted from the sale of ecclesiastical honours; and the indigent bishop of Leucadia [18] was made responsible for a pension of one hundred pieces of gold. [19]

Cities and revenue of Peloponnesus

But the wealth of the province, and the trust of the revenue, were founded on the fair and plentiful produce of trade and manufactures; and some symptoms of liberal policy may be traced in a law which exempts from all personal taxes the mariners of Peloponnesus and the workmen in parchment and purple. This denomination may be fairly applied or extended to the manufactures of linen, woollen, and more especially of silk: the two former of which had flourished in Greece since the days of Homer; and the last was introduced perhaps as early as the reign of Justinian. These arts, which were exercised at Corinth, Thebes, and Argos, afforded food and occupation to a numerous people; the men, women and children were distributed according to their age and strength; and, if many of

Manufactures, especially of silk,

[17] Constantin. de Administrando Imperio, l. ii. c. 50, 51,52.

[18] The rock of Leucate was the southern promontory of his island and diocese. Had he been the exclusive guardian of the Lover's Leap, so well known to the readers of Ovid (Epist. Sappho) and the Spectator, he might have been the richest prelate of the Greek church.

[19] Leucatensis mihi juravit episcopus, quotannis ecclesiam suam debere Nicephoro aureos centum persolvere, similiter et ceteras plus minusve secundum vires suas (Liutprand in Legat. p. 489 [c. 63]).

these were domestic slaves, their masters, who directed the work and enjoyed the profit, were of a free and honourable condition. The gifts which a rich and generous matron of Peloponnesus presented to the emperor Basil, her adopted son, were doubtless fabricated in the Grecian looms. Danielis bestowed a carpet of fine wool, of a pattern which imitated the spots of a peacock's tail, of a magnitude to overspread the floor of a new church, erected in the triple name of Christ, of Michael the archangel, and the prophet Elijah. She gave six hundred pieces of silk and linen, of various use and denomination : the silk was painted with the Tyrian die, and adorned by the labours of the needle ; and the linen was so exquisitely fine that an entire piece might be rolled in the hollow of a cane.[20] In his description of the Greek manufactures, an historian of Sicily discriminates their price according to the weight and quality of the silk, the closeness of the texture, the beauty of the colours, and the taste and materials of the embroidery. A single, or even a double or treble, thread was thought sufficient for ordinary sale ; but the union of six threads composed a piece of stronger and more costly workmanship. Among the colours, he celebrates, with affectation of eloquence, the fiery blaze of the scarlet, and the softer lustre of the green. The embroidery was raised either in silk or gold ; the more simple ornament of stripes or circles was surpassed by the nicer imitation of flowers ; the vestments that were fabricated for the palace or the altar often glittered with precious stones ; and the figures were delineated in strings of Oriental pearls.[21] Till the twelfth century, Greece alone, of all the countries of Christendom, was possessed of the insect who is taught by nature, and of the workmen who are instructed by art, to prepare this elegant luxury. But the secret had been stolen by the dexterity and diligence of the Arabs ; the caliphs of the East and West scorned to borrow from the unbelievers their furniture and apparel ; and two cities of Spain, Almeria and

[20] See Constantine (in Vit. Basil. c. 74, 75, 76, p. 195, 197, in Script. post Theophanem), who allows himself to use many technical or barbarous words : barbarous, says he, τῇ τῶν πολλῶν ἀμαθίᾳ, καλὸν γὰρ ἐπὶ τούτοις κοινολεκτεῖν. Ducange labours on some ; but he was not a weaver.

[21] The manufactures of Palermo, as they are described by Hugo Falcandus (Hist. Sicula in proem. in Muratori, Script. Rerum Italicarum, tom. v. p. 256), are a copy of those of Greece. Without transcribing his declamatory sentences, which I have softened in the text, I shall observe, that in this passage, the strange word *exarentasmata* is very properly changed for *exanthemata* by Carisius, the first editor. Falcandus lived about the year 1190.

Lisbon, were famous for the manufacture, the use, and perhaps the exportation of silk. It was first introduced into Sicily by the Normans ; and this emigration of trade distinguishes the victory of Roger from the uniform and fruitless hostilities of every age. After the sack of Corinth, Athens, and Thebes, his lieutenant embarked with a captive train of weavers and artificers of both sexes, a trophy glorious to their master and disgraceful to the Greek emperor.[22] The king of Italy was not insensible of the value of the present ; and, in the restitution of the prisoners, he exempted only the male and female manufacturers of Thebes and Corinth, who labour, says the Byzantine historian, under a barbarous lord, like the old Eretrians in the service of Darius.[23] A stately edifice, in the palace of Palermo, was erected for the use of this industrious colony ;[24] and the art was propagated by their children and disciples to satisfy the increasing demand of the western world. The decay of the looms of Sicily may be ascribed to the troubles of the island and the competition of the Italian cities. In the year thirteen hundred and fourteen, Lucca alone, among her sister republics, enjoyed the lucrative monopoly.[25] A domestic revolution dispersed the manufactures of Florence, Bologna, Venice, Milan, and even the countries beyond the Alps ; and, thirteen years after this event, the statutes of Modena enjoin the plant-

transported from Greece to Italy

[22] Inde ad interiora Græciæ progressi, Corinthum, Thebas, Athenas, antiquâ nobilitate celebres, expugnant , et, maximâ ibidem prædâ direptâ, opifices etiam, qui sericos pannos texere solent, ob ignominiam Imperatoris illius suique principis gloriam captivos deducunt. Quos Rogerius, in Palermo Siciliæ metropoli collocans, artem texendi suos edocere præcepit ; et exhinc prædicta ars illa, prius a Græcis tantum inter Christianos habita, Romanis patere cœpit ingeniis (Otho Frisingen. de Gestis Frederici I. l. i. c. 33, in Muratori, Script. Ital. tom. vi. p. 668). This exception allows the bishop to celebrate Lisbon and Almeria in sericorum pannorum opificio prænobilissimæ (in Chron. apud Muratori, Annali d'Italia, tom. ix. p. 415). [On the manufacture of silk and the regulation of the silk trade and guilds of silk merchants at Constantinople, much light is thrown by the so-called 'Επαρχικὸν βιβλίον, or Book of the Prefect of the City—an Imperial Edict published by M. Jules Nicole of Geneva in 1893, and attributed by him, without sufficient proof, to Leo VI. Cp. sects. iv.-viii. We find distinguished the vestiopratai who sold silk dresses ; the prandiopratai who sold dresses imported from Syria or Cilicia ; the metaxopratai, silk merchants ; the katartarioi, silk manufacturers ; and serikarioi, silk weavers.]

[23] Nicetas in Manuel, l. ii. c. 8, p. 65. He describes these Greeks as skilled εὐητρίους ὀθόνας ὑφαίνειν, as ἱστῷ προσανέχοντας τῶν ἐξαμίτων καὶ χρυσοπάστων στολῶν.

[24] Hugo Falcandus styles them nobiles officinas. The Arabs had not introduced silk, though they had planted canes and made sugar in the plain of Palermo.

[25] See the Life of Castruccio Casticani, not by Machiavel, but by his more authentic biographer Nicholas Tegrimi. Muratori, who has inserted it in the xith volume of his Scriptores, quotes this curious passage in his Italian Antiquities (tom. i. dissert. xxv. p. 378).

ing of mulberry trees and regulate the duties on raw silk.[26]
The northern climates are less propitious to the education of
the silk-worm ; but the industry of France and England [27] is
supplied and enriched by the productions of Italy and China.

I must repeat the complaint that the vague and scanty memorials of the times will not afford any just estimate of the
taxes, the revenue, and the resources of the Greek empire.
From every province of Europe and Asia the rivulets of gold
and silver discharged into the Imperial reservoir a copious and
perennial stream.[28]  The separation of the branches from the
trunk increased the relative magnitude of Constantinople ; and
the maxims of despotism contracted the state to the capital,
the capital to the palace, and the palace to the royal person.
A Jewish traveller, who visited the East in the twelfth century,
is lost in his admiration of the Byzantine riches.  " It is here,"
says Benjamin of Tudela, " in the queen of cities, that the
tributes of the Greek empire are annually deposited, and the
lofty towers are filled with precious magazines of silk, purple
and gold.  It is said that Constantinople pays each day to her
sovereign twenty thousand pieces of gold ; which are levied on
the shops, taverns, and markets, on the merchants of Persia
and Egypt, of Russia and Hungary, of Italy and Spain, who
frequent the capital by sea and land." [29]  In all pecuniary
matters, the authority of a Jew is doubtless respectable ; but,
as the three hundred and sixty-five days would produce a
yearly income exceeding seven millions sterling, I am tempted
to retrench at least the numerous festivals of the Greek calendar.  The mass of treasure that was saved by Theodora and
Basil the Second will  suggest a splendid though indefinite
idea of their supplies and resources.  The mother of Michael,
before she retired to a cloister, attempted to check or expose
the prodigality of her ungrateful son by a free and faithful

[26] From the Ms. statutes, as they are quoted by Muratori in his Italian Antiquities (tom. ii. dissert. xxx. p. 46-48).

[27] The broad silk manufacture was established in England in the year 1620
(Anderson's Chronological Deduction, vol. ii. p. 4) ; but it is to the revocation of
the Edict of Nantes that we owe the Spitalfields colony.

[28] [And from the reign of Leo the Great in the 5th, to the capture of Constantinople at the beginning of the 13th, the gold coinage was never depreciated.]

[29] Voyage de Benjamin de Tudèle, tom. i. c. 5, p. 44-52.  The Hebrew text has
been translated into French by that marvellous child Baratier, who has added a
volume of crude learning.  The errors and fictions of the Jewish rabbi are not a
sufficient ground to deny the reality of his travels.  [Benjamin's Itinerary has been
edited and translated by A. Asher, 2 vols., 1840.  For his statements concerning
Greece, cp. Gregorovius, Gesch. der Stadt Athen im Mittelalter, i. p. 200.]

account of the wealth which he inherited : one hundred and nine thousand pounds of gold, and three hundred thousand of silver, the fruits of her own economy and that of her deceased husband.[30]  The avarice of Basil is not less renowned than his valour and fortune : his victorious armies were paid and rewarded without breaking into the mass of two hundred thousand pounds of gold (about eight millions sterling) which he had buried in the subterraneous vaults of the palace.[31]  Such accumulation of treasure is rejected by the theory and practice of modern policy ; and we are more apt to compute the national riches by the use and abuse of the public credit.  Yet the maxims of antiquity are still embraced by a monarch formidable to his enemies ; by a republic respectable to her allies ; and both have attained their respective ends, of military power and domestic tranquillity.

Whatever might be consumed for the present wants, or reserved for the future use, of the state, the first and most sacred demand was for the pomp and pleasure of the emperor; and his discretion only could define the measure of his private expense.  The princes of Constantinople were far removed from the simplicity of nature ; yet, with the revolving seasons, they were led by taste or fashion to withdraw to a purer air from the smoke and tumult of the capital.  They enjoyed, or affected to enjoy, the rustic festival of the vintage ; their leisure was amused by the exercise of the chase, and the calmer occupation of fishing ; and in the summer heats they were shaded from the sun and refreshed by the cooling breezes from the sea.  The coasts and islands of Asia and Europe were covered with their magnificent villas ; but, instead of the modest art which secretly strives to hide itself and to decorate the scenery of nature, the marble structure of their gardens served only to expose the riches of the lord and the labours of the architect.  The successive casualties of inheritance and forfeiture had rendered the sovereign proprietor of many stately houses in the city and suburbs, of which twelve were appropriated to the ministers of state ; but the great palace, [32] the centre of the Imperial resi-

*Pomp and luxury of the emperors*

*The palace of Constantinople*

[30] See the continuator of Theophanes (l. iv. p. 107 [p. 172, ed. Bonn]), Cedrenus (p. 544 [ii. p. 158, ed. Bonn]), and Zonaras (tom. ii. l. xvi. p. 157 [c. 2]).

[31] Zonaras (tom. ii. l. xvii. p. 225 [c. 8]), instead of pounds, uses the more classic appellation of talents, which, in a literal sense and strict computation, would multiply sixty-fold the treasure of Basil.

[32] For a copious and minute description of the Imperial palace, see the Constantinop. Christiana (l. ii. c. 4, p. 113-123) of Ducange, the Tillemont of the middle

dence, was fixed during eleven centuries to the same position,
between the hippodrome, the cathedral of St. Sophia, and the
gardens, which descended by many a terrace to the shores of
the Propontis. The primitive edifice of the first Constantine
was a copy or rival of ancient Rome ; the gradual improvements
of his successors aspired to emulate the wonders of the old
world,[33] and in the tenth century the Byzantine palace excited
the admiration, at least of the Latins, by an unquestionable
pre-eminence of strength, size, and magnificence.[34] But the
toil and treasure of so many ages had produced a vast and
irregular pile ; each separate building was marked with the
character of the times and of the founder; and the want of
space might excuse the reigning monarch who demolished,
perhaps with secret satisfaction, the works of his predecessors.
The economy of the emperor Theophilus allowed a more free
and ample scope for his domestic luxury and splendour. A
favourite ambassador, who had astonished the Abbassides themselves by his pride and liberality, presented on his return the
model of a palace, which the caliph of Bagdad had recently

ages. Never has laborious Germany produced two antiquarians more laborious
and accurate than these two natives of lively France. [For recent works on the
reconstruction of the Imperial Palace, based on the Ceremonies of Constantine
Porphyrogennetos, see above, vol. 2, p. 546. All attempts to reconstruct the plan
must be fanciful until the site is excavated. The following facts emerge as certain
from the investigations of Labarte and Bieliaiev. There were two ways from the
Chrysotriklinos (see below, n. 36) to the Hippodrome. By the northern part of the
palace, the Emperor could reach the cathisma at the north of the Hippodrome ;
but the (probably) shorter way led through the southern rooms of the palace, (a)
the Lausiac triklinos and (b) the triklinos of Justinian (II.), commonly called "the
Justinian ". The Justinian opened into the Skyla (a vestibule), from which there
was a door into the Hippodrome (eastern side) ; and, as the Justinian ran from
east to west, we can conclude that the Chrysotriklinos, the chief throne-room of the
Older Palace, with the adjoining private rooms of the Emperor, was *east* of the
Hippodrome. The other way, which the Emperor followed when he went to St.
Sophia or to the cathisma of the Hippodrome, led through the palace of Theophilus (the Trikonchon, see below) and the palace of Daphne. We know the names
of all the rooms, &c., through which he passed, but we have no clue to the direction. We can only say that (1) all these palaces and halls were north of the Justinian ; (2) the Trikonchon lay between the Gold Triklinos and the palace of
Daphne ; (3) the palace of Magnaura lay north of the palace of Daphne.]

[33] The Byzantine palace surpasses the Capitol, the palace of Pergamus, the
Rufinian wood (φαιδρὸν ἄγαλμα), the temple of Hadrian at Cyzicus, the Pyramids,
the Pharus, &c., according to an epigram (Antholog. Græc. l. iv. p. 488, 489.
Brodæi, apud Wechel) ascribed to Julian, ex-præfect of Egypt. Seventy-one of
his epigrams, some lively, are collected in Brunck (Analect. Græc. tom. ii. p. 493-
510) ; but this is wanting.

[34] Constantinopolitanum Palatium non pulchritudine solum, verum etiam forti-
tudine, omnibus quas unquam videram [*leg.* perspexerim] munitionibus præstat
(Liutprand, Hist. l. v. c. 9 [ = c. 21], p. 465).

constructed on the banks of the Tigris. The model was instantly copied and surpassed; the new buildings of Theophilus [35] were accompanied with gardens, and with five churches, one of which was conspicuous for size and beauty; it was crowned with three domes, the roof, of gilt brass, reposed on columns of Italian marble, and the walls were encrusted with marbles of various colours. In the face of the church, a semi-circular portico, of the figure and name of the Greek *sigma*, was supported by fifteen columns of Phrygian marble, and the subterraneous vaults were of a similar construction. The square before the sigma was decorated with a fountain, and the margin of the bason was lined and encompassed with plates of silver. In the beginning of each season, the bason, instead of water, was replenished with the most exquisite fruits, which were abandoned to the populace for the entertainment of the prince. He enjoyed this tumultuous spectacle from a throne resplendent with gold and gems, which was raised by a marble staircase to the height of a lofty terrace. Below the throne were seated the officers of his guards, the magistrates, the chiefs of the factions of the circus; the inferior steps were occupied by the people, and the place below was covered with troops of dancers, singers, and pantomimes. The square was surrounded by the hall of justice, the arsenal, and the various offices of business and pleasure; and the *purple* chamber was named from the annual distribution of robes of scarlet and purple by the hand of the empress herself. The long series of the apartments was adapted to the seasons, and decorated with marble and porphyry, with painting, sculpture, and mosaics, with a profusion of gold, silver, and precious stones. His fanciful magnificence employed the skill and patience of such artists as the times could afford; but the taste of Athens would have despised their frivolous and costly labours: a golden tree, with its leaves and branches, which sheltered a multitude of birds, warbling their artificial notes, and two lions of massy gold, and of the natural size, who

[The Mystic Phiale]

---

[35] See the anonymous continuator of Theophanes (p. 59, 61, 86 [p. 94, 98, 139, ed. Bonn]), whom I have followed in the neat and concise abstract of Le Beau (Hist. du Bas. Empire, tom. xiv. p. 436, 438). [The great building of Theophilus was the Trikonchon (so called from its three apses) with a semicircular peristyle called the Sigma. The building had an understorey, which from its acoustic property of rendering whispers audible was called Μυστήριον—" The Whispering Room". Theophilus was so pleased with his new edifice that he made considerable changes in the ceremonies of the Court; transferring to the Trikonchon many solemnities and receptions which used to be held in other rooms. See Theoph. Contin. p. 142, ed. Bonn.]

looked and roared like their brethren of the forest. The successors of Theophilus, of the Basilian and Comnenian dynasties, were not less ambitious of leaving some memorial of their residence ; and the portion of the palace most splendid and august was dignified with the title of the golden *triclinium*.[36]

Furniture and attendance With becoming modesty, the rich and noble Greeks aspired to imitate their sovereign, and, when they passed through the streets on horseback, in their robes of silk and embroidery, they were mistaken by the children for kings.[37] A matron of Peloponnesus,[38] who had cherished the infant fortunes of Basil the Macedonian, was excited by tenderness or vanity to visit the greatness of her adopted son. In a journey of five hundred miles from Patras to Constantinople, her age or indolence declined the fatigue of an horse or carriage ; the soft litter or bed of Danielis was transported on the shoulders of ten robust slaves ; and, as they were relieved at easy distances, a band of three hundred was selected for the performance of this service. She was entertained in the Byzantine palace with filial reverence and the honours of a queen ; and, whatever might be the origin of her wealth, her gifts were not unworthy of the regal dignity. I have already described the fine and curious manufactures of Peloponnesus, of linen, silk, and woollen ; but the most acceptable of her presents consisted in three hundred beautiful youths, of whom one hundred were eunuchs ;[39] "for she was not

[36] In aureo triclinio quæ præstantior est pars potentissime (*the usurper Romanus*) degens cæteras partes (*filiis*) distribuerat (Liutprand. Hist. l. v. c. 9 [ = c. 21 ], p. 469). For this lax signification of Triclinium (ædificium tria vel plura κλίνη scilicet στέγη complectens) see Ducange (Gloss. Græc. et Observations sur Joinville, p. 240) and Reiske (ad Constantinum de Ceremoniis, p. 7). [The Gold Room (Χρυσοτρίκλινος), being near the imperial chambers, was more convenient for ordinary ceremonies than the more distant throne-rooms which were used only on specially solemn occasions. It was built by Justin II., and was probably modelled on the design of the Church of St. Sergius and Bacchus built by Justinian. (For the plan of this church see plate 5 in the atlas to Salzenberg's Altchristliche Baudenkmale von Cpel. ; cp. Labarte, *op. cit.* p. 161 ; Bieliaiev, *op. cit.* p. 12.) Ducange, Constant. Christ. II. p. 94-95, confounds the Chrysotriklinos with the Augusteus, another throne-room which was in the Daphne palace. The Chrysotriklinos was domed and had eight καμάραι or recesses off the central room.]

[37] In equis vecti (says Benjamin of Tudela) regum filiis videntur persimiles. I prefer the Latin version of Constantine l'Empereur (p. 46) to the French of Baratier (tom. i. p. 49).

[38] See the account of her journey, munificence, and testament in the Life of Basil, by his grandson Constantine (c. 74, 75, 76, p. 195-197).

[39] *Carsamatium* [*leg.* carzimasium] (καρξιμάδες, Ducange, Gloss.) Græci vocant, amputatis viril ibus et virgâ, puerum eunuchum quos [*leg.* quod] Verdunenses mercatores ob immensum lucrum facere solent et in Hispaniam ducere (Liutprand, l. vi. c. 3, p. 470).—The last abomination of the abominable slave-trade ! Yet I am surprised to find in the xth century such active speculations of commerce in Lorraine.

ignorant," says the historian, "that the air of the palace is more congenial to such insects than a shepherd's dairy to the flies of the summer". During her lifetime, she bestowed the greater part of her estates in Peloponnesus, and her testament instituted Leo, the son of Basil, her universal heir. After the payment of the legacies, fourscore villas or farms were added to the Imperial domain; and three thousand slaves of Danielis were enfranchised by their new lord, and transplanted as a colony to the Italian coast. From this example of a private matron, we may estimate the wealth and magnificence of the emperors. Yet our enjoyments are confined by a narrow circle; and, whatsoever may be its value, the luxury of life is possessed with more innocence and safety by the master of his own, than by the steward of the public, fortune.

In an absolute government, which levels the distinctions of noble and plebeian birth, the sovereign is the sole fountain of honour; and the rank, both in the palace and the empire, depends on the titles and offices which are bestowed and resumed by his arbitrary will. Above a thousand years, from Vespasian to Alexius Comnenus,[40] the *Cæsar* was the second person, or at least the second degree, after the supreme title of *Augustus* was more freely communicated to the sons and brothers of the reigning monarch. To elude without violating his promise to a powerful associate, the husband of his sister, and, without giving himself an equal, to reward the piety of his brother Isaac, the crafty Alexius interposed a new and supereminent dignity. The happy flexibility of the Greek tongue allowed him to compound the names of Augustus and emperor (Sebastos and Autocrator), and the union produced the sonorous title of *Sebastocrator*. He was exalted above the Cæsar on the first step of the throne; the public acclamations repeated his name; and he was only distinguished from the sovereign by some peculiar ornaments of the head and feet. The emperor alone could assume the purple or red buskins, and the close diadem or tiara, which imitated the fashion of the Persian kings.[41]  It was an high pyramidal cap of

*Honours and titles of the Imperial family*

[40] See the Alexiad (l. iii. p. 78, 79 [c. 4]) of Anna Comnena, who, except in filial piety, may be compared to Mademoiselle de Montpensier. In her awful reverence for titles and forms, she styles her father Ἐπιστημονάρχης, the inventor of this royal art, the τέχνη τεχνῶν, and ἐπιστήμη ἐπιστημῶν.

[41] Στέμμα, στέφανος, διάδημα; see Reiske, ad Ceremoniale, p, 14, 15. Ducange has given a learned dissertation on the crowns of Constantinople, Rome, France, &c. (sur Joinville, xxv. p. 289-303), but of his thirty-four models none exactly tally with Anna's description. [The Imperial costume may be best studied in Byzantine miniatures. It does not seem correct to describe the crown as a "high pyramidal

cloth or silk, almost concealed by a profusion of pearls and jewels: the crown was formed by an horizontal circle and two arches of gold ; at the summit, the point of their intersection, was placed a globe or cross, and two strings or lappets of pearl depended on either cheek.   Instead of red, the buskins of the Sebastocrator and Cæsar were green ; and on their *open* coronets or crowns the precious gems were more sparingly distributed.   Beside and below the Cæsar, the fancy of Alexius created the *Panhyper-sebastos* and the *Protosebastos,* whose sound and signification will satisfy a Grecian ear.   They imply a superiority and a priority above the simple name of Augustus ; and this sacred and primitive title of the Roman prince was degraded to the kinsmen and servants of the Byzantine court.   The daughter of Alexius applauds, with fond complacency, this artful gradation of hopes and honours ; but the science of words is accessible to the meanest capacity ; and this vain dictionary was easily enriched by the pride of his successors.   To their favourite sons or brothers, they imparted the more lofty appellation of Lord or *Despot,* which was illustrated with new ornaments and prerogatives, and placed immediately after the person of the emperor himself.   The five titles of 1. *Despot ;* 2. *Sebastocrator ;* 3. *Cæsar ;* 4. *Panhypersebastos ;* and, 5. *Protosebastos ;* were usually confined to the princes of his blood ; they were the emanations of his majesty ; but, as they exercised no regular functions, their existence was useless, and their authority precarious.

Offices of the palace, the state, and the army But in every monarchy the substantial powers of government must be divided and exercised by the ministers of the palace and treasury, the fleet and army.   The titles alone can differ ; and in

cap " ; the crowns represented in the paintings are not high or pyramidal.  The diadems of the Empresses had not the cross or the pearl pendants.  As Gibbon says, it was only the crown and the red boots which distinguished the Emperor ; there were no distinctively Imperial robes.   (1) On great state occasions the Emperor wore a long tunic (not necessarily purple) called a *divetesion* (διβητήσιον) ; and over it either a heavy mantle (χλαμύς) or a scarf (λῶρος) wound over the shoulders and round the arms.   (2) As a sort of half-dress costume and always when he was riding the Emperor wore a different tunic, simpler and more convenient called the *scaramangion* (σκαραμάγγιον) and over it a lighter cloak (σαγίον).  (3) There was yet another lighter dress, the *colovion* (κολόβιον), a tunic with short sleeves to the elbow or no sleeves at all, which he wore on some occasions.  All these official tunics were worn over the ordinary tunic (χιτών) of private life.  The only satisfactory discussions of these Imperial costumes are to be found in Bieliaiev Ezhednevnye i Voskresnye Priemy viz. Tsarei ( = Byzantina Bk. ii., 1893) : for the σκαραμάγγιον, p. 8 ; κολόβιον, p. 26 ; διβητήσιον, p. 51-56 ; λῶρος (which corresponded to the Roman *trabea*), p. 213, 214, 301.   For the θωράκιον which was worn on certain occasions instead of the διβητήσιον see *ib.* 197-8 (Basil ii. in the miniature mentioned below, note 54, seems to wear a gold θωράκιον).   Bieliaiev explains the origin of διβητήσιον (διβιτήσιον) satisfactorily from Lat. *divitense* (p. 54).]

the revolution of ages, the counts and præfects, the prætor and quæstor, insensibly descended, while their servants rose above their heads to the first honours of the state. 1. In a monarchy, which refers every object to the person of the prince, the care and ceremonies of the palace form the most respectable department. The *Curopalata*,[42] so illustrious in the age of Justinian, was supplanted by the *Protovestiare*, whose primitive functions were limited to the custody of the wardrobe. From thence his jurisdiction was extended over the numerous menials of pomp and luxury; and he presided with his silver wand at the public and private audience. 2. In the ancient system of Constantine, the name of *Logothete*, or accountant, was applied to the receivers of the finances: the principal officers were distinguished as the Logothetes of the domain, of the posts, the army, the private and public treasure; and the *great Logothete*, the supreme guardian of the laws and revenues, is compared with the chancellor of the Latin monarchies.[43] His discerning eye pervaded

---

[42] Pars exstans curis, solo diademate dispar,
    Ordine pro rerum vocitatus *Cura-Palati;*

says the African Corippus (de Laudibus Justini, l. i. 136), and in the same century (the sixth) Cassiodorius represents him, who, virgâ aureâ decoratus, inter numerosa obsequia primus ante pedes regios incederet (Variar. vii. 5). But this great officer (unknown) ἀνεπίγνωστος, exercising no function, νῦν δὲ οὐδεμίαν, was cast down by the modern Greeks to the xvth rank (Codin. c. 5, p. 65 [p. 35, ed. Bonn]). [It is not correct to say that the place of the Curopalates was taken by the protovestiarios. This office of Curopalates still existed, but his functions and the entire responsibility of the care of the Palace were devolved upon the Great Papias (ὁ μέγας παπίας), who was always an eunuch and held the rank of protospathar. He was a very important official, and had an assistant (also an eunuch) called " the Second " (ὁ δεύτερος). Under him were all the palace servants: (1) the diaetarii, attendants attached to the various rooms ; (2) the lûstai, bath-attendants ; (3) the lamp-lighters (κανδηλάπται) ; (4) the stove-heaters (καμηνάδες, καλδάριοι) ; (5) the horo-logoi, who looked after the palace clocks, and (6) the mysterious ζαράβαι. Under the Second, who was specially concerned with the wardrobe, were the *vestitores*, &c. The protovestiarios is totally distinct. He was a sort of chamberlain, next in rank apparently to the Præpositus sacri cubiculi, and holding an office of great trust. Bieliaiev (to whom we owe a valuable essay on all these offices in Byzantina, i. p. 145 *sqq.*) conjectures that the duty of the Protovestiary was to take care of a private treasury (in which not only ornaments but money was kept) in the Imperial bed-chamber (p. 176-7). As for the Curopalates he still remained one of the highest dignitaries, though it is not clear what duties he performed. Probably his post was honorary. In rank he was the highest person at court next to the nobilissimus, who came immediately after the Cæsar. (Philotheus, ap. Const. Porph. de Cer. ii. 52, p. 711.) Only six persons were deemed worthy of sitting at the same table as the Emperor and Empress, namely, the Patriarch of Constantinople, the Cæsar, the Nobilissimus, the Curopalates, the Basileopator (cp. above, vol. v. p. 206), and the Zostê patricia or highest maid of honour. See Philotheus, *ib.* p. 726.]

[43] Nicetas (in Manuel. l. vii. c. i. [p. 262, ed. Bonn]) defines him ὡς ἡ Λατίνων [βούλεται] φωνὴ Καγκελάριον, ὡς δ' Ἕλληνες εἴποιεν Λογοθέτην. Yet the epithet of μέγας was added by the elder Andronicus (Ducange, tom. i. p. 822, 823). [This is the Logothete τοῦ γενικοῦ who corresponded to the old Count of the Sacred Largesses

the civil administration; and he was assisted, in due subordination, by the eparch or præfect of the city, the first secretary, and the keepers of the privy seal, the archives, and the red or purple ink which was reserved for the sacred signature of the emperor alone.[44]   The introductor and interpreter of foreign ambassadors were the great *Chiauss* [45] and the *Dragoman*,[46] two names of Turkish origin, and which are still familiar to the Sublime Porte. 3. From the humble style and service of guards, the *Domestics* insensibly rose to the station of generals; the military themes of the East and West, the legions of Europe and Asia, were often divided, till the *great Domestic* was finally invested with the universal and absolute command of the land forces.[47]   The *Protostrator*, in his original functions, was the assistant of the emperor when he mounted on horseback; he gradually became the lieutenant of the great Domestic in the field; and his jurisdiction extended over the stables, the cavalry, and the royal train of hunting and hawking.   The *Stratopedarch* was the great judge of the camp; the *Protospathaire* [48] commanded the guards; the *Constable*,[49] the *great Æteriarch*,[50] and the *Acolyth* [51] were the

(τὸ γενικόν = the Exchequer.   For the history of the financial bureaux, compare Bury, *Later Roman Empire*, ii. p. 324, note).   But there were other Logothetes: the Logothete of the military chest (τοῦ στρατιωτικοῦ); the Logothete of the Dromos or Imperial post—a name which first occurs in the 8th century; the Logothete of the pastures (τῶν αγελῶν, "of the flocks").]

[44] From Leo I. (A.D. 470) the Imperial ink, which is still visible on some original acts, was a mixture of vermillion and cinnabar or purple.   The Emperor's guardians, who shared in this prerogative, always marked in green ink the indiction and the month.   See the Dictionnaire Diplomatique (tom. i. p. 511, 513), a valuable abridgment.

[45] The Sultan sent a Σιαούς to Alexius (Anna Comnena, l. vi. p. 170 [c. 9]; Ducange *ad loc.*), and Pachymer often speaks of the μέγας τζαούς (l. vii. c. 1, l. xii. c. 30, l. xiii. c. 22).   The Chiaoush basha is now at the head of 700 officers (Rycaut's *Ottoman Empire*, p. 349, octavo edition).

[46] *Tagerman* is the Arabic name of an interpreter (d'Herbelot, p. 854, 855); πρῶτος τῶν ἑρμηνέων οὓς κοινῶς ὀνομάζουσι δραγομάνους, says Codinus (c. v. No. 70, p. 67).   See Villehardouin (No. 96), Busbequius (Epist. iv. p. 338), and Ducange (Observations sur Villehardouin and Gloss. Græc. et Latin).

[47] [There were various offices (7 in the 10th century) with the title Domestic. The three chief were the Domestic of the Schools, the Domestic of the Excubiti, and the Domestic of the Imperials.   Cp. Philotheus apud Const. Porph. i. p. 713.]

[48] [The Πρωτοσπαθάριος τῶν βασιλικῶν.   But *protospatharios* was also a rank, not a title; it was the rank below that of patrician and above that of *spatharocandidatus* (which in turn was superior to that of *spatharios*).]

[49] Κονόσταυλος, or κοντόσταυλος, a corruption from the Latin Comes stabuli, or the French Connétable.   In a military sense, it was used by the Greeks in the xith century, at least as early as in France.

[50] [ὁ ἑταιρειάρχης, cp. above, vol. v. p. 208, note 45.]

[51] [ἀκόλουθός, and if anglicized should be *acoluth*.   ἀκολουθία meant a ceremony.]

separate chiefs of the Franks, the barbarians, and the Varangi, or English, the mercenary strangers, who, in the decay of the national spirit, formed the nerve of the Byzantine armies. 4. The naval powers were under the command of the *great Duke*; in his absence they obeyed the *great Drungaire* of the fleet; and, in *his* place, the *Emir*, or *admiral*, a name of Saracen extraction,[52] but which has been naturalised in all the modern languages of Europe. Of these officers, and of many more whom it would be useless to enumerate, the civil and military hierarchy was framed. Their honours and emoluments, their dress and titles, their mutual salutations and respective pre-eminence, were balanced with more exquisite labour than would have fixed the constitution of a free people; and the code was almost perfect when this baseless fabric, the monument of pride and servitude, was for ever buried in the ruins of the empire.[53]

The most lofty titles and the most humble postures, which devotion has applied to the Supreme Being, have been prostituted by flattery and fear to creatures of the same nature with ourselves. The mode of *adoration*,[54] of falling prostrate on the ground and kissing the feet of the emperor, was borrowed by Diocletian from Persian servitude; but it was continued and aggravated till the last age of the Greek monarchy. Excepting only on Sundays, when it was waved, from a motive of religious pride, this humiliating reverence was exacted from all who entered the royal presence, from the princes invested with the diadem and purple, and from the ambassadors who represented their independent sovereigns, the caliphs of Asia, Egypt, or Spain, the kings of France and Italy, and the Latin emperors of ancient

*Adoration of the emperor*

[52] It was directly borrowed from the Normans. In the xiith century, Giannone reckons the admiral of Sicily among the great officers.

[53] This sketch of honours and offices is drawn from George Codinus Curopalata, who survived the taking of Constantinople by the Turks; his elaborate though trifling work (de Officiis Ecclesiæ et Aulæ C. P.) has been illustrated by the notes of Goar, and the three books of Gretser, a learned Jesuit. [For Codinus see Appendix 1.—Following "Codinus," Ducange and Gibbon, in the account in the text, have given a description of the ministers and officials of the Byzantine court which confounds different periods in a single picture. The functions and the importance of these dignitaries were constantly changing; but the history of each office has still to be written.]

[54] The respectful salutation of carrying the hand to the mouth, *ad os*, is the root of the Latin word, *adoro adorare*. [This is to go too far back. *Adoro* comes directly from *oro*.] See our learned Selden (vol. iii. p. 143-145, 942), in his Titles of Honour. It seems, from the first books of Herodotus, to be of Persian origin. [The adoration of the Basileus is vividly represented in a fine miniature in a Venetian psalter, which shows the Emperor Basil II. in grand costume and men grovelling at his feet. There is a coloured reproduction in Schlumberger's Nicéphore Phocas, p. 304.]

Rome. In his transactions of business, Liutprand, bishop of Cremona,[55] asserted the free spirit of a Frank and the dignity of
his master Otho. Yet his sincerity cannot disguise the abasement of his first audience. When he approached the throne,
the birds of the golden tree began to warble their notes, which
were accompanied by the roarings of the two lions of gold.
With his two companions, Liutprand was compelled to bow and
to fall prostrate; and thrice he touched the ground with his
forehead. He arose; but, in the short interval, the throne had
been hoisted by an engine from the floor to the ceiling, the
Imperial figure appeared in new and more gorgeous apparel,
and the interview was concluded in haughty and majestic
silence. In this honest and curious narrative, the bishop of
Cremona represents the ceremonies of the Byzantine court,
which are still practised in the Sublime Porte, and which were
preserved in the last age by the dukes of Moscovy or Russia.
After a long journey by the sea and land, from Venice to Constantinople, the ambassador halted at the golden gate, till he
was conducted by the formal officers to the hospitable palace
prepared for his reception; but this palace was a prison, and its
jealous keepers prohibited all social intercourse, either with
strangers or natives. At his first audience, he offered the gifts
of his master, slaves, and golden vases, and costly armour. The
ostentatious payment of the officers and troops displayed before
his eyes the riches of the empire: he was entertained at a
royal banquet,[56] in which the ambassadors of the nations were
marshalled by the esteem or contempt of the Greeks: from his
own table, the emperor, as the most signal favour, sent the
plates which he had tasted; and his favourites were dismissed
with a robe of honour.[57] In the morning and evening of each
day, his civil and military servants attended their duty in the

[55] The two embassies of Liutprand to Constantinople, all that he saw or suffered
in the Greek capital, are pleasantly described by himself (Hist. l. vi. c. 1-4, p. 469-
471. Legatio ad Nicephorum Phocam, p. 479-489).

[56] Among the amusements of the feast, a boy balanced, on his forehead, a pike,
or pole, twenty-four feet long, with a cross bar of two cubits a little below the top.
Two boys, naked, though cinctured (*campestrati*), together and singly, climbed,
stood, played, descended, &c., ita me stupidum reddidit; utrum mirabilius nescio
(p. 470 [vi. c. 9]). At another repast, an homily of Chrysostom on the Acts of the
Apostles was read elata voce non Latine (p. 483 [c. 29. The words *non Latine* do
not occur in the text; but there is a variant *Latina* for *elata*]).

[57] *Gala* is not improbably derived from Cala, or Caloat, in Arabic, a robe of
honour (Reiske, Not. in Ceremon. p. 84). [*Gala* seems to be connected with
*gallant*, O. Fr. *galant;* and it is supposed that both words may be akin to N.H.G.
*geil*, Gothic *gailjan* (to rejoice), χαίρω.]

palace; their labour was repaid by the sight, perhaps by the smile, of their lord; his commands were signified by a nod or a sign; but all earthly greatness *stood* silent and submissive in his presence. In his regular or extraordinary processions through the capital, he unveiled his person to the public view; the rites of policy were connected with those of religion, and his visits to the principal churches were regulated by the festivals of the Greek calendar. On the eve of these processions, the gracious or devout intention of the monarch was proclaimed by the heralds. The streets were cleared and purified; the pavement was strewed with flowers; the most precious furniture, the gold and silver plate, and silken hangings were displayed from the windows and balconies, and a severe discipline restrained and silenced the tumult of the populace. The march was opened by the military officers at the head of their troops; they were followed in long order by the magistrates and ministers of the civil government: the person of the emperor was guarded by his eunuchs and domestics, and at the church door he was solemnly received by the patriarch and his clergy. The task of applause was not abandoned to the rude and spontaneous voices of the crowd. The most convenient stations were occupied by the bands of the blue and green factions of the circus; [58] and their furious conflicts, which had shaken the capital, were insensibly sunk to an emulation of servitude. From either side they echoed in responsive melody the praises of the emperor; their poets and musicians directed the choir, and *long life* [59] and victory were the burden of every song. The same acclamations were performed at the audience, the banquet, and the church; and, as an evidence of boundless sway, they were repeated in the Latin, [60] Gothic, Persian, French, and even English language, [61] by the mercenaries who sustained the real or fictitious character of those nations. By the pen of Constantine Porphyrogenitus this science of form and flattery has been reduced into a pom-

*Processions and acclamations*

---

[58] [See above, vol. iv., Appendix 10, p. 531-2.]

[59] Πολυχρονίζειν is explained by εὐφημίζειν (Codin. c. 7, Ducange, Gloss. Græc. tom. i. p. 1199).

[60] Κωνσέρβετ Δέους ἠμπέριουμ βέστρουμ — βίκτωρ σῆς σέμπερ — βήβητε Δόμηνι Ἠμπεράτορες ἦν μούλτος ἄννος (Ceremon. [i.] c. 75, p. 215). The want of the Latin V obliged the Greeks to employ their β [it was not a shift; the pronunciation of β was then, as it is now, the same as that of v]; nor do they regard quantity. Till he recollected the true language, these strange sentences might puzzle a professor.

[61] Βάραγγοι κατὰ τὴν πατρίαν γλῶσσαν καὶ οὗτοι, ἤγουν Ἰγκλινιστὶ πολυχρονίζουσι (Codin. p. 90 [p. 57, ed. Bonn]). I wish he had preserved the words, however corrupt, of their English acclamation.

pous and trifling volume,[62] which the vanity of succeeding times might enrich with an ample supplement. Yet the calmer reflection of a prince would surely suggest that the same acclamations were applied to every character and every reign ; and, if he had risen from a private rank, he might remember that his own voice had been the loudest and most eager in applause, at the very moment when he envied the fortune, or conspired against the life, of his predecessor.[63]

*Marriage of the Cæsars with foreign nations*

The princes of the North, of the nations, says Constantine, without faith or fame, were ambitious of mingling their blood with the blood of the Cæsars, by their marriage with a royal virgin, or by the nuptials of their daughters with a Roman prince.[64] The aged monarch, in his instructions to his son, reveals the secret maxims of policy and pride ; and suggests the most decent reasons for refusing these insolent and unreasonable demands. Every animal, says the discreet emperor, is prompted by nature to seek a mate among the animals of his own species ; and the human species is divided into various tribes, by the distinction of language, religion, and manners. A just regard to the purity of descent preserves the harmony of public and private life ; but the mixture of foreign blood is the fruitful source of disorder and discord. Such has ever been the opinion and practice of the sage Romans ; their jurisprudence proscribed the marriage of a citizen and a stranger ; in the days of freedom and virtue, a senator would have scorned to match his daughter with a king ; the glory of Mark Anthony was sullied by an Egyptian wife ;[65] and the emperor Titus was compelled, by popular censure, to dismiss with reluctance the reluctant Bernice.[66] This

[62] For all these ceremonies, see the professed work of Constantine Porphyrogenitus, with the notes, or rather dissertations, of his German editors, Leich and Reiske. For the rank of the *standing* courtiers, p. 80 [c. 23 *ad fin.*], not. 23, 62, for the adoration, except on Sundays, p. 95, 240 [c. 39 ; c. 91 (p. 414, ed. Bonn)], not. 131, the processions, p. 2 [c. 1], &c., not. p. 3, &c., the acclamations, *passim*, not. 25, &c., the factions and Hippodrome, p. 177-214 [c. 68—c. 73], not. 9, 93, &c., the Gothic games, p. 221 [c. 83], not. 111, vintage, p. 217 [c. 78], not. 109. Much more information is scattered over the work.

[63] Et privato Othoni et nuper eadem dicenti nota adulatio (Tacit. Hist. i. 85).

[64] The xiiith chapter, de Administratione Imperii, may be explained and rectified by the Familiæ Byzantinæ of Ducange.

[65] Sequiturque nefas ! Ægyptia conjunx (Virgil, Æneid. viii. 688 [*leg.* 686]). Yet this Egyptian wife was the daughter of a long line of kings. Quid te mutavit (says Antony in a private letter to Augustus)? an quod reginam ineo ? Uxor mea est (Sueton. in August. c. 69). Yet I much question (for I cannot stay to inquire) whether the triumvir ever dared to celebrate his marriage either with Roman or Egyptian rites.

[66] Berenicem invitus invitam dimisit (Suetonius in Tito, c. 7). Have I observed elsewhere that this Jewish beauty was at this time above fifty years of age? The judicious Racine has most discreetly suppressed both her age and her country.

perpetual interdict was ratified by the fabulous sanction of the great Constantine. The ambassadors of the nations, more especially of the unbelieving nations, were solemnly admonished that such strange alliances had been condemned by the founder of the church and city. The irrevocable law was inscribed on the altar of St. Sophia; and the impious prince who should stain the majesty of the purple was excluded from the civil and ecclesiastical communion of the Romans. If the ambassadors were instructed by any false brethren in the Byzantine history, they might produce three memorable examples of the violation of this imaginary law: the marriage of Leo, or rather of his father, Constantine the Fourth, with the daughter of the king of the Chozars, the nuptials of the grand-daughter of Romanus with a Bulgarian prince, and the union of Bertha of France or Italy with young Romanus, the son of Constantine Porphyrogenitus himself. To these objections three answers were prepared, which solved the difficulty and established the law. I. The deed and the guilt of Constantine Copronymus were acknowledged. The Isaurian heretic, who sullied the baptismal font and declared war against the holy images, had indeed embraced a barbarian wife. By this impious alliance he accomplished the measure of his crimes, and was devoted to the just censure of the church and of posterity. II. Romanus could not be alleged as a legitimate emperor; he was a plebeian usurper, ignorant of the laws, and regardless of the honour, of the monarchy. His son Christopher, the father of the bride, was the third in rank in the college of princes, at once the subject and the accomplice of a rebellious parent. The Bulgarians were sincere and devout Christians; and the safety of the empire, with the redemption of many thousand captives, depended on this preposterous alliance. Yet no consideration could dispense from the law of Constantine: the clergy, the senate, and the people disapproved the conduct of Romanus; and he was reproached, both in his life and death, as the author of the public disgrace. III. For the marriage of his own son with the daughter of Hugo, king of Italy, a more honourable defence is contrived by the wise Porphyrogenitus. Constantine, the great and holy, esteemed the fidelity and valour of the Franks;[67] and his pro-

*Imaginary law of Constantine*

*The first exception. A.D. 733*

*The second. A.D. 941*

*The third. A.D. 943*

---

[67] Constantine was made to praise the εὐγένεια and περιφάνεια of the Franks, with whom he claimed a private and public alliance. The French writers (Isaac Casaubon in Dedicat. Polybii) are highly delighted with these compliments. [A Monodia is extant which is composed by Imperial order for the young Romanus and dedicated by him to Bertha. It has been published by S. Lambros in the Bulletin de Correspondance hellénique, ii., 266 sqq. (1878).]

phetic spirit beheld the vision of their future greatness. They alone were excepted from the general prohibition: Hugo king of France was the lineal descendant of Charlemagne; [68] and his daughter Bertha inherited the prerogatives of her family and nation. The voice of truth and malice insensibly betrayed the fraud or error of the Imperial court. The patrimonial estate of Hugo was reduced from the monarchy of France to the simple county of Arles; though it was not denied that, in the confusion of the times, he had usurped the sovereignty of Provence and invaded the kingdom of Italy. His father was a private noble: and, if Bertha derived her female descent from the Carlovingian line, every step was polluted with illegitimacy or vice. The grand-mother of Hugo was the famous Valdrada, the concubine, rather than the wife, of the second Lothair; whose adultery, divorce, and second nuptials had provoked against him the thunders of the Vatican. His mother, as she was styled, the great Bertha, was successively the wife of the count of Arles and the marquis of Tuscany: France and Italy were scandalized by her gallantries; and, till the age of threescore, her lovers, of every degree, were the zealous servants of her ambition. The example of maternal incontinence was copied by the king of Italy; and the three favourite concubines of Hugo were decorated with the classic names of Venus, Juno, and Semele.[69] The daughter of Venus was granted to the solicitations of the Byzantine court; her name of Bertha was changed to that of Eudoxia; and she was wedded, or rather betrothed, to young Romanus, the future heir of the empire of the East. The consummation of this foreign alliance was sus-pended by the tender age of the two parties; and, at the end of five years, the union was dissolved by the death of the virgin spouse. The second wife of the emperor Romanus was a maiden of ple-beian, but of Roman birth; and their two daughters, Theophano and Anne, were given in marriage to the princes of the earth. The eldest was bestowed, as the pledge of peace, on the eldest son of the great Otho, who had solicited this alliance with arms

[Death of Bertha. A.D. 949]

Otho of Germany. A.D. 972

[68] Constantine Porphyrogenitus (de Administrat. Imp. c. 26) exhibits a pedigree and life of the illustrious king Hugo (περιβλέπτου ῥῆγος Οὐγωνος). A more correct idea may be formed from the Criticism of Pagi, the Annals of Muratori, and the Abridgment of St. Marc, A.D. 925-946.

[69] After the mention of the three goddesses, Liutprand very naturally adds, et quoniam non rex solus iis abutebatur, earum nati ex incertis patribus originem ducunt (Hist. l. iv. c. 6 [= c. 14]); for the marriage of the younger Bertha see Hist. l. v. c. 5 [= c. 14]; for the incontinence of the elder, dulcis exercitio Hymenæi, l. ii. c. 15 [= c. 55]; for the virtues and vices of Hugo, l. iii. c. 5 [= c. 19]. Yet it must not be forgot that the bishop of Cremona was a lover of scandal.

and embassies. It might legally be questioned how far a Saxon was entitled to the privilege of the French nation; but every scruple was silenced by the fame and piety of a hero who had restored the empire of the West. After the death of her father-in-law and husband, Theophano governed Rome, Italy, and Germany during the minority of her son, the third Otho; and the Latins have praised the virtues of an empress, who sacrificed to a superior duty the remembrance of her country.[70] In the nuptials of her sister Anne, every prejudice was lost, and every consideration of dignity was superseded, by the stronger argument of necessity and fear. A Pagan of the North, Wolodomir, great prince of Russia, aspired to a daughter of the Roman purple; and his claim was enforced by the threats of war, the promise of conversion, and the offer of a powerful succour against a domestic rebel. A victim of her religion and country, the Grecian princess was torn from the palace of her fathers, and condemned to a savage reign and an hopeless exile on the banks of the Borysthenes, or in the neighbourhood of the Polar circle.[71] Yet the marriage of Anne was fortunate and fruitful; the daughter of her grandson Jeroslaus was recommended by her Imperial descent; and the king of France, Henry I., sought a wife on the last borders of Europe and Christendom.[72]

*Wolodomir of Russia [Vladimir of Kiev] A.D. 988 [989]*

*[Iaroslav]*

In the Byzantine palace, the emperor was the first slave of the ceremonies which he imposed, of the rigid forms which regulated each word and gesture, besieged him in the palace, and violated the leisure of his rural solitude. But the lives and fortunes of millions hung on his arbitrary will; and the firmest

*Despotic power*

[70] Licet illa Imperatrix Græca sibi et aliis fuisset satis utilis, et optima, &c., is the preamble of an inimical writer, apud Pagi, tom. iv. A.D. 989, No. 3. Her marriage and principal actions may be found in Muratori, Pagi, and St. Marc, under the proper years. [For the question as to the identity of Theophano, see above, vol. v. p. 211, note 49. For her remarkably capable regency (a striking contrast to that of Agnes of Poictiers, mother of the Emperor Henry IV.) see Giesebrecht, Gesch. der deutschen Kaiserzeit, i. p. 611 sqq.]

[71] Cedrenus, tom. ii. p. 699 [ii. p. 444, ed. Bonn]; Zonaras, tom. ii. p. 221 [xvii. 7]; Elmacin, Hist. Saracenica, l. iii. c. 6; Nestor apud Levesque, tom. ii. p. 112 [Chron. Nestor, c. 42]; Pagi, Critica, A.D. 987, No. 6; a singular concourse! Wolodomir and Anne are ranked among the saints of the Russian church. Yet we know his vices, and are ignorant of her virtues. [For the date of Vladimir's marriage and conversion see below, chap. lv. p. 164, note 100.]

[72] Henricus primus duxit uxorem Scythicam [et] Russam, filiam regis Jeroslai. An embassy of bishops was sent into Russia, and the father gratanter filiam cum multis donis misit. This event happened in the year 1051. See the passages of the original chronicles in Bouquet's Historians of France (tom. xi. p. 29, 159, 161, 319, 384, 481). Voltaire might wonder at this alliance; but he should not have owned his ignorance of the country, religion, &c., of Jeroslaus—a name so conspicuous in the Russian annals.

minds, superior to the allurements of pomp and luxury, may be
seduced by the more active pleasure of commanding their
equals. The legislative and executive power were centered in
the person of the monarch, and the last remains of the authority
of the senate were finally eradicated by Leo the Philosopher.[73]
A lethargy of servitude had benumbed the minds of the Greeks;
in the wildest tumults of rebellion they never aspired to the
idea of a free constitution; and the private character of the
prince was the only source and measure of their public happiness. Superstition riveted their chains; in the church of St.
Sophia, he was solemnly crowned by the patriarch; at the foot
of the altar, they pledged their passive and unconditional
obedience to his government and family. On his side he
engaged to abstain as much as possible from the capital punishments of death and mutilation; his orthodox creed was subscribed with his own hand, and he promised to obey the decrees
of the seven synods, and the canons of the holy church.[74] But
the assurance of mercy was loose and indefinite: he swore, not
to his people, but to an invisible judge, and, except in the
inexpiable guilt of heresy, the ministers of heaven were always
prepared to preach the indefeasible right, and to absolve the
venial transgressions, of their sovereign. The Greek ecclesiastics
were themselves the subjects of the civil magistrate; at the nod
of a tyrant, the bishops were created, or transferred, or deposed,
or punished with an ignominious death: whatever might be their
wealth or influence, they could never succeed like the Latin
clergy in the establishment of an independent republic; and the
patriarch of Constantinople condemned, what he secretly envied,
the temporal greatness of his Roman brother. Yet the exercise
of boundless despotism is happily checked by the laws of nature
and necessity. In proportion to his wisdom and virtue, the
master of an empire is confined to the path of his sacred and
laborious duty. In proportion to his vice and folly, he drops
the sceptre too weighty for his hands; and the motions of the
royal image are ruled by the imperceptible thread of some
minister or favourite, who undertakes for his private interest to

Coronation
oath

[73] A constitution of Leo the philosopher (lxxviii. [Zachariä, Jus Græco-Rom.
iii. p. 175]), ne senatus consulta amplius fiant, speaks the language of naked
despotism, ἐξ οὗ τὸ μόναρχον κράτος τὴν τούτων ἀνῆπται διοίκησιν, καὶ ἄκαιρον καὶ μάταιον
τὸ [leg. τὸν] ἄχρηστον μετὰ τῶν χρείαν παρεχομένων συνάπτεσθαι [leg. συντάττεσθαι].

[74] Codinus (de Officiis, c. xvii. p. 120, 121 [p. 87, ed. Bonn]) gives an idea of
this oath so strong to the church πιστὸς καὶ γνήσιος δοῦλος καὶ υἱὸς τῆς ἁγίας ἐκκλησίας,
so weak to the people καὶ ἀπέχεσθαι φόνων καὶ ἀκρωτηριασμῶν καὶ [τῶν] ὁμοίων τούτοις
κατὰ τὸ δυνατόν.

exercise the task of the public oppression. In some fatal moment, the most absolute monarch may dread the reason or the caprice of a nation of slaves; and experience has proved that whatever is gained in the extent, is lost in the safety and solidity, of regal power.

Whatever titles a despot may assume, whatever claims he may assert, it is on the sword that he must ultimately depend to guard him against his foreign and domestic enemies. From the age of Charlemagne to that of the Crusades, the world (for I overlook the remote monarchy of China) was occupied and disputed by the three great empires or nations of the Greeks, the Saracens, and the Franks. Their military strength may be ascertained by a comparison of their courage, their arts and riches, and their obedience to a supreme head, who might call into action all the energies of the state. The Greeks, far inferior to their rivals in the first, were superior to the Franks, and at least equal to the Saracens, in the second and third of these warlike qualifications.

*Military force of the Greeks, the Saracens, and the Franks*

The wealth of the Greeks enabled them to purchase the service of the poorer nations, and to maintain a naval power for the protection of their coasts and the annoyance of their enemies.[75] A commerce of mutual benefit exchanged the gold of Constantinople for the blood of the Sclavonians and Turks, the Bulgarians and Russians: their valour contributed to the victories of Nicephorus and Zimisces; and, if an hostile people pressed too closely on the frontier, they were recalled to the defence of their country and the desire of peace by the well managed attack of a more distant tribe.[76] The command of the Mediterranean, from the mouth of the Tanais to the columns of Hercules, was always claimed, and often possessed, by the successors of Constantine. Their capital was filled with naval stores and dexterous artificers; the situation of Greece and Asia, the long coasts, deep gulfs, and numerous islands

*Navy of the Greeks*

---

[75] If we listen to the threats of Nicephorus to the ambassador of Otho : Nec est in mari domino tuo classium numerus. Navigantium fortitudo mihi soli inest, qui eum classibus aggrediar, bello maritimas ejus civitates demoliar ; et quæ fluminibus sunt vicina redigam in favillam (Liutprand in Legat. ad Nicephorum Phocam, in Muratori, Scriptores Rerum Italicarum, tom. ii. pars i. p. 481 [c. 11]). He observes in another place [c. 45], qui cæteris præstant Venetici sunt et Amalphitani.

[76] Nec ipsa capiet eum (the emperor Otho) in quâ ortus est pauper et [gunnata, id est] pellicea Saxonia ; pecuniâ quâ pollemus omnes nationes super eum [ipsum] invitabimus ; et quasi Keramicum confringemus (Liutprand in Legat. p. 487 [c. 53]). The two books, De administrando Imperio, perpetually inculcate the same policy.

accustomed their subjects to the exercise of navigation ; and tne trade of Venice and Amalfi supplied a nursery of seamen to the Imperial fleet.[77]   Since the time of the Peloponnesian and Punic wars, the sphere of action had not been enlarged ; and the science of naval architecture appears to have declined.   The art of constructing those stupendous machines which displayed three, or six, or ten, ranges of oars, rising above, or falling behind, each other, was unknown to the ship-builders of Constantinople, as well as to the mechanicians of modern days.[78] The *Dromones* [79] or light galleys of the Byzantine empire were content with two tier of oars ; each tier was composed of five and twenty benches ; and two rowers were seated on each bench, who plied their oars on either side of the vessel.   To these we must add the captain or centurion, who, in time of action, stood erect with his armour-bearer on the poop, two steersmen at the helm, and two officers at the prow, the one to manage the anchor, the other to point and play against the enemy the tube of liquid fire.   The whole crew, as in the infancy of the art, performed the double service of mariners and soldiers ; they were provided with defensive and offensive arms, with bows and arrows, which they used from the upper deck, with long pikes, which they pushed through the port-holes of the lower tier. Sometimes, indeed, the ships of war were of a larger and more solid construction ; and the labours of combat and navigation were more regularly divided between seventy soldiers and two hundred and thirty mariners.   But for the most part they were of the light and manageable size ; and, as the cape of Malea in Peloponnesus was still clothed with its ancient terrors, an Imperial fleet was transported five miles over land across the Isthmus of Corinth.[80]   The principles of maritime tactics had

[77] The xixth chapter of the Tactics of Leo (Meurs. Opera, tom. vi. p. 825-848), which is given more correct from a manuscript of Gudius, by the laborious Fabricius (Bibliot. Græc. tom. vi. p. 372-379), relates to the *Naumachia* or naval war.   [On the Byzantine navy, compare Appendix 5.]

[78] Even of fifteen or sixteen rows of oars, in the navy of Demetrius Poliorcetes. These were for real use ; the forty rows of Ptolemy Philadelphus were applied to a floating palace, whose tonnage, according to Dr. Arbuthnot (Tables of Ancient Coins, &c., p. 231-236), is compared as 4½ to one, with an English 100-gun ship.

[79] The Dromones of Leo, &c., are so clearly described with two tier of oars that I must censure the version of Meursius and Fabricius, who pervert the sense by a blind attachment to the classic appellation of *Triremes*.   The Byzantine historians are sometimes guilty of the same inaccuracy.

[80] Constantin. Porphyrogen. in Vit. Basil. c. lxi. p. 185.   He calmly praises the stratagem as a βουλὴν συνετὴν καὶ σοφήν ; but the sailing round Peloponnesus is described by his terrified fancy as a circumnavigation of a thousand miles.

not undergone any change since the time of Thucydides: a squadron of galleys still advanced in a crescent, charged to the front, and strove to impel their sharp beaks against the feeble sides of their antagonists. A machine for casting stones and darts was built of strong timbers in the midst of the deck ; and the operation of boarding was effected by a crane that hoisted baskets of armed men. The language of signals, so clear and copious in the naval grammar of the moderns, was imperfectly expressed by the various positions and colours of a commanding flag. In the darkness of the night the same orders to chase, to attack, to halt, to retreat, to break, to form, were conveyed by the lights of the leading galley. By land, the fire-signals were repeated from one mountain to another ; a chain of eight stations commanded a space of five hundred miles ; and Constantinople in a few hours was apprised of the hostile motions of the Saracens of Tarsus.[81] Some estimate may be formed of the power of the Greek emperors, by the curious and minute detail of the armament which was prepared for the reduction of Crete. A fleet [A.D. 902] of one hundred and twelve galleys, and seventy-five vessels of the Pamphylian style, was equipped in the capital, the islands of the Ægean sea, and the sea-ports of Asia, Macedonia, and Greece. It carried thirty-four thousand marines, seven thousand three hundred and forty soldiers, seven hundred Russians, and five thousand and eighty-seven Mardaites, whose fathers had been transplanted from the mountains of Libanus. Their pay, most probably of a month, was computed at thirty-four centenaries of gold, about one hundred and thirty-six thousand pounds sterling. Our fancy is bewildered by the endless recapitulation of arms and engines, of clothes and linen, of bread for the men and forage for the horses, and of stores and utensils of every description, inadequate to the conquest of a petty island, but amply sufficient for the establishment of a flourishing colony.[82]

---

[81] The continuator of Theophanes (l. iv. p. 122, 123 [c. 35]) names the successive stations, the castle of Lulum near Tarsus, mount Argæus, Isamus, Ægilus, the hill of Mamas, Cyrisus [Cyrizus], Mocilus, the hill of Auxentius, the sun-dial of the Pharus of the great palace. He affirms that the news were transmitted ἐν ἀκαρεῖ, n an indivisible moment of time. Miserable amplification, which, by saying too much, says nothing. How much more forcible and instructive would have been the definition of three or six or twelve hours ! [See above, vol. v. p. 200, note.]

[82] See the Ceremoniale of Constantine Porphyrogenitus, l. ii. c. 44, p. 176-192 [eg. 376-392]. A critical reader will discern some inconsistencies in different parts of this account ; but they are not more obscure or more stubborn than the establishment and effectives, the present and fit for duty, the rank and file and the private, of a modern return, which retain in proper hands the knowledge of these profitable mysteries. [See above, p. 57, note 135.]

The invention of the Greek fire did not, like that of gun-powder, produce a total revolution in the art of war. To these liquid combustibles the city and empire of Constantinople owed their deliverance ; and they were employed in sieges and sea-fights with terrible effect. But they were either less improved or less susceptible of improvement ; the engines of antiquity, the catapultæ, balistæ, and battering-rams, were still of most frequent and powerful use in the attack and defence of fortifica-tions ; nor was the decision of battles reduced to the quick and heavy *fire* of a line of infantry, whom it were fruitless to protect with armour against a similar fire of their enemies. Steel and iron were still the common instruments of destruction and safety ; and the helmets, cuirasses, and shields of the tenth century did not, either in form or substance, essentially differ from those which had covered the companions of Alexander or Achilles.[83] But, instead of accustoming the modern Greeks, like the legionaries of old, to the constant and easy use of this salutary weight, their armour was laid aside in light chariots, which followed the march, till, on the approach of an enemy, they resumed with haste and reluctance the unusual incum-brance. Their offensive weapons consisted of swords, battle-axes, and spears ; but the Macedonian pike was shortened a fourth of its length, and reduced to the more convenient measure of twelve cubits or feet. The sharpness of the Scythian and Arabian arrows had been severely felt ; and the emperors lament the decay of archery as a cause of the public misfortunes, and recommend, as an advice and a command, that the military youth, till the age of forty, should assiduously practise the exercise of the bow.[84] The *bands,* or regiments, were usually three hundred strong ; and, as a medium between the extremes of four and sixteen, the foot-soldiers of Leo and Constantine were formed eight deep ; but the cavalry charged in four ranks, from the reasonable consideration that the weight of the front could not be increased by any pressure of the hindmost horses. If the ranks of the infantry or cavalry were sometimes doubled, this cautious array betrayed a secret distrust of the courage of

---

[83] See the fifth, sixth and seventh chapters, περὶ ὅπλων, περὶ ὁπλίσεως and περὶ γυμν-ασίας, in the Tactics of Leo, with the corresponding passages in those of Constantine. [On the organization and tactics of the Byzantine army see Mr. Oman's Art of War, ii. Bk. iv. chaps. ii. and iii.]

[84] They observe τῆς γὰρ τοξείας παντελῶς ἀμεληθείσης . . . ἐν τοῖς Ῥωμάνοις τὰ πολλὰ νῦν εἴωθε σφάλματα γίνεσθαι (Leo, Tactic. p. 581 [6, § 5]; Constantin. p. 1216). Yet such were not the maxims of the Greeks and Romans, who despised the loose and distant practice of archery.

the troops, whose numbers might swell the appearance of the line, but of whom only a chosen band would dare to encounter the spears and swords of the barbarians. The order of battle must have varied according to the ground, the object, and the adversary; but their ordinary disposition, in two lines and a reserve, presented a succession of hopes and resources most agreeable to the temper as well as the judgment of the Greeks.[85] In case of a repulse, the first line fell back into the intervals of the second; and the reserve, breaking into two divisions, wheeled round the flanks to improve the victory or cover the retreat. Whatever authority could enact was accomplished, at least in theory, by the camps and marches, the exercises and evolutions, the edicts and books, of the Byzantine monarch.[86] Whatever art could produce from the forge, the loom, or the laboratory, was abundantly supplied by the riches of the prince and the industry of his numerous workmen. But neither authority nor art could frame the most important machine, the soldier himself; and, if the *ceremonies* of Constantine always suppose the safe and triumphal return of the emperor,[87] his *tactics* seldom soar above the means of escaping a defeat and procrastinating the war.[88] Notwithstanding some transient success, the Greeks were sunk in their own esteem and that of their neighbours. A cold hand and a loquacious tongue was the vulgar description of the nation; the author of the Tactics was besieged in his capital; and the last of the barbarians, who trembled at the name of the Saracens or Franks, could proudly exhibit the medals of gold and silver which they had extorted from the feeble sovereign of Constantinople. What spirit their government and character denied, might have been inspired in some degree by the influence of religion; but the religion of the Greeks could only teach them to suffer and to yield. The emperor Nicephorus, who restored for a moment the discipline

---

[85] Compare the passages of the Tactics, p. 669 and 721 with the xiiith chapter. [The strength of the army lay in the heavy cavalry.]

[86] In the preface to his Tactics, Leo very freely deplores the loss of discipline and the calamities of the times, and repeats without scruple (Proem. p. 537) the reproaches of ἀμέλεια, ἀταξία, ἀγυμνασία, δειλία, &c., nor does it appear that the same censures were less deserved in the next generation by the disciples of Constantine.

[87] See in the Ceremonial (l. ii. c. 19, p. 353) the form of the emperor's trampling on the necks of the captive Saracens, while the singers chanted, "thou hast made my enemies my footstool!" and the people shouted forty times the kyrie eleison.

[88] Leo observes (Tactic. p. 668) that a fair open battle against any nation whatsoever is ἐπισφαλές and ἐπικίνδυνον; the words are strong and the remark is true; yet, if such had been the opinion of the old Romans, Leo had never reigned on the shores of the Thracian Bosphorus.

and glory of the Roman name, was desirous of bestowing the
honours of martyrdom on the Christians, who lost their lives
in an holy war against the infidels. But this political law was
defeated by the opposition of the patriarch, the bishops, and
the principal senators ; and they strenuously urged the canons
of St. Basil, that all who were polluted by the bloody trade of
a soldier should be separated, during three years, from the
communion of the faithful.[89]

Character
and tactics of
the Saracens

These scruples of the Greeks have been compared with the
tears of the primitive Moslems when they were held back from
battle ; and this contrast of base superstition and high-spirited
enthusiasm unfolds to a philosophic eye the history of the rival
nations. The subjects of the last caliphs[90] had undoubtedly
degenerated from the zeal and faith of the companions of the
prophet. Yet their martial creed still represented the Deity as
the author of war ;[91] the vital though latent spark of fanaticism still glowed in the heart of their religion, and among the
Saracens who dwelt on the Christian borders it was frequently
rekindled to a lively and active flame. Their regular force was
formed of the valiant slaves who had been educated to guard
the person and accompany the standard of their lord ; but the
Musulman people of Syria and Cilicia, of Africa and Spain, was
awakened by the trumpet which proclaimed an holy war
against the infidels. The rich were ambitious of death or
victory in the cause of God ; the poor were allured by the
hopes of plunder ; and the old, the infirm, and the women assumed their share of meritorious service by sending their
substitutes, with arms and horses, into the field. These
offensive and defensive arms were similar in strength and
temper to those of the Romans, whom they far excelled in the
management of the horse and the bow ; the massy silver of
their belts, their bridles, and their swords, displayed the
magnificence of a prosperous nation, and, except some black

[89] Zonaras (tom. ii. l. xvi. p. 202, 203 [c. 25]) and Cedrenus (Compend. p. 688
[ii. p. 369, ed. Bonn]), who relate the design of Nicephorus, most unfortunately apply
the epithet of γενναίως to the opposition of the patriarch.

[90] The xviiith chapter of the tactics of the different nations is the most
historical and useful of the whole collection of Leo. The manners and arms of
the Saracens (Tactic. p. 809-817, and a fragment from the Medicean Ms. in the
preface of the vith volume of Meursius) the Roman emperor was too frequently
called upon to study.

[91] Παντὸς δὲ καὶ κακοῦ ἔργου τὸν Θεὸν αἴτιον ὑποτίθενται, καὶ πολέμοις χαίρειν λέγουσι
τὸν Θεὸν τὸν διασκόρπιζοντα ἔθνη τὰ τοὺς πολέμους θέλοντα. Leon. Tactic. p. 809 [c. 18,
§ 111].

archers of the South, the Arabs disdained the naked bravery of
their ancestors. Instead of waggons, they were attended by a
long train of camels, mules, and asses; the multitude of these
animals, whom they bedecked with flags and streamers, appeared
to swell the pomp and magnitude of their host; and the
horses of the enemy were often disordered by the uncouth
figure and odious smell of the camels of the East. Invincible
by their patience of thirst and heat, their spirits were frozen by
a winter's cold, and the consciousness of their propensity to
sleep exacted the most rigorous precautions against the sur-
prises of the night. Their order of battle was a long square of
two deep and solid lines: the first of archers, the second of
cavalry. In their engagements by sea and land, they sustained with patient firmness the fury of the attack, and seldom
advanced to the charge till they could discern and oppress the
lassitude of their foes. But, if they were repulsed and broken,
they knew not how to rally or renew the combat; and their
dismay was heightened by the superstitious prejudice that God
had declared himself on the side of their enemies. The decline
and fall of the caliphs countenanced this fearful opinion; nor
were there wanting, among the Mahometans and Christians,
some obscure prophecies [92] which prognosticated their alternate
defeats. The unity of the Arabian empire was dissolved, but
the independent fragments were equal to populous and powerful kingdoms; and in their naval and military armaments an
emir of Aleppo or Tunis might command no despicable fund of
skill and industry and treasure. In their transactions of peace
and war with the Saracens, the princes of Constantinople too
often felt that these barbarians had nothing barbarous in their
discipline; and that, if they were destitute of original genius,
they had been endowed with a quick spirit of curiosity and
imitation. The model was indeed more perfect than the copy;
their ships, and engines, and fortifications were of a less skilful
construction; and they confess, without shame, that the same
God, who has given a tongue to the Arabians, had more nicely
fashioned the hands of the Chinese and the heads of the
Greeks. [93]

[92] Liutprand (p. 484, 485 [c. 39]) relates and interprets the oracles of the Greeks
and Saracens, in which, after the fashion of prophecy, the past is clear and historical, the future is dark, ænigmatical, and erroneous. From this boundary of light
and shade an impartial critic may commonly determine the date of the composition.

[93] The sense of this distinction is expressed by Abulpharagius (Dynast. p. 2, 62,
101); but I cannot recollect the passage in which it is conveyed by this lively
apophthegm.

The Franks
or Latins

A name of some German tribes between the Rhine and the
Weser had spread its victorious influence over the greatest part
of Gaul, Germany, and Italy ; and the common appellation of
FRANKS [94] was applied by the Greeks and Arabians to the
Christians of the Latin church, the nations of the West, who
stretched beyond *their* knowledge to the shores of the Atlantic
Ocean. The vast body had been inspired and united by the
soul of Charlemagne ; but the division and degeneracy of his
race soon annihilated the Imperial power, which would have
rivalled the Cæsars of Byzantium and revenged the indignities
of the Christian name. The enemies no longer feared, nor
could the subjects any longer trust, the application of a public
revenue, the labours of trade and manufactures in the military
service, the mutual aid of provinces and armies, and the naval
squadrons which were regularly stationed from the mouth of
the Elbe to that of the Tiber. In the beginning of the tenth
century, the family of Charlemagne had almost disappeared ;
his monarchy was broken into many hostile and independent
states ; the regal title was assumed by the most ambitious
chiefs ; their revolt was imitated in a long subordination of
anarchy and discord ; and the nobles of every province disobeyed
their sovereign, oppressed their vassals, and exercised perpetual
hostilities against their equals and neighbours. Their private
wars, which overturned the fabric of government, fomented the
martial spirit of the nation. In the system of modern Europe,
the power of the sword is possessed, at least in fact, by five or
six mighty potentates ; their operations are conducted on a
distant frontier by an order of men who devote their lives to
the study and practice of the military art ; the rest of the country
and community enjoys in the midst of war the tranquillity of
peace, and is only made sensible of the change by the aggravation or decrease of the public taxes. In the disorders of the
tenth and eleventh centuries, every peasant was a soldier, and
every village a fortification ; each wood or valley was a scene
of murder and rapine ; and the lords of each castle were compelled to assume the character of princes and warriors. To
their own courage and policy they boldly trusted for the safety

[94] Ex Francis, quo nomine tam Latinos quam Teutones comprehendit, ludum
habuit (Liutprand in Legat. ad Imp. Nicephorum, p. 483, 484 [c. 33]). This extension of the name may be confirmed from Constantine (de administrando Imperio,
l. ii. c. 27, 28) and Eutychius (Annal. tom. i. p. 55, 56), who both lived before the
crusades. The testimonies of Abulpharagius (Dynast. p. 69) and Abulfeda
(Prefat. ad Geograph.) are more recent.

of their family, the protection of their lands, and the revenge of their injuries ; and, like the conquerors of a larger size, they were too apt to transgress the privilege of defensive war. The powers of the mind and body were hardened by the presence of danger and the necessity of resolution ; the same spirit refused to desert a friend and to forgive an enemy ; and, instead of sleeping under the guardian care of the magistrate, they proudly disdained the authority of the laws. In the days of feudal anarchy, the instruments of agriculture and art were converted into the weapons of bloodshed : the peaceful occupations of civil and ecclesiastical society were abolished or corrupted ; and the bishop who exchanged his mitre for an helmet was more forcibly urged by the manners of the times than by the obligation of his tenure.[95]

The love of freedom and of arms was felt, with conscious pride, by the Franks themselves, and is observed by the Greeks with some degree of amazement and terror. "The Franks," says the emperor Constantine, "are bold and valiant to the verge of temerity ; and their dauntless spirit is supported by the contempt of danger and death. In the field and in close onset, they press to the front, and rush headlong against the enemy, without deigning to compute either his numbers or their own. Their ranks are formed by the firm connexions of consanguinity and friendship ; and their martial deeds are prompted by the desire of saving or revenging their dearest companions. In their eyes a retreat is a shameful flight, and flight is indelible infamy."[96] A nation endowed with such high and intrepid spirit must have been secure of victory, if these advantages had not been counterbalanced by many weighty defects. The decay of their naval power left the Greeks and Saracens in possession of the sea, for every purpose of annoyance and supply. In the age which preceded the institution of knighthood, the Franks were rude and unskilful

*Their character and tactics*

[95] On this subject of ecclesiastical and beneficiary discipline, Father Thomassin (tom. iii. l. i. c. 40, 45, 46, 47) may be usefully consulted. A general law of Charlemagne exempted the bishops from personal service ; but the opposite practice, which prevailed from the ixth to the xvth century, is countenanced by the example or silence of saints and doctors. . . . You justify your cowardice by the holy canons, says Rutherius of Verona ; the canons likewise forbid you to whore, and yet——

[96] In the xviiith chapter of his Tactics, the emperor Leo has fairly stated the military vices and virtues of the Franks (whom Meursius ridiculously translates by *Galli*) and the Lombards, or Langobards. See likewise the xxvith Dissertation of Muratori de Antiquitatibus Italiæ medii Ævi.

in the service of cavalry; [97] and in all perilous emergencies
their warriors were so conscious of their ignorance that they
chose to dismount from their horses and fight on foot.  Un-
practised in the use of pikes or of missile weapons, they were
encumbered by the length of their swords, the weight of their
armour, the magnitude of their shields, and, if I may repeat
the satire of the meagre Greeks, by their unwieldy intemperance.  Their independent spirit disdained the yoke of subordination, and abandoned the standard of their chief, if he attempted to keep the field beyond the term of their stipulation
or service.  On all sides they were open to the snares of an
enemy, less brave, but more artful, than themselves.  They
might be bribed, for the barbarians were venal ; or surprised
in the night, for they neglected the precautions of a close encampment or vigilant sentinels.  The fatigues of a summer's
campaign exhausted their strength and patience, and they
sunk in despair if their voracious appetite was disappointed of
a plentiful supply of wine and of food.  This general character
of the Franks was marked with some national and local shades,
which I should ascribe to accident rather than to climate, but
which were visible both to natives and to foreigners.  An ambassador of the great Otho declared, in the palace of Constantinople, that the Saxons could dispute with swords better than
with pens ; and that they preferred inevitable death to the
dishonour of turning their backs to an enemy.[98]  It was the
glory of the nobles of France that, in their humble dwellings,
war and rapine were the only pleasure, the sole occupation, of
their lives.  They affected to deride the palaces, the banquets,
the polished manners, of the Italians, who, in the estimate of
the Greeks themselves, had degenerated from the liberty and
valour of the ancient Lombards.[99]

[97] Domini tui milites (says the proud Nicephorus) equitandi ignari pedestris
pugnæ sunt inscii ; scutorum magnitudo, loricarum gravitudo, ensium longitudo,
galearumque pondus neutrâ parte pugnare eos sinit ; ac subridens, impedit, inquit,
ac eos [leg. eos et] gastrimargia hoc est ventris ingluvies, &c. Liutprand in Legat.
p. 480, 481 [c. 11].

[98] In Saxoniâ certe scio . . . decentius ensibus pugnare quam calamis, et prius
mortem obire quam hostibus terga dare (Liutprand, p. 482 [c. 22]).

[99] Φράγγοι τοίνυν καὶ Λογγίβαρδοι λόγον ἐλευθερίας περὶ πολλοῦ ποιοῦνται, ἀλλ' οἱ μὲν
Λογγίβαρδοι τὸ πλέον τῆς τοιαύτης ἀρετῆς νῦν ἀπώλεσαν.  Leonis Tactica, c. 18 [§ 80],
p. 805.  The emperor Leo died A.D. 911 ; an historical poem, which ends in 916,
and appears to have been composed in 940 [between 915 and 922], by a native of
Venetia, discriminates in these verses the manners of Italy and France :—

——Quid inertia bello
Pectora (Ubertus ait) duris prætenditis armis,
O Itali ?  Potius vobis sacra pocula cordi

By the well-known edict of Caracalla, his subjects, from Britain Oblivion of to Egypt, were entitled to the name and privilege of Romans, the Latin language and their national sovereign might fix his occasional or permanent residence in any province of their common country.  In the division of the East and West an ideal unity was scrupulously preserved, and in their titles, laws, and statutes the successors of Arcadius and Honorius announced themselves as the inseparable colleagues of the same office, as the joint sovereigns of the Roman world and city, which were bounded by the same limits.  After the fall of the Western monarchy, the majesty of the purple resided solely in the princes of Constantinople ; and of these Justinian was the first, who, after a divorce of sixty years, regained the dominion of ancient Rome and asserted, by the right of conquest, the august title of Emperor of the Romans.[100]  A motive of vanity or discontent solicited one of his successors, Constans the Second, to abandon the Thracian Bosphorus and to restore the pristine honours of the Tiber : an extravagant project (exclaims the malicious Byzantine), as if he had despoiled a beautiful and blooming virgin, to enrich, or rather to expose, the deformity of a wrinkled and decrepit matron.[101]  But the sword of the Lombards opposed his settlement in Italy ; he entered Rome, not as a conqueror, but as a fugitive, and, after a visit of twelve days, he pillaged, and for ever deserted, the ancient capital of the world.[102]  The final revolt and separation of Italy

> Sæpius et stomachum nitidis laxare saginis
> Elatasque domos rutilo fulcire metallo.
> Non eadem Gallos similis vel cura remordet ;
> Vicinas quibus est studium devincere terras
> Depressumque larem spoliis hinc inde coactis
> Sustentare——

(Anonym. Carmen Panegyricum de Laudibus Berengarii Augusti, l. ii. in Muratori, Script. Rerum Italic. tom. ii. pars i. p. 393 [*leg.* 395] [in Pertz Monum., iv. p. 189 *sqq.* New ed. by Dümmler, 1871]).

[100] Justinian, says the Historian Agathias (l. v. p. 157 [c. 14]), πρῶτος Ῥωμαίων αὐτοκράτωρ ὀνόματι καὶ πράγματι.  Yet the specific title of Emperor of the Romans was not used at Constantinople, till it had been claimed by the French and German emperors of old Rome.

[101] Constantine Manasses reprobates this design in his barbarous verse [3836 *sqq.*]:

> Τὴν πόλιν τὴν βασιλείαν ἀποκοσμῆσαι θέλων,
> Καὶ τὴν ἀρχὴν χαρίσασθαι [τῇ] τριπεμπέλῳ Ῥώμῃ,
> Ὡς εἴτις ἀβροστόλιστον ἀποκοσμήσει νύμφην,
> Καὶ γραῦν τινα τρικόρωνον ὡς κόρην ὡράϊσει.

and it is confirmed by Theophanes, Zonaras, Cedrenus, and the Historia Miscella : Voluit in urbem Romam Imperium transferre (l. xix. p. 157, in tom. i. pars i. of the Scriptores Rer. Ital. of Muratori).

[102] Paul. Diacon. l. v. c. 11, p. 480.  Anastasius in Vitis Pontificum, in Muratori's Collection, tom. iii. pars i. p. 141.

was accomplished about two centuries after the conquests of Justinian, and from his reign we may date the gradual oblivion of the Latin tongue. That legislator had composed his Institutes, his Code, and his Pandects, in a language which he celebrates as the proper and public style of the Roman government, the consecrated idiom of the palace and senate of Constantinople, of the camps and tribunals of the East.[103] But this foreign dialect was unknown to the people and soldiers of the Asiatic provinces, it was imperfectly understood by the greater part of the interpreters of the laws and the ministers of the state. After a short conflict, nature and habit prevailed over the obsolete institutions of human power : for the general benefit of his subjects, Justinian promulgated his novels in the two languages ; the several parts of his voluminous jurisprudence were successively translated ; [104] the original was forgotten, the version was studied, and the Greek, whose intrinsic merit deserved indeed the preference, obtained a legal as well as popular establishment in the Byzantine monarchy. The birth and residence of succeeding princes estranged them from the Roman idiom : Tiberius by the Arabs,[105] and Maurice by the Italians,[106] are distinguished as the first of the Greek Cæsars, as the founders of a new dynasty and empire ; the silent revolution was accomplished before the death of Heraclius ; and the ruins of the Latin speech were darkly preserved in the terms of jurisprudence and the acclamations of the palace. After the restoration

---

[103] Consult the preface of Ducange (ad Gloss. Græc. medii Ævi) and the Novels of Justinian (vii. lxvi.). The Greek language was κοινός, the Latin was πάτριος to himself, κυριώτατος to the πολιτείας σχῆμα, the system of government.

[104] Οὐ μὴν ἀλλὰ καὶ Λατινικὴ λέξις καὶ φράσις εἰσέτι τοὺς νόμους [κρύπτουσα] τοὺς συνεῖναι ταύτην μὴ δυναμένους ἰσχυρῶς ἀπετείχιξε (Matth. Blastares, Hist. Juris. apud Fabric. Bibliot. Græc. tom. xii. p. 369). The Code and Pandects (the latter by Thalelæus) were translated in the time of Justinian (p. 358, 366). Theophilus, one of the original triumvirs, has left an elegant, though diffuse, paraphrase of the Institutes. On the other hand, Julian, antecessor of Constantinople (A.D. 570), cxx. Novellas Græcas eleganti Latinitate donavit (Heineccius, Hist. J. R. p. 396), for the use of Italy and Africa.

[105] Abulpharagius assigns the viith Dynasty to the Franks or Romans, the viiith to the Greeks, the ixth to the Arabs. A tempore Augusti Cæsaris donec imperaret Tiberius Cæsar spatio circiter annorum 600 fuerunt Imperatores C. P. Patricii, et præcipua pars exercitus Romani ; extra quod, consiliarii, scribæ et populus, omnes Græci fuerunt ; deinde regnum etiam Græcanicum factum est (p. 96, vers. Pocock). The Christian and ecclesiastical studies of Abulpharagius gave him some advantage over the more ignorant Moslems.

[106] Primus ex Græcorum genere in Imperio confirmatus est [the right reading] ; or, according to another Ms. of Paulus Diaconus (l. iii. c. 15, p. 443), in Græcorum Imperio.

of the Western empire by Charlemagne and the Othos, the names of Franks and Latins acquired an equal signification and extent; and these haughty barbarians asserted, with some justice, their superior claim to the language and dominion of Rome. They insulted the aliens of the East who had renounced the dress and idiom of Romans; and their reasonable practice will justify the frequent appellation of Greeks.[107] But this contemptuous appellation was indignantly rejected by the prince and people to whom it is applied. Whatsoever changes had been introduced by the lapse of ages, they alleged a lineal and unbroken succession from Augustus and Constantine; and, in the lowest period of degeneracy and decay, the name of ROMANS adhered to the last fragments of the empire of Constantinople.[108] The Greek emperors and their subjects retain and assert the name of Romans

While the government of the East was transacted in Latin, the Greek was the language of literature and philosophy; nor could the masters of this rich and perfect idiom be tempted to envy the borrowed learning and imitative taste of their Roman disciples. After the fall of paganism, the loss of Syria and Egypt, and the extinction of the schools of Alexandria and Athens, the studies of the Greeks insensibly retired to some regular monasteries, and above all to the royal college of Constantinople, which was burnt in the reign of Leo the Isaurian.[109] In the pompous style of the age, the president of that foundation was named the Sun of Science: his twelve associates, the professors in the different arts and faculties, were the twelve signs of the zodiac; a library of thirty-six thousand five hundred volumes was open to their inquiries; and they could shew an ancient manuscript of Homer, on a roll of parchment one hundred and twenty feet in length, the intestines, as it was fabled, of a Period of ignorance

---

[107] Quia linguam, mores, vestesque mutâstis, putavit Sanctissimus Papa (an audacious irony), ita vos [vobis] displicere Romanorum nomen. His nuncios, rogabant Nicephorum Imperatorem Græcorum, ut cum Othone Imperatore Romanorum amicitiam faceret (Liutprand in Legatione, p. 486 [c. 47]). [The citation is *verbally* inaccurate.]

[108] By Laonicus Chalcocondyles, who survived the last siege of Constantinople, the account is thus stated (l. i. p. 3 [p. 6, ed. Bonn]): Constantine transplanted his Latins of Italy to a Greek city of Thrace: they adopted the language and manners of the natives, who were confounded with them under the name of Romans. The kings of Constantinople, says the historian, ἐπὶ τῷ σφᾶς αὐτοὺς σεμνύνεσθαι Ῥωμαίων βασιλεῖς τε καὶ αὐτοκράτορας ἀποκαλεῖν, Ἑλλήνων δὲ βασιλεῖς οὐκέτι οὐδαμῇ ἀξιοῦν.

[109] See Ducange (C. P. Christiana, l. ii. p. 150, 151), who collects the testimonies, not of Theophanes, but at least of Zonaras (tom. ii. l. xv. p. 104 [c. 3]), Cedrenus (p. 454 [i. 795, ed. Bonn]), Michael Glycas (p. 281 [p. 522, ed. Bonn]), Constantine Manasses (p. 87 [l. 4257]). After refuting the absurd charge against the emperor, Spanheim (Hist. Imaginum, p. 90-111), like a true advocate, proceeds to doubt or deny the reality of the fire, and almost of the library.

prodigious serpent.[110]   But the seventh and eighth centuries
were a period of discord and darkness ; the library was burnt, the
college was abolished, the Iconoclasts are represented as the
foes of antiquity ; and a savage ignorance and contempt of letters
has disgraced the princes of the Heraclean and Isaurian dynasties.[111]

Revival of
Greek learn-
ing

In the ninth century we trace the first dawnings of the restoration of science.[112]   After the fanaticism of the Arabs had subsided, the caliphs aspired to conquer the arts, rather than the
provinces, of the empire : their liberal curiosity rekindled the
emulation of the Greeks, brushed away the dust from their
ancient libraries, and taught them to know and reward the
philosophers, whose labours had been hitherto repaid by the
pleasure of study and the pursuit of truth.   The Cæsar Bardas,
the uncle of Michael the Third, was the generous protector of
letters, a title which alone has preserved his memory and excused his ambition.   A particle of the treasures of his nephew
was sometimes diverted from the indulgence of vice and folly ;
a school was opened in the palace of Magnaura ; and the presence
of Bardas excited the emulation of the masters and students.
At their head, was the philosopher Leo, archbishop of Thessalonica ; his profound skill in astronomy and the mathematics was admired by the strangers of the East ; and this occult science was
magnified by vulgar credulity, which modestly supposes that all
knowledge superior to its own must be the effect of inspiration
or magic.   At the pressing entreaty of the Cæsar, his friend, the
celebrated Photius,[113] renounced the freedom of a secular and
studious life, ascended the patriarchal throne, and was alternately excommunicated and absolved by the synods of the East
and West.   By the confession even of priestly hatred, no art or
science, except poetry, was foreign to this universal scholar, who

[110] According to Malchus (apud Zonar. l. xiv. p. 53 [*leg.* 52 ; c. 2]) this Homer
was burnt in the time of Basiliscus.   The Ms. might be renewed—but on a serpent's skin ?   Most strange and incredible !

[111] The ἀλογία of Zonaras, the ἀργία καὶ ἀμαθία of Cedrenus, are strong words,
perhaps not ill suited to these reigns.

[112] See Zonaras (l. xvi. p. 160, 161 [c. 4]) and Cedrenus (p. 549, 550 [ii. 168-9, ed.
Bonn]).   Like Friar Bacon, the philosopher Leo has been transformed by ignorance
into a conjurer ; yet not so undeservedly, if he be the author of the oracles more
commonly ascribed to the emperor of the same name.   The physics of Leo in Ms.
are in the library of Vienna (Fabricius, Bibliot. Græc. tom. vi. p. 366, tom. xii. p.
781).   Quiescant !   [On the mathematical studies of Leo see Heiberg, der byzant.
Mathematiker Leon, in Bibliot. Mathematica, N. F. i. 33 *sqq.* 1887.]

[113] The ecclesiastical and literary character of Photius is copiously discussed by
Hanckius (de Scriptoribus Byzant. p. 269-396) and Fabricius.   [See Appendix 1.]

was deep in thought, indefatigable in reading, and eloquent in diction. Whilst he exercised the office of protospathaire, or captain of the guards, Photius was sent ambassador to the caliph of Bagdad.[114] The tedious hours of exile, perhaps of confinement, were beguiled by the hasty composition of his *Library*, a living monument of erudition and criticism. Two hundred and fourscore writers, historians, orators, philosophers, theologians, are reviewed without any regular method : he abridges their narrative or doctrine, appreciates their style and character, and judges even the fathers of the church with a discreet freedom, which often breaks through the superstition of the times. The emperor Basil, who lamented the defects of his own education, entrusted to the care of Photius his son and successor Leo the Philosopher ; and the reign of that prince and of his son Constantine Porphyrogenitus forms one of the most prosperous æras of the Byzantine literature. By their munificence the treasures of antiquity were deposited in the Imperial library ; by their pens, or those of their associates, they were imparted in such extracts and abridgments as might amuse the curiosity, without oppressing the indolence, of the public. Besides the *Basilics*, or code of laws, the arts of husbandry and war, of feeding or destroying the human species, were propagated with equal diligence ; and the history of Greece and Rome was digested into fifty-three heads or titles, of which two only (of embassies, and of virtues and vices) have escaped the injuries of time. In every station, the reader might contemplate the image of the past world, apply the lesson or warning of each page, and learn to admire, perhaps to imitate, the examples of a brighter period. I shall not expatiate on the works of the Byzantine Greeks, who, by the assiduous study of the ancients, have deserved in some measure the remembrance and gratitude of the moderns. The scholars of the present age may still enjoy the benefit of the philosophical common-place book of Stobæus, the grammatical and historical lexicon of Suidas, the Chiliads of Tzetzes, which comprise six hundred narratives in twelve thousand verses, and the commentaries on Homer of Eustathius, archbishop of Thessalonica, who, from his horn of plenty, has poured the

---

[114] Εἰς Ἀσσυρίους can only mean Bagdad, the seat of the caliph ; and the relation of his embassy might have been curious and instructive. But how did he procure his books ? A library so numerous could neither be found at Bagdad, nor transported with his baggage, nor preserved in his memory. Yet the last, however incredible, seems to be affirmed by Photius himself, ὅσας αὐτῶν ἡ μνήμη διέσωζε. Camusat (Hist. Critique des Journaux, p. 87-94) gives a good account of the Myriobiblon.

names and authorities of four hundred writers.  From these
originals, and from the numerous tribe of scholiasts and critics,[115]
some estimate may be formed of the literary wealth of the
twelfth century ; Constantinople was enlightened by the genius
of Homer and Demosthenes, of Aristotle and Plato ; and in
the enjoyment or neglect of our present riches, we must envy
the generation that could still peruse the history of Theopompus,
the orations of Hyperides, the comedies of Menander,[116] and the
odes of Alcæus and Sappho.  The frequent labour of illustration
attests not only the existence but the popularity of the Grecian
classics ; the general knowledge of the age may be deduced from
the example of two learned females, the empress Eudocia, and
the princess Anna Comnena, who cultivated, in the purple, the
arts of rhetoric and philosophy.[117]  The vulgar dialect of the

[115] Of these modern Greeks, see the respective articles in the Bibliotheca Græca
of Fabricius : a laborious work, yet susceptible of a better method and many improvements : of Eustathius (tom. i. p. 289-292, 306-329 [for Eustathius see App. 1.
and below, cap. lvi. p. 218]), of the Pselli (a diatribe of Leo Allatius, ad calcem
tom. v. [reprinted in Migne, P. G. vol. 122]), of Constantine Porphyrogenitus (tom.
vi. p. 486-509), of John Stobæus (tom. viii. 665-728), of Suidas (tom. ix. p. 620-827),
John Tzetzes (tom. xii. p. 245-273).  Mr. Harris, in his Philological Arrangements,
opus senile, has given a sketch of this Byzantine learning (p. 287-300).  [The elder
Psellus (flor. c. init. saec. ix.) is a mere name.  For the life of the younger Psellus,
see above, vol. v. Appendix 1.  John of Stoboi belongs to the 6th century.  Of
Suidas (a Thessalian name) nothing is known, but his lexicographical work was
compiled in the 10th century.  Its great importance is due to its biographical
notices and information on literary history.  Much of the author s knowledge was
obtained at second hand through the collections of Constantine Porphyrogennetos.
Cp. Krumbacher, op. cit. p. 567.  Best ed. by G. Bernhardy (1834-53).  The only
certain work of Isaac Tzetzes is a treatise on the metres of Pindar.  He and his
younger brother John lived in the 12th century.  John wrote, among other things,
an exegesis on Homer ; scholia on Hesiod, Aristophanes, the Alexandra of Lyco-
phron, and the Halicutica of Oppian ; a commentary on Porphyry's Eisagoge.
Most famous are his Chiliads (βίβλος ἱστορίας) in 12,674 political verses, containing
600 historical anecdotes, mythological stories, &c., and provided with marginal
scholia (ed. T. Kiessling, 1826).  Extant letters of Tzetzes have been collected by
T. Pressel (1851).]

[116] From obscure and hearsay evidence, Gerard Vossius (de Poetis Græcis, c. 6)
and Le Clerc (Bibliothèque Choisie, tom. xix. p. 285) mention a commentary of
Michael Psellus on twenty-four plays of Menander, still extant in Ms. at Constantinople.  Yet such classic studies seem incompatible with the gravity or dulness of
a schoolman, who pored over the categories (de Psellis, p. 42), and Michael has
probably been confounded with Homerus Sellius, who wrote arguments to the
comedies of Menander.  In the xth century, Suidas quotes fifty plays, but he often
transcribes the old scholiast of Aristophanes.  [In the present century several
speeches of Hyperides have been recovered from tombs in Egypt.]

[117] Anna Comnena may boast of her Greek style (τὸ Ἑλληνίζειν ἐς ἄκρον ἐσπουδακυιᾶ),
and Zonaras, her contemporary, but not her flatterer, may add with truth, γλῶτται
εἶχεν ἀκριβῶς Ἀττικίζουσαν.  The princess was conversant with the artful dialogues
of Plato ; and had studied the τετρακτύς, or quadrivium of astrology, geometry,
arithmetic, and music (see her preface to the Alexiad, with Ducange's notes).

city was gross and barbarous : a more correct and elaborate style distinguished the discourse, or at least the compositions, of the church and palace, which sometimes affected to copy the purity of the Attic models.

In our modern education, the painful though necessary attainment of two languages, which are no longer living, may consume the time and damp the ardour of the youthful student. The poets and orators were long imprisoned in the barbarous dialects of our Western ancestors, devoid of harmony or grace ; and their genius, without precept or example, was abandoned to the rude and native powers of their judgment and fancy. But the Greeks of Constantinople, after purging away the impurities of their vulgar speech, acquired the free use of their ancient language, the most happy composition of human art, and a familiar knowledge of the sublime masters who had pleased or instructed the first of nations. But these advantages only tend to aggravate the reproach and shame of a degenerate people. They held in their lifeless hands the riches of their fathers, without inheriting the spirit which had created and improved that sacred patrimony : they read, they praised, they compiled, but their languid souls seemed alike incapable of thought and action. In the revolution of ten centuries, not a single discovery was made to exalt the dignity or promote the happiness of mankind. Not a single idea has been added to the speculative systems of antiquity, and a succession of patient disciples became in their turn the dogmatic teachers of the next servile generation. Not a single composition of history, philosophy, or literature, has been saved from oblivion by the intrinsic beauties of style or sentiment, of original fancy, or even of successful imitation. In prose, the least offensive of the Byzantine writers are absolved from censure by their naked and unpresuming simplicity ; but the orators, most eloquent [118] in their own conceit, are the farthest removed from the models whom they affect to emulate. In every page our taste and reason are wounded by the choice of gigantic and obsolete words, a stiff and intricate phraseology,

*Decay of taste and genius*

[Eudocia Macrembolitissa, the wife of Constantine X., must be deposed from the place which she has hitherto occupied in Byzantine literature, since it has been established that the Ἰωνιά (Violarium) was not compiled by her, but nearly five centuries later (c. 1543) by Constantine Palaeokappa. See P. Pulch, de Eudociae quod fertur Violario (Strassburg, 1880) and Konstantin Palaeocappa, in Hermes 17, 177 sqq. (1882). Cp. Krumbacher, op. cit. p. 579.]

[118] To censure the Byzantine taste, Ducange (Prefat. Gloss. Græc. p. 17) strings the authorities of Aulus Gellius, Jerom, Petronius, George Hamartolus, Longinus ; who give at once the precept and the example.

the discord of images, the childish play of false or unseasonable ornament, and the painful attempt to elevate themselves, to astonish the reader, and to involve a trivial meaning in the smoke of obscurity and exaggeration. Their prose is soaring to the vicious affectation of poetry: their poetry is sinking below the flatness and insipidity of prose. The tragic, epic, and lyric muses were silent and inglorious; the bards of Constantinople seldom rose above a riddle or epigram, a panegyric or tale; they forgot even the rules of prosody; and, with the melody of Homer yet sounding in their ears, they confound all measure of feet and syllables in the impotent strains which have received the name of *political* or city verses.[119] The minds of the Greeks were bound in the fetters of a base and imperious superstition, which extends her dominion round the circle of profane science. Their understandings were bewildered in metaphysical controversy; in the belief of visions and miracles, they had lost all principles of moral evidence; and their taste was vitiated by the homilies of the monks, an absurd medley of declamation and scripture. Even these contemptible studies were no longer dignified by the abuse of superior talents; the leaders of the Greek church were humbly content to admire and copy the oracles of antiquity, nor did the schools or pulpit produce any rivals of the fame of Athanasius and Chrysostom.[120]

Want of national emulation

In all the pursuits of active and speculative life, the emulation of states and individuals is the most powerful spring of the efforts and improvements of mankind. The cities of ancient Greece were cast in the happy mixture of union and independence, which is repeated on a larger scale, but in a looser form, by the nations of modern Europe: the union of language, re-

---

[119] The *versus politici*, those common prostitutes, as, from their easiness, they are styled by Leo Allatius, usually consist of fifteen syllables. They are used by Constantine Manasses, John Tzetzes, &c. (Ducange, Gloss. Latin. tom. iii. p. i. p. 345, 346, edit. Basil, 1762). [All the verses which abandoned prosody and considered only accent may be called *political*; but the most common form was the line of fifteen syllables with a diæresis after the eighth syllable; the rhythm was :—

$$\smile\!\smile\;\smile\!\smile\;\smile\!\smile\;\smile\!\smile \mid \smile\!\smile\;\smile\!\smile\;\smile\!\smile$$

Proverbs in this form existed as early as the sixth century; and in the Ceremonies of Constantine Porphyrogennetos we find a popular spring song in political verse, beginning (p. 367):—

ἰδὲ τὸ ἔαρ τὸ γλυκὺ | πάλιν ἐπανατέλλει.

The question has been much debated whether this kind of verse arose out of the ancient trochaic, or the ancient iambic, tetrameter. Cp. Krumbacher, *op. cit.* p. 650-1.]

[120] As St. Bernard of the Latin, so St. John Damascenus in the viiith century is revered as the last father of the Greek, church.

ligion, and manners, which renders them the spectators and judges of each other's merit; [121] the independence of government and interest, which asserts their separate freedom, and excites them to strive for pre-eminence in the career of glory. The situation of the Romans was less favourable; yet in the early ages of the republic, which fixed the national character, a similar emulation was kindled among the states of Latium and Italy; and, in the arts and sciences, they aspired to equal or surpass their Grecian masters. The empire of the Cæsars undoubtedly checked the activity and progress of the human mind; its magnitude might, indeed, allow some scope for domestic competition; but, when it was gradually reduced, at first to the East, and at last to Greece and Constantinople, the Byzantine subjects were degraded to an abject and languid temper, the natural effect of their solitary and insulated state. From the North they were oppressed by nameless tribes of barbarians, to whom they scarcely imparted the appellation of men. The language and religion of the more polished Arabs were an unsurmountable bar to all social intercourse. The conquerors of Europe were their brethren in the Christian faith; but the speech of the Franks or Latins was unknown, their manners were rude, and they were rarely connected, in peace or war, with the successors of Heraclius. Alone in the universe, the self-satisfied pride of the Greeks was not disturbed by the comparison of foreign merit; and it is no wonder if they fainted in the race, since they had neither competitors to urge their speed nor judges to crown their victory. The nations of Europe and Asia were mingled by the expeditions to the Holy Land; and it is under the Comnenian dynasty that a faint emulation of knowledge and military virtue was rekindled in the Byzantine empire.

[121] Hume's Essays, vol. i. p. 125.

## CHAPTER LIV

*Origin and Doctrine of the Paulicians—Their Persecution by the
Greek Emperors—Revolt in Armenia, &c.—Transplantation into
Thrace—Propagation in the West—The Seeds, Character, and
Consequences, of the Reformation*

Supine super-
stition of the
Greek church
IN the profession of Christianity, the variety of national characters may be clearly distinguished.  The natives of Syria and
Egypt abandoned their lives to lazy and contemplative devotion ;
Rome again aspired to the dominion of the world ; and the wit
of the lively and loquacious Greeks was consumed in the disputes of metaphysical theology.  The incomprehensible mysteries
of the Trinity and Incarnation, instead of commanding their
silent submission, were agitated in vehement and subtle controversies, which enlarged their faith, at the expense, perhaps,
of their charity and reason.  From the council of Nice to the
end of the seventh century, the peace and unity of the church
was invaded by these spiritual wars ; and so deeply did they
affect the decline and fall of the empire that the historian has
too often been compelled to attend the synods, to explore the
creeds, and to enumerate the sects, of this busy period of ecclesiastical annals.  From the beginning of the eighth century to
the last ages of the Byzantine empire the sound of controversy
was seldom heard ; curiosity was exhausted, zeal was fatigued,
and, in the decrees of six councils, the articles of the Catholic
faith had been irrevocably defined.  The spirit of dispute, however vain and pernicious, requires some energy and exercise of
the mental faculties ; and the prostrate Greeks were content to
fast, to pray, and to believe, in blind obedience to the patriarch
and his clergy.  During a long dream of superstition, the Virgin
and the Saints, their visions and miracles, their relics and images,
were preached by the monks and worshipped by the people ;
and the appellation of people might be extended without injustice to the first ranks of civil society.  At an unseasonable
moment the Isaurian emperors attempted somewhat rudely to

awaken their subjects : under their influence, reason might obtain some proselytes, a far greater number was swayed by interest
or fear ; but the Eastern world embraced or deplored their visible
deities, and the restoration of images was celebrated as the feast [A.D. 843]
of orthodoxy.  In this passive and unanimous state the ecclesiastical rulers were relieved from the toil, or deprived of the
pleasure, of persecution.  The Pagans had disappeared ; the
Jews were silent and obscure ; the disputes with the Latins
were rare and remote hostilities against a national enemy ; and
the sects of Egypt and Syria enjoyed a free toleration, under
the shadow of the Arabian caliphs.  About the middle of the
seventh century, a branch of Manichæans was selected as the
victims of spiritual tyranny : their patience was at length exasperated to despair and rebellion ; and their exile has scattered
over the West the seeds of reformation.  These important events
will justify some inquiry into the doctrine and story of the
PAULICIANS : [1] and, as they cannot plead for themselves, our
candid criticism will magnify the *good*, and abate or suspect
the *evil*, that is reported by their adversaries.

The Gnostics, who had distracted the infancy, were oppressed Origin of the
by the greatness and authority, of the church.  Instead of emu- disciples of
lating or surpassing the wealth, learning, and numbers of the St. Paul.
Catholics, their obscure remnant was driven from the capitals A.D. 660, &c.
of the East and West, and confined to the villages and mountains
along the borders of the Euphrates.  Some vestige of the Marcionites may be detected in the fifth century ; [2] but the numerous
sects were finally lost in the odious name of the Manichæans ;
and these heretics, who presumed to reconcile the doctrines of
Zoroaster and Christ, were pursued by the two religions with
equal and unrelenting hatred.  Under the grandson of Heraclius,
in the neighbourhood of Samosata, more famous for the birth
of Lucian than for the title of a Syrian kingdom, a reformer
arose, esteemed by the *Paulicians* as the chosen messenger of

---

[1] The errors and virtues of the Paulicians are weighed, with his usual judgment
and candour, by the learned Mosheim (Hist. Ecclesiast. seculum ix. p. 311, &c.).
He draws his original intelligence from Photius (contra Manichæos, l. i.) and
Peter Siculus (Hist. Manichæorum).  The first of these accounts has not fallen
into my hands ; the second, which Mosheim prefers, I have read in a Latin version
inserted in the Maxima Bibliotheca Patrum (tom. xvi. p. 754-764) from the edition
of the Jesuit Raderus (Ingolstadii, 1604, in 4to).  [See Appendix 6.]

[2] In the time of Theodoret, the diocese of Cyrrhus, in Syria, contained eight
hundred villages.  Of these, two were inhabited by Arians and Eunomians, and
eight by *Marcionites*, whom the laborious bishop reconciled to the Catholic church
(Dupin, Bibliot. Ecclésiastique, tom. iv. p. 81, 82).  [The existence of Marcionites
at the end of the 6th century is attested by Theophylactus Simocatta.]

truth. In his humble dwelling of Mananalis,[3] Constantine entertained a deacon, who returned from Syrian captivity, and
received the inestimable gift of the New Testament, which was
already concealed from the vulgar by the prudence of the Greek,
and perhaps of the Gnostic, clergy.[4] These books became the
measure of his studies and the rule of his faith ; and the Catholics, who dispute his interpretation, acknowledge that his text
was genuine and sincere. But he attached himself with peculiar
devotion to the writings and character of St. Paul : the name of
the Paulicians is derived by their enemies from some unknown
and domestic teacher ; but I am confident that they gloried in
their affinity to the apostle of the Gentiles.[5] His disciples,
Titus, Timothy, Sylvanus, Tychicus, were represented by Constantine and his fellow-labourers : the names of the apostolic
churches were applied to the congregations which they assembled
in Armenia and Cappadocia ; and this innocent allegory revived
the example and memory of the first ages.[6] In the gospel, and

*Their Bible*

[3] [The text of Petros Hegumenos (see Appendix 6) gives Καμάναλις, a mere misprint (notwithstanding Karapet Ter-Mkrttschian, Die Paulikianer, p. 5). For the
identification of Mananalis with Karachoban, on the Kinis Chai, S.E. of Erzerum,
see Conybeare, Key of Truth, Introd. p. lxix.]

[4] Nobis profanis ista (*sacra Evangelia*) legere non licet sed sacerdotibus duntaxat,
was the first scruple of a Catholic when he was advised to read the Bible (Petr.
Sicul. p. 761).

[5] [Three derivations of *Paulician* were alleged. (1) From Paul of Samosata,
son of a Manichæan woman ; he was said to be the founder of the heresy ; but
the Paulicians themselves did not admit this and said that Silvanus was their true
founder. See all the sources (cp. Appendix 6). But cp. Conybeare, *op. cit.* p. cvi.
(2) This Paul was said to have a brother John ; and, perhaps from a consciousness of the difficulty of deriving Paulician from Paulos (cp. Friedrich, Bericht über
die Paulikianer, p. 93), it was proposed (see Photius, ed. Migne, P.G., 102, p. 17)
to regard the word as a corruption of Παυλοιωάννης, "Paul-John". (3) From St.
Paul (see Pseudo-Phot., ap. Migne, *ib.* p. 109).—The word is curiously formed ;
"followers of Paul" ought to be *Paulianoi*. It seems highly probable that the
name *Paulician* was not used by the heretics themselves. George Mon. says "they
call themselves Christians, but us Romans". "Paulikianos" must be formed from
"Paulikios," an Armenian diminutive somewhat contemptuous (compare Kour-
tikios, &c.). It might then be suggested that the hypothetical Paulikios from whom
the sect derived their nickname, is to be identified with Paul the Armenian, father
of Gegnaesius, the third head of the Paulician church (see Photius, c. Man. p. 53
ap. Migne, P.G. 102 ; Petrus Sic. p. 1284, *ib.* 104).]

[6] [The seven teachers of the Paulicians were : (1) Constantine = Silvanus ; (2)
Simeon = Titus ; (3) Gegnesius = Timotheus (an Armenian) ; (4) Joseph = Epaph-
roditus ; (5) Zacharias, rejected by some, and named the hireling Shepherd ; (6)
Baanes (an Armenian name, Vahan), nicknamed the Dirty; (7) Sergius = Tychicus.
Their six churches were : (1) "Macedonia" = Cibossa near Colonea (founded by
Silvanus and Titus) ; (2) "Achaia" = Mananalis (founded by Timotheus) ; (3)
"the Philippians" (where?) (founded by Epaphroditus and Zacharias) ; (4) "the
Laodiceans" = Argaus ; (5) "the Ephesians" = Mopsuestia ; (6) "the Colossians" = Κυνοχωρῖται or Κοινοχωρῖται (apparently like the Ἀστατοι, a particular
sect). The 4th and 6th churches are thus given by George Mon. p. 607 (ed. Muralt),
but Peter Sic. connects the Colossians with Argaus and equates the Laodiceans
with the Kunochorites (those who dwell in τὴν τοῦ κυνὸς χώραν).]

the epistles of St. Paul, his faithful follower investigated the
creed of primitive Christianity ; and, whatever might be the
success, a Protestant reader will applaud the spirit of the inquiry.
But, if the scriptures of the Paulicians were pure, they were not
perfect. Their founders rejected the two epistles of St. Peter,[7]
the apostle of the circumcision, whose dispute with their favourite
for the observance of the law could not easily be forgiven.[8]
They agreed with their Gnostic brethren in the universal contempt for the Old Testament, the books of Moses and the
prophets, which have been consecrated by the decrees of the
Catholic church. With equal boldness, and doubtless with more
reason, Constantine, the new Sylvanus, disclaimed the visions
which, in so many bulky and splendid volumes, had been published
by the Oriental sects ;[9] the fabulous productions of the Hebrew
patriarchs and the sages of the East ; the spurious gospels,
epistles, and acts, which in the first age had overwhelmed the
orthodox code ; the theology of Manes and the authors of the
kindred heresies ; and the thirty generations, or æons, which
had been created by the fruitful fancy of Valentine. The
Paulicians sincerely condemned the memory and opinions of
the Manichæan sect, and complained of the injustice which
impressed that invidious name on the simple votaries of St.
Paul and of Christ.[10]

Of the ecclesiastical chain, many links had been broken by the
Paulician reformers ; and their liberty was enlarged, as they reduced the number of masters at whose voice profane reason must
bow to mystery and miracle. The early separation of the Gnostics had preceded the establishment of the Catholic worship ; and
against the gradual innovations of discipline and doctrine they

*The sim-
plicity of
their belief
and worship*

---

[7] In rejecting the *second* epistle of St. Peter, the Paulicians are justified by some of
the most respectable of the ancients and moderns (see Wetstein ad loc.; Simon, Hist.
Critique du Nouveau Testament, c. 17). They likewise overlooked the Apocalypse
(Petr. Sicul. p. 756 [p. 1256, ap. Migne, P. G. 104]) ; but, as such neglect is not imputed as a crime, the Greeks of the ixth century must have been careless of the
credit and honour of the Revelations.

[8] This contention, which has not escaped the malice of Porphyry, supposes some
error and passion in one or both of the apostles. By Chrysostom, Jerom, and
Erasmus, it is represented as a sham quarrel, a pious fraud, for the benefit of the
Gentiles and the correction of the Jews (Middleton's Works, vol. ii. p. 1-20).

[9] Those who are curious of this heterodox library may consult the researches of
Beausobre (Hist. Critique du Manichéisme, tom. i. p. 385-437). Even in Africa,
St. Austin could describe the Manichæan books, tam multi, tam grandes, tam
pretiosi codices (contra Faust. xiii. 14) ; but he adds, without pity, Incendite
omnes illas membranas : and his advice has been rigorously followed.

[10] [The Greeks included the Paulicians, like the Marcionites, under the general
title of Manichæans, because they supposed them to be dualists, assuming two first
principles.]

were as strongly guarded by habit and aversion as by the silence
of St. Paul and the evangelists.  The objects which had been
transformed by the magic of superstition appeared to the eyes
of the Paulicians in their genuine and naked colours.  An image
made without hands was the common workmanship of a mortal
artist, to whose skill alone the wood and canvas must be indebted for their merit or value.  The miraculous relics were an
heap of bones and ashes, destitute of life or virtue, or of any
relation, perhaps, with the person to whom they were ascribed.
The true and vivifying cross was a piece of sound or rotten
timber ; the body and blood of Christ, a loaf of bread and a cup
of wine, the gifts of nature and the symbols of grace.  The
mother of God was degraded from her celestial honours and
immaculate virginity ; and the saints and angels were no longer
solicited to exercise the laborious office of mediation in heaven
and ministry upon earth.  In the practice, or at least in the
theory, of the sacraments, the Paulicians were inclined to abolish
all visible objects of worship, and the words of the gospel were,
in their judgment, the baptism and communion of the faithful.
They indulged a convenient latitude for the interpretation of
scripture ; and, as often as they were pressed by the literal sense,
they could escape to the intricate mazes of figure and allegory.
Their utmost diligence must have been employed to dissolve the
connexion between the Old and the New Testament ; since they
adored the latter as the oracles of God, and abhorred the former
as the fabulous and absurd invention of men or dæmons.  We
cannot be surprised that they should have found in the gospel
the orthodox mystery of the Trinity ; but, instead of confessing
the human nature and substantial sufferings of Christ, they
amused their fancy with a celestial body that passed through
the virgin like water through a pipe ; with a fantastic crucifixion
that eluded the vain and impotent malice of the Jews.  A creed
thus simple and spiritual was not adapted to the genius of the
times ; [11] and the rational Christian, who might have been contented with the light yoke and easy burthen of Jesus and his
apostles, was justly offended that the Paulicians should dare to
violate the unity of God, the first article of natural and revealed

They hold
the two
principles
of the Ma-
gians and
Manichæans

---

[11] The six capital errors of the Paulicians are defined by Peter Siculus (p. 756
[c. 10, p. 1253, 1256-7, ed. Migne]) with much prejudice and passion.  [In the
following order : (1) The two principles ; (2) the exclusion of the Virgin Mary from
the number of " Good Folk " (cp. the Perfect of the Bogomils ; see Appendix 6) ;
and the doctrine that Christ's body came down from Heaven ; (3) the rejection of
the Sacrament and (4) the Cross, and (5) the Old Testament, &c. ; (6) the rejection of the elders of the Church.]

religion.  Their belief and their trust was in the Father of
Christ, of the human soul, and of the invisible world.  But they
likewise held the eternity of matter : a stubborn and rebellious
substance, the origin of a second principle, of an active being,
who has created this visible world and exercises his temporal
reign till the final consummation of death and sin.[12]  The appearances of moral and physical evil had established the two principles in the ancient philosophy and religion of the East ; from
whence this doctrine was transfused to the various swarms of
the Gnostics.  A thousand shades may be devised in the nature
and character of *Ahriman*, from a rival god to a subordinate
dæmon, from passion and frailty to pure and perfect malevolence :
but, in spite of our efforts, the goodness and the power of Ormusd
are placed at the opposite extremities of the line ; and every step
that approaches the one must recede in equal proportion from the
other.[13]

The apostolic labours of Constantine-Sylvanus soon multiplied
the number of his disciples, the secret recompense of spiritual
ambition.  The remnant of the Gnostic sects, and especially the
Manichæans of Armenia, were united under his standard ; many
Catholics were converted or seduced by his arguments ; and he
preached with success in the regions of Pontus[14] and Cappadocia,
which had long since imbibed the religion of Zoroaster.  The
Paulician teachers were distinguished only by their scriptural
names, by the modest title of fellow-pilgrims, by the austerity
of their lives, their zeal or knowledge, and the credit of some
extraordinary gifts of the Holy Spirit.  But they were incapable
of desiring, or at least of obtaining, the wealth and honours of
the Catholic prelacy : such antichristian pride they bitterly censured ; and even the rank of elders or presbyters was condemned
as an institution of the Jewish synagogue.  The new sect was

*The establish-
ment of the
Paulicians
in Armenia,
Pontus, &c.*

---

[12] Primum illorum axioma est, duo rerum esse principia ; Deum malum et Deum
bonum aliumque hujus mundi conditorem et principem, et alium futuri ævi (Petr.
Sicul. p. 756 [c. 10, p. 1253, ed. Migne]).  [One god was the Heavenly Father,
who has not authority in this world but in the world to come ; the other was the
world-maker (cosmopoiêtês), who governs the present world.  Cp. George Mon.,
p. 607, ed. Muralt.]

[13] Two learned critics, Beausobre (Hist. Critique du Manichéisme, l. i. 4, 5, 6)
and Mosheim (Institut. Hist. Eccles. and de Rebus Christianis ante Constantinum,
sec. i. ii. iii.), have laboured to explore and discriminate the various systems of the
Gnostics on the subject of the two principles.

[14] The countries between the Euphrates and the Halys were possessed above
350 years by the Medes (Herodot. l. i. c. 103) and Persians ; and the kings of
Pontus were of the royal race of the Achæmenides (Sallust. Fragment. l. iii. with
the French supplement, and notes of the President de Brosses).

loosely spread over the provinces of Asia Minor to the westward
of the Euphrates; six of their principal congregations represented
the churches to which St. Paul had addressed his epistles; and
their founder chose his residence in the neighbourhood of
Colonia,[15] in the same district of Pontus which had been celebrated by the altars of Bellona [16] and the miracles of Gregory.[17]
After a mission of twenty-seven years, Sylvanus, who had retired
from the tolerating government of the Arabs, fell a sacrifice to

Persecution<br>of the Greek<br>emperors

Roman persecution.   The laws of the pious emperors, which
seldom touched the lives of less odious heretics, proscribed without mercy or disguise the tenets, the books, and the persons of
the Montanists and Manichæans : the books were delivered to
the flames ; and all who should presume to secrete such writings,
or to profess such opinions, were devoted to an ignominious
death.[18]   A Greek minister, armed with legal and military
powers, appeared at Colonia to strike the shepherd, and to re-
claim, if possible, the lost sheep.   By a refinement of cruelty,
Simeon placed the unfortunate Sylvanus before a line of his disciples, who were commanded, as the price of their pardon and
the proof of their repentance, to massacre their spiritual father.
They turned aside from the impious office ; the stones dropped
from their filial hands ; and of the whole number only one executioner could be found, a new David, as he is styled by the
Catholics, who boldly overthrew the giant of heresy.   This

[15] Most probably founded by Pompey after the conquest of Pontus.  This
Colonia, on the Lycus above Neo-Cæsarea, is named by the Turks Couleihisar, or
Chonac, a populous town in a strong country (d'Anville, Géographie Ancienne,
tom. ii. p. 34 ; Tournefort, Voyage du Levant, tom. iii. lettre xxi. p. 293).  [Professor
Ramsay is inclined to identify Colonea with Kara Hissar (= Black Castle, Μαυρό-
καστρον, Attaliates, p. 125) ; Asia Minor, p. 267, and cp. p. 57.]

[16] The temple of Bellona at Comana, in Pontus, was a powerful and wealthy
foundation, and the high priest was respected as the second person in the kingdom.
As the sacerdotal office had been occupied by his mother's family, Strabo (l. xii. p.
809 [2, § 3], 835, 836, 837 [3, § 32 sqq.]) dwells with peculiar complacency on the
temple, the worship, and festival, which was twice celebrated every year.   But the
Bellona of Pontus had the features and character of the goddess, not of war, but
of love.

[17] Gregory, bishop of Neo-Cæsarea (A.D. 240-265), surnamed Thaumaturgus or
the Wonder-worker.   An hundred years afterwards, the history or romance of his
life was composed by Gregory of Nyssa, his namesake and countryman, the brother
of the great St. Basil.

[18] Hoc cæterum ad sua egregia facinora divini atque orthodoxi Imperatores
addiderunt, ut Manichæos Montanosque capitali puniri sententiâ juberent, eorum-
que libros, quocunque in loco inventi essent, flammis tradi ; quod siquis uspiam
eosdem occultasse deprehenderetur, hunc eundem mortis pœnæ addici, ejusque
bona in fiscum inferri (Petr. Sicul. p. 759).   What more could bigotry and persecution desire?

apostate, Justus was his name, again deceived and betrayed his unsuspecting brethren, and a new conformity to the acts of St. Paul may be found in the conversion of Simeon : like the apostle, he embraced the doctrine which he had been sent to persecute, renounced his honours and fortunes, and acquired among the Paulicians the fame of a missionary and a martyr.  They were not ambitious of martyrdom,[19] but, in a calamitous period of one hundred and fifty years, their patience sustained whatever zeal could inflict ; and power was insufficient to eradicate the obstinate vegetation of fanaticism and reason.  From the blood and ashes of the first victims, a succession of teachers and congregations repeatedly arose ; amidst their foreign hostilities, they found leisure for domestic quarrels ; they preached, they disputed, they suffered ; and the virtues, the apparent virtues, of Sergius, in a [Sergius of pilgrimage of thirty-three years, are reluctantly confessed by Tavia] the orthodox historians.[20]  The native cruelty of Justinian the Second was stimulated by a pious cause ; and he vainly hoped to extinguish, in a single conflagration, the name and memory of the Paulicians.  By their primitive simplicity, their abhorrence of popular superstition, the Iconoclast princes might have been reconciled to some erroneous doctrines ; but they themselves were exposed to the calumnies of the monks, and they chose to be the tyrants, lest they should be accused as the accomplices, of the Manichæans.  Such a reproach has sullied the clemency of Nicephorus, who relaxed in their favour the severity of the penal statutes, nor will his character sustain the honour of a more liberal motive.  The feeble Michael the First, the rigid Leo the Armenian, were foremost in the race of persecution ; but the prize must doubtless be adjudged to the sanguinary

---

[19] It should seem that the Paulicians allowed themselves some latitude of equivocation and mental reservation ; till the Catholics discovered the pressing questions, which reduced them to the alternative of apostacy or martyrdom (Petr. Sicul. p. 760).

[20] The persecution is told by Petrus Siculus (p. 579-763) with satisfaction and pleasantry.  Justus *justa* persolvit.  Simeon was not τίτος but κῆτος [cp. Petrus, c. 27, p. 1281, ed. Migne] (the pronunciation of the two vowels must have been nearly the same), a great whale that drowned the mariners who mistook him for an island.  See likewise Cedrenus (p. 432-435 [i. 766 *sqq.*, ed. B.]).  [Sergius seems to have lived about the end of the eighth and beginning of the ninth century ; but there are some difficulties and confusions in the chronology.  Cp. Ter-Mkrttschian, Die Paulikianer, p. 17 *sqq.*  There seems no reason to question the date assigned to the founder Sylvanus by George Monachus, *viz.*, the reigns of Constans II. and Constantine IV.  And in that case there is no reason why Gegnæsius, the third head of the Paulician Church, should not have lived under Leo III. (see Photius, p. 53, ap. Migne, P. G. 102 ; Petrus Sic., p. 1284, *ib.* 104).  The chronology holds together.]

devotion of Theodora, who restored the images to the Oriental church.  Her inquisitors explored the cities and mountains of the lesser Asia, and the flatterers of the empress have affirmed that, in a short reign, one hundred thousand Paulicians were extirpated by the sword, the gibbet, or the flames.  Her guilt or merit has perhaps been stretched beyond the measure of truth ; but, if the account be allowed, it must be presumed that many simple Iconoclasts were punished under a more odious name ; and that some, who were driven from the church, unwillingly took refuge in the bosom of heresy.

Revolt of the Paulicians. A.D. 845-880

The most furious and desperate of rebels are the sectaries of a religion long persecuted, and at length provoked.  In an holy cause they are no longer susceptible of fear or remorse : the justice of their arms hardens them against the feelings of humanity ; and they revenge their fathers' wrongs on the children of their tyrants.  Such have been the Hussites of Bohemia and the Calvinists of France, and such, in the ninth century, were the Paulicians of Armenia and the adjacent provinces.[21]  They were first awakened to the massacre of a governor and bishop, who exercised the Imperial mandate of converting or destroying the heretics ; and the deepest recesses of mount Argæus protected their independence and revenge. A more dangerous and consuming flame was kindled by the persecution of Theodora, and the revolt of Carbeas, a valiant

[General of the Anatolic Theme]

Paulician, who commanded the guards of the general of the East.  His father had been impaled by the Catholic inquisitors ; and religion, or at least nature, might justify his desertion and revenge.  Five thousand of his brethren were united by the same motives ; they renounced the allegiance of anti-christian Rome ; a Saracen emir introduced Carbeas to the caliph ; and the commander of the faithful extended his sceptre to the im-

They fortify Tephrice

placable enemy of the Greeks.  In the mountains between Siwas [22] and Trebizond he founded or fortified the city of Tephrice, [23] which is still occupied by a fierce and licentious

---

[21] Petrus Siculus (p. 763, 764), the continuator of Theophanes (l. iv. c. 4, p. 103, 104), Cedrenus (p. 541, 542, 545 [ii. 153 sqq., ed. B.]), and Zonaras (tom. ii. l. xvi. p. 156 [c. 2]) describe the revolt and exploits of Carbeas and his Paulicians.

[22] [Sebastea.]

[23] Otter (Voyage en Turquie et en Perse, tom. ii.) is probably the only Frank who has visited the independent Barbarians of Tephrice, now Divrigni [Devrik], from whom he fortunately escaped in the train of a Turkish officer. [The Paulicians first occupied and fortified (with the help of the Emir of Melitene) Argaûs and Amara (Theoph. Cont., iv. 16, p. 166, ed. Bonn).  Argaûs has been identified with Argovan, on a tributary of the Euphrates, due north of Melitene, by Mr. J. G. C.

people, and the neighbouring hills were covered with the Paulician fugitives, who now reconciled the use of the Bible and the sword. During more than thirty years, Asia was afflicted by the calamities of foreign and domestic war; in their hostile inroads the disciples of St. Paul were joined with those of Mahomet; and the peaceful Christians, the aged parent and tender virgin, who were delivered into barbarous servitude, might justly accuse the intolerant spirit of their sovereign. So urgent was the mischief, so intolerable the shame, that even the dissolute Michael, the son of Theodora, was compelled to march in person against the Paulicians: he was defeated under the walls of Samosata; and the Roman emperor fled before the heretics whom his mother had condemned to the flames.[24] The Saracens fought under the same banners, but the victory was ascribed to Carbeas; and the captive generals, with more than an hundred tribunes, were either released by his avarice or tortured by his fanaticism. The valour and ambition of Chrysocheir,[25] his successor, embraced a wider circle of rapine and revenge. In alliance with his faithful Moslems, he boldly penetrated into the heart of Asia; the troops of the frontier and the palace were repeatedly overthrown; the edicts of persecution were answered by the pillage of Nice and Nicomedia, of Ancyra and Ephesus; nor could the apostle St. John protect from violation his city and sepulchre. The cathedral of Ephesus was turned into a stable for mules and horses; and the Paulicians vied with the Saracens in their contempt and abhorrence of images and relics. It is not unpleasing to observe the triumph of rebellion over the same despotism which has disdained the prayers of an injured people. The emperor Basil, the Macedonian, was reduced to sue for peace, to offer a ransom for the captives, and to request, in the language of moderation and charity, that Chrysocheir would spare his fellow-Christians, *and pillage Asia Minor*

named (*opprobrious by the worshippers of images*, *but trade an*

Anderson (Journal of Hell. Studies, xvii. p. 27, 1897); and he places Amara (or Abara) on a high pass on the road from Sebastea to Lycandus, nearly due south of Sebastea. Tephrice lay S.E. from Sebastea on the road from that city to Satala. " The secluded position of Divreky made it the seat of an almost independent band of Kurds, when it was visited by Otter in 1743. Voyage en Turquie et en Perse, ii. 306." Finlay, ii. p. 169, note. See further, for the site, Mr. Guy Le Strange in Journ. R. Asiat. Soc. vol. 28 (1896). The Arabic name was Abrik.]

[24] [For this expedition see Theoph. Contin. iv. c. 23.]

[25] In the history of Chrysocheir, Genesius (Chron. p. 67-70. edit. Venet. [*leg.* 57-60, p. 121 *sqq.*, ed. Bonn]) has exposed the nakedness of the empire. Constantine Porphyrogenitus (in Vit. Basil. c. 37-43, p. 166-171) has displayed the glory of his grandfather. Cedrenus (p. 570-573 [ii. p. 209 *sqq.*, ed. B.]) is without their passions or their knowledge.

and content himself with a royal donative of gold and silver and silk-garments. "If the emperor," replied the insolent fanatic, "be desirous of peace, let him abdicate the East, and reign without molestation in the West. If he refuse, the servants of the Lord will precipitate him from the throne." The reluctant Basil suspended the treaty, accepted the defiance, and led his army into the land of heresy, which he wasted with [c. A.D. 871-2] fire and sword. The open country of the Paulicians was exposed to the same calamities which they had inflicted ; but, when he had explored the strength of Tephrice, the multitude of the barbarians, and the ample magazines of arms and provisions, he desisted with a sigh from the hopeless siege.[26]     On his return to Constantinople he laboured, by the foundation of convents and churches, to secure the aid of his celestial patrons, of Michael the archangel and the prophet Elijah ; and it was his daily prayer that he might live to transpierce, with three arrows, the head of his impious adversary. Beyond his expectations, the wish was accomplished : after a successful inroad, Chryso-cheir was surprised and slain in his retreat ; and the rebel's [A.D. 874-5] head was triumphantly presented at the foot of the throne. On the reception of this welcome trophy, Basil instantly called for his bow, discharged three arrows with unerring aim, and accepted the applause of the court, who hailed the victory of the royal Their decline archer. With Chrysocheir, the glory of the Paulicians faded and withered ;[27] on the second expedition of the emperor, the impregnable Tephrice was deserted by the heretics, who sued for mercy or escaped to the borders. The city was ruined, but the spirit of independence survived in the mountains ; the Paulicians defended, above a century, their religion and liberty, infested the Roman limits, and maintained their perpetual alliance with the enemies of the empire and the gospel.

Their trans-plantation from Ar-menia to Thrace     About the middle of the eighth century, Constantine, sur-named Copronymus by the worshippers of images, had made an expedition into Armenia, and found, in the cities of Melitene

[26] [In regard to this campaign of Basil (in 871 or 872) it was generally supposed that he crossed the Euphrates, as the Continuator of Theophanes states (p. 269). But Mr. J. G. C. Anderson has shown that this must be a mistake and that the scene of the whole campaign was west of the Euphrates (Classical Review, April, 1896, p. 139). Basil's object (after his failure at Tephrice) was to capture Meli-tene, the chief Saracen stronghold of the Cis-Euphratesian territory in Asia Minor. Theoph. Contin. *ib.*]

[27] Συναπεμαράνθη πᾶσα ἡ ἀνθοῦσα τῆς Τεφρικῆς εὐανδρία [p. 212]. How elegant is the Greek tongue, even in the mouth of Cedrenus ! [Cp. George Mon. p. 841, ed. Bonn.]

and Theodosiopolis, a great number of Paulicians, his kindred heretics. As a favour or punishment, he transplanted them from the banks of the Euphrates to Constantinople and Thrace ; and by this emigration their doctrine was introduced and diffused in Europe.[28] If the sectaries of the metropolis were soon mingled with the promiscuous mass, those of the country struck a deep root in a foreign soil. The Paulicians of Thrace resisted the storms of persecution, maintained a secret correspondence with their Armenian brethren, and gave aid and comfort to their preachers, who solicited, not without success, the infant faith of the Bulgarians.[29] In the tenth century, they were restored and multiplied by a more powerful colony, which John Zimisces [30] transported from the Chalybian hills to the valleys of Mount Hæmus. The Oriental clergy, who would have preferred the destruction, impatiently sighed for the absence, of the Manichæans ; the warlike emperor had felt and esteemed their valour ; their attachment to the Saracens was pregnant with mischief ; but, on the side of the Danube, against the barbarians of Scythia, their service might be useful and their loss would be desirable. Their exile in a distant land was softened by a free toleration ; the Paulicians held the city of Philippopolis and the keys of Thrace ; the Catholics were their subjects ; the Jacobite emigrants their associates : they occupied a line of villages and castles in Macedonia and Epirus ; and many native Bulgarians were associated to the communion of arms and heresy. As long as they were awed by power and treated with moderation, their voluntary bands were distinguished in the armies of the empire ; and the courage of these *dogs*, ever greedy of war, ever thirsty of human blood, is noticed with astonishment, and almost with reproach, by the pusillanimous Greeks. The same spirit ren-

---

[28] Copronymus transported his συγγενεῖς, heretics ; and thus ἐπλατύνθη ἡ αἵρεσις Παυλικιανῶν, says Cedrenus (p. 463 [ii. p. 10]), who has copied the annals of Theophanes. [*Sub* A.M. 6247.]

[29] Petrus Siculus, who resided nine months at Tephrice (A.D. 870) for the ransom of captives (p. 764), was informed of their intended mission, and addressed his preservative, the Historia Manichæorum, to the new archbishop of the Bulgarians (p. 754 [p. 1241, ed. Migne]). [For Petrus Siculus, cp. Appendix 6.]

[30] The colony of Paulicians and Jacobites, transplanted by John Zimisces (A.D. 970) from Armenia to Thrace, is mentioned by Zonaras (tom. ii. l. xvii. p. 209 [c. 1]) and Anna Comnena (Alexiad, l. xiv. p. 450, &c. [c. 8]). [This colonisation must have taken place *after* the conquest of Eastern Bulgaria and the war with Sviatoslav ; and therefore not before A.D. 973. Cp. Schlumberger, L'épopée byzantine, p. 181. Scylitzes (= Cedrenus ii. p. 382) says that it was Thomas, Patriarch of Antioch, who suggested the transplantation. He realised that in the Eastern provinces the Paulicians were dangerous allies of the Saracens.]

dered them arrogant and contumacious : they were easily provoked by caprice or injury ; and their privileges were often
violated by the faithless bigotry of the government and clergy.
In the midst of the Norman war, two thousand five hundred
Manichæans deserted the standard of Alexius Comnenus,[31] and
retired to their native homes.   He dissembled till the moment
of revenge ; invited the chiefs to a friendly conference; and
punished the innocent and guilty by imprisonment, confiscation,
and baptism.   In an interval of peace, the emperor undertook
the pious office of reconciling them to the church and state : his
winter quarters were fixed at Philippopolis; and the thirteenth
apostle, as he is styled by his pious daughter, consumed whole
days and nights in theological controversy.   His arguments were
fortified, their obstinacy was melted, by the honours and rewards
which he bestowed on the most eminent proselytes ; and a new
city, surrounded with gardens, enriched with immunities, and
dignified with his own name, was founded by Alexius, for the
residence of his vulgar converts.   The important station of
Philippopolis was wrested from their hands ; the contumacious
leaders were secured in a dungeon or banished from their country ;
and their lives were spared by the prudence, rather than the
mercy, of an emperor at whose command a poor and solitary
[A.D. 1111]   heretic was burnt alive before the church of St. Sophia.[32]   But
the proud hope of eradicating the prejudices of a nation was
speedily overturned by the invincible zeal of the Paulicians, who
ceased to dissemble or refused to obey.   After the departure
and death of Alexius, they soon resumed their civil and religious
laws.   In the beginning of the thirteenth century, their pope
or primate (a manifest corruption) resided on the confines of
Bulgaria, Croatia, and Dalmatia, and governed by his vicars the

---

[31] The Alexiad of Anna Comnena (l. v. p. 131 [c. 3], l. vi. p. 154, 155 [c. 2], l.
xiv. p. 450-457 [c. 8, 9], with the annotations of Ducange) records the transactions
of her apostolic father with the Manichæans, whose abominable heresy she was
desirous of refuting.

[32] Basil, a monk, and the author of the Bogomiles, a sect of Gnostics, who soon
vanished (Anna Comnena, Alexiad, l. xv. p. 486-494 [c. 8, 9, 10]; Mosheim, Hist.
Ecclesiastica, p. 420).   [This Basil was not "the author of the Bogomils".
*Bogomil* is the Slavonic equivalent of the Greek name *Theophilos ;* and Bogomil,
who founded the sect, lived in the tenth century under the Bulgarian prince Peter
(regn. 927-969).   There arose soon two Bogomil churches : the Bulgarian, and that
of the Dragoviči ; and from these two all the other later developments started.
Rački seeks the name of the second church among the Macedonian Dragoviči on
the Vardar ; while Golubinski identifies them with Dragoviči in the neighbourhood
of Philippopolis.   See Jireček, Gesch. der Bulgaren, p. 176.   For the Bogomilian
doctrines, see Appendix 6.]

filial congregations of Italy and France.[33]  From that æra, a
minute scrutiny might prolong and perpetuate the chain of tradition.   At the end of the last age, the sect or colony still inhabited the valleys of mount Hæmus, where their ignorance and
poverty were more frequently tormented by the Greek clergy
than by the Turkish government.   The modern Paulicians have
lost all memory of their origin ; and their religion is disgraced
by the worship of the cross, and the practice of bloody sacrifice,
which some captives have imported from the wilds of Tartary.[34]

In the West, the first teachers of the Manichæan theology *Their in-troduction into Italy and France*
had been repulsed by the people, or suppressed by the prince.
The favour and success of the Paulicians in the eleventh and
twelfth centuries must be imputed to the strong, though secret,
discontent which armed the most pious Christians against the
church of Rome.   Her avarice was oppressive, her despotism
odious ; less degenerate perhaps than the Greeks in the worship
of saints and images, her innovations were more rapid and
scandalous ; she had rigorously defined and imposed the doctrine
of transubstantiation : the lives of the Latin clergy were more
corrupt, and the Eastern bishops might pass for the successors
of the apostles, if they were compared with the lordly prelates
who wielded by turns the crosier, the sceptre, and the sword.
Three different roads might introduce the Paulicians into the
heart of Europe.   After the conversion of Hungary, the pilgrims
who visited Jerusalem might safely follow the course of the
Danube ; in their journey and return they passed through Philippopolis , and the sectaries, disguising their name and heresy,
might accompany the French or German caravans to their respective countries.   The trade and dominion of *Venice* pervaded
the coast of the Adriatic, and the hospitable republic opened
her bosom to foreigners of every climate and religion.   Under
the Byzantine standard, the Paulicians were often transported to
the Greek provinces of Italy and Sicily ; in peace and war they
freely conversed with strangers and natives, and their opinions
were silently propagated in Rome, Milan, and the kingdoms beyond the Alps.[35]   It was soon discovered that many thousand

[33] Matt. Paris, Hist. Major, p. 267.   This passage of our English historian is
alleged by Ducange in an excellent note on Villehardouin (No. 208), who found the
Paulicians at Philippopolis the friends of the Bulgarians.

[34] See Marsigli, Stato Militare dell' Impero Ottomano, p. 24.

[35] The introduction of the Paulicians into Italy and France is amply discussed
by Muratori (Antiquitat. Italiæ medii Ævi, tom. v. dissert. lx. p. 81-152) and
Mosheim (p. 379-382, 419-422).   Yet both have overlooked a curious passage of

Catholics of every rank, and of either sex, had embraced the
Manichæan heresy; and the flames which consumed twelve
canons of Orleans was the first act and signal of persecution.
The Bulgarians,[36] a name so innocent in its origin, so odious in
its application, spread their branches over the face of Europe.
United in common hatred of idolatry and Rome, they were connected by a form of episcopal and presbyterian government;
their various sects were discriminated by some fainter or darker
shades of theology; but they generally agreed in the two principles: the contempt of the Old Testament, and the denial of
the body of Christ, either on the cross or in the eucharist. A
confession of simple worship and blameless manners is extorted
from their enemies; and so high was their standard of perfection
that the increasing congregations were divided into two classes
of disciples, of those who practised and of those who aspired.

Persecution<br>of the Albi-<br>geois. A.D.<br>1200, &c. It was in the country of the Albigeois,[37] in the southern provinces of France, that the Paulicians were most deeply implanted;
and the same vicissitudes of martyrdom and revenge which had
been displayed in the neighbourhood of the Euphrates were repeated in the thirteenth century on the banks of the Rhone.
The laws of the Eastern emperors were revived by Frederic the
Second. The insurgents of Tephrice were represented by the
barons and cities of Languedoc: Pope Innocent III. surpassed
the sanguinary fame of Theodora. It was in cruelty alone that
her soldiers could equal the heroes of the crusades, and the

---

William the Apulian, who clearly describes them in a battle between the Greeks
and Normans, A.D. 1040 (in Muratori, Script. Rerum Ital. tom. v. p. 256).

> Cum Græcis aderant quidam quos pessimus error
> Fecerat amentes, et ab ipso nomen habebant.

But he is so ignorant of their doctrine as to make them a kind of Sabellians or
Patripassians. [It is thought that the Bogomilian doctrine travelled westward chiefly
by the provinces of southern Italy; Jireček, *op. cit.* p. 212.]

[36] *Bulgari, Boulgres, Bougres*, a national appellation, has been applied by the
French as a term of reproach to usurers and unnatural sinners. The *Paterini*, or
*Patelini*, has been made to signify a smooth and flattering hypocrite, such as
*l'Avocat Patelin* of that original and pleasant farce (Ducange, Gloss. Latinitat.
medii et infimi Ævi). [The word is said to be derived from Pataria, a suburb of
Milan.] The Manichæans were likewise named *Cathari*, or the pure, by corruption, *Gazari*, &c.

[37] Of the laws, crusade, and persecution against the Albigeois, a just, though
general, idea is expressed by Mosheim (p. 477-481). The detail may be found in
the ecclesiastical historians, ancient and modern, Catholics and Protestants; and
among these Fleury is the most impartial and moderate. [C. Schmidt, Histoire et
doctrine de la secte des Cathares, 2 vols., 1849. Rački, Bogomili i Catareni,
Agram, 1869. These sectaries begin to appear in southern Gaul about A.D. 1017.
Their chief seat was Toulouse; they were called *Albigeois* from the town of Albi,
and *Tisserands* because many weavers embraced the doctrine. For the Ritual of the
Albigeois, preserved in a Lyons Ms., see Conybeare, Key of Truth, App. vi. Cp.
below, App. 6.]

cruelty of her priests was far excelled by the founders of the inquisition:[38] an office more adapted to confirm, than to refute, the belief of an evil principle. The visible assemblies of the Paulicians, or Albigeois, were extirpated by fire and sword; and the bleeding remnant escaped by flight, concealment, or catholic conformity. But the invincible spirit which they had kindled still lived and breathed in the Western world. In the state, in the church, and even in the cloister, a latent succession was preserved of the disciples of St. Paul; who protested against the tyranny of Rome, embraced the Bible as the rule of faith, and purified their creed from all the visions of the Gnostic theology. The struggles of Wickliff in England, of Huss in Bohemia, were premature and ineffectual; but the names of Zuinglius, Luther, and Calvin are pronounced with gratitude as the deliverers of nations.

A philosopher, who calculates the degree of their merit and the value of their reformation, will prudently ask from what articles of faith, *above* or *against* our reason, they have enfranchised the Christians; for such enfranchisement is doubtless a benefit so far as it may be compatible with truth and piety. After a fair discussion we shall rather be surprised by the timidity, than scandalized by the freedom, of our first reformers.[39] With the Jew, they adopted the belief and defence of all the Hebrew scriptures, with all their prodigies, from the garden of Eden to the visions of the prophet Daniel; and they were bound, like the Catholics, to justify against the Jews the abolition of a divine law. In the great mysteries of the Trinity and Incarnation the reformers were severely orthodox: they freely adopted the theology of the four or the six first councils; and, with the Athanasian creed, they pronounced the eternal damnation of all who did not believe the Catholic faith. Transubstantiation, the invisible change of the bread and wine into the body and

*Character and consequences of the reformation*

---

[38] The Acts (Liber Sententiarum) of the Inquisition of Toulouse (A.D. 1307-1323) have been published by Limborch (Amstelodami, 1692), with a previous History of the Inquisition in general. They deserved a more learned and critical editor. As we must not calumniate even Satan, or the Holy Office, I will observe that, of a list of criminals which fills nineteen folio pages, only fifteen men and four women were delivered to the secular arm. [In an annotation on this note Dr. Smith says: "Dr. Maitland, in his Facts and Documents Relating to the Ancient Albigenses and Waldenses, remarks (p. 217, note) that Gibbon ought to have said *thirty-two* men and *eight* women".]

[39] The opinions and proceedings of the reformers are exposed in the second part of the general history of Mosheim; but the balance, which he has held with so clear an eye, and so steady an hand, begins to incline in favour of his Lutheran brethren.

blood of Christ, is a tenet that may defy the power of argument
and pleasantry; but, instead of consulting the evidence of their
senses, of their sight, their feeling, and their taste, the first
Protestants were entangled in their own scruples, and awed by
the words of Jesus in the institution of the sacrament. Luther
maintained a *corporeal*, and Calvin a *real*, presence of Christ in
the eucharist; and the opinion of Zuinglius, that it is no more
than a spiritual communion, a simple memorial, has slowly prevailed in the reformed churches.[40]   But the loss of one mystery
was amply compensated by the stupendous doctrines of original
sin, redemption, faith, grace, and predestination, which have
been strained from the epistles of St. Paul. These subtle
questions had most assuredly been prepared by the fathers and
schoolmen; but the final improvement and popular use may be
attributed to the first reformers, who enforced them as the absolute and essential terms of salvation. Hitherto the weight of
supernatural belief inclines against the Protestants; and many a
sober Christian would rather admit that a wafer is God, than
that God is a cruel and capricious tyrant.

Yet the services of Luther and his rival are solid and important; and the philosopher must own his obligations to these
fearless enthusiasts.[41]   I. By their hands the lofty fabric of
superstition, from the abuse of indulgences to the intercession
of the Virgin, has been levelled with the ground. Myriads of
both sexes of the monastic profession were restored to the
liberty and labours of social life. An hierarchy of saints and
angels, of imperfect and subordinate deities, were stripped of
their temporal power, and reduced to the enjoyment of celestial
happiness; their images and relics were banished from the
church; and the credulity of the people was no longer nourished
with the daily repetition of miracles and visions. The imitation
of Paganism was supplied by a pure and spiritual worship of
prayer and thanksgiving, the most worthy of man, the least
unworthy of the Deity. It only remains to observe whether
such sublime simplicity be consistent with popular devotion;
whether the vulgar, in the absence of all visible objects, will

[40] Under Edward VI. our reformation was more bold and perfect: but in the
fundamental articles of the church of England a strong and explicit declaration
against the real presence was obliterated in the original copy, to please the people,
or the Lutherans, or Queen Elizabeth (Burnet's History of the Reformation, vol.
ii. p. 82, 128, 302).

[41] " Had it not been for such men as Luther and myself," said the fanatic Whiston
to Halley the philosopher, "you would now be kneeling before an image of St.
Winifred."

not be inflamed by enthusiasm, or insensibly subside in languor and indifference. II. The chain of authority was broken, which restrains the bigot from thinking as he pleases, and the slave from speaking as he thinks; the popes, fathers, and councils were no longer the supreme and infallible judges of the world; and each Christian was taught to acknowledge no law but the scriptures, no interpreter but his own conscience. This freedom, however, was the consequence, rather than the design, of the Reformation. The patriot reformers were ambitious of succeeding the tyrants whom they had dethroned. They imposed with equal rigour their creeds and confessions; they asserted the right of the magistrate to punish heretics with death. The pious or personal animosity of Calvin proscribed in Servetus [42] the guilt of his own rebellion; [43] and the flames of Smithfield, in which he was afterwards consumed, had been kindled for the Anabaptists by the zeal of Cranmer. [44] The nature of the tiger was the same, but he was gradually deprived of his teeth and fangs. A spiritual and temporal kingdom was possessed by the Roman pontiff; the Protestant doctors were subjects of an humble rank, without revenue or jurisdiction. His decrees were consecrated by the antiquity of the Catholic church; their arguments and disputes were submitted to the people; and their appeal to private judgment was accepted, beyond their

---

[42] The article of *Servet* in the Dictionnaire Critique of Chauffepié is the best account which I have seen of this shameful transaction. See likewise the Abbé d'Artigny, Nouveaux Mémoires d'Histoire, &c., ii. p. 55-154. [The remarkable theological heresies of Servet were as obnoxious to the Protestants as to the Catholics. For an account of his system see H. Tollin's Das Lehrsystem Michael Servets, in 3 vols. (1876-8). The documents of the trial of Servet may be conveniently consulted in the edition of Calvin's works by Baum, Cunitz, and Reuss, vol. 8. There is a good account of the transaction in Roget's Histoire du peuple de Genève, vol. 4 (1877).]

[43] I am more deeply scandalized at the single execution of Servetus, than at the hecatombs which have blazed in the Auto da Fés of Spain and Portugal. 1. The zeal of Calvin seems to have been envenomed by personal malice, and perhaps envy. He accused his adversary before their common enemies, the judges of Vienna, and betrayed, for his destruction, the sacred trust of a private correspondence. 2. The deed of cruelty was not varnished by the pretence of danger to the church or state. In his passage through Geneva, Servetus was an harmless stranger, who neither preached, nor printed, nor made proselytes. 3. A Catholic inquisitor yields the same obedience which he requires, but Calvin violated the golden rule of doing as he would be done by: a rule which I read in a moral treatise of Isocrates (in Nicole, tom. i. p. 93, edit. Battie), four hundred years before the publication of the gospel. Ἃ πάσχοντες ὑφ' ἑτέρων ὀργίζεσθε, ταῦτα τοῖς ἄλλοις μὴ ποιεῖτε. [The part taken by Calvin in the transaction seems to have been chiefly the furnishing of the documents on which Servetus was condemned.]

[44] See Burnet, vol. ii. p. 84-86. The sense and humanity of the young king were oppressed by the authority of the primate.

wishes, by curiosity and enthusiasm.   Since the days of Luther
and Calvin, a secret reformation has been silently working in
the bosom of the reformed churches; many weeds of prejudice
were eradicated ; and the disciples of Erasmus [45] diffused a spirit
of freedom and moderation.   The liberty of conscience has been
claimed as a common benefit, an inalienable right ; [46] the free
governments of Holland [47] and England [48] introduced the practice
of toleration ; and the narrow allowance of the laws has been
enlarged by the prudence and humanity of the times.   In the
exercise, the mind has understood the limits of its powers, and
the words and shadows that might amuse the child can no longer
satisfy his manly reason.   The volumes of controversy are overspread with cobwebs ; the doctrine of a Protestant church is far
removed from the knowledge or belief of its private members ;
and the forms of orthodoxy, the articles of faith, are subscribed
with a sigh or a smile by the modern clergy.   Yet the friends
of Christianity are alarmed at the boundless impulse of inquiry
and scepticism.   The predictions of the Catholics are accomplished ; the web of mystery is unravelled by the Arminians,
Arians, and Socinians, whose numbers must not be computed
from their separate congregations ; and the pillars of revelation
are shaken by those men who preserve the name without the
substance of religion, who indulge the licence without the temper
of philosophy.[49]

[45] Erasmus may be considered as the father of rational theology.   After a
slumber of an hundred years, it was revived by the Arminians of Holland, Grotius,
Limborch, and Le Clerc ; in England by Chillingworth, the latitudinarians of
Cambridge (Burnet, Hist. of own Times, vol. i. p. 261-268, octavo edition),
Tillotson, Clarke, Hoadley, &c.

[46] I am sorry to observe that the three writers of the last age, by whom the rights
of toleration have been so nobly defended, Bayle, Leibnitz, and Locke, are all
laymen and philosophers.

[47] See the excellent chapter of Sir William Temple on the Religion of the United
Provinces.   I am not satisfied with Grotius (de Rebus Belgicis, Annal. l. i. p. 13, 14,
edit. in 12mo), who improves the Imperial laws of persecution, and only condemns
the bloody tribunal of the inquisition.

[48] Sir Walter Blackstone (Commentaries, vol. iv. p. 33, 54) explains the law of
England as it was fixed at the Revolution.   The exceptions of Papists, and of those
who deny the Trinity, would still leave a tolerable scope for persecution, if the
national spirit were not more effectual than an hundred statutes.

[49] I shall recommend to public animadversion two passages in Dr. Priestly, which
betray the ultimate tendency of his opinions.   At the first of these (Hist. of the
Corruptions of Christianity, vol. i. p. 275, 276) the priest, at the second (vol. ii. p.
484) the magistrate, may tremble !

## CHAPTER LV

*The Bulgarians—Origin, Migrations, and Settlement of the Hungarians—Their inroads in the East and West—The monarchy of Russia—Geography and Trade—Wars of the Russians against the Greek Empire—Conversion of the Barbarians*

UNDER the reign of Constantine the grandson of Heraclius, the ancient barrier of the Danube, so often violated and so often restored, was irretrievably swept away by a new deluge of barbarians. Their progress was favoured by the caliphs, their unknown and accidental auxiliaries · the Roman legions were occupied in Asia, and, after the loss of Syria, Egypt, and Africa, the Cæsars were twice reduced to the danger and disgrace of defending their capital against the Saracens. If, in the account of this interesting people, I have deviated from the strict and original line of my undertaking, the merit of the subject will hide my transgression or solicit my excuse. In the East, in the West, in war, in religion, in science, in their prosperity, and in their decay, the Arabians press themselves on our curiosity: the first overthrow of the church and empire of the Greeks may be imputed to their arms ; and the disciples of Mahomet still hold the civil and religious sceptre of the Oriental world. But the same labour would be unworthily bestowed on the swarms of savages who, between the seventh and the twelfth century, descended from the plains of Scythia, in transient inroad or perpetual emigration.[1] Their names are uncouth, their origins doubtful, their actions obscure, their superstition was blind, their valour brutal, and the uniformity of their

---

[1] *All* the passages of the Byzantine history which relate to the barbarians are compiled, methodized, and transcribed, in a Latin version, by the laborious John Gotthelf Stritter, in his " Memoriæ Populorum ad Danubium, Pontum Euxinum, Paludem Mæotidem, Caucasum, Mare Caspium, et inde magis ad Septemtriones incolentium ". Petropoli, 1771-1779 ; in four tomes, or six volumes, in 4to. But the fashion has not enhanced the price of these raw materials.

public and private lives was neither softened by innocence nor refined by policy. The majesty of the Byzantine throne repelled and survived their disorderly attacks ; the greater part of these barbarians has disappeared without leaving any memorial of their existence, and the despicable remnant continues, and may long continue, to groan under the dominion of a foreign tyrant. From the antiquities of, I. *Bulgarians*, II. *Hungarians*, and III. *Russians*, I shall content myself with selecting such facts as yet deserve to be remembered. The conquests of the, IV., Normans, and the monarchy of the, V., Turks, will naturally terminate in the memorable Crusades to the Holy Land, and the double fall of the city and empire of Constantine.

Emigration of the Bulgarians. A.D. 680, &c.
I. In his march to Italy, Theodoric [2] the Ostrogoth had trampled on the arms of the Bulgarians. After this defeat, the name and the nation are lost during a century and a half ; [3] and it may be suspected that the same or a similar appellation was revived by strange colonies from the Borysthenes, the Tanais, or the Volga. A king of the ancient Bulgaria [4] bequeathed to his five sons a last lesson of moderation and concord. It was received as youth has ever received the counsels of age and experience : the five princes buried their father ; divided his subjects and cattle ; forgot his advice ; separated from each other ; and wandered in quest of fortune, till we find the most adventurous in the heart of Italy, under the protection of the exarch of Ravenna. [5] But the stream of emigration was directed or impelled towards the capital. The modern Bulgaria, along the southern banks of the Danube, was stamped with the name and image which it has retained to the present hour ; the new conquerors successively

[2] [Above] Hist. vol. iv. p. 177.

[3] [The Bulgarians continued to live north of the Danube and formed part of the Avar empire in the latter half of the sixth century. They appear as the subjects of the Chagan in Theophylactus Simocatta.]

[4] Theophanes, p. 296-299 [*sub* A.M. 6171]. Anastasius, p. 113 [p. 225 *sqq*. ed. de Boor]. Nicephorus, C. P. p. 22, 23 [p. 33, 34, ed. de Boor]. Theophanes places the old Bulgaria on the banks of the Atell or Volga [old Bulgaria lay between the rivers Volga and Kama. There is still a village called Bolgary in the province of Kazan] ; but he deprives himself of all geographical credit by discharging that river into the Euxine Sea. [For the legend of King Krovat's sons see Appendix 7.]

[5] Paul. Diacon. de Gestis Langobard. l. v. c. 29, p. 881, 882. The apparent difference between the Lombard historian and the above-mentioned Greeks is easily reconciled by Camillo Pellegrino (de Ducatu Beneventano, dissert. vii. in the Scriptores Rerum Ital. tom. v. p. 186, 187) and Beretti (Chorograph. Italiæ medii Ævi, p. 273, &c.). This Bulgarian colony was planted in a vacant district of Samnium [at Bovianum, Sergna, and Sipicciano], and learned the Latin, without forgetting their native language.

acquired, by war or treaty, the Roman provinces of Dardania, Thessaly, and the two Epirus'; [6] the ecclesiastical supremacy was translated from the native city of Justinian ; and, in their prosperous age, the obscure town of Lychnidus, or Achrida, was honoured with the throne of a king and a patriarch.[7] The unquestionable evidence of language attests the descent of the Bulgarians from the original stock of the Sclavonian, or more properly Slavonian, race ; [8] and the kindred bands of Servians, Bosnians, Rascians, Croatians, Walachians,[9] &c. followed either the standard or the example of the leading tribe. From the Euxine to the Adriatic, in the state of captives or subjects, or allies or enemies, of the Greek empire, they overspread the land ; and the national appellation of the SLAVES [10] has been degraded

[6] These provinces of the Greek idiom and empire are assigned to the Bulgarian kingdom in the dispute of ecclesiastical jurisdiction between the patriarchs of Rome and Constantinople (Baronius, Annal. Eccles. A.D. 869, No. 75).

[7] The situation and royalty of Lychnidus, or Achrida, are clearly expressed in Cedrenus (p. 713 [ii. p. 468, ed. B.]). The removal of an archbishop or patriarch from Justinianea prima, to Lychnidus, and at length to Ternovo, has produced some perplexity in the ideas or language of the Greeks (Nicephorus Gregoras, l. ii. c. 2, p. 14, 15 ; Thomassin, Discipline de l'Eglise, tom. i. l. i. c. 19, 23) ; and a Frenchman (d'Anville) is more accurately skilled in the geography of their own country (Hist. de l'Academie des Inscriptions, tom. xxxi.).

[8] Chalcocondyles, a competent judge, affirms the identity of the language of the Dalmatians, Bosnians, Servians, *Bulgarians*, Poles (de Rebus Turcicis, l. x. p. 283 [p. 530, ed. Bonn]), and elsewhere of the Bohemians (l. ii. p. 38 [p 73, *ib.*]). The same author has marked the separate idiom of the Hungarians. [The Bulgarian conquerors adopted the language of their Slavonic subjects, but they were not Slavs. See Appendix 8.]

[9] See the work of John Christopher de Jordan, de Originibus Sclavicis, Vindobonæ, 1745, in four parts, or two volumes in folio. His collections and researches are useful to elucidate the antiquities of Bohemia and the adjacent countries : but his plan is narrow, his style barbarous, his criticism shallow, and the Aulic counsellor is not free from the prejudices of a Bohemian. [The statement in the text can partly stand, if it is understood that " kindred bands " means kindred to the Slavs who formed the chief population of the Bulgarian Kingdom—not to the Bulgarian conquerors. The Servians, Croatians, &c., were Slavs. But in no case does it apply to the Walachians, who ethnically were probably Illyrians—descended at least from those people who inhabited Dacia and Illyricum, before the coming of the Slavs. There was a strong Walachian population in the Bulgarian kingdom which extended north of the Danube (see Appendix 11) ; and it has been conjectured that the Walachians even gave the Bulgarians a king—*Sabinos*, a name of Latin sound. But this seems highly doubtful ; and compare Appendix 9.]

[10] Jordan subscribes to the well-known and probable derivation from *Slava, laus, gloria*, a word of familiar use in the different dialects and parts of speech, and which forms the termination of the most illustrious names (de Originibus Sclavicis, pars i. p. 40, pars iv. p. 101, 102). [This derivation has been generally abandoned, and is obviously unlikely. Another, which received the approbation of many, explained the name Slovanie (sing. Slovanjn) from *slovo*, "a word," in the sense of ὁμόγλωττοι, people who speak one language—opposed to Niemi, "the dumb" (non-Slavs, Germans). But this too sounds improbable, and has been

by chance or malice from the signification of glory to that of servitude.[11]  Among these colonies, the Chrobatians,[12] or Croats, who now attend the motions of an Austrian army, are the descendants of a mighty people, the conquerors and sovereigns of Dalmatia.  The maritime cities, and of these the infant republic of Ragusa, implored the aid and instructions of the Byzantine court : they were advised by the magnanimous Basil to reserve a small acknowledgment of their fidelity to the Roman empire, and to appease, by an annual tribute, the wrath of these irresistible barbarians.  The kingdom of Croatia was shared by eleven *Zoupans,* or feudatory lords ; and their united forces were numbered at sixty thousand horse and one hundred thousand foot.  A long sea-coast, indented with capacious harbours, covered with a string of islands, and almost in sight of the Italian shores, disposed both the natives and strangers to the practice of navigation.  The boats or brigantines of the Croats were constructed after the fashion of the old Liburnians ; one hundred and eighty vessels may excite the idea of a respectable navy ; but our seamen will smile at the allowance of ten, or twenty, or forty, men for each of these ships of war.  They were gradually converted to the more honourable service of commerce ; yet the Sclavonian pirates were still frequent and dangerous ; and it was not before the close of the tenth century that the freedom and sovereignty of the Gulf were effectually vindicated

*Croats or Sclavonians of Dalmatia. A.D. 900, &c.*

rightly rejected by Schafarik, who investigates the name at great length (Slawische Alterthümer, ii. p. 25 *sqq.*).  The original form of the name was Slované or Slovené.  The form "Sclavonian," which is still often used in English books, ought to be discarded (as Gibbon suggests) ; the guttural does not belong to the word, but was inserted by the Greeks, Latins, and Orientals (Σκλάβος, Sclavus, Saklab, Sakalibé, &c.).  By the analogy of other names similarly formed, Schafarik shows convincingly that the name was originally local, meaning "the folk who dwelled in Slovy," cp. p. 43-45.  The discovery of this hypothetical Slovy is another question.  In the Chronicle of Nestor, Slovene is used in the special sense of a tribe about Novgorod, as well as in the general sense of Slav.]

[11] This conversion of a national into an appellative name appears to have arisen in the viiith century, in the Oriental France [*i.e.* East Francia, or Franconia : towards the end of the eighth century, cp. Schafarik, *op. cit.*, ii. p. 325-6] ; where the princes and bishops were rich in Sclavonian captives, not of the Bohemian (exclaims Jordan) but of Sorabian race.  From thence the word was extended to general use, to the modern languages, and even to the style of the last Byzantines (see the Greek and Latin Glossaries of Ducange).  The confusion of the Σέρβλοι, or Servians, with the Latin *Servi* was still more fortunate and familiar (Constant. Porphyr. de Administrando Imperio, c. 32, p. 99).  [Serb is supposed to have been the oldest national name of the Slavs, on the evidence of Procopius (B. G. iii. 14), who says that the Slavs and Antæ had originally one name, Σπόροι, which is frequently explained as = Srbs.  Schafarik, *op. cit.*, i. p. 93-99.]

[12] The emperor Constantine Porphyrogenitus, most accurate for his own times, most fabulous for preceding ages, describes the Sclavonians of Dalmatia (c. 29-36).

by the Venetian republic.[13]    The ancestors of these Dalmatian kings were equally removed from the use and abuse of navigation ; they dwelt in the White Croatia, in the inland regions of Silesia and Little Poland, thirty days' journey, according to the Greek computation, from the sea of darkness.

The glory of the Bulgarians[14] was confined to a narrow scope both of time and place.    In the ninth and tenth centuries they reigned to the south of the Danube ; but the more powerful nations that had followed their emigration repelled all return to the north and all progress to the west.    Yet, in the obscure catalogue of their exploits, they might boast an honour which had hitherto been appropriated to the Goths : that of slaying in battle one of the successors of Augustus and Constantine.    The emperor Nicephorus had lost his fame in the Arabian, he lost his life in the Sclavonian, war.    In his first operations he advanced with boldness and success into the centre of Bulgaria, and burnt the *royal court*, which was probably no more than an edifice and village of timber.    But, while he searched the spoil and refused all offers of treaty, his enemies collected their spirits and their forces ; the passes of retreat were insuperably barred ; and the trembling Nicephorus was heard to exclaim : " Alas, alas ! unless we could assume the wings of birds, we cannot hope to escape ".    Two days he waited his fate in the inactivity of despair ; but, on the morning of the third, the Bulgarians surprised the camp ; and the Roman prince, with the great officers of the empire, were slaughtered in their tents.    The body of Valens had been saved from insult , but the head of Nicephorus was exposed on a spear, and his skull, enchased with gold, was often replenished in the feasts of victory.    The Greeks bewailed the dishonour of the throne ; but they acknowledged the just punishment of avarice and cruelty.    This savage cup was deeply tinctured with the manners of the Scythian wilderness ; but they were softened before the end of the same century by a peaceful

*[marginalia: First kingdom of the Bulgarians. A.D. 640-1017]*

*[marginalia: A.D.]*

*[marginalia: The war of Nicephorus with Krum]*

*[marginalia: A.D. 811]*

[13] See the anonymous Chronicle of the xith century, ascribed to John Sagorninus (p. 94-102), and that composed in the xivth by the Doge Andrew Dandolo (Script. Rerum Ital. tom. xii. p. 227-230) : the two oldest monuments of the history of Venice.

[14] The first kingdom of the Bulgarians may be found, under the proper dates, in the Annals of Cedrenus and Zonaras.    The Byzantine materials are collected by Stritter (Memoriæ Populorum, tom. ii. pars ii. p. 441-647), and the series of their kings is disposed and settled by Ducange (Fam. Byzant. p. 305-318).    [For an ancient Bulgarian list of the early Bulgarian kings see Appendix 9.    For the migration and establishment south of the Danube, and extent of the kingdom, cp. Appendix 8.]

## 134        THE DECLINE AND FALL

intercourse with the Greeks, the possession of a cultivated region, and the introduction of the Christian worship.[15]  The nobles of Bulgaria were educated in the schools and palace of Constantinople ; and Simeon,[16] a youth of the royal line, was instructed in the rhetoric of Demosthenes and the logic of Aristotle.  He relinquished the profession of a monk for that of a
A.D. 888-927, or 922 king and warrior ; and in his reign, of more than forty years,[17] Bulgaria assumed a rank among the civilised powers of the earth. The Greeks, whom he repeatedly attacked, derived a faint consolation from indulging themselves in the reproaches of perfidy
[A.D. 893] and sacrilege.  They purchased the aid of the Pagan Turks ;
[Turks=Hungarians] but Simeon, in a second battle, redeemed the loss of the first, at a time when it was esteemed a victory to elude the arms of that formidable nation.  The Servians [18] were overthrown, made
[A.D. 924] captive, and dispersed ; and those who visited the country before

[15] [In the year after his victory over Nicephorus, the Bulgarian prince Krum or Krumn captured the towns of Mesembria and Develtus, and in the following year inflicted a crushing defeat on Michael I. at Versinicia near Hadrianople (June, 813) and proceeded to besiege Constantinople. He retired having devastated the country, but prepared to besiege the capital again in 815.  His death was a relief to the Emperor Leo V. (see above, vol. 5, p. 194), who then took the field and gained at Mesembria a bloody victory over the Bulgarians.  The prince Giom Omortag, who came to the throne about 817 or 818, made a treaty with Leo for 30 years ; and peace was maintained for more than 75 years, till the accession of Simeon.  Omortag is called *Mortagon* by the Greek chroniclers, and Ombritag by Theophylactus of Ochrida ; but the right form of the name is furnished by his own curious inscription which was discovered at Trnovo (see Appendix 10).  Omortag had three sons, and it is to be noticed that all three had Slavonic names ; this marks a stage in the growth of Slavonic influence in the kingdom.  The youngest, Malomir, came to the throne.  He was succeeded by his nephew Boris (circa A.D. 852-888), whose reign is memorable for the conversion of Bulgaria to Christianity (see Appendix 12).]

[16] Simeonem [emi-argon, id est] semi-Græcum esse aiebant, eo quod a pueritiâ Byzantii Demosthenis rhetoricam et Aristotelis syllogismos didicerat [*leg.* didicerit] (Liutprand, l. iii. c. 8 [= c. 29]).  He says in another place, Simeon, fortis, bellator, Bulgariæ [*leg.* Bulgariis] præerat ; Christianus sed vicinis Græcis valde inimicus (l. i. c. 2 [= c. 5]).  [It is important to notice that native Slavonic literature flourished under Simeon—the result of the invention of Slavonic alphabets (see Appendix 12). Simeon himself—anticipating Constantine Porphyrogennetos—instituted the compilation of a Sbornik or encyclopædia (theological, philosophical, historical), extracted from 20 Greek writers.  The Presbyter Grigori translated the chronicle of John Malalas into Slavonic.   John the Exarch wrote a *Shestodnev* (Hexaemeron), an account of the Creation.  The monk Chrabr wrote a valuable little treatise on the invention of the Cyrillic alphabet (cp. App. 12) ; and other works (chiefly theological) of the same period are extant.]

[17] [Simeon came to the throne in 893, and died May 27, 927.]

[18] [That is, *Servia* in the strict sense, excluding the independent Servian principalities of Zachlumia, Trevunia, Diocletia, as well as the Narentans.  See Const. Porph., De Adm. Imp., chaps. 32-36.  The boundary of Bulgaria against Servia in Simeon's time seems to have followed the Drin ; it left Belgrade, Prishtina, Nitzch and Lipljan in Bulgaria.]

their restoration could discover no more than fifty vagrants, without women or children, who extorted a precarious subsistence from the chase. On classic ground, on the banks of the Achelöus, the Greeks were defeated; their horn was broken by [A.D. 917, Aug. 20] the strength of the barbaric Hercules.[19] He formed the siege of Constantinople; and, in a personal conference with the emperor, Simeon imposed the conditions of peace. They met with the most jealous precautions; the royal galley was drawn close to an artificial and well-fortified platform; and the majesty of the purple was emulated by the pomp of the Bulgarian. "Are you a Christian?" said the humble Romanus. "It is your duty to abstain from the blood of your fellow-Christians. Has the thirst of riches seduced you from the blessings of peace? Sheathe your sword, open your hand, and I will satiate the utmost measure of your desires." The reconciliation was sealed by a domestic alliance;[20] the freedom of trade was granted or restored; the first honours of the court were secured to the friends of Bulgaria, above the ambassadors of enemies or strangers;[21] and her princes

---

[19] ——Rigidum fera dextera cornu
Dum tenet, infregit truncâque a fronte revellit.

Ovid (Metamorph. ix. 1-100) has boldly painted the combat of the river-god and the hero; the native and the stranger. [The battle was fought near Anchialos in Bulgaria (Leo Diac. p. 124). There was a river named Achelous in the neighbourhood (Theoph. Contin. p. 389; cp. Pseudo-Sym. Mag. p. 724), and the name misled Gibbon. Cp. Finlay, ii. p. 288 note.]

[20] [The peace was concluded after Simeon's death in A.D. 927. Th. Uspenski has published (in the Lietopis ist. phil. obschestva, of the Odessa University. Viz. Otd. ii., 1894, p. 48 sqq.) a curious jubilant sermon preached at Constantinople on the occasion of the conclusion of the peace. It presents great difficulties, owing to the allusiveness of its style, which has been ingeniously discussed by Uspenski, who is tempted to identify the anonymous author with Nicolaus Mysticus, the Patriarch, a correspondent of the Tsar Simeon. But chronology seems to exclude this supposition; for Nicolaus died in 925; and, though the preliminaries to the peace may have occupied a considerable time, the sermon must have been composed after the death of Simeon in 927 (as M. Uspenski seems to forget in his concluding remarks, p. 123).]

[21] The ambassador of Otho was provoked by the Greek excesses, cum Christophori filiam Petrus Bulgarorum *Vasileus* conjugem duceret, *Symphona*, id est consonantia, scripto [*al.* consonantia scripta], juramento firmata sunt, ut omnium gentium *Apostolis*, id est nunciis, penes nos Bulgarorum Apostoli præponantur, honorentur, diligantur (Liutprand in Legatione, p. 482 [c. 19]). See the Ceremoniale of Constantine of Porphyrogenitus, tom. i. p. 82 [c. 24, p. 139, ed. Bonn], tom. ii. p. 429, 430, 434, 435, 443, 444, 446, 447 [c. 52, p. 740, 742, 743, 749, 751, 767, 771, 772, 773], with the annotations of Reiske. [Bulgarian rulers before Simeon were content with the title Knęz. Simeon first assumed the title tsar (from *tsesar*, *ts'sar*;=Cæsar). It may have been remembered that Terbel had been made a Cæsar by Justinian II. (Nicephorus, p. 42, ed. de Boor). The Archbishopric of Bulgaria was raised to the dignity of a Patriarchate. Simeon's residence was Great Peristhlava; see below, p. 160, note 90.]

were dignified with the high and invidious title of *basileus*, or emperor. But this friendship was soon disturbed : after the death of Simeon, the nations were again in arms ; his feeble
**A.D. 950, &c.** successors were divided [22] and extinguished ; and, in the beginning of the eleventh century, the second Basil, who was born in the purple, deserved the appellation of conqueror of the Bulgarians.[23] His avarice was in some measure gratified by a treasure of four hundred thousand pounds sterling (ten thousand pounds weight of gold) which he found in the palace of Lychnidus. His cruelty inflicted a cool and exquisite vengeance on fifteen thousand captives who had been guilty of the defence of their

[22] [In A.D. 963 Shishman of Trnovo revolted, and founded an independent kingdom in Macedonia and Albania. Thus there were now two Bulgarian kingdoms and two tsars.]

[23] [The kingdom of Eastern Bulgaria had been conquered first by the Russians and then by the Emperor Tzimisces (see below, p. 161), but Western Bulgaria survived, and before 980, Samuel, son of Shishman, came to the throne. His capital was at first Prespa, but he afterwards moved to Ochrida. His aim was to recover Eastern Bulgaria and conquer Greece ; and for thirty-five years he maintained a heroic struggle against the Empire. Both he and his great adversary Basil were men of iron, brave, cruel, and unscrupulous ; and Basil was determined not merely to save Eastern, but to conquer Western, Bulgaria. In the first war (976-986) the Bulgarians were successful. Samuel pushed southward and, after repeated attempts which were repulsed, captured Larissa in Thessaly and pushed on to the Isthmus. This was in A.D. 986. To cause a diversion and relieve Greece, Basil marched on Sophia, but was caught in a trap, and having endured immense losses escaped with difficulty. After this defeat Eastern Bulgaria was lost to the Empire. (The true date of the capture of Larissa and the defeat of Basil, A.D. 986, has been established, against the old date 981, by the evidence of the Strategikon of Kekaumenos,—for which see above, vol. 5, p. 505. Cp. Schlumberger, L'épopée Byzantine, p. 636. On this first Bulgarian war, see also the Vita Niconis, ap. Martène et Durand, ampl. Coll. 6, 837 *sqq.* ; and a contemporary poem of John Geometres, Migne, P. G. vol. 106, p. 934, and cp. p. 920, a piece on the *Cometopulos*, *i.e.* Samuel, with a pun on κομήτης, " comet ".) There was a cessation of hostilities for ten years. The second war broke out in A.D. 996. Samuel invaded Greece, but returning he was met by a Greek army in the plain of the Spercheios north of Thermopylæ, and his whole host was destroyed in a night surprise. In A.D. 1000 Basil recovered Eastern Bulgaria, and in the following year South-western Macedonia (Vodena, Berrœa). Again hostilities languished for over ten years ; Basil was occupied in the east. In A.D. 1014, the third war began ; on July 29 Nicephorus Xiphias gained a brilliant victory over the Bulgarian army at Bielasica (somewhere in the neighbourhood of the river Strumica) ; Samuel escaped to Prilêp, but died six weeks later. The struggle was sustained weakly under Gabriel Roman (Samuel's son) and John Vladislav, his murderer and successor, last Tsar of Ochrida, who fell, besieging Durazzo, in 1018. The Bulgarians submitted, and the whole Balkan peninsula was once more imperial. If Samuel had been matched with a less able antagonist than Basil, he would have succeeded in effecting what was doubtless his great aim, the union of all the Slavs south of the Danube into a great empire. For a fuller account of these wars see Finlay, vol. ii. ; and for the first war, Schlumberger, *op. cit.*, chap. x. Jireček, Gesch. der Bulgaren, p. 192-8, is remarkably brief. There is a fuller study of the struggle by Rački in the Croatian tongue (1875).]

country : they were deprived of sight ; but to one of each
hundred a single eye was left, that he might conduct his blind
century to the presence of their king.  Their king is said to [Death of Tsar
have expired of grief and horror ; the nation was awed by this Samuel. A.D. 1014, Sept. 15]
terrible example ; the Bulgarians were swept away from their
settlements, and circumscribed within a narrow province ; the
surviving chiefs bequeathed to their children the advice of
patience and the duty of revenge.

II. When the black swarm of Hungarians first hung over Emigration of
Europe, about nine hundred years after the Christian æra, they Hungarians. the Turks or
were mistaken by fear and superstition for the Gog and Magog A.D. 884
of the Scriptures, the signs and forerunners of the end of the
world.[24]  Since the introduction of letters, they have explored
their own antiquities with a strong and laudable impulse of
patriotic curiosity.[25]  Their rational criticism can no longer be
amused with a vain pedigree of Attila and the Huns ; but they
complain that their primitive records have perished in the Tartar war ; that the truth or fiction of their rustic songs is long
since forgotten ; and that the fragments of a rude chronicle [26]
must be painfully reconciled with the contemporary though
foreign intelligence of the Imperial geographer.[27]  *Magiar* is [Magyar]
the national and Oriental denomination of the Hungarians ;
but, among the tribes of Scythia, they are distinguished by the

[24] A bishop of Wurtzburg [*leg.* Verdun] submitted this opinion to a reverend
abbot ; but *he* more gravely decided that Gog and Magog were the spiritual persecutors of the church ; since Gog signifies the roof, the pride of the Heresiarchs, and
Magog what comes from the roof, the propagation of their sects.  Yet these men
once commanded the respect of mankind (Fleury, Hist. Eccles. tom. xi. p. 594,
&c.).

[25] The two national authors, from whom I have derived the most assistance, are
George Pray (Dissertationes ad Annales veterum Hungarorum, &c., Vindobonæ,
1775, in folio) and Stephen Katona (Hist. Critica Ducum et Regum Hungariæ
stirpis Arpadianæ, Pæstini, 1778-1781, 5 vols. in octavo).  The first embraces a
large and often conjectural space ; the latter, by his learning, judgment, and perspicuity, deserves the name of a critical historian.

[26] The author of this Chronicle is styled the notary of king Béla.  Katona has
assigned him to the twelfth century, and defends his character against the hyper-
criticism of Pray.  This rude annalist must have transcribed some historical records,
since he could affirm with dignity, rejectis falsis fabulis rusticorum, et garrulo cantu
joculatorum.   In the xvth century, these fables were collected by Thurotzius,
and embellished by the Italian Bonfinius.  See the Preliminary Discourse in the
Hist. Critica Ducum, p. 7-33.  [Cp. Appendix 13.]

[27] See Constantine de Administrando Imperio, c. 3, 4, 13, 38-42. Katona has
nicely fixed the composition of this work to the years 949, 950, 951 (p. 4-7).  [Cp.
App. 4.]   The critical historian (p. 34-107) endeavours to prove the existence,
and to relate the actions, of a first duke *Almus*, the father of Arpad, who is tacitly
rejected by Constantine.  [Constantine, c 38, says that Arpad was elected chief,
and not his father *Salmutzes* (Almos).]

Greeks under the proper and peculiar name of *Turks*, as the descendants of that mighty people who had conquered and reigned from China to the Volga. The Pannonian colony preserved a correspondence of trade and amity with the eastern Turks on the confines of Persia; and, after a separation of three hundred and fifty years, the missionaries of the king of Hungary discovered and visited their ancient country near the banks of the Volga. They were hospitably entertained by a people of pagans and savages, who still bore the name of Hungarians; conversed in their native tongue, recollected a tradition of their long-lost brethren, and listened with amazement to the marvellous tale of their new kingdom and religion. The zeal of conversion was animated by the interest of consanguinity; and one of the greatest of their princes had formed the generous, though fruitless, design of replenishing the solitude of Pannonia by this domestic colony from the heart of Tartary.[28] From this primitive country they were driven to the West by the tide of war and emigration, by the weight of the more distant tribes, who at the same time were fugitives and conquerors. Reason or fortune directed their course towards the frontiers of the Roman empire; they halted in the usual stations along the banks of the great rivers; and in the territories of Moscow, Kiow, and Moldavia some vestiges have been discovered of their temporary residence. In this long and various peregrination, they could not always escape the dominion of the stronger; and the purity of their blood was improved or sullied by the mixture of a foreign race; from a motive of compulsion or choice, several tribes of the Chazars were associated to the standard of their ancient vassals; introduced the use of a second language;[29] and obtained by their superior renown the most honourable place in the front of battle. The military force of the Turks and their allies marched in seven equal and artificial divisions; each division was formed of thirty thousand eight hundred and fifty-seven warriors, and the proportion of women, children, and servants supposes and requires at least a million of emigrants. Their public counsels were directed by seven *vayvods*,[30] or hereditary chiefs; but the experience of discord and weakness recommended the more simple and vigorous administration of a

[28] Pray (Dissert. p. 37-39, &c.) produces and illustrates the original passages of the Hungarian missionaries, Bonfinius and Æneas Silvius.

[29] [Cp. Appendix 13.]

[30] [Voivods, " war-leaders," a Slavonic word. Cp. Appendix 13.]

single person. The sceptre which had been declined by the modest Lebedias, was granted to the birth or merit of Almus and his son Arpad, and the authority of the supreme khan of the Chazars confirmed the engagement of the prince and people : of the people to obey his commands, of the prince to consult their happiness and glory.

With this narrative we might be reasonably content, if the *Their Fennic origin* penetration of modern learning had not opened a new and larger prospect of the antiquities of nations. The Hungarian language stands alone, and as it were insulated, among the Sclavonian dialects ; but it bears a close and clear affinity to the idioms of the *Fennic* race,[31] of an obsolete and savage race, which formerly occupied the northern regions of Asia and Europe. The genuine appellation of *Ugri* or *Igours* is found on the Western confines of China,[32] their migration to the banks of the Irtish is attested by Tartar evidence,[33] a similar name and language are detected in the southern parts of Siberia,[34] and the remains of the Fennic tribes are widely, though thinly, scattered from the sources of the Oby to the shores of Lapland.[35] The consanguinity of the Hungarians and Laplanders would display the powerful energy of climate on the children of a common parent ; the lively contrast between the bold adventurers who are intoxicated with the wines of the Danube, and the wretched fugitives who are immersed beneath the snows of the polar circle. Arms and freedom have ever been the

---

[31] Fischer, in the Quæstionos Petropollianæ de Origine Ungrorum, and Pray, Dissertat. i. ii. iii. &c., have drawn up several comparative tables of the Hungarian with the Fennic dialects. The affinity is indeed striking, but the lists are short ; the words are purposely chosen ; and I read in the learned Bayer (Comment. Academ. Betropol. tom. x. p. 374) that, although the Hungarian has adopted many Fennic words (innumeras voces), it essentially differs toto genio et naturâ. [Cp. Appendix 13.]

[32] In the region of Turfan, which is clearly and minutely described by the Chinese geographers (Gaubil, Hist. du Grand Gengiscan, p. 13 ; De Guignes, Hist. des Huns, tom. ii. p. 31, &c.).

[33] Hist. Généalogique des Tartars, par Abulghazi Bahadur Khan, partie ii. p. 90-98.

[34] In their journey to Pekin, both Isbrand Ives (Harris's Collection of Voyages and Travels, vol. ii. p. 920, 921) and Bell (Travels, vol. i. p. 174) found the Vogulitz in the neighbourhood of Tobolsky. By the tortures of the etymological art, *Ugur* and *Vogul* are reduced to the same name ; the circumjacent mountains really bear the appellation of *Ugrian ;* and of all the Fennic dialects the Vogulian is the nearest to the Hungarian (Fischer, Dissert. i. p. 20-30. Pray, Dissert. ii. p. 31-34). [It is quite true that the Vogulian comes closest to the Hungarian.]

[35] The eight tribes of the Fennic race are described in the curious work of M. Levesque (Hist. des Peuples soumis à la Domination de la Russie, tom. i. p. 361-561).

ruling, though too often the unsuccessful, passion of the Hungarians, who are endowed by nature with a vigorous constitution of soul and body.[36]  Extreme cold has diminished the stature and congealed the faculties of the Laplanders; and the Arctic tribes, alone among the sons of men, are ignorant of war and unconscious of human blood : an happy ignorance, if reason and virtue were the guardians of their peace ![37]

Tactics and manners of the Hungarians and Bulgarians. A.D. 900, &c.

It is the observation of the Imperial author of the Tactics[38] that all the Scythian hordes resembled each other in their pastoral and military life, that they all practised the same means of subsistence, and employed the same instruments of destruction. But he adds that the two nations of Bulgarians and Hungarians were superior to their brethren, and similar to each other, in the improvements, however rude, of their discipline and government; their visible likeness determines Leo to confound his friends and enemies in one common description; and the picture may be heightened by some strokes from their contemporaries of the tenth century.  Except the merit and fame of military prowess, all that is valued by mankind appeared vile and contemptible to these barbarians, whose native fierceness was stimulated by the consciousness of numbers and freedom.  The tents of the Hungarians were of leather, their garments of fur ; they shaved their hair and scarified their faces ; in speech they were slow, in action prompt, in treaty perfidious ; and they shared the common reproach of barbarians, too ignorant to conceive the importance of truth, too proud to deny or palliate the breach of their most solemn engagements.  Their simplicity has been praised ; yet they abstained only from the luxury they had never known ; whatever they saw, they coveted ; their desires were insatiate, and their sole industry was the hand of violence and rapine.

[36] This picture of the Hungarians and Bulgarians is chiefly drawn from the Tactics of Leo, p. 796-801 [c. 18], and the Latin Annals, which are alleged by Baronius, Pagi, and Muratori, A.D. 889, &c.

[37] Buffon, Hist. Naturelle, tom. v. p. 6, in 12mo.  Gustavus Adolphus attempted, without success, to form a regiment of Laplanders.  Grotius says of these Arctic tribes, arma arcus et pharetra, sed adversus feras (Annal. l. iv. p. 236) ; and attempts, after the manner of Tacitus, to varnish with philosophy their brutal ignorance.

[38] Leo has observed that the government of the Turks was monarchical, and that their punishments were rigorous (Tactics, p. 896 [18, § 46], ἀπηνεῖς καὶ βαρείας). Regino (in Chron. A.D. 889) mentions theft as a capital crime, and his jurisprudence is confirmed by the original code of St. Stephen (A.D. 1016).  If a slave were guilty, he was chastised, for the first time, with the loss of his nose, or a fine of five heifers ; for the second, with the loss of his ears, or a similar fine ; for the third, with death ; which the freeman did not incur till the fourth offence, as his first penalty was the loss of liberty (Katona, Hist. Regum Hungar. tom. i. p. 231, 232).

By the definition of a pastoral nation, I have recalled a long description of the economy, the warfare, and the government that prevail in that stage of society; I may add that to fishing as well as to the chase the Hungarians were indebted for a part of their subsistence; and, since they *seldom* cultivated the ground, they must, at least in their new settlements, have sometimes practised a slight and unskilful husbandry. In their emigrations, perhaps in their expeditions, the host was accompanied by thousands of sheep and oxen, which increased the cloud of formidable dust, and afforded a constant and wholesome supply of milk and animal food. A plentiful command of forage was the first care of the general, and, if the flocks and herds were secure of their pastures, the hardy warrior was alike insensible of danger and fatigue. The confusion of men and cattle that overspread the country exposed their camp to a nocturnal surprise, had not a still wider circuit been occupied by their light cavalry, perpetually in motion to discover and delay the approach of the enemy. After some experience of the Roman tactics, they adopted the use of the sword and spear, the helmet of the soldier, and the iron breast-plate of his steed; but their native and deadly weapon was the Tartar bow; from the earliest infancy, their children and servants were exercised in the double science of archery and horsemanship; their arm was strong; their aim was sure; and, in the most rapid career, they were taught to throw themselves backwards, and to shoot a volley of arrows into the air. In open combat, in secret ambush, in flight or pursuit, they were equally formidable; an appearance of order was maintained in the foremost ranks, but their charge was driven forwards by the impatient pressure of succeeding crowds. They pursued, headlong and rash, with loosened reins and horrific outcries; but, if they fled, with real or dissembled fear, the ardour of a pursuing foe was checked and chastised by the same habits of irregular speed and sudden evolution. In the abuse of victory, they astonished Europe, yet smarting from the wounds of the Saracen and the Dane; mercy they rarely asked, and more rarely bestowed; both sexes were accused as equally inaccessible to pity, and their appetite for raw flesh might countenance the popular tale that they drank the blood and feasted on the hearts of the slain. Yet the Hungarians were not devoid of those principles of justice and humanity which nature has implanted in every bosom. The licence of public and private injuries was restrained by laws and punishments; and in the security of an open camp theft is the most tempting and most dangerous offence. Among the barbarians, there were many whose spontaneous virtue supplied their laws and corrected their manners, who performed the duties, and sympathized with the affections, of social life.

After a long pilgrimage of flight or victory, the Turkish hordes approached the common limits of the French and Byzantine empires. Their first conquests and final settlements extended on either side of the Danube above Vienna, below Belgrade, and beyond the measure of the Roman province of Pannonia, or the modern kingdom of Hungary.[39] That ample and fertile land was loosely occupied by the Moravians, a Sclavonian name and tribe, which were driven by the invaders into the compass of a narrow province. Charlemagne had stretched a vague and nominal empire as far as the edge of Transylvania ; but, after the failure of his legitimate line, the dukes of Moravia forgot their obedience and tribute to the monarchs of Oriental France.[40] The bastard Arnulph was provoked to invite the arms of the Turks ; they rushed through the real or figurative wall which his indiscretion had thrown open ; and the king of Germany has been justly reproached as a traitor to the civil and ecclesiastical society of the Christians. During the life of Arnulph, the Hungarians were checked by gratitude or fear ; but in the infancy of his son Lewis they discovered and invaded Bavaria ; and such was their Scythian speed that, in a single day, a circuit of fifty miles was stripped and consumed. In the battle of Augsburg, the Christians maintained their advantage till the seventh hour of the day ; they were deceived and vanquished by the flying stratagems of the Turkish cavalry. The conflagration spread over the provinces of Bavaria, Swabia, and Franconia ; and the Hungarians[41] promoted the reign of anarchy by forcing the

[39] See Katona, Hist. Ducum Hungar. p. 321-352. [One of the most important consequences of the Hungarian invasion and final settlement in these regions was the permanent separation of the Northern from the Southern Slavs. In the eighth and ninth centuries the Slavs formed an unbroken line from the Baltic to the Cretan sea. This line was broken by the Magyar wedge.]

[40] [In the latter part of the ninth century, Moravia under Sviatopolk or Svatopluk was a great power, the most formidable neighbour of the Western Empire. It looked as if he were going to found a great Slavonic empire. For the adoption of the Christian faith see Appendix 12. He died in 894, and under his incompetent son the power of Great Moravia declined, and was blotted out from the number of independent states by the Hungarians about A.D. 906. The annihilation of Moravia might be a relief to the Franks who had originally (before Svatopluk's death) called in the Magyars against the Moravians, but they found—at least for some time to come—more terrible foes in the Magyars.]

[41] Hungarorum gens, cujus omnes fere nationes expertæ [sunt] sævitiam, &c., is the preface of Liutprand (l. i. c. 2 [= c. 5]), who frequently expatiates on the calamities of his own times. See l. i. c. 5 [= c. 13]; l. ii. c. 1, 2, 4, 5, 6, 7 [= c. 2-5, 8 sqq. 21];

stoutest barons to discipline their vassals and fortify their castles.
The origin of walled towns is ascribed to this calamitous period ;
nor could any distance be secure against an enemy who, almost
at the same instant, laid in ashes the Helvetian monastery of St.
Gall, and the city of Bremen on the shores of the northern
ocean. Above thirty years the Germanic empire, or kingdom,
was subject to the ignominy of tribute ; and resistance was disarmed by the menace, the serious and effectual menace, of dragging the women and children into captivity and of slaughtering
the males above the age of ten years. I have neither power nor
inclination to follow the Hungarians beyond the Rhine ; but I
must observe with surprise that the southern provinces of France
were blasted by the tempest, and that Spain, behind her Pyrenees,
was astonished at the approach of these formidable strangers.[42]
The vicinity of Italy had tempted their early inroads ; but, from A.D. 900
their camp on the Brenta, they beheld with some terror the
apparent strength and populousness of the new-discovered
country. They requested leave to retire ; their request was
proudly rejected by the Italian king ; and the lives of twenty
thousand Christians paid the forfeit of his obstinacy and rashness.
Among the cities of the West, the royal Pavia was conspicuous
in fame and splendour ; and the pre-eminence of Rome itself
was only derived from the relics of the apostles. The Hungarians appeared ; Pavia was in flames ; forty-three churches A.D. 924
were consumed ; and, after the massacre of the people, they
spared about two hundred wretches who had gathered some
bushels of gold and silver (a vague exaggeration) from the smoking ruins of their country. In these annual excursions from the
Alps to the neighbourhood of Rome and Capua, the churches,
that yet escaped, resounded with a fearful litany : " Oh ! save
and deliver us from the arrows of the Hungarians ! " But the
saints were deaf or inexorable ; and the torrent rolled forwards,
till it was stopped by the extreme land of Calabria.[43] A com-

---

l. iii. c. 1, &c. ; l. v. c. 8 [= c. 19], 15 [= c. 33], in Legat. p. 485 [c. 45]. His colours
are glaring, but his chronology must be rectified by Pagi and Muratori. [For these
early invasions of the Western Empire by the Hungarians see E. Dümmler,
Geschichte des ostfränkischen Reichs, ii. 437 *sqq.*, 543 *sqq.* The terrible defeat of
the Bavarians under Margrave Liutpold took place on July 5, 907.]

[42] The three bloody reigns of Arpad, Zoltan, and Toxus are critically illustrated
by Katona (Hist. Ducum, &c. p. 107-499). His diligence has searched both
natives and foreigners ; yet to the deeds of mischief, or glory, I have been able to
add the destruction of Bremen (Adam Bremensis, i. 43 [*leg.* 54]).

[43] Muratori has considered with patriotic care the danger and resources of Modena.
The citizens besought St Geminianus, their patron, to avert, by his intercession,
the *rabies, flagellum*, &c.

position was offered and accepted for the head of each Italian subject; and ten bushels of silver were poured forth in the Turkish camp. But falsehood is the natural antagonist of violence; and the robbers were defrauded both in the numbers of the assessment and the standard of the metal. On the side of the East the Hungarians were opposed in doubtful conflict by the equal arms of the Bulgarians, whose faith forbade an alliance with the Pagans, and whose situation formed the barrier of the Byzantine empire. The barrier was overturned; the emperor of Constantinople beheld the waving banners of the Turks; and one of their boldest warriors presumed to strike a battle-axe into the golden gate. The arts and treasures of the Greeks diverted the assault; but the Hungarians might boast, on their retreat, that they had imposed a tribute on the spirit of Bulgaria and the majesty of the Cæsars.[44] The remote and rapid operations of the same campaign appear to magnify the powers and numbers of the Turks; but their courage is most deserving of praise, since a light troop of three or four hundred horse would often attempt and execute the most daring inroads to the gates of Thessalonica and Constantinople. At this disastrous æra of the ninth and tenth centuries, Europe was afflicted by a triple scourge from the North, the East, and the South; the Norman, the Hungarian, and the Saracen sometimes trod the same ground of desolation; and these savage foes might have been compared by Homer to the two lions growling over the carcase of a mangled stag.[45]

The deliverance of Germany and Christendom was achieved by the Saxon princes, Henry the Fowler and Otho the Great,

A.D. 924

Victory of Henry the Fowler. A.D. 934 [933]

Nunc te rogamus, licet servi pessimi,
Ab Ungerorum nos defendas jaculis.

The bishop erected walls for the public defence, not contra dominos serenos (Antiquitat. Ital. med. Ævi, tom. i. dissertat. i. p. 21, 22), and the song of the nightly watch is not without elegance or use (tom. iii. diss. xl. p. 709). The Italian annalist has accurately traced the series of their inroads (Annali d'Italia, tom. vii. p. 365, 367, 393, 401, 437, 440; tom. viii. p. 19, 41, 52, &c.).

[44] Both the Hungarian and Russian annals suppose that they besieged, or attacked, or insulted Constantinople (Pray, dissertat. x. p. 239; Katona, Hist. Ducum, p. 354-360), and the fact is *almost* confessed by the Byzantine historian (Leo Grammaticus, p. 506 [p. 322, ed. Bonn]; Cedrenus, tom. ii. p. 629 [ii. p. 316 ed. Bonn]), yet, however glorious to the nation, it is denied or doubted by the critical historian, and even by the notary of Béla. Their scepticism is meritorious; they could not safely transcribe or believe the rusticorum fabulas; but Katona might have given due attention to the evidence of Liutprand; Bulgarorum gentem atque *Graecorum* tributariam fecerant (Hist. l. ii. c. 4, p. 435 [= c. 7]).

[45] ―――― λέονθ' ὥς δηρινθήτην,
῎Ωτ' ὄρεος κορυφῇσι περὶ κταμένης ἐλάφοιο
῎Αμφω πεινάοντε μέγα φρονέοντε μάχεσθον.    [Il. 16, 756.]

who, in two memorable battles, for ever broke the power of the Hungarians.[46] The valiant Henry was roused from a bed of sickness by the invasion of his country; but his mind was vigorous and his prudence successful. "My companions," said he on the morning of the combat, "maintain your ranks, receive on your bucklers the first arrows of the Pagans, and prevent their second discharge by the equal and rapid career of your lances." They obeyed, and conquered; and the historical picture of the castle of Merseburg expressed the features, or at least the character, of Henry, who, in an age of ignorance, entrusted to the finer arts the perpetuity of his name.[47] At the end of twenty years, the children of the Turks who had fallen by his sword invaded the empire of his son; and their force is defined, in the lowest estimate, at one hundred thousand horse. They were invited by domestic faction; the gates of Germany were treacherously unlocked; and they spread, far beyond the Rhine and the Meuse, into the heart of Flanders. But the vigour and prudence of Otho dispelled the conspiracy; the princes were made sensible that, unless they were true to each other, their religion and country were irrecoverably lost; and the national powers were reviewed in the plains of Augsburg. They marched and fought in eight legions,[48] according to the division of provinces and tribes; the first, second, and third were composed of Bavarians; the fourth of Franconians; the fifth of Saxons, under the immediate command of the monarch; the sixth and seventh consisted of Swabians; and the eighth

*[Battle of Riada]*

*of Otho the Great. A.D. 955 [August 10]*

*[Battle of the Lechfeld]*

[46] They are amply and critically discussed by Katona (Hist. Ducum, p. 360-368, 427-470). Liutprand (l. ii. c. 8, 9 [= c. 24-31]) is the best evidence for the former, and Witichind (Annal. Saxon. l. iii. [c. 34-49]) of the latter; but the critical historian will not even overlook the horn of a warrior, which is said to be preserved at Jazberin.

[47] Hunc vero triumphum, tam laude quam memoriâ dignum, ad Meresburgum rex in superiori cœnaculo domus per ζωγραφίαν, id est, picturam, notari [*leg.* notare] præcepit, adeo ut rem veram potius quam verisimilem videas: an high encomium (Liutprand, l. ii. c. 9 [= c. 31]). Another palace in Germany had been painted with holy subjects by the order of Charlemagne; and Muratori may justly affirm, nulla sæcula fuere in quibus pictores desiderati fuerint (Antiquitat. Ital. medii Ævi, tom. ii. dissert. xxiv. p. 360, 361). Our domestic claims to antiquity of ignorance and original imperfection (Mr. Walpole's lively words) are of a much more recent date (Anecdotes of Painting, vol. i. p. 2, &c.). [This victory is commonly called the battle of Merseburg; but it was fought at Riada (according to Widukind, i. 38, who in such a matter is the best authority), and Riada probably corresponds to Rietheburg, where the streams of the Unstrut and Helme meet. The event should be called the battle of Riada. The Italian Liutprand who names Merseburg is not such a good witness as the Saxon historian.]

[48] [Giesebrecht has made it probable that by legion Widukind (iii. 44) meant a company of 1000 men. Gesch. der deutschen Kaiserzeit, i. p. 831.]

legion, of a thousand Bohemians, closed the rear of the host. The resources of discipline and valour were fortified by the arts of superstition, which, on this occasion, may deserve the epithets of generous and salutary. The soldiers were purified with a fast; the camp was blessed with the relics of saints and martyrs; and the Christian hero girded on his side the sword of Constantine, grasped the invincible spear of Charlemagne, and waved the banner of St. Maurice, the præfect of the Thebæan legion. But his firmest confidence was placed in the holy lance,[49] whose point was fashioned of the nails of the cross, and which his father had extorted from the king of Burgundy by the threats of war and the gift of a province. The Hungarians were expected in the front;[50] they secretly passed the Lech, a river of Bavaria that falls into the Danube; turned the rear of the Christian army; plundered the baggage and disordered the legions of Bohemia and Swabia. The battle was restored by the Franconians, whose duke, the valiant Conrad, was pierced with an arrow as he rested from his fatigues; the Saxons fought under the eyes of their king; and his victory surpassed, in merit and importance, the triumphs of the last two hundred years. The loss of the Hungarians was still greater in the flight than in the action; they were encompassed by the rivers of Bavaria; and their past cruelties excluded them from the hope of mercy. Three captive princes were hanged at Ratisbon, the multitude of prisoners was slain or mutilated, and the fugitives, who presumed to appear in the face of their country, were condemned to everlasting poverty and disgrace.[51] Yet the spirit of the nation was humbled, and the most accessible passes of Hungary were fortified with a ditch and rampart. Adversity suggested the counsels of moderation and peace; the robbers of the West acquiesced in a sedentary life; and the next generation was taught, by a discerning prince, that far more might be gained by multiplying and exchanging the produce of a fruitful soil. The native race, the Turkish or Fennic blood, was mingled with

A.D. 972

[49] See Baronius, Annal. Eccles. A.D. 929, No. 2-5. The lance of Christ is taken from the best evidence, Liutprand (l. iv. c. 12 [= c. 25]), Sigebert, and the acts of St. Gerard; but the other military relics depend on the faith of the Gesta Anglorum post Bedam, l. ii. c. 8.

[50] [The best account of the battle is in Widukind. The other sources are Annales Sangallenses majores; Flodoard; Continuator Reginonis; Ruotger; and a later but noteworthy account in the Vita Udalrici by Gerhard. See E. Dümmler, Kaiser Otto der Grosse (in the Jahrbb. der deutschen Geschichte), 1876 (p. 256 sqq.), and Giesebrecht, op. cit. (p. 418 sqq.), for details of the battle.]

[51] Katona, Hist. Ducum Hungariæ, p. 500, &c.

new colonies of Scythian or Sclavonian origin ;[52] many thousands of robust and industrious captives had been imported from all the countries of Europe ;[53] and, after the marriage of Geisa with a Bavarian princess, he bestowed honours and estates on the nobles of Germany.[54]   The son of Geisa was invested with the regal title, and the house of Arpad reigned three hundred years in the kingdom of Hungary.   But the freeborn barbarians were not dazzled by the lustre of the diadem, and the people asserted their indefeasible right of choosing, deposing, and punishing the hereditary servant of the state.

III. The name of RUSSIANS [55] was first divulged, in the ninth century, by an embassy from Theophilus, emperor of the East, to the emperor of the West, Lewis, the son of Charlemagne. The Greeks were accompanied by the envoys of the great duke, or chagan, or *czar*, of the Russians.   In their journey to Con-

*Origin of the Russian monarchy*

---

[52] Among these colonies we may distinguish, 1. The Chazars, or Cabari, who joined the Hungarians on their march (Constant. de Admin. Imp. c. 39, 40, p. 108, 109).   [The name of the Kabars, a Khazar people, survives in the name of the two Kabar-dahs (Kabar-hills).]   2. The Jazyges, Moravians, and Siculi, whom they found in the land ; the last were [according to Simon de Kéza, c. 4] *perhaps* a remnant of the Huns of Attila, and were entrusted with the guard of the borders. [Siculus (*Zaculus* in Simon de Kéza) is the equivalent, in chroniclers' Latin, of Székely (plural, Székelyek), which is generally derived from *szék*, seat, abode. Hunfalvy (Magyarország Ethnographiája, p. 302) explains the word as "beyond the habitations," a name which might be applied to people of a march district. The word would thus be formed like Erdély (= Erdö-elv, beyond the forest), the Hungarian name of Transylvania.   Their German neighbours call the Székelyek Szeklers.]   3. The Russians, who, like the Swiss in France, imparted a general name to the royal porters   4   The Bulgarians, whose chiefs (A.D. 956) were in vited, cum magnâ multitudine *Hismahelitarum*.   Had any of these Sclavonians embraced the Mahometan religion ?   5. The Bisseni and Cumans, a mixed multitude of Patzinacites, Uzi, Chazars, &c. who had spread to the lower Danube. [Bisseni = Patzinaks ; Cumans = Uzi.]   The last colony of 40,000 Cumans, A.D. 1239, was received and converted by the kings of Hungary, who derived from that tribe a new regal appellation (Pray, Dissert. vi. vii. p. 109-173 ; Katona, Hist. Ducum, p. 95-99, 252-264, 476, 479-483, &c.).

[53] Christiani autem, quorum pars major populi est, qui ex omni parte mundi illuc tracti sunt captivi, &c.   Such was the language of Piligrinus, the first missionary who entered Hungary, A.D. 973.   Pars major is strong.   Hist. Ducum, p. 517.

[54] The fideles Teutonici of Geisa are authenticated in old charters ; and Katona, with his usual industry, has made a fair estimate of these colonies, which had been so loosely magnified by the Italian Ranzanus (Hist. Critic. Ducum. p. 667-681).

[55] Among the Greeks, this national appellation has a singular form 'Ρῶς, as an undeclinable word, of which many fanciful etymologies have been suggested.   [Cp. Appendix 14.]   I have perused, with pleasure and profit, a dissertation de Origine Russorum (Comment. Academ. Petropolitanæ, tom. viii. p. 388-436) by Theophilus Sigefrid Bayer, a learned German, who spent his life and labours in the service of Russia.   A geographical tract of d'Anville, de l'Empire de Russie, son Origine, et ses Accroissemens (Paris, 1772, in 12mo), has likewise been of use.

stantinople, they had traversed many hostile nations; and they hoped to escape the dangers of their return by requesting the French monarch to transport them by sea to their native country. A closer examination detected their origin: they were the brethren of the Swedes and Normans, whose name was already odious and formidable in France; and it might justly be apprehended that these Russian strangers were not the messengers of peace but the emissaries of war. They were detained, while the Greeks were dismissed; and Lewis expected a more satisfactory account, that he might obey the laws of hospitality or prudence, according to the interest of both empires.[56] The Scandinavian origin of the people, or at least the princes of Russia, may be confirmed and illustrated by the national annals [57] and the general history of the North. The Normans, who had so long been concealed by a veil of impenetrable darkness, suddenly burst forth in the spirit of naval and military enterprise. The vast, and, as it is said, the populous, regions of Denmark, Sweden, and Norway were crowded with independent chieftains and desperate adventurers, who sighed in the laziness of peace, and smiled in the agonies of death. Piracy was the exercise, the trade, the glory and the virtue, of the Scandinavian youth. Impatient of a bleak climate and narrow limits, they started from the banquet, grasped their arms, sounded their horn, ascended their vessels, and explored every coast that promised either spoil or settlement. The Baltic was the first scene of their naval achievements; they visited the eastern shores, the silent residence of Fennic and Sclavonian tribes, and the primitive Russians of the lake Ladoga paid a tribute, the skins of white squirrels, to these strangers, whom they saluted with the title of *Varangians*,[58] or Corsairs. Their superiority in

[56] See the entire passage (dignum, says Bayer, ut aureis in tabulis figatur) in the Annales Bertiniani Francorum (in Script. Ital. Muratori, tom ii. pars i. p. 525 [Pertz, Mon. i. 434]), A.D. 839, twenty-two years before the æra of Ruric. In the tenth century, Liutprand (Hist. l. v. c. 6 [= c. 15]) speaks of the Russians and Normans as the same Aquilonares homines of a red complexion.

[57] My knowledge of these annals is drawn from M. Levesque, Histoire de Russie. Nestor, the first and best of these ancient annalists, was a monk of Kiow, who died in the beginning of the twelfth century; but his chronicle was obscure, till it was published at Petersburgh, 1767, in 4to. Levesque, Hist. de Russie, tom. i. p. 16. Coxe's Travels, vol. ii. p. 184. [See Appendix 1.]

[58] Theophil. Sig. Bayer de Varagis (for the name is differently spelt), in Comment. Academ. Petropolitanæ, tom. iv. p. 275-311. [The Varangians, in the proper and original sense of the word, meant the Scandinavians. In the chronicle of Nestor, the Baltic Sea is the sea of the Variazi (c. 4). Endless attempts have been made, chiefly by Russian scholars, to find other identifications (such as Slavs, Khazars

arms, discipline, and renown, commanded the fear and reverence
of the natives. In their wars against the more inland savages,
the Varangians condescended to serve as friends and auxiliaries,
and gradually, by choice or conquest, obtained the dominion of
a people whom they were qualified to protect. Their tyranny
was expelled, their valour was again recalled, till at length,
Ruric,[59] a Scandinavian chief, became the father of a dynasty A.D. 862
which reigned above seven hundred years. His brothers extended his influence; the example of service and usurpation was
imitated by his companions[60] in the southern provinces of
Russia; and their establishments, by the usual methods of war
and assassination, were cemented into the fabric of a powerful
monarchy.

As long as the descendants of Ruric were considered as aliens The Varan-
and conquerors, they ruled by the sword of the Varangians, gians of Con-
distributed estates and subjects to their faithful captains, and stantinople
supplied their numbers with fresh streams of adventurers from
the Baltic coast.[61] But, when the Scandinavian chiefs had
struck a deep and permanent root into the soil, they mingled
with the Russians in blood, religion, and language, and the first
Waladimir had the merit of delivering his country from these
foreign mercenaries. They had seated him on the throne; his
riches were insufficient to satisfy their demands; but they
listened to his pleasing advice that they should seek, not a
more grateful, but a more wealthy master; that they should
embark for Greece, where, instead of the skins of squirrels, silk

Finns); but all these attempts were eminently unsuccessful. The geographical
meaning of Varangia has been brought out most clearly in a passage in the Book
of Advice which is annexed to the Strategicon of Cecaumenos (see above, vol. 5, p.
505). In § 246 (p. 97, ed. Vasilievski and Jernstedt) Harold Hardrada is called the
" son of the king of Varangia " i.e. Norway. The formation of the Varangian
guard at Constantinople, and the inclusion in it of other Teutons (Danes, English,
&c.), led to an extension of the meaning of Varangian from its original limitation to
Norwegians or Scandinavians. Schafarik (ii. 72) derives the name from *vara, vaere*,
a compact; the meaning would be *fœderati*.]

[59] [The name is Scandinavian (old Norse Hraerikr). Riuric founded Novgorod
(Nestor, c. 15); died in 879.]

[60] [This refers to the story of Oskold and Dir, boyars of Riuric, and their establishment at Kiev; see Nestor, c. 15, 16, 18. Oleg, who succeeded Riuric at Novgorod, is stated in this chronicle to have marched against Kiev and put Oskold and
Dir to death (A.D. 881). It was doubtless Oleg who united Novgorod and Kiev,
but it has been questioned whether Oskold and Dir were real personages. The
Arabic writer Masūdī mentions " Dir " as a powerful Slav king.]

[61] Yet, as late as the year 1018, Kiow and Russia were still guarded ex fugiti-
vorum servorum robore confluentium, et maxime Danorum. Bayer, who quotes
(p. 292) the Chronicle of Dithmar [Thietmar] of Merseburg, observes that it was
unusual for the Germans to enlist in a foreign service.

and gold would be the recompense of their service. At the same time, the Russian prince admonished his Byzantine ally to disperse and employ, to recompense and restrain, these impetuous children of the North. Contemporary writers have recorded the introduction, name, and character of the *Varangians* : each day they rose in confidence and esteem ; the whole body was assembled at Constantinople to perform the duty of guards ; and their strength was recruited by a numerous band of their countrymen from the island of Thule. On this occasion the vague appellation of Thule is applied to England ; and the new Varangians were a colony of English and Danes who fled from the yoke of the Norman conqueror. The habits of pilgrimage and piracy had approximated the countries of the earth ; these exiles were entertained in the Byzantine court ; and they preserved, till the last age of the empire, the inheritance of spotless loyalty and the use of the Danish or English tongue. With their broad and double-edged battle-axes on their shoulders, they attended the Greek emperor to the temple, the senate, and the hippodrome ; he slept and feasted under their trusty guard ; and the keys of the palace, the treasury, and the capital were held by the firm and faithful hands of the Varangians.[62]

Geography and trade of Russia. A.D. 950    In the tenth century, the geography of Scythia was extended far beyond the limits of ancient knowledge ; and the monarchy of the Russians obtains a vast and conspicuous place in the map of Constantine.[63] The sons of Ruric were masters of the spacious province of Wolodomir, or Moscow ; and, if they were confined on that side by the hordes of the East, their western frontier in those early days was enlarged to the Baltic sea and the country of the Prussians. Their northern reign ascended above the sixtieth degree of latitude, over the Hyperborean regions, which fancy had peopled with monsters, or clouded with eternal dark-

[62] Ducange has collected from the original authors the state and history of the Varangi at Constantinople (Glossar. Med. et Infimæ Græcitatis, sub voce Βάραγγοι Med. et Infimæ Latinitatis, sub voce *Vagri ;* Not. ad Alexiad. Annæ Comnenæ, p. 256, 257, 258 ; Notes sur Villehardouin, p. 296-299). See likewise the annotations of Reiske to the Ceremoniale Aulæ Byzant. of Constantine, tom. ii. p. 149, 150. Saxo Grammaticus affirms that they spoke Danish ; but Codinus maintains them till the fifteenth century in the use of their native English : Πολυχρονίζουσι οἱ Βάραγγοι κατὰ τὴν πάτριον γλῶσσαν αὐτῶν ἤτοι Ἰγκλινιστί.

[63] The original record of the geography and trade of Russia is produced by the emperor Constantine Porphyrogenitus (de Administrat. Imperii, c. 2, p. 55, 56, c. 9, p. 59-61, c. 13, p. 63-67, c. 37, p. 106, c. 42, p. 112, 113), and illustrated by the diligence of Bayer (de Geographiâ Russiæ vicinarumque Regionum circiter A.C. 948, in Comment. Academ. Petropol. tom. ix. p. 367-422, tom. x. p. 371-421), with the aid of the chronicles and traditions of Russia, Scandinavia, &c.

ness.  To the south they followed the course of the Borysthenes,
and approached with that river the neighbourhood of the Euxine
Sea.  The tribes that dwelt, or wandered, in this ample circuit
were obedient to the same conqueror, and insensibly blended
into the same nation.  The language of Russia is a dialect of
the Sclavonian ; but, in the tenth century, these two modes
of speech were different from each other ; and, as the Sclavonian
prevailed in the South, it may be presumed that the original
Russians of the North, the primitive subjects of the Varangian
chief, were a portion of the Fennic race.[64]  With the emigration,
union, or dissolution of the wandering tribes, the loose and indefinite picture of the Scythian desert has continually shifted.
But the most ancient map of Russia affords some places which
still retain their name and position ; and the two capitals, Novogorod [65] and Kiow,[66] are coeval with the first age of the monarchy.
Novogorod had not yet deserved the epithet of great, nor the
alliance of the Hanseatic league, which diffused the streams of
opulence and the principles of freedom.  Kiow could not yet
boast of three hundred churches, an innumerable people, and a
degree of greatness and splendour, which was compared with
Constantinople by those who had never seen the residence of
the Cæsars.  In their origin, the two cities were no more than
camps or fairs, the most convenient stations in which the barbarians might assemble for the occasional business of war or
trade.  Yet even these assemblies announce some progress in
the arts of society ; a new breed of cattle was imported from the
southern provinces ; and the spirit of commercial enterprise per-

[64] [There were peoples of Finnic race in Livonia and Ingria, between Novgorod
and the Baltic ; and east of Novgorod the Finnic circle reached down to the Oka,
south of Moskowa.  The most southerly of these peoples were the Muromians,
whose town was Murom ; north of these were the Merians, whose town was Rostov ;
and further north were the Ves, who lived about the White Lake (Bielo-ozero).
The Muromians, the Merians, and Ves were in loose subjection to Riuric (Nestor,
c. 15).]

[65] The haughty proverb : " Who can resist God and the great Novogorod ? " is
applied by M. Levesque (Hist. de Russie, tom. i. p. 60) even to the times that preceded the reign of Ruric.  In the course of his history he frequently celebrates this
republic, which was suppressed A.D. 1475 (tom ii. p. 252-266).  That accurate
traveller, Adam Olearius, describes (in 1635) the remains of Novogorod, and the
route by sea and land of the Holstein ambassadors (tom. i. p. 123-129).

[66] In hâc magnâ civitate, quæ est caput regni, plus trecentæ ecclesiæ habentur
et nundinæ octo, populi etiam ignota manus (Eggehardus ad A.D. 1018, apud
Bayer, tom. ix. p. 412 [Ekkehardus Uraugiensis, Chronicon, ap. Pertz, Mon. vi.]).
He likewise quotes (tom. x. p. 397) the words of the Saxon annalist [Adam of
Bremen, ii. c. 19], Cujus (Russiae) metropolis est Chive, æmula sceptri Constantino-
politani quæ est clarissimum decus Græciæ.  The fame of Kiow, especially in the
xith century, had reached the German and the Arabian geographers.

vaded the sea and land from the Baltic to the Euxine, from the
mouth of the Oder to the port of Constantinople. In the days
of idolatry and barbarism, the Sclavonic city of Julin was fre-
quented and enriched by the Normans, who had prudently
secured a free mart of purchase and exchange.[67] From this
harbour, at the entrance of the Oder, the corsair, or merchant,
sailed in forty-three days to the eastern shores of the Baltic,
the most distant nations were intermingled, and the holy groves
of Curland *are said* to have been decorated with *Grecian* and
Spanish gold.[68] Between the sea and Novogorod an easy intercourse was discovered: in the summer, through a gulf, a lake,
and a navigable river; in the winter season, over the hard and
level surface of boundless snows. From the neighbourhood of
that city, the Russians descended the streams that fall into the
Borysthenes; their canoes, of a single tree, were laden with
slaves of every age, furs of every species, the spoil of their bee-
hives, and the hides of their cattle; and the whole produce of
the North was collected and discharged in the magazines of
Kiow. The month of June was the ordinary season of the
departure of the fleet; the timber of the canoes was framed
into the oars and benches of more solid and capacious boats;
and they proceeded without obstacle down the Borysthenes, as
far as the seven or thirteen ridges of rocks, which traverse the
bed, and precipitate the waters, of the river. At the more
shallow falls it was sufficient to lighten the vessels; but the
deeper cataracts were impassable; and the mariners, who
dragged their vessels and their slaves six miles over land, were
exposed in this toilsome journey to the robbers of the desert.[69]

[67] In Odoræ ostio quâ Scythicas alluit paludes, nobilissima civitas Julinum [*leg.*
Jumne], celeberrimam Barbaris et Græcis qui sunt in circuitu præstans stationem ;
est sane maxima omnium quas Europa claudit civitatum (Adam Bremensis, Hist.
Eccles. p. 19 [ii. 19]). A strange exaggeration even in the xith century. The
trade of the Baltic, and the Hanseatic league, are carefully treated in Anderson's
Historical Deduction of Commerce ; at least in *our* language, I am not acquainted
with any book so satisfactory. [Jumne lies near Wollin.]

[68] According to Adam of Bremen (de Situ Daniæ, p. 58), the old Curland extended eight days' journey along the coast ; and by Peter Teutoburgicus (p. 68, A.D.
1326) Memel is defined as the common frontier of Russia, Curland, and Prussia.
Aurum ibi plurimum (says Adam) [ . . . ] divinis auguribus atque necromanticis
omnes domus sunt plenæ . . . a toto orbe ibi responsa petuntur maxime ab
Hispanis (forsan *Zupanis*, id est regulis Lettoviæ [other conjectures are : *Cispanis*
and *his paganis*]) et Græcis [c. 16]. The name of Greeks was applied to the
Russians even before their conversion : an imperfect conversion, if they still consulted the wizards of Curland (Bayer, tom. x. p. 378, 402, &c.; Grotius, Prolegomen.
ad Hist. Goth. p. 99).

[69] Constantine [de adm. Imp. c. 9] only reckons seven cataracts, of which he

At the first island below the falls, the Russians celebrated the festival of their escape ; at a second, near the mouth of the river, they repaired their shattered vessels for the longer and more perilous voyage of the Black Sea. If they steered along the coast, the Danube was accessible ; with a fair wind they could reach in thirty-six or forty hours the opposite shores of Anatolia ; and Constantinople admitted the annual visit of the strangers of the North. They returned at the stated season with a rich cargo of corn, wine, and oil, the manufactures of Greece, and the spices of India. Some of their countrymen resided in the capital and provinces ; and the national treaties protected the persons, effects, and privileges of the Russian merchant.[70]

But the same communication which had been opened for the benefit, was soon abused for the injury, of mankind. In a period of one hundred and ninety years, the Russians made four attempts to plunder the treasures of Constantinople ; the event was various, but the motive, the means, and the object were the same in these naval expeditions.[71] The Russian traders

*Naval expeditions of the Russians against Constantinople*

[70] Nestor apud Levesque, Hist. de Russie, tom. i. p. 78-80 [caps. 21, 22, 27, 35]. From the Dnieper or Borysthenes, the Russians went to Black Bulgaria, Chazaria, and *Syria*. To Syria, how? where? when? May we not, instead of Συρία, read Συανία? (de Administrat. Imp. c. 42, p. 113). The alteration is slight ; the position of Suania, between Chazaria and Lazica, is perfectly suitable ; and the name was still used in the xith century (Cedren. tom. ii. p. 770). [Four treaties are cited in the old Russian chronicle : (1) A.D. 907 (Nestor, c. 21) with Oleg; (2) A.D. 911 (*ib.* c. 22) with Oleg; (3) A.D. 945 (*ib.* c. 27) with Igor ; (4) A.D. 970 (*ib.* c. 36) with Sviatoslav. There is no doubt that the texts of the last three treaties inserted by the chronicler are genuine. According to custom, duplicates of the documents in Greek and in the language of the other contracting party were drawn up. These treaties have attracted much attention from Russian scholars. Two investigations deserve special mention : a paper of Sergieevich in the January No. of the Zhurnal Minist. Nar. prosv., 1882, and an article of Dimitriu in Viz. Vremenn. ii. p. 531 *sqq.* (1893). The transaction of A.D. 907, before the walls of Constantinople, was merely a convention, not a formal treaty ; and Dimitriu shows that the negotiation of A.D. 911 was doubtless intended to convert the spirit of this convention into an international treaty, signed and sealed. But he also makes it probable that this treaty of A.D. 911 did not receive its final ratification from Oleg and his boyars, and consequently was not strictly binding. But it proved a basis for the treaty of 945, which was completed with the full diplomatic forms and which refers back to it.]

[71] The wars of the Russians and Greeks in the ixth, xth, and xith centuries are related in the Byzantine Annals, especially those of Zonaras and Cedrenus ; and all their testimonies are collected in the *Russica* of Stritter, tom. ii. pars ii. p. 939-1044.

had seen the magnificence and tasted the luxury of the city of
the Cæsars. A marvellous tale, and a scanty supply, excited
the desires of their savage countrymen : they envied the gifts
of nature which their climate denied ; they coveted the works
of art which they were too lazy to imitate and too indigent to
purchase : the Varangian princes unfurled the banners of piratical adventure, and their bravest soldiers were drawn from the
nations that dwelt in the northern isles of the ocean.[72] The
image of their naval armaments was revived in the last century
in the fleets of the Cossacks, which issued from the Borysthenes
to navigate the same seas for a similar purpose.[73] The Greek
appellation of *monoxyla*, or single canoes, might be justly applied
to the bottom of their vessels. It was scooped out of the long
stem of a beech or willow, but the slight and narrow foundation
was raised and continued on either side with planks, till it attained the length of sixty, and the height of about twelve, feet.
These boats were built without a deck, but with two rudders
and a mast ; to move with sails and oars ; and to contain from
forty to seventy men, with their arms, and provisions of fresh
water and salt fish. The first trial of the Russians was made
with two hundred boats ; but, when the national force was
exerted, they might arm against Constantinople a thousand or
twelve hundred vessels. Their fleet was not much inferior to
the royal navy of Agamemnon, but it was magnified in the
eyes of fear to ten or fifteen times the real proportion of its
strength and numbers. Had the Greek emperors been endowed
with foresight to discern, and vigour to prevent, perhaps they
might have sealed with a maritime force the mouth of the Borysthenes. Their indolence abandoned the coast of Anatolia to
the calamities of a piratical war, which, after an interval of six
hundred years, again infested the Euxine ; but, as long as the
capital was respected, the sufferings of a distant province escaped
the notice both of the prince and the historian. The storm,
which had swept along from the Phasis and Trebizond, at length
burst on the Bosphorus of Thrace : a strait of fifteen miles,
in which the rude vessels of the Russian might have been
stopped and destroyed by a more skilful adversary. In their

The first.
A.D. 865 [860]

[72] Προσεταιρισάμενος δὲ καὶ συμμαχικὸν οὐκ ὀλίγον ἀπὸ τῶν κατοικούντων ἐν τοῖς
προσαρκτίοις τοῦ Ὠκεανοῦ νήσοις ἐθνῶν. Cedrenus, in Compend. p. 758 [ii. 551, ed. B.].

[73] See Beauplan (Description de l'Ukraine, p. 54-61). His descriptions are
lively, his plans accurate, and, except the circumstance of fire-arms, we may read
old Russians for modern Cossacks.

first enterprise [74] under the prince of Kiow, they passed without opposition, and occupied the port of Constantinople in the absence of the emperor Michael, the son of Theophilus. Through [Michael iii.] a crowd of perils he landed at the palace stairs, and immediately repaired to a church of the Virgin Mary.[75] By the advice of the patriarch, her garment, a precious relic, was drawn from the sanctuary and dipped in the sea; and a seasonable tempest, which determined the retreat of the Russians, was devoutly ascribed to the Mother of God.[76] The silence of the Greeks [The second. A.D. 904 [907]] may inspire some doubt of the truth, or at least of the importance, of the second attempt of Oleg, the guardian of the sons of Ruric.[77] A strong barrier of arms and fortifications defended the Bosphorus: they were eluded by the usual expedient of drawing the boats over the isthmus; and this simple operation is described in the national chronicles as if the Russian fleet had sailed over dry land with a brisk and favourable gale. The [The third. A.D. 941]

[74] It is to be lamented that Bayer has only given a Dissertation de Russorum *primâ* Expeditione Constantinopolitanâ (Comment. Academ. Petropol. tom. vi. p. 365-391). After disentangling some chronological intricacies, he fixes it in the years 864 or 865, a date which might have smoothed some doubts and difficulties in the beginning of M. Levesque's history. [The true date of the Russian attack on Constantinople is given in a short Chronicle first printed by F. Cumont in "Anecdota Bruxellensia I. Chroniques quelques byzantines du Mscr. 11376"; and has been established demonstratively by C. de Boor (Byz. Zeitsch. iv. p. 445 *sqq.*). It is June 18, 860; the old date 865 or 866 was derived from the Chronicle of Pseudo-Symeon (p. 674, ed. Bonn: cp. above, vol. 5, p. 503), but it has been proved by Hirsch that the dates of this chronicle had no authority. The same source which gives the right date asserts that the Russians were defeated and annihilated (ἠφανίσθησαν) by the Christians with the help of the Virgin. It seems certain that they experienced a severe defeat *after* their retreat from the walls. Two homilies delivered by Photius on the occasion of this attack were published by Nauck in 1867 and again by C. Müller in Frag. Hist. Graec. v. 2, p. 162 *sqq.* The first was spoken in the moment of terror before the Emperor's arrival; the second after the rescue. But the second makes no mention of the destruction of the hostile armament; hence de Boor shows that it must have been delivered immediately after the relief of the barbarians from the walls, but before their destruction. Another contemporary notice of the event is found in the life of Ignatius by Nicetas (see above, vol. 5, p. 502), Migne, P. G. 105, p. 512. The chronicle of Nestor makes Oskold and Dir (see above, note 60) the leaders of the expedition.]

[75] When Photius wrote his encyclic epistle on the conversion of the Russians, the miracle was not yet sufficiently ripe; he reproaches the nation as εἰς ὠμότητα καὶ μιαιφονίαν [πάντας] δευτέρους ταττόμενον. [See Photii Epistolæ, ed. Valettas, p. 178.]

[76] Leo Grammaticus, p. 463, 464 [p. 241, ed. B.]. Constantini Continuator, in Script. post Theophanem, p. 121, 122 [p. 196-7, ed. B.]. Simeon Logothet. p. 445, 446 [p. 674-5, ed. B.]. Georg. Monach. p. 535, 536 [826, ed. B.]. Cedrenus, tom. ii. p. 551 [ii. 173, ed. B.]. Zonaras, tom. ii. p. 162 [xvi. 5].

[77] See Nestor [c. 21] and Nicon, in Levesque's Hist. de Russie, tom. i. p. 74-80. Katona (Hist. Ducum, p. 75-79) uses his advantage to disprove this Russian victory, which would cloud the siege of Kiow by the Hungarians.

leader of the third armament, Igor, the son of Ruric, had chosen a moment of weakness and decay, when the naval powers of the empire were employed against the Saracens. But, if courage be not wanting, the instruments of defence are seldom deficient. Fifteen broken and decayed galleys were boldly launched against the enemy; but, instead of the single tube of Greek fire usually planted on the prow, the sides and stern of each vessel were abundantly supplied with that liquid combustible. The engineers were dexterous; the weather was propitious; many thousand Russians, who chose rather to be drowned than burnt, leaped into the sea; and those who escaped to the Thracian shore were inhumanly slaughtered by the peasants and soldiers. Yet one third of the canoes escaped into shallow water; and the next spring Igor was again prepared to retrieve his disgrace and claim his revenge.[78] After a long peace, Jaroslaus, the great-grandson of Igor, resumed the same project of a naval invasion. A fleet, under the command of his son, was repulsed at the entrance of the Bosphorus by the same artificial flames. But in the rashness of pursuit the vanguard of the Greeks was encompassed by an irresistible multitude of boats and men; their provision of fire was probably exhausted; and twenty-four galleys were either taken, sunk, or destroyed.[79]

Yet the threats or calamities of a Russian war were more frequently diverted by treaty than by arms. In these naval hostilities every disadvantage was on the side of the Greeks; their savage enemy afforded no mercy; his poverty promised no spoil; his impenetrable retreat deprived the conqueror of the hopes of revenge; and the pride or weakness of empire indulged an opinion that no honour could be gained or lost in the intercourse with barbarians. At first their demands were high and inadmissible, three pounds of gold for each soldier or mariner of the fleet; the Russian youth adhered to the design of conquest and glory; but the counsels of moderation were recommended by the hoary sages. "Be content," they said, "with the liberal offers of Cæsar; is it not far better to obtain without a combat

*The fourth. A.D. 1043*

*Negotiations and prophecy*

*[A.D. 944]*

[78] Leo Grammaticus, p. 506, 507 [p. 323, ed. B.]; Incert. Contin. p. 263, 264 [p. 424]; Simeon Logothet. p. 490, 491 [p. 746-7, ed. B.]; Georg. Monach. p. 588, 589 [p. 914, ed. B.]; Cedren. tom. ii. p. 629 [ii. 316, ed. B.]; Zonaras, tom. ii. p. 190, 191 [xvi. 19]; and Liutprand, l. v. c. 6 [= c. 15], who writes from the narratives of his father-in-law, then ambassador at Constantinople, and corrects the vain exaggeration of the Greeks. [Nestor, c. 26.]

[79] I can only appeal to Cedrenus (tom. ii. p. 758, 759 [ii. 551, ed. B.]) and Zonaras (tom. ii. p. 253, 254 [xvii. 24]), but they grow more weighty and credible as they draw near to their own times. [Cp. Nestor, c. 56.]

the possession of gold, silver, silks, and all the objects of our desires? Are we sure of victory? Can we conclude a treaty with the sea? We do not tread on the land; we float on the abyss of water, and a common death hangs over our heads." [80] The memory of these Arctic fleets that seemed to descend from the Polar circle left a deep impression of terror on the Imperial city. By the vulgar of every rank, it was asserted and believed that an equestrian statue in the square of Taurus was secretly inscribed with a prophecy, how the Russians, in the last days, should become masters of Constantinople. [81] In our own time, a Russian armament, instead of sailing from the Borysthenes, has circumnavigated the continent of Europe; and the Turkish capital has been threatened by a squadron of strong and lofty ships of war, each of which, with its naval science and thundering artillery, could have sunk or scattered an hundred canoes, such as those of their ancestors. Perhaps the present generation may yet behold the accomplishment of the prediction, of a rare prediction, of which the style is unambiguous and the date unquestionable.

By land the Russians were less formidable than by sea; and, as they fought for the most part on foot, their irregular legions must often have been broken and overthrown by the cavalry of the Scythian hordes. Yet their growing towns, however slight and imperfect, presented a shelter to the subject and a barrier to the enemy: the monarchy of Kiow, till a fatal partition, assumed the dominion of the North; and the nations from the Volga to the Danube were subdued or repelled by the arms of Swatoslaus, [82] the son of Igor, the son of Oleg, the son of Ruric.

Reign of Swatoslaus. A.D. 955-970

[Sviatoslav. A.D. 945-972]

---

[80] Nestor, apud Levesque, Hist. de Russie, tom. i. p. 87. [This advice was given by his counsellors to Igor in A.D. 944. See Nestor, c. 27; p. 25, ed. Miklosich.]

[81] This brazen statue, which had been brought from Antioch, and was melted down by the Latins, was supposed to represent either Joshua or Bellerophon, an odd dilemma. See Nicetas Choniates (p. 413, 414 [p. 848, ed. Bonn]), Codinus (de Originibus [*leg.* de Signis] C. P. p. 24 [p. 43, ed. B.]), and the anonymous writer de Antiquitat. C. P. (Banduri, Imp. Orient. tom. i. p. 17, 18) who lived about the year 1100. They witness the belief of the prophecy; the rest is immaterial. [The prophecy is not mentioned in the passage of Nicetas; and "Codinus" is merely a copyist of the anonymous Πάτρια τῆς Κωνσταντινουπόλεως edited by G. Banduri (see Appendix 1). Therefore (as Smith rightly pointed out in his annotation to this note) there is only one witness.]

[82] The life of Swatoslaus, or Sviateslaf, or Sphendosthlabus [the form in Greek writers], is extracted from the Russian Chronicles by M. Levesque (Hist. de Russie, tom. i. p. 94-107). [Nestor, c. 32-36. Sviatoslav was born in A.D. 942 (cp. Nestor, c. 27); his independent reign began about A.D. 965, in which year he made an expedition against the Khazars (*ib.* 32).]

The vigour of his mind and body was fortified by the hardships of a military and savage life. Wrapt in a bear-skin Swatoslaus usually slept on the ground, his head reclining on a saddle; his diet was coarse and frugal, and, like the heroes of Homer,[83] his meat (it was often horse-flesh) was broiled or roasted on the coals. The exercise of war gave stability and discipline to his army; and it may be presumed that no soldier was permitted to transcend the luxury of his chief. By an embassy from Nicephorus, the Greek emperor, he was moved to undertake the conquest of Bulgaria, and a gift of fifteen hundred pounds of gold was laid at his feet to defray the expense, or reward the toils, of the expedition.[84] An army of sixty thousand men was assembled and embarked; they sailed from the Borysthenes to the Danube; their landing was effected on the Mæsian shore; and, after a sharp encounter, the swords of the Russians prevailed against the arrows of the Bulgarian horse. The vanquished king sunk into the grave; his children were made captive;[85] and

[A.D. 967]

[Circa £67,000]

[Jan. 30, A.D. 969]

[83] This resemblance may be clearly seen in the ninth book of the Iliad (205-221), in the minute detail of the cookery of Achilles. By such a picture a modern epic poet would disgrace his work and disgust his reader; but the Greek verses are harmonious; a dead language can seldom appear low or familiar; and at the distance of two thousand seven hundred years we are amused with the primitive manners of antiquity.

[84] [The Bulgarian Tsar Peter, successor of Simeon, made a treaty with the Empire in A.D.927. He stipulated to prevent the Hungarians from invading the Empire, and in return he was to receive an annual subsidy; and the contract was sealed by his marriage with the granddaughter of Romanus. Peter, a feeble prince, wished to preserve the treaty, but he was not able to prevent some Magyar invasions (A.D. 959, 962, 967); and the strong and victorious Nicephorus refused to pay the subsidies any longer. He saw that the time had come to reassert the power of the Empire against Bulgaria. He advanced against Peter in 967 (this is the right date; others place it in 966), but unaccountably retreated without accomplishing anything. He then sent Calocyres to Kiev to instigate Sviatoslav against Bulgaria. The envoy was a traitor, and conceived the idea of making Sviatoslav's conquest of Bulgaria a means of ascending himself the throne of Constantinople. Sviatoslav conquered the north of Bulgaria in the same year (Nestor, c. 32), and established his residence at Peristhlava (near Tulcea, on south arm of the Danube delta; to be distinguished from Great Peristhlava, see below, note 90). Drster (Silistria) alone held out against the Russians. Sviatoslav wintered at Peristhlava, but was obliged to return to Russia in the following year (968) to deliver Kiev, which was besieged by the Patzinaks (Nestor, c. 33). A few months later his mother Olga died (ib. c. 34), and then Sviatoslav returned to Bulgaria, which he purposed to make the centre of his dominions. Leo Diaconus (v. c. 2, 3; p. 77-79) and the Greek writers do not distinguish the first and second Russian invasions of Sviatoslav; hence the narrative of Gibbon is confused. For these events see Jireček, Gesch. der Bulgaren, p. 186-7; Hilferding, Gesch. der Bulgaren, i. 126; and (very fully told in) Schlumberger, Nicéphore Phocas, c. xii. and c. xv.]

[85] [Before Peter's death, in Jan. A.D. 969, Nicephorus, aware of the treachery of his ambassador Calocyres who had remained with Sviatoslav, and afraid of the ambition of the Russian prince, changed his policy; and, though he had called Russia in to

his dominions as far as mount Hæmus, were subdued or ravaged by the northern invaders. But, instead of relinquishing his prey and performing his engagements, the Varangian prince was more disposed to advance than to retire ; and, had his ambition been crowned with success, the seat of empire in that early period might have been transferred to a more temperate and fruitful climate. Swatoslaus enjoyed and acknowledged the advantages of his new position, in which he could unite, by exchange or rapine, the various productions of the earth. By an easy navigation he might draw from Russia the native commodities of furs, wax, and hydromel ; Hungary supplied him with a breed of horses and the spoils of the West ; and Greece abounded with gold, silver, and the foreign luxuries which his poverty had affected to disdain. The bands of Patzinacites, Chozars, and Turks repaired to the standard of victory ; and the ambassador [Calocyros] of Nicephorus betrayed his trust, assumed the purple, and promised to share with his new allies the treasures of the Eastern world. From the banks of the Danube the Russian prince pursued his march as far as Hadrianople ; a formal summons to evacuate the Roman province was dismissed with contempt ; and Swatoslaus fiercely replied that Constantine might soon expect the presence of an enemy and a master.

Nicephorus could no longer expel the mischief which he had introduced ; [86] but his throne and wife were inherited by John

subdue Bulgaria, he now formed a treaty with Bulgaria to keep Russia out. The basis of this treaty (Leo Diac. p. 7-9) was a contract of marriage between the two young Emperors, Basil and Constantine, and two Bulgarian princesses. Then the death of Peter supervened. David the son of Shishman the Tsar of western Bulgaria (cp. above, p. 136, note 22) made an attempt to seize eastern Bulgaria, but was anticipated by Peter's young son, Boris. Then Sviatoslav returned to Bulgaria (see last note). During his absence Little Peristhlava seems to have been regained by the Bulgarians and he had to recapture it. Then he went south and took Great Peristhlava ; and captured Boris and his brother Romanus, A.D. 969.]

[86] [Nicephorus was assassinated Dec. 10, A.D. 969. Lines of his admirer John Geometres, bishop of Melitene, written soon after his death, attest the apprehensions of the people of Constantinople at the threatening Russian invasions. "Rise up," he cries to the dead sovereign, "gather thine army ; for the Russian host is speeding against us ; the Scythians are throbbing for carnage," &c. The piece is quoted by Scylitzes (Cedrenus, ii. p. 378, ed. Bonn) and is printed in Hase's ed. of Leo Diac. (p. 453, ed. B.). Evidently these verses were written just after the capture of Philippopolis by the Russians, and the horrible massacre of the inhabitants, in early spring A.D. 970, when the Russian plunderers were already approaching the neighbourhood of the capital. John Tzimisces, before he took the field, sent two embassies to Sviatoslav, commanding him to leave not only the Imperial provinces but Bulgaria (cp. Lambin in the Mémoires de l'Acad. de St. Petersburg, 1876, p. 119 sqq.). In preparing for his campaign, Tzimisces formed a new regiment of chosen soldiers, which he called the *Immortals* (Leo Diac. p. 107). For the Russian wars of Tzimisces see Schlumberger, L'épopée Byzantine, chaps i., ii., iii. ; and Bielov's study (cited below, note 88).]

His defeat by
JohnZimisces.
A.D. 970-973

[A.D. 972]

Zimisces,[87] who, in a diminutive body, possessed the spirit and abilities of an hero. The first victory of his lieutenants deprived the Russians of their foreign allies, twenty thousand of whom were either destroyed by the sword or provoked to revolt or tempted to desert.[88] Thrace was delivered, but seventy thousand barbarians were still in arms; and the legions that had been recalled from the new conquests of Syria prepared, with the return of the spring, to march under the banners of a warlike prince, who declared himself the friend and avenger of the injured Bulgaria. The passes of mount Hæmus had been left unguarded; they were instantly occupied; the Roman vanguard was formed of the *immortals* (a proud imitation of the Persian style); the emperor led the main body of ten thousand five hundred foot;[89] and the rest of his forces followed in slow and cautious array with the baggage and military engines. The first exploit of Zimisces was the reduction of Marcianopolis, or Peristhlaba,[90] in two days: the trumpets sounded; the walls were scaled; eight thousand five hundred Russians were put to the sword;[91] and

---

[87] This singular epithet is derived from the Armenian language, and Τζιμισκῆς is interpreted in Greek by μουζακίτζης, or μοιρακίτζης. As I profess myself equally ignorant of *these* words, I may be indulged in the question in the play, "Pray which of you is the interpreter?" From the context they seem to signify *Adolescentulus* (Leo Diacon. l. iv. Ms. apud Ducange, Glossar. Græc. p. 1570 [Bk. v. c. 9, p. 92, ed Bonn]). [*Tshemshkik* would be the Armenian form. It is supposed to be derived from a phrase meaning a red boot.]

[88] [The first victory was gained by the general Bardas Sclerus in the plains near Arcadiopolis; it saved Constantinople. M. Bielov in a study of this war (Zhurnal Min. vol. 170, 1876, p. 168 *sqq.*) tried to show that the Russians were victorious, but (as M. Schlumberger rightly thinks) he is unsuccessful in proving this thesis.]

[89] [For the date (A.D. 972) of this splendid expedition of Tzimisces cp. Schlumberger, *op. cit.* p. 82. Nestor places it in A.D. 971 (c. 36).]

[90] In the Sclavonic tongue, the name of Peristhlaba implied the great or illustrious city, μεγάλη καὶ οὖσα καὶ λεγομένη, says Anna Comnena (Alexiad, l. vii. p. 194 [c. 3]). From its position between mount Hæmus and the lower Danube, it appears to fill the ground, or at least the station, of Marcianopolis. The situation of Durostolus, or Dristra, is well known and conspicuous (Comment. Academ. Petropol. tom. ix. p. 415, 416; D'Anville, Geographie Ancienne, tom. i. p. 307, 311). [Great Peristhlava was situated at Eski Stambul, 22 kilometres south of Shumla. Marcianopolis was much farther east; some of its ruins have been traced near the modern village of Dievna (about 30 kils. west of Varna as the crow flies). Tzimisces called Peristhlava after himself Joannopolis, but the city rapidly decayed after this period. He called Drster Theodoropolis, in honour of St. Theodore the Megalomartyr, who was supposed to have fought in the Roman ranks in the last great fight at Drster on July 23. Thereby hangs a problem. The Greek writers say that the day of the battle was the feast of St. Theodore; but his feast falls on June 8. Cp. Muralt, Essai de Chron. byz. ad ann.]

[91] [The Greek sources for the capture of Peristhlava (and for the whole campaign) are Leo the Deacon and Scylitzes. The numbers (given by Scylitzes) are very doubtful.]

the sons of the Bulgarian king were rescued from an ignominious prison, and invested with a nominal diadem. After these repeated losses, Swatoslaus retired to the strong post of Dristra, on the banks of the Danube, and was pursued by an enemy who alternately employed the arms of celerity and delay. The Byzantine galleys ascended the river; the legions completed a line of circumvallation; [92] and the Russian prince was encompassed, assaulted, and famished, in the fortifications of the camp and city. Many deeds of valour were performed; several desperate sallies were attempted; nor was it till after a siege of sixty-five days that Swatoslaus yielded to his adverse fortune. The liberal terms which he obtained announce the prudence of the victor, who respected the valour, and apprehended the despair, of an unconquered mind. The great duke of Russia bound himself by solemn imprecations to relinquish all hostile designs; a safe passage was opened for his return; the liberty of trade and navigation was restored; a measure of corn was distributed to each of his soldiers; and the allowance of twenty-two thousand measures attests the loss and the remnant of the barbarians. [93] After a painful voyage, they again reached the mouth of the Borysthenes; but their provisions were exhausted; the season was unfavourable; they passed the winter on the ice; and, before they could prosecute their march, Swatoslaus was surprised and oppressed by the neighbouring tribes, with whom the Greeks entertained a perpetual and useful correspondence. [94] Far different was the return of Zimisces, who was received in his capital like Camillus or Marius, the saviours of ancient Rome. But the merit of the victory was attributed by the pious emperor to the Mother of God; and the image of the Virgin Mary, with the divine infant in her arms, was placed on a triumphal car, adorned with the spoils of war and the ensigns of Bulgarian royalty. Zimisces made his public entry on horseback; the diadem on his head, a crown of laurel in his hand; and Constantinople was astonished to applaud the martial virtues of her sovereign. [95]

[Siege of Drster begins April 25]

[July 25]

[92] [A battle was fought outside Silistria and the Russians discomfited, in April 23, before the siege began.]

[93] [For the treaty see above, p. 153, note 7.]

[94] The political management of the Greeks, more especially with the Patzinacites, is explained in the seven first chapters de Administratione Imperii.

[95] In the narrative of this war, Leo the Deacon (apud Pagi, Critica, tom. iv. A.D. 968-973 [Bk. vi. c. 3-13]) is more authentic and circumstantial than Cedrenus (tom. ii. p. 660-683) and Zonaras (tom. ii. p. 205-214 [xvi. 27-xvii. 3]). These declaimers have multiplied to 308,000 and 330,000 men those Russian forces of which the contemporary had given a moderate and consistent account.

# THE DECLINE AND FALL

Photius of Constantinople, a patriarch whose ambition was equal to his curiosity, congratulates himself and the Greek church on the conversion of the Russians.[96] Those fierce and bloody barbarians had been persuaded by the voice of reason and religion, to acknowledge Jesus for their God, the Christian missionaries for their teachers, and the Romans for their friends and brethren. His triumph was transient and premature. In the various fortune of their piratical adventures, some Russian chiefs might allow themselves to be sprinkled with the waters of baptism; and a Greek bishop, with the name of metropolitan, might administer the sacraments in the church of Kiow to a congregation of slaves and natives. But the seed of the Gospel was sown on a barren soil: many were the apostates, the converts were few; and the baptism of Olga may be fixed as the æra of Russian Christianity.[97] A female, perhaps of the basest origin, who could revenge the death, and assume the sceptre, of her husband Igor, must have been endowed with those active virtues which command the fear and obedience of barbarians. In a moment of foreign and domestic peace, she sailed from Kiow to Constantinople; and the emperor Constantine Porphyrogenitus has described with minute diligence the ceremonial of her reception in his capital and palace. The steps, the titles, the salutations, the banquet, the presents, were exquisitely adjusted, to gratify the vanity of the stranger, with due reverence to the superior majesty of the purple.[98] In the sacrament of baptism, she received the venerable name of the empress Helena; and her conversion might be preceded or followed by her uncle, two interpreters, sixteen damsels, of an higher, and eighteen of a lower, rank, twenty-two domestics or ministers, and forty-four Russian merchants, who composed the retinue of the great princess Olga. After her return to Kiow and Novogorod, she firmly persisted

[96] Phot. Epistol. ii. No. 35, p. 58, edit. Montacut [Ep. 4, ed. Valettas, p. 178]. It was unworthy of the learning of the editor to mistake the Russian nation, τὸ Ῥῶς, for a war-cry of the Bulgarians; nor did it become the enlightened patriarch to accuse the Sclavonian idolaters τῆς Ἑλληνικῆς καὶ ἀθέου δόξης. They were neither Greeks nor atheists.

[97] M. Levesque has extracted, from old chronicles and modern researches, the most satisfactory account of the religion of the *Slavi*, and the conversion of Russia (Hist. de Russie, tom. i. p. 35-54, 59, 92, 93, 113-121, 124-129, 148, 149, &c.). [Nestor, c. 31.]

[98] See the Ceremoniale Aulæ Byzant. tom. ii. c. 15, p. 343-345: the style of Olga, or Elga [Old Norse, *Helga*], is Ἀρχόντισσα Ῥωσίας. For the chief of barbarians the Greeks whimsically borrowed the title of an Athenian magistrate, with a female termination which would have astonished the ear of Demosthenes. [In the account of the Ceremony of Olga's reception her baptism is not mentioned; it was indeed irrelevant.]

in her new religion ; but her labours in the propagation of the
Gospel were not crowned with success ; and both her family
and nation adhered with obstinacy or indifference to the gods
of their fathers. Her son Swatoslaus was apprehensive of
the scorn and ridicule of his companions ; and her grandson
Wolodomir devoted his youthful zeal to multiply and decorate
the monuments of ancient worship. The savage deities of the
North were still propitiated with human sacrifices : in the choice
of the victim, a citizen was preferred to a stranger, a Christian
to an idolater ; and the father who defended his son from the
sacerdotal knife was involved in the same doom by the rage of
a fanatic tumult. Yet the lessons and example of the pious
Olga had made a deep though secret impression on the minds
of the prince and people : the Greek missionaries continued to
preach, to dispute, and to baptize ; and the ambassadors or
merchants of Russia compared the idolatry of the woods with
the elegant superstition of Constantinople. They had gazed
with admiration on the dome of St. Sophia : the lively pictures
of saints and martyrs, the riches of the altar, the number and
vestments of the priests, the pomp and order of the ceremonies ;
they were edified by the alternate succession of devout silence
and harmonious song ; nor was it difficult to persuade them that
a choir of angels descended each day from heaven to join in the
devotion of the Christians.[99]  But the conversion of Wolodomir <sub>Of Wolodomir.</sub>
was determined, or hastened, by his desire of a Roman bride.   At A.D. 988 [989]
the same time, and in the city of Cherson, the rites of baptism and
marriage were celebrated by the Christian pontiff ; the city he
restored to the emperor Basil, the brother of his spouse ; but the
brazen gates were transported, as it is said, to Novogorod, and
erected before the first church as a trophy of his victory and
faith.[100]   At his despotic command, Peroun, the god of thunder,

[99] See an anonymous fragment published by Banduri (Imperium Orientale, tom.
ii. p. 112, 113), de Conversione Russorum.  [Reprinted in vol. iii. of Bonn ed. of
Constantine Porph. p. 357 *sqq.* ; but since published in a fuller form from a
Patmos Ms. by W. Regel in Analecta Byzantino-Russica, p. 44 *sqq.* (1891).  But
the narrative is a later compilation and mixes up together (Regel, *op. cit.* p. xxi.)
the story of the earlier conversion by Photius, and the legend of the introduction
of the Slavonic alphabet by Cyril and Methodius.]

[100] Cherson, or Corsun, is mentioned by Herberstein (apud Pagi, tom. iv. p.
56) as the place of Wolodomir's baptism and marriage ; and both the tradition and
the gates are still preserved at Novogorod.  Yet an observing traveller transports
the brazen gates from Magdeburg in Germany (Coxe's Travels into Russia, &c.
vol. i. p. 452), and quotes an inscription, which seems to justify his opinion.  The
modern reader must not confound this old Cherson of the Tauric or Crimæan
peninsula [situated on the southern shore of the bay of Sebastopol] with a new city

whom he had so long adored, was dragged through the streets of Kiow ; and twelve sturdy barbarians battered with clubs the misshapen image, which was indignantly cast into the waters of the Borysthenes.   The edict of Wolodomir had proclaimed that all who should refuse the rites of baptism would be treated as the enemies of God and their prince ; and the rivers were instantly filled with many thousands of obedient Russians, who acquiesced in the truth and excellence of a doctrine which had been embraced by the great duke and his boyars.[101]   In the next generation the relics of paganism were finally extirpated ; but, as the two brothers of Wolodomir had died without baptism, their bones were taken from the grave and sanctified by an irregular and posthumous sacrament.

Christianity of the North.
A.D. 800-1100

In the ninth, tenth, and eleventh centuries of the Christian æra, the reign of the gospel and of the church was extended over Bulgaria, Hungary, Bohemia, Saxony, Denmark, Norway, Sweden, Poland, and Russia.[102]   The triumphs of apostolic zeal were repeated in the iron age of Christianity ; and the northern and eastern regions of Europe submitted to a religion more different in theory than in practice from the worship of their native idols.   A laudable ambition excited the monks, both of Germany and Greece, to visit the tents and huts of the barbarians ; poverty, hardships, and dangers, were the lot of the first missionaries ; their courage was active and patient ; their motive pure and meritorious ; their present reward consisted in

of the same name, which had arisen near the mouth of the Borysthenes, and was lately honoured by the memorable interview of the empress of Russia with the emperor of the West.   [Till recently, the date of the marriage and conversion of Vladimir was supposed to be A.D. 988.   The authority is the Russian chronicle of " Nestor," which contains the fullest (partly legendary) account (c. 42).   Vladimir captured Cherson, and sent an embassy, demanding the hand of the princess Anne, and threatening to attack Constantinople if it were refused.   Vasilievski showed (in a paper in the Zhurnal Min., 184 (1876), p. 156) from the notice in Leo Diaconus (p. 175, ed. Bonn), and the Baron von Rosen (in his book of extracts from the annals of Yahia (1883), note 169), that Cherson was captured in A.D. 989 (c. June) ; and it follows that the marriage and conversion cannot have been celebrated before the autumn of 989.   The fragment which is sometimes called " Notes of the Greek toparch of Gothia," which was published by Hase (notes to Leo Diaconus, p. 496 sqq. ed. Bonn), does not belong to this period nor concern the neighbourhood of Cherson ; but probably refers to events which happened on the lower Don in the early part of the 10th century.   This explanation has been proposed by Th. Uspenski in the Kievskaia Starina of 1889 (see Schlumberger, L'épopée Byzantine, p. 767, note).]

101 [The adoption of Christianity in Russia was facilitated by the fact that there was no sacerdotal caste to oppose it.   This point is insisted on by Kostomarov, Russische Geschichte in Biographien, i. 5.]

102 Consult the Latin text, or English version, of Mosheim's excellent History of the Church, under the first head or section of each of these centuries.

the testimony of their conscience and the respect of a grateful people ; but the fruitful harvest of their toils was inherited and enjoyed by the proud and wealthy prelates of succeeding times. The first conversions were free and spontaneous : an holy life and an eloquent tongue were the only arms of the missionaries ; but the domestic fables of the pagans were silenced by the miracles and visions of the strangers ; and the favourable temper of the chiefs was accelerated by the dictates of vanity and interest. The leaders of nations, who were saluted with the titles of kings and saints,[103] held it lawful and pious to impose the Catholic faith on their subjects and neighbours : the coast of the Baltic, from Holstein to the gulf of Finland, was invaded under the standard of the cross ; and the reign of idolatry was closed by the conversion of Lithuania in the fourteenth century. Yet truth and candour must acknowledge that the conversion of the North imparted many temporal benefits both to the old and the new Christians. The rage of war, inherent to the human species, could not be healed by the evangelic precepts of charity and peace ; and the ambition of Catholic princes has renewed in every age the calamities of hostile contention. But the admission of the barbarians into the pale of civil and ecclesiastical society delivered Europe from the depredations, by sea and land, of the Normans, the Hungarians, and the Russians, who learned to spare their brethren and cultivate their possessions.[104] The establishment of law and order was promoted by the influence of the clergy ; and the rudiments of art and science were introduced into the savage countries of the globe. The liberal piety of the Russian princes engaged in their service the most skilful of the Greeks, to decorate the cities and instruct the inhabitants ; the dome and the paintings of St. Sophia were rudely copied in the churches of Kiow [105] and Novogorod ; the writ-

[103] In the year 1000, the ambassadors of St. Stephen received from pope Sylvester the title of King of Hungary, with a diadem of Greek workmanship. It had been designed for the duke of Poland ; but the Poles, by their own confession, were yet too barbarous to deserve an *angelical* and *apostolical* crown (Katona, Hist. Critic. Regum Stirpis Arpadianæ, tom. i. p. 1-20).

[104] Listen to the exultations of Adam of Bremen (A.D. 1080), of which the substance is agreeable to truth : Ecce illa ferocissima Danorum, &c. natio . . . jamdudum novit in Dei laudibus Alleluia resonare . . . Ecce populus ille piraticus . . . suis nunc finibus contentus est. Ecce patria [illa] horribilis semper inaccessa propter cultum idolorum . . . prædicatores veritatis ubique certatim admittit, &c. &c. (de Situ Daniæ, &c. p. 40, 41, edit. Elzevir [c. 42] : a curious and original prospect of the north of Europe, and the introduction of Christianity).

[105] [The great monument of Yaroslav's reign is the church of St. Sophia at Kiev, built by Greek masons. A smaller church, also dedicated to the Holy Wisdom,

ings of the fathers were translated into the Sclavonic idiom ; and
three hundred noble youths were invited or compelled to attend
the lessons of the college of Jaroslaus.[106]  It should appear that
Russia might have derived an early and rapid improvement from
her peculiar connection with the church and state of Constantinople [107] which in that age so justly despised the ignorance of
the Latins.  But the Byzantine nation was servile, solitary, and
verging to an hasty decline ; after the fall of Kiow, the navigation of the Borysthenes was forgotten ; the great princes of
Wolodomir and Moscow were separated from the sea and
Christendom ; and the divided monarchy was oppressed by the
ignominy and blindness of Tartar servitude.[108]  The Sclavonic and
Scandinavian kingdoms, which had been converted by the Latin
missionaries, were exposed, it is true, to the spiritual jurisdiction
and temporal claims of the popes ; [109] but they were united, in
language and religious worship, with each other, and with Rome ;
they imbibed the free and generous spirit of the European republic, and gradually shared the light of knowledge which arose
on the western world.

was built at Novgorod on the pattern of the Kiev church by his son Vladimir in
1045.]

[106] [For Yaroslav's taste for books, see Nestor, c. 55.]

[107] [It is important to notice the growth of monasticism in Russia in the 11th
century.  The original hearth and centre of the movement was at Kiev in the
Pestcherski or Crypt Monastery, famous for the Saint Theodosius [ob. 1074] whose
biography was written by Nestor.  Kostomarov (*op. cit.* p. 18 *sqq.*) has a readable
chapter on the subject.]

[108] The great princes removed in 1156 from Kiow, which was ruined by the
Tartars in 1240.  Moscow became the seat of empire in the xivth century.
See the first and second volumes of Levesque's History, and Mr. Coxe's Travels
into the North, tom. i. p. 241, &c.

[109] The ambassadors of St. Stephen had used the reverential expressions of
*regnum oblatum, debitam obedientiam*, &c. which were most rigorously interpreted
by Gregory VII. ; and the Hungarian Catholics are distressed between the sanctity
of the pope and the independence of the crown (Katona, Hist. Critica, tom. i. p.
20-25, tom. ii. p. 304, 346, 360, &c.).

CHAPTER LVI

*The Saracens, Franks, and Greeks, in Italy—First Adventures and
Settlement of the Normans—Character and Conquests of Robert
Guiscard, Duke of Apulia—Deliverance of Sicily by his Brother
Roger—Victories of Robert over the Emperors of the East and
West—Roger, king of Sicily, invades Africa and Greece—The
Emperor Manuel Comnenus—Wars of the Greeks and Normans
—Extinction of the Normans*

THE three great nations of the world, the Greeks, the Saracens, Conflict of the
and the Franks, encountered each other on the theatre of Italy.[1] Latins, and
The southern provinces, which now compose the kingdom of Greeks, in
Naples, were subject, for the most part, to the Lombard dukes 840-1017
and princes of Beneventum :[2] so powerful in war that they
checked for a moment the genius of Charlemagne ; so liberal in
peace that they maintained in their capital an academy of thirty-
two philosophers and grammarians.    The division of this flourishing state produced the rival principalities of Benevento, Salerno,
and Capua ;[3] and the thoughtless ambition or revenge of the

[1] For the general history of Italy in the ixth and xth centuries, I may properly
refer to the vth, vith, and viith books of Sigonius de Regno Italiæ (in the
second volume of his works, Milan, 1732) ; the Annals of Baronius, with the
Criticism of Pagi ; the viith and viiith books of the Istoria Civile del Regno di
Napoli of Giannone ; the viith and viiith volumes (the octavo edition) of the
Annali d'Italia of Muratori, and the iid volume of the Abrégé Chronologique
of M. de St. Marc, a work which, under a superficial title, contains much genuine
learning and industry.  But my long accustomed reader will give me credit for
saying that I myself have ascended to the fountain-head, as often as such ascent
could be either profitable or possible ; and that I have diligently turned over the
originals in the first volumes of Muratori's great collection of the *Scriptores Rerum
Italicarum.*

[2] Camillo Pellegrino, a learned Capuan of the last century, has illustrated the
history of the duchy of Beneventum, in his two books, Historia Principum Longo-
bardorum, in the Scriptores of Muratori, tom. ii. pars i. p. 221-345, and tom. v.
p. 159-245.

[3] [The duchy of Beneventum first split up into two parts, an eastern and a
western—the western under the name of the Principality of Salerno.  Soon after this
the Count of Capua threw off his allegiance to the Prince of Salerno ; so that the

competitors invited the Saracens to the ruin of their common
inheritance.   During a calamitous period of two hundred years
Italy was exposed to a repetition of wounds, which the invaders
were not capable of healing by the union and tranquillity of a
perfect conquest.   Their frequent and almost annual squadrons
issued from the port of Palermo, and were entertained with too
much indulgence by the Christians of Naples ; the more formidable fleets were prepared on the African coast ; and even the
Arabs of Andalusia were sometimes tempted to assist or oppose
the Moslems of an adverse sect.   In the revolution of human
events, a new ambuscade was concealed in the Caudine forks,
the fields of Cannæ were bedewed a second time with the blood
of the Africans, and the sovereign of Rome again attacked or
defended the walls of Capua and Tarentum.   A colony of
Saracens had been planted at Bari, which commands the entrance of the Adriatic Gulf; and their impartial depredations
provoked the resentment, and conciliated the union, of the two
emperors.   An offensive alliance was concluded between Basil
the Macedonian, the first of his race, and Lewis, the great-
grandson of Charlemagne ;[4] and each party supplied the defi-
ciencies of his associate.   It would have been imprudent in the
Byzantine monarch to transport his stationary troops of Asia to
an Italian campaign ; and the Latin arms would have been
insufficient, if *his* superior navy had not occupied the mouth of
the Gulf.   The fortress of Bari was invested by the infantry of
the Franks, and by the cavalry and galleys of the Greeks ; and,
after a defence of four years, the Arabian emir submitted to the
clemency of Lewis, who commanded in person the operations of
the siege.   This important conquest had been achieved by the
concord of the East and West ; but their recent amity was soon
embittered by the mutual complaints of jealousy and pride.
The Greeks assumed as their own the merit of the conquest
and the pomp of the triumph ; extolled the greatness of their
powers, and affected to deride the intemperance and sloth of
the handful of barbarians who appeared under the banners of
the Carlovingian prince.   His reply is expressed with the eloquence of indignation and truth : " We confess the magnitude
of your preparations," says the great-grandson of Charlemagne.

*Conquest of
Bari.  A.D. 871*

old duchy of Beneventum was represented by three independent states.   For the
history of Salerno see Schipa, Storia del principato Longobardo in Salerno, in the
Arch. storico per le cose prov. Nap., 12 (1887).]

[4] See Constantin. Porphyrogen. de Thematibus, l. ii. c. xi. in Vit. Basil. c. 55,
p. 181.

"Your armies were indeed as numerous as a cloud of summer locusts, who darken the day, flap their wings, and, after a short flight, tumble weary and breathless to the ground. Like them, ye sunk after a feeble effort; ye were vanquished by your own cowardice; and withdrew from the scene of action to injure and despoil our Christian subjects of the Sclavonian coast. We were few in number, and why were we few? Because, after a tedious expectation of your arrival, I had dismissed my host, and retained only a chosen band of warriors to continue the blockade of the city. If they indulged their hospitable feasts in the face of danger and death, did these feasts abate the vigour of their enterprise? Is it by your fasting that the walls of Bari have been overturned? Did not these valiant Franks, diminished as they were by languor and fatigue, intercept and vanquish the three most powerful emirs of the Saracens? and did not their defeat precipitate the fall of the city? Bari is now fallen; Tarentum trembles; Calabria will be delivered; and, if we command the sea, the island of Sicily may be rescued from the hands of the infidels. My brother (a name most offensive to the vanity of the Greek), accelerate your naval succours, respect your allies, and distrust your flatterers." [5]

These lofty hopes were soon extinguished by the death of Lewis, and the decay of the Carlovingian house; and, whoever might deserve the honour, the Greek emperors, Basil and his son Leo, secured the advantage, of the reduction of Bari. The Italians of Apulia and Calabria were persuaded or compelled to acknowledge their supremacy, and an ideal line from mount Garganus to the bay of Salerno leaves the far greater part of the kingdom of Naples under the dominion of the eastern empire. Beyond that line, the dukes or republics of Amalphi [6] and Naples, who had never forfeited their voluntary allegiance, rejoiced in the neighbourhood of their lawful sovereign; and Amalphi was enriched by supplying Europe with the produce and manufactures of Asia. But the Lombard princes of Benevento, Salerno, and Capua [7] were reluctantly torn from the communion of the Latin

New province of the Greeks in Italy. A.D. 890

[Bari won by the Greeks. A.D. 876]

---

[5] The original epistle of the emperor Lewis II. to the emperor Basil, a curious record of the age, was first published by Baronius (Annal. Eccles. A.D. 871, No. 51-71) from the Vatican Ms. of Erchempert, or rather of the anonymous historian of Salerno. [Printed also in Duchesne, Hist. Fr. scr. iii. p. 555.]

[6] See an excellent dissertation de Republicâ Amalphitanâ in the Appendix (p. 1-42) of Henry Brenckmann's Historia Pandectarum (Trajecti ad Rhenum, 1722, in 40). [Materials for the history of Naples are collected in Capasso's Monumenta ad Neap. duc. histor. pertinentia, vol. i. 1881; vol. ii. 1, 1885, 2, 1892.]

[7] Your master, says Nicephorus, has given aid and protection principibus

world, and too often violated their oaths of servitude and tribute. The city of Bari rose to dignity and wealth, as the metropolis of the new theme or province of Lombardy; the title of patrician, and afterwards the singular name of *Catapan*,[8] was assigned to the supreme governor; and the policy both of the church and state was modelled in exact subordination to the throne of Constantinople. As long as the sceptre was disputed by the princes of Italy, their efforts were feeble and adverse; and the Greeks resisted or eluded the forces of Germany, which descended from the Alps under the Imperial standard of the Othos. The first and greatest of those Saxon princes was compelled to relinquish the siege of Bari: the second, after the loss of his stoutest bishops and barons, escaped with honour from the bloody field of Crotona. On that day the scale of war was turned against the Franks by the valour of the Saracens.[9] These corsairs had indeed been driven by the

[Theme of Lagubardia]

Defeat of Otho III. [II.] A.D. 983 [982]

Capuano et Beneventano, servis meis, quos oppugnare dispono . . . Nova (potius *nota*) res est quod eorum patres et avi nostro Imperio tributa dederunt (Liutprand, in Legat. p. 484). Salerno is not mentioned, yet the prince changed his party about the same time, and Camillo Pellegrino (Script. Rer. Ital. tom. ii. pars i. p. 285) has nicely discerned this change in the style of the anonymous chronicle. Or the rational ground of history and language, Liutprand (p. 480) had asserted the Latin claim to Apulia and Calabria. [The revival of East-Roman influence in Southern Italy in the last years of the ninth century is illustrated by the fact that an Imperial officer (of the rank of protospathar) resided at the court of the Dukes of Beneventum from A.D. 891. The allegiance of Naples, Amalfi, and Gaeta was indeed little more than nominal. For the history of Gaeta the chief source is the Codex Caietanus, published in the Tabularium Casinense (1890, 1892).]

[8] See the Greek and Latin Glossaries of Ducange (Κατεπάνω, *catapanus*), and his notes on the Alexias (p. 275). Against the contemporary notion, which derive it from Κατὰ πᾶν, *juxta omne*, he treats it as a corruption of the Latin *capitaneus* Yet M. de St. Marc has accurately observed (Abrégé Chronologique, tom. ii. p. 924) that in this age the capitanei were not *captains*, but only nobles of the firs rank, the great valvassors of Italy. [The Theme of Italy extended from the Ofante in the north and the Bradano in the west to the southern point of Apulia, and in cluded the south of Calabria (the old Bruttii). It must not be confounded with the Capitanata. It was probably about the year 1000 that the governors of the Theme of Italy conquered the land on the north side of their province, betwee the Ofanto and Fortore (see Heinemann, Gesch. der Normannen in Unter-Italie und Sicilien, i. p. 20). From the title of the governors, Katepanô, this conques was called the Catepanata, and this became (through the influence of popula etymology) Capitanata.]

[9] Οὐ μόνον διὰ πολέμων ἀκριβῶς ἐκτεταγμένων τὸ τοιοῦτον ὑπήγαγε τὸ ἔθνος (the Lom bards), ἀλλὰ καὶ ἀγχινοίᾳ χρησάμενος καὶ δικαιοσύνῃ καὶ χρηστότητι, ἐπιεικῶς τε τοῖ προσερχομένοις προσφερόμενος, καὶ τὴν ἐλευθερίαν αὐτοῖς πάσης τε δουλείας καὶ τῶν ἄλλω φορολογιῶν χαριζόμενος (Leon. Tactic. c. xv. p. 741). The little Chronicle of Bene ventum (tom. ii. pars i. p. 280) gives a far different character of the Greeks durin the five years (A.D. 891-896) that Leo was master of the city. [For good accoun of the expedition and defeat of Otto II. see Giesebrecht, Gesch. der deutsche Kaiserzeit, i. p. 595 *sqq.*, and Schlumberger, L'épopée byzantine, p. 502 *sqq.* Th battle was fought in July 982, near Stilo, south of Croton.]

Byzantine fleets from the fortresses and coasts of Italy; but a sense of interest was more prevalent than superstition or resentment, and the caliph of Egypt had transported forty thousand Moslems to the aid of his Christian ally. The successors of Basil amused themselves with the belief that the conquest of Lombardy had been achieved, and was still preserved, by the justice of their laws, the virtues of their ministers, and the gratitude of a people whom they had rescued from anarchy and oppression. A series of rebellions might dart a ray of truth into the palace of Constantinople; and the illusions of flattery were dispelled by the easy and rapid success of the Norman adventurers.

The revolution of human affairs had produced in Apulia and Calabria a melancholy contrast between the age of Pythagoras and the tenth century of the Christian æra. At the former period, the coast of Great Greece (as it was then styled) was planted with free and opulent cities: these cities were peopled with soldiers, artists and philosophers; and the military strength of Tarentum, Sybaris, or Crotona was not inferior to that of a powerful kingdom. At the second æra, these once-flourishing provinces were clouded with ignorance, impoverished by tyranny, and depopulated by barbarian war; nor can we severely accuse the exaggeration of a contemporary that a fair and ample district was reduced to the same desolation which had covered the earth after the general deluge.[10] Among the hostilities of the Arabs, the Franks, and the Greeks, in the southern Italy, I shall select two or three anecdotes expressive of their national manners. 1. It was the amusement of the Saracens to profane, as well as to pillage, the monasteries and churches. At the siege of Salerno, a Musulman chief spread his couch on the communion table, and on that altar sacrificed each night the virginity of a Christian nun. As he wrestled with a reluctant maid, a beam in the roof was accidentally or dexterously thrown down on his head; and the death of the lustful emir was imputed to the wrath of Christ, which was at length awakened to the defence of his faithful spouse.[11] 2. The Saracens besieged the cities of Beneventum

*(margin note: Anecdotes)*

*(margin note: A.D. 873)*

*(margin note: A.D. 874)*

---

[10] Calabriam adeunt, eamque inter se divisam reperientes funditus depopulati unt (or depopularunt), ita ut deserta sit velut in diluvio. Such is the text of Ierempert, or Erchempert, according to the two editions of Carraccioli (Rer. Italic. Script. tom. v. p. 23), and of Camillo Pellegrino (tom. ii. p. 246). Both were extremely scarce, when they were reprinted by Muratori.

[11] Baronius (Annal. Eccles. A.D. 874, No. 2) has drawn this story from a Ms. of Erchempert who died at Capua only fifteen years after the event. But the

and Capua : after a vain appeal to the successors of Charlemagne
the Lombards implored the clemency and aid of the Greek
emperor.[12]  A fearless citizen dropped from the walls, passed
the intrenchments, accomplished his commission, and fell into
the hands of the barbarians, as he was returning with the welcome news.  They commanded him to assist their enterprise, and
deceive his countrymen, with the assurance that wealth and
honours should be the reward of his falsehood, and that his sincerity would be punished with immediate death.  He affected to yield
but, as soon as he was conducted within hearing of the Christians
on the rampart, " Friends and brethren," he cried with a loud
voice, " be bold and patient, maintain the city ; your sovereign
is informed of your distress, and your deliverers are at hand.  I
know my doom, and commit my wife and children to your
gratitude."  The rage of the Arabs confirmed his evidence ; and
the self-devoted patriot was transpierced with an hundred spears.
He deserves to live in the memory of the virtuous, but the repetition of the same story in ancient and modern times may sprinkle
A.D. 930 some doubts on the reality of this generous deed.[13]   3. The recital of the third incident may provoke a smile amidst the horrors
of war.  Theobald, marquis of Camerino and Spoleto,[14] supported
the rebels of Beneventum ; and his wanton cruelty was not incompatible in that age with the character of an hero.  His captives of the Greek nation or party were castrated without mercy,
and the outrage was aggravated by a cruel jest, that he wished
to present the emperor with a supply of eunuchs, the most

cardinal was deceived by a false title, and we can only quote the anonymous
Chronicle of Salerno (Paralipomena, c. 110), composed towards the end of the xth
century, and published in the second volume of Muratori's Collection.  See the
Dissertations of Camillo Pellegrino (tom. ii. pars i. 231-281, &c.).

[12] Constantine Porphyrogenitus (in Vit. Basil. c. 58, p. 183) is the original author
of this story.  He places it under the reigns of Basil and Lewis II. ; yet the reduction of Beneventum by the Greeks is dated A.D. 891, after the decease of both of
those princes.

[13] In the year 663, the same tragedy is described by Paul the Deacon (de Gestis
Langobard. l. v. c. 7, 8, p. 870, 871, edit. Grot), under the walls of the same city
of Beneventum.  But the actors are different, and the guilt is imputed to the Greeks
themselves, which in the Byzantine edition is applied to the Saracens.  In the late
war in Germany, M. d'Assas, a French officer of the regiment of Auvergne, is said
to have devoted himself in a similar manner.  His behaviour is the more heroic, as
mere silence was required by the enemy who had made him prisoner (Voltaire
Siècle de Louis XV. c. 33, tom. ix. p. 172).

[14] Theobald, who is styled Heros by Liutprand, was properly duke of Spoleto
and marquis of Camerino, from the year 926 to 935.  The title and office of
marquis (commander of the march or frontier) was introduced into Italy by the
French emperors (Abrégé Chronologique, tom. ii. p. 645-732, &c.).

precious ornaments of the Byzantine court. The garrison of the castle had been defeated in a sally, and the prisoners were sentenced to the customary operation. But the sacrifice was disturbed by the intrusion of a frantic female, who, with bleeding cheeks, dishevelled hair, and importunate clamours, compelled the marquis to listen to her complaint. " It is thus," she cried, " ye magnanimous heroes, that ye wage war against women, against women who have never injured ye, and whose only arms are the distaff and the loom ? " Theobald denied the charge, and protested that, since the Amazons, he had never heard of a female war. "And how," she furiously exclaimed, " can you attack us more directly, how can you wound us in a more vital part, than by robbing our husbands of what we most dearly cherish, the source of our joys, and the hope of our posterity ? The plunder of our flocks and herds I have endured without a murmur, but this fatal injury, this irreparable loss, subdues my patience, and calls aloud on the justice of heaven and earth." A general laugh applauded her eloquence ; the savage Franks, inaccessible to pity, were moved by her ridiculous, yet rational despair ; and, with the deliverance of the captives, she obtained the restitution of her effects. As she returned in triumph to the castle, she was overtaken by a messenger, to inquire, in the name of Theobald, what punishment should be inflicted on her husband, were he again taken in arms ? "Should such," she answered without hesitation, " be his guilt and misfortune, he has eyes, and a nose, and hands, and feet. These are his own, and these he may deserve to forfeit by his personal offences. But let my lord be pleased to spare what his little handmaid presumes to claim as her peculiar and lawful property." [15]

The establishment of the Normans in the kingdoms of Naples and Sicily [16] is an event most romantic in its origin, and in its consequences most important both to Italy and

*Origin of the Normans in Italy. A.D. 1016*

[15] Liutprand, Hist. l. iv. c. iv. in the Rerum Italic. Script. tom. i. pars i. p. 453, 454. Should the licentiousness of the tale be questioned, I may exclaim, with poor Sterne, that it is hard if I may not transcribe with caution what a bishop could write without scruple ! What if I had translated, ut viris certetis testiculos amputare, in quibus nostri corporis refocillatio, &c. ?

[16] The original monuments of the Normans in Italy are collected in the vth volume of Muratori, and among these we may distinguish the poem of William Apulus (p. 245-278), and the history of Galfridus (*Jeffery*) Malaterra (p. 537-607). Both were natives of France, but they wrote on the spot, in the age of the first conquerors (before A.D. 1100), and with the spirit of freemen. It is needless to recapitulate the compilers and critics of Italian history, Sigonius, Baronius, Pagi, Giannone, Muratori, St. Marc, &c. whom I have always consulted and never copied. [See Appendix 1.]

the Eastern empire.    The broken provinces of the Greeks,
Lombards, and Saracens were exposed to every invader, and
every sea and land were invaded by the adventurous spirit of
the Scandinavian pirates.    After a long indulgence of rapine
and slaughter, a fair and ample territory was accepted, occupied,
and named, by the Normans of France ; they renounced their
gods for the God of the Christians ; [17] and the dukes of Normandy acknowledged themselves the vassals of the successors of
Charlemagne and Capet.    The savage fierceness which they had
brought from the snowy mountains of Norway was refined, without being corrupted, in a warmer climate ; the companions of
Rollo insensibly mingled with the natives ; they imbibed the
manners, language,[18] and gallantry of the French nation ; and,
in a martial age, the Normans might claim the palm of valour
and glorious achievements.    Of the fashionable superstitions,
they embraced with ardour the pilgrimages of Rome, Italy, and
the Holy Land.    In this active devotion, their minds and bodies
were invigorated by exercise : danger was the incentive, novelty
the recompense ; and the prospect of the world was decorated
by wonder, credulity, and ambitious hope.    They confederated
for their mutual defence ; and the robbers of the Alps, who had
been allured by the garb of a pilgrim, were often chastised by
the arm of a warrior.    In one of these pious visits [19] to the cavern
of mount Garganus in Apulia, which had been sanctified by the
apparition of the archangel Michael,[20] they were accosted by a

[17] Some of the first converts were baptized ten or twelve times, for the sake of the
white garment usually given at this ceremony.    At the funeral of Rollo, the gifts
to monasteries, for the repose of his soul, were accompanied by a sacrifice of one
hundred captives.    But in a generation or two the national change was pure and
general.

[18] The Danish language was still spoken by the Normans of Bayeux on the sea-
coast, at a time (A.D. 940) when it was already forgotten at Rouen, in the court
and capital.    Quem (Richard I.) confestim pater Baiocas mittens Botoni militiæ
suæ principi nutriendum tradidit, ut, ubi *linguâ* eruditus *Danicâ*, suis exterisque
hominibus sciret aperte dare responsa (Wilhelm. Gemeticensis de Ducibus Nor-
mannis, l. iii. c. 8, p. 623, edit. Camden).    Of the vernacular and favourite idiom
of William the Conqueror (A.D. 1035) Selden (Opera, tom. ii. p. 1640-1656) has
given a specimen, obsolete and obscure even to antiquarians and lawyers.

[19] [In A.D. 1016 as a Saracen fleet besieged Salerno, 40 Roman knights returning
from the Holy Land disembarked in the neighbourhood, and hearing that the place
was hard pressed offered their services to Prince Waimar.    Their bravery delivered
the town, and laden with rich presents they returned to Normandy, promising to
induce their countrymen to visit the south and help in the defence of the land against
the unbelievers.    See Aimé, Ystorie de li Normant, i. c. 17 (and cp. H. Bresslau,
Heinrich, ii. 3, Excurs. 4).    Before the year was over, a certain Rudolf with his four
brothers started to seek their fortune in the south ; when they reached Italy, they
came to terms with Melus, the rebel of Bari, through the mediation of the Pope.]

[20] See Leandro Alberti (Descrizione d'Italia, p. 250) and Baronius (A.D. 493, No.

tranger in the Greek habit, but who soon revealed himself as a
ebel, a fugitive, and a mortal foe of the Greek empire. His
ame was Melo: [21] a noble citizen of Bari, who, after an unsuc- [Melus]
essful revolt, was compelled to seek new allies and avengers of
is country. The bold appearance of the Normans revived the
opes and solicited his confidence: they listened to the com-
laints, and still more to the promises, of the patriot. The as-
urance of wealth demonstrated the justice of his cause; and
hey viewed, as the inheritance of the brave, the fruitful land
vhich was oppressed by effeminate tyrants. On their return to
Normandy, they kindled a spark of enterprise; and a small but
ntrepid band was freely associated for the deliverance of Apulia.
They passed the Alps by separate roads, and in the disguise of
ilgrims; but in the neighbourhood of Rome they were saluted
y the chief of Bari, who supplied the more indigent with arms
nd horses, and instantly led them to the field of action. In the [A.D. 1017]
rst conflict, their valour prevailed; [22] but, in the second engage-
nent, they were overwhelmed by the numbers and military
ngines of the Greeks, and indignantly retreated with their faces [A.D. 1018]
o the enemy. The unfortunate Melo ended his life, a suppliant [Death of Melus. A.D. 1020]
t the court of Germany: his Norman followers, excluded from
heir native and their promised land, wandered among the hills
nd valleys of Italy, and earned their daily subsistence by the
word. To that formidable sword the princes of Capua, Beneven-
um, Salerno, and Naples, alternately appealed in their domestic
uarrels; the superior spirit and discipline of the Normans gave
ictory to the side which they espoused; and their cautious
olicy observed the balance of power, lest the preponderance of
ny rival state should render their aid less important and their
ervice less profitable. Their first asylum was a strong camp in
he depth of the marshes of Campania; but they were soon
ndowed by the liberality of the duke of Naples with a more
lentiful and permanent seat. Eight miles from his residence, Foundation of Aversa. A.D.
s a bulwark against Capua, the town of Aversa was built and 1029 [1030]

). If the archangel inherited the temple and oracle, perhaps the cavern, of old
alchas the soothsayer (Strab. Geograph. l. vi. p. 435, 436), the Catholics (on this
ccasion) have surpassed the Greeks in the elegance of their superstition.

[21] [Melus was the leader of the anti-Greek party in Bari. His first revolt was for
time successful, but was put down in 1010 by the Catepan Basil Mesardonites.]

[22] [There were three battles. Melus and the Normans invaded the Capitanate in
17. They gained a victory at Arenula on the river Fortore, and a second, more
ecisive, at Vaccaricia (near Troja). See Heinemann, op. cit. p. 36 (and Appendix).
n the following year they suffered the great defeat on the plain of Cannæ, at the
nds of the Catepan Basil Bojannes.]

fortified for their use ; [23] and they enjoyed as their own the corn and fruits, the meadows and groves, of that fertile district. The report of their success attracted every year new swarms of pilgrims and soldiers ; the poor were urged by necessity ; the rich were excited by hope ; and the brave and active spirits of Normandy were impatient of ease and ambitious of renown. The independent standard of Aversa afforded shelter and encouragement to the outlaws of the province, to every fugitive who had escaped from the injustice or justice of his superiors : and these foreign associates were quickly assimilated in manners and language to the Gallic colony. The first leader of the Normans was count Rainulf ; and, in the origin of society, preeminence of rank is the reward and the proof of superior merit. [24]

The Normans serve in Sicily. A.D. 1038.

Since the conquest of Sicily by the Arabs, the Grecian emperors had been anxious to regain that valuable possession ; but their efforts, however strenuous, had been opposed by the distance and the sea. Their costly armaments, after a gleam of success, added new pages of calamity and disgrace to the Byzantine annals ; twenty thousand of their best troops were lost in a single expedition ; and the victorious Moslems derided the policy of a nation, which entrusted eunuchs not only with the custody of their women, but with the command of their men. [25] After a reign of two hundred years, the Saracens were ruined by their divisions. [26] The emir disclaimed the authority of the king of

[23] [The settlement was assigned to Rainulf—one of Rudolph's brothers—by Duke Sergius IV. of Naples. Aversa was founded in 1030 (Heinemann, *op. cit.* p. 58, note 2). Rainulf married the sister of Sergius, but after her death he deserted the cause of Naples and went over to the interests of the foe, Pandulf of Capua, married his niece and became his vassal,—Aversa being disputed territory between Naples and Capua. But, when the Emperor Conrad visited Southern Italy in 1038, Pandulf was deposed, and the county of Aversa was united with the principality of Salerno. This, as Heinemann observes (p. 69), was a political event of the first importance. The Roman settlement was formally recognized by the Emperor,—taken as it were under the protection of the Western Empire.]

[24] See the first book of William Appulus. His words are applicable to every swarm of barbarians and freebooters :

Si vicinorum quis *pernitiosus* ad illos
Confugiebat, eum gratanter suscipiebant ;
Moribus et linguâ quoscumque venire videbant
Informant propriâ ; gens efficiatur ut una.

And elsewhere, of the native adventurers of Normandy :

Pars parat, exiguæ vel opes aderant quia nullæ ;
Pars, quia de magnis majora subire volebant.

[25] Liutprand in Legatione, p. 485. Pagi has illustrated this event from the Ms history of the deacon Leo (tom. iv. A.D. 965, No. 17-19).

[26] See the Arabian Chronicle of Sicily, apud Muratori, Script. Rerum Ital. tom i. p. 253.

Tunis; the people rose against the emir; the cities were usurped
by the chiefs; each meaner rebel was independent in his village
or castle; and the weaker of two rival brothers implored the
friendship of the Christians.[27] In every service of danger the
Normans were prompt and useful: and five hundred *knights*, or
warriors on horseback, were enrolled by Arduin, the agent and
interpreter of the Greeks, under the standard of Maniaces, governor of Lombardy.[28] Before their landing, the brothers were re- [A.D. 1038]
conciled; the union of Sicily and Africa were restored; and the
Island was guarded to the water's edge. The Normans led the [Capture of Messina]
van, and the Arabs of Messina felt the valour of an untried foe.
In a second action, the emir of Syracuse was unhorsed and trans- [Battle of Rametta. A.D. 1038]
pierced by the *iron arm* of William of Hauteville. In a third
engagement, his intrepid companions discomfited the host of [Battle of Troina. A.D. 1039]
sixty thousand Saracens, and left the Greeks no more than the
labour of the pursuit: a splendid victory; but of which the pen of
the historian may divide the merit with the lance of the Normans. It is, however, true that they essentially promoted the
success of Maniaces, who reduced thirteen cities, and the greater
part of Sicily, under the obedience of the emperor. But his
military fame was sullied by ingratitude and tyranny. In the
division of the spoil the deserts of his brave auxiliaries were
forgotten; and neither their avarice nor their pride could brook
this injurious treatment. They complained by the mouth of
their interpreter; their complaint was disregarded; their interpreter was scourged; the sufferings were *his*; the insult and resentment belonged to *those* whose sentiments he had delivered.
Yet they dissembled till they had obtained, or stolen, a safe

[27] [It was the emir Akhal who appealed to the Greeks to help him against his
brother, Abū Hafs, who headed the Sicilian rebels. The latter were supported by
the Zayrid Sultan of Tunis (Muizz ben Bādīs), and Akhal though he was supported
by the Catepan of Italy and a Greek army in 1037 was shut up in Palermo, where
he was murdered by his own followers. The statement in the text that "the
brothers were reconciled" is misleading; but a prospect of such a reconciliation
seems to have induced the Catepan to return to Italy without accomplishing much.
Cp. Cedrenus, ii. p. 516; and Heinemann, *op. cit.* p. 74. Meanwhile preparations
had been made in Constantinople for an expedition to recover Sicily; and Maniaces
arrived in Apulia and crossed over to the island in 1038.]

[28] [For a personal description of George Maniaces, a Hercules of colossal height
(εἰς δέκατον ἀνεστηκὼς πόδα), see Psellus, Hist. p. 137-8 (ed. Sathas). According to
Vámbéry the name *Maniakes* is Turkish and means *noble*. His memory survives
at Syracuse in the Castel Maniaci, at the south point of Ortygia commanding the
entrance to the Great Harbour. Maniaces was accompanied by another famous
warrior, Harald Hardrada (brother of King Olaf of Norway), who was slain a
quarter of a century later on English soil. Maniaces was the general of the expedition: he was not governor of the Theme of Lombardy.]

passage to the Italian continent; their brethren of Aversa sympathized in their indignation, and the province of Apulia was invaded as the forfeit of the debt.[29]   Above twenty years after the
first emigration, the Normans took the field with no more than
seven hundred horse and five hundred foot; and, after the recall
of the Byzantine legions [30] from the Sicilian war, their numbers
are magnified to the amount of threescore thousand men.  Their
herald proposed the option of battle or retreat; " Of battle," was
the unanimous cry of the Normans; and one of their stoutest
warriors, with a stroke of his fist, felled to the ground the horse
of the Greek messenger.  He was dismissed with a fresh horse;
the insult was concealed from the Imperial troops; but in two
successive battles [31] they were more fatally instructed of the
prowess of their adversaries.  In the plains of Cannæ, the Asiatics fled from the adventurers of France; the duke of Lombardy
was made prisoner; the Apulians acquiesced in a new dominion;
and the four places of Bari, Otranto, Brundusium, and Tarentum
were alone saved in the shipwreck of the Grecian fortunes.
From this æra we may date the establishment of the Norman
power, which soon eclipsed the infant colony of Aversa.  Twelve
counts [32] were chosen by the popular suffrage; and age, birth,

*Their con-
quest of
Apulia.
1040-1043* A.D.

[A.D. 1041]

[May 4]

[29] Jeffrey Malaterra, who relates the Sicilian war and the conquest of Apulia (l.
i. c. 7, 8, 9, 19).   The same events are described by Cedrenus (tom. ii. p. 741-
743, 755, 756) and Zonaras (tom. ii. p. 237, 238); and the Greeks are so hardened
to disgrace that their narratives are impartial enough.

[30] Cedrenus specifies the τάγμα of the Obsequium (Phrygia) and the μέρος of the
Thracesians (Lydia; consult Constantine de Thematibus, i. 3, 4, with Delisle's
map), and afterwards names the Pisidians and Lycaonians with the foederati.
[The Normans under Rainulf were acting in common with, and at the instigation
of, the Lombard Arduin.   They seized Melfi while the Catepan Michael Doceanus
was in Sicily seeking to retrieve the losses which the Greek cause had suffered since
the recall of Maniaces.   From Melfi they conquered Ascoli and other places, and
Michael was forced to return to Italy.   All this happened in A.D. 1040.  Heinemann, *op. cit.* p. 84.]

[31] [(1) On the Olivento (a tributary of the Ofanto), March 17, (2) near Monte
Maggiore, in the plain of Cannæ, May 4, and (3) at Montepeloso, Sept. 3, 1041.
See Heinemann, *op. cit.* p. 358-61.]

[32] Omnes conveniunt; et bis sex nobiliores,
       Quos genus et gravitas morum decorabat et ætas,
       Elegere duces.   Provectis ad comitatum
       His alii parent.   Comitatus nomen honoris
       Quo donantur erat.   Hi totas undique terras
       Divisere sibi, ni sors inimica repugnet;
       Singula proponunt loca quæ contingere sorte
       Cuique duci debent, et quæque tributa locorum.

And, after speaking of Melphi, William Appulus adds,

       Pro numero comitum bis sex statuere plateas,
       Atque domus comitum totidem fabricantur in urbe.

and merit were the motives of their choice. The tributes of their peculiar districts were appropriated to their use ; and each count erected a fortress in the midst of his lands, and at the head of his vassals. In the centre of the province, the common habitation of Melphi was reserved as the metropolis and citadel of the republic ; an house and separate quarter was allotted to each of the twelve counts ; and the national concerns were regulated by this military senate. The first of his peers, their president and general, was entitled count of Apulia ; and this dignity was conferred on William of the Iron Arm, who, in the [A.D. 1042] language of the age, is styled a lion in battle, a lamb in society, and an angel in council.[33] The manners of his countrymen are fairly delineated by a contemporary and national historian.[34] "The Normans," says Malaterra, "are a cunning and revengeful Character of the Normans people ; eloquence and dissimulation appear to be their hereditary qualities : they can stoop to flatter ; but, unless they are curbed by the restraint of law, they indulge the licentiousness of nature and passion. Their princes affect the praise of popular munificence ; the people observe the medium, or rather blend the extremes, of avarice and prodigality ; and, in their eager thirst of wealth and dominion, they despise whatever they possess, and hope whatever they desire. Arms and horses, the luxury of dress, the exercises of hunting and hawking,[35] are the delight of the Normans ; but on pressing occasions they can endure with

Leo Ostiensis (l. ii. c. 67) enumerates the divisions of the Apulian cities, which it is needless to repeat.

[33] Gulielm. Appulus, l. ii. c. 12, according to the reference of Giannone (Istoria Civile di Napoli, tom. ii. p. 31), which I cannot verify in the original. The Apulian praises indeed his *validas vires, probitas animi*, and *vivida virtus ;* and declares that, had he lived, no poet could have equalled his merits (l. i. p. 258, l. ii. p. 259). He was bewailed by the Normans, quippe qui tanti consilii virum (says Malaterra, l. i. c. 12, p. 552) tam armis strenuum, tam sibi munificum, affabilem, morigeratum, ulterius se habere diffidebant. [Having elected William, the Normans placed themselves under the suzerainty of Waimar of Salerno, who assumed the title of Prince of Apulia and Calabria. William, Rainulf, and Waimar then proceeded to Melfi and divided the conquests. Rainulf received, as an honorary present, Siponto and Mount Garganus ; William got Ascoli ; his brother, Drogo, Venosa, &c. &c., Aimé, Ystorie de li Normant, ii. 29, 30. The extent of the Norman conquest in this first stage corresponds (Heinemann observes, p. 94) to the towns in the regions of the rivers Ofanto and Bradano. "The valleys of these rivers were the natural roads to penetrate from Melfi eastward and southward into Greek territory."]

[34] The gens astutissima, injuriarum ultrix . . . adulari sciens . . . eloquentiis inserviens, of Malaterra (l. i. c. 3, p. 550) are expressive of the popular and proverbial character of the Normans.

[35] The hunting and hawking more properly belong to the *descendants* of the Norwegian sailors ; though they might import from Norway and Iceland the finest casts of falcons.

incredible patience the inclemency of every climate and the toil and abstinence of a military life." [36]

Oppression of Apulia. A.D. 1046, &c. The Normans of Apulia were seated on the verge of the two empires; and, according to the policy of the hour, they accepted the investiture of their lands from the sovereigns of Germany or Constantinople. [37] But the firmest title of these adventurers was the right of conquest: they neither loved nor trusted; they were neither trusted nor beloved; the contempt of the princes was mixed with fear, and the fear of the natives was mingled with hatred and resentment. Every object of desire, an horse, a woman, a garden, tempted and gratified the rapaciousness of the strangers; [38] and the avarice of their chiefs was only coloured by the more specious names of ambition and glory. The twelve counts were sometimes joined in a league of injustice: in their domestic quarrels, they disputed the spoils of the people; the virtues of William were buried in his grave; and Drogo, his brother and successor, was better qualified to lead the valour, than to restrain the violence, of his peers. Under the reign of Constantine Monomachus, the policy, rather than benevolence, of the Byzantine court attempted to relieve Italy from this adherent mischief, more grievous than a flight of barbarians; [39] and Argyrus, the son of Melo, was invested for this purpose with the most lofty titles [40] and the most ample commission. The

[36] We may compare this portrait with that of William of Malmsbury (de Gestis Anglorum, l. iii. p. 101, 102), who appreciates, like a philosophic historian, the vices and virtues of the Saxons and Normans. England was assuredly a gainer by the conquest.

[37] [The visit of the Emperor Henry III. to southern Italy in A.D. 1047 was of special importance. He restored to Pandulf the principality of Capua, which Conrad II. had transferred to Waimar of Salerno. Waimar had to resign his title of Prince of Apulia and Calabria, and his suzerainty over the Normans; while the Norman princes, Rainulf of Aversa and Drogo (William's successor), Count of Apulia, were elevated to be immediate vassals of the Empire.]

[38] The biographer of St. Leo IX. pours his holy venom on the Normans. Videns indisciplinatam et alienam gentem Normannorum, crudeli et inaudita rabie, et plusquam Pagana impietate, adversus ecclesias Dei insurgere, passim Christianos trucidare, &c. (Wibert, c. 6). The honest Apulian (l. ii. p. 259) says calmly of their accuser, Veris commiscens fallacia.

[39] The policy of the Greeks, revolt of Maniaces, &c. must be collected from Cedrenus (tom. ii. p. 757, 758), William Appulus (l. i. p. 257, 258, l. ii. p. 259), and the two Chronicles of Bari, by Lupus Protospata (Muratori, Script. Ital. tom. v. p. 42, 43, 44), and an anonymous writer (Antiquitat. Italiæ medii Ævi, tom. i. p. 31-35). [This anonymous chronicle, called the Annales Barenses, compiled before A.D. 1071, is printed in Pertz, Mon. V. p. 51-56, with the corresponding text of "Lupus" opposite.] This last is a fragment of some value.

[40] Argyrus received, says the anonymous Chronicle of Bari, Imperial letters, Fœderatus et Patriciatus, et Catapani et Vestatus. In his Annals, Muratori (tom.

memory of his father might recommend him to the Normans; and he had already engaged their voluntary service to quell the revolt of Maniaces, and to avenge their own and the public injury. It was the design of Constantine to transplant this warlike colony from the Italian provinces to the Persian war; and the son of Melo distributed among the chiefs the gold and manufactures of Greece, as the first fruits of the Imperial bounty. But his arts were baffled by the sense and spirit of the conquerors of Apulia: his gifts, or at least his proposals, were rejected; and they unanimously refused to relinquish their possessions and their hopes for the distant prospect of Asiatic fortune. After the means of persuasion had failed, Argyrus resolved to compel or to destroy: the Latin powers were solicited against the common enemy; and an offensive alliance was formed of the pope and the two emperors of the East and West. The throne of St. Peter was occupied by Leo the Ninth, a simple saint,[41] of a temper most apt to deceive himself and the world, and whose venerable character would consecrate with the name of piety the measures least compatible with the practice of religion. His humanity was affected by the complaints, perhaps the calumnies, of an injured people; the impious Normans had interrupted the payment of tithes; and the temporal sword might be lawfully unsheathed against the sacrilegious robbers, who were deaf to the censures of the church. As a German of noble birth and royal kindred, Leo had free access to the court and confidence of the emperor Henry the Third; and in search of arms and allies his ardent zeal transported him from Apulia to Saxony, from the Elbe to the Tiber. During these hostile preparations, Argyrus indulged himself in the use of secret and guilty weapons; a crowd of Normans became the victims of public or private revenge; and the valiant Drogo was murdered in a church. But his spirit survived in his brother Humphrey, the third count of Apulia. The assassins were chastised; and the son of Melo, overthrown and wounded, was driven from the

League of the pope and the two empires. A.D. 1049-1054

A.D. 1051

---

viii. p. 426) very properly reads, or interprets, *Sevestatus*, the title of Sebastos or Augustus. But in his Antiquities, he was taught by Ducange to make it a palatine office, master of the wardrobe.

[41] A life of St. Leo IX., deeply tinged with the passions and prejudices of the age, has been composed by Wibert, printed at Paris, 1615, in octavo, and since inserted in the Collections of the Bollandists, of Mabillon, and of Muratori. [J. May, Untersuchungen über die Abfassungszeit und Glaubwürdigheit von Wiberts Vita Leonis IX. (Offenburg, 1889).] The public and private history of that pope is diligently treated by M. de St. Marc (Abrégé, tom. ii. p. 140-210, and p. 25-95, second column).

field to hide his shame behind the walls of Bari, and to await the tardy succour of his allies.

Expedition of
pope Leo IX.
against the
Normans.
A.D. 1053
But the power of Constantine was distracted by a Turkish war; the mind of Henry was feeble and irresolute; and the pope, instead of passing the Alps with a German army, was accompanied only by a guard of seven hundred Swabians and some volunteers of Lorraine. In his long progress from Mantua to Beneventum, a vile and promiscuous multitude of Italians was enlisted under the holy standard;[42] the priest and the robber slept in the same tent; the pikes and crosses were intermingled in the front; and the natural saint repeated the lessons of his youth in the order of march, of encampment, and of combat. The Normans of Apulia could muster in the field no more than three thousand horse, with an handful of infantry; the defection of the natives intercepted their provisions and retreat; and their spirit, incapable of fear, was chilled for a moment by superstitious awe. On the hostile approach of Leo, they knelt without disgrace or reluctance before their spiritual father. But the pope was inexorable; his lofty Germans affected to deride the diminutive stature of their adversaries; and the Normans were informed that death or exile was their only alternative. Flight they disdained, and, as many of them had been three days without tasting food, they embraced the assurance of a more easy and honourable death. They climbed the hill of Civitella, descended into the plain, and charged in three divisions the army of the pope. On the left and in the centre, Richard count of Aversa, and Robert the famous Guiscard, attacked, broke, routed, and pursued the Italian multitudes, who fought without discipline and fled without shame. A harder trial was reserved for the valour of count Humphrey, who led the cavalry of the right wing. The Germans[43] have been described as unskilful in the management of the horse and lance; but on foot they formed a strong and impenetrable

[Battle of
Civitate]

His defeat and
captivity.
June 18

---

[42] See the expedition of Leo IX. against the Normans. See William Appulus (l. ii. p. 259-261) and Jeffrey Malaterra (l. i. c. 13, 14, 15, p. 253) [and Aimé, iii. c. 40]. They are impartial, as the national is counterbalanced by the clerical prejudice. [For details, cp. Heinemann, *op. cit.*, Appendix, p. 366 *sqq.*]

[43] Teutonici, quia cæsaries et forma decoros
    Fecerat egregie proceri corporis illos,
    Corpora derident Normannica, quæ breviora
    Esse videbantur.

The verses of the Apulian are commonly in this strain, though he heats himself a little in the battle. Two of his similes from hawking and sorcery are descriptive of manners.

# OF THE ROMAN EMPIRE 183

phalanx ; and neither man nor steed nor armour could resist the
weight of their long and two-handed swords.  After a severe
conflict, they were encompassed by the squadrons returning
from the pursuit ; and died in their ranks with the esteem
of their foes and the satisfaction of revenge.  The gates of
Civitella were shut against the flying pope, and he was overtaken by the pious conquerors, who kissed his feet, to implore his blessing and the absolution of their sinful victory.
The soldiers beheld in their enemy and captive the vicar of
Christ ; and, though we may suppose the policy of the chiefs,
it is probable that they were infected by the popular superstition.  In the calm of retirement, the well-meaning pope
deplored the effusion of Christian blood, which must be imputed
to his account ; he felt, that he had been the author of sin and
scandal ; and, as his undertaking had failed, the indecency of
his military character was universally condemned.[44]  With these
dispositions, he listened to the offers of a beneficial treaty ;[45]
deserted an alliance which he had preached as the cause of
God ; and ratified the past and future conquests of the Normans.
By whatever hands they had been usurped, the provinces of
Apulia and Calabria were a part of the donation of Constantine
and the patrimony of St. Peter ; the grant and the acceptance
confirmed the mutual claims of the pontiff and the adventurers.
They promised to support each other with spiritual and temporal arms ; a tribute or quit-rent of twelvepence was afterwards
stipulated for every plough-land ; and since this memorable
transaction the kingdom of Naples has remained above seven
hundred years a fief of the Holy See.[46]

Origin of the
papal investi-
ture to the
Normans

[44] Several respectable censures or complaints produced by M. de St. Marc (tom.
ii. p. 200-204).  As Peter Damianus, the oracle of the times, had denied the popes
the right of making war, the hermit (lugens eremi incola) is arraigned by the cardinal, and Baronius (Annal. Eccles. A.D. 1053, No. 10-17) most strenuously asserts
the two swords of St. Peter.

[45] [We have no contemporary evidence for the conditions which the Normans
imposed on Leo, whom they detained in Beneventum.  Heinemann thinks it probable (p. 143) that they required him to renounce the papal pretensions to sovereignty
over territory in Apulia and Calabria, and to abandon his alliance with the Eastern
Emperor.  Leo, unable to bring himself to consent, remained at Beneventum till
March, 1054 ; a severe illness (which proved fatal) filled him with a desire to return
to Rome and induced him to consent to the Norman demands.  He died on April
19.  During his sojourn at Beneventum, he was engaged on a correspondence in
connexion with the ecclesiastical quarrel—the final breach—with the Greek Church,
see below, cap. lx.]

[46] The origin and nature of the papal investitures are ably discussed by Giannone
(Istoria Civile di Napoli, tom. ii. p. 37-49, 57-66) as a lawyer and antiquarian.
Yet he vainly strives to reconcile the duties of patriot and Catholic, adopts an

Birth and
character of
Robert Guis-
card.    A.D.
1020-1085

The pedigree of Robert Guiscard[47] is variously deduced from the peasants and the dukes of Normandy : from the peasants, by the pride and ignorance of a Grecian princess ;[48] from the dukes by the ignorance and flattery of the Italian subjects.[49] His genuine descent may be ascribed to the second or middle order of private nobility.[50] He sprang from a race of *valvassors* or *bannerets* of the diocese of the Coutances, in the lower Normandy ; the castle of Hauteville was their honourable seat ; his father Tancred was conspicuous in the court and army of the duke ; and his military service was furnished by ten soldiers or knights. Two marriages, of a rank not unworthy of his own, made him the father of twelve sons, who were educated at home by the impartial tenderness of his second wife. But a narrow patrimony was insufficient for this numerous and daring progeny ; they saw around the neighbourhood the mischiefs of poverty and discord, and resolved to seek in foreign wars a more glorious inheritance. Two only remained to perpetuate the race and cherish their father's age ; their ten brothers, as they successively attained the vigour of manhood, departed from the castle, passed the Alps, and joined the Apulian camp of the Normans. The elder were prompted by native spirit ; their success encouraged their younger brethren ; and the three first in seniority, William, Drogo, and Humphrey, deserved to be the chiefs of their nation, and

empty distinction of " Ecclesia Romana non dedit sed accepit," and shrinks from an honest but dangerous confession of the truth.

[47] The birth, character, and first actions of Robert Guiscard may be found in Jeffrey Malaterra (l. i. c. 3, 4, 11, 16, 17, 18, 38, 39, 40), William Appulus (l. ii. p. 260-262), William Gemeticensis or of Jumiegès (l. xi, c. 30, p. 663, 664, edit. Camden), and Anna Comnena (Alexiad. l. i. p. 23-27 [c. 10, 11], l. vi. p. 165, 166), with the annotations of Ducange (Not. in Alexiad. p. 230-232, 320), who has swept all the French and Latin Chronicles for supplemental intelligence.

[48] Ὁ δὲ Ῥομπέρτος (a Greek corruption [μπ is the regular symbol for the *b* sound in mediæval and modern Greek ; β would represent *v*]) οὗτος ἦν Νορμάννος τὸ γένος, τὴν τύχην ἄσημος [i. c. 10]. . . . Again, ἐξ ἀφανοῦς πάνυ τύχης περιφανές. And elsewhere (l. iv. p. 84 [c. 1]), ἀπὸ ἐσχάτης πενίας καὶ τύχης ἀφανοῦς. Anna Comnena was born in the purple ; yet her father was no more than a private though illustrious subject, who raised himself to the empire.

[49] Giannone (tom. ii. p. 2) forgets all his original authors, and rests this princely descent on the credit of Inveges, an Augustine monk of Palermo, in the last century. They continue the succession of dukes from Rollo to William II. the Bastard or Conqueror, whom they hold (communemente si tiene) to be the father of Tancred of Hauteville ; a most strange and stupendous blunder ! The sons of Tancred fought in Apulia, before William II. was three years old (A.D. 1037).

[50] The judgment of Ducange is just and moderate : Certe humilis fuit ac tenuis Roberti familia, si ducalem et regium spectemus apicem, ad quem postea pervenit ; quæ honesta tamen et præter nobilium vulgarium statum et conditionem illustris habita est, " quæ nec humi reperet nec altum quid tumeret " (Wilhelm Malmsbur. de Gestis Anglorum, l. iii. p. 107 ; Not. ad Alexiad. p. 230).

the founders of the new republic. Robert was the eldest of the seven sons of the second marriage; and even the reluctant praise of his foes has endowed him with the heroic qualities of a soldier and a statesman. His lofty stature surpassed the tallest of his army; his limbs were cast in the true proportion of strength and gracefulness; and to the decline of life he maintained the patient vigour of health and the commanding dignity of his form. His complexion was ruddy, his shoulders were broad, his hair and beard were long and of a flaxen colour, his eyes sparkled with fire, and his voice, like that of Achilles, could impress obedience and terror amidst the tumult of battle. In the ruder ages of chivalry, such qualifications are not below the notice of the poet or historian; they may observe that Robert, at once, and with equal dexterity, could wield in the right hand his sword, his lance in the left; that in the battle of Civitella, he was thrice unhorsed; and that in the close of that memorable day he was adjudged to have borne away the prize of valour from the warriors of the two armies.[51] His boundless ambition was founded on the consciousness of superior worth; in the pursuit of greatness, he was never arrested by the scruples of justice and seldom moved by the feelings of humanity; though not insensible of fame, the choice of open or clandestine means was determined only by his present advantage. The surname of *Guiscard*[52] was applied to this master of political wisdom, which is too often confounded with the practice of dissimulation and deceit; and Robert is praised by the Apulian poet for excelling the cunning of Ulysses and the eloquence of Cicero. Yet these arts were disguised by an appearance of military frankness: in his highest fortune, he was accessible and courteous to his fellow-soldiers; and, while he indulged the prejudices of his new subjects, he affected in his dress and manners to maintain the ancient fashion of his country.

---

[51] I shall quote with pleasure some of the best lines of the Apulian (l. ii. p. 270).

> Pugnat utrâque manû, nec lancea cassa nec ensis
> Cassus erat, quocunque manu deducere vellet.
> Ter dejectus equo, ter viribus ipse resumptis,
> Major in arma redit ; stimulos furor ipse ministrat.
> Ut Leo cum frendens, &c.

>     .    .    .    .    .    .    .    .
> Nullus in hoc bello sicuti post bella probatum est
> Victor vel victus, tam magnos edidit ictus.

[52] The Norman writers and editors most conversant with their own idiom interpret *Guiscard*, or *Wiscard*, by *Callidus*, a cunning man. The root (*wise*) is familiar to our ear; and in the old word *Wiseacre* I can discern something of a similar sense and termination. Τὴν ψυχὴν πανουργότατος is no bad translation of the surname and character of Robert.

He grasped with a rapacious, that he might distribute with a liberal, hand ; his primitive indigence had taught the habits of frugality ; the gain of a merchant was not below his attention ; and his prisoners were tortured with slow and unfeeling cruelty [c. A.D. 1046] to force a discovery of their secret treasure.  According to the Greeks, he departed from Normandy with only five followers on horseback and thirty on foot ; yet even this allowance appears too bountiful ; the sixth son of Tancred of Hauteville passed the Alps as a pilgrim ; and his first military band was levied among the adventurers of Italy.  His brothers and countrymen had divided the fertile lands of Apulia ; but they guarded their shares with the jealousy of avarice ; the aspiring youth was driven forwards to the mountains of Calabria, and in his first exploits against the Greeks and the natives it is not easy to discriminate the hero from the robber.  To surprise a castle or a convent, to ensnare a wealthy citizen, to plunder the adjacent villages for necessary food, were the obscure labours which formed and exercised the powers of his mind and body.  The volunteers of Normandy adhered to his standard ; and, under his command, the peasants of Calabria assumed the name and character of Normans.

His ambition and success. A.D. 1054-1080    As the genius of Robert expanded with his fortune, he awakened the jealousy of his elder brother, by whom, in a transient quarrel, his life was threatened and his liberty restrained.  After the death of Humphrey, the tender age of his sons excluded them from the command ; they were reduced to a private estate by the ambition of their guardian and uncle ; [A.D. 1057]   and Guiscard was exalted on a buckler, and saluted count of Apulia and general of the republic.  With an increase of authority and of force, he resumed the conquest of Calabria, and soon aspired to a rank that should raise him for ever above the heads of his equals.  By some acts of rapine or sacrilege he had incurred a papal excommunication : but Nicholas the Second was easily persuaded that the divisions of friends could terminate only in their mutual prejudice ; that the Normans were the faithful champions of the Holy See ; and it was safer to trust [Synod of Melfi.  A.D. 1059, August 23]   the alliance of a prince than the caprice of an aristocracy.  A synod of one hundred bishops was convened at Melphi ; and the count interrupted an important enterprise to guard the person and execute the decrees of the Roman pontiff.  His gratitude and policy conferred on Robert and his posterity the ducal title,[53]

───────────

[53] The acquisition of the ducal title by Robert Guiscard is a nice and obscure business.  With the good advice of Giannone, Muratori, and St. Marc, I have endeavoured to form a consistent and probable narrative.

with the investiture of Apulia, Calabria, and all the lands, both
in Italy and Sicily, which his sword could rescue from the schismatic Greeks and the unbelieving Saracens.[54] This apostolic
sanction might justify his arms ; but the obedience of a free and
victorious people could not be transferred without their consent ;
and Guiscard dissembled his elevation till the ensuing campaign
had been illustrated by the conquest of Consenza and Reggio.
In the hour of triumph, he assembled his troops, and solicited
the Normans to confirm by their suffrage the judgment of the
vicar of Christ ; the soldiers hailed with joyful acclamations their
valiant duke ; and the counts, his former equals, pronounced
the oath of fidelity, with hollow smiles and secret indignation.
After this inauguration, Robert styled himself, " By the grace of
God and St. Peter, duke of Apulia, Calabria, and hereafter of
Sicily " ; and it was the labour of twenty years to deserve
and realise these lofty appellations.    Such tardy progress, in a
narrow space, may seem unworthy of the abilities of the chief
and the spirit of the nation ; but the Normans were few in
number ; their resources were scanty ; their service was voluntary and precarious.    The bravest designs of the Duke were
sometimes opposed by the free voice of his parliament of barons ;
the twelve counts of popular election conspired against his
authority ; and against their perfidious uncle the sons of Humphrey demanded justice and revenge.    By his policy and vigour,
Guiscard discovered their plots, suppressed their rebellions, and
punished the guilty with death or exile ; but in these domestic
feuds his years, and the national strength, were unprofitably
consumed.    After the defeat of his foreign enemies, the Greeks,
Lombards, and Saracens, their broken forces retreated to the
strong and populous cities of the sea coast.    They excelled in
the arts of fortification and defence ; the Normans were accustomed to serve on horseback in the field, and their rude attempts
could only succeed by the efforts of persevering courage.    The
resistance of Salerno was maintained above eight months ; the

*Duke of Apulia. A.D 1060*

*[May-Dec., A.D. 1076]*

---

[54] Baronius (Annal. Eccles. A.D. 1059, No. 69) has published the original act.
He professes to have copied it from the *Liber Censuum*, a Vatican Ms.    Yet a
Liber Censuum of the twelfth century has been printed by Muratori (Antiquit.
medii Ævi, tom. v. p. 851-908), and the names of Vatican and Cardinal awaken
the suspicions of a Protestant, and even of a philosopher.    [The Liber Censuum,
composed at the end of the 12th century (1192), contains the rent-roll of the Roman
Church and various original documents, and the Lives of Popes beginning with
Leo IX.    The oldest Ms. does not contain the Lives.    Muratori printed the whole
compilation in Scr. Rer. Ital., 3, i. p. 277 *sqq. ;* the edition in the Ant. Med.
Ev. does not include the Lives.]

# 188        THE DECLINE AND FALL

siege or blockade of Bari lasted near four years.[55]   In these
actions the Norman duke was the foremost in every danger,
in every fatigue the last and most patient.   As he pressed the
citadel of Salerno, an huge stone from the rampart shattered
one of his military engines ; and by a splinter he was wounded
in the breast.   Before the gates of Bari, he lodged in a miserable
hut or barrack, composed of dry branches, and thatched with
straw : a perilous station, on all sides open to the inclemency of
the winter and the spears of the enemy.[56]

His Italian
conquests

The Italian conquests of Robert correspond with the limits of
the present kingdom of Naples ; and the countries united by
his arms have not been dissevered by the revolutions of seven
hundred years.[57]   The monarchy has been composed of the
Greek provinces Calabria and Apulia, of the Lombard principality of Salerno, the republic of Amalphi,[58] and the inland
dependencies of the large and ancient duchy of Beneventum.
Three districts only were exempted from the common law of
subjection : the first for ever, and the two last till the middle of
the succeeding century.   The city and immediate territory of
Benevento had been transferred, by gift or exchange, from the
German emperor to the Roman pontiff; and, although this holy
land was sometimes invaded, the name of St. Peter was finally
more potent than the sword of the Normans.   Their first colony
of Aversa subdued and held the state of Capua ; and her princes
were reduced to beg their bread before the palace of their
fathers.   The dukes of Naples, the present metropolis, maintained the popular freedom, under the shadow of the Byzantine
empire.   Among the new acquisitions of Guiscard, the science
of Salerno,[59] and the trade of Amalphi,[60] may detain for a

[55] [Not so long : August, 1068—April, 1071.  The best source for the siege is
Aimé, v. 27.   Immediately before he laid siege to Bari, Robert captured Otranto.]

[56] Read the life of Guiscard in the second and third books of the Apulian, the
first and second books of Malaterra.

[57] The conquests of Robert Guiscard and Roger I., the exemption of Benevento
and the twelve provinces of the kingdom, are fairly exposed by Giannone in the
second volume of his Istoria Civile, l. ix., x., xi. and l. xvii. p. 460-470.  This
modern division was not established before the time of Frederic II.

[58] [Amalfi acknowledged the lordship of Robert (" Duke of Amalfi ") from A.D.
1073.  Cp. Heinemann, op. cit. p. 268.]

[59] Giannone (tom. ii. p. 119-127), Muratori (Antiquitat. medii Ævi, tom. ii.
dissert. xliv. p. 935, 936), and Tiraboschi (Istoria della Letteratura Italiana) have
given an historical account of these physicians ; their medical knowledge and
practice must be left to our physicians.

[60] At the end of the Historia Pandectarum of Henry Brenckmann (Trajecti ad
Rhenum, 1722, in 4to), the indefatigable author has inserted two dissertations, de

moment the curiosity of the reader.   I.  Of the learned faculties jurisprudence implies the previous establishment of laws and property; and theology may perhaps be superseded by the full light of religion and reason.   But the savage and the sage must alike implore the assistance of physic; and, if *our* diseases are inflamed by luxury, the mischiefs of blows and wounds would be more frequent in the ruder ages of society.  The treasures of Grecian medicine had been communicated to the Arabian colonies of Africa, Spain, and Sicily; and in the intercourse of peace and war a spark of knowledge had been kindled and cherished at Salerno, an illustrious city, in which the men were honest and the women beautiful.[61]    A school, the first that arose in the darkness of Europe, was consecrated to the healing art; [62] the conscience of monks and bishops were reconciled to that salutary and lucrative profession; and a crowd of patients, of the most eminent rank and most distant climates, invited or visited the physicians of Salerno.   They were protected by the Norman conquerors; and Guiscard, though bred in arms, could discern the merit and value of a philosopher.  After a pilgrimage of thirty-nine years, Constantine, an African Christian, returned from Bagdad, a master of the language and learning of the Arabians; and Salerno was enriched by the practice, the lessons

Republicâ Amalphitanâ, and de Amalphi a Pisanis direptâ, which are built on the estimonies of one hundred and forty writers.   Yet he has forgotten two most important passages of the embassy of Liutprand (A.D. 969), which compare the trade and navigation of Amalphi with that of Venice.

[61] Urbs Latii non est hâc delitiosior urbe,
Frugibus arboribus vinoque redundat ; et unde
Non tibi poma, nuces, non pulchra palatia desunt,
Non species muliebris abest probitasque virorum.
(Gulielmus Appulus, l. iii. p. 267.)

It has been commonly maintained that the medical school of Salerno owed its rise and development to Arabic influence.   This view seems to be mistaken ; documents published in De Renzi's *Collectio Salernitana* (1852) seem decidedly against it.  See Mr. Rashdall's Universities in the Middle Ages, vol. i. p. 78 (chap. , p. 75 *sqq.* is devoted to Salerno).   Mr. Rashdall is inclined to connect the revival of medical science in the 11th century at Salerno with the survival of the Greek language in those regions.  Salerno went back to Hippocrates independently of Arabia ; and it was when the Arabic methods in medicine became popular in the 13th century that the Salerno school declined.]

[62] [At the beginning of the 12th cent. Ordericus Vitalis describes the medica school of Salerno as existing *ab antiquo tempore* (Hist. Ecc. ii., Bk. 3, 11 in Migne, Patr. Lat., vol. 188, p. 260) ; see Rashdall, p. 77.   The place was famous for its physicians in the 10th cent., and we have works of medical writers of Salerno from the early part of the 11th (*e.g.*, Gariopontus).   The fullest account of the school is De Renzi's Storia documentata della scuola medica di Salerno.   The school was first recognized by Frederick II., whose edict in 1231 appointed it as the examining body for candidates who desired to obtain the royal licence which he made compulsory for the practice of medicine.]

and the writings, of the pupil of Avicenna. The school of
medicine has long slept in the name of an university ;[63] but her
precepts are abridged in a string of aphorisms, bound together
in the Leonine verses, or Latin rhymes, of the twelfth century.[64]

Trade of
Amalphi

II. Seven miles to the west of Salerno, and thirty to the south
of Naples, the obscure town of Amalphi displayed the power and
rewards of industry. The land, however fertile, was of narrow
extent ; but the sea was accessible and open ; the inhabitants
first assumed the office of supplying the western world with the
manufactures and productions of the East ; and this useful traffic
was the source of their opulence and freedom. The government
was popular under the administration of a duke and the supremacy of the Greek emperor. Fifty thousand citizens were
numbered in the walls of Amalphi ; nor was any city more
abundantly provided with gold, silver, and the objects of precious
luxury. The mariners who swarmed in her port excelled in the
theory and practice of navigation and astronomy ; and the discovery of the compass, which has opened the globe, is due to
their ingenuity or good fortune. Their trade was extended to
the coasts, or at least to the commodities, of Africa, Arabia, and
India ; and their settlements in Constantinople, Antioch, Jerusalem, and Alexandria acquired the privileges of independent
colonies.[65] After three hundred years of prosperity, Amalphi

[63] [It was a school of doctors, in no way resembling a university. As Mr. Rashdall observes (loc. cit., p. 82) : "Salerno remains a completely isolated factor in the
academic polity of the Middle Ages. While its position as a school of medicine
was, for two centuries at least, as unique as that of Paris in Theology and that of
Bologna in Law, while throughout the Middle Ages no school of medicine except
Montpellier rivalled its fame, it remained without influence in the development of
academic institutions."]

[64] Muratori carries their antiquity above the year (1066) of the death of Edward
the Confessor, the rex Anglorum to whom they are addressed. Nor is this date
affected by the opinion, or rather mistake, of Pasquier (Recherches de la France,
l. vii. c. 2) and Ducange (Glossar. Latin.). The practice of rhyming, as early as
the seventh century, was borrowed from the languages of the North and East
(Muratori, Antiquitat. tom. iii. dissert. xl. p. 686-708). [Constantine translated
the Aphorisms of Hippocrates from the Arabic version, c. A.D. 1080.]

[65] The description of Amalphi, by William the Apulian (l. iii. p. 267), contains
much truth and some poetry ; and the third line may be applied to the sailor's
compass :

> Nulla magis locuples argento, vestibus, auro
> Partibus innumeris ; hâc plurimus urbe moratur
> Nauta *maris caelique vias aperire peritus.*
> Huc et Alexandri diversa feruntur ab urbe
> Regis, et Antiochi. Gens hæc freta plurima transit.
> His [hic] Arabes, Indi, Siculi nascuntur et Afri.
> Hæc gens est totum prope nobilitata per orbem,
> Et mercanda ferens, et amans mercata referre.

was oppressed by the arms of the Normans, and sacked by the jealousy of Pisa ; but the poverty of one thousand fishermen is yet dignified by the remains of an arsenal, a cathedral, and the palaces of royal merchants.

Roger, the twelfth and last of the sons of Tancred, had been long detained in Normandy by his own and his father's age. He accepted the welcome summons ; hastened to the Apulian camp ; and deserved at first the esteem, and afterwards the envy, of his elder brother. Their valour and ambition were equal ; but the youth, the beauty, the elegant manners, of Roger engaged the disinterested love of his soldiers and people. So scanty was his allowance, for himself and forty followers, that he descended from conquest to robbery, and from robbery to domestic theft ; and so loose were the notions of property that, by his own historian, at his special command, he is accused of stealing horses from a stable at Melphi.[66] His spirit emerged from poverty and disgrace ; from these base practices he rose to the merit and glory of a holy war ; and the invasion of Sicily was seconded by the zeal and policy of his brother Guiscard. After the retreat of the Greeks, the *idolaters*, a most audacious reproach of the Catholics, had retrieved their losses and possessions ; but the deliverance of the island, so vainly undertaken by the forces of the Eastern empire, was achieved by a small and private band of adventurers.[67] In the first attempt Roger braved, in an open boat, the real and fabulous dangers of Scylla and Charyb-lis ; landed with only sixty soldiers on a hostile shore ; drove the Saracens to the gates of Messina ; and safely returned with the spoils of the adjacent country. In the fortress of Trani, his active and patient courage were equally conspicuous. In his old age he related with pleasure, that, by the distress of the

Conquest of
Sicily by
count Roger.
A.D. 1060-1090

[A.D. 1060]

[Troina]

[A.D. 1062]

[66] Latrocinio armigerorum suorum in multis sustentabatur, quod quidem ad ejus gnominiam non dicimus ; sed ipso ita præcipiente adhuc viliora et reprehensibiliora dicturi [*leg.* de ipso scripturi] sumus ut pluribus patescat quam laboriose et cum quantâ augustiâ a profundâ paupertate ad summum culmen divitiarum vel honoris attigerit. Such is the preface of Malaterra (l. i. c. 25) to the horse-stealing. From the moment (l. i. c. 19) that he has mentioned his patron Roger, the elder brother inks into the second character. Something similar in Velleius Paterculus may be observed of Augustus and Tiberius.

[67] Duo sibi proficua deputans, animæ scilicet et corporis, si terram idolis deditam ad cultum divinum revocaret (Galfrid Malaterra, l. ii. c. 1). The conquest of Sicily is related in the three last books, and he himself has given an accurate summary of the chapters (p. 544-546). [The Brevis historia liberationis Messanae, printed in Muratori, Scr. rer. It. 6, p. 614 *sqq.*, which ascribes the capture of Messina to this first descent of Roger, has been shown by Amari to be a concoction of the 18th century (Stor. dei Musulmani di Sicilia, iii. 56). Messina was taken in the following year—1061, May.]

siege, himself and the countess his wife had been reduced to a single cloak or mantle, which they wore alternately; that in a sally his horse had been slain, and he was dragged away by the Saracens; but that he owed his rescue to his good sword, and had retreated with his saddle on his back, lest the meanest trophy might be left in the hands of the miscreants. In the siege of Trani, three hundred Normans withstood and repulsed the forces of the island. In the field of Ceramio,[68] fifty thousand horse and foot were overthrown by one hundred and thirty-six Christian soldiers, without reckoning St. George, who fought on horseback in the foremost ranks. The captive banners, with four camels, were reserved for the successors of St. Peter; and had these barbaric spoils been exposed not in the Vatican, but in the Capitol, they might have revived the memory of the Punic triumphs. These insufficient numbers of the Normans most probably denote their knights, the soldiers of honourable and equestrian rank, each of whom was attended by five or six followers in the field;[69] yet, with the aid of this interpretation, and after every fair allowance on the side of valour, arms, and reputation, the discomfiture of so many myriads will reduce the prudent reader to the alternative of a miracle or a fable. The Arabs of Sicily derived a frequent and powerful succour from their countrymen of Africa: in the siege of Palermo, the Norman cavalry was assisted by the galleys of Pisa; and, in the hour of action, the envy of the two brothers was sublimed to a generous and invincible emulation. After a war of thirty years,[70] Roger, with the title of great count, obtained the sovereignty of the largest and most fruitful island of the Mediterranean; and his administration displays a liberal and enlightened mind above the limits of his age and education. The Moslems were maintained in the free enjoyment of their religion and property;[71] a philosopher and physician of Mazara, of the race of Mahomet, harangued the conqueror, and was invited to court; his geo

*Troina]*

*[A.D. 1063]*

*[A.D. 1071-2]*

---

[68] [The fortress of Cerami was not far from Troina.]

[69] See the word *milites* in the Latin Glossary of Ducange.

[70] Of odd particulars, I learn from Malaterra that the Arabs had introduced into Sicily the use of camels (l. i. c. 33) and of carrier pigeons (c. 42), and that the bit of the tarantula provokes a windy disposition, quæ per anum inhoneste crepitand emergit: a symptom most ridiculously felt by the whole Norman army in their camp near Palermo (c. 36). I shall add an etymology not unworthy of the eleventh century: *Messana* is derived from *Messis*, the place from whence the harvests of the isle were sent in tribute to Rome (l. ii. c. 1).

[71] See the capitulation of Palermo in Malaterra, l. ii. c. 45, and Giannone, wh remarks the general toleration of the Saracens (tom. ii. p. 72).

graphy of the seven climates was translated into Latin ; and
Roger, after a diligent perusal, preferred the work of the Arabian
to the writings of the Grecian Ptolemy.[72]   A remnant of Christian
natives had promoted the success of the Normans ; they
were rewarded by the triumph of the cross.   The island was
restored to the jurisdiction of the Roman pontiff; new bishops
were planted in the principal cities ; and the clergy was satisfied
by a liberal endowment of churches and monasteries.   Yet the
Catholic hero asserted the rights of the civil magistrate.   Instead
of resigning the investiture of benefices, he dexterously applied
to his own profit the papal claims :  the supremacy of the crown
was secured and enlarged by the singular bull which declares
the princes of Sicily hereditary and perpetual legates of the
Holy See.[73]

To Robert Guiscard, the conquest of Sicily was more glorious
than beneficial ; the possession of Apulia and Calabria was inadequate
to his ambition ; and he resolved to embrace or create
the first occasion of invading, perhaps of subduing, the Roman
empire of the East.[74]   From his first wife, the partner of his
humble fortunes, he had been divorced under the pretence of
consanguinity ; and her son Bohemond was destined to imitate,
rather than to succeed, his illustrious father.   The second wife
of Guiscard was the daughter of the princes of Salerno ; the
Lombards acquiesced in the lineal succession of their son Roger ;
their five daughters were given in honourable nuptials,[75] and

*Robert invades the Eastern empire. A.D. 1081*

*[Sigelgaita]*

[72] John Leo Afer, de Medicis et Philosophis Arabibus, c. 14, apud Fabric.
Bibliot. Græc. tom. xiii. p. 278, 279.   This philosopher is named Esseriph Essachalli,
and he died in Africa, A.H. 516—A.D. 1122.   Yet this story bears a strange
resemblance to the Sherif al Edrissi, who presented his book (Geographia Nubiensis,
see preface, p. 88, 90, 170) to Roger king of Sicily, A.H. 548—A.D. 1153 (d'Herbelot,
Bibliothèque Orientale, p. 786 ; Prideaux's Life of Mahomet, p. 188 ; Petit de la
Croix, Hist. de Gengiscan, p. 535, 536 ; Casiri, Bibliot. Arab. Hispan. tom. ii. p.
9-13), and I am afraid of some mistake.

[73] Malaterra remarks the foundation of the bishoprics (l. iv. c. 7) and produces
the original of the bull (l. iv. c. 29).   Giannone gives a rational idea of this privilege,
and the tribunal of the monarchy of Sicily (tom. ii. p. 95-102) ; and St. Marc (Abrégé,
tom. iii. p. 217-301, 1st column) labours the case with the diligence of a Sicilian
lawyer.

[74] In the first expedition of Robert against the Greeks, I follow Anna Comnena
(the 1st, iiird, ivth, and vth books of the Alexiad), William Appulus (l. ivth
and vth, p. 270-275), and Jeffrey Malaterra (l. iii. c. 13, 14, 24-29, 39).   Their
information is contemporary and authentic, but none of them were eye-witnesses of
the war. [Monograph :  Schwarz, Die Feldzüge Robert Guiscards gegen das
byzantinische Reich, 1854.]

[75] One of them was married to Hugh, the son of Azzo, or Axo, a marquis of
Lombardy, rich, powerful, and *noble* (Gulielm. Appul. l. iii. p. 267), in the xith
century, and whose ancestors in the xth and ixth are explored by the critical in-

[Helena] one of them was betrothed, in a tender age, to Constantine, a beautiful youth, the son and heir of the emperor Michael.[76] But the throne of Constantinople was shaken by a revolution ; the imperial family of Ducas was confined to the palace or the cloister ; and Robert deplored, and resented, the disgrace of his daughter and the expulsion of his ally. A Greek, who styled himself the father of Constantine, soon appeared at Salerno, and related the adventures of his fall and flight. That unfortunate friend was acknowledged by the duke, and adorned with the pomp and titles of Imperial dignity : in his triumphal progress through Apulia and Calabria, Michael[77] was saluted with the tears and acclamations of the people ; and pope Gregory the Seventh exhorted the bishops to preach, and the Catholics to fight, in the pious work of his restoration.[78] His conversations with Robert were frequent and familiar ; and their mutual promises were justified by the valour of the Normans and the treasures of the East. Yet this Michael, by the confession of the Greeks and Latins, was a pageant and an impostor : a monk who had fled from his convent, or a domestic who had served in the palace. The fraud had been contrived by the subtle Guiscard ;[79] and he trusted that, after this pretender had given a decent colour to his arms, he would sink, at the nod of the conqueror, into his primitive obscurity. But victory was the

dustry of Leibnitz and Muratori. From the two elder sons of the marquis Azzo are derived the illustrious lines of Brunswick and Este. See Muratori, Antichità Estense.

[76] Anna Comnena, somewhat too wantonly, praises and bewails that handsome boy, who, after the rupture of his barbaric nuptials (l. i. p. 23 [c. 10]), was betrothed as her husband ; he was ἄγαλμα φύσεως . . . Θεοῦ χειρῶν φιλοτίμημα . . . χρυσοῦ γένους ἀπορροή, &c. (p. 27 [c. 12]). Elsewhere, she describes the red and white of his skin, his hawk's eyes, &c. l. iii. p. 71 [c. 1]. [It had been proposed originally that Helena should marry another Constantine, a brother of Michael ; and there are extant two letters of this Emperor to Robert Guiscard, concerning the projected alliance, dating from 1073 (in the correspondence of Psellus, published by Sathas, Bibl. Gr. Med. Æv., 5, p. 385 sqq.). For criticism see Seger, Nikephorus Bryennios, p. 123-4 : Heinemann, op. cit. p. 394-6.]

[77] Anna Comnena, l. i. p. 28, 29 ; Gulielm. Appul. l. iv. p. 271 ; Galfrid Malaterra, l. iii. c. 13, p. 579, 580. Malaterra is more cautious in his style ; but the Apulian is bold and positive.

——Mentitus se Michaelem
Venerat a Danais quidam seductor ad illum.

As Gregory VII. had believed, Baronius, almost alone, recognises the empero Michael (A.D. 1080, No. 44).

[78] [Registrum Epistolarum, of Gregory VII. (ap. Jaffé, Bibl. rer. Germ. ii.), viii. 6, p. 435.]

[79] [So the Greeks said. But probably this was not so. Robert saw through the imposture and took advantage of it ; but probably did not invent it.]

only argument that could determine the belief of the Greeks ; and the ardour of the Latins was much inferior to their credulity : the Norman veterans wished to enjoy the harvest of their toils, and the unwarlike Italians trembled at the known and unknown dangers of a transmarine expedition. In his new levies, Robert exerted the influence of gifts and promises, the terrors of civil and ecclesiastical authority ; and some acts of violence might justify the reproach that age and infancy were pressed without distinction into the service of their unrelenting prince. After two years' incessant preparations, the land and naval forces were assembled at Otranto, at the heel or extreme promontory of Italy; and Robert was accompanied by his wife, who fought by his side, his son Bohemond, and the representative of the emperor Michael. Thirteen hundred knights [80] of Norman race or discipline formed the sinews of the army, which might be swelled to thirty thousand [81] followers of every denomination. The men, the horses, the arms, the engines, the wooden towers, covered with raw hides, were embarked on board one hundred and fifty vessels ; the transports had been built in the ports of Italy, and the galleys were supplied by the alliance of the republic of Ragusa.

At the mouth of the Adriatic gulf, the shores of Italy and Epirus incline towards each other. The space between Brundusium and Durazzo, the Roman passage, is no more than one hundred miles ; [82] at the last station of Otranto, it is contracted to fifty ; [83] and this narrow distance had suggested to Pyrrhus and Pompey the sublime or extravagant idea of a bridge. Before the general embarkation, the Norman duke dispatched Bohemond with fifteen galleys to seize or threaten the isle of Corfu, to

Siege of Durazzo. A.D. 1081, June 17

[May, A.D. 1081]

---

[80] Ipse armatæ militiæ non plusquam MCCC milites secum habuisse, ab eis qui eidem negotio interfuerunt attestatur (Malaterra, l. iii. c. 24, p. 583). These are the same whom the Apulian (l. iv. p. 273) styles the equestris gens ducis, equites de gente ducis.

[81] Εἰς τριάκοντα χιλιάδας, says Anna Comnena (Alexias, l. i. p. 37 [c. 16]), and her account tallies with the number and lading of the ships. Ivit in [leg. contra] Dyrrachium cum xv millibus hominum, says the Chronicon Breve Normannicum (Muratori, Scriptores, tom. v. p. 278). I have endeavoured to reconcile these reckonings.

[82] The Itinerary of Jerusalem (p. 609, edit. Wesseling) gives a true and reasonable space of a thousand stadia, or one hundred miles, which is strangely doubled by Strabo (l. vi. p. 433 [3, § 8]) and Pliny (Hist. Natur. iii. 16).

[83] Pliny (Hist. Nat. iii. 6, 16) allows quinquaginta millia for this brevissimus cursus, and agrees with the real distance from Otranto to La Vallona, or Aulon (d'Anville, Analyse de la Carte des Côtes de la Grèce, &c., p. 3-6). Hermolaus Barbarus, who substitutes centum (Harduin, Not. lxvi. in Plin. l. iii.), might have been corrected by every Venetian pilot who had sailed out of the gulf.

survey the opposite coast, and to secure an harbour in the neighbourhood of Vallona for the landing of the troops.   They passed
and landed without perceiving an enemy ; and this successful experiment displayed the neglect and decay of the naval power of
the Greeks.   The islands of Epirus and the maritime towns were
subdued by the arms or the name of Robert, who led his fleet and
army from Corfu (I use the modern appellation) [84] to the siege of
Durazzo.   That city, the western key of the empire, was guarded
by ancient renown and recent fortifications, by George Palæologus, a patrician, victorious in the Oriental wars, and a numerous
garrison of Albanians and Macedonians, who, in every age, have
maintained the character of soldiers.   In the prosecution of his
enterprise, the courage of Guiscard was assailed by every form of
danger and mischance.   In the most propitious season of the year,
as his fleet passed along the coast, a storm of wind and snow un-
expectedly arose : the Adriatic was swelled by the raging blast
of the south, and a new shipwreck confirmed the old infamy of
the Acroceraunian rocks. [85]   The sails, the masts, and the oars
were shattered or torn away ; the sea and shore were covered
with the fragments of vessels, with arms and dead bodies ; and
the greatest part of the provisions were either drowned or
damaged.   The ducal galley was laboriously rescued from the
waves, and Robert halted seven days on the adjacent cape, to
collect the relics of his loss and revive the drooping spirits of his
soldiers.   The Normans were no longer the bold and experienced
mariners who had explored the ocean from Greenland to Mount
Atlas, and who smiled at the petty dangers of the Mediterranean.
They had wept during the tempest ; they were alarmed by the
hostile approach of the Venetians, who had been solicited by the
prayers and promises of the Byzantine court.   The first day's
action was not disadvantageous to Bohemond, a beardless youth, [86]
who led the naval powers of his father.   All night the galleys of
the republic lay on their anchors in the form of a crescent ; and

[84] [Corfu, of course, is not a corruption of Kerkyra, but is the mediæval Greek
name Κορυφώ, which, originally applied to the hill-town (κορυφή), was extended to
designate the island.]

[85] Infames scopulos Acroceraunia, Horat. carm. i. 3.   The præcipitem Africum
decertantem Aquilonibus et rabiem Noti, and the monstra natantia of the Adriatic,
are somewhat enlarged ; but Horace trembling for the life of Virgil is an interesting
moment in the history of poetry and friendship.

[86] Τῶν δὲ εἰς τὸν πώγωνα αὐτοῦ ἐφυβρισάντων (Alexias, l. iv. p. 106 [c. 2]).   Yet the
Normans shaved, and the Venetians wore their beards ; they must have derided the
no-beard of Bohemond : an harsh interpretation ! (Ducange, Not. ad Alexiad. p.
283).

the victory of the second day was decided by the dexterity of their evolutions, the station of their archers, the weight of their javelins, and the borrowed aid of the Greek fire. The Apulian and Ragusian vessels fled to the shore, several were cut from their cables and dragged away by the conqueror ; and a sally from the town carried slaughter and dismay to the tents of the Norman duke. A seasonable relief was poured into Durazzo, and, as soon as the besiegers had lost the command of the sea, the islands and maritime towns withdrew from the camp the supply of tribute and provision. That camp was soon afflicted with a pestilential disease ; five hundred knights perished by an inglorious death ; and the list of burials (if all could obtain a decent burial) amounted to ten thousand persons. Under these calamities, the mind of Guiscard alone was firm and invincible : and, while he collected new forces from Apulia and Sicily, he battered, or scaled, or sapped, the walls of Durazzo. But his industry and valour were encountered by equal valour and more perfect industry. A moveable turret, of a size and capacity to contain five hundred soldiers, had been rolled forwards to the foot of the rampart ; but the descent of the door or draw-bridge was checked by an enormous beam, and the wooden structure was instantly consumed by artificial flames.

While the Roman empire was attacked by the Turks in the East and the Normans in the West, the aged successor of Michael surrendered the sceptre to the hands of Alexius, an illustrious captain, and the founder of the Comnenian dynasty. The princess Anne, his daughter and historian, observes, in her affected style, that even Hercules was unequal to a double combat ; and, on this principle, she approves an hasty peace with the Turks, which allowed her father to undertake in person the relief of Durazzo. On his accession, Alexius found the camp without soldiers, and the treasury without money ; yet such were the vigour and activity of his measures that, in six months, he assembled an army of seventy thousand men,[87] and performed a march of five hundred miles. His troops were levied in Europe

The army and march of the emperor Alexius. April-September

---

[87] Muratori (Annali d'Italia, tom. ix. p. 136, 137) observes that some authors (Petrus Diacon. Chron. Casinen. l. iii. c. 49) compose the Greek army of 170,000 men, but that the *hundred* may be struck off, and that Malaterra reckons only 70,000 : a slight inattention. The passage to which he alludes is in the Chronicle of Lupus Protospata (Script. Ital. tom. v. p. 45). Malaterra (l. iv. c. 27) speaks in high, but indefinite, terms of the emperor, cum copiis innumerabilibus ; like the Apulian poet (l. iv. p. 272).

More locustarum montes et plana teguntur.

and Asia, from Peloponnesus to the Black Sea ; his majesty was
displayed in the silver arms and rich trappings of the companies
of horseguards ; and the emperor was attended by a train of
nobles and princes, some of whom, in rapid succession, had been
clothed with the purple, and were indulged by the lenity of the
times in a life of affluence and dignity.   Their youthful ardour
might animate the multitude ; but their love of pleasure and contempt of subordination were pregnant with disorder and mischief ;
and their importunate clamours for speedy and decisive action
disconcerted the prudence of Alexius, who might have surrounded
and starved the besieging army.   The enumeration of provinces
recalls a sad comparison of the past and present limits of the
Roman world : the raw levies were drawn together in haste and
terror ; and the garrisons of Anatolia, or Asia Minor, had been
purchased by the evacuation of the cities which were immediately
occupied by the Turks.   The strength of the Greek army consisted in the Varangians, the Scandinavian guards, whose numbers
were recently augmented by a colony of exiles and volunteers
from the British island of Thule.   Under the yoke of the Norman
conqueror, the Danes and English were oppressed and united :
a band of adventurous youths resolved to desert a land of slavery ;
the sea was open to their escape ; and, in their long pilgrimage,
they visited every coast that afforded any hope of liberty and
revenge.   They were entertained in the service of the Greek
emperor ; and their first station was in a new city on the Asiatic
shore : but Alexius soon recalled them to the defence of his
person and palace ; and bequeathed to his successors the inheritance of their faith and valour.[88]   The name of a Norman invader
revived the memory of their wrongs: they marched with alacrity
against the national foe, and panted to regain in Epirus the glory
which they had lost in the battle of Hastings.  The Varangians were
supported by some companies of Franks or Latins ; and the rebels,
who had fled to Constantinople from the tyranny of Guiscard,
were eager to signalise their zeal and gratify their revenge.   In
this emergency, the emperor had not disdained the impure aid
of the Paulicians or Manichæans of Thrace and Bulgaria ; and
these heretics united with the patience of martyrdom the spirit
and discipline of active valour.[89]   The treaty with the sultan had

[88] See William of Malmsbury, de Gestis Anglorum, l. ii. p. 92.   Alexius fidem
Anglorum suscipiens præcipuis familiaritatibus suis eos applicabat, amorem eorum
filio transcribens.   Ordericus Vitalis (Hist. Eccles. l. iv. p. 508, l. vii. p. 641) relates
their emigration from England, and their service in Greece.

[89] See the Apulian, l. i. p. 256.   The character and story of these Manichæans
has been the subject of the livth chapter.

procured a supply of some thousand Turks ; and the arrows of
the Scythian horse were opposed to the lances of the Norman
cavalry. On the report and distant prospect of these formidable
numbers, Robert assembled a council of his principal officers.
" You behold," said he, " your danger ; it is urgent and inevitable.
The hills are covered with arms and standards ; and the emperor
of the Greeks is accustomed to wars and triumphs. Obedience
and union are our only safety ; and I am ready to yield the command to a more worthy leader." The vote and acclamation,
even of his secret enemies, assured him, in that perilous moment,
of their esteem and confidence ; and the duke thus continued :
" Let us trust in the rewards of victory, and deprive cowardice of
the means of escape. Let us burn our vessels and our baggage,
and give battle on this spot, as if it were the place of our nativity
and our burial." The resolution was unanimously approved ; and,
without confining himself to his lines, Guiscard awaited in battle-
array the nearer approach of the enemy. His rear was covered
by a small river ; his right wing extended to the sea ; his left to
the hills ; nor was he conscious, perhaps, that on the same ground
Cæsar and Pompey had formerly disputed the empire of the
world.[90]

Against the advice of his wisest captains, Alexius resolved
to risk the event of a general action, and exhorted the garrison
of Durazzo to assist their own deliverance by a well-timed sally
from the town. He marched in two columns to surprise the
Normans before day-break on two different sides : his light
cavalry was scattered over the plain ; the archers formed the
second line ; and the Varangians claimed the honours of the
vanguard. In the first onset, the battle-axes of the strangers
made a deep and bloody impression on the army of Guiscard,
which was now reduced to fifteen thousand men. The Lombards
and Calabrians ignominiously turned their backs ; they fled towards the river and the sea ; but the bridge had been broken
down to check the sally of the garrison, and the coast was lined
with the Venetian galleys, who played their engines among the
disorderly throng. On the verge of ruin, they were saved by
the spirit and conduct of their chiefs. Gaita, the wife of Robert, [Sigelgaita]
is painted by the Greeks as a warlike Amazon, a second Pallas ;
less skilful in arts, but not less terrible in arms, than the Athenian

*(margin note: Battle of Durazzo. A.D. 1081, October 18)*

---

[90] See the simple and masterly narrative of Cæsar himself (Comment. de Bell.
Civil. iii. 41-75). It is a pity that Quintus Icilius (M. Guischard) did not live to
analyse these operations, as he has done the campaigns of Africa and Spain.

goddess : [91] though wounded by an arrow, she stood her ground, and strove, by her exhortation and example, to rally the flying troops.[92] Her female voice was seconded by the more powerful voice and arm of the Norman duke, as calm in action as he was magnanimous in council : "Whither," he cried aloud, "whither do ye fly ? your enemy is implacable ; and death is less grievous than servitude." The moment was decisive : as the Varangians advanced before the line, they discovered the nakedness of their flanks ; the main battle of the duke, of eight hundred knights, stood firm and entire ; they couched their lances, and the Greeks deplore the furious and irresistible shock of the French cavalry.[93] Alexius was not deficient in the duties of a soldier or a general ; but he no sooner beheld the slaughter of the Varangians and the flight of the Turks, than he despised his subjects and despaired of his fortune. The princess Anne, who drops a tear on this melancholy event, is reduced to praise the strength and swiftness of her father's horse, and his vigorous struggle, when he was almost overthrown by the stroke of a lance, which had shivered the Imperial helmet. His desperate valour broke through a squadron of Franks who opposed his flight ; and, after wandering two days and as many nights in the mountains, he found some repose of body, though not of mind, in the walls of Lychnidus. The victorious Robert reproached the tardy and feeble pursuit which had suffered the escape of so illustrious a prize ; but he consoled his disappointment by the trophies and standards of the field, the wealth and luxury of the Byzantine camp, and the glory of defeating an army five times

---

[91] Παλλας αλλη καν μη Αθηνη [Anna Comn., iv. c. 6], which is very properly translated by the president Cousin (Hist. de Constantinople, tom. iv. p. 131 in 12mo), qui combattoit comme une Pallas, quoiqu' elle ne fût pas aussi savante que celle d'Athènes. The Grecian goddess was composed of two discordant characters, of Neith, the workwoman of Sais in Egypt, and of a virgin Amazon of the Tritonian Lake in Libya (Banier, Mythologie, tom. iv. p. 1-31 in 12mo).

[92] Anna Comnena (l. iv. p. 116 [c. 6]) admires, with some degree of terror, her masculine virtues. They were more familiar to the Latins ; and, though the Apulian (l. iv. p. 273) mentions her presence and her wound, he represents her as far less intrepid.

Uxor in hoc bello Roberti forte sagittâ
Quâdam læsa fuit ; quo vulnere *territa* nullam
Dum sperabat opem se pœne *subegerat* hosti.

The last is an unlucky word for a female prisoner.

[93] Απο της [μετα] του Ρομπερτου προηγησαμενης μαχης, γινωσκων την πρωτην κατα των εναντιων ιππασιαν των Κελτων ανυποιστον (Anna, l. v. p. 133 [c. 3]), and elsewhere και γαρ Κελτος ανηρ πας εποχουμενος μεν ανυποιστος την ορμην και την θεαν εστιν (p. 140 [c. 6]). The pedantry of the princess in the choice of classic appellations encouraged Ducange to apply to his countrymen the characters of the ancient Gauls.

more numerous than his own. A multitude of Italians had been the victims of their own fears; but only thirty of his knights were slain in this memorable day. In the Roman host, the loss of Greeks, Turks, and English amounted to five or six thousand : [94] the plain of Durazzo was stained with noble and royal blood ; and the end of the impostor Michael was more honourable than his life.

It is more than probable that Guiscard was not afflicted by the loss of a costly pageant, which had merited only the contempt and derision of the Greeks. After their defeat, they still persevered in the defence of Durazzo ; and a Venetian commander supplied the place of George Palæologus, who had been imprudently called away from his station. The tents of the besiegers were converted into barracks, to sustain the inclemency of the winter ; and in answer to the defiance of the garrison Robert insinuated that his patience was at least equal to their obstinacy.[95] Perhaps he already trusted to his secret correspondence with a Venetian noble, who sold the city for a rich and honourable marriage. At the dead of night several rope-ladders were dropped from the walls ; the light Calabrians ascended in silence ; and the Greeks were awakened by the name and trumpets of the conqueror. Yet they defended the street three days against an enemy already master of the rampart ; and near seven months elapsed between the first investment and the final surrender of the place. From Durazzo the Norman duke advanced into the heart of Epirus or Albania ; traversed the first mountains of Thessaly ; surprised three hundred English in the city of Castoria ; approached Thessalonica ; and made Constantinople tremble. A more pressing duty suspended the prosecution of his ambitious designs. By shipwreck, pestilence, and the sword, his army was reduced to a third of the original numbers ; and, instead of being recruited from Italy, he was informed, by plaintive epistles, of the mischiefs and dangers which had been produced by his absence : the revolt of the cities and barons of Apulia ; the distress of the pope ; and the approach or invasion of Henry king of Germany. Highly presuming that

Durazzo taken. A.D. 1082, Feb. 8 [21]

---

[94] Lupus Protospata (tom. iii. p. 45) says 6000 ; William the Apulian more than 5000 (l. iv. p. 273). Their modesty is singular and laudable : they might with so little trouble have slain two or three myriads of schismatics and infidels !

[95] The Romans had changed the inauspicious name of *Epi-damnus* to Dyrrachium (Plin. iii. 26), and the vulgar corruption of Duracium (see Malaterra) bore some affinity to *hardness*. One of Robert's names was Durand, *a durando :* Poor wit ! (Alberic. Monach. in Chron. apud Muratori, Annali d' Italia, tom. ix. p. 137).

Return of
Robert [A.D.
1082], and
actions of
Bohemond
his person was sufficient for the public safety, he repassed the
sea in a single brigantine, and left the remains of the army
under the command of his son and the Norman counts, exhorting
Bohemond to respect the freedom of his peers, and the counts
to obey the authority of their leader. The son of Guiscard trod
in the footsteps of his father ; and the two destroyers are compared, by the Greeks, to the caterpillar and the locust, the last
of whom devours whatever has escaped the teeth of the former.[96]
After winning two battles against the emperor, he descended
into the plain of Thessaly, and besieged Larissa, the fabulous
realm of Achilles,[97] which contained the treasure and magazines
of the Byzantine camp. Yet a just praise must not be refused
to the fortitude and prudence of Alexius, who bravely struggled
with the calamities of the times. In the poverty of the state,
he presumed to borrow the superfluous ornaments of the churches ;
the desertion of the Manichæans was supplied by some tribes of
Moldavia ; a reinforcement of seven thousand Turks replaced
and revenged the loss of their brethren ; and the Greek soldiers
were exercised to ride, to draw the bow, and to the daily practice
of ambuscades and evolutions. Alexius had been taught by
experience that the formidable cavalry of the Franks on foot
was unfit for action, and almost incapable of motion ; [98] his
archers were directed to aim their arrows at the horse rather
than the man ; and a variety of spikes and snares was scattered
over the ground on which he might expect an attack. In the
neighbourhood of Larissa the events of war were protracted and
balanced. The courage of Bohemond was always conspicuous,
and often successful ; but his camp was pillaged by a stratagem
of the Greeks ; the city was impregnable ; and the venal or discontented counts deserted his standard, betrayed their trusts,
and enlisted in the service of the emperor. Alexius returned to

---

[96] Βρούχους καὶ ἀκρίδας εἶπεν ἄν τις αὐτοὺς [τὸν] πατέρα καὶ [τὸν] υἱόν (Anna, l. i. p.
35 [c. 14]). By these similes, so different from those of Homer, she wishes to inspire
contempt as well as horror for the little noxious animal, a conqueror. Most unfortunately, the common sense, or common nonsense, of mankind resists her laudable design.

[97] Prodiit hâc auctor Trojanæ cladis Achilles.

The supposition of the Apulian (l. v. p. 275) may be excused by the more classic
poetry of Virgil (Æneid II. 197), Larissæus Achilles, but it is not justified by the
geography of Homer.

[98] The τῶν πεδίλων προάλματα, which incumbered the knights on foot, have been
ignorantly translated spurs (Anna Comnena, Alexias, l. v. p. 140 [c. 6]). Ducange
has explained the true sense by a ridiculous and inconvenient fashion, which lasted
from the xith to the xvth century. These peaks, in the form of a scorpion,
were sometimes two feet, and fastened to the knee with a silver chain.

Constantinople with the advantage, rather than the honour, of victory. After evacuating the conquests which he could no longer defend, the son of Guiscard embarked for Italy, and was embraced by a father who esteemed his merit and sympathized in his misfortune.

Of the Latin princes, the allies of Alexius and enemies of Robert, the most prompt and powerful was Henry, the Third or Fourth, king of Germany and Italy, and future emperor of the West. The epistle of the Greek monarch [99] to his brother is filled with the warmest professions of friendship, and the most lively desire of strengthening their alliance by every public and private tie. He congratulates Henry on his success in a just and pious war, and complains that the prosperity of his own empire is disturbed by the audacious enterprises of the Norman Robert. The list of his presents expresses the manners of the age, a radiated crown of gold, a cross set with pearls to hang on the breast, a case of relics with the names and titles of the saints, a vase of crystal, a vase of sardonyx, some balm, most probably of Mecca, and one hundred pieces of purple. To these he added a more solid present, of one hundred and forty-four thousand Byzantines of gold, with a further assurance of two hundred and sixteen thousand, so soon as Henry should have entered in arms the Apulian territories, and confirmed by an oath the league against the common enemy. The German,[100] who was already in Lombardy at the head of an army and a faction, accepted these liberal offers and marched towards the south : his speed was checked by the sound of the battle of Durazzo ; but the influence of his arms or name, in the hasty return of Robert, was a full equivalent for the Grecian bribe. Henry was the severe adversary of the Normans, the allies and vassals of Gregory the Seventh, his implacable foe. The long quarrel of the throne and mitre had been recently kindled by the zeal and ambition of that haughty priest : [101] the king and the pope had degraded each

The emperor Henry III.<br>[IV.] invited by the Greeks.<br>A.D. 1081

---

[99] The epistle itself (Alexias, l. iii. p. 93, 94, 95 [c. 10]) well deserves to be read. There is one expression, ἀστροπέλεκυν δεδεμένον μετὰ χρυσαφίου, which Ducange does not understand ; I have endeavoured to grope out a tolerable meaning ; χρυσάφιον, is a golden crown ; ἀστροπέλεκυς, is explained by Simon Portius (in Lexico Græco-Barbar.) by κεραυνός, πρηστήρ, a flash of lightning. [Heinemann has shown that this letter reached Henry IV. at Rome in June, 1081 (op. cit. p. 396-8). The embassy is mentioned in Benzo's Panegyricus rhythmicus, probably composed at end of 1081 (printed in Pertz, Mon. xi. p. 591 sqq.).]

[100] For these general events I must refer to the general historians Sigonius, Baronius, Muratori, Mosheim, St. Marc, &c.

[101] The lives of Gregory VII. are either legends or invectives (St. Marc, Abrégé, tom. iii. p. 235, &c.), and his miraculous or magical performances are alike in-

other ; and each had seated a rival on the temporal or spiritual throne of his antagonist. After the defeat and death of his Swabian rebel, Henry descended into Italy, to assume the Imperial crown, and to drive from the Vatican the tyrant of the church.[102] But the Roman people adhered to the cause of Gregory: their resolution was fortified by supplies of men and money from Apulia ; and the city was thrice ineffectually besieged by the king of Germany. In the fourth year he corrupted, as it is said, with Byzantine gold the nobles of Rome whose estates and castles had been ruined by the war. The gates, the bridges, and fifty hostages were delivered into his hands : the antipope, Clement the Third, was consecrated in the Lateran : the grateful pontiff crowned his protector in the Vatican ; and the emperor Henry fixed his residence in the Capitol, as the lawful successor of Augustus and Charlemagne. The ruins of the Septizonium were still defended by the nephew of Gregory : the pope himself was invested in the castle of St. Angelo ; and his last hope was in the courage and fidelity of his Norman vassal. Their friendship had been interrupted by some reciprocal injuries and complaints ; but, on this pressing occasion, Guiscard was urged by the obligation of his oath, by his interest, more potent than oaths, by the love of fame, and his enmity to the two emperors. Unfurling the holy banner, he resolved to fly to the relief of the prince of the apostles : the most numerous of his armies, six thousand horse and thirty thousand foot, was instantly assembled ; and his march from Salerno to Rome was animated by the public applause and the promise of the divine favour. Henry, invincible in sixty-six battles, trembled at his approach ; recollected some indispensable affairs that required his presence in Lombardy ;

*Besieges Rome. A.D. 1081-1084;*

*A.D. 1084, March 21, 24, 31*

*Flies before Robert; May*

credible to a modern reader. He will, as usual, find some instruction in Le Clerc (Vie de Hildebrand, Bibliot. ancienne et moderne, tom. viii.) and much amusement in Bayle (Dictionnaire Critique, *Grégoire* VII.). That pope was undoubtedly a great man, a second Athanasius, in a more fortunate age of the church. May I presume to add that the portrait of Athanasius is one of the passages of my history (vol. ii. p. 361 *sqq.*), with which I am the least dissatisfied ? [The present century has produced an enormous Hildebrandine literature. The pioneer work was that of Johannes Voigt in 1815 ; Hildebrand als Papst Gregor VII. und sein Zeitalter. The Protestant author represented Gregory in the light of a reformer. Voigt's work led to an English monograph by J. W. Bowden : The Life and Pontificate of Gregory VII. 1840. Spörer's study in 7 vols. appeared 20 years later (Papst Gregorius VII. und sein Zeitalter, 1859-61).]

[102] Anna, with the rancour of a Greek schismatic, calls him [ὁ] κατάπτυστος οὗτος Πάπας (l. i. p. 32 [c. 13]), a pope, or priest, worthy to be spit upon ; and accuses him of scourging, shaving, perhaps of castrating, the ambassadors of Henry (p. 31, 33). But this outrage is improbable and doubtful (see the sensible preface of Cousin).

exhorted the Romans to persevere in their allegiance; and hastily retreated three days before the entrance of the Normans. In less than three years, the son of Tancred of Hauteville enjoyed the glory of delivering the pope, and of compelling the two emperors of the East and West to fly before his victorious arms.[103] But the triumph of Robert was clouded by the calamities of Rome. By the aid of the friends of Gregory, the walls had been perforated or scaled; but the Imperial faction was still powerful and active; on the third day, the people rose in a furious tumult; and an hasty word of the conqueror, in his defence or revenge, was the signal of fire and pillage.[104] The Saracens of Sicily, the subjects of Roger, and auxiliaries of his brother, embraced this fair occasion of rifling and profaning the holy city of the Christians: many thousands of the citizens, in the sight, and by the allies, of their spiritual father, were exposed to violation, captivity, or death; and a spacious quarter of the city, from the Lateran to the Coliseum, was consumed by the flames and devoted to perpetual solitude.[105] From a city, where he was now hated and might be no longer feared, Gregory retired to end his days in the palace of Salerno. The artful pontiff might flatter the vanity of Guiscard with the hope of a Roman or Imperial crown; but this dangerous measure, which would have inflamed the ambition of the Norman, must for ever have alienated the most faithful princes of Germany.

The deliverer and scourge of Rome might have indulged himself in a season of repose; but, in the same year of the flight of the German emperor, the indefatigable Robert resumed the design of his eastern conquests. The zeal or gratitude of Gregory had promised to his valour the kingdoms of Greece

Second expedition of Robert into Greece. A.D. 1084, October

---

[103] Sic uno tempore victi
    Sunt terræ Domini duo : rex Alemannicus iste,
    Imperii rector Romani maximus ille.
    Alter ad arma ruens armis superatur ; et alter
    Nominis auditi solâ formidine cessit.

It is singular enough that the Apulian, a Latin, should distinguish the Greek as the ruler of the Roman empire (l. iv. p. 274).

[104] The narrative of Malaterra (l. iii. c. 37, p. 587, 588) is authentic, circumstantial, and fair. Dux ignem exclamans urbe incensâ, &c. The Apulian softens the mischief (inde quibusdam ædibus exustis), which is again exaggerated in some partial Chronicles (Muratori, Annali, tom. ix. p. 147).

[105] After mentioning this devastation, the Jesuit Donatus (de Româ veteri et novâ, l. iv. c. 8, p. 489) prettily adds, Duraret hodieque in Cœlio monte interque ipsum et Capitolium miserabilis facies prostratæ urbis, nisi in hortorum vinetorumque amœnitatem Roma resurrexisset ut perpetuâ viriditate contegeret vulnera et ruinas suas.

and Asia; [106] his troops were assembled in arms, flushed with
success, and eager for action. Their numbers, in the language
of Homer, are compared by Anna to a swarm of bees; [107] yet
the utmost and moderate limits of the powers of Guiscard have
been already defined ; they were contained on this second occasion in one hundred and twenty vessels ; and, as the season
was far advanced, the harbour of Brundusium [108] was preferred
to the open road of Otranto. Alexius, apprehensive of a second
attack, had assiduously laboured to restore the naval forces of
the empire; and obtained from the republic of Venice an important succour of thirty-six transports, fourteen galleys, and
nine galeots or ships of extraordinary strength and magnitude.
Their services were liberally paid by the licence or monopoly of
trade, a profitable gift of many shops and houses in the port
of Constantinople, and a tribute to St. Mark, the more acceptable, as it was the produce of a tax on their rivals of Amalphi.[109]
By the union of the Greeks and Venetians, the Adriatic was
covered with an hostile fleet; but their own neglect, or the
vigilance of Robert, the change of a wind, or the shelter of a
mist, opened a free passage ; and the Norman troops were safely
disembarked on the coast of Epirus. With twenty strong and
well-appointed galleys, their intrepid duke immediately fought
the enemy, and, though more accustomed to fight on horseback,
he trusted his own life, and the lives of his brother and two
sons, to the event of a naval combat. The dominion of the
sea was disputed in three engagements, in sight of the island
of Corfu ; in the two former, the skill and numbers of the allies

[106] The royalty of Robert, either promised or bestowed by the pope (Anna, l. i.
p. 32 [c. 13]), is sufficiently confirmed by the Apulian (l. iv. p. 270).

> Romani regni sibi promisisse coronam
> Papa ferebatur.

Nor can I understand why Gretser, and the other papal advocates, should be displeased with this new instance of apostolic jurisdiction.

[107] See Homer, Iliad B (I hate this pedantic mode of quotation by the letters
of the Greek alphabet), 87, &c. His bees are the image of a disorderly crowd ;
their discipline and public works seem to be the ideas of a later age (Virgil, Æneid,
l. i.).

[108] Gulielm. Appulus, l. v. p. 276. The admirable port of Brundusium was
double ; the outward harbour was a gulf covered by an island, and narrowing by
degrees, till it communicated by a small gullet with the inner harbour, which embraced the city on both sides. Cæsar and nature have laboured for its ruin ; and
against such agents, what are the feeble efforts of the Neapolitan government ?
(Swinburne's Travels in the two Sicilies, vol. i. p. 384-390).

[109] [The golden Bull is printed in Tafel and Thomas, Urkunden zur älteren
Handels-und Staatsgeschichte der Republik Venedigs, in Fontes rer. Aust. ii. 12,
No. 23.]

were superior; but in the third the Normans obtained a final
and complete victory.[110]   The light brigantines of the Greeks
were scattered in ignominious flight; the nine castles of the
Venetians maintained a more obstinate conflict; seven were
sunk, two were taken; two thousand five hundred captives
implored in vain the mercy of the victor; and the daughter
of Alexius deplores the loss of thirteen thousand of his subjects
or allies.   The want of experience had been supplied by the
genius of Guiscard; and each evening, when he had sounded
a retreat, he calmly explored the causes of his repulse, and
invented new methods how to remedy his own defects and to
baffle the advantages of the enemy.   The winter season suspended his progress; with the return of spring he again aspired
to the conquest of Constantinople; but, instead of traversing
the hills of Epirus, he turned his arms against Greece and the
islands, where the spoils would repay the labour, and where the
land and sea forces might pursue their joint operations with
vigour and effect.   But, in the isle of Cephalonia, his projects
were fatally blasted by an epidemical disease; Robert himself, His death.
in the seventieth year of his age, expired in his tent, and a A.D. 1085, July 17
suspicion of poison was imputed, by public rumour, to his wife,
or to the Greek emperor.[111]   This premature death might allow

[110] William of Apulia (l. v. p. 276) describes the victory of the Normans, and
forgets the two previous defeats, which are diligently recorded by Anna Comnena
(l. vi. p. 159, 160, 161 [c. 5]).   In her turn, she invents or magnifies a fourth action,
to give the Venetians revenge and rewards.   Their own feelings were far different,
since they deposed their doge, propter excidium stoli (Dandulus in Chron. in
Muratori, Script. Rerum Italicarum, tom. xii. p. 249).

[111] The most authentic writers, William of Apulia (l. v. 277), Jeffrey Malaterra
(l. iii. c. 41, p. 589), and Romuald of Salerno (Chron. in Muratori, Script. Rerum
Ital. tom. vii.), are ignorant of this crime so apparent to our countrymen William
of Malmesbury (l. iii. p. 107) and Roger de Hoveden (p. 710 in Script. post Bedam),
and the latter can tell how the just Alexius married, crowned, and burnt alive, his
female accomplice.   The English historian is indeed so blind that he ranks Robert
Guiscard, or Wiscard, among the knights of Henry I. who ascended the throne
fifteen years after the duke of Apulia's death.   [When he died, Robert was on the
point of sailing to Cephalonia, but he did not die in the island.   He died (where
he had made his winter quarters) at Bundicia on the river Glykys, on the coast of
Epirus.   Heinemann (op. cit. p. 401-3) treats the question in an acute appendix,
and makes it probable that this Glykys is to be connected with the Γλυκὺς λιμήν,
the name given by Strabo to the bay into which the Acheron flows—now called the
bay of Phanari.   He conjectures that Bundicia is the ancient Pandosia.   The
Chronicon breve Nortmannicum, sub ann., states that Guiscard died in Cassiopi
and Romuald of Salerno says apud insulam Cassiopam; hence it has been supposed that the place was Cassiope, on the north side of the island of Corfu.
Heinemann would connect " Cassiopa " with Cassopia in Epirus.   The statement
that he died in Cephalonia is due to Anna Comnena (vi. 6) and Anon. Bar. sub
ann., but is irreconcilable with the rest of the story.]

a boundless scope for the imagination of his future exploits : and the event sufficiently declares that the Norman greatness was founded on his life.[112] Without the appearance of an enemy, a victorious army dispersed or retreated in disorder and consternation ; and Alexius, who had trembled for his empire, rejoiced in his deliverance. The galley which transported the remains of Guiscard was shipwrecked on the Italian shore; but the duke's body was recovered from the sea, and deposited in the sepulchre of Venusia,[113] a place more illustrious for the birth of Horace [114] than for the burial of the Norman heroes. Roger, his second son and successor, immediately sunk to the humble station of a duke of Apulia : the esteem or partiality of his father left the valiant Bohemond to the inheritance of his sword. The national tranquillity was disturbed by his claims, till the first crusade against the infidels of the East opened a more splendid field of glory and conquest.[115]

Reign and ambition of Roger, great count of Sicily. A.D. 1101-1154, Feb. 26

Of human life the most glorious or humble prospects are alike and soon bounded by the sepulchre. The male line of Robert Guiscard was extinguished, both in Apulia and at Antioch, in the second generation; but his younger brother became the father of a line of kings; and the son of the great count was endowed with the name, the conquests, and the spirit of the first Roger.[116] The heir of that Norman adventurer was born in Sicily : and, at the age of only four years, he succeeded to the sovereignty of the island, a lot which reason might

[112] The joyful Anna Comnena scatters over some flowers over the grave of an enemy (Alexiad. l. vi. p. 162-166 [c. 6, 7]), and his best praise is the esteem and envy of William the Conqueror, the sovereign of his family. Græcia (says Malaterra) hostibus recedentibus libera læta quievit : Apulia tota sive Calabria turbatur.

[113] Urbs Venusina nitet tantis decorata sepulchris,

is one of the last lines of the Apulian's poem (l. v. p. 278). William of Malmesbury (l. iii. p. 107) inserts an epitaph on Guiscard, which is not worth transcribing.

[114] Yet Horace had few obligations to Venusia : he was carried to Rome in his childhood (Serm. i. 6), and his repeated allusions to the doubtful limit of Apulia and Lucania (Carm. iii. 4 ; Serm. ii. 1) are unworthy of his age and genius.

[115] See Giannone (tom. ii. p. 88-93) and the historians of the first crusade.

[116] The reign of Roger, and the Norman kings of Sicily, fills four books of the Istoria Civile of Giannone (tom. ii. l. xi.-xiv. p. 136-340), and is spread over the ninth and tenth volumes of the Italian Annals of Muratori. In the Bibliothèque Italique (tom. i. p. 175-222) I find an useful abstract of Capecelatro, a modern Neapolitan, who has composed, in two volumes, the history of his country from Roger I. to Frederic II. inclusive. [The old collection of authorities for Sicilian history by Fazellus (1579) was reissued at Catania in 1749-52. The Neapolitan collection of G. Del Re in 2 vols. (see below, note 118) includes some Sicilians. Some chronicles written in the Sicilian tongue were collected by Vincenzo de' Giovanni and published in 1865 (Cronache Siciliane dei secoli xiii.-xiv. c. xv.).]

envy, could she indulge for a moment the visionary, though virtuous, wish of dominion. Had Roger been content with his fruitful patrimony, an happy and grateful people might have blessed their benefactor; and, if a wise administration could have restored the prosperous times of the Greek colonies,[117] the opulence and power of Sicily alone might have equalled the widest scope that could be acquired and desolated by the sword of war. But the ambition of the great count was ignorant of these noble pursuits; it was gratified by the vulgar means of violence and artifice. He sought to obtain the undivided possession of Palermo, of which one moiety had been ceded to the elder branch; struggled to enlarge his Calabrian limits beyond the measure of former treaties; and impatiently watched the declining health of his cousin William of Apulia, the grandson of Robert. On the first intelligence of his premature death, Roger sailed from Palermo with seven galleys, cast anchor in the bay of Salerno, received, after ten days' negotiation, an oath of fidelity from the Norman capital, commanded the submission of the barons, and extorted a legal investiture from the reluctant popes, who could not long endure either the friendship or enmity of a powerful vassal. The sacred spot of Benevento was respectfully spared, as the patrimony of St. Peter; but the reduction of Capua and Naples completed the design of his uncle Guiscard; and the sole inheritance of the Norman conquests was possessed by the victorious Roger. A conscious superiority of power and merit prompted him to disdain the titles of duke and of count; and the isle of Sicily, with a third perhaps of the continent of Italy, might form the basis of a kingdom [118] which would only yield to the monarchies of France and England. The chiefs of the nation who attended his coronation at Palermo might doubtless pronounce under what name he should reign over them; but the example of a Greek tyrant or a Saracen emir were insufficient to justify his regal character; and the nine kings

*Duke of Apulia. A.D. 1127*

---

[117] According to the testimony of Philistus and Diodorus, the tyrant Dionysius of Syracuse could maintain a standing force of 10,000 horse, 100,000 foot, and 400 galleys. Compare Hume (Essays, vol. i. p. 268, 435) and his adversary Wallace (Numbers of Mankind, p. 306, 307). The ruins of Agrigentum are the theme of every traveller, d'Orville, Reidesel, Swinburne, &c.

[118] A contemporary historian of the acts of Roger, from the year 1127 to 1135, founds his title on merit and power, the consent of the barons, and the ancient royalty of Sicily and Palermo, without introducing pope Anacletus (Alexand. Cœnobii Telesini Abbatis de Rebus gestis Regis Rogerii, lib. iv. in Muratori, Script. Rerum Ital. tom. v. p. 607-645 [printed, with Italian translation, in Del Re's Cronisti e scrittori sincroni Napolitani, vol. i. p. 85 *sqq.* (1845)]).

of the Latin world [119] might disclaim their new associate, unless
he were consecrated by the authority of the supreme pontiff.
The pride of Anacletus was pleased to confer a title which the
pride of the Norman had stooped to solicit; [120] but his own
legitimacy was attacked by the adverse election of Innocent
the Second; and, while Anacletus sat in the Vatican, the successful fugitive was acknowledged by the nations of Europe.
The infant monarchy of Roger was shaken, and almost overthrown, by the unlucky choice of an ecclesiastical patron; and
the sword of Lothaire the Second of Germany, the excommunica-
tions of Innocent, the fleets of Pisa, and the zeal of St. Bernard,
were united for the ruin of the Sicilian robber. After a gallant
resistance, the Norman prince was driven from the continent of
Italy; a new duke of Apulia was invested by the pope and the
emperor, each of whom held one end of the *gonfanon*, or flag-
staff, as a token that they asserted their right and suspended
their quarrel. But such jealous friendship was of short and
precarious duration; the German armies soon vanished in disease
and desertion; [121] the Apulian duke, with all his adherents, was
exterminated by a conqueror who seldom forgave either the
dead or the living; like his predecessor Leo the Ninth, the
feeble though haughty pontiff became the captive and friend
of the Normans; and their reconciliation was celebrated by the
eloquence of Bernard, who now revered the title and virtues of
the king of Sicily.

As a penance for his impious war against the successor of St.
Peter, that monarch might have promised to display the banner
of the cross, and he accomplished with ardour a vow so propitious
to his interest and revenge. The recent injuries of Sicily might
provoke a just retaliation on the heads of the Saracens; the
Normans, whose blood had been mingled with so many subject
streams, were encouraged to remember and emulate the naval

*First king of Sicily. A.D. 1130, Dec. 25 —A.D. 1139, July 25*

*His conquests in Africa. A.D. 1122-1152*

[119] The kings of France, England, Scotland, Castile, Arragon, Navarre, Sweden,
Denmark, and Hungary. The three first were more ancient than Charlemagne;
the three next were created by their sword, the three last by their baptism;
and of these the king of Hungary alone was honoured or debased by a papal
crown.

[120] Fazellus, and a crowd of Sicilians, had imagined a more early and independent coronation (A.D. 1130, May 1), which Giannone unwillingly rejects (tom. ii.
p. 137-144). This fiction is disproved by the silence of contemporaries; nor can
it be restored by a spurious charter of Messina (Muratori, Annali d'Italia, tom. ix.
p. 340; Pagi, Critica, tom. iv. p. 467, 468).

[121] Roger corrupted the second person of Lothaire's army, who sounded, or
rather cried, a retreat; for the Germans (says Cinnamus, l. iii. c. i. p. 51) are ignorant of the use of trumpets. Most ignorant himself! [Cinnamus says that they
did not use a trumpet; not that they were ignorant of it.]

trophies of their fathers, and in the maturity of their strength they contended with the decline of an African power. When the Fatimite caliph departed for the conquest of Egypt, he rewarded the real merit and apparent fidelity of his servant Joseph with a gift of his royal mantle and forty Arabian horses, his palace, with its sumptuous furniture, and the government of the kingdoms of Tunis and Algiers. The Zeirides,[122] the descendants of Joseph, forgot their allegiance and gratitude to a distant benefactor, grasped and abused the fruits of prosperity; and, after running the little course of an Oriental dynasty, were now fainting in their own weakness. On the side of the land, they were pressed by the Almohades, the fanatic princes of Morocco, while the sea-coast was open to the enterprises of the Greeks and Franks, who, before the close of the eleventh century, had extorted a ransom of two hundred thousand pieces of gold. By the first arms of Roger, the island or rock of Malta, which has been since ennobled by a military and religious colony, was inseparably annexed to the crown of Sicily. Tripoli,[123] a strong and maritime city, was the next object of his attack; and the slaughter of the males, the captivity of the females, might be justified by the frequent practice of the Moslems themselves. The capital of the Zeirides was named Africa from the country, and Mahadia [124] from the Arabian founder; it is strongly built on a neck of land, but the imperfection of the harbour is not compensated by the fertility of the adjacent plain. Mahadia was besieged by George the Sicilian admiral, with a fleet of one hundred and fifty galleys, amply provided with men and the instruments of mischief; the sovereign had fled, the Moorish governor refused to capitulate, declined the last and irresistible assault, and, secretly escaping with the Moslem inhabitants, abandoned the place and its treasures to the rapacious Franks. In successive expeditions, the king of Sicily or his lieutenants reduced the cities of Tunis,

---

[122] See de Guignes, Hist. Générale des Huns, tom. i. p. 369-373, and Cardonne, Hist. de l'Afrique, &c. sous la Domination des Arabes, tom. ii. p. 70-144. Their common original appears to be Novairi.

[123] Tripoli (says the Nubian geographer, or more properly the Sherif al Edrisi) urbs fortis, saxeo muro vallata, sita prope littus maris. Hanc expugnavit Rogerius, qui mulieribus captivis ductis, viros peremit.

[124] See the geography of Leo Africanus (in Ramusio, tom. i. fol. 74, verso, fol. 5, recto) and Shaw's Travels (p. 110), the viith book of Thuanus, and the 11th of the Abbé de Vertot. The possession and defence of the place was offered by Charles V. and wisely declined by the knights of Malta.

Safax, Capsia, Bona, and a long tract of the sea-coast ;[125] the
fortresses were garrisoned, the country was tributary, and a
boast, that it held Africa in subjection, might be inscribed with
some flattery on the sword of Roger.[126]    After his death, that
sword was broken; and these transmarine possessions were
neglected, evacuated, or lost, under the troubled reign of his
successor.[127]    The triumphs of Scipio and Belisarius have proved
that the African continent is neither inaccessible nor invincible
yet the great princes and powers of Christendom have repeatedly
failed in their armaments against the Moors, who may still glory
in the easy conquest and long servitude of Spain.

His invasion
of Greece.
A.D. 1146

Since the decease of Robert Guiscard, the Normans had re
linquished, above sixty years, their hostile designs against the
empire of the East.    The policy of Roger solicited a public and
private union with the Greek princes, whose alliance would
dignify his regal character ; he demanded in marriage a daughter
of the Comnenian family, and the first steps of the treaty seemed
to promise a favourable event.    But the contemptuous treatment
of his ambassadors exasperated the vanity of the new monarch
and the insolence of the Byzantine court was expiated, accord
ing to the laws of nations, by the sufferings of a guiltless people.[12]
With a fleet of seventy galleys George the admiral of Sicily ap
peared before Corfu ; and both the island and city were delivered
into his hands by the disaffected inhabitants, who had yet t
learn that a siege is still more calamitous than a tribute.    I
this invasion, of some moment in the annals of commerce, th
Normans spread themselves by sea, and over the provinces o
Greece ; and the venerable age of Athens, Thebes, and Corinth
was violated by rapine and cruelty.    Of the wrongs of Athens
no memorial remains.    The ancient walls, which encompassed
without guarding, the opulence of Thebes, were scaled by th

[125] Pagi has accurately marked the African conquests of Roger ; and his criticis
was supplied by his friend the Abbé Longuerue with some Arabic memorials (A.
1147, No. 26, 27, A.D. 1148, No. 16, A.D. 1153, No. 16).

[126] Appulus et Calaber, Siculus mihi servit et Afer.

A proud inscription, which denotes that the Norman conquerors were still di
criminated from their Christian and Moslem subjects.

[127] Hugo Falcandus (Hist. Sicula, in Muratori, Script. tom. vii. p. 270, 271) a
cribes these losses to the neglect or treachery of the admiral Majo.

[128] The silence of the Sicilian historians, who end too soon or begin too lat
must be supplied by Otho of Frisingen, a German (de Gestis Frederici I. l. i.
33, in Muratori, Script. tom. vi. p. 668), the Venetian Andrew Dandulus (id. to
xii. p. 282, 283), and the Greek writers Cinnamus (l. iii. c. 2-5) and Nicetas (
Manuel. l. ii. c. 2-6).

Latin Christians; but their sole use of the gospel was to sanctify an oath that the lawful owners had not secreted any relic of their inheritance or industry. On the approach of the Normans the lower town of Corinth was evacuated : the Greeks retired to the citadel, which was seated on a lofty eminence abundantly watered by the classic fountain of Pirene : an impregnable fortress, if the want of courage could be balanced by any advantages of art or nature. As soon as the besiegers had surmounted the labour (their sole labour) of climbing the hill, their general, from the commanding eminence, admired his own victory, and testified his gratitude to heaven by tearing from the altar the precious image of Theodore the tutelary saint. The silk weavers of both sexes, whom George transported to Sicily, composed the most valuable part of the spoil, and, in comparing the skilful industry of the mechanic with the sloth and cowardice of the soldier, he was heard to exclaim that the distaff and loom were the only weapons which the Greeks were capable of using. The progress of this naval armament was marked by two conspicuous events, the rescue of the king of France and the insult of the Byzantine capital. In his return by sea from an unfortunate crusade, Louis the Seventh was intercepted by the Greeks, who basely violated the laws of honour and religion. The unfortunate encounter of the Norman fleet delivered the royal captive ; and, after a free and honourable entertainment in the court of Sicily, Louis continued his journey to Rome and Paris.[129] In the absence of the emperor, Constantinople and the Hellespont were left without defence and without the suspicion of danger. The clergy and people, for the soldiers had followed the standard of Manuel, were astonished and dismayed at the hostile appearance of a line of galleys, which boldly cast anchor in the front of the Imperial city. The forces of the Sicilian admiral were inadequate to the siege or assault of an immense and populous metropolis ; but George enjoyed the glory of humbling the Greek arrogance, and of marking the path of conquest to the navies of the West. He landed some soldiers to rifle the fruits of the royal gardens, and pointed with silver, or more probably with fire, the arrows which he discharged against the palace of the Cæsars.[130] This playful

*His admiral delivers Louis VII., of France*

*Insults Constantinople*

---

[129] To this imperfect capture and speedy rescue, I apply the παρ᾽ ὀλίγον ἦλθε τοῦ λῶναι of Cinnamus, l. ii. c. 19, p. 49. Muratori, on tolerable evidence (Annali d'Italia, tom. ix. p. 420, 421), laughs at the delicacy of the French, who maintain, marisque nullo impediente periculo ad regnum proprium reversum esse : yet I observe that their advocate, Ducange, is less positive as the commentator on Cinnamus than as the editor of Joinville.

[130] In palatium regium sagittas igneas injecit, says Dandulus ; but Nicetas, l. ii.

The emperor
Manuel re-
pulses the
Normans.
A.D. 1148, 1149 outrage of the pirates of Sicily, who had surprised an unguarded
moment, Manuel affected to despise, while his martial spirit
and the forces of the empire were awakened to revenge. The
Archipelago and Ionian sea were covered with his squadrons and
those of Venice ; but I know not by what favourable allowance
of transports, victuallers, and pinnaces, our reason, or even fancy,
can be reconciled to the stupendous account of fifteen hundred
vessels, which is proposed by a Byzantine historian. These operations were directed with prudence and energy ; in his home-
ward voyage George lost nineteen of his galleys, which were
separated and taken ; after an obstinate defence, Corfu implored
the clemency of her lawful sovereign ; nor could a ship, a soldier
of the Norman prince, be found, unless as a captive, within the
limits of the Eastern empire. The prosperity and the health of
Roger were already in a declining state ; while he listened in his
palace of Palermo to the messengers of victory or defeat, the invincible Manuel, the foremost in every assault, was celebrated
by the Greeks or Latins as the Alexander or Hercules of the
age.

He reduces
Apulia and
Calabria.
A.D. 1155     A prince of such a temper could not be satisfied with having
repelled the insolence of a barbarian. It was the right and
duty, it might be the interest and glory, of Manuel to restore
the ancient majesty of the empire, to recover the provinces
of Italy and Sicily, and to chastise this pretended king, the
grandson of a Norman vassal.[131] The natives of Calabria were
still attached to the Greek language and worship, which had
been inexorably proscribed by the Latin clergy : after the loss
of her dukes, Apulia was chained as a servile appendage to
the crown of Sicily ; the founder of the monarchy had ruled by
the sword ; and his death had abated the fear, without healing
the discontent, of his subjects ; the feudal government was always
pregnant with the seeds of rebellion ; and a nephew of Roger himself invited the enemies of his family and nation. The majesty
of the purple, and a series of Hungarian and Turkish wars, prevented Manuel from embarking his person in the Italian expedition. To the brave and noble Palæologus, his lieutenant, the

c. 8, p. 66, transforms them into βέλη ἀργεντέους ἔχοντα ἀτρακτούς, and adds that
Manuel styled this insult παίγνιον and γέλωτα . . . λῃστεύοντα. These arrows, by the
compiler, Vincent de Beauvais, are again transmuted into gold.

[131] For the invasion of Italy, which is almost overlooked by Nicetas, see the more
polite history of Cinnamus (l. iv. c. 1-15, p. 78-101), who introduces a diffuse narrative by a lofty profession, περὶ τῆς Σικελίας τε καὶ τῆς Ἰταλῶν ἐσκέπτετο γῆς, ὡς καὶ ταῦτα
Ῥωμαίοις ἀνασώσαιτο [iii. 5].

Greek monarch entrusted a fleet and army; the siege of Bari was his first exploit; and, in every operation, gold as well as steel was the instrument of victory. Salerno, and some places along the Western coast, maintained their fidelity to the Norman king; but he lost in two campaigns the greater part of his continental possessions; and the modest emperor, disdaining all flattery and falsehood, was content with the reduction of three hundred cities or villages of Apulia and Calabria, whose names and titles were inscribed on all the walls of the palace. The His design of prejudices of the Latins were gratified by a genuine or fictitious Italy and the donation under the seal of the German Cæsars; [132] but the suc- pire. A.D. cessor of Constantine soon renounced this ignominious pretence, 1155-1174, &c. claimed the indefeasible dominion of Italy, and professed his design of chasing the barbarians beyond the Alps. By the artful speeches, liberal gifts, and unbounded promises of their Eastern ally, the free cities were encouraged to persevere in their generous struggle against the despotism of Frederic Barbarossa; the walls of Milan were rebuilt by the contributions of Manuel; and he poured, says the historian, a river of gold into the bosom of Ancona, whose attachment to the Greeks was fortified by the jealous enmity of the Venetians. [133] The situation and trade of Ancona rendered it an important garrison in the heart of Italy; it was twice besieged by the arms of Frederic; the Imperial forces were twice repulsed by the spirit of freedom; that spirit was animated by the ambassador of Constantinople; and the most intrepid patriots, the most faithful servants, were rewarded by the wealth and honours of the Byzantine court. [134] The pride of Manuel disdained and rejected a barbarian colleague; his ambition was excited by the hope of stripping the purple from the German usurpers, and of establishing, in the West, as in the East, his lawful title of sole emperor of the Romans. With this view, he solicited the alliance of the people and the

[132] The Latin, Otho (de Gestis Frederici I. l. ii. c. 30, p. 734), attests the forgery; the Greek, Cinnamus (l. i. c. 4, p. 78), claims a promise of restitution from Conrad and Frederic. An act of fraud is always credible when it is told of the Greeks.

[133] Quod Anconitani Græcum imperium nimis diligerent . . . Veneti speciali odio Anconam oderunt. The cause of love, perhaps of envy, were the beneficia, flumen aureum of the emperor; and the Latin narrative is confirmed by Cinnamus (l. iv. c. 14, p. 98).

[134] Muratori mentions the two sieges of Ancona: the first, in 1167, against Frederic I. in person (Annali, tom. x. p. 39, &c.), the second, in 1173, against his lieutenant Christian, archbishop of Mentz, a man unworthy of his name and office (p. 76, &c.). It is of the second siege that we possess an original narrative, which he has published in his great collection (tom. vi. p. 921-946).

bishop of Rome. Several of the nobles embraced the cause of the Greek monarch; the splendid nuptials of his niece with Odo Frangipani secured the support of that powerful family,[135] and his royal standard or image was entertained with due reverence in the ancient metropolis.[136] During the quarrel between Frederic and Alexander the Third, the pope twice received in the Vatican the ambassadors of Constantinople. They flattered his piety by the long-promised union of the two churches, tempted the avarice of his venal court, and exhorted the Roman pontiff to seize the just provocation, the favourable moment, to humble the savage insolence of the Alemanni, and to acknowledge the true representative of Constantine and Augustus.[137]

**Failure of his designs**

But these Italian conquests, this universal reign, soon escaped from the hand of the Greek emperor. His first demands were eluded by the prudence of Alexander the Third, who paused on this deep and momentous revolution,[138] nor could the pope be seduced by a personal dispute to renounce the perpetual inheritance of the Latin name. After his re-union with Frederic, he spoke a more peremptory language, confirmed the acts of his predecessors, excommunicated the adherents of Manuel, and pronounced the final separation of the churches, or at least the empires, of Constantinople and Rome.[139] The free cities of Lombardy no longer remembered their foreign benefactor, and, without preserving the friendship of Ancona, he soon incurred the enmity of Venice.[140] By his own avarice, or the complaints of his subjects, the Greek emperor was provoked to arrest the persons, and confiscate the effects, of the Venetian merchants. This violation of the public faith exasperated a free and commer-

---

[135] We derive this anecdote from an anonymous chronicle of Fossa Nova, published by Muratori (Script. Ital. tom. vii. p. 874). [ = Annales Ceccanenses, in Pertz, Mon. xix. 276 sqq.]

[136] The Βασίλειον σημεῖον of Cinnamus (l. iv. c. 14, p. 99) is susceptible of this double sense. A standard is more Latin, an image more Greek.

[137] Nihilominus quoque petebat, ut quia occasio justa et tempus opportunum et acceptabile se obtulerant, Romani corona imperii a sancto apostolo sibi redderetur ; quoniam non ad Frederici Alamanni, sed ad suum jus asseruit pertinere (Vit. Alexandri III. a Cardinal. Arragoniæ, in Script. Rerum Ital. tom. iii. par. i. p. 458). His second embassy was accompanied cum immensâ multitudine pecuniarum.

[138] Nimis alta et perplexa sunt (Vit. Alexandri III. p. 460, 461), says the cautious pope.

[139] Μηδὲν μέσον εἶναι λέγων Ῥώμῃ τῇ νεωτέρᾳ πρὸς τὴν πρεσβυτέραν πάλαι ἀπορραγεισῶν (Cinnamus, l. iv. c. 14, p. 99).

[140] In his vith book, Cinnamus describes the Venetian war, which Nicetas has not thought worthy of his attention. The Italian accounts, which do not satisfy our curiosity, are reported by the annalist Muratori, under the years 1171, &c.

cial people : one hundred galleys were launched and armed in as many days ; they swept the coasts of Dalmatia and Greece ; but, after some mutual wounds, the war was terminated by an agreement, inglorious to the empire, insufficient for the republic ; and a complete vengeance of these and of fresh injuries was reserved for the succeeding generation. The lieutenant of Manuel had informed his sovereign that he was strong enough to quell any domestic revolt of Apulia and Calabria ; but that his forces were inadequate to resist the impending attack of the king of Sicily. His prophecy was soon verified ; the death of Palæologus devolved the command on several chiefs, alike eminent in rank, alike defective in military talents ; the Greeks were oppressed by land and sea ; and a captive remnant, that escaped the swords of the Normans and Saracens, abjured all future hostility against the person or dominions of their conqueror.[141] Yet the king of Sicily esteemed the courage and constancy of Manuel, who had landed a second army on the Italian shore ; he respectfully addressed the new Justinian, solicited a peace or truce of thirty years, accepted as a gift the regal title, and acknowledged himself the military vassal of the Roman empire.[142] The Byzantine Cæsars acquiesced in this shadow of dominion, without expecting, perhaps without desiring, the service of a Norman army ; and the truce of thirty years was not disturbed by any hostilities between Sicily and Constantinople. About the end of that period, the throne of Manuel was usurped by an inhuman tyrant, who had deserved the abhorrence of his country and mankind : the sword of William the Second, the grandson of Roger, was drawn by a fugitive of the Comnenian race ; and the subjects of Andronicus might salute the strangers as friends, since they detested their sovereign as the worst of enemies. The Latin historians[143] expatiate on the rapid progress of the four counts who invaded

*Peace with the Normans. A.D. 1156*

*Last war of the Greeks and Normans A.D. 1185*

[141] This victory is mentioned by Romuald of Salerno (in Muratori, Script. Ital. om. vii. p. 198). It is whimsical enough that in the praise of the king of Sicily Cinnamus (l. iv. c. 13, p. 97, 98) is much warmer and more copious than Falcandus p. 268, 270). But the Greek is fond of description, and the Latin historian is not ond of William the Bad.

[142] For the epistle of William I. see Cinnamus (l. iv. c. 15, p. 101, 102) and Nicetas (l. ii. c. 8). It is difficult to affirm whether these Greeks deceived themselves, or the public, in these flattering portraits of the grandeur of the empire.

[143] I can only quote of original evidence, the poor chronicles of Sicard of Cremona (p. 603), and of Fossa Nova (p. 875), as they are published in the viith tome of Muratori's historians. The king of Sicily sent his troops contra nequitiam Antronici . . . ad acquirendum imperium C. P. They were capti aut confusi . . . ecepti captique, by Isaac.

Romania with a fleet and army, and reduced many castles and
cities to the obedience of the king of Sicily. The Greeks [144]
accuse and magnify the wanton and sacrilegious cruelties that
were perpetrated in the sack of Thessalonica, the second city
of the empire. The former deplore the fate of those invincible
but unsuspecting warriors, who were destroyed by the arts of a
vanquished foe. The latter applaud, in songs of triumph, the
repeated victories of their countrymen on the sea of Marmora
or Propontis, on the banks of the Strymon, and under the walls
of Durazzo. A revolution, which punished the crimes of Andronicus, had united against the Franks the zeal and courage
of the successful insurgents : ten thousand were slain in battle,
and Isaac Angelus, the new emperor, might indulge his vanity
or vengeance in the treatment of four thousand captives. Such
was the event of the last contest between the Greeks and Normans : before the expiration of twenty years, the rival nations
were lost or degraded in foreign servitude ; and the successors
of Constantine did not long survive to insult the fall of the
Sicilian monarchy.

William I.,
the Bad, king
of Sicily. A.D.
1154, Feb. 26
—A.D. 1166,
May 7
The sceptre of Roger successively devolved to his son and
grandson : they might be confounded under the name of
William ; they are strongly discriminated by the epithets of the
*bad* and the *good ;* but these epithets, which appear to describe
the perfection of vice and virtue, cannot strictly be applied to
either of the Norman princes. When he was roused to arms
by danger and shame, the first William did not degenerate
from the valour of his race ; but his temper was slothful ; his
manners were dissolute ; his passions headstrong and mischievous ; and the monarch is responsible, not only for his personal
vices, but for those of Majo, the great admiral, who abused
the confidence, and conspired against the life, of his benefactor.
From the Arabian conquest, Sicily had imbibed a deep tincture
of Oriental manners ; the despotism, the pomp, and even the
harem, of a sultan ; and a Christian people was oppressed and insulted by the ascendant of the eunuchs, who openly professed,
or secretly cherished, the religion of Mahomet. An eloquent

---

[144] By the failure of Cinnamus, we are now reduced to Nicetas (in Andronico, l.
i. c. 7, 8, 9, l. ii. c. i. in Isaac. Angelo, l. i. c. 1-4), who now becomes a respectable
contemporary. As he survived the emperor and the empire, he is above flattery ;
but the fall of Constantinople exasperated his prejudices against the Latins. For the
honour of learning I shall observe that Homer's great Commentator, Eustathius,
archbishop of Thessalonica, refused to desert his flock. [For Eustathius and his
work on the siege of Thessalonica see Appendix 1.]

historian of the times [145] has delineated the misfortunes of
his country : [146] the ambition and fall of the ungrateful Majo ;
the revolt and punishment of his assassins ; the imprisonment
and deliverance of the king himself ; the private feuds that arose
from the public confusion ; and the various forms of calamity
and discord which afflicted Palermo, the island, and the continent, during the reign of William the First, and the minority
of his son.  The youth, innocence, and beauty of William the
Second [147] endeared him to the nation : the factions were reconciled ; the laws were revived ; and, from the manhood to the premature death of that amiable prince, Sicily enjoyed a short
season of peace, justice, and happiness, whose value was enhanced
by the remembrance of the past and the dread of futurity.  The
legitimate male posterity of Tancred of Hauteville was extinct in
the person of the second William ; but his aunt, the daughter of
Roger, had married the most powerful prince of the age ; and
Henry the Sixth, the son of Frederic Barbarossa, descended from
the Alps, to claim the Imperial crown and the inheritance of his
wife.  Against the unanimous wish of a free people, this inheritance could only be acquired by arms ; and I am pleased to transcribe the style and sense of the historian Falcandus, who writes
at the moment and on the spot, with the feelings of a patriot, and
the prophetic eye of a statesman.  "Constantia, the daughter of
Sicily, nursed from her cradle in the pleasures and plenty, and

William II.,
the Good.
A.D. 1166, May
7—A.D. 1189,
Nov. 16

Lamentation
of the his-
torian Fal-
candus

---

[145] The Historia Sicula of Hugo Falcandus, which properly extends from 1154 to
1169, is inserted in the viith volume of Muratori's Collection (tom. vii. p. 259-
344), and preceded by an eloquent preface or epistle (p. 251-258) de Calamitatibus
Siciliæ.  [Re-edited by Del Re in Cronisti e scrittori sincroni napoletani, 1845.]
Falcandus has been styled the Tacitus of Sicily ; and, after a just but immense
abatement, from the first to the twelfth century, from a senator to a monk, I would
not strip him of his title : his narrative is rapid and perspicuous, his style bold and
elegant, his observation keen ; he had studied mankind, and feels like a man.  I
can only regret the narrow and barren field on which his labours have been cast.
[Cp. App. 1.  For the history of Sicily from the accession of William the Bad to
1177 see F. Holzach, Die auswärtige Politik des Königreichs Sicilien 1154-1177
(1892).]

[146] The laborious Benedictines (l'Art de vérifier les Dates, p. 896) are of opinion
that the true name of Falcandus is Fulcandus, or Foucault.  According to them,
Hugues Foucault, a Frenchman by birth, and at length abbot of St. Denys, had
followed into Sicily his patron Stephen de la Perche, uncle to the mother of William
II. archbishop of Palermo, and great chancellor of the kingdom.  Yet Falcandus
has all the feelings of a Sicilian ; and the title of *Alumnus* (which he bestows on
himself) appears to indicate that he was born, or at least educated, in the island.
[See Appendix 1.]

[147] Falcand. p. 303.  Richard de St. Germano begins his history from the death
and praises of William II.  After some unmeaning epithets, he thus continues :
Legis et justitiæ cultus tempore suo vigebat in regno ; suâ erat quilibet sorte contentus (were they mortals ?) ; ubique pax, ubique securitas, nec latronum metuebat
viator insidias, nec maris nauta offendicula piratarum (Script. Rerum Ital. tom.
vii. p. 969).

educated in the arts and manners, of this fortunate isle, departed long since to enrich the barbarians with our treasures,
and now returns with her savage allies, to contaminate the
beauties of her venerable parent. Already I behold the swarms
of angry barbarians; our opulent cities, the places flourishing
in a long peace, are shaken with fear, desolated by slaughter,
consumed by rapine, and polluted by intemperance and lust.
I see the massacre or captivity of our citizens, the rapes of our
virgins and matrons.[148] In this extremity (he interrogates a
friend) how must the Sicilians act? By the unanimous election
of a king of valour and experience, Sicily and Calabria might
yet be preserved;[149] for in the levity of the Apulians, ever
eager for new revolutions, I can repose neither confidence nor
hope.[150] Should Calabria be lost, the lofty towers, the numerous
youth, and the naval strength, of Messina[151] might guard the
passage against a foreign invader. If the savage Germans
coalesce with the pirates of Messina; if they destroy with fire
the fruitful region, so often wasted by the fires of mount Ætna,[152]
what resource will be left for the interior parts of the island,
these noble cities which should never be violated by the hostile
footsteps of a barbarian?[153] Catana has again been overwhelmed
by an earthquake; the ancient virtue of Syracuse expires in
poverty and solitude;[154] but Palermo is still crowned with a
diadem, and her triple walls inclose the active multitudes of
Christians and Saracens. If the two nations, under one king,

---

[148] Constantia, primis a cunabulis in deliciarum tuarum affluentiâ diutius edu-
cata, tuisque institutis [instituta], doctrinis et moribus informata, tandem opibus tuis
Barbaros delatura [ditatura] discessit ; et nunc cum ingentibus copiis [. . .]
revertitur, ut pulcherrima [pulcherrimæ] nutricis ornamenta [. . .] barbaricâ
fœditate contaminet . . . Intueri mihi jam videor turbulentas barbarorum acies
. . . civitates opulentas et loca diuturnâ pace florentia, metu concutere, cæde
vastare, rapinis atterere, et fœdare luxuriâ : [occurrunt] hinc cives aut [resistendo]
gladiis intercepti, aut [. . .] servitute depressi [illinc], virgines [. . .] constupratæ,
matronæ, &c. [p. 253-4].

[149] Certe si regem [sibi] non dubiæ virtutis elegerint, nec a Saracenis Christiani
[leg. a Christianis Saraceni] dissentiant, poterit rex creatus rebus licet quasi desperatis
et [fere] perditis subvenire, et incursus hostium, si prudenter egerit, propulsare.

[150] In Apulis, qui, semper novitate gaudentes, novarum rerum studiis aguntur,
nihil arbitror spei aut fiduciæ reponendum.

[151] Si civium tuorum virtutem et audaciam attendas, . . . murorum etiam ambi-
tum densis turribus circumseptum.

[152] Cum crudelitate piraticâ Theutonum confligat atrocitas, et inter ambustos
lapides, et Æthnæ flagrantis incendia, &c.

[153] Eam partem, quam nobilissimarum civitatum fulgor illustrat, quæ et toti
regno singulari meruit privilegio præeminere, nefarium esset . . . vel barbarorum
ingressu pollui. I wish to transcribe his florid, but curious, description of the
palace, city, and luxuriant plain of Palermo.

[154] Vires non suppetunt, et conatus tuos tam inopia civium, quam paucitas bella-
torum elidunt.

can unite for their common safety, they may rush on the barbarians with invincible arms. But, if the Saracens, fatigued by a repetition of injuries, should now retire and rebel; if they should occupy the castles of the mountains and sea-coast, the unfortunate Christians, exposed to a double attack, and placed as it were between the hammer and the anvil, must resign themselves to hopeless and inevitable servitude." [155] We must not forget that a priest here prefers his country to his religion; and that the Moslems, whose alliance he seeks, were still numerous and powerful in the state of Sicily.

The hopes, or at least the wishes, of Falcandus were at first gratified by the free and unanimous election of Tancred, the grandson of the first king, whose birth was illegitimate, but whose civil and military virtues shone without a blemish. During four years, the term of his life and reign, he stood in arms on the farthest verge of the Apulian frontier, against the powers of Germany; and the restitution of a royal captive, of Constantia herself, without injury or ransom, may appear to surpass the most liberal measure of reason. After his decease, the kingdom of his widow and infant son fell without a struggle; and Henry pursued his victorious march from Capua to Palermo. The political balance of Italy was destroyed by his success; and, if the pope and the free cities had consulted their obvious and real interest, they would have combined the powers of earth and heaven to prevent the dangerous union of the German empire with the kingdom of Sicily. But the subtle policy, for which the Vatican has so often been praised or arraigned, was on this occasion blind and inactive; and, if it were true that Celestine the Third had kicked away the Imperial crown from the head of the prostrate Henry,[156] such an act of impotent pride could

*Conquest of the kingdom of Sicily by the emperor Henry VI. A.D. 1194*

---

[155] At vero, quia difficile est Christianos in tanto rerum turbine, sublato regis timore Saracenos non opprimere, si Saraceni [. . .] injuriis fatigati ab eis cœperint dissidere, et castella forte maritima vel montanas munitiones occupaverint; ut hinc cum Theutonicis summâ [sit] virtute pugnandum illinc Saracenis crebris insultibus occurrendum, quid putas acturi sunt Siculi inter has depressi angustias, et velut inter malleum et incudem multo cum discrimine constituti? hoc utique agent quod poterunt, ut se Barbaris miserabili conditione dedentes, in eorum se conferant potestatem. Outinam plebis et [ac] procerum, Christianorum et Saracenorum vota conveniant; ut regem sibi concorditer eligentes, [irruentes] barbaros totis viribus, toto conanime, totisque desideriis proturbare contendant. The Normans and Sicilians appear to be confounded.

[156] The testimony of an Englishman, of Roger de Hoveden (p. 689), will lightly weigh against the silence of German and Italian history (Muratori, Annali d'Italia, om. x. p. 156). The priests and pilgrims, who returned from Rome, exalted, by every tale, the omnipotence of the holy father.

serve only to cancel an obligation and provoke an enemy. The Genoese, who enjoyed a beneficial trade and establishment in Sicily, listened to the promise of his boundless gratitude and speedy departure ; [157] their fleet commanded the straits of Messina, and opened the harbour of Palermo ; and the first act of this government was to abolish the privileges, and to seize the property, of these imprudent allies. The last hope of Falcandus was defeated by the discord of the Christians and Mahometans : they fought in the capital; several thousands of the latter were slain; but their surviving brethren fortified the mountains, and disturbed above thirty years the peace of the island. By the policy of Frederic the Second, sixty thousand Saracens were transplanted to Nocera in Apulia. In their wars against the Roman church, the emperor and his son Mainfroy were strengthened and disgraced by the service of the enemies of Christ ; and this national colony maintained their religion and manners in the heart of Italy, till they were extirpated, at the end of the thirteenth century, by the zeal and revenge of the house of Anjou.[158] All the calamities which the prophetic orator had deplored were surpassed by the cruelty and avarice of the German conqueror. He violated the royal sepulchres, and explored the secret treasures of the palace, Palermo, and the whole kingdom : the pearls and jewels, however precious, might be easily removed ; but one hundred and sixty horses were laden with the gold and silver of Sicily.[159] The young king, his mother and sisters, and the nobles of both sexes, were separately confined in the fortresses of the Alps ; and, on the slightest rumour of rebellion, the captives were deprived of life, of their eyes, or of the hope of posterity. Constantia herself was touched with sympathy for the miseries of her country ; and the heiress of the Norman line

[157] Ego enim in eo cum Teutonicis manere non debeo (Caffari, Annal. Genuenses, in Muratori, Script. Rerum Italicarum, tom. vi. p. 367, 368).

[158] For the Saracens of Sicily and Nocera, see the Annals of Muratori (tom. x. p. 149, and A.D. 1223, 1247), Giannone (tom. ii. p. 385), and of the originals, in Muratori's Collection, Richard de St. Germano (tom. vii. p. 996), Matteo Spinelli de Giovenazzo (tom. vii. p. 1064), Nicholas de Jamsilla (tom. x. p. 494), and Matteo Villani (tom. xiv. l. vii. p. 103). The last of these insinuates that, in reducing the Saracens of Nocera, Charles II. of Anjou employed rather artifice than violence.

[159] Muratori quotes a passage from Arnold of Lubec (l. iv. c. 20). Reperit thesauros absconditos, et omnem lapidum pretiosorum et gemmarum gloriam, ita ut oneratis 160 somariis gloriose ad terram suam redierit. Roger de Hoveden, who mentions the violation of the royal tomb and corpses, computes the spoil of Salerno at 200,000 ounces of gold (p. 746). On these occasions, I am almost tempted to exclaim with the listening maid in La Fontaine, " Je voudrois bien avoir ce qui manque ".

might struggle to check her despotic husband, and to save the patrimony of her new-born son, of an emperor so famous in the next age under the name of Frederic the Second. Ten years after this revolution, the French monarchs annexed to their crown the duchy of Normandy ; the sceptre of her ancient dukes had been transmitted, by a grand-daughter of William the Conqueror, to the house of Plantagenet ; and the adventurous Normans, who had raised so many trophies in France, England, and Ireland, in Apulia, Sicily, and the East, were lost, either in victory or servitude, among the vanquished nations.

*Final extinction of the Normans. A.D. 1204*

## CHAPTER LVII

*The Turks of the House of Seljuk—Their Revolt against Mahmud, Conqueror of Hindostan—Togrul subdues Persia, and protects the Caliphs—Defeat and Captivity of the Emperor Romanus Diogenes by Alp Arslan—Power and Magnificence of Malek Shah—Conquest of Asia Minor and Syria—State and Oppression of Jerusalem—Pilgrimages to the Holy Sepulchre*

The Turks    FROM the isle of Sicily the reader must transport himself beyond the Caspian Sea, to the original seat of the Turks or Turkmans, against whom the first crusade was principally directed. Their Scythian empire of the sixth century was long since dissolved ; but the name was still famous among the Greeks and Orientals ; and the fragments of the nation, each a powerful and independent people, were scattered over the desert from China to the Oxus and the Danube : the colony of Hungarians was admitted into the republic of Europe, and the thrones of Asia were occupied by slaves and soldiers of Turkish extraction. While Apulia and Sicily were subdued by the Norman lance, a swarm of these northern shepherds overspread the kingdoms of Persia : their princes of the race of Seljuk erected a splendid and solid empire from Samarcand to the confines of Greece and Egypt ; and the Turks have maintained their dominion in Asia Minor till the victorious crescent has been planted on the dome of St. Sophia.

Mahmud, the Gaznevide. A.D. 997-1028    One of the greatest of the Turkish princes was Mamood or Mahmud,[1] the Gaznevide, who reigned in the eastern provinces

---

[1] I am indebted for his character and history to d'Herbelot (Bibliothèque Orientale, *Mahmud*, p. 533-537), M. de Guignes (Histoire des Huns, tom. iii. p. 155-173), and our countryman, Colonel Alexander Dow (vol. i. p. 23-83). In the two first volumes of his History of Hindostan, he styles himself the translator of the Persian Ferishta ; but in his florid text it is not easy to distinguish the version and the original. [This work of Dow has been superseded by the translation of Colonel Briggs : " History of the Mahomedan Power in India till the year 1612, translated from the original Persian of Mohamed Kasim Ferishta," in 4 vols., 1829. Cp. his remarks on Dow's work in the Preface, vol. i. p. vi, vii.]

of Persia one thousand years after the birth of Christ. His
father Sebectagi was the slave of the slave of the slave of the [Subuktigīn]
commander of the faithful. But in this descent of servitude,
the first degree was merely titular, since it was filled by the
sovereign of Transoxiana and Chorasan, who still paid a nominal
allegiance to the caliph of Bagdad. The second rank was that
of a minister of state, a lieutenant of the Samanides,[2] who broke,
by his revolt, the bonds of political slavery. But the third step
was a state of real and domestic servitude in the family of that
rebel; from which Sebectagi, by his courage and dexterity,
ascended to the supreme command of the city and province of
Gazna,[3] as the son-in-law and successor of his grateful master.
The falling dynasty of the Samanides was at first protected, and
at last overthrown, by their servants; and, in the public disorders, the fortune of Mahmud continually increased. For him,
the title of *sultan*[4] was first invented; and his kingdom was
enlarged from Transoxiana to the neighbourhood of Ispahan,
from the shores of the Caspian to the mouth of the Indus. But
the principal source of his fame and riches was the holy war
which he waged against the Gentoos of Hindostan. In this
foreign narrative I may not consume a page; and a volume
would scarcely suffice to recapitulate the battles and sieges of His twelve ex-
his twelve expeditions. Never was the Musulman hero dis- peditions into Hindostan

---

[2] The dynasty of the Samanides continued 125 years, A.D. 874-999, under ten
princes. See their succession and ruin, in the Tables of M. de Guignes (Hist. des
Huns, tom. i. p. 404-406). They were followed [south of the Oxus] by the
Gaznevides, A.D. 999-1183. (See tom. i. p. 239, 240.) His division of nations
often disturbs the series of time and place.

[3] Gaznah hortos non habet; est emporium et domicilium mercaturæ Indicæ.
Abulfedæ Geograph. Reiske, tab. xxiii. p. 349; d'Herbelot, p. 364. It has not
been visited by any modern traveller. [Subuktigīn conquered Bŭst and Kusdār
in A.D. 978. For the story of his rise, cp. Nizām al-Mulk, Siasset Nameh, tr.
Schefer, p. 140 *sqq.*]

[4] By the ambassador of the caliph of Bagdad, who employed an Arabian or
Chaldaic word that signifies *lord* and *master* (d'Herbelot, p. 825). It is interpreted
Αὐτοκράτωρ, Βασιλεὺς Βασιλέων, by the Byzantine writers of the eleventh century; and
the name (Σουλτανός, Soldanus) is familiarly employed in the Greek and Latin
languages, after it had passed from the Gaznevides to the Seljukides, and other
emirs of Asia and Egypt. Ducange (Dissertation xvi. sur Joinville, p. 238-240,
Gloss. Græc. et Latin.) labours to find the title of sultan in the ancient kingdom
of Persia; but his proofs are mere shadows; a proper name in the Themes of
Constantine (ii. 11), an anticipation of Zonaras, &c. and a medal of Kai Khosrou,
not (as he believes) the Sassanide of the vith, but the Seljukide of Iconium of the
xiiith, century (de Guignes, Hist. des Huns, tom. i. p. 246). [The title *sultan*,
for the captain of the bodyguard, was introduced at least as early as the reign of
Mutawakkil, in the middle of the 9th century. It has been conjectured (by Vámbéry) that the name of one of the sons of the Hungarian chief Arpad, Ζάλτας, is
really *sultan*. The old Vienna chronicle gives his name as *Zoltan*, and the scribe
of King Béla, as *Zulta*.]

mayed by the inclemency of the seasons, the height of the mountains, the breadth of the rivers, the barrenness of the desert, the multitudes of the enemy, or the formidable array of their elephants of war.[5] The sultan of Gazna surpassed the limits of the conquests of Alexander; after a march of three months, over the hills of Cashmir and Thibet, he reached the famous city of Kinnoge,[6] on the Upper Ganges; and, in a naval combat on one of the branches of the Indus, he fought and vanquished four thousand boats of the natives. Delhi, Lahor, and Multan were compelled to open their gates; the fertile kingdom of Guzarat attracted his ambition and tempted his stay; and his avarice indulged the fruitless project of discovering the golden and aromatic isles of the Southern Ocean. On the payment of a tribute, the *rajahs* preserved their dominions; the people, their lives and fortunes; but to the religion of Hindostan the zealous Musulman was cruel and inexorable; many hundred temples, or pagodas, were levelled with the ground; many thousand idols were demolished; and the servants of the prophet were stimulated and rewarded by the precious materials of which they were composed. The pagoda of Sumnat was situated on the promontory of Guzarat, in the neighbourhood of Diu, one of the last remaining possessions of the Portuguese.[7] It was endowed with the revenue of two thousand villages; two thousand Brahmins were consecrated to the service of the Deity, whom they washed each morning and evening in water from the distant Ganges: the subordinate ministers consisted of three hundred musicians, three hundred barbers, and five hundred dancing girls, conspicuous for their birth and beauty. Three sides of the temple were protected by the ocean, the narrow isthmus

[Kanauj]

[Somnath.
A.D. 1024]

---

[5] Ferishta (apud Dow, Hist. of Hindostan, vol. i. p. 49) mentions the report of a *gun* in the Indian army. But, as I am slow in believing this premature (A.D. 1008) use of artillery, I must desire to scrutinise first the text and then the authority of Ferishta, who lived in the Mogul court in the last century. [Briggs (*op. cit.* vol. i. p. 47) translates, in the passage to which Gibbon refers, "naphtha-balls" and "arrows"; the original words being *nupth* and *khudung*. But in other Mss. the variants are formed: *tope* (a gun) and *toofung* (a musket). These readings must be due to interpolators. Probably Bābar first introduced guns into Upper India in 1526. Cp. the note of Briggs.]

[6] Kinnoge or Canouge (the old Palimbothra) is marked in latitude 27° 3′ longitude 80° 13′. See d'Anville (Antiquité de l'Inde, p. 60-62), corrected by the local knowledge of Major Rennell (in his excellent Memoir on his map of Hindostan, p. 37-43), 300 jewellers, 30,000 shops for the areca nut, 60,000 bands of musicians, &c. (Abulfed. Geograph. tab. xv. p. 274; Dow, vol. i. p. 16) will allow an ample deduction. [Palimbothra is supposed to be Patna.]

[7] The idolaters of Europe, says Ferishta (Dow, vol. i. p. 66). Consult Abulfed (p. 272) and Rennell's map of Hindostan.

was fortified by a natural or artificial precipice ; and the city and adjacent country were peopled by a nation of fanatics. They confessed the sins and the punishment of Kinnoge and Delhi ; but, if the impious stranger should presume to approach *their* holy precincts, he would surely be overwhelmed by a blast of the divine vengeance. By this challenge the faith of Mahmud was animated to a personal trial of the strength of this Indian deity. Fifty thousand of his worshippers were pierced by the spear of the Moslems : the walls were scaled ; the sanctuary was profaned ; and the conqueror aimed a blow of his iron mace at the head of the idol. The trembling Brahmins are said to have offered ten millions sterling [8] for his ransom ; and it was urged by the wisest counsellors that the destruction of a stone image would not change the hearts of the Gentoos, and that such a sum might be dedicated to the relief of the true believers. " Your reasons," replied the Sultan, " are specious and strong ; but never in the eyes of posterity shall Mahmud appear as a merchant of idols." He repeated his blows, and a treasure of pearls and rubies, concealed in the belly of the statue, explained in some degree the devout prodigality of the Brahmins. The fragments of the idol were distributed to Gazna, Mecca, and Medina. Bagdad listened to the edifying tale ; and Mahmud was saluted by the caliph with the title of guardian of the fortune and faith of Mahomet.

From the paths of blood, and such is the history of nations, His character cannot refuse to turn aside to gather some flowers of science or virtue. The name of Mahmud the Gaznevide is still venerable in the East : his subjects enjoyed the blessings of prosperity and peace ; his vices were concealed by the veil of religion ; and two familiar examples will testify his justice and magnanimity. I. As he sat in the Divan, an unhappy subject bowed before the throne to accuse the insolence of a Turkish soldier who had driven him from his house and bed. " Suspend your clamours," said Mahmud, " inform me of his next visit, and ourself in person will judge and punish the offender." The sultan followed his guide, invested the house with his guards, and, extinguishing the torches, pronounced the death of the criminal, who had been seized in the act of rapine and adultery. After the execution of his sentence, the lights were rekindled, Mahmud fell prostrate in prayer, and, rising from the ground, demanded some homely fare,

[8] [Not ten millions sterling, but " crores of gold ". Briggs, p. 72, translates a quantity of gold ".]

which he devoured with the voraciousness of hunger.    The poor
man, whose injury he had avenged, was unable to suppress his
astonishment and curiosity ; and the courteous monarch condescended to explain the motives of this singular behaviour.    " I
had reason to suspect that none except one of my sons could dare
to perpetrate such an outrage ; and I extinguished the lights,
that my justice might be blind and inexorable.    My prayer was
a thanksgiving on the discovery of the offender ; and so painful
was my anxiety that I had passed three days without food since
the first moment of your complaint."    II. The sultan of Gazna
had declared war against the dynasty of the Bowides, the sovereigns of the western Persia ; he was disarmed by an epistle of
the sultana mother, and delayed his invasion till the manhood of
her son.[9]    " During the life of my husband," said the artful regent, " I was ever apprehensive of your ambition ; he was a
prince and a soldier worthy of your arms.    He is now no more ;
his sceptre has passed to a woman and a child, and you *dare not*
attack their infancy and weakness.    How inglorious would be
your conquest, how shameful your defeat ! and yet the event of
war is in the hand of the Almighty."    Avarice was the only
defect that tarnished the illustrious character of Mahmud ; and
never has that passion been more richly satisfied.    The Oriental
exceed the measure of credibility in the account of millions of
gold and silver, such as the avidity of man has never accumulated
in the magnitude of pearls, diamonds, and rubies, such as have
never been produced by the workmanship of nature.[10]    Yet the
soil of Hindostan is impregnated with precious minerals ; her
trade, in every age, has attracted the gold and silver of the
world ; and her virgin spoils were rifled by the first of the
Mahometan conquerors.    His behaviour, in the last days of his
life, evinces the vanity of these possessions, so laboriously won,
so dangerously held, and so inevitably lost.    He surveyed the
vast and various chambers of the treasury of Gazna ; burst into
tears ; and again closed the doors, without bestowing any portion
of the wealth which he could no longer hope to preserve.    The
following day he reviewed the state of his military force : one

[9] D'Herbelot, Bibliothèque Orientale, p. 527.    Yet these letters, apophthegm
&c., are rarely the language of the heart, or the motives of public action.

[10] For instance, a ruby of four hundred and fifty miskals (Dow, vol. i. p. 53)
six pounds three ounces : the largest in the treasury of Delhi weighed seventee
miskals (Voyages de Tavernier, partie ii. p. 280).    It is true that in the East a
coloured stones are called rubies (p. 355), and that Tavernier saw three larger an
more precious among the jewels de notre grand roi, le plus puissant et plus ma
nifique de tous les Rois de la terre (p. 376).

hundred thousand foot, fifty-five thousand horse, and thirteen hundred elephants of battle.[11]   He again wept the instability of human greatness ; and his grief was embittered by the hostile progress of the Turkmans, whom he had introduced into the heart of his Persian kingdom.

In the modern depopulation of Asia, the regular operation of government and agriculture is confined to the neighbourhood of cities ; and the distant country is abandoned to the pastoral tribes of Arabs, Curds, and *Turkmans*.[12]   Of the last-mentioned people, two considerable branches extend on either side of the Caspian Sea : the western colony can muster forty thousand soldiers ; the eastern, less obvious to the traveller, but more strong and populous, has increased to the number of one hundred thousand families.   In the midst of civilised nations, they preserve the manners of the Scythian desert, remove their encampments with the change of seasons, and feed their cattle among the ruins of palaces and temples.   Their flocks and herds are their only riches ; their tents, either black or white, according to the colour of the banner, are covered with felt, and of a circular form ; their winter apparel is a sheep-skin ; a robe of cloth or cotton their summer garment : the features of the men are harsh and ferocious ; the countenance of their women is soft and pleasing. Their wandering life maintains the spirit and exercise of arms ; they fight on horseback ; and their courage is displayed in frequent contests with each other and with their neighbours.   For the licence of pasture they pay a slight tribute to the sovereign of the land ; but the domestic jurisdiction is in the hands of the chiefs and elders.   The first emigration of the eastern Turkmans, the most ancient of their race, may be ascribed to the tenth century of the Christian æra.[13]   In the decline of the caliphs, and the weakness of their lieutenants, the barrier of the Jaxartes was often violated : in each invasion, after the victory or retreat

*(marginal note:)* Manners and emigration of the Turks or Turkmans. A.D. 980-1028

---

[11] Dow, vol, i. p. 65.  The sovereign of Kinnoge is said to have possessed 2500 elephants (Abulfed. Geograph. tab. xv. p. 274).  From these Indian stories the reader may correct a note in my first volume (p. 209) ; or from that note he may correct these stories.

[12] See a just and natural picture of these pastoral manners, in the history of William, archbishop of Tyre (l. i. c. vii. in the Gesta Dei per Francos, p. 633, 634), and a valuable note by the editor of the Histoire Généalogique des Tatars, p. 535-538.

[13] The first emigrations of the Turkmans, and doubtful origin of the Seljukians, may be traced in the laborious history of the Huns, by M. de Guignes (tom. i. tables Chronologiques, l. v. tom. iii. l. vii. ix. x.), and the Bibliothèque Orientale d'Herbelot (p. 799-802, 897-901), Elmacin (Hist. Saracen. p. 331-333), and Abul-pharagius (Dynast. p. 221, 222).

of their countrymen, some wandering tribe, embracing the
Mahometan faith, obtained a free encampment in the spacious
plains and pleasant climate of Transoxiana and Carizme. The
Turkish slaves who aspired to the throne encouraged these emigrations, which recruited their armies, awed their subjects and
rivals, and protected the frontier against the wilder natives of
Turkestan; and this policy was abused by Mahmud the Gaznevide
beyond the example of former times. He was admonished of his
error by a chief of the race of Seljuk, who dwelt in the territory of
Bochara. The sultan had enquired what supply of men he could
furnish for military service. " If you send," replied Ismael, " one
of these arrows into our camp, fifty thousand of your servants
will mount on horseback." " And if that number," continued
Mahmud, " should not be sufficient ? " " Send this second arrow
to the horde of Balik, and you will find fifty thousand more."
" But," said the Gaznevide, dissembling his anxiety, " if I should
stand in need of the whole force of your kindred tribes ? " " Dispatch my bow," was the last reply of Ismael, " and, as it is
circulated around, the summons will be obeyed by two hundred
thousand horse." The apprehension of such formidable friendship induced Mahmud to transport the most obnoxious tribes
into the heart of Chorasan, where they would be separated from
their brethren by the river Oxus, and inclosed on all sides by the
walls of obedient cities. But the face of the country was an object of temptation rather than terror; and the vigour of government was relaxed by the absence and death of the sultan of
Gazna. The shepherds were converted into robbers; the band
of robbers were collected into an army of conquerors; as far
as Ispahan and the Tigris, Persia was afflicted by their predatory inroads; and the Turkmans were not ashamed or afraid to
measure their courage and numbers with the proudest sovereign
of Asia. Massoud, the son and successor of Mahmud, had too
[Emirs]
long neglected the advice of his wisest Omrahs. " Your enemies,"
they repeatedly urged, " were in their origin a swarm of ants;
they are now little snakes; and, unless they be instantly crushed,
they will acquire the venom and magnitude of serpents." After
some alternatives of truce and hostility, after the repulse or partial
success of his lieutenants, the sultan marched in person against the
Turkmans, who attacked him on all sides with barbarous shouts
and irregular onset. " Massoud," says the Persian historian,

[14] Dow, Hist. of Hindostan, vol. i. p. 89, 95-98. I have copied this passage
a specimen of the Persian manner; but I suspect that by some odd fatality t

"plunged singly to oppose the torrent of gleaming arms, exhibiting such acts of gigantic force and valour as never king had before displayed. A few of his friends, roused by his words and actions, and that innate honour which inspires the brave, seconded their lord so well that, wheresoever he turned his fatal sword, the enemies were mowed down or retreated before him. But now, when victory seemed to blow on his standard, misfortune was active behind it ; for, when he looked round, he beheld almost his whole army, excepting that body he commanded in person, devouring the paths of flight." The Gaznevide was abandoned by the cowardice or treachery of some generals of Turkish race ; and this memorable day of Zendecan [15] founded in Persia the dynasty of the shepherd kings.[16]

They defeat the Gaznevides, and subdue Persia. A.D.1038 [1039] [Battle of Damghan]

The victorious Turkmans immediately proceeded to the election of a king ; and, if the probable tale of a Latin historian [17] deserves any credit, they determined by lot the choice of their new master. A number of arrows were successively inscribed with the name of a tribe, a family, and a candidate ; they were drawn from the bundle by the hand of a child ; and the important prize was obtained by Togrul Beg, the son of Michael, the son of Seljuk, whose surname was immortalised in the greatness of his posterity. The sultan Mahmud, who valued himself on his skill in national genealogy, professed his ignorance of the family of Seljuk ; yet the father of that race appears to have been a chief of power and renown.[18] For a

Dynasty of the Seljukians. A.D. 1038-1152

style of Ferishta has been improved by that of Ossian. [The translation of Briggs, i. 110, is as follows : " The king undismayed even by the defection of his officers gallantly rode his horse to the spot where he perceived the conflict most bloody, performing prodigies of valour, unequalled perhaps by any sovereign ; but his efforts were vain ; for, when he looked round, he beheld nearly the whole of his army, excepting the body which he commanded in person, in full flight ".]

[15] The Zendekan of d'Herbelot (p. 1028), the Dindaka of Dow (vol. i. p. 97), is probably the Dandanekan of Abulfeda (Geograph. p. 345, Reiske), a small town of Chorasan, two days' journey from Marû [Persian, Merv], and renowned through the East for the production and manufacture of cotton.

[16] The Byzantine historians (Cedrenus, tom. ii. p. 766, 767 [ii. p. 566, ed. Bonn] ; Zonaras, tom. ii. p. 255 [xvii. 25] ; Nicephorus Bryennius, p. 21 [p. 26, ed. B.]) have confounded, in this revolution, the truth of time and place, of names and persons, of causes and events. The ignorance and errors of these Greeks (which I shall not stop to unravel) may inspire some distrust of the story of Cyaxares and Cyrus, as it is told by their most eloquent predecessors.

[17] Willerm. Tyr. l. i. c. 7, p. 633 [ed. Bongars.]. The divination by arrows is ancient and famous in the East.

[18] D'Herbelot, p. 801. Yet, after the fortune of his posterity, Seljuk became the thirty-fourth in lineal descent from the great Afrasiab, emperor of Touran (p. 800). The Tartar pedigree of the house of Zingis gave a different cast to flattery and fable ; and the historian Mirkhond derives the Seljukides from Alankavah,

daring intrusion into the harem of his prince, Seljuk was banished from Turkestan ; with a numerous tribe of his friends and vassals, he passed the Jaxartes, encamped in the neighbourhood of Samarcand, embraced the religion of Mahomet,[19] and acquired the crown of martyrdom in a war against the infidels. His age, of an hundred and seven years, surpassed the life of his son, and Seljuk adopted the care of his two grandsons, Togrul

and Jaafar ; the eldest of whom, at the age of forty-five, was invested with the title of sultan, in the royal city of Nishabur.

The blind determination of chance was justified by the virtues of the successful candidate.    It would be superfluous to praise the valour of a Turk ; and the ambition of Togrul [20] was equal to his valour.    By his arms, the Gaznevides were expelled from the eastern kingdoms of Persia, and gradually driven to the banks of the Indus, in search of a softer and more wealthy conquest. In the West he annihilated the dynasty of the Bowides ; and the sceptre of Irak passed from the Persian to the Turkish nation. The princes who had felt, or who feared, the Seljukian arrows, bowed their heads in the dust ; by the conquest of Aderbijan,

or Media, he approached the Roman confines ; and the shepherd presumed to dispatch an ambassador, or herald, to demand the tribute and obedience of the emperor of Constantinople.[21]    In his own dominions, Togrul was the father of his soldiers and people ; by a firm and equal administration Persia was relieved from the evils of anarchy ; and the same hands which had been imbrued in blood became the guardians of justice and the public peace.    The more rustic, perhaps the wisest, portion of the Turkmans [22] continued to dwell in the tents of their ancestors ;

the virgin mother (p. 801, col. 2). If they be the same as the *Zalzuts* of Abulghazi Bahader Khan (Hist. Généalogique, p. 148), we quote in their favour the most weighty evidence of a Tartar prince himself, the descendant of Zingis, Alankavah, or Alancu, and Oguz Khan.

[19] [The Seljūks were possibly Christians, before they were converted to Islamism ; the names Michael, Jonas, Moses, which some of them bore, may point to this. Cp. Cahun, Intr. à l'histoire de l'Asie, p. 170.]

[20] By a slight corruption, Togrul Beg is the Tangroli-pix of the Greeks.    His reign and character are faithfully exhibited by d'Herbelot (Bibliothèque Orientale, p. 1027, 1028) and de Guignes (Hist. des Huns, tom. iii. p. 189-201).

[21] Cedrenus, tom. ii. p. 774, 775 [ii. p. 580, ed. B.].    Zonaras, tom. ii. p. 257 [xvii. 25].    With their usual knowledge of Oriental affairs, they describe the ambassador as a *sherif*, who, like the syncellus of the patriarch, was the vicar and successor of the caliph.

[22] From William of Tyre, I have borrowed this distinction of Turks and Turkmans, which at least is popular and convenient.    The names are the same, and the addition of *man* is of the same import in the Persic and Teutonic idioms. Few critics will adopt the etymology of James de Vitry (Hist. Hierosol. l. i. c. 11, p. 1061), of Turcomani, quasi *Turci* et *Comani*, a mixed people.

and, from the Oxus to the Euphrates, these military colonies were protected and propagated by their native princes. But the Turks of the court and city were refined by business and softened by pleasure; they imitated the dress, language, and manners of Persia; and the royal palaces of Nishabur and Rei displayed the order and magnificence of a great monarchy. The most deserving of the Arabians and Persians were promoted to the honours of the state; and the whole body of the Turkish nation embraced with fervour and sincerity the religion of Mahomet. The northern swarms of barbarians, who overspread both Europe and Asia, have been irreconcilably separated by the consequences of a similar conduct. Among the Moslems, as among the Christians, their vague and local traditions have yielded to the reason and authority of the prevailing system, to the fame of antiquity, and the consent of nations. But the triumph of the Koran is more pure and meritorious, as it was not assisted by any visible splendour of worship which might allure the Pagans by some resemblance of idolatry. The first of the Seljukian sultans was conspicuous by his zeal and faith: each day he repeated the five prayers which are enjoined to the true believers; of each week, the two first days were consecrated by an extraordinary fast; and in every city a mosch was completed, before Togrul presumed to lay the foundations of a palace.[23]

With the belief of the Koran, the son of Seljuk imbibed a lively reverence for the successor of the prophet. But that sublime character was still disputed by the caliphs of Bagdad and Egypt, and each of the rivals was solicitous to prove his title in the judgment of the strong, though illiterate, barbarians. Mahmud the Gaznevide had declared himself in favour of the line of Abbas; and had treated with indignity the robe of honour which was presented to the Fatimite ambassador. Yet the ungrateful Hashemite had changed with the change of fortune; he applauded the victory of Zendecan, and named the Seljukian sultan his temporal vicegerent over the Moslem world. As Togrul executed and enlarged this important trust, he was called to the deliverance of the caliph Cayem, and obeyed the holy [Al-Kaim] summons, which gave a new kingdom to his arms.[24] In the palace of Bagdad, the commander of the faithful still slumbered, a venerable phantom. His servant or master, the prince of the

*He delivers the caliph of Bagdad. A.D. 1055*

---

[23] Hist. Générale des Huns, tom. iii. p. 165, 166, 167. M. de Guignes quotes Abulmahasen, an historian of Egypt.

[24] Consult the Bibliothèque Orientale, in the articles of the *Abbassides, Caher,* and *Caiem,* and the Annals of Elmacin and Abulpharagius.

Bowides, could no longer protect him from the insolence of meaner tyrants; and the Euphrates and Tigris were oppressed by the revolt of the Turkish and Arabian emirs. The presence of a conqueror was implored as a blessing; and the transient mischiefs of fire and sword were excused as the sharp but salutary remedies which alone could restore the health of the republic. At the head of an irresistible force, the sultan of Persia marched from Hamadan : the proud were crushed, the prostrate were spared; the prince of the Bowides disappeared; the heads of the most obstinate rebels were laid at the feet of Togrul; and he inflicted a lesson of obedience on the people of Mosul and Bagdad. After the chastisement of the guilty and the restoration His investi- of peace, the royal shepherd accepted the reward of his labours ; ture and a solemn comedy represented the triumph of religious prejudice over barbarian power.[25] The Turkish sultan embarked on the Tigris, landed at the gate of Racca, and made his public entry on horseback. At the palace-gate he respectfully dismounted, and walked on foot, preceded by his emirs without arms. The caliph was seated behind his black veil ; the black garment of the Abbassides was cast over his shoulders, and he held in his hand the staff of the apostle of God. The conqueror of the East kissed the ground, stood some time in a modest posture, and was led towards the throne by the vizir and an interpreter. After Togrul had seated himself on another throne, his commission was publicly read, which declared him the temporal lieutenant of the vicar of the prophet. He was successively invested with seven robes of honour, and presented with seven slaves, the natives of the seven climates of the Arabian empire. His mystic veil was perfumed with musk; two crowns were placed on his head ; two scymetars were girded on his side, as the symbols of a double reign over the East and West. After this inauguration, the sultan was prevented from prostrating himself a second time ; but he twice kissed the hand of the commander of the faithful, and his titles were proclaimed by the voice of heralds and the applause of the Moslems.[26] In a second visit to Bagdad, the Seljukian prince again rescued the caliph from his enemies; and devoutly, on foot, led the bridle of his mule from the prison to the palace. Their alliance was cemented

[25] For this curious ceremony, I am indebted to M. de Guignes (tom. iii. p. 197, 198), and that learned author is obliged to Bondari, who composed in Arabic the history of the Seljukides (tom. v. p. 365). I am ignorant of his age, country and character.

[26] [Weil, Gesch. der Chalifen, iii. p. 99.]

by the marriage of Togrul's sister with the successor of the prophet. Without reluctance he had introduced a Turkish virgin into his harem ; but Cayem proudly refused his daughter to the sultan, disdained to mingle the blood of the Hashemites with the blood of a Scythian shepherd ; and protracted the negotiation many months, till the gradual diminution of his revenue admonished him that he was still in the hands of a master. The royal nuptials were followed by the death of Togrul himself ; [27] as he left no children, his nephew Alp Arslan succeeded to the title and prerogatives of sultan ; and his name, after that of the caliph, was pronounced in the public prayers of the Moslems. Yet in this revolution the Abbassides acquired a larger measure of liberty and power. On the throne of Asia, the Turkish monarchs were less jealous of the domestic administration of Bagdad ; and the commanders of the faithful were relieved from the ignominious vexations to which they had been exposed by the presence and poverty of the Persian dynasty.

and death.
A.D. 1063

Since the fall of the caliphs, the discord and degeneracy of the Saracens respected the Asiatic provinces of Rome ; which, by the victories of Nicephorus, Zimisces, and Basil, had been extended as far as Antioch and the eastern boundaries of Armenia. Twenty-five years after the death of Basil, his successors were suddenly assaulted by an unknown race of barbarians, who united the Scythian valour with the fanaticism of new proselytes and the art and riches of a powerful monarchy.[28] The myriads of Turkish horse overspread a frontier of six hundred miles from Taurus to Arzeroum, and the blood of one hundred and thirty thousand Christians was a grateful sacrifice to the Arabian prophet. Yet the arms of Togrul did not make any deep or lasting impression on the Greek empire. The torrent rolled away from the open country ; the sultan retired without glory or success from the siege of an Armenian city ; the obscure hostilities were continued or suspended with a vicissitude of

The Turks invade the Roman empire. A.D. 1050

[27] Eodem anno (A.H. 455) obiit princeps Togrulbecus . . . rex fuit clemens, prudens, et peritus regnandi, cujus terror corda mortalium invaserat, ita ut obedirent ei reges atque ad ipsum scriberent. Elmacin, Hist. Saracen. p. 342, vers. Erpenii.

[28] For these wars of the Turks and Romans, see in general the Byzantine histories of Zonaras and Cedrenus, Scylitzes the continuator of Cedrenus, and Nicephorus Bryennius Cæsar. The two first of these were monks, the two latter statesmen ; yet such were the Greeks that the difference of style and character is scarcely discernible. For the Orientals, I draw as usual on the wealth of d'Herbelot (see titles of the first Seljukides) and the accuracy of de Guignes (Hist. des Huns, tom. iii. l. x.).

events ; and the bravery of the Macedonian legions renewed
the fame of the conqueror of Asia.[29]    The name of Alp Arslan,
the valiant lion, is expressive of the popular idea of the perfection of man ; and the successor of Togrul displayed the fierceness
and generosity of the royal animal.  He passed the Euphrates
at the head of the Turkish cavalry, and entered Cæsarea, the
metropolis of Cappadocia, to which he had been attracted by
the fame and wealth of the temple of St. Basil.  The solid
structure resisted the destroyer ; but he carried away the doors
of the shrine incrusted with gold and pearls, and profaned the
relics of the tutelar saint, whose mortal frailties were now

covered by the venerable rust of antiquity.    The final conquest
of Armenia and Georgia was achieved by Alp Arslan.    In Armenia, the title of a kingdom and the spirit of a nation [30] were
annihilated ; the artificial fortifications were yielded by the
mercenaries of Constantinople ; by strangers without faith, veterans without pay or arms, and recruits without experience or
discipline.  The loss of this important frontier was the news of
a day ; and the Catholics were neither surprised nor displeased
that a people so deeply infected with the Nestorian and Euty-
chian errors had been delivered by Christ and his mother into
the hands of the infidels.[31]    The woods and valleys of mount
Caucasus were more strenuously defended by the native Georgians [32] or Iberians : but the Turkish sultan and his son Malek

---

[29] Ἐφέρετο γὰρ ἐν Τούρκοις λόγος, ὡς εἴη πεπρωμένον καταστραφῆναι τὸ Τούρκων γένος
ἀπὸ τῆς τοιαύτης δυνάμεως, ὁποίαν ὁ Μακεδὼν Ἀλέξανδρος ἔχων κατεστρέψατο Πέρσας.
Cedrenus, tom. ii. p. 791 [ii. p. 611, ed. B.].    The credulity of the vulgar is always
probable ; and the Turks had learned from the Arabs the history or legend of
Escander Dulcarnein (d'Herbelot, p. 317, &c.).

[30] [And the culture.  Ani which had passed under the dominion of the Empire
in 1046 was captured by Alp Arslan in 1064 (July 6).    Kars was then ceded by its
trembling prince to the Empire in exchange for Camendav in the mountains of
Cilicia ; but it had hardly been occupied by the Imperialists before it was taken by
the Turks.]

[31] Οἳ καὶ [leg. τὴν] Ἰβηρίαν καὶ Μεσοποταμίαν καὶ Ἀρμενίαν οἰκοῦσιν· [leg. καὶ
Μεσοποταμίαν μέχρι Λυκανδοῦ καὶ Μελιτηνῆς καὶ τὴν παρακειμένην οἰκοῦσιν Ἀρμενίαν] καὶ
οἳ τὴν Ἰουδαικὴν τοῦ Νεστορίου καὶ τῶν Ἀκεφάλων θρησκεύουσιν αἵρεσιν (Scylitzes, ad
calcem Cedreni, tom. ii. p. 834 [ii. p. 687, ed. B.], whose ambiguous construction
shall not tempt me to suspect that he confounded the Nestorian and Monophysite
heresies).  He familiarly talks of the μῆνις, χόλος, ὀργή, Θεοῦ, qualities, as I should
apprehend, very foreign to the perfect Being ; but his bigotry is forced to confess
that they were soon afterwards discharged on the orthodox Romans.

[32] Had the name of Georgians been known to the Greeks (Stritter, Memoriæ
Byzant. tom. iv. Iberica), I should derive it from their agriculture, as the Σκύθαι
γεωργοί of Herodotus (l. iv. c. 18, p. 289, edit. Wesseling).    But it appears only
since the crusades, among the Latins (Jac. a Vitriaco, Hist. Hierosol. c. 79, p.
1095) and Orientals (d'Herbelot, p. 407), and was devoutly borrowed from St.
George of Cappadocia.

were indefatigable in this holy war; their captives were compelled to promise a spiritual as well as temporal obedience;
and, instead of their collars and bracelets, an iron horse-shoe,
a badge of ignominy, was imposed on the infidels who still adhered to the worship of their fathers. The change, however,
was not sincere or universal; and, through ages of servitude,
the Georgians have maintained the succession of their princes
and bishops. But a race of men, whom nature has cast in her
most perfect mould, is degraded by poverty, ignorance, and
vice; their profession, and still more their practice, of Christianity is an empty name; and, if they have emerged from
heresy, it is only because they are too illiterate to remember a
metaphysical creed.[33]

The false or genuine magnanimity of Mahmud the Gaznevide
was not imitated by Alp Arslan; and he attacked, without scruple,
the Greek empress Eudocia and her children. His alarming
progress compelled her to give herself and her sceptre to the
hand of a soldier; and Romanus Diogenes was invested with
the Imperial purple. His patriotism, and perhaps his pride,
urged him from Constantinople within two months after his
accession; and the next campaign he most scandalously took
the field during the holy festival of Easter. In the palace,
Diogenes was no more than the husband of Eudocia; in the
camp, he was the emperor of the Romans, and he sustained
that character with feeble resources and invincible courage.
By his spirit and success, the soldiers were taught to act, the
subjects to hope, and the enemies to fear. The Turks had
penetrated into the heart of Phrygia; but the sultan himself
had resigned to his emirs the prosecution of the war; and their
numerous detachments were scattered over Asia in the security
of conquest. Laden with spoil and careless of discipline, they
were separately surprised and defeated by the Greeks; the activity of the emperor seemed to multiply his presence; and,
while they heard of his expedition to Antioch, the enemy felt
his sword on the hills of Trebizond. In three laborious campaigns, the Turks were driven beyond the Euphrates;[34] in the

*The emperor Romanus Diogenes. A.D. 1068-107*

*[1st campaign, A.D. 1069; 2nd campaign, A.D. 1069]*

---

[33] Mosheim, Institut. Hist. Eccles. p. 632. See in Chardin's Travels (tom. i.
p. 171-175) the manners and religion of this handsome but worthless nation. See
the pedigree of their princes from Adam to the present century, in the Tables of
M. de Guignes (tom. i. p. 433-438).

[34] [In the first two campaigns Romanus led the army himself. For the geo-
graphy of these military operations see Mr. J. G. C. Anderson's paper in Journal of
Hellenic Studies, xvii. p. 36-39 (1897). In the third campaign (A.D. 1070) Manuel
Comnenus was entrusted with the command.]

fourth and last, Romanus undertook the deliverance of Armenia.
The desolation of the land obliged him to transport a supply
of two months' provisions; and he marched forwards to the
siege of Malazkerd,[35] an important fortress in the midway
between the modern cities of Arzeroum and Van.  His army
amounted, at the least, to one hundred thousand men.  The
troops of Constantinople were reinforced by the disorderly multitudes of Phrygia and Cappadocia ; but the real strength was
composed of the subjects and allies of Europe, the legions of
Macedonia, and the squadrons of Bulgaria ; the Uzi, a Molda-
vian horde, who were themselves of the Turkish race ;[36] and,
above all, the mercenary and adventurous bands of French and
Normans.  Their lances were commanded by the valiant Ursel
of Baliol, the kinsman or father of the Scottish kings,[37] and were
allowed to excel in the exercise of arms, or, according to the
Greek style, in the practice of the Pyrrhic dance.

[35] This city is mentioned by Constantine Porphyrogenitus (de Administrat. Imperii, l. ii. c. 44, p. 119) and the Byzantines of the xith century, under the
name of Mantzikierte, and by some is confounded with Theodosiopolis ; but
Delisle, in his notes and maps, has very properly fixed the situation.  Abulfeda
(Geograph. tab. xviii. p. 310) describes Malasgerd as a small town, built with black
stone, supplied with water, without trees, &c.  [Manzikert is on the Murad Tchai,
north of Lake Van.]

[36] The Uzi of the Greeks (Stritter, Memor. Byzant. tom. iii. p. 923-948) are the
Gozz of the Orientals (Hist. des Huns, tom. ii. p. 522, tom. iii. p. 133, &c.).  They
appear on the Danube and the Volga, in Armenia, Syria, and Chorasan, and the
name seems to have been extended to the whole Turkman race.  [The Uzi were a
Turkish horde akin to the Patzinaks.  They are mentioned by Constantine Porphyrogennetos (in the De Adm. Imp.) as living in his time beyond the Patzinaks and
the Khazars.  They are the same as the Cumani (*Komanoi* in Anna Comnena,
&c.) ; and are called Polovtsi in the old Russian Chronicle.  The Hungarians call
them Kúnok.  They first appeared in Russia in A.D. 1055 (Nestor, c. 59).  Then
they drove the Patzinaks out of Atelkuzu, the land of which *they* had formerly
dispossessed the Hungarians into Walachia.  Sixty thousand of them crossed the
Danube in 1065, but were for the most part cut to pieces, with the help of the
Patzinaks ; some of the remnant were settled in Macedonia.  A glossary of the
Cumanian language has been accidentally preserved in a Ms. which Petrarch presented to the Library of St. Mark.  It was published by Klaproth in Mémoires
relatifs à l'Asia, iii. (title : Alphabetum Persicum Comanicum et Latinum) and
has been edited by Count Géza Kuun, Codex Cumanicus, 1880.  It establishes the
Turkish character of the Uzes.]

[37] Urselius (the Russelius of Zonaras) is distinguished by Jeffrey Malaterra (l. i.
c. 33) among the Norman conquerors of Sicily, and with the surname of *Baliol ;*
and our own historians will tell how the Baliols came from Normandy to Durham,
built Bernard's Castle on the Tees, married an heiress of Scotland, &c.  Ducange
(Not. ad Nicephor. Bryennium, l. ii. No. 4) has laboured the subject in honour of
the president de Bailleul, whose father had exchanged the sword for the gown.
[For the history of Ursel and his Norman realm in Asia Minor see Nicephorus
Bryennius, p. 73 *sqq.*, and Attaleiates, p. 184 *sqq.*  Cp. Hirsch, Forschungen zur
deutschen Geschichte, 8, p. 332 *sqq.*]

On the report of this bold invasion, which threatened his Defeat of the Romans. A.D. 1071, August hereditary dominions, Alp Arslan flew to the scene of action at the head of forty thousand horse.[38]  His rapid and skilful evolutions distressed and dismayed the superior numbers of the Greeks ; [Battle of Manzikert] and in the defeat of Basilacius, one of their principal generals, he displayed the first example of his valour and clemency.  The imprudence of the emperor had separated his forces after the reduction of Malazkerd.  It was in vain that he attempted to recal the mercenary Franks : they refused to obey his summons ; he disdained to await their return ; the desertion of the Uzi filled his mind with anxiety and suspicion ; and against the most salutary advice he rushed forward to speedy and decisive action.  Had he listened to the fair proposals of the sultan, Romanus might have secured a retreat, perhaps a peace ; but in these overtures he supposed the fear or weakness of the enemy, and his answer was conceived in the tone of insult and defiance.  " If the barbarian wishes for peace, let him evacuate the ground which he occupies for the encampment of the Romans, and surrender his city and palace of Rei as a pledge of his sincerity."  Alp Arslan smiled at the vanity of the demand, but he wept the death of so many faithful Moslems ; and, after a devout prayer, proclaimed a free permission to all who were desirous of retiring from the field.  With his own hand she tied up his horse's tail, exchanged his bow and arrow for a mace and scymetar, clothed himself in a white garment, perfumed his body with musk, and declared that, if he were vanquished, that spot should be the place of his burial.[39]  The sultan himself had affected to cast away his missile weapons ; but his hopes of victory were placed in the arrows of the Turkish cavalry, whose squadrons were loosely distributed in the form of a crescent.  Instead of the successive lines and reserves of the Grecian tactics, Romanus led his army in a single and solid phalanx, and pressed with vigour

---

[38] Elmacin (p. 343, 344) assigns this probable number, which is reduced by Abulpharagius to 15,000 (p. 227) and by d'Herbelot (p. 102) to 12,000 horse.  But the same Elmacin gives 300,000 men to the emperor, of whom Abulpharagius says, cum centum hominum millibus, multisque equis et magnâ pompâ instructus.  The Greeks abstain from any definition of numbers.  [The Byzantine army was not prepared to cope with the extraordinarily rapid motions of the Turks ; Gibbon brings this point out.  But it should be added that the army in any case was inclined to be insubordinate, and Romanus had difficulty in handling it.  Moreover there was treachery in his camp.  There seems no doubt however that he fought the battle rashly.  Cp. Finlay, iii. 33 ; and C. W. Oman, Hist. of the Art of War, vol. 2, p. 217-19.]

[39] The Byzantine writers do not speak so distinctly of the presence of the sultan ; he committed his forces to an eunuch, had retired to a distance, &c.  Is it ignorance, or jealousy, or truth ?

and impatience the artful and yielding resistance of the barbarians.  In this desultory and fruitless combat, he wasted the
greater part of a summer's day, till prudence and fatigue compelled him to return to his camp.  But a retreat is always
perilous in the face of an active foe ; and no sooner had the
standard been turned to the rear than the phalanx was broken
by the base cowardice, or the baser jealousy, of Andronicus, a
rival prince, who disgraced his birth and the purple of the
Cæsars.[40]  The Turkish squadrons poured a cloud of arrows on
this moment of confusion and lassitude ; and the horns of their
formidable crescent were closed in the rear of the Greeks.  In
the destruction of the army and pillage of the camp, it would be
needless to mention the number of the slain or captives.  The
Byzantine writers deplore the loss of an inestimable pearl : they
forget to mention that, in this fatal day, the Asiatic provinces
of Rome were irretrievably sacrificed.

Captivity and
deliverance of
the emperor

As long as a hope survived, Romanus attempted to rally and
save the relics of his army.  When the centre, the Imperial
station, was left naked on all sides, and encompassed by the
victorious Turks, he still, with desperate courage, maintained
the fight till the close of day, at the head of the brave and
faithful subjects who adhered to his standard.  They fell around
him ; his horse was slain ; the emperor was wounded ; yet he
stood alone and intrepid, till he was oppressed and bound by the
strength of multitudes.  The glory of this illustrious prize was
disputed by a slave and a soldier : a slave who had seen him
on the throne of Constantinople, and a soldier whose extreme
deformity had been excused on the promise of some signal
service.  Despoiled of his arms, his jewels, and his purple,
Romanus spent a dreary and perilous night on the field of
battle, amidst a disorderly crowd of the meaner barbarians.  In
the morning the royal captive was presented to Alp Arslan, who
doubted of his fortune, till the identity of the person was
ascertained by the report of his ambassadors, and by the more
pathetic evidence of Basilacius, who embraced with tears the
feet of his unhappy sovereign.  The successor of Constantine,
in a plebeian habit, was led into the Turkish divan, and commanded to kiss the ground before the lord of Asia.  He

---

[40] He was the son of the Cæsar John Ducas, brother of the emperor Constantine (Ducange, Fam. Byzant. p. 165).  Nicephorus Bryennius applauds his virtues,
and extenuates his faults (l. i. p. 30, 38, l. ii. p. 53 [p. 41, 54, 76, ed. B.]).  Yet he
owns his enmity to Romanus, οὐ πάνυ δὲ φιλίως ἔχων πρὸς βασιλέα.  Scylitzes speaks
more explicitly of his treason.

reluctantly obeyed ; and Alp Arslan, starting from his throne, is said to have planted his foot on the neck of the Roman emperor.[41]   But the fact is doubtful ; and, if, in this moment of insolence, the sultan complied with a national custom, the rest of his conduct has extorted the praise of his bigoted foes, and may afford a lesson to the most civilised ages.  He instantly raised the royal captive from the ground ; and, thrice clasping his hand with tender sympathy, assured him that his life and dignity should be inviolate in the hands of a prince who had learned to respect the majesty of his equals and the vicissitudes of fortune.  From the divan Romanus was conducted to an adjacent tent, where he was served with pomp and reverence by the officers of the sultan, who, twice each day, seated him in the place of honour at his own table.  In a free and familiar conversation of eight days, not a word, not a look, of insult escaped from the conqueror ; but he severely censured the unworthy subjects who had deserted their valiant prince in the hour of danger, and gently admonished his antagonist of some errors which he had committed in the management of the war. In the preliminaries of negotiation, Alp Arslan asked him what treatment he expected to receive, and the calm indifference of the emperor displays the freedom of his mind.  "If you are cruel," said he, "you will take my life ; if you listen to pride, you will drag me at your chariot wheels ; if you consult your interest, you will accept a ransom, and restore me to my country."  "And what," continued the sultan, "would have been your own behaviour, had fortune smiled on your arms ?" The reply of the Greek betrays a sentiment, which prudence, and even gratitude, should have taught him to suppress.  "Had I vanquished," he fiercely said, "I would have inflicted on thy body many a stripe."  The Turkish conqueror smiled at the insolence of his captive ; observed that the Christian law inculcated the love of enemies and forgiveness of injuries ; and nobly declared that he would not imitate an example which he condemned.  After mature deliberation, Alp Arslan dictated the terms of liberty and peace, a ransom of a million, an annual tribute of three hundred and sixty thousand pieces of gold,[42]

---

[41] This circumstance, which we read and doubt in Scylitzes and Constantine Manasses, is more prudently omitted by Nicephorus and Zonaras. [The reader may remember how the Emperor Justinian II. placed his feet on the necks of his rivals Leontius and Apsimar.  Finlay (iii. 34) rebukes Gibbon for his scepticism here.]

[42] The ransom and tribute are attested by reason and the Orientals.  The other Greeks are modestly silent ; but Nicephorus Bryennius dares to affirm that the

the marriage of the royal children, and the deliverance of all
the Moslems who were in the power of the Greeks. Romanus,
with a sigh, subscribed this treaty, so disgraceful to the
majesty of the empire; he was immediately invested with a
Turkish robe of honour; his nobles and patricians were restored
to their sovereign; and the sultan, after a courteous embrace,
dismissed him with rich presents and a military guard. No
sooner did he reach the confines of the empire than he was
informed that the palace and provinces had disclaimed their
allegiance to a captive: a sum of two hundred thousand pieces
was painfully collected; and the fallen monarch transmitted
this part of his ransom, with a sad confession of his impotence
and disgrace. The generosity, or perhaps the ambition, of the
sultan prepared to espouse the cause of his ally; but his designs were prevented by the defeat, imprisonment, and death
of Romanus Diogenes.[43]

Death of Alp
Arslan. A.D.
1072
In the treaty of peace it does not appear that Alp Arslan
extorted any province or city from the captive emperor; and
his revenge was satisfied with the trophies of his victory, and
the spoils of Anatolia from Antioch to the Black Sea. The
fairest part of Asia was subject to his laws; twelve hundred
princes, or the sons of princes, stood before his throne; and
two hundred thousand soldiers marched under his banners.
The sultan disdained to pursue the fugitive Greeks; but he
meditated the more glorious conquest of Turkestan, the original
seat of the house of Seljuk. He moved from Bagdad to the
banks of the Oxus; a bridge was thrown over the river; and
twenty days were consumed in the passage of his troops. But
the progress of the great king was retarded by the governor of
Berzem; and Joseph the Carizmian presumed to defend his
fortress against the powers of the East. When he was produced

terms were οὐκ ἀναξίας Ῥωμαίων ἀρχῆς, and that the emperor would have preferred
death to a shameful treaty.
[43] The defeat and captivity of Romanus Diogenes may be found in John Scylitze
ad calcem Cedreni, tom. ii. p. 835-843 [ii. p. 689 sqq. ed. B.]. Zonaras, tom. ii
p. 281-284 [xvii. 13, 14, 15]. Nicephorus Bryennius, l. i. p. 25-32 [p. 33 sqq. ed
B.]. Glycas, p. 325-327 [p. 607 sqq. ed. B.]. Constantine Manasses, p. 134 [p
280, ed. B.]. Elmacin, Hist. Saracen. p. 343, 344. Abulpharag. Dynast. p. 227
D'Herbelot, p. 102, 103. De Guignes, tom. iii. p. 207-211. Besides my old ac
quaintance, Elmacin and Abulpharagius, the historian of the Huns has consulted
Abulfeda, and his epitomizer, Benschounah, a Chronicle of the Caliphs, by Soyouth
Abulmahasen of Egypt, and Novairi of Africa. [See also the Chronicle of Michae
Attaleiates, p. 152 sqq. ed. Bonn. On the battle Finlay, vol. iii. p. 32-4, an
Gfrörer, Byzantinische Geschichten, vol. iii. chap. 28; Oman, cited above, no
38; cp. too Seger, Nikephoros Bryennios, p. 41 sqq. Gfrörer insists (p. 785) o
the statement of Elmacin that the battle was fought at Zahra (Zareshad? east c
Manzikert).]

a captive in the royal tent, the sultan, instead of praising his valour, severely reproached his obstinate folly ; and the insolent replies of the rebel provoked a sentence, that he should be fastened to four stakes and left to expire in that painful situation. At this command the desperate Carizmian, drawing a dagger, rushed headlong towards the throne : the guards raised their battle-axes ; their zeal was checked by Alp Arslan, the most skilful archer of the age ; he drew his bow, but his foot slipped, the arrow glanced aside, and he received in his breast the dagger of Joseph, who was instantly cut in pieces.     The wound was mortal ; and the Turkish prince bequeathed a dying admonition to the pride of kings. " In my youth," said Alp Arslan, " I was advised by a sage to humble myself before God ; to distrust my own strength ; and never to despise the most contemptible foe.     I have neglected these lessons ; and my neglect has been deservedly punished.     Yesterday, as from an eminence I beheld the numbers, the discipline, and the spirit of my armies, the earth seemed to tremble under my feet ; and I said in my heart, surely thou art the king of the world, the greatest and most invincible of warriors.     These armies are no longer mine ; and, in the confidence of my personal strength, I now fall by the hand of an assassin." [44]     Alp Arslan possessed the virtues of a Turk and a Musulman ; his voice and stature commanded the reverence of mankind ; his face was shaded with long whiskers ; and his ample turban was fashioned in the shape of a crown.     The remains of the sultan were deposited in the tomb of the Seljukian dynasty ; and the passenger might read and meditate this useful inscription : [45] " O YE WHO HAVE SEEN THE GLORY OF ALP ARSLAN EXALTED TO THE HEAVENS, REPAIR TO MARU, AND YOU WILL BEHOLD IT BURIED IN THE DUST ! "     The annihilation of the inscription, and the tomb itself, more forcibly proclaims the instability of human greatness.

During the life of Alp Arslan, his eldest son had been acknowledged as the future sultan of the Turks.     On his father's death, the inheritance was disputed by an uncle, a cousin, and a brother : they drew their scymetars, and assembled their followers ; and

Reign and prosperity of Malek Shah. A.D. 1072-1092

---

[44] This interesting death is told by d'Herbelot (p. 103, 104) and M. de Guignes (tom. iii. p. 212, 213) from their Oriental writers ; but neither of them have transfused the spirit of Elmacin (Hist. Saracen. p. 344, 345).

[45] A critique of high renown (the late Dr. Johnson), who has severely scrutinised the epitaphs of Pope, might cavil in this sublime inscription at the words, "repair to Maru," since the reader must already be at Maru before he could peruse the inscription.

the triple victory of Malek Shah [46] established his own reputation and the right of primogeniture. In every age, and more especially in Asia, the thirst of power has inspired the same passions and occasioned the same disorders; but, from the long series of civil war, it would not be easy to extract a sentiment more pure and magnanimous than is contained in a saying of the Turkish prince. On the eve of the battle, he performed his devotions at Thous, before the tomb of the Imam Riza. As the sultan rose from the ground, he asked his vizir Nizam, who had knelt beside him, what had been the object of his secret petition : "That your arms may be crowned with victory," was the prudent and most probably the sincere answer of the minister. "For my part," replied the generous Malek, "I implored the Lord of Hosts that he would take from me my life and crown, if my brother be more worthy than myself to reign over the Moslems." The favourable judgment of heaven was ratified by the caliph ; and for the first time the sacred title of Commander of the Faithful was communicated to a barbarian.[46a] But this barbarian, by his personal merit and the extent of his empire, was the greatest prince of his age. After the settlement of Persia and Syria, he marched at the head of innumerable armies to achieve the conquest of Turkestan, which had been undertaken by his father. In his passage of the Oxus, the boatmen, who had been employed in transporting some troops, complained that their payment was assigned on the revenues of Antioch. The sultan frowned at this preposterous choice, but he smiled at the artful flattery of his vizir. "It was not to postpone their reward that I selected those remote places, but to leave a memorial to posterity that under your reign Antioch and the Oxus were subject to the same sovereign." But this description of his limits was unjust and parsimonious : beyond the Oxus, he reduced to his obedience the cities of Bochara, Carizme, and Samarcand, and crushed each rebellious slave, or independent savage, who dared to resist. Malek passed the Sihon or Jaxartes, the last boundary of Persian civilisation : the lords of Turkestan yielded to his supremacy ; his name was inserted on the coins, and in the prayers, of Cashgar, a Tartar kingdom on the extreme borders of China. From the Chinese frontier, he stretched his immediate jurisdiction or feudatory sway to the west and south, as far as the

[Tus]

[46] The Bibliothèque Orientale has given the text of the reign of Malek (p. 542, 543, 544, 654, 655), and the Histoire Générale des Huns (tom. iii. p. 214-224) has added the usual measure of repetition, emendation, and supplement. Without these two learned Frenchmen, I should be blind indeed in the Eastern world.

[46a] [Not Commander of the Faithful (title reserved for Caliphs); but "Partner of the Commander of the Faithful".]

mountains of Georgia, the neighbourhood of Constantinople, the holy city of Jerusalem, and the spicy groves of Arabia Felix. Instead of resigning himself to the luxury of his harem, the shepherd king, both in peace and war, was in action and in the field. By the perpetual motion of the royal camp, each province was successively blessed with his presence; and he is said to have perambulated twelve times the wide extent of his dominions, which surpassed the *Asiatic* reign of Cyrus and the caliphs. Of these expeditions, the most pious and splendid was the pilgrimage of Mecca; the freedom and safety of the caravans were protected by his arms; the citizens and pilgrims were enriched by the profusion of his alms; and the desert was cheered by the places of relief and refreshment, which he instituted for the use of his brethren. Hunting was the pleasure, and even the passion, of the sultan, and his train consisted of forty-seven thousand horses; but, after the massacre of a Turkish chase, for each piece of game, he bestowed a piece of gold on the poor, a slight atonement, at the expense of the people, for the cost and mischief of the amusement of kings. In the peaceful prosperity of his reign, the cities of Asia were adorned with palaces and hospitals, with mosques and colleges; few departed from his divan without reward, and none without justice. The language and literature of Persia revived under the house of Seljuk;[47] and, if Malek emulated the liberality of a Turk less potent than himself,[48] his palace might resound with the songs of an hundred poets. The sultan bestowed a more serious and learned care on the reformation of the calendar, which was effected by a general assembly of the astronomers of the East. By a law of the prophet, the Moslems are confined to the irregular course of the lunar months; in Persia, since the age of Zoroaster, the revolution of the sun has been known and celebrated as an annual festival;[49] but, after the fall of the Magian empire, the intercalation had been neglected; the fractions of minutes and hours were multiplied into days; and the date of the Spring was removed

[47] See an excellent discourse at the end of Sir William Jones's History of Nadir Shah, and the articles of the poets, Amak, Anvari, Raschadi, &c. in the Bibliothèque Orientale.
[48] His name was Kheder Khan. Four bags were placed round his sopha, and, as he listened to the song, he cast handfuls of gold and silver to the poets (d Herbelot, p. 107). All this may be true; but I do not understand how he could reign in Transoxiana in the time of Malek Shah, and much less how Kheder could surpass him in power and pomp. I suspect that the beginning, not the end, of the xith century is the true æra of his reign. [Kadr Khān (one of the Turki Ilak Khāns) ruled at Kāshghar and Yarkand at beginning of xith cent.; his coins exist.]
[49] See Chardin, Voyages en Perse, tom. ii. p. 235.

from the sign of Aries to that of Pisces. The reign of Malek was illustrated by the *Gelalæan* æra ; and all errors, either past or future, were corrected by a computation of time, which surpasses the Julian, and approaches the accuracy of the Gregorian, style.[50]

His death.
A.D. 1092

[A.D. 1063-1092]

In a period when Europe was plunged in the deepest barbarism, the light and splendour of Asia may be ascribed to the docility rather than the knowledge of the Turkish conquerors. An ample share of their wisdom and virtue is due to a Persian vizir, who ruled the empire under the reign of Alp Arslan and his son. Nizam, one of the most illustrious ministers of the East, was honoured by the caliph as an oracle of religion and science ; [51] he was trusted by the sultan as the faithful vicegerent of his power and justice. After an administration of thirty years, the fame of the vizir, his wealth, and even his services, were transformed into crimes. He was overthrown by the insidious arts of a woman and a rival ; and his fall was hastened by a rash declaration that his cap and ink-horn, the badges of his office, were connected by the divine decree with the throne and diadem of the sultan. At the age of ninety-three years, the venerable statesman was dismissed by his master, accused by his enemies, and murdered by a fanatic : the last words of Nizam attested his innocence, and the remainder of Malek's life was short and inglorious. From Ispahan, the scene of this disgraceful transaction, the sultan moved to Bagdad, with the design of transplanting the caliph, and of fixing his own residence in the capital of the Moslem world. The feeble successor of Mahomet obtained a respite of ten days ; and, before the expiration of the term, the barbarian was summoned by the angel of death. His ambassadors at Constantinople had asked in marriage a Roman princess ; but the

[50] The Gelalæan æra (Gelaleddin, Glory of the Faith, was one of the names or titles of Malek Shah) is fixed to the 15th of March, A.H. 471, A.D. 1079. Dr. Hyde has produced the original testimonies of the Persians and Arabians (de Religione veterum Persarum, c. 16, p. 200-211). [The reform of the calendar was the work of Malik's minister, Nizãm al-Mulk.]

[51] [Nizãm has left a memorial of himself in the Siasset Nameh or " book of government," which has been published with a translation by Schefer. It throws great light on the history of the time and shows us how the Seljūks were already changing under the influence of Iranian civilisation and Islamism. In this respect it is very interesting to compare it with the *Kudatker Bilik* or Art of Government, a contemporary work (written c. 1069 at Kashgar) which shows the pure Turk spirit of central Asia. The comparison is drawn by Cahun (*op. cit.* p. 182 *sqq.*). Among the Turks, for instance, women had great influence ; but in the Siasset Nameh " religion is much, woman is nothing ". For a sketch of the vizierate of Nizãm, see Mr. Stanley Lane-Poole's *Saladin* (1898), chap. i.]

proposal was decently eluded; and the daughter of Alexius, who might herself have been the victim, expresses her abhorrence of this unnatural conjunction.[52]  The daughter of the sultan was bestowed on the caliph Moctadi, with the imperious condition that, renouncing the society of his wives and concubines, he should for ever confine himself to this honourable alliance.

The greatness and unity of the Turkish empire expired in the person of Malek Shah.  His vacant throne was disputed by his brother and his four sons; and, after a series of civil wars, the treaty which reconciled the surviving candidates confirmed a lasting separation in the *Persian* dynasty, the eldest and principal branch of the house of Seljuk.  The three younger dynasties were those of *Kerman*, of *Syria*, and of *Roum* : the first of these commanded an extensive, though obscure,[53] dominion on the shores of the Indian Ocean;[54] the second expelled the Arabian princes of Aleppo and Damascus; and the third, our peculiar care, invaded the Roman provinces of Asia Minor.  The generous policy of Malek contributed to their elevation; he allowed the princes of his blood, even those whom he had vanquished in the field, to seek new kingdoms worthy of their ambition; nor was he displeased that they should draw away the more ardent spirits who might have disturbed the tranquillity of his reign.  As the supreme head of his family and nation, the great sultan of Persia commanded the obedience and tribute of his royal brethren; the throne of Kerman and Nice, of Aleppo and Damascus; the Atabeks, and emirs of Syria and Mesopotamia, erected their standards under the shadow of his sceptre;[55] and the hordes of Turkmans overspread the plains of the western

Division of the Seljukian empire

[52] She speaks of this Persian royalty as ἀπάσης κακοδαιμονέστερον πενίας.  Anna Comnena was only nine years old at the end of the reign of Malek Shah (A.D. 1092), and, when she speaks of his assassination, she confounds the sultan with the vizir (Alexias, l. vi. p. 177, 178 [c. 12]).

[53] So obscure that the industry of M. de Guignes could only copy (tom. i. p. 244, tom. iii. part i. p. 269, &c.) the history, or rather list, of the Seljukides of Kerman, in Bibliothèque Orientale.  They were extinguished before the end of the xiith century.  [For the succession of the Seljūks of Kirmān, A.D. 1041-1187, see S. Lane-Poole, Mohammadan Dynasties, p. 153.  The main line of the Seljūks, with a nominal overlordship over the younger branches, continued to rule in Irāk Ajam and Khurāsān and expired with Sinjar in A.D. 1157.]

[54] Tavernier, perhaps the only traveller who has visited Kerman, describes the capital as a great ruinous village, twenty-five days' journey from Ispahan, and twenty-seven from Ormus, in the midst of a fertile country (Voyages en Turquie et en Perse, p. 107, 110).

[55] It appears from Anna Comnena that the Turks of Asia Minor obeyed the signet and chiauss of the great sultan (Alexias, l. vi. p. 170 [c. 9]) and that the two sons of Soliman were detained in his court (p. 180 [c. 12]).

Asia. After the death of Malek, the bands of union and subordination were relaxed and finally dissolved; the indulgence of the house of Seljuk invested their slaves with the inheritance of kingdoms; and, in the Oriental style, a crowd of princes arose from the dust of their feet.[56]

Conquest of Asia Minor by the Turks. A.D. 1074-1084

A prince of the royal line, Cutulmish, the son of Izrail, the son of Seljuk, had fallen in a battle against Alp Arslan; and the humane victor had dropped a tear over his grave. His five sons, strong in arms, ambitious of power, and eager for revenge, unsheathed their scymetars against the son of Alp Arslan. The two armies expected the signal, when the caliph, forgetful of the majesty which secluded him from vulgar eyes, interposed his venerable mediation. "Instead of shedding the blood of your brethren, your brethren both in descent and faith, unite your forces in an holy war against the Greeks, the enemies of God and his apostle." They listened to his voice; the sultan embraced his rebellious kinsmen; and the eldest, the valiant Soliman, accepted the royal standard, which gave him the free conquest and hereditary command of the provinces of the Roman empire, from Arzeroum to Constantinople and the unknown regions of the West.[57] Accompanied by his four brothers, he passed the Euphrates: the Turkish camp was soon seated in the neighbourhood of Kutaieh, in Phrygia; and his flying cavalry laid waste the country as far as the Hellespont and the Black Sea. Since the decline of the empire, the peninsula of Asia Minor had been exposed to the transient though destructive inroads of the Persians and Saracens; but the fruits of a lasting conquest were reserved for the Turkish sultan; and his arms were introduced by the Greeks, who aspired to reign on the ruins of their country. Since the captivity of Romanus, six years the feeble son of Eudocia had trembled under the weight of the Imperial crown, till the provinces of the East and West were lost in the same month by a double rebellion: of either chief Nicephorus was the common name; but the surnames of

[Cotyæum]

[A.D. 1078]

[56] This expression is quoted by Petit de la Croix (Vie de Gengiscan, p. 161) from some poet, most probably a Persian. [The slaves who were to conduct the affairs of the Seljûk princes generally became the governors or regents, *atâbegs*, for their sons or heirs, and thus got the supreme power into their hands.]

[57] On the conquest of Asia Minor, M. de Guignes has derived no assistance from the Turkish or Arabian writers, who produce a naked list of the Seljukides of Roum. The Greeks are unwilling to expose their shame, and we must extort some hints from Scylitzes (p. 860, 863 [p. 731, 736, ed. B.]), Nicephorus Bryennius (p. 88, 91, 92, &c. 103, 104 [p. 130, p. 136, 137, p. 158 *sqq.* ed. B.]), and Anna Comnena (Alexias, p. 91, 92, &c. [iii. c. 9], 168, &c. [vi. c. 9]) [and the History of Michael Attaleiates].

Bryennius and Botoniates distinguish the European and Asiatic candidates. Their reasons, or rather their promises, were weighed in the divan; and, after some hesitation, Soliman declared himself in favour of Botoniates, opened a free passage to his troops in their march from Antioch to Nice, and joined the banner of the crescent to that of the cross. After his ally had ascended the throne of Constantinople, the sultan was hospitably entertained in the suburb of Chrysopolis or Scutari; and a body of two thousand Turks was transported into Europe, to whose dexterity and courage the new emperor was indebted for the defeat and captivity of his rival Bryennius. But the conquest of Europe was dearly purchased by the sacrifice of Asia: Constantinople was deprived of the obedience and revenue of the provinces beyond the Bosphorus and Hellespont; and the regular progress of the Turks, who fortified the passes of the rivers and mountains, left not a hope of their retreat or expulsion. Another candidate implored the aid of the sultan: [58] Melissenus, [A.D. 1079] in his purple robes and red buskins, attended the motions of the Turkish camp; and the desponding cities were tempted by the summons of a Roman prince, who immediately surrendered them into the hands of the barbarians. These acquisitions were [A.D. 1081] confirmed by a treaty of peace with the emperor Alexius; his fear of Robert compelled him to seek the friendship of Soliman; and it was not till after the sultan's death that he extended as far as Nicomedia, about sixty miles from Constantinople, the eastern boundary of the Roman world. Trebizond alone, defended on either side by the sea and mountains, preserved at the extremity of the Euxine the ancient character of a Greek colony, and the future destiny of a Christian empire.

Since the first conquests of the caliphs, the establishment of the Turks in Anatolia, or Asia Minor, was the most deplorable loss which the church and empire had sustained. By the propagation of the Moslem faith, Soliman deserved the name of *Gazi*, a holy champion; and his new kingdom of the Romans, or of *Roum*, was added to the tables of Oriental geography. It is described as extending from the Euphrates to Constantinople, from the Black Sea to the confines of Syria; pregnant with mines of silver and iron, of alum and copper, fruitful in corn and wine, and productive of cattle and excellent horses.[59] The wealth of Lydia,

*The Seljukian kingdom of Roum*

[58] [It was Melissenus who yielded Nicaea to Sulaiman.]
[59] Such is the description of Roum by Haiton the Armenian, whose Tartar history may be found in the collections of Ramusio and Bergeron [and in L. de Backer's L'extrême orient au moyen âge, p. 125 *sqq.* 1877] (see Abulfeda, Geograph. climat. xvii. p. 301-305 [and P. Paris, in Hist. littéraire de France, t. 25, p. 479 *sqq.* 1869]).

the arts of the Greeks, the splendour of the Augustan age, existed
only in books and ruins, which were equally obscure in the eyes
of the Scythian conquerors.   Yet, in the present decay, Anatolia
still contains *some* wealthy and populous cities ;   and, under the
Byzantine empire, they were far more flourishing in numbers,
size, and opulence.   By the choice of the sultan, Nice, the metropolis of Bithynia, was preferred for his palace and fortress : the
seat of the Seljukian dynasty of Roum was planted one hundred
miles from Constantinople ;   and the divinity of Christ was denied
and derided in the same temple in which it had been pronounced
by the first general synod of the Catholics.   The unity of God
and the mission of Mahomet were preached in the mosques ;   the
Arabian learning was taught in the schools ;   the Cadhis judged
according to the law of the Koran ;   the Turkish manners and
language prevailed in the cities ;   and Turkman camps were
scattered over the plains and mountains of Anatolia.   On the
hard conditions of tribute and servitude, the Greek Christians
might enjoy the exercise of their religion ;   but their most holy
churches were profaned ;   their priests and bishops were insulted ; [60] they were compelled to suffer the triumph of the
*pagans* and the apostacy of their brethren ;   many thousand
children were marked by the knife of circumcision ;   and many
thousand captives were devoted to the service or the pleasures
of their masters. [61]   After the loss of Asia, Antioch still maintained her primitive allegiance to Christ and Cæsar ;   but the
solitary province was separated from all Roman aid, and surrounded on all sides by the Mahometan powers.   The despair of
Philaretus the governor prepared the sacrifice of his religion and
loyalty, had not his guilt been prevented by his son, who hastened
to the Nicene palace, and offered to deliver this valuable prize
into the hands of Soliman.   The ambitious sultan mounted on
horseback, and in twelve nights (for he reposed in the day) performed a march of six hundred miles.   Antioch was oppressed

[60] Dicit eos quendam abusione Sodomiticâ intervertisse episcopum (Guibert.
Abbat. Hist. Hierosol. l. i. p. 468).   It is odd enough that we should find a parallel
passage of the same people in the present age.   '' Il n'est point d'horreur que ces
Turcs n'ayent commis, et semblables aux soldats effrenés, qui dans la sac d'une
ville non contens de disposer de tout à leur gré pretendent encore aux succès les
moins désirables, quelques Sipahis ont porté leurs attentats sur la personne du
vieux rabbi de la synagogue, et celle de l'Archévêque Grec '' (Mémoires du Baron
de Tott, tom. ii. p. 193).

[61] The emperor, or abbot, describe the scenes of a Turkish camp as if they had
been present.   Matres correptæ in conspectu filiarum multipliciter repetitis diver-
sorum coitibus vexabantur (is that the true reading ?), cum filiæ assistentes carmina
præcinere saltando cogerentur.   Mox eadem passio ad filias, &c.

by the speed and secrecy of his enterprise ; and the dependent cities, as far as Laodicea and the confines of Aleppo,[62] obeyed the example of the metropolis. From Laodicea to the Thracian Bosphorus, or arm of St. George, the conquests and reign of Soliman extended thirty days' journey in length, and in breadth about ten or fifteen, between the rocks of Lycia and the Black Sea.[63] The Turkish ignorance of navigation protected, for a while, the inglorious safety of the emperor ; but no sooner had a fleet of two hundred ships been constructed by the hands of the captive Greeks, than Alexius trembled behind the walls of his capital. His plaintive epistles were dispersed over Europe, to excite the compassion of the Latins, and to paint the danger, the weakness, and the riches, of the city of Constantine.[64]

But the most interesting conquest of the Seljukian Turks was that of Jerusalem,[65] which soon became the theatre of nations. In their capitulation with Omar, the inhabitants had stipulated the assurance of their religion and property ; but the articles were interpreted by a master against whom it was dangerous to dispute ; and in the four hundred years of the reign of the

State and pilgrimage of Jerusalem. A.D. 638-1099

---

[62] See Antioch, and the death of Soliman, in Anna Comnena (Alexias, l. vi. p. 168, 169 [c. 9]), with the notes of Ducange.

[63] William of Tyre (l. i. c. 9, 10, p. 635) gives the most authentic and deplorable account of these Turkish conquests.

[64] In his epistle to the count of Flanders, Alexius seems to fall too low beneath his character and dignity ; yet it is approved by Ducange (Not. ad Alexiad. p. 335, &c.) and paraphrased by the abbot Guibert, a contemporary historian. The Greek text no longer exists ; and each translator and scribe might say with Guibert (p. 475), verbis vestita meis, a privilege of most indefinite latitude. [Guibert incorporates the substance of this letter, Recueil, H. Occ. iv. p. 131 *sqq.* The best edition of the text (preserved only in Latin) is that of the Count de Riant (1877 and again 1879). A controversy has raged over the genuineness of the document. Riant rejects it as spurious (like Wilken, Raumer, and others). But it was accepted as genuine by Sybel, and has been defended more recently by Vasilievski (Zhurn. Min. Nar. Prosv. 164, p. 325 *sqq.* 1872) and Hagenmeyer (Byz. Ztsch. vi. 1 *sqq.* 1897). It is doubtless genuine. The objections brought against it are not weighty ; and the critics who condemn it have offered no theory of its origin that is in the least probable. It is perfectly incredible that it was composed as a deliberate forgery in the year 1098-9 in the camp of the Crusaders, as Riant tries to establish. Its contents are absolutely inconsistent with this theory. It was probably written long *before* the First Crusade ; and Hagenmeyer is probably right in assigning it to 1088, when the Empire was in danger from the Patzinaks, and some months after the personal interview of Alexius with Robert of Flanders at Berrœa. The letter, of course, has suffered seriously in the process of its translation into Latin.]

[65] Our best fund for the history of Jerusalem from Heraclius to the crusades is contained in two large and original passages of William, archbishop of Tyre (l. i. c. 1-10, l. xviii. c. 5, 6), the principal author of the Gesta Dei per Francos. M. de Guignes has composed a very learned Mémoire sur le Commerce des François dans le Levant avant les Croisades, &c. (Mém. de l'Académie des Inscriptions, tom. xxxvii. p. 467-500).

caliphs, the political climate of Jerusalem was exposed to the
vicissitudes of storms and sunshine.[66]   By the increase of proselytes and population, the Mahometans might excuse their usurpation of three-fourths of the city ; but a peculiar quarter was
reserved for the patriarch with his clergy and people ; a tribute
of two pieces of gold was the price of protection ; and the sepulchre of Christ, with the church of the Resurrection, was still left in
the hands of his votaries.   Of these votaries, the most numerous
and respectable portion were strangers to Jerusalem : the pilgrimages to the Holy Land had been stimulated, rather than
suppressed, by the conquest of the Arabs ; and the enthusiasm
which had always prompted these perilous journeys was nourished
by the congenial passions of grief and indignation.   A crowd of
pilgrims from the East and West continued to visit the holy
sepulchre and the adjacent sanctuaries, more especially at the
festival at Easter ; and the Greeks and Latins, the Nestorians
and Jacobites, the Copts and Abyssinians, the Armenians and
Georgians, maintained the chapels, the clergy, and the poor of
their respective communions.   The harmony of prayer in so many
various tongues, the worship of so many nations in the common
temple of their religion, might have afforded a spectacle of edification and peace ; but the zeal of the Christian sects was embittered by hatred and revenge ; and in the kingdom of a
suffering Messiah, who had pardoned his enemies, they aspired
to command and persecute their spiritual brethren.   The pre-
eminence was asserted by the spirit and numbers of the Franks ;
and the greatness of Charlemagne [67] protected both the Latin
pilgrims, and the Catholics of the East.   The poverty of Carthage,
Alexandria, and Jerusalem was relieved by the alms of that pious
emperor ;  and many monasteries of Palestine were founded or restored by his liberal devotion.   Harun Alrashid, the greatest of
the Abbassides, esteemed in his Christian brother a similar supremacy of genius and power ;  their friendship was cemented by
a frequent intercourse of gifts and embassies ; and the caliph,
without resigning the substantial dominion, presented the em-

[66] Secundum Dominorum dispositionem plerumque lucida plerumque nubila rece-
pit intervalla, et ægrotantis more temporum praesentium gravabatur aut respirabat
qualitate (l. i. c. 3, p. 630).   The Latinity of William of Tyre is by no means contemptible ; but in his account of 490 years, from the loss to the recovery of Jerusalem, he exceeds the true account by thirty years.

[67] For the transactions of Charlemagne with the Holy Land, see Eginhard (de
Vitâ Caroli Magni, c. 16, p. 79-82), Constantine Porphyrogenitus (de Administratione Imperii, l. ii. c. 26, p. 80), and Pagi (Critica, tom. iii. A.D. 800, No. 13, 14,
15).

peror with the keys of the holy sepulchre, and perhaps of the city of Jerusalem. In the decline of the Carlovingian monarchy, the republic of Amalphi promoted the interest of trade and religion in the East. Her vessels transported the Latin pilgrims to the coasts of Egypt and Palestine, and deserved, by their useful imports, the favour and alliance of the Fatimite caliphs : [68] an annual fair was instituted on mount Calvary ; and the Italian merchants founded the convent and hospital of St. John of Jerusalem, the cradle of the monastic and military order, which has since reigned in the isles of Rhodes and of Malta. Had the Christian pilgrims been content to revere the tomb of a prophet, the disciples of Mahomet, instead of blaming, would have imitated, their piety ; but these rigid *Unitarians* were scandalized by a worship which represents the birth, death, and resurrection, of a God ; the Catholic images were branded with the name of idols ; and the Moslems smiled with indignation [69] at the miraculous flame, which was kindled on the eve of Easter in the holy sepulchre.[70] This pious fraud, first devised in the ninth century,[71] was devoutly cherished by the Latin crusaders, and is annually repeated by the clergy of the Greek, Armenian, and Coptic sects,[72] who impose on the credulous spectators [73] for their own benefit and that of their tyrants. In every age, a principle of toleration has been fortified by a sense of interest ; and the revenue of the prince and his emir was increased each year by the expense and tribute of so many thousand strangers.

---

[68] The caliph granted his privileges, Amalphitanis viris amicis et utilium introductoribus (Gesta Dei, p. 934). The trade of Venice to Egypt and Palestine cannot produce so old a title, unless we adopt the laughable translation of a Frenchman who mistook the two factions of the circus (Veneti et Prasini) for the Venetians and Parisians.

[69] An Arabic chronicle of Jerusalem (apud Asseman. Bibliot. Orient. tom. i. p. 628, tom. iv. p. 368) attests the unbelief of the caliph and the historian ; yet Cantacuzene presumes to appeal to the Mahometans themselves for the truth of this perpetual miracle.

[70] In his Dissertations on Ecclesiastical History, the learned Mosheim has separately discussed this pretended miracle (tom. ii. p. 214-306), de lumine sancti sepulchri.

[71] William of Malmsbury (l. iv. c. ii. p. 209) quotes the Itinerary of the monk Bernard, an eye-witness, who visited Jerusalem A.D. 870. The miracle is confirmed by another pilgrim some years older ; and Mosheim ascribes the invention to the Franks soon after the decease of Charlemagne.

[72] Our travellers, Sandys (p. 134), Thévenot (p. 621-627), Maundrell (p. 94, 95), &c., describe this extravagant farce. The Catholics are puzzled to decide *when* the miracle ended and the trick began.

[73] The Orientals themselves confess the fraud, and plead necessity and edification (Mémoires du Chevalier d'Arvieux, tom. ii. p. 140 ; Joseph Abudacni, Hist. Copt. c. 20) ; but I will not attempt, with Mosheim, to explain the mode. Our travellers have failed with the blood of St. Januarius at Naples.

Under the
Fatimite
caliphs. A.D.
969-1076
The revolution which transferred the sceptre from the Abbassides to the Fatimites was a benefit, rather than an injury,
to the Holy Land.  A sovereign resident in Egypt was more
sensible of the importance of Christian trade ; and the emirs
of Palestine were less remote from the justice and power of
the throne.  But the third of these Fatimite caliphs was the
[Succeeds in
Egypt. A.D.
996]
famous Hakem,[74] a frantic youth, who was delivered by his impiety and despotism from the fear either of God or man ; and
whose reign was a wild mixture of vice and folly.  Regardless
of the most ancient customs of Egypt, he imposed on the women
an absolute confinement : the restraint excited the clamours of
both sexes ; their clamours provoked his fury ; a part of Old
Cairo was delivered to the flames ; and the guards and citizens
were engaged many days in a bloody conflict.  At first the
caliph declared himself a zealous Musulman, the founder or
benefactor of mosques and colleges : twelve hundred and ninety
copies of the Koran were transcribed at his expense in letters of
gold ; and his edict extirpated the vineyards of the Upper Egypt.
[Assumes
divinity.
A.D. 1017]
But his vanity was soon flattered by the hope of introducing a
new religion ; he aspired above the fame of a prophet, and styled
himself the visible image of the Most High God, who, after nine
apparitions on earth, was at length manifest in his royal person.
At the name of Hakem, the lord of the living and the dead,
every knee was bent in religious adoration : his mysteries were
performed on a mountain near Cairo ; sixteen thousand converts
had signed his profession of faith ; and at the present hour, a
free and warlike people, the Druses of mount Libanus, are persuaded of the life and divinity of a madman and tyrant.[75]  In
his divine character, Hakem hated the Jews and Christians, as
the servants of his rivals ; while some remains of prejudice or
prudence still pleaded in favour of the law of Mahomet.[76]  Both

[74] See d'Herbelot (Bibliot. Orientale, p. 411), Renaudot (Hist. Patriarch. Alex. p.
390, 397, 400, 401), Elmacin (Hist. Saracen. p. 321-323), and Marei (p. 384-386), an
historian of Egypt, translated by Reiske from Arabic into German, and verbally
interpreted to me by a friend.  [Al-Hākim Abū-Alī al-Mansūr reigned in Egypt
from 996 to 1020.]

[75] The religion of the Druses is concealed by their ignorance and hypocrisy.  Their
secret doctrines are confined to the elect who profess a contemplative life ; and
the vulgar Druses, the most indifferent of men, occasionally conform to the worship
of the Mahometans and Christians of their neighbourhood.  The little that is, or
deserves to be, known may be seen in the industrious Niebuhr (Voyages, tom. ii. p.
354-357) and the second volume of the recent and instructive Travels of M. de Volney.  [The religion of the Druses has been thoroughly investigated by Silvestre de
Sacy in his Exposé de la religion des Druses, in two volumes, 1838.]

[76] [" It was not in his ' divine character ' that Hakem ' hated the Jews and
Christians,' but in that of a Mahometan bigot, which he displayed in the earlier

in Egypt and Palestine, his cruel and wanton persecution made some martyrs and many apostates: the common rights and special privileges of the sectaries were equally disregarded; and a general interdict was laid on the devotion of strangers and natives. The temple of the Christian world, the church of the Resurrection, was demolished to its foundations; the luminous prodigy of Easter was interrupted, and much profane labour was exhausted to destroy the cave in the rock, which properly constitutes the holy sepulchre. At the report of this sacrilege, the nations of Europe were astonished and afflicted; but, instead of arming in the defence of the Holy Land, they contented themselves with burning or banishing the Jews, as the secret advisers of the impious barbarian.[77] Yet the calamities of Jerusalem were in some measure alleviated by the inconstancy or repentance of Hakem himself; and the royal mandate was sealed for the restitution of the churches, when the tyrant was assassinated by the emissaries of his sister. The succeeding caliphs resumed the maxims of religion and policy; a free toleration was again granted; with the pious aid of the emperor of Constantinople the holy sepulchre arose from its ruins; and, after a short abstinence, the pilgrims returned with an increase of appetite to the spiritual feast.[78] In the sea-voyage of Palestine, the dangers were frequent and the opportunities rare: but the conversion of Hungary opened a safe communication between Germany and Greece. The charity of St. Stephen, the apostle of his kingdom, relieved and conducted his itinerant brethren;[79] and from Belgrade to Antioch they traversed fifteen hundred miles of a Christian empire. Among the Franks, the zeal of pilgrimage prevailed beyond the example of former times; and the roads were covered with multitudes of either sex and of every rank, who professed their contempt of life, so soon as they should

*Sacrilege of Hakem. A.D. 1009*

*Increase of pilgrimages. A.D. 1024, &c.*

years of his reign. His barbarous persecutions and the burning of the church of the Resurrection at Jerusalem belong entirely to that period; and his assumption of divinity was followed by an edict of toleration to Jews and Christians. The Mahometans, whose religion he then treated with hostility and contempt, being far the most numerous, were his most dangerous enemies, and therefore the objects of his most inveterate hatred " (Milman, note to this passage).]

[77] See Glaber, l. iii. c. 7, and the Annals of Baronius and Pagi, A.D. 1009.

[78] Per idem tempus ex universo orbe tam innumerabilis multitudo cœpit confluere ad sepulchrum Salvatoris Hierosolymis, quantum nullus hominum prius sperare poterat. Ordo inferioris plebis . . . mediocres . . . reges et comites . . . præsules . . . mulieres multæ nobiles cum pauperioribus . . . Pluribus enim erat mentis desiderium mori priusquam ad propria reverterentur (Glaber, l. iv. c. 6; Bouquet, Historians of France, tom. x. p. 50).

[79] Glaber, l. iii. c. 1. Katona (Hist. Critic. Regum Hungariæ, tom. i. p. 304-311) examines whether St. Stephen founded a monastery at Jerusalem.

have kissed the tomb of their Redeemer. Princes and prelates abandoned the care of their dominions; and the numbers of these pious caravans were a prelude to the armies which marched in the ensuing age under the banner of the cross. About thirty years before the first crusade, the archbishop of Mentz, with the bishops of Utrecht, Bamberg, and Ratisbon, undertook this laborious journey from the Rhine to the Jordan; and the multitude of their followers amounted to seven thousand persons. At Constantinople, they were hospitably entertained by the emperor; but the ostentation of their wealth provoked the assault of the wild Arabs; they drew their swords with scrupulous reluctance, and sustained a siege in the village of Capernaum, till they were rescued by the venal protection of the Fatimite emir. After visiting the holy places, they embarked for Italy, but only a remnant of two thousand arrived in safety in their native land. Ingulphus, a secretary of William the Conqueror, was a companion of this pilgrimage; he observes that they sallied from Normandy, thirty stout and well-appointed horsemen; but that they repassed the Alps, twenty miserable palmers, with the staff in their hand, and the wallet at their back.[80]

Conquest of
Jerusalem by
the Turks.
A.D. 1076-1096

[Hims =
Emesa]
After the defeat of the Romans, the tranquillity of the Fatimite caliphs was invaded by the Turks.[81] One of the lieutenants of Malek Shah, Atsiz the Carizmian, marched into Syria at the head of a powerful army, and reduced Damascus by famine and the sword. Hems, and the other cities of the province, acknowledged the caliph of Bagdad and the sultan of Persia; and the victorious emir advanced without resistance to the banks of the Nile; the Fatimite was preparing to fly into the heart of Africa; but the negroes of his guard and the inhabitants of Cairo made a desperate sally, and repulsed the Turk from the confines of Egypt. In his retreat, he indulged the licence of slaughter and rapine; the judge and notaries of Jerusalem were invited to his camp; and their execution was followed by the massacre of three thousand citizens. The cruelty or the defeat of Atsiz was soon punished by the sultan Toucush, the brother of Malek Shah, who, with a higher title and more formidable powers, asserted the dominion of Syria and

[80] Baronius (A.D. 1064, No. 43-56) has transcribed the greater part of the original narratives of Ingulphus, Marianus, and Lambertus. [Descriptions of the Holy Land by pilgrims of the 12th century, translated into English, will be found in vols. iv. and v. of the Library of the Palestine Pilgrims' Text Society.]

[81] See Elmacin (Hist. Saracen. p. 349, 350) and Abulpharagius (Dynast. p. 237, vers. Pocock). M. de Guignes (Hist. des Huns, tom. iii. part i. p. 215, 216) adds the testimonies, or rather the names, of Abulfeda and Novairi.

Palestine. The house of Seljuk reigned about twenty years in
Jerusalem ;[82] but the hereditary command of the holy city and
territory was entrusted or abandoned to the emir Ortok, the
chief of a tribe [82a] of Turkmans, whose children, after their expulsion from Palestine, formed two dynasties on the borders of
Armenia and Assyria.[83] The Oriental Christians and the Latin
pilgrims deplored a revolution, which, instead of the regular
government and old alliance of the caliphs, imposed on their
necks the iron yoke of the strangers of the north.[84] In his
court and camp the great sultan had adopted in some degree
the arts and manners of Persia ; but the body of the Turkish
nation, and more especially the pastoral tribes, still breathed
the fierceness of the desert. From Nice to Jerusalem, the
western countries of Asia were a scene of foreign and domestic
hostility ; and the shepherds of Palestine, who held a precarious
sway on a doubtful frontier, had neither leisure nor capacity to
await the slow profits of commercial and religious freedom.
The pilgrims, who, through innumerable perils, had reached
the gates of Jerusalem, were the victims of private rapine or
public oppression, and often sunk under the pressure of famine
and disease, before they were permitted to salute the holy
sepulchre. A spirit of native barbarism, or recent zeal,
prompted the Turkmans to insult the clergy of every sect ;
the patriarch was dragged by the hair along the pavement
and cast into a dungeon, to extort a ransom from the sympathy of his flock ; and the divine worship in the church of
the Resurrection was often disturbed by the savage rudeness
of its masters. The pathetic tale excited the millions of

---

[82] From the expedition of Isar Atsiz (A.H. 469, A.D. 1076) to the expulsion of
the Ortokides (A.D. 1096). Yet William of Tyre (l. i, c, 6, p. 633) asserts that
Jerusalem was thirty-eight years in the hands of the Turks ; and an Arabic chronicle,
quoted by Pagi (tom. iv. p. 202), supposes that the city was reduced by a Carizmian
general to the obedience of the caliph of Bagdad, A.H. 463, A.D. 1070. These
early dates are not very compatible with the general history of Asia ; and I am
sure that, as late as A.D. 1064, the regnum Babylonicum (of Cairo) still prevailed
in Palestine (Baronius, A.D. 1064, No. 56). [See Mujīr ad-Dīn, Hist. de Jérusalem,
transl. Sauvaire (1876), p. 69-70 ; who states that Atsīz ibn Auk (the Khwarizmian
governor of Damascus) took Jerusalem in 1070-1 and the Abbāsid caliph was proclaimed there two years later, and the Ortokids expelled in 1096.]

[82a] [Family.]

[83] De Guignes, Hist. des Huns, tom. i. p. 249-252.

[84] Willerm. Tyr. l. i. c. 8, p. 634, who strives hard to magnify the Christian
grievances. The Turks exacted an *aureus* from each pilgrim ! The *caphar* of
the Franks is now fourteen dollars ; and Europe does not complain of this volun
tary tax.

the West to march under the standard of the Cross to the relief of the Holy Land; and yet how trifling is the sum of these accumulated evils, if compared with the single act of the sacrilege of Hakem, which had been so patiently endured by the Latin Christians! A slighter provocation inflamed the more irascible temper of their descendants: a new spirit had arisen of religious chivalry and papal dominion; a nerve was touched of exquisite feeling; and the sensation vibrated to the heart of Europe.

## CHAPTER LVIII

*Origin and Numbers of the First Crusade—Characters of the Latin Princes—Their March to Constantinople—Policy of the Greek Emperor Alexius—Conquest of Nice, Antioch, and Jerusalem, by the Franks—Deliverance of the Holy Sepulchre—Godfrey of Bouillon, first King of Jerusalem—Institutions of the French or Latin Kingdom*

ABOUT twenty years after the conquest of Jerusalem by the Turks, the holy sepulchre was visited by an hermit of the name of Peter, a native of Amiens, in the province of Picardy [1] in France. His resentment and sympathy were excited by his own injuries and the oppression of the Christian name; he mingled his tears with those of the patriarch, and earnestly inquired if no hopes of relief could be entertained from the Greek emperors of the East. The patriarch exposed the vices and weakness of the successors of Constantine. "I will rouse," exclaimed the hermit, "the martial nations of Europe in your cause;" and Europe was obedient to the call of the hermit. The astonished patriarch dismissed him with epistles of credit and complaint; and no sooner did he land at Bari than Peter hastened to kiss the feet of the Roman Pontiff. His stature was small, his appearance contemptible; but his eye was keen and lively; and he possessed that vehemence of speech which seldom fails to impart the persuasion of the soul.[2] He was born of a gentle-

The first<br>crusade. A.D.<br>1095-1099.<br>Peter the<br>Hermit

---

[1] Whimsical enough is the origin of the name of *Picards*, and from thence of *Picardie*, which does not date earlier than A.D. 1200. It was an academical joke, an epithet first applied to the quarrelsome humour of those students, in the university of Paris, who came from the frontier of France and Flanders (Valesii Notitia Galliarum, p. 447; Longuerue, Description de la France, p. 54).

[2] William of Tyre (l. i. c. 11, p. 637, 638) thus describes the hermit: Pusillus, persona contemptibilis, vivacis ingenii, et oculum habens perspicacem gratumque, et sponte fluens ei non deerat eloquium. See Albert Aquensis, p. 185. Guibert, p. 482. Anna Comnena in Alexiad. l. x. p. 284 [c. 5], &c. with Ducange's notes, p. 349. [In the writers who are contemporary with the First Crusade there is not a word of Peter the Hermit instigating Pope Urban, nor is he mentioned as present

man's family (for we must now adopt a modern idiom), and his
military service was under the neighbouring counts of Boulogne,
the heroes of the first crusade.   But he soon relinquished the
sword and the world ; and, if it be true that his wife, however
noble, was aged and ugly, he might withdraw, with the less
reluctance, from her bed to a convent, and at length to an her-
mitage.   In this austere solitude, his body was emaciated, his
fancy was inflamed ; whatever he wished, he believed ; whatever
he believed, he *saw* in dreams and revelations.   From Jerusalem
the pilgrim returned an accomplished fanatic; but, as he excelled
in the popular madness of the times, Pope Urban the Second
received him as a prophet, applauded his glorious design, promised to support it in a general council, and encouraged him to
proclaim the deliverance of the Holy Land.   Invigorated by
the approbation of the Pontiff, his zealous missionary traversed,
with speed and success, the provinces of Italy and France.   His
diet was abstemious, his prayers long and fervent, and the alms
which he received with one hand, he distributed with the other;
his head was bare, his feet naked, his meagre body was wrapt in
a coarse garment; he bore and displayed a weighty crucifix; and
the ass on which he rode was sanctified in the public eye by the
service of the man of God.   He preached to innumerable crowds
in the churches, the streets, and the high-ways : the hermit
entered with equal confidence the palace and the cottage ; and
the people, for all was people, were impetuously moved by his
call to repentance and arms.   When he painted the sufferings
of the natives and pilgrims of Palestine, every heart was melted
to compassion ; every breast glowed with indignation, when he
challenged the warriors of the age to defend their brethren and
rescue their Saviour : his ignorance of art and language was compensated by sighs, and tears, and ejaculations ; and Peter supplied the deficiency of reason by loud and frequent appeals to
Christ and his mother, to the saints and angels of paradise, with
whom he had personally conversed.   The most perfect orator of
Athens might have envied the success of his eloquence : the
rustic enthusiast inspired the passions which he felt, and Christendom expected with impatience the counsels and decrees of the
supreme Pontiff.

at the Council of Clermont.   The story first appears in Albert of Aix and a little
later in the Chanson d'Antioche (of the Pilgrim Richard, c. 1145), which has been
edited by P. Paris, 1848.   See Hagenmeyer, Peter der Eremite, 1879.   After the
Council of Clermont Peter was active in preaching the Crusade in his own country
in the north-east of France, as we know from Guibertus.]

The magnanimous spirit of Gregory the Seventh had already embraced the design of arming Europe against Asia; the ardour of his zeal and ambition still breathes in his epistles.  From either side of the Alps, fifty thousand Catholics had enlisted under the banner of St. Peter;[3] and his successor reveals *his* intention of marching at their head against the impious sectaries of Mahomet.  But the glory or reproach of executing, though not in person, this holy enterprise was reserved for Urban the Second,[4] the most faithful of his disciples.  He undertook the conquest of the East, whilst the larger portion of Rome was possessed and fortified by his rival, Guibert of Ravenna, who contended with Urban for the name and honours of the pontificate. He attempted to unite the powers of the West, at a time when the princes were separated from the church, and the people from their princes, by the excommunication which himself and his predecessors had thundered against the emperor and the king of France.  Philip the First, of France, supported with patience the censures which he had provoked by his scandalous life and adulterous marriage.  Henry the Fourth, of Germany, asserted the right of investitures, the prerogative of confirming his bishops by the delivery of the ring and crosier.  But the emperor's party was crushed in Italy by the arms of the Normans and the Countess Mathilda; and the long quarrel had been recently envenomed by the revolt of his son Conrad, and the shame of his wife,[5] who, in the synods of Constance and Placentia, confessed the manifold prostitutions to which she had been exposed by an husband regardless of her honour and his

---

[3] Ultra quinquaginta millia, si me possunt in expeditione pro duce et pontifice habere, armatâ manu volunt in inimicos Dei insurgere, et ad sepulchrum Domini ipso ducente pervenire (Gregor. vii. epist. ii. 31, in tom. xii. p. 322, concil.).

[4] See the original lives of Urban II. by Pandulphus Pisanus and Bernardus Guido [in his Vitae Pontificum Romanorum ; Bernard flourished at the beginning of the 14th century], in Muratori, Rer. Ital. Script. tom. iii. pars i. p. 352, 353. [The continuation of the Liber Pontificalis from Gregory VII. to Honorius II. was ascribed by Baronius to Pandulfus of Pisa, and this view was adopted in Muratori's edition.  But Giesebrecht has shown that the lives of Gregory VII., Victor III., and Urban II. are independent compositions and probably the work of the Cardinal Petrus Pisanus.  The lives of Gelasius II., Calixtus II., and Honorius II. were written by Pandulf, the nephew of Hugh of Alatri.  See Giesebrecht, Allgemeine Monatschrift, 1852, p. 260 *sqq.*, and Gesch. der deutschen Kaiserzeit, iii. p. 1067-8 (5th ed.).—On Urban II. cp. M. F. Stern, Biographie des Papstes Urban II., 1883.]

[5] She is known by the different names of Praxes, Eupræcia, Eufrasia, and Adelais [generally called Praxedis in the sources]; and was the daughter of a Russian prince [Vsevlad of Kiev], and the widow of a Margrave of Brandenburg. Struv. Corpus Hist. Germanicæ, p. 340.

own.[6]  So popular was the cause of Urban, so weighty was his
influence, that the council which he summoned at Placentia [7]
was composed of two hundred bishops of Italy, France, Burgundy, Swabia, and Bavaria.  Four thousand of the clergy, and
thirty thousand of the laity, attended this important meeting ;
and, as the most spacious cathedral would have been inadequate
to the multitude, the session of seven days was held in a plain
adjacent to the city.  The ambassadors of the Greek emperor,
Alexius Comnenus, were introduced to plead the distress of their
sovereign, and the danger of Constantinople, which was divided
only by a narrow sea from the victorious Turks, the common
enemy of the Christian name.  In their suppliant address, they
flattered the pride of the Latin princes ; and, appealing at once
to their policy and religion, exhorted them to repel the barbarians on the confines of Asia rather than to expect them in
the heart of Europe.  At the sad tale of the misery and perils
of their Eastern brethren, the assembly burst into tears ; the
most eager champions declared their readiness to march ; and
the Greek ambassadors were dismissed with the assurance of a
speedy and powerful succour.  The relief of Constantinople was
included in the larger and most distant project of the deliverance of Jerusalem ; but the prudent Urban adjourned the final
decision to a second synod, which he proposed to celebrate in
some city of France in the autumn of the same year.  The short
delay would propagate the flame of enthusiasm ; and his firmest
hope was in a nation of soldiers,[8] still proud of the pre-eminence

[6] Henricus odio eam cœpit habere : ideo incarceravit eam, et concessit ut
plerique vim ei inferrent ; imo filium hortans ut eam subagitaret (Dodechin,
Continuat. Marian. Scot. [*i.e.* the Annales S. Disibodi falsely ascribed to a certain
Abbot Dodechin and erroneously supposed to be a continuation of the Chronicle of
Marianus Scotus] apud Baron. A.D. 1093, No. 4).  In the synod of Constance, she
is described by Bertholdus, rerum inspector : quæ se tantas et tam inauditas
fornicationum spurcitias, et a tantis passam fuisse conquesta est, &c.  And again
at Placentia : satis misericorditer suscepit, eo quod ipsam tantas spurcitias non
tam commississe quam invitam pertulisse pro certo cognoverit Papa cum sanctâ
synodo.  Apud Baron. A.D. 1093, No. 4, 1094, No. 3.  A rare subject for the infallible decision of a Pope and council !  These abominations are repugnant to
every principle of human nature, which is not altered by a dispute about rings and
crosiers.  Yet it should seem that the wretched woman was tempted by the priests
to relate or subscribe some infamous stories of herself and her husband.

[7] See the narrative and acts of the synod of Placentia, Concil. tom. xii. p. 821,
&c.  [Mansi, Concil. xx. p. 804, and cp. Pertz, Mon. 8, p. 474, for a notice appended
to the Acts.]

[8] Guibert himself, a Frenchman, praises the piety and valour of the French
nation, the author and example of the crusades :  Gens nobilis, prudens, bellicosa,
dapsilis, et nitida.——Quos enim Britones, *Anglos*, Ligures, si bonis eos moribus

of their name, and ambitious to emulate their hero Charlemagne,[9] who, in the popular romance of Turpin,[10] had achieved the conquest of the Holy Land. A latent motive of affection or vanity might influence the choice of Urban. He was himself a native of France, a monk of Clugny, and the first of his countrymen who ascended the throne of St. Peter. The Pope had illustrated his family and province. Nor is there perhaps a more exquisite gratification than to revisit, in a conspicuous dignity, the humble and laborious scenes of our youth.

It may occasion some surprise that the Roman pontiff should erect, in the heart of France, the tribunal from whence he hurled his anathemas against the king ; but our surprise will vanish, so soon as we form a just estimate of a king of France of the eleventh century.[11] Philip the First was the great-grandson of Hugh Capet, the founder of the present race, who, in the decline of Charlemagne's posterity, added the regal title to his patrimonial estates of Paris and Orleans. In this narrow compass he was possessed of wealth and jurisdiction ; but, in the rest of France, Hugh and his first descendants were no more than the feudal lords of about sixty dukes and counts, of independent and hereditary power,[12] who disdained the control of

videamus, non illico *Francos homines* appellemus? (p. 478). He owns, however, that the vivacity of the French degenerates into petulance among foreigners (p. 483), and vain loquaciousness (p. 502).

[9] Per viam quam jamdudum Carolus Magnus, mirificus rex Francorum [*leg.* Franciae], aptari fecit usque C. P. (Gesta Francorum, p. 1, Robert. Monach. Hist. Hieros. l. i. p. 33, &c.).

[10] John Tilpinus, or Turpinus, was Archbishop of Rheims, A.D. 773. After the year 1000, this romance was composed in his name by a monk of the borders of France and Spain ; and such was the idea of ecclesiastical merit that he describes himself as a fighting and drinking priest ! Yet the book of lies was pronounced authentic by Pope Calixtus II. (A.D. 1122), and is respectfully quoted by the abbot Suger, in the great Chronicles of St. Denys (Fabric. Bibliot. Latin. medii Ævi, edit. Mansi, tom. iv. p. 161). [The most important critical work on Turpin's romance (Historia de vita Caroli Magni et Rolandi eius nepotis, is the title) is that of Gaston Paris, De Pseudo-Turpino (1865), who makes it probable that the first part (cc. 1-5) was composed in the 11th century by a Spaniard, and the second part (c. 1110) by a monk at Vienne. The most recent edition is that of F. Castets, 1880. There were several old French translations. One, for instance, was edited by F. A. Wulff (Chronique dite de Turpin, 1881), and two others by T. Auracher (1876, 1877). There is an English translation by T. Rodd (History of Charles the Great and Orlando ascribed to Turpin, 1812, 2 vols.).]

[11] See Etat de la France, by the Count de Boulainvilliers, tom. i. p. 180-182, and the second volume of the Observations sur l'Histoire de France, by the Abbé de Mably.

[12] In the provinces to the south of the Loire, the first *Capetians* were scarcely allowed a feudal supremacy. On all sides, Normandy, Bretagne, Aquitain, Burgundy, Lorraine, and Flanders contracted the name and limits of the *proper* France. See Hadrian Vales. Notitia Galliarum.

laws and legal assemblies, and whose disregard of their sovereign was revenged by the disobedience of their inferior vassals. At Clermont, in the territories of the count of Auvergne,[13] the pope might brave with impunity the resentment of Philip; and the council which he convened in that city was not less numerous or respectable than the synod of Placentia.[14] Besides his court and council of Roman cardinals, he was supported by thirteen archbishops and two hundred and twenty-five bishops;[15] the number of mitred prelates was computed at four hundred; and the fathers of the church were blessed by the saints, and enlightened by the doctors, of the age. From the adjacent kingdoms a martial train of lords and knights of power and renown attended the council,[16] in high expectation of its resolves; and such was the ardour of zeal and curiosity that the city was filled, and many thousands, in the month of November, erected their tents or huts in the open field. A session of eight days produced some useful or edifying canons for the reformation of manners; a severe censure was pronounced against the licence of private war; the Truce of God [17] was confirmed, a suspension of hostilities during four days of the week; women and priests were placed under the safeguard of the church; and a protection of three years was extended to husbandmen and merchants, the defenceless victims of military rapine. But a law, however venerable be the sanction, cannot suddenly transform the temper of the times; and the benevolent efforts of Urban deserve the less praise, since he laboured to appease some domestic quarrels that he might spread the flames of war from the Atlantic to the Euphrates. From the synod of Placentia the rumour of his

[13] These counts, a younger branch of the dukes of Aquitain, were at length despoiled of the greatest part of their country by Philip Augustus. The bishops of Clermont gradually became princes of the city. Mélanges, tirés d'une grande Bibliothèque, tom. xxxvi. p. 288, &c.

[14] See the acts of the council of Clermont, Concil. tom. xii. p. 829, &c. [Mansi, Concilia, xx. p. 815 sqq.]

[15] [Thirteen archbishops, eighty bishops, and ninety abbots, Giesebrecht, iii. p. 667, following Cencius Camerarius (Mansi, xx. 908), and the Pope himself (ib., 829).]

[16] Confluxerunt ad concilium e multis regionibus viri, potentes et honorati, innumeri quamvis cingulo laicalis militiæ superbi (Baldric, an eye-witness, p. 86-88. Robert. Mon. p. 31, 32. Will. Tyr. i. 14, 15, p. 639-641. Guibert, p. 478-480. Fulcher. Caront. p. 382).

[17] The Truce of God (Treva, or Treuga Dei) was first invented in Aquitain, A.D. 1032; blamed by some bishops as an occasion of perjury, and rejected by the Normans as contrary to their privileges (Ducange, Gloss. Latin. tom. vi. p. 682-685). [Kluckhohn, Geschichte des Gottesfriedens.]

great design had gone forth among the nations ; the clergy, on their return, had preached in every diocese the merit and glory of the deliverance of the Holy Land ; and, when the pope ascended a lofty scaffold in the market-place of Clermont, his eloquence was addressed to a well-prepared and impatient audience. His topics were obvious, his exhortation was vehement, his success inevitable. The orator was interrupted by the shout of thousands, who with one voice, and in their rustic idiom, exclaimed aloud, " God wills it, God wills it ! " [18] " It is indeed the will of God," replied the pope ; " and let this memorable word, the inspiration surely of the Holy Spirit, be for ever adopted as your cry of battle, to animate the devotion and courage of the champions of Christ. His cross is the symbol of your salvation ; wear it, a red, a bloody cross, as an external mark on your breasts or shoulders, as a pledge of your sacred and irrevocable engagement." The proposal was joyfully accepted ; great numbers both of the clergy and laity impressed on their garments the sign of the cross,[19] and solicited the pope to march at their head. This dangerous honour was declined by the more prudent successor of Gregory, who alleged the schism of the church, and the duties of his pastoral office, recommending to the faithful, who were disqualified by sex or profession, by age or infirmity, to aid, with their prayers and alms, the personal service of their robust brethren. The name and powers of his legate he devolved on Adhemar, bishop of Puy, the first who had received the cross at his hands. The foremost of the temporal chiefs was Raymond, count of Toulouse, whose ambassadors in the council excused the absence, and pledged the honour, of their master. After the confession and absolution of their sins, the champions of the cross were dismissed with a superfluous admonition to invite their countrymen and friends ;

---

[18] *Deus vult, Deus vult !* was the pure acclamation of the clergy who understood Latin (Robert. Mon. l. i. p. 32). By the illiterate laity, who spoke the *Provincial* or *Limousin* idiom, it was corrupted to *Deus lo volt*, or *Diex el volt.* See Chron. Casinense, l. iv. c. 11. p. 497, in Muratori, Script. Rerum Ital. tom. iv., and Ducange (Dissertat. xi. p. 207 sur Joinville, and Gloss. Lat. tom. ii. p. 690), who, in his preface, produces a very difficult specimen of the dialect of Rovergue, A.D. 1100, very near, both in time and place, to the council of Clermont (p. 15, 16). [See Sybel, Geschichte des ersten Kreuzzuges, p. 185 *sqq.*]

[19] Most commonly on their shoulders, in gold, or silk, or cloth, sewed on their garments. In the first crusade, all were red ; in the third, the French alone preserved that colour, while green crosses were adopted by the Flemings, and white by the English (Ducange, tom. ii. p. 651). Yet in England the red ever appears the favourite, and, as it were, the national, colour of our military ensigns and uniforms.

and their departure for the Holy Land was fixed to the festival of the Assumption, the fifteenth of August, of the ensuing year.[20]

Justice of the Crusades

So familiar, and as it were so natural, to man is the practice of violence that our indulgence allows the slightest provocation, the most disputable right, as a sufficient ground of national hostility. But the name and nature of an *holy war* demands a more rigorous scrutiny; nor can we hastily believe that the servants of the Prince of Peace would unsheath the sword of destruction, unless the motives were pure, the quarrel legitimate, and the necessity inevitable. The policy of an action may be determined from the tardy lessons of experience; but, before we act, our conscience should be satisfied of the justice and propriety of our enterprise. In the age of the crusades, the Christians, both of the East and West, were persuaded of their lawfulness and merit; their arguments are clouded by the perpetual abuse of scripture and rhetoric; but they seem to insist on the right of natural and religious defence, their peculiar title to the Holy Land, and the impiety of their Pagan and Mahometan foes.[21] I. The right of a just defence may fairly include our civil and spiritual allies : it depends on the existence of danger; and that danger must be estimated by the twofold

[20] Bongarsius, who has published the original writers of the crusades, adopts, with much complacency, the fanatic title of Guibertus, Gesta DEI per Francos though some critics propose to read Gesta *Diaboli* per Francos (Hanoviæ, 1611 two vols. in folio). I shall briefly enumerate, as they stand in this collection [superseded by the Recueil des historiens des Croisades ; Historiens occidentaux vols. 1-5, 1841-1895], the authors whom I have used for the first crusade. I. Gesta Francorum [Recueil, 3, p. 121 *sqq.*]. II. Robertus Monachus [*ib.* 3, p. 717 *sqq.*]. III. Baldricus [*ib.* 4, p. 1 *sqq.*]. IV. Raimundus de Agiles [*ib.* 3, p. 235 *sqq.*]. V. Albertus Aquensis [*ib.* 4, p. 265 *sqq.*]. VI. Fulcherius Carnotensis [*ib.* 3, p. 311 *sqq.*]. VII. Guibertus [*ib.* 4, p. 113 *sqq.*]. VIII. Willielmus Tyriensis [*ib.* 1 No. 3]. Muratori has given us, IX. Radulphus Cadomensis de Gestis Tancred (Script. Rer. Ital. tom. v. p. 285-333 [Recueil, 3, p. 603 *sqq.*]), and X. Bernardus Thesaurarius de Acquisitione Terræ Sanctæ (tom. vii. p. 664-848 [*ib.* 2, p. 483 *sqq.*]) The last of these was unknown to a late French historian, who has given a large and critical list of the writers of the crusades (Esprit des Croisades, tom. i. p. 13-141) and most of whose judgments my own experience will allow me to ratify. It was late before I could obtain a sight of the French historians collected by Duchesne. I Petri Tudebodi Sacerdotis Sivracensis [of Sivrai in Poitou ; flor. c. A.D. 1100 Historia de Hierosolymitano Itinere (tom. iv. p. 773-815 [Recueil, 3, p. 1 *sqq.* French translation by S. de Goy, 1878]) has been transfused into the first anony mous writer of Bongarsius [rather, the Gesta Francorum were incorporated and augmented by Peter. So Sybel ; but otherwise Klein in his monograph Raimund von Aguilers, 1892]. II. The Metrical History of the First Crusade, in vii. book (p. 890-912), is of small value or account.

[21] If the reader will turn to the first scene of the First Part of Henry IV., he will see in the text of Shakespeare the natural feelings of enthusiasm ; and in the note of Dr. Johnson the workings of a bigoted though vigorous mind, greedy of every pretence to hate and persecute those who dissent from his creed.

consideration of the malice and the power of our enemies. A pernicious tenet has been imputed to the Mahometans, the duty of *extirpating* all other religions by the sword. This charge of ignorance and bigotry is refuted by the Koran, by the history of the Musulman conquerors, and by their public and legal toleration of the Christian worship. But it cannot be denied that the Oriental churches are depressed under their iron yoke ; that, in peace and war, they assert a divine and indefeasible claim of universal empire ; and that, in their orthodox creed, the unbelieving nations are continually threatened with the loss of religion or liberty. In the eleventh century, the victorious arms of the Turks presented a real and urgent apprehension of these losses. They had subdued, in less than thirty years, the kingdoms of Asia, as far as Jerusalem and the Hellespont ; and the Greek empire tottered on the verge of destruction. Besides an honest sympathy for their brethren, the Latins had a right and interest in the support of Constantinople, the most important barrier of the West ; and the privilege of defence must reach to prevent, as well as to repel, an impending assault. But this salutary purpose might have been accomplished by a moderate succour ; and our calmer reason must disclaim the innumerable hosts and remote operations which overwhelmed Asia and depopulated Europe. II. Palestine could add nothing to the strength or safety of the Latins ; and fanaticism alone could pretend to justify the conquest of that distant and narrow province. The Christians affirmed that their inalienable title to the promised land had been sealed by the blood of their divine Saviour : it was their right and duty to rescue their inheritance from the unjust possessors, who profaned his sepulchre and oppressed the pilgrimage of his disciples. Vainly would it be alleged that the pre-eminence of Jerusalem and the sanctity of Palestine have been abolished with the Mosaic law ; that the God of the Christians is not a local deity ; and that the recovery of Bethlehem or Calvary, his cradle or his tomb, will not atone for the violation of the moral precepts of the gospel. Such arguments glance aside from the leaden shield of superstition ; and the religious mind will not easily relinquish its hold on the sacred ground of mystery and miracle. III. But the holy wars which have been waged in every climate of the globe, from Egypt to Livonia, and from Peru to Hindostan, require the support of some more general and flexible tenet. It has been often supposed, and sometimes affirmed, that a difference of religion is a worthy cause of hostility ; that obstinate unbelievers may be slain or sub-

dued by the champions of the cross; and that grace is the sole
fountain of dominion as well as of mercy. Above four hundred
years before the first crusade, the eastern and western provinces
of the Roman empire had been acquired about the same time
and in the same manner, by the barbarians of Germany and
Arabia. Time and treaties had legitimated the conquests of the
*Christian* Franks: but, in the eyes of their subjects and neighbours, the Mahometan princes were still tyrants and usurpers
who, by the arms of war or rebellion, might be lawfully driven
from their unlawful possession.[22]

Spiritual<br>motives and<br>indulgences
As the manners of the Christians were relaxed, their discipline
of penance [23] was enforced; and, with the multiplication of sins,
the remedies were multiplied. In the primitive church, a voluntary and open confession prepared the work of atonement. In
the middle ages, the bishops and priests interrogated the
criminal; compelled him to account for his thoughts, words,
and actions; and prescribed the terms of his reconciliation with
God. But, as this discretionary power might alternately be
abused by indulgence and tyranny, a rule of discipline was
framed, to inform and regulate the spiritual judges. This mode
of legislation was invented by the Greeks; their *penitentials*
were translated, or imitated, in the Latin church; and, in the
time of Charlemagne, the clergy of every diocese were provided
with a code, which they prudently concealed from the knowledge
of the vulgar. In this dangerous estimate of crimes and punishments, each case was supposed, each difference was remarked
by the experience or penetration of the monks; some sins are
enumerated which innocence could not have suspected, and
others which reason cannot believe; and the more ordinary
offences of fornication and adultery, of perjury and sacrilege, of
rapine and murder, were expiated by a penance which, according to the various circumstances, was prolonged from forty days

[22] The Sixth Discourse of Fleury on Ecclesiastical History (p. 223-261) contains
an accurate and rational view of the causes and effects of the crusades.

[23] The penance, indulgences, &c. of the middle ages are amply discussed by
Muratori (Antiquitat. Italiæ medii Ævi, tom. v. dissert. lxviii. p. 709-768) and by
M. Chais (Lettres sur les Jubilés et les Indulgences, tom. ii. lettres 21 and 22,
478-556), with this difference, that the abuses of superstition are mildly, perhaps
faintly, exposed by the learned Italian, and peevishly magnified by the Dutch
minister.

[24] Schmidt (Histoire des Allemands, tom. ii. p. 211-220, 452-462) gives an abstract of the Penitential of Rhegino [ed. Wasserschleben, 1840] in the ixth [c. A.
906], and of Burchard [Migne, Patr. Lat. 140, p. 537 *sqq.*] in the xth, century.
In one year, five and thirty murders were perpetrated at Worms.

o seven years. During this term of mortification, the patient
vas healed, the criminal was absolved, by a salutary regimen of
asts and prayers; the disorder of his dress was expressive of
rief and remorse; and he humbly abstained from all the
usiness and pleasure of social life. But the rigid execution of
hese laws would have depopulated the palace, the camp, and
he city; the barbarians of the West believed and trembled;
ut nature often rebelled against principle; and the magistrate
aboured without effect to enforce the jurisdiction of the priest.
A literal accomplishment of penance was indeed impracticable:
he guilt of adultery was multiplied by daily repetition; that of
omicide might involve the massacre of a whole people; each
ct was separately numbered; and, in those times of anarchy
nd vice, a modest sinner might easily incur a debt of three
undred years. His insolvency was relieved by a commutation,
r *indulgence*: a year of penance was appreciated at twenty-six
*olidi* [25] of silver, about four pounds sterling, for the rich; at
hree solidi, or nine shillings, for the indigent: and these alms
vere soon appropriated to the use of the church, which derived,
rom the redemption of sins, an inexhaustible source of opulence
nd dominion. A debt of three hundred years, or twelve
undred pounds, was enough to impoverish a plentiful fortune;
he scarcity of gold and silver was supplied by the alienation of
and; and the princely donations of Pepin and Charlemagne are
xpressly given for the *remedy* of their soul. It is a maxim of
he civil law, That whosoever cannot pay with his purse must
ay with his body; and the practice of flagellation was adopted
y the monks, a cheap, though painful, equivalent. By a fan-
astic arithmetic, a year of penance was taxed at three thousand
ashes; [26] and such was the skill and patience of a famous hermit,
t. Dominic of the Iron Cuirass, [27] that in six days he could dis-
harge an entire century, by a whipping of three hundred
housand stripes. His example was followed by many penitents

[25] Till the xiith century, we may support the clear account of xii *denarii*,
pence, to the *solidus*, or shilling; and xx *solidi* to the pound weight of
lver, about the pound sterling. Our money is diminished to a third, and the
rench to a fiftieth, of this primitive standard.

[26] Each century of lashes was sanctified with the recital of a psalm; and the
hole psalter, with the accompaniment of 15,000 stripes, was equivalent to five
ears.

[27] The Life and Achievements of St. Dominic Loricatus was composed by his
iend and admirer, Peter Damianus [Acta Sanctorum, 14th October, 6; p. 621
*q.*]. See Fleury, Hist. Ecclés. tom. xiii. p. 96-104; Baronius, A.D. 1056, No.
, who observes from Damianus, how fashionable, even among ladies of quality
ublimis generis), this expiation (purgatorii genus) was grown.

of both sexes; and, as a vicarious sacrifice was accepted, a sturdy
disciplinarian might expiate on his own back the sins of his benefactors.[28] These compensations of the purse and the person
introduced, in the eleventh century, a more honourable mode of
satisfaction. The merit of military service against the Saracens
of Africa and Spain had been allowed by the predecessors of
Urban the Second. In the council of Clermont, that Pope proclaimed a plenary indulgence to those who should enlist under
the banner of the cross: the absolution of *all* their sins, and a
full receipt for *all* that might be due of canonical penance.[29]
The cold philosophy of modern times is incapable of feeling the
impression that was made on a sinful and fanatic world. At
the voice of their pastor, the robber, the incendiary, the homicide
arose by thousands to redeem their souls, by repeating on the
infidels the same deeds which they had exercised against their
Christian brethren; and the terms of atonement were eagerly
embraced by offenders of every rank and denomination. None
were pure; none were exempt from the guilt and penalty of
sin; and those who were the least amenable to the justice of
God and the church were the best entitled to the temporal
and eternal recompense of their pious courage. If they fell, the
spirit of the Latin clergy did not hesitate to adorn their tomb
with the crown of martyrdom;[30] and, should they survive, they
could expect without impatience the delay and increase of their
heavenly reward. They offered their blood to the Son of God,
who had laid down his life for their salvation: they took up the
cross, and entered with confidence into the way of the Lord.
His providence would watch over their safety; perhaps his
visible and miraculous power would smooth the difficulties of
their holy enterprise. The cloud and pillar of Jehovah had
marched before the Israelites into the promised land. Might
not the Christians more reasonably hope that the rivers would
open for their passage; that the walls of the strongest cities

[28] At a quarter, or even half, a rial a lash, Sancho Panza was a cheaper and
possibly not a more dishonest workman. I remember, in Père Labat (Voyages en
Italie, tom. vii. p. 16-29), a very lively picture of the *dexterity* of one of these
artists.

[29] Quicunque pro solâ devotione, non pro honoris vel pecuniæ adeptione, ad
liberandam ecclesiam Dei Jerusalem profectus fuerit, iter illud pro omni pœnitent
reputetur. Canon. Concil. Claromont. ii. p. 829. Guibert styles it, novum
salutis genus (p. 471), and is almost philosophical on the subject.

[30] Such at least was the belief of the crusaders, and such is the uniform style
of the historians (Esprit des Croisades, tom. iii. p. 477); but the prayers for the
repose of their souls is inconsistent in orthodox theology with the merits of martyrdom.

would fall at the sound of their trumpets; and that the sun would be arrested in his mid-career, to allow them time for the destruction of the infidels?

Of the chiefs and soldiers who marched to the holy sepulchre, I will dare to affirm that *all* were prompted by the spirit of enthusiasm, the belief of merit, the hope of reward, and the assurance of divine aid. But I am equally persuaded that in *many* it was not the sole, that in *some* it was not the leading, principle of action. The use and abuse of religion are feeble to stem, they are strong and irresistible to impel, the stream of national manners. Against the private wars of the barbarians, their bloody tournaments, licentious loves, and judicial duels, the popes and synods might ineffectually thunder. It is a more easy task to provoke the metaphysical disputes of the Greeks, to drive into the cloister the victims of anarchy or despotism, to sanctify the patience of slaves and cowards, or to assume the merit of the humanity and benevolence of modern Christians. War and exercise were the reigning passions of the Franks or Latins; they were enjoined, as a penance, to gratify those passions, to visit distant lands, and to draw their swords against the nations of the East. Their victory, or even their attempt, would immortalise the names of the intrepid heroes of the cross; and the purest piety could not be insensible to the most splendid prospect of military glory. In the petty quarrels of Europe, they shed the blood of their friends and countrymen, for the acquisition perhaps of a castle or a village. They could march with alacrity against the distant and hostile nations who were devoted to their arms: their fancy already grasped the golden sceptres of Asia; and the conquest of Apulia and Sicily by the Normans might exalt to royalty the hopes of the most private adventurer. Christendom, in her rudest state, must have yielded to the climate and cultivation of the Mahometan countries; and their natural and artificial wealth had been magnified by the tales of pilgrims and the gifts of an imperfect commerce. The vulgar, both the great and small, were taught to believe every wonder, of lands flowing with milk and honey, of mines and treasures, of gold and diamonds, of palaces of marble and jasper, and of odoriferous groves of cinnamon and frankincense. In this earthly paradise each warrior depended on his sword to carve a plenteous and honourable establishment, which he measured only by the extent of his wishes.[31] Their vassals and

> Temporal and carnal motives

---

[31] The same hopes were displayed in the letters of the adventurers, ad animandos qui in Franciâ resederant. Hugh de Reiteste could boast that his share

soldiers trusted their fortunes to God and their master : the
spoils of a Turkish emir might enrich the meanest follower of
the camp ; and the flavour of the wines, the beauty of the Grecian women,[32] were temptations more adapted to the nature, than
to the profession, of the champions of the cross. The love of
freedom was a powerful incitement to the multitudes who were
oppressed by feudal or ecclesiastical tyranny. Under this holy
sign, the peasants and burghers, who were attached to the
servitude of the glebe, might escape from an haughty lord,
and transplant themselves and their families to a land of liberty.
The monk might release himself from the discipline of his convent ; the debtor might suspend the accumulation of usury and
the pursuit of his creditors ; and outlaws and malefactors of
every cast might continue to brave the laws and elude the
punishment of their crimes.[33]

Influence of
example

These motives were potent and numerous : when we have
singly computed their weight on the mind of each individual,
we must add the infinite series, the multiplying powers of
example and fashion. The first proselytes became the warmest
and most effectual missionaries of the cross : among their friends
and countrymen they preached the duty, the merit, and the
recompense of their holy vow ; and the most reluctant hearers
were insensibly drawn within the whirlpool of persuasion and
authority. The martial youths were fired by the reproach or
suspicion of cowardice ; the opportunity of visiting with an army
the sepulchre of Christ was embraced by the old and infirm, by
women and children, who consulted rather their zeal than their
strength ; and those who in the evening had derided the folly of
their companions were the most eager, the ensuing day, to tread
in their footsteps. The ignorance, which magnified the hopes,
diminished the perils, of the enterprise. Since the Turkish conquest, the paths of pilgrimage were obliterated ; the chiefs themselves had an imperfect notion of the length of the way and the

amounted to one abbey and ten castles, of the yearly value of 1500 marks, and
that he should acquire an hundred castles by the conquest of Aleppo (Guibert, p.
554, 555).

[32] In his genuine or fictitious letter to the Count of Flanders, Alexius mingles
with the danger of the church, and the relics of saints, the auri et argenti amor
and pulcherrimarum fœminarum voluptas (p. 476) ; as if, says the indignant
Guibert, the Greek women were handsomer than those of France. [For the letter
see above, p. 251, note 64.]

[33] See the privileges of the Crucesignati, freedom from debt, usury, injury, secular
justice, &c. The pope was their perpetual guardian (Ducange, tom. ii. p. 651
652).

state of their enemies ; and such was the stupidity of the people that, at the sight of the first city or castle beyond the limits of their knowledge, they were ready to ask, whether that was not the Jerusalem, the term and object of their labours. Yet the more prudent of the crusaders, who were not sure that they should be fed from heaven with a shower of quails or manna, provided themselves with those precious metals which, in every country, are the representatives of every commodity. To defray, according to their rank, the expenses of the road, princes alienated their provinces, nobles their lands and castles, peasants their cattle and the instruments of husbandry. The value of property was depreciated by the eager competition of multitudes ; while the price of arms and horses was raised to an exorbitant height, by the wants and impatience of the buyers.[34] Those who remained at home, with sense and money, were enriched by the epidemical disease : the sovereigns acquired at a cheap rate the domains of their vassals ; and the ecclesiastical purchasers completed the payment by the assurance of their prayers. The cross, which was commonly sewed on the garment, in cloth or silk, was inscribed by some zealots on their skin ; an hot iron, or indelible liquor, was applied to perpetuate the mark ; and a crafty monk, who showed the miraculous impression on his breast, was repaid with the popular veneration and the richest benefices of Palestine.[35]

The fifteenth of August had been fixed in the council of Clermont for the departure of the pilgrims ; but the day was anticipated by the thoughtless and needy crowd of plebeians ; and I shall briefly dispatch the calamities which they inflicted and suffered, before I enter on the more serious and successful enterprise of the chiefs. Early in the spring, from the confines of France and Lorraine, about sixty thousand of the populace of both sexes flocked round the first missionary of the crusade, and pressed him with clamorous importunity to lead them to the holy sepulchre. The hermit, assuming the character, without the talents or authority, of a general, impelled or obeyed the forward impulse of his votaries along the banks of the Rhine and Danube. Their wants and numbers soon compelled them to

*Departure of the first crusaders. A.D. 1096, March, May &c.*

---

[34] Guibert (p. 481) paints in lively colours this general emotion. He was one of the few contemporaries who had genius enough to feel the astonishing scenes that were passing before their eyes. Erat itaque videre miraculum caro omnes emere, atque vili vendere, &c.

[35] Some instances of these *stigmata* are given in the Esprit des Croisades (tom. iii. p. 169, &c.), from authors whom I have not seen.

separate, and his lieutenant, Walter the Pennyless,[36] a valiant though needy soldier, conducted a vanguard of pilgrims, whose condition may be determined from the proportion of eight horsemen to fifteen thousand foot. The example and footsteps of Peter were closely pursued by another fanatic, the monk Godescal, whose sermons had swept away fifteen or twenty thousand peasants from the villages of Germany. Their rear was again pressed by an herd of two hundred thousand, the most stupid and savage refuse of the people, who mingled with their devotion a brutal licence of rapine, prostitution, and drunkenness. Some counts and gentlemen, at the head of three thousand horse, attended the motions of the multitude to partake in the spoil ; but their genuine leaders (may we credit such folly ?) were a goose and a goat, who were carried in the front, and to whom these worthy Christians ascribed an infusion of the divine Spirit.[37] Of these and of other bands of enthusiasts, the first and most easy warfare was against the Jews, the murderers of the Son of God. In the trading cities of the Moselle and the Rhine, their colonies were numerous and rich ; and they enjoyed, under the protection of the emperor and the bishops, the free exercise of their religion.[38] At Verdun, Treves, Mentz, Spires, Worms, many thousands of that unhappy people were pillaged and massacred ;[39] nor had they felt a more bloody stroke since the persecution of Hadrian. A remnant was saved by the firmness of their bishops, who accepted a feigned and transient conversion ; but the more obstinate Jews opposed their fanaticism to the fanaticism of the Christians, barricadoed their houses, and, precipitating themselves, their families, and their wealth, into the rivers or the flames, disappointed the malice, or at least the avarice, of their implacable foes.

[36] [Along with his uncle Walter de Poissy.]

[37] Fuit et aliud scelus detestabile in hâc congregatione pedestris populi stulti et vesanæ levitatis, ... *anserem* quendam divino Spiritu asserebant afflatum, et *capellam* non minus eodem repletam, et has sibi duces [hujus] secundæ viæ fecerant, &c. (Albert. Aquensis, l. i, c. 31, p. 196). Had these peasants founded an empire, they might have introduced, as in Egypt, the worship of animals, which their philosophic descendants would have glossed over with some specious and subtle allegory.

[38] Benjamin of Tudela describes the state of his Jewish brethren from Cologne along the Rhine : they were rich, generous, learned, hospitable, and lived in the eager hope of the Messiah (Voyage, tom. i. p. 243-245, par Baratier). In seventy years (he wrote about A.D. 1170) they had recovered from these massacres.

[39] These massacres and depredations on the Jews, which were renewed at each crusade, are *coolly* related. It is true that St. Bernard (epist. 363, tom. i. p. 329) admonishes the Oriental Franks, non sunt persequendi Judæi, non sunt trucidandi. The contrary doctrine had been preached by a *rival* monk.

Between the frontiers of Austria and the seat of the Byzan- Their destruction in Hungary and Asia. A.D. 1096
tine monarchy, the crusaders were compelled to traverse an
interval of six hundred miles; the wild and desolate countries
of Hungary [40] and Bulgaria. The soil is fruitful, and intersected
with rivers; but it was then covered with morasses and forests,
which spread to a boundless extent, whenever man has ceased
to exercise his dominion over the earth. Both nations had imbibed the rudiments of Christianity; the Hungarians were ruled
by their native princes; the Bulgarians by a lieutenant of the
Greek emperor; but on the slightest provocation, their ferocious
nature was rekindled, and ample provocation was afforded by
the disorders of the first pilgrims. Agriculture must have
been unskilful and languid among a people, whose cities were
built of reeds and timber, which were deserted in the summer-
season for the tents of hunters and shepherds. A scanty
supply of provisions was rudely demanded, forcibly seized, and
greedily consumed; and, on the first quarrel, the crusaders gave [In Servia]
a loose to indignation and revenge. But their ignorance of the
country, of war, and of discipline exposed them to every snare.
The Greek præfect of Bulgaria commanded a regular force; at
the trumpet of the Hungarian king, the eighth or the tenth of
his martial subjects bent their bows and mounted on horseback; their policy was insidious, and their retaliation on these
pious robbers was unrelenting and bloody.[41] About a third of
the naked fugitives, and the hermit Peter was of the number,
escaped to the Thracian mountains; and the emperor, who
respected the pilgrimage and succour of the Latins, conducted
them by secure and easy journeys to Constantinople, and advised [Arrival at Constantinople. Aug. 1, A.D. 1096]
them to wait the arrival of their brethren. For a while they
remembered their faults and losses; but no sooner were they

[40] See the contemporary description of Hungary in Otho of Frisingen [Gesta
Friderici], l. ii. c. 31, in Muratori, Script. Rerum Italicarum, tom. vi. p. 665, 666.
[This work of Otto, along with the continuation by Rahewin, has been edited in
Pertz, Mon. xx. p. 347 sqq. ; and (by G. Waitz) in Scr. rer. Germ. 1884.]

[41] The old Hungarians, without excepting Turotzius, are ill informed of the
first crusade, which they involve in a single passage. Katona, like ourselves, can
only quote the writers of France; but he compares with local science the ancient
and modern geography. Ante portam Cyperon, is Sopron, or Poson; Mallevilla,
Zemlin; Fluvius Maroe, Savus; Lintax, Leith; Mesebroch, or Marseburg, Ouar,
or Moson; Tollenburg, Pragg (De Regibus Hungariæ, tom. iii. p. 19-53). [The
Hungarian king Caloman treated the pilgrims well. But a few stragglers belonging to the host of Walter were plundered at Semlin, and their arms were hung up
on the wall. The army of Peter the Hermit, arriving later, saw the arms of their
forerunners, and took vengeance by attacking and occupying the town. Both the
host of Peter and that of Walter lost a great many men in conflicts in Bulgaria.]

revived by the hospitable entertainment than their venom was
again inflamed ; they stung their benefactor, and neither gardens
nor palaces nor churches [41a] were safe from their depredations.
For his own safety, Alexius allured them to pass over to the
Asiatic side of the Bosphorus ; but their blind impetuosity
soon urged them to desert the station which he had assigned,[41b]
and to rush headlong against the Turks, who occupied the road
of Jerusalem.   The hermit, conscious of his shame, had withdrawn from the camp to Constantinople ; and his lieutenant,

[Gualterius Sinehabere]

Walter the Pennyless, who was worthy of a better command,
attempted, without success, to introduce some order and prudence among the herd of savages.   They separated in quest
of prey, and themselves fell an easy prey to the arts of the
Sultan.   By a rumour that their foremost companions were

[leg. Kilij Arslan]

rioting in the spoils of his capital, Soliman tempted the main
body to descend into the plain of Nice ; they were overwhelmed
by the Turkish arrows ; and a pyramid of bones [42] informed
their companions of the place of their defeat.   Of the first
crusaders, three hundred thousand had already perished, before
a single city was rescued from the infidels, before their graver
and more noble brethren had completed the preparations of
their enterprise.[43]

[41a] [In the suburbs ; they were not admitted into the city.]

[41b] [Their station was Nicomedia and its neighbourhood (Gesta Fr. ii. 4), including
Civetot (Albert, i. 16 ; Gesta Fr. ii. 8) and Helenopolis (Anna, x. 6).]

[42] Anna Comnena (Alexias, l. x. p. 287 [c. 6]) describes this ὀστῶν κολωνός as a
mountain, ὑψηλὸν καὶ βάθος καὶ πλάτος ἀξιολογώτατον [ἀπολαμβάνον].   In the siege of
Nice, such were used by the Franks themselves as the materials of a wall.   [It was
near the river Dracon, which had been fixed as the boundary between the Empire
and Rūm.]

[43] [See table on opposite page.]

43 To save time and space, I shall represent in a short table, the particular references to the great events of the first crusade. [In cases where the author cites by the *pages* of Bongarsius, the chapters are added within square brackets, so that the reader may be able easily to refer to the Recueil des historiens de Croisades, or any other text In the case of Baldric the pages of the edition in the Recueil (Hist. Occ. vol. iv.) are given.]

| | The Crowd. | The Chiefs. | The Road to Constantinople. | Alexius. | Nice and Asia Minor. | Edessa. | Antioch. | The Battle. | The Holy Lance. | Conquest of Jerusalem. |
|---|---|---|---|---|---|---|---|---|---|---|
| I. Gesta Francorum | p. 1, 2 [i. 1, 2] | p. 2 [i. 2, 3] | p. 2, 3 [i. 3, 4] | p. 4, 5 [ii. 1-4] | p. 5-7 [ii. 7-iv. 2] | — | p. 9-15 [iv. 5-27] | p. 15-22 [iv. 28-40] | p. 18-20 [iv. 35. 38] | p. 26-29 [iv. 49-55] |
| II. Robertus Monachus | p. 33, 34 [i. 4, 5] | p. 35, 36 [ii. 1-5] | p. 36, 37 [ii. 7-14] | p. 37, 38 [ii. 14-19] | p. 39-45 [iii. 1-2E] | — [cp. iii. 23] | p. 45-55 [iii. 29-v. 14] | p. 56-66 [vi. 4-vii. 19] | p. 61, 62 [vii. 1-3] | p. 74-81 [ix. 1-26] |
| III. Baldricus | p. 89 [p. 17] | [p. 17] | p. 91-93 [p. 20-23] | p. 91-94 [p. 20-25] | p. 94-101 [p. 26-35] | — | p. 101, 111 [p. 39-58] | p. 111-122 [p. 59-79] | p. 116-119 [p. 67-68, 73, 75] | p. 130-138 [p. 96-111] |
| IV. Raimundus des Agiles | — | — | p. 139, 140 [c. 1, 2] | p. 140, 141 [c. 2, 3] | p. 142 [c. 3, 4] | — | p. 142-149 [c. 5-9] | p. 149-155 [c. 10-17] | p. 150, 152, 156 [c. 10, 13, 18] | p. 173-183 [c. 20, 21] |
| V. Albertus Aquensis | l. i. c. 7-31 [seg. 30] | [ii. 1] | l. ii. c. 1-8 | {l. ii. c. 9-19} | {l. ii. c. 20-43}<br>{l. iii. c. 1-4} | {l. iii. c. 5-32}<br>{l. iv. 9-12}<br>{l. v. 15-22} | {l. iii. c. 33-66; iv. 1-26} | l. iv. c. 7-56 | l. iv. c. 43 | {l. v. c. 45, 46}<br>{l. vi. 1-50} |
| VI. Fulcherius Carnotensis | p. 384 [i. 2] | [i. 6] | p. 385, 386 [i. 6-8] | p. 386 [i. 9] | p. 387-389 [i. 9-18] | p. 389, 390 [i. 14] | p. 390-392 [i. 15-17] | p. 392-395 [i. 19-23] | p. 392 [i. 18] | p. 396-400 [i. 25-28] |
| VII. Guibertus | p. 482, 485 [ii. 8-11] | [485-7] [ii. 12-19] | p. 485, 489 [ii. 12-iii. 3] | p. 485-490 [ii. 12-iii. 4] | p. 491-496, 498 [iii. 4-8; iv. 2] | p. 496, 497 [iii. 13] | p. 498, 506, 512 [iv. 3, 14; v. 8] | p. 512-523 [v. 9-vi. 10] | p. 520, 530, 533 [vi. 1, 22, 34] | p. 543-537 [vi. 11-vii. 11] |
| VIII. Willermus Tyrensis | l. i. c. 18-30 | l. i. c. 17 | {l. ii. c. 1-4, 13, 17, 22} | l. ii. c. 5-23 | {l. iii. c. 1-12}<br>{l. iv. c. 13-25} | l. iv. c. 1-6 | {l. iv. 9-24}<br>{l. v. 1-23} | {l. vi. c. 1-23} | l. vi. c. 14. | {l. vii. c. 1-25}<br>{l. viii. c. 1-24} |
| IX. Radulphus Cadomensis | — | c. i. 3, 15 | c. 4-7, 17 | {c. 8-13, 18, 19} | c. 14-16, 21-47 | — | c. 48-71 | c. 72-91 | c. 100-109 | c. 111-138 |
| X. Bernardus Thesaurarius | c. 7-11 | — | c. 11-20 | c. 11-20 | c. 21-25 | c. 26 | c. 27-38 | c. 39-52 | c. 45 | c. 54-77 |

The chiefs of the first crusade

None of the great sovereigns of Europe embarked their persons in the first crusade. The emperor Henry the Fourth was not disposed to obey the summons of the pope ; Philip the First of France was occupied by his pleasures ; William Rufus of England by a recent conquest ; the kings of Spain were engaged in a domestic war against the Moors ; and the northern monarchs of Scotland, Denmark,[44] Sweden, and Poland, were yet strangers to the passions and interests of the South. The religious ardour was more strongly felt by the princes of the second order, who held an important place in the feudal system. Their situation will naturally cast, under four distinct heads, the review of their names and characters ; but I may escape some needless repetition by observing at once that courage and the exercise of arms are the common attribute of these Christian adventurers. I. The first rank both in war and council is justly due to Godfrey of Bouillon ; and happy would it have been for the crusaders, if they had trusted themselves to the sole conduct of that accomplished hero, a worthy representative of Charlemagne, from whom he was descended in the female line. His father was of the noble race of the counts of Boulogne : Brabant, the lower province of Lorraine,[45] was the inheritance of his mother ; and, by the emperor's bounty, he was himself invested with that ducal title, which has been improperly transferred to his lordship of Bouillon in the Ardennes.[46] In the service of Henry the Fourth he bore the great standard of the empire, and pierced with his lance the breast of Rodolph, the rebel king : Godfrey was the first who ascended the walls of Rome ; and his sickness, his vow, perhaps his remorse for bearing arms against the Pope, confirmed an early resolution of visiting the holy sepulchre, not as a pilgrim, but a deliverer. His valour was matured by prudence and moderation ; his piety, though blind,

I. Godfrey of Bouillon

[44] The author of the Esprit des Croisades has doubted, and might have disbelieved, the crusade and tragic death of Prince Sueno, with 1500 or 15,000 Danes, who was cut off by Sultan Soliman in Cappadocia, but who still lives in the poem of Tasso (tom. iv. p. 111-115).

[45] The fragments of the kingdoms of Lotharingia, or Lorraine, were broken into the two duchies, of the Moselle, and of the Meuse ; the first has preserved its name, which in the latter has been changed into that of Brabant (Vales. Notit. Gall. p. 283-288). [Lothringen had been divided into Upper and Lower in the latter part of the reign of Otto I. The two duchies were again united, under Conrad II., in the hands of Duke Gozelo ; but on his death in 1044 were separated, going to his two sons, by permission of Henry III.]

[46] See, in the description of France, by the Abbé de Longuerue, the articles of *Boulogne*, part i. p. 54 ; *Brabant*, part ii. p. 47, 48 ; *Bouillon*, p. 134. On his departure, Godfrey sold or pawned Bouillon to the church for 1300 marks.

was sincere ; and, in the tumult of a camp, he practised the real
and fictitious virtues of a convent. Superior to the private factions of the chiefs, he reserved his enmity for the enemies of
Christ ; and, though he gained a kingdom by the attempt, his
pure and disinterested zeal was acknowledged by his rivals.
Godfrey of Bouillon [47] was accompanied by his two brothers,
by Eustace the elder, who had succeeded to the county of
Boulogne, and by the younger, Baldwin, a character of more ambiguous virtue. The Duke of Lorraine was alike celebrated
on either side of the Rhine ; from birth and education, he
was equally conversant with the French and Teutonic languages :
the barons of France, Germany, and Lorraine assembled their
vassals ; and the confederate force that marched under his
banner was composed of fourscore thousand foot and about
ten thousand horse. 11. In the parliament that was held
at Paris, in the king's presence, about two months after the
council of Clermont, Hugh, count of Vermandois, was the most
conspicuous of the princes who assumed the cross. But the
appellation of *the Great* was applied, not so much to his merit or
possessions (though neither were contemptible), as to the royal
birth of the brother of the king of France.[48] Robert, duke
of Normandy, was the eldest son of William the Conqueror ;
but on his father's death he was deprived of the kingdom of
England, by his own indolence and the activity of his brother
Rufus. The worth of Robert was degraded by an excessive
levity and easiness of temper ; his cheerfulness seduced him to
the indulgence of pleasure ; his profuse liberality impoverished
the prince and people ; his indiscriminate clemency multiplied
the number of offenders ; and the amiable qualities of a
private man became the essential defects of a sovereign. For
the trifling sum of ten thousand marks he mortgaged Normandy during his absence to the English usurper ;[49] but his

> II. Hugh of
> Vermandois.
> Robert of
> Normandy,
> Robert of
> Flanders,
> Stephen of
> Chartres, &c.

---

[47] See the family character of Godfrey in William of Tyre, l. ix. c. 5-8 ; his
previous design in Guibert (p. 485) ; his sickness and vow in Bernard. Thesaur.
(c. 78).

[48] Anna Comnena supposes that Hugh [Οὖβος] was proud of his nobility, riches,
and power (l. x. p. 288 [c. 7]) ; the two last articles appear more equivocal ; but
an εὐγένεια, which, seven hundred years ago, was famous in the palace of Constantinople, attests the ancient dignity of the Capetian family of France.

[49] Will. Gemeticensis [of Jumièges ; c. A.D. 1027 ; the end of Bk. 7 and Bk. 8
are not by William], l. vii. c. 7, p. 672, 673, in Camden. Normanicis [in Migne, Pat.
Lat. 149, p. 779 *sqq.*]. He pawned the duchy for one hundredth part of the
present yearly revenue. Ten thousand marks may be equal to five hundred
thousand livres, and Normandy annually yields fifty-seven millions to the king
(Necker, Administration des Finances, tom. i. p. 287).

engagement and behaviour in the holy war announced in Robert
a reformation of manners, and restored him in some degree to
the public esteem. Another Robert was count of Flanders, a
royal province, which, in this century, gave three queens to the
thrones of France, England, and Denmark. He was surnamed
the Sword and Lance of the Christians ; but in the exploits of a
soldier he sometimes forgot the duties of a general. Stephen,
count of Chartres, of Blois, and of Troyes, was one of the richest
princes of the age ; and the number of his castles has been compared to the three hundred and sixty-five days of the year. His
mind was improved by literature ; and, in the council of the
chiefs, the eloquent Stephen [50] was chosen to discharge the office
of their president. These four were the principal leaders of the
French, the Normans, and the pilgrims of the British isles ; but
the list of the barons, who were possessed of three or four towns,
would exceed, says a contemporary, the catalogue of the Trojan

**III. Raymond of Toulouse** war.[51]    III. In the south of France, the command was assumed
by Adhemar, bishop of Puy, the Pope's legate, and by Raymond,
count of St. Giles and Toulouse, who added the prouder titles
of duke of Narbonne and marquis of Provence. The former
was a respectable prelate, alike qualified for this world and the
next. The latter was a veteran warrior, who had fought against
the Saracens of Spain, and who consecrated his declining age,
not only to the deliverance, but to the perpetual service, of the
holy sepulchre. His experience and riches gave him a strong
ascendant in the Christian camp, whose distress he was often
able, and sometimes willing, to relieve. But it was easier for
him to extort the praise of the infidels than to preserve the
love of his subjects and associates. His eminent qualities were
clouded by a temper, haughty, envious, and obstinate ; and,
though he resigned an ample patrimony for the cause of God,
his piety, in the public opinion, was not exempt from avarice
and ambition.[52]    A mercantile rather than a martial spirit pre-

[50] His original letter to his wife [Adela] is inserted in the Spicilegium of Dom.
Luc. d'Acheri, tom. iv. and quoted in the Esprit des Croisades, tom. i. p. 63.
[This and another letter (entitled Ep. ex castris obsidionis Nicaenae anno 1098) are
printed in the Recueil, Hist. Occ. 3, p. 883 *sqq.*]

[51] Unius enim, duum, trium, seu quatuor oppidorum dominos quis numeret ?
quorum tanta fuit copia, ut non vix totidem Trojana obsidio coegisse putetur.
(Ever the lively and interesting Guibert, p. 486.)

[52] It is singular enough that Raymond of St. Giles, a second character in the
genuine history of the crusades, should shine as the first of heroes in the writings
of the Greeks (Anna Comnen. Alexiad. l. x. xi. [Anna calls him *Isangeles*]) and
the Arabians (Longueruana, p. 129).

vailed among his *provincials*,[53] a common name, which included the natives of Auvergne and Languedoc,[54] the vassals of the kingdom of Burgundy or Arles. From the adjacent frontier of Spain he drew a band of hardy adventurers; as he marched through Lombardy, a crowd of Italians flocked to his standard; and his united force consisted of one hundred thousand horse and foot. If Raymond was the first to enlist, and the last to depart, the delay may be excused by the greatness of his preparation and the promise of an everlasting farewell. IV. The name of Bohemond, the son of Robert Guiscard, was already famous by his double victory over the Greek emperor; but his father's will had reduced him to the principality of Tarentum and the remembrance of his Eastern trophies, till he was awakened by the rumour and passage of the French pilgrims. It is in the person of this Norman chief that we may seek for the coolest policy and ambition, with a small allay of religious fanaticism. His conduct may justify a belief that he had secretly directed the design of the pope, which he affected to second with astonishment and zeal. At the siege of Amalphi, his example and discourse inflamed the passions of a confederate army; he instantly tore his garment, to supply crosses for the numerous candidates, and prepared to visit Constantinople and Asia at the head of ten thousand horse and twenty thousand foot. Several princes of the Norman race accompanied this veteran general; and his cousin Tancred [55] was the partner, rather than the servant, of the war. In the accomplished character of Tancred we discover all the virtues of a perfect knight,[56] the true spirit of chivalry, which inspired

IV. Bohemond and Tancred

---

[53] Omnes de Burgundiâ, et Alverniâ, et Vasconiâ, et Gothi (of *Languedoc*), provinciales appellabantur cæteri vero Francigenæ, et hoc in exercitu; inter hostes autem Franci dicebantur. Raymond de Agiles, p. 144.

[54] The town of his birth, or first appanage, was consecrated to St. Ægidius, whose name, as early as the first crusade, was corrupted by the French into St. Gilles, or St. Giles. It is situate in the Lower Languedoc, between Nismes and the Rhone, and still boasts a collegiate church of the foundation of Raymond (Mélanges tirés d'une grande Bibliothèque, tom. xxxvii. p. 51).

[55] The mother of Tancred was Emma, sister of the great Robert Guiscard; his father, the marquis Odo the Good. It is singular enough that the family and country of so illustrious a person should be unknown; but Muratori reasonably conjectures that he was an Italian, and perhaps of the race of the marquises of Montferrat in Piedmont (Script. tom. v. p. 281, 282). [But see below, p. 296, n. 86.]

[56] To gratify the childish vanity of the house of Este, Tasso has inserted in his poem, and in the first crusade, a fabulous hero, the brave and amorous Rinaldo (x. 75, xvii. 66-94). He might borrow his name from a Rinaldo, with the Aquila bianca Estense, who vanquished, as the standard-bearer of the Roman church,

the generous sentiments and social offices of man far better than the base philosophy, or the baser religion, of the times.

Chivalry

Between the age of Charlemagne and that of the crusades, a revolution had taken place among the Spaniards, the Normans, and the French, which was gradually extended to the rest of Europe. The service of the infantry was degraded to the plebeians ; the cavalry formed the strength of the armies, and the honourable name of *miles,* or soldier, was confined to the gentlemen [57] who served on horseback and were invested with the character of knighthood. The dukes and counts, who had usurped the rights of sovereignty, divided the provinces among their faithful barons : the barons distributed among their vassals the fiefs or benefices of their jurisdiction ; and these military tenants, the peers of each other and of their lord, composed the noble or equestrian order, which disdained to conceive the peasant or burgher as of the same species with themselves. The dignity of their birth was preserved by pure and equal alliances ; their sons alone, who could produce four quarters or lines of ancestry, without spot or reproach, might legally pretend to the honour of knighthood ; but a valiant plebeian was sometimes enriched and ennobled by the sword, and became the father of a new race. A single knight could impart, according to his judgment, the character which he received ; and the warlike sovereigns of Europe derived more glory from this personal distinction than from the lustre of their diadem. This ceremony, of which some traces may be found in Tacitus and the woods of Germany,[58] was in its origin simple and profane ; the candidate, after some previous trial, was invested with the sword and spurs ; and his cheek or shoulder was touched with a slight blow, as an emblem of the last affront which it was lawful for him to endure. But superstition mingled in every public and private action of life ; in the holy wars, it sanctified the profes-

the emperor Frederic I. (Storia Imperiale di Ricobaldo, in Muratori, Script. Ital. tom. ix. p. 360 ; Ariosto, Orlando Furioso, iii. 30). But, 1. The distance of sixty years between the youth of the two Rinaldos destroys their identity. 2. The Storia Imperiale is a forgery of the Conte Boyardo, at the end of the xvth century (Muratori, p. 281-289). 3. This Rinaldo and his exploits are not less chimerical than the hero of Tasso (Muratori, Antichità Estense, tom. i. p. 350).

[57] Of the words, *gentilis, gentilhomme, gentleman,* two etymologies are produced : 1. From the barbarians of the fifth century, the soldiers, and at length the conquerors, of the Roman empire, who were vain of their foreign nobility ; and, 2. From the sense of the civilians, who consider *gentilis* as synonymous with *ingenuus.* Selden inclines to the first, but the latter is more pure, as well as probable.

[58] Framea scutoque juvenem ornant. Tacitus, Germania, c. 13.

sion of arms ; and the order of chivalry was assimilated in its rights and privileges to the sacred orders of priesthood. The bath and white garment of the novice were an indecent copy of the regeneration of baptism ; his sword, which he offered on the altar, was blessed by the ministers of religion ; his solemn reception was preceded by fasts and vigils ; and he was created a knight, in the name of God, of St. George, and of St. Michael the arch-angel. He swore to accomplish the duties of his profession ; and education, example, and the public opinion were the inviolable guardians of his oath. As the champion of God and the ladies (I blush to unite such discordant names), he devoted himself to speak the truth ; to maintain the right ; to protect the distressed; to practise *courtesy,* a virtue less familiar to the ancients ; to pursue the infidels ; to despise the allurements of ease and safety ; and to vindicate in every perilous adventure the honour of his character. The abuse of the same spirit provoked the illiterate knight to disdain the arts of industry and peace ; to esteem himself the sole judge and avenger of his own injuries ; and proudly to neglect the laws of civil society and military discipline. Yet the benefits of this institution, to refine the temper of barbarians, and to infuse some principles of faith, justice, and humanity, were strongly felt, and have been often observed. The asperity of national prejudice was softened ; and the community of religion and arms spread a similar colour and generous emulation over the face of Christendom. Abroad in enterprise and pilgrimage, at home in martial exercise, the warriors of every country were perpetually associated ; and impartial taste must prefer a Gothic tournament to the Olympic games of classic antiquity.[59] Instead of the naked spectacles which corrupted the manners of the Greeks and banished from the stadium the virgins and the matrons, the pompous decoration of the lists was crowned with the presence of chaste and high-born beauty, from whose hands the conqueror received the prize of his dexterity and courage. The skill and strength that were exerted in wrestling and boxing bear a distant and doubtful relation to the merit of a soldier ; but the tournaments, as they were invented in France and eagerly adopted both in the East and West, presented a lively image of the business of the field.

---

[59] The athletic exercises, particularly the cœstus and pancratium, were condemned by Lycurgus, Philopœmen, and Galen, a lawgiver, a general, and a physician. Against their authority and reasons, the reader may weigh the apology of Lucian, in the character of Solon. See West on the Olympic Games, in his Pindar, vol. ii. p. 86-96, 245-248.

The single combats, the general skirmish, the defence of a pass or castle, were rehearsed as in actual service ; and the contest, both in real and mimic war, was decided by the superior management of the horse and lance.   The lance was the proper and peculiar weapon of the knight ; his horse was of a large and heavy breed ; but this charger, till he was roused by the approaching danger, was usually led by an attendant, and he quietly rode a pad or palfrey of a more easy pace.   His helmet and sword, his greaves and buckler, it would be superfluous to describe ; but I may remark that at the period of the crusades the armour was less ponderous than in later times ; and that, instead of a massy cuirass, his breast was defended by an hauberk or coat of mail.   When their long lances were fixed in the rest, the warriors furiously spurred their horses against the foe ; and the light cavalry of the Turks and Arabs could seldom stand against the direct and impetuous weight of their charge.   Each knight was attended to the field by his faithful squire, a youth of equal birth and similar hopes ; he was followed by his archers and men at arms, and four, or five, or six soldiers were computed as the furniture of a complete *lance*.   In the expeditions to the neighbouring kingdoms or the Holy Land, the duties of the feudal tenure no longer subsisted ; the voluntary service of the knights and their followers was either prompted by zeal or attachment, or purchased with rewards and promises ; and the numbers of each squadron were measured by the power, the wealth, and the fame of each independent chieftain.   They were distinguished by his banner, his armorial coat, and his cry of war ; and the most ancient families of Europe must seek in these achievements the origin and proof of their nobility.   In this rapid portrait of chivalry, I have been urged to anticipate on the story of the crusades, at once an effect, and a cause, of this memorable institution.[60]

March of the princes to Constantinople. A.D. 1096, August 15—A.D. 1097, May     Such were the troops, and such the leaders, who assumed the cross for the deliverance of the holy sepulchre.   As soon as they were relieved by the absence of the plebeian multitude, they encouraged each other, by interviews and messages, to accomplish their vow and hasten their departure.   Their wives and sisters were desirous of partaking the danger and merit of

[60] On the curious subject of knighthood, knights' service, nobility, arms, cry of war, banners, and tournaments, an ample fund of information may be sought in Selden (Opera, tom. iii. part I.   Titles of Honour, part ii. c. 1, 3, 5, 8), Ducange (Gloss. Latin. tom. iv. p. 398-412, &c.), Dissertations sur Joinville (i. vi.-xii. p. 127-142 ; p. 165-222), and M. de St. Palaye (Mémoires sur la Chevalerie).   [Here the author anticipates a later age.   At the time of the First Crusade, there was no chivalry, as here meant ; knight signified a trooper.]

the pilgrimage ; their portable treasures were conveyed in bars
of silver and gold ; and the princes and barons were attended
by their equipage of hounds and hawks, to amuse their leisure
and to supply their table. The difficulty of procuring subsistence for so many myriads of men and horses engaged them
to separate their forces ; their choice or situation determined
the road ; and it was agreed to meet in the neighbourhood of
Constantinople, and from thence to begin their operations
against the Turks. From the banks of the Meuse and the
Moselle, Godfrey of Bouillon followed the direct way of Germany, Hungary, and Bulgaria ; and, as long as he exercised the
sole command, every step afforded some proof of his prudence
and virtue. On the confines of Hungary he was stopped three
weeks by a Christian people, to whom the name, or at least the
abuse, of the cross was justly odious. The Hungarians still
smarted with the wounds which they had received from the
first pilgrims; in their turn they had abused the right of defence
and retaliation ; and they had reason to apprehend a severe
revenge from an hero of the same nation, and who was engaged
in the same cause. But, after weighing the motives and the
events, the virtuous duke was content to pity the crimes and
misfortunes of his worthless brethren ; and his twelve deputies,
the messengers of peace, requested in his name a free passage
and an equal market. To remove their suspicions, Godfrey
trusted himself, and afterwards his brother, to the faith of
Carloman, king of Hungary, who treated them with a [Caloman]
simple but hospitable entertainment : the treaty was sanctified
by their common gospel ; and a proclamation, under pain of
death, restrained the animosity and licence of the Latin
soldiers. From Austria to Belgrade, they traversed the plains
of Hungary, without enduring or offering an injury ; and the
proximity of Carloman, who hovered on their flanks with his
numerous cavalry, was a precaution not less useful for their
safety than for his own. They reached the banks of the Save ;
and no sooner had they passed the river than the king of
Hungary restored the hostages and saluted their departure with
the fairest wishes for the success of their enterprise. With the
same conduct and discipline, Godfrey pervaded the woods of
Bulgaria and the frontiers of Thrace ; and might congratulate
himself that he had almost reached the first term of his pilgrimage without drawing his sword against a Christian adversary.
After an easy and pleasant journey through Lombardy, from
Turin to Aquileia, Raymond and his provincials marched forty

days through the savage country of Dalmatia [61] and Sclavonia.
The weather was a perpetual fog ; the land was mountainous
and desolate ; the natives were either fugitive or hostile ; loose
in their religion and government, they refused to furnish provisions or guides ; murdered the stragglers ; and exercised by
night and day the vigilance of the count, who derived more
security from the punishment of some captive robbers than from
his interview and treaty with the prince of Scodra.[62]    His
march between Durazzo and Constantinople was harassed, without being stopped, by the peasants and soldiers of the Greek
emperor ; and the same faint and ambiguous hostility was prepared for the remaining chiefs, who passed the Adriatic from
the coast of Italy.    Bohemond had arms and vessels, and foresight and discipline ; and his name was not forgotten in the
provinces of Epirus and Thessaly.    Whatever obstacles he
encountered were surmounted by his military conduct and the
valour of Tancred ; and, if the Norman prince affected to spare
the Greeks, he gorged his soldiers with the full plunder of an
heretical castle.[63]    The nobles of France pressed forwards with
the vain and thoughtless ardour of which their nation has been
sometimes accused.    From the Alps to Apulia, the march of
Hugh the Great, of the two Roberts, and of Stephen of Chartres,
through a wealthy country, and amidst the applauding Catholics,
was a devout or triumphant progress : they kissed the feet of
the Roman pontiff ; and the golden standard of St. Peter was
delivered to the brother of the French monarch.[64]    But in this
visit of piety and pleasure they neglected to secure the season
and the means of their embarkation : the winter was insensibly

[61] The Familiæ Dalmaticæ of Ducange are meagre and imperfect ; the national
historians are recent and fabulous, the Greeks remote and careless.    In the year
1104, Coloman reduced the maritime country as far as Trau and Salona (Katona,
Hist. Crit. tom. iii. p. 195-207).    [For the journey see Knapp, Reisen durch die
Balkanhalbinsel während des Mittelalters, in the Mittheilungen der k. k. geograph.
Gesellschaft in Wien, xxiii., 1880.]

[62] Scodras appears in Livy as the capital and fortress of Gentius, king of the
Illyrians, arx munitissima, afterwards a Roman colony (Cellarius, tom. i. p. 393,
394).    It is now called Iscodar, or Scutari (d'Anville, Géographie Ancienne, tom.
i. p. 164).    The sanjiak (now a pasha) of Scutari, or Schendeire, was the viiith
under the Beglerbeg, of Romania, and furnished 600 soldiers on a revenue of
78,787 rix dollars (Marsigli, Stato Militare del Impero Ottomano, p. 128).

[63] In Pelagoniâ castrum hæreticum . . . spoliatum cum suis habitatoribus
igne combussere.    Nec id eis injuriâ contigit : quia illorum detestabilis sermo et
cancer serpebat, jamque circumjacentes regiones suo pravo dogmate fœdaveram
(Robert. Mon. p. 36, 37).    After coolly relating the fact, the archbishop Baldric
adds, as a phrase, Omnes siquidem illi viatores, Judaeos, hæreticos, Saracenos
æqualiter habent exosos ; quos omnes appellant inimicos Dei (p. 92).

[64] Ἀναλαβόμενος ἀπὸ Ῥώμης τὴν χρυσῆν τοῦ Ἁγίου Πέτρου σημαίαν (Alexiad, l. x. p.
288 [c. 7]).

lost ; their troops were scattered and corrupted in the towns of
Italy. They separately accomplished their passage, regardless
of safety or dignity : and within nine months from the feast of
the Assumption, the day appointed by Urban, all the Latin
princes had reached Constantinople. But the Count of Vermandois was produced as a captive ; his foremost vessels were
scattered by a tempest ; and his person, against the law of
nations, was detained by the lieutenants of Alexius. Yet the
arrival of Hugh had been announced by four-and-twenty knights
in golden armour, who commanded the emperor to revere the
general of the Latin Christians, the brother of the King of
kings.[65]

In some Oriental tale I have read the fable of a shepherd,
who was ruined by the accomplishment of his own wishes : he
had prayed for water ; the Ganges was turned into his grounds ;
and his flock and cottage were swept away by the inundation.
Such was the fortune, or at least the apprehension, of the Greek
emperor, Alexius Comnenus, whose name has already appeared
in this history, and whose conduct is so differently represented
by his daughter Anna [66] and by the Latin writers.[67]  In the
council of Placentia, his ambassadors had solicited a moderate
succour, perhaps of ten thousand soldiers ; but he was astonished
by the approach of so many potent chiefs and fanatic nations.
The emperor fluctuated between hope and fear, between timidity
and courage ; but in the crooked policy which he mistook for
wisdom I cannot believe, I cannot discern, that he maliciously
conspired against the life or honour of the French heroes.  The

*Policy of the emperor Alexius Comnenus. A.D. 1096, December—A.D. 1097, May*

---

[65] Ὁ Βασιλεὺς τῶν βασιλέων [Anna, x. c. 7, ad init. in Hugo's letter or message to
Alexius], καὶ ἀρχηγὸς τοῦ Φραγγικοῦ στρατεύματος ἅπαντος [ib. c. 7, med., in the an-
nouncement of the four and twenty knights to the Duke of Dyrrachium]. This
Oriental pomp is extravagant in a count of Vermandois ; but the patriot Ducange
repeats with much complacency (Not. ad Alexiad, p. 352, 353 ; Dissert. xxvii. sur
Joinville, p. 315) the passages of Matthew Paris (A.D. 1254) and Froissard (vol. iv.
p. 201), which style the King of France rex regum and chef de tous les rois
Chrétiens.

[66] Anna Comnena was born on the 1st of December, A.D. 1083, indiction vii.
Alexiad, l. vi. p. 166, 167 [c. 8]). At thirteen, the time of the first crusade, she
was nubile, and perhaps married to the younger Nicephorus Bryennius, whom she
fondly styles τὸν ἐμὸν Καίσαρα (l. x. p. 295, 296 [c. 9]). Some moderns have
*imagined* that her enmity to Bohemond [Βαϊμοῦντος] was the fruit of disappointed
love. In the transactions of Constantinople and Nice, her partial accounts (Alex.
x. xi. p. 283-317) may be opposed to the partiality of the Latins ; but in their
subsequent exploits she is brief and ignorant. [Cp. above, vol. 5, p. 506.]

[67] In their views of the character and conduct of Alexius, Maimbourg has
favoured the *Catholic* Franks, and Voltaire has been partial to the *schismatic*
Greeks. The prejudice of a philosopher is less excusable than that of a Jesuit.

promiscuous multitudes of Peter the Hermit were savage beasts, alike destitute of humanity and reason ; nor was it possible for Alexius to prevent or deplore their destruction. The troops of Godfrey and his peers were less contemptible, but not less suspicious, to the Greek emperor. Their motives *might* be pure and pious ; but he was equally alarmed by his knowledge of the ambitious Bohemond and his ignorance of the Transalpine chiefs: the courage of the French was blind and headstrong ; they might be tempted by the luxury and wealth of Greece, and elated by the view and opinion of their invincible strength ; and Jerusalem might be forgotten in the prospect of Constantinople. After a long march and painful abstinence, the troops of Godfrey encamped in the plains of Thrace ; they heard with indignation that their brother, the count of Vermandois, was imprisoned by the Greeks ; and their reluctant Duke was compelled to indulge them in some freedom of retaliation and rapine. They were appeased by the submission of Alexius ; he promised to supply their camp ; and, as they refused, in the midst of winter, to pass the Bosphorus, their quarters were assigned among the gardens and palaces on the shores of that narrow sea. But an incurable jealousy still rankled in the minds of the two nations, who despised each other as slaves and barbarians. Ignorance is the ground of suspicion, and suspicion was inflamed into daily provocations ; prejudice is blind, hunger is deaf ; and Alexius is accused of a design to starve or assault the Latins on a dangerous post, on all sides encompassed with the waters.[68] Godfrey sounded his trumpets, burst the net, overspread the plain, and insulted the suburbs ; but the gates of Constantinople were strongly fortified ; the ramparts were lined with archers ; and, after a doubtful conflict, both parties listened to the voice of peace and religion. The gifts and promises of the emperor insensibly soothed the fierce spirit of the western strangers ; as a Christian warrior, he rekindled their zeal for the prosecution of their holy enterprise, which he engaged to second with his troops and treasures. On the return of spring, Godfrey was persuaded to occupy a pleasant and plentiful camp in Asia ; and

[Jan. 1097]    no sooner had he passed the Bosphorus, than the Greek vessels

---

[68] Between the Black Sea, the Bosphorus, and the river Barbyses, which is deep in summer, and runs fifteen miles through a flat meadow. Its communication with Europe and Constantinople is by the stone-bridge of the *Blachernae* [close to St. Callinicus], which in successive ages was restored by Justinian and Basil (Gyllius de Bosphoro Thracio, l. ii. c. 3 ; Ducange, C. P. Christiana, l. iv. c. 2, p. 179).

were suddenly recalled to the opposite shore.   The same policy
was repeated with the succeeding chiefs, who were swayed by
the example, and weakened by the departure, of their foremost
companions.   By his skill and diligence, Alexius prevented the
union of any two of the confederate armies at the same moment
under the walls of Constantinople ; and, before the feast of the
Pentecost, not a Latin pilgrim was left on the coast of Europe.

The same arms which threatened Europe might deliver Asia *He obtains*
and repel the Turks from the neighbouring shores of the *the homage of the crusaders*
Bosphorus and Hellespont.   The fair provinces from Nice to
Antioch were the recent patrimony of the Roman emperor ; and
his ancient and perpetual claim still embraced the kingdoms
of Syria and Egypt.   In his enthusiasm, Alexius indulged, or
affected, the ambitious hope of leading his new allies to subvert
the thrones of the East ; but the calmer dictates of reason and
temper dissuaded him from exposing his royal person to the
faith of unknown and lawless barbarians.   His prudence, or his
pride, was content with extorting from the French princes an
oath of homage and fidelity, and a solemn promise that they
would either restore, or hold, their Asiatic conquests as the
humble and loyal vassals of the Roman empire.   Their independent spirit was fired at the mention of this foreign and
voluntary servitude ; they successively yielded to the dextrous
application of gifts and flattery ; and the first proselytes became
the most eloquent and effectual missionaries to multiply the
companions of their shame.   The pride of Hugh of Vermandois
was soothed by the honours of his captivity ; and in the brother
of the French king the example of submission was prevalent
and weighty.   In the mind of Godfrey of Bouillon, every human
consideration was subordinate to the glory of God and the
success of the crusade.   He had firmly resisted the temptations
of Bohemond and Raymond, who urged the attack and conquest
of Constantinople.   Alexius esteemed his virtues, deservedly
named him the champion of the empire, and dignified his
homage with the filial name and the rights of adoption.[69]  The *[Arrival of Bohemond. April, 26, 1097]*
hateful Bohemond was received as a true and ancient ally ; and,
if the emperor reminded him of former hostilities, it was only to
praise the valour that he had displayed, and the glory that he
had acquired, in the fields of Durazzo and Larissa.   The son of

[69] There were two sorts of adoption, the one by arms, the other by introducing
the son between the shirt and skin of his father.   Ducange (sur Joinville, diss. xxii.
p. 270) supposes Godfrey's adoption to have been of the latter sort.  [The adoption
is mentioned by Albert, ii. 16.]

Guiscard was lodged and entertained, and served with Imperial pomp : one day, as he passed through the gallery of the palace, a door was carelessly left open to expose a pile of gold and silver, of silk and gems, of curious and costly furniture, that was heaped in seeming disorder from the floor to the roof of the chamber. "What conquests," exclaimed the ambitious miser, " might not be achieved by the possession of such a treasure ! " " It is your own," replied a Greek attendant, who watched the motions of his soul ; and Bohemond, after some hesitation, condescended to accept this magnificent present. The Norman was flattered by the assurance of an independent principality ; and Alexius eluded, rather than denied, his daring demand of the office of great domestic, or general, of the East. The two Roberts, the son of the conqueror of England and the kinsman of three queens,[70] bowed in their turn before the Byzantine throne. A private letter of Stephen of Chartres attests his admiration of the emperor, the most excellent and liberal of men, who taught him to believe that he was a favourite, and promised to educate and establish his youngest son. In his southern province, the count of St. Giles and Toulouse faintly recognised the supremacy of the king of France, a prince of a foreign nation and language. At the head of an hundred thousand men, he declared that he was the soldier and servant of Christ alone, and that the Greek might be satisfied with an equal treaty of alliance and friendship. His obstinate resistance enhanced the value and the price of his submission ; and he shone, says the princess Anne, among the barbarians, as the sun amidst the stars of heaven. His disgust of the noise and insolence of the French, his suspicions of the designs of Bohemond, the emperor imparted to his faithful Raymond ; and that aged statesman might clearly discern that, however false in friendship, he was sincere in his enmity.[71] The spirit of chivalry was last subdued in the person of Tancred ; and none could deem themselves dishonoured by the imitation of that gallant knight. He disdained the gold and flattery of the Greek monarch ; assaulted in his presence an insolent patrician ; escaped to Asia in the habit of a private soldier ; and yielded with a sigh to the authority of Bohemond and the interest of the Christian cause. The best and most ostensible reason was the impossibility of passing the sea and accomplishing their vow, without the licence and the vessels of

---

[70] After his return, Robert of Flanders became the *man* of the King of England, for a pension of 400 marks. See the first act in Rymer's Fœdera.

[71] Sensit vetus regnandi, falsos in amore, odia non fingere. Tacit. vi. 44.

Alexius; but they cherished a secret hope that, as soon as they trode the continent of Asia, their swords would obliterate their shame, and dissolve the engagement, which on his side might not be very faithfully performed. The ceremony of their homage was grateful to a people who had long since considered pride as the substitute of power. High on his throne, the emperor sat mute and immoveable : his majesty was adored by the Latin princes; and they submitted to kiss either his feet or his knees, an indignity which their own writers are ashamed to confess and unable to deny.[72]

Private or public interest suppressed the murmurs of the dukes and counts ; but a French baron (he is supposed to be Robert of Paris [73]) presumed to ascend the throne, and to place himself by the side of Alexius. The sage reproof of Baldwin provoked him to exclaim, in his barbarous idiom, " Who is this rustic, that keeps his seat, while so many valiant captains are standing round him ? " The emperor maintained his silence, dissembled his indignation, and questioned his interpreter concerning the meaning of the words, which he partly suspected from the universal language of gesture and countenance. Before the departure of the pilgrims, he endeavoured to learn the name and condition of the audacious baron. " I am a Frenchman," replied Robert, " of the purest and most ancient nobility of my country. All that I know is, that there is a church in my neighbourhood,[74] the resort of those who are desirous of approving their valour in single combat. Till an enemy appears, they address their prayers to God and his saints. That church I have frequently visited, but never have I found an antagonist who dared to accept my defiance." Alexius dismissed the challenger with some prudent

Insolence of the Franks

[72] The proud historians of the crusades slide and stumble over this humiliating step. Yet, since the heroes knelt to salute the emperor as he sat motionless on his throne, it is clear that they must have kissed either his feet or knees. It is only singular that Anna should not have amply supplied the silence or ambiguity of the Latins. The abasement of their princes would have added a fine chapter to the Ceremoniale Aulæ Byzantinæ.

[73] He called himself Φράγγος καθαρὸς τῶν εὐγενῶν (Alexias, l. x. p. 301 [c. 11]). What a title of *noblesse* of the xith century, if any one could now prove his inheritance ! Anna relates, with visible pleasure, that the swelling barbarian, Λατῖνος τετυφωμένος, was killed, or wounded, after fighting in the front in the battle of Dorylæum (l. xi. p. 317). This circumstance may justify the suspicion of Ducange (Not. p. 362) that he was no other than Robert of Paris, of the district most peculiarly styled the Duchy or Island of France (*L'Isle de France*).

[74] With the same penetration, Ducange discovers his church to be that of St. Drausus, or Drosin, of Soissons, quem duello dimicaturi solent invocare : pugiles qui ad memoriam ejus (*his tomb*) pernoctant invictos reddit, ut et de Burgundiâ et Italiâ tali necessitate confugiatur ad eum. Joan. Sariburiensis, epist. 139.

advice for his conduct in the Turkish warfare ; and history repeats with pleasure this lively example of the manners of his age and country.

The conquest of Asia was undertaken and achieved by Alexander, with thirty-five thousand Macedonians and Greeks;[75] and his best hope was in the strength and discipline of his phalanx of infantry.  The principal force of the crusaders consisted in their cavalry ; and, when that force was mustered in the plains of Bithynia, the knights and their martial attendants on horseback amounted to one hundred thousand fighting men completely armed with the helmet and coat of mail.  The value of these soldiers deserved a strict and authentic account ; and the flower of European chivalry might furnish, in a first effort, this formidable body of heavy horse.  A part of the infantry might be enrolled for the service of scouts, pioneers, and archers ; but the promiscuous crowd were lost in their own disorder ; and we depend not on the eyes or knowledge, but on the belief and fancy, of a chaplain of count Baldwin,[76] in the estimate of six hundred thousand pilgrims able to bear arms, besides the priests and monks, the women and children, of the Latin camp.  The reader starts ; and, before he is recovered from his surprise, I shall add, on the same testimony, that if all who took the cross had accomplished their vow, above six millions would have migrated from Europe to Asia.  Under this oppression of faith, I derive some relief from a more sagacious and thinking writer,[77] who, after the same review of the cavalry, accuses the credulity of the priest of Chartres, and even doubts whether the *Cisalpine* regions (in the geography of a Frenchman) were sufficient to produce and pour forth such incredible multitudes.  The coolest scepticism will remember that of these religious volunteers great numbers never beheld Constantinople and Nice.  Of enthusiasm the influence is irregular and transient ; many were detained at home by reason or cowardice, by poverty or weakness ; and many were repulsed by the obstacles of the way, the more in-

[75] There is some diversity on the numbers of his army ; but no authority can be compared with that of Ptolemy, who states it at five thousand horse and thirty thousand foot (see Usher's Annales, p. 152).

[76] Fulcher. Carnotensis, p. 387.   He enumerates nineteen nations of different names and languages (p. 389) ; but I do not clearly apprehend his difference between the *Franci* and *Galli, Itali* and *Apuli*.   Elsewhere (p. 385) he contemptuously brands the deserters.

[77] Guibert, p. 556.   Yet even his gentle opposition implies an immense multitude.   By Urban II., in the fervour of his zeal, it is only rated at 300,000 pilgrims (Epist. xvi. Concil. tom. xii. p. 731).

superable as they were unforeseen to these ignorant fanatics. The savage countries of Hungary and Bulgaria were whitened with their bones; their vanguard was cut in pieces by the Turkish sultan; and the loss of the first adventure, by the sword, or climate, or fatigue, has already been stated at three hundred thousand men. Yet the myriads that survived, that marched, that pressed forwards on the holy pilgrimage were a subject of astonishment to themselves and to the Greeks. The copious energy of her language sinks under the efforts of the princess Anne; [78] the images of locusts, of leaves and flowers, of the sands of the sea, or the stars of heaven, imperfectly represent what she had seen and heard; and the daughter of Alexius exclaims that Europe was loosened from its foundations and hurled against Asia. The ancient hosts of Darius and Xerxes labour under the same doubt of a vague and indefinite magnitude; but I am inclined to believe that a larger number has never been contained within the lines of a single camp than at the siege of Nice, the first operation of the Latin princes. Their motives, their characters, and their arms have been already displayed. Of their troops, the most numerous portion were natives of France; the Low Countries, the banks of the Rhine, and Apulia, sent a powerful reinforcement; some bands of adventurers were drawn from Spain, Lombardy, and England; [79] and from the distant bogs and mountains of Ireland or Scotland [80]

[78] Alexias, l. x. p. 283 [c. 5], 305 [c. 11]. Her fastidious delicacy complains of their strange and inarticulate names; and indeed there is scarcely one that she has not contrived to disfigure with the proud ignorance, so dear and familiar to a polished people. I shall select only one example, *Sangeles*, for the count of St. Giles. [Sangeles would be a near enough equivalent for St. Gilles, but it is *Isangeles*; and the form of the corruption seems to have been determined by an etymology complimentary to the count,—ἰσάγγελος, angelic. A reader, ignorant of the pronunciation of modern Greek, might easily do injustice to Anna. The modern Greek alphabet has no letters equivalent to *b* and *d* (β represents *v*, and δ is aspirated *dh*); and in order to reproduce these sounds they resort to the devices of μπ and ντ. Thus *Robert* is quite correctly Ῥομπέρτος, and Γοντοφρέ is a near transliteration of Godfrey (Godefroi).]

[79] William of Malmesbury (who wrote about the year 1130) has inserted in his history (l. iv. p. 130-154) a narrative of the first crusade; but I wish that, instead of listening to the tenue murmur which had passed the British ocean (p. 143), he had confined himself to the numbers, families, and adventures of his countrymen. I find in Dugdale that an English Norman, Stephen, Earl of Albemarle and Holdernesse, led the rear-guard with Duke Robert, at the battle of Antioch (Baronage, part i. p. 61).

[80] Videres Scotorum apud se ferocium alias imbellium cuneos (Guibert, p. 471); the *crus intectum*, and *hispida chlamys*, may suit the Highlanders; but the *finibus uliginosis* may rather apply to the Irish bogs. William of Malmesbury expressly mentions the Welsh and Scots, &c. (l. iv. p. 133), who quitted, the former venationem saltuum, the latter familiaritatem pulicum.

issued some naked and savage fanatics, ferocious at home, but unwarlike abroad. Had not superstition condemned the sacrilegious prudence of depriving the poorest or weakest Christian of the merit of the pilgrimage, the useless crowd, with mouths but without hands, might have been stationed in the Greek empire, till their companions had opened and secured the way of the Lord. A small remnant of the pilgrims, who passed the Bosphorus, was permitted to visit the holy sepulchre. Their northern constitution was scorched by the rays, and infected by the vapours, of a Syrian sun. They consumed, with heedless prodigality, their stores of water and provisions; their numbers exhausted the inland country; the sea was remote, the Greeks were unfriendly, and the Christians of every sect fled before the voracious and cruel rapine of their brethren. In the dire necessity of famine, they sometimes roasted and devoured the flesh of their infant or adult captives. Among the Turks and Saracens, the idolaters of Europe were rendered more odious by the name and reputation of cannibals; the spies who introduced themselves into the kitchen of Bohemond were shewn several human bodies turning on the spit; and the artful Norman encouraged a report, which increased at the same time the abhorrence and the terror of the infidels.[81]

Siege of Nice. A.D. 1097, May 14—June 20 [19] I have expatiated with pleasure on the first steps of the crusaders, as they paint the manners and character of Europe; but I shall abridge the tedious and uniform narrative of their blind achievements, which were performed by strength and are described by ignorance. From their first station in the neighbourhood of Nicomedia, they advanced in successive divisions, passed the contracted limit of the Greek empire, opened a road through the hills, and commenced, by the siege of his capital, their pious warfare against the Turkish sultan. His kingdom of Roum extended from the Hellespont to the confines of Syria and barred the pilgrimage of Jerusalem; his name was Kilidge-Arslan, or Soliman,[82] of the race of Seljuk, and son

---

[81] This cannibal hunger, sometimes real, more frequently an artifice or a lie, may be found in Anna Comnena (Alexias, l. x. p. 288 [c. 7]), Guibert (p. 546), Radulph. Cadom. (c. 97). The stratagem is related by the author of the Gesta Francorum, the monk Robert Baldric, and Raymond des Agiles, in the siege and famine of Antioch. [In the Romance of Richard Cœur de Lion (edited by Weber) Richard eats the heads of Saracens.]

[82] His Musulman appellation of Soliman is used by the Latins, and his character is highly embellished by Tasso. His Turkish name of Kilidge-Arslan (A.H. 485-500, A.D. 1192-1206; see de Guignes's Tables, tom. i. p. 245) is employed by the Orientals, and with some corruption by the Greeks; but little more than his name can be found in the Mahometan writers, who are dry and sulky on the

of the first conqueror ; and, in the defence of a land which
the Turks considered as their own, he deserved the praise
of his enemies, by whom alone he is known to posterity.
Yielding to the first impulse of the torrent, he deposited his
family and treasure in Nice, retired to the mountains with fifty
thousand horse, and twice descended to assault the camps or
quarters of the Christian besiegers, which formed an imperfect
circle of above six miles. The lofty and solid walls of Nice
were covered by a deep ditch, and flanked by three hundred
and seventy towers ; and on the verge of Christendom the
Moslems were trained in arms and inflamed by religion. Before
this city, the French princes occupied their stations, and prosecuted their attacks without correspondence or subordination ;
emulation prompted their valour ; but their valour was sullied
by cruelty, and their emulation degenerated into envy and civil
discord. In the siege of Nice the arts and engines of antiquity
were employed by the Latins ; the mine and the battering-ram,
the tortoise, and the belfry or moveable turret, artificial fire, and
the *catapult* and *balist*, the sling, and the cross bow for the casting
of stones and darts.[83] In the space of seven weeks much labour
and blood were expended, and some progress, especially by
Count Raymond, was made on the side of the besiegers. But
the Turks could protract their resistance and secure their escape,
as long as they were masters of the lake Ascanius,[84] which
stretches several miles to the westward of the city. The means
of conquest were supplied by the prudence and industry of
Alexius ; a great number of boats was transported on sledges
from the sea to the lake ; they were filled with the most dextrous of his archers ; the flight of the sultana was intercepted ;
Nice was invested by land and water ; and a Greek emissary
persuaded the inhabitants to accept his master's protection, and
to save themselves, by a timely surrender, from the rage of the

subject of the first crusade (de Guignes, tom. iii. p. ii. p. 10-30). [This is not quite
correct. Sulaimān died in 1086. After an interregnum of six years Kilij-Arslān,
his son, succeeded in 1092, and reigned till 1106. The western historians confuse
the two.]

[83] On the fortifications, engines, and sieges of the middle ages, see Muratori
(Antiquitat. Italiæ, tom. ii. dissert. xxvi. p. 452-524). The *belfredus*, from whence
our belfry, was the moveable tower of the ancients (Ducange, tom. i. p. 608).
[See description of the *berefridus* in the Itinerarium regis Ricardi, iii. c. 6 (ed.
Stubbs), and of the κριοφόρος χελώνη in Anna Comnena, xiii. c. 3 ; they are the
same engine. Compare on the whole subject, Oman, Art of War, ii. p. 131
*sqq.*]

[84] I cannot forbear remarking the resemblance between the siege and lake of
Nice, with the operations of Hernan Cortez before Mexico. See Dr. Robertson,
Hist. of America, l. v.

294

savages of Europe.  In the moment of victory, or at least of
hope, the crusaders, thirsting for blood and plunder, were awed
by the Imperial banner that streamed from the citadel, and
Alexius guarded with jealous vigilance this important conquest.
The murmurs of the chiefs were stifled by honour or interest ;
and, after an halt of nine days, they directed their march towards
[June 27] Phrygia, under the guidance of a Greek general, whom they
suspected of secret connivance with the sultan.  The consort
and the principal servants of Soliman had been honourably
restored without ransom, and the emperor's generosity to the
*miscreants* [85] was interpreted as treason to the Christian cause.

Battle of Dorylæum. A.D. 1097, July 4 [1]     Soliman was rather provoked than dismayed by the loss of his
capital ; he admonished his subjects and allies of this strange
invasion of the western barbarians ; the Turkish emirs obeyed
the call of loyalty or religion ; the Turkman hordes encamped
round his standard ; and his whole force is loosely stated by the
Christians at two hundred, or even three hundred and sixty
thousand horse.   Yet he patiently waited till they had left behind them the sea and the Greek frontier, and, hovering on the
flanks, observed their careless and confident progress in two
columns, beyond the view of each other.  Some miles before
[Eskishehr] they could reach Dorylæum in Phrygia, the left and least
numerous division was surprised, and attacked, and almost
oppressed, by the Turkish cavalry.[86]  The heat of the weather,
the clouds of arrows, and the barbarous onset overwhelmed the
crusaders ; they lost their order and confidence, and the fainting
fight was sustained by the personal valour, rather than by the
military conduct, of Bohemond, Tancred, and Robert of Normandy.   They were revived by the welcome banners of duke
Godfrey, who flew to their succour, with the count of Vermandois and sixty thousand horse, and was followed by Raymond
of Toulouse, the bishop of Puy, and the remainder of the sacred
army.   Without a moment's pause they formed in new order,
and advanced to a second battle.   They were received with

[85] *Mécréant*, a word invented by the French crusaders, and confined in that
language to its primitive sense.    It should seem that the zeal of our ancestors
boiled higher, and that they branded every unbeliever as a rascal.  A similar prejudice still lurks in the minds of many who think themselves Christians.

[86] Baronius has produced a very doubtful letter to his brother Roger (A.D. 1098,
No. 15).   The enemies consisted of Medes, Persians, Chaldeans ; be it so.   The
first attack was, cum nostro incommodo ; true and tender.   But why Godfrey of
Bouillon and Hugh *brothers ?*   Tancred is styled *filius ;* of whom ? certainly not ot
Roger, nor of Bohemond.  [Tancred was a nephew of Bohemond, and a grand-
nephew of Roger.  His mother was Emma, Robert Guiscard's daughter ; his
father Marchisus (Gest. Fr. iv. 2 Marchisi filius), which conceivably does not mean
a western Marquis but refers to the name of a Saracen emir, as P. Paris suggests,
Chanson d'Antioch, ii. 372 ; but it is not easy to find a likely name.]

equal resolution ; and, in their common disdain for the unwar-like people of Greece and Asia, it was confessed on both sides that the Turks and the Franks were the only nations entitled to the appellation of soldiers.[87] Their encounter was varied and balanced by the contrast of arms and discipline ; of the direct charge, and wheeling evolutions ; of the couched lance, and the brandished javelin ; of a weighty broad-sword, and a crooked sabre ; of cumbrous armour, and thin flowing robes ; [87a] and of the long Tartar bow, and the *arbalist* or cross-bow, a deadly weapon, yet unknown to the Orientals.[88] As long as the horses were fresh and the quivers full, Soliman maintained the advantage of the day ; and four thousand Christians were pierced by the Turkish arrows. In the evening, swiftness yielded to strength ; on either side, the numbers were equal, or at least as great as any ground could hold or any generals could manage ; but in turning the hills the last division of Raymond and his *pro-vincials* was led, perhaps without design, on the rear of an exhausted enemy ; and the long contest was determined. Be-sides a nameless and unaccounted multitude, three thousand *pagan* knights were slain in the battle and pursuit ; the camp of Soliman was pillaged ; and in the variety of precious spoil the curiosity of the Latins was amused with foreign arms and apparel, and the new aspect of dromedaries and camels. The importance of the victory was proved by the hasty retreat of the sultan : reserving ten thousand guards of the relics of his army, Soliman evacuated the kingdom of Roum, and hastened to implore the aid, and kindle the resentment, of his Eastern brethren. In a march of five hundred miles, the crusaders tra- March through the Lesser Asia. July-September versed the Lesser Asia, through a wasted land and deserted towns, without either finding a friend or an enemy. The geo-grapher [89] may trace the position of Dorylæum, Antioch of

---

[87] Veruntamen dicunt se esse de Francorum generatione ; et quia nullus homo naturaliter debet esse miles nisi Franci et Turci (Gesta Francorum, p. 7). The same community of blood and valour is attested by Archbishop Baldric (p. 99).

[87a] [The painted windows of the Church of St. Denys, made by order of the abbot Suger in the 12th cent., reproduced in Montfaucon's Monuments, plate li., &c., illustrated the armour of the Saracens.]

[88] *Balista, Balestra, Arbalestre.* See Muratori, Antiq. tom. ii. p. 517-524. Ducange, Gloss. Latin. tom. i. p. 531, 532. In the time of Anna Comnena, this weapon, which she describes under the name of *tzangra*, was unknown in the East (l. x. p. 291 [c. 8]). By an humane inconsistency, the pope strove to pro-ibit it in Christian wars.

[89] The curious reader may compare the classic learning of Cellarius and the geographical science of D'Anville. William of Tyre is the only historian of the crusades who has any knowledge of antiquity ; and M. Otter trode almost in the footsteps of the Franks from Constantinople to Antioch (Voyage en Turquie et en Perse, tom. i. p. 35-88).

Pisidia, Iconium, Archelais, and Germanicia, and may compare those classic appellations with the modern names of Eskishehr the old city, Akshehr the white city, Cogni, Erekli,[89a] and Marash. As the pilgrims passed over a desert, where a draught of water is exchanged for silver, they were tormented by intolerable thirst; and on the banks of the first rivulet their haste and intemperance were still more pernicious to the disorderly throng. They climbed with toil and danger the steep and slippery sides of mount Taurus; many of the soldiers cast away their arms to secure their footsteps; and, had not terror preceded their van, the long and trembling file might have been driven down the precipice by an handful of resolute enemies. Two of their most respectable chiefs, the duke of Lorraine and the count of Toulouse, were carried in litters; Raymond was raised, as it is said, by miracle, from an hopeless malady; and Godfrey had been torn by a bear, as he pursued that rough and perilous chase in the mountains of Pisidia.

*Baldwin founds the principality of Edessa. A.D. 1097-1151*

To improve the general consternation, the cousin of Bohemond and the brother of Godfrey were detached from the main army, with their respective squadrons of five and of seven hundred knights. They over-ran, in a rapid career, the hills and sea-coast of Cilicia, from Cogni to the Syrian gates; the Norman standard was first planted on the walls of Tarsus and Malmistra; but the proud injustice of Baldwin at length provoked the patient and generous Italian, and they turned their consecrated swords against each other in a private and profane quarrel. Honour was the motive, and fame the reward, of Tancred; but fortune smiled on the more selfish enterprise of his rival.[90] He was called to the assistance of a Greek or Armenian tyrant, who had been suffered under the Turkish yoke to reign over the Christians of Edessa. Baldwin accepted the character of his son and champion; but no sooner was he introduced into the city than he inflamed [91] the people to the massacre of his father, occupied the throne and treasure, ex

*[Thoros]*

---

[89a] [Eregli is the ancient Heraclea, about 30 hours south-east of Iconium (Kōniya). It was here that Tancred and Baldwin separated from the main army. Gesta Fr. x. 5.]

[90] This detached conquest of Edessa is best represented by Fulcherius Carnotensis, or of Chartres (in the collections of Bongarsius, Duchesne, and Martenne' the valiant chaplain of Count Baldwin (Esprit des Croisades, tom. i. p. 13-14). In the disputes of that prince with Tancred, his partiality is encountered by the partiality of Radulphus Cadomensis, the soldier and historian of the gallant marquis. [See the Chronicle of Matthew of Edessa, tr. Dulaurier, p. 218-221.]

[91] [In the account of Matthew of Edessa, ib. p. 219-220, Baldwin did not influence the people, but conspirators induced him to consent to their plan of assassinating Thoros. The deed, however, was done, not by a band of conspirators, but by "the inhabitants" in a mass; ib. p. 220.]

tended his conquests over the hills of Armenia and the plain of Mesopotamia, and founded the first principality of the Franks or Latins, which subsisted fifty-four years beyond the [*leg.* forty-six] Euphrates.[92]

Before the Franks could enter Syria, the summer, and even the autumn, were completely wasted : the siege of Antioch, or the separation and repose of the army during the winter season, was strongly debated in their council ; the love of arms and the holy sepulchre urged them to advance, and reason perhaps was on the side of resolution, since every hour of delay abates the fame and force of the invader and multiplies the resources of defensive war. The capital of Syria was protected by the river Orontes, and the *iron bridge* of nine arches derives its name from the massy gates of the two towers which are constructed at either end.[93] They were opened by the sword of the duke of Normandy : his victory gave entrance to three hundred thousand crusaders, an account which may allow some scope for losses and desertion, but which clearly detects much exaggeration in the review of Nice. In the description of Antioch [94] it is not easy to define a middle term between her ancient magnificence, under the successors of Alexander and Augustus, and the modern aspect of Turkish desolation. The Tetrapolis, or four cities, if they retained their name and position, must have left a large vacuity in a circumference of twelve miles ; and that measure, as well as the number of four hundred towers, are not perfectly consistent with the five gates, so often mentioned in the history of the siege. Yet Antioch must have still flourished as a great and populous capital. At the head of the Turkish emirs, Baghisian, a veteran chief, commanded in the place ; his [Yaghisiyan] garrison was composed of six or seven thousand horse and fifteen or twenty thousand foot : one hundred thousand Moslems are said to have fallen by the sword, and their numbers were probably inferior to the Greeks, Armenians, and Syrians, who had been no more than fourteen years the slaves of the house of Seljuk. From the remains of a solid and stately wall it appears to have arisen to the height of threescore feet in the valleys ;

*Marginal notes:* Siege of Antioch. A.D. 1097, October 21—A.D. 1098, June 3

[92] See de Guignes, Hist. des Huns, tom. i. p. 456. [Edessa was taken in 1144 by Imād ad-dīn Zangī.]

[93] [About 3½ hrs. east of Antioch. See Hagenmeyer's note on Gesta Fr. xii. 1. Compare Le Strange, Palestine under the Muslims, p. 60.]

[94] For Antioch, see Pococke (Description of the East, vol. ii. p. i. p. 188-193), Otter (Voyage en Turquie, &c., tom. i. p. 81, &c.), the Turkish geographer (in Otter's notes), the Index Geographicus of Schultens (ad calcem Bohadin. Vit. Saladin.), and Abulfeda (Tabula Syriæ, p. 115-116, vers. Reiske). [Le Strange, Palestine under the Muslims, p. 367-377.]

and wherever less art and labour had been applied, the ground was supposed to be defended by the river, the morass, and the mountains. Notwithstanding these fortifications, the city had been repeatedly taken by the Persians, the Arabs, the Greeks, and the Turks ; [95] so large a circuit must have yielded many pervious points of attack ; and, in a siege that was formed about the middle of October, the vigour of the execution could alone justify the boldness of the attempt. Whatever strength and valour could perform in the field, was abundantly discharged by the champions of the cross : in the frequent occasions of sallies, of forage, of the attack and defence of convoys, they were often victorious ; and we can only complain that their exploits are sometimes enlarged beyond the scale of probability and truth. The sword of Godfrey [96] divided a Turk from the shoulder to the haunch, and one half of the infidel fell to the ground, while the other was transported by his horse to the city gate. As Robert of Normandy rode against his antagonist, " I devote thy head," he piously exclaimed, " to the dæmons of hell," and that head was instantly cloven to the breast by the resistless stroke of his descending faulchion. But the reality or report of such gigantic prowess [97] must have taught the Moslems to keep within their walls, and against those walls of earth or stone the sword and the lance were unavailing weapons. In the slow and successive labours of a siege the crusaders were supine and ignorant, without skill to contrive, or money to purchase, or industry to use the artificial engines and implements of assault. In the conquest of Nice they had been powerfully assisted by the wealth and knowledge of the Greek emperor : his absence was poorly supplied by some Genoese and Pisan vessels that were attracted by religion or trade to the coast of Syria ; the stores were scanty, the return precarious, and the communica-

[95] [One of the most important fortifications for a besieger of Antioch to seize was the tower of Bagrās, or St. Luke, which commanded the pass over Mount Amanus to Alexandretta. It was fortified strongly by Nicephorus Phocas, when he besieged the city in 968.]

[96] Ensem elevat, eumque a sinistrâ parte scapularum tantâ virtute intorsit, ut quod pectus medium disjunxit spinam et vitalia interrupit ; et sic lubricus ensis super crus dextrum integer exivit ; sicque caput integrum cum dextrâ parte corporis immersit gurgite, partemque quæ equo præsidebat remisit civitati (Robert Mon. p. 50). Cujus ense trajectus, Turcus duo factus est Turci ; ut inferior alter in urbem equitaret, alter arcitenens in flumine nataret (Radulph. Cadom. c. 53, p. 304). Yet he justifies the deed by the *stupendis* viribus of Godfrey ; and William of Tyre covers it by obstupuit populus facti novitate . . . mirabilis (l. v. c. 6, p. 701). Yet it must not have appeared incredible to the knights of that age.

[97] See the exploits of Robert, Raymond, and the modest Tancred, who imposed silence on his squire (Radulph. Cadom. c. 53).

tion difficult and dangerous. Indolence or weakness had prevented the Franks from investing the entire circuit ; and the perpetual freedom of two gates relieved the wants, and recruited the garrison, of the city. At the end of seven months, after the ruin of their cavalry, and an enormous loss by famine, desertion, and fatigue, the progress of the crusaders was imperceptible, and their success remote, if the Latin Ulysses, the artful and ambitious Bohemond, had not employed the arms of cunning and deceit. The Christians of Antioch were numerous and discontented : Phirouz, a Syrian renegado, had acquired the favour of the emir, and the command of three towers; and the merit of his repentance disguised to the Latins, and perhaps to himself, the foul design of perfidy and treason. A secret correspondence, for their mutual interest, was soon established between Phirouz and the prince of Tarento ; and Bohemond declared in the council of the chiefs that he could deliver the city into their hands. But he claimed the sovereignty of Antioch as the reward of his service ; and the proposal which had been rejected by the envy, was at length extorted from the distress, of his equals. The nocturnal surprise was executed by the French and Norman princes, who ascended in person the scaling-ladders that were thrown from the walls ; their new proselyte, after the murder of his too scrupulous brother, embraced and introduced the servants of Christ : the army rushed through the gates ; and the Moslems soon found that, although mercy was hopeless, resistance was impotent. But the citadel still refused to surrender ; and the victors themselves were speedily encompassed and besieged by the innumerable forces of Kerboga, prince of Mosul, who, with twenty-eight Turkish emirs, advanced to the deliverance of Antioch. Five and twenty days the Christians spent on the verge of destruction ; and the proud lieutenant of the caliph and the sultan left them only the choice of servitude or death.[98] In this extremity they collected the relics of their strength, sallied from the town, and in a single memorable day annihilated or dispersed the host of Turks and Arabians, which they might safely report to have consisted of six hundred thousand men.[99] Their supernatural

*[Firur]*

*Victory of the crusaders. A.D. 1098, June 28*

[98] After mentioning the distress and humble petition of the Franks, Abulpharagius adds the haughty reply of Codbuka, or Kerboga [Kawām ad-Dawla (pillar of the realm) Kurbughā] ; " Non evasuri estis nisi per gladium " (Dynast. p. 242). [In the Chanson d'Antioche, Kurbughā is mysteriously called Carbaran *d'Oliferne*.]

[99] In describing the host of Kerboga, most of the Latin historians, the author of the Gesta (p. 17), Robert Monachus (p. 56), Baldric (p. 111), Fulcherius Carnotensis (p. 392), Guibert (p. 512), William of Tyre (l. vi. c. iii. p. 714), Bernard

allies I shall proceed to consider : the human causes of the victory of Antioch were the fearless despair of the Franks ; and the surprise, the discord, perhaps the errors, of their unskilful and presumptuous adversaries.  The battle is described with as much disorder as it was fought ; but we may observe the tent of Kerboga, a moveable and spacious palace, enriched with the luxury of Asia, and capable of holding above two thousand persons ; we may distinguish his three thousand guards, who were cased, the horses as well as men, in complete steel.

Their famine and distress at Antioch

In the eventful period of the siege and defence of Antioch, the crusaders were, alternately, exalted by victory or sunk in despair ; either swelled with plenty or emaciated with hunger. A speculative reasoner might suppose that their faith had a strong and serious influence on their practice ; and that the soldiers of the cross, the deliverers of the holy sepulchre, prepared themselves by a sober and virtuous life for the daily contemplation of martyrdom.   Experience blows away this charitable illusion ; and seldom does the history of profane war display such scenes of intemperance and prostitution as were exhibited under the walls of Antioch.   The grove of Daphne no longer flourished ; but the Syrian air was still impregnated with the same vices ; the Christians were seduced by every temptation [100] that nature either prompts or reprobates ; the authority of the chiefs was despised ; and sermons and edicts were alike fruitless against those scandalous disorders, not less pernicious to military discipline than repugnant to evangelic purity.   In the first days of the siege and the possession of Antioch, the Franks consumed with wanton and thoughtless prodigality the frugal subsistence of weeks and months ; the desolate country no longer yielded a supply ; and from that country they were at length excluded by the arms of the besieging Turks.   Disease, the faithful companion of want, was envenomed by the rains of the winter, the summer heats, unwholesome food, and the close imprisonment of multitudes.   The pictures of famine and pestilence are always the same, and always disgustful ; and our

Thesaurarius (c. 39, p. 695), are content with the vague expressions of *infinita multitudo, immensum agmen, innumerae copiae*, or *gentes,* which correspond with the μετὰ ἀναριθμήτων χιλιάδων of Anna Comnena (Alexias, l. xi. p. 318-320 [c. 4]). The numbers of the Turks are fixed by Albert Aquensis at 200,000 (l. iv. c. x. p. 242), and by Radulphus Cadomensis at 400,000 horse (c. lxxii. p. 309).  [Much larger figures are given by Matthew of Edessa, c. clv. p. 221.]

[100] See the tragic and scandalous fate of an archdeacon of royal birth, who was slain by the Turks as he reposed in an orchard, playing at dice with a Syrian concubine.

imagination may suggest the nature of their sufferings and their resources. The remains of treasure or spoil were eagerly lavished in the purchase of the vilest nourishment ; and dreadful must have been the calamities of the poor, since, after paying three marks of silver for a goat, and fifteen for a lean camel,[101] the count of Flanders was reduced to beg a dinner, and duke Godfrey to borrow an horse. Sixty thousand horses had been reviewed in the camp ; before the end of the siege they were diminished to two thousand, and scarcely two hundred fit for service could be mustered on the day of battle. Weakness of body and terror of mind extinguished the ardent enthusiasm of the pilgrims ; and every motive of honour and religion was sub-dued by the desire of life.[102] Among the chiefs three heroes may be found without fear or reproach : Godfrey of Bouillon was supported by his magnanimous piety ; Bohemond by ambition and interest ; and Tancred declared, in the true spirit of chivalry, that, as long as he was at the head of forty knights, he would never relinquish the enterprise of Palestine. But the count of Toulouse and Provence was suspected of a voluntary indisposi-tion ; the duke of Normandy was recalled from the sea-shore by the censures of the church ; Hugh the Great, though he led the vanguard of the battle, embraced an ambiguous opportunity of returning to France ; and Stephen, count of Chartres, basely deserted the standard which he bore, and the council in which he presided. The soldiers were discouraged by the flight of William, viscount of Melun, surnamed the *Carpenter*, from the weighty strokes of his axe ; and the saints were scandalized by the fall of Peter the Hermit, who, after arming Europe against Asia, attempted to escape from the penance of a necessary fast. Of the multitude of recreant warriors, the names (says an his-torian) are blotted from the book of life ; and the opprobrious epithet of the rope-dancers was applied to the deserters who dropt in the night from the walls of Antioch. The emperor Alexius,[103] who seemed to advance to the succour of the Latins,

---

[101] The value of an ox rose from five solidi (fifteen shillings) at Christmas to two marks (four pounds), and afterwards much higher : a kid or lamb, from one shilling to eighteen of our present money : in the second famine, a loaf of bread, or the head of an animal, sold for a piece of gold. More examples might be pro-duced ; but it is the ordinary, not the extraordinary, prices that deserve the notice of the philosopher.

[102] Alii multi quorum nomina non tenemus ; quia, deleta de libro vitæ, præsenti operi non sunt inserenda (Will. Tyr. l. vi. c. v. p. 715). Guibert (p. 518-523) attempts to excuse Hugh the Great, and even Stephen of Chartres.

[103] See the progress of the crusade, the retreat of Alexius, the victory of Antioch, and the conquest of Jerusalem, in the Alexiad, l. xi. p. 317-327 [c. 3-6]. Anna was so prone to exaggeration that she magnifies the exploits of the Latins.

was dismayed by the assurance of their hopeless condition. They expected their fate in silent despair ; oaths and punishments were tried without effect ; and, to rouse the soldiers to the defence of the walls, it was found necessary to set fire to their quarters.

Legend of the Holy Lance For their salvation and victory, they were indebted to the same fanaticism which had led them to the brink of ruin. In such a cause, and in such an army, visions, prophecies, and miracles were frequent and familiar. In the distress of Antioch, they were repeated with unusual energy and success ; St. Ambrose had assured a pious ecclesiastic that two years of trial must precede the season of deliverance and grace ; the deserters were stopped by the presence and approaches of Christ himself ; the dead had promised to arise and combat with their brethren ; the Virgin had obtained the pardon of their sins ; and their confidence was revived by a visible sign, the seasonable and splendid discovery of the HOLY LANCE. The policy of their chiefs has on this occasion been admired and might surely be excused ; but a pious fraud is seldom produced by the cool conspiracy of many persons ; and a voluntary impostor might depend on the support of the wise and the credulity of the people. Of the diocese of Marseilles, there was a priest of low cunning and loose manners, and his name was Peter Bartholemy. He presented himself at the door of the council-chamber, to disclose an apparition of St. Andrew, which had been thrice reiterated in his sleep, with a dreadful menace if he presumed to suppress the commands of Heaven. "At Antioch," said the apostle, " in the church of my brother St. Peter, near the high altar, is concealed the steel head of the lance that pierced the side of our Redeemer. In three days, that instrument of eternal, and now of temporal, salvation will be manifested to his disciples. Search, and ye shall find ; bear it aloft in battle ; and that mystic weapon shall penetrate the souls of the miscreants." The pope's legate, the bishop of Puy, affected to listen with coldness and distrust ; but the revelation was eagerly accepted by count Raymond, whom his faithful subject, in the name of the apostle, had chosen for the guardian of the holy lance. The experiment was resolved ; and on the third day, after a due preparation of prayer and fasting, the priest of Marseilles introduced twelve trusty spectators, among whom were the count and his chaplain; and the church doors were barred against the impetuous multitude. The ground was opened in the appointed place ; but the workmen, who relieved each other, dug to the depth of twelve feet without discovering the object of their search. In the evening, when count Raymond had withdrawn to his post, and the weary assistants began to murmur, Bartholemy, in his shirt and without his shoes, boldly descended into the pit; the darkness of the hour and of the place enabled him to secrete and deposit the head of a Saracen lance, and the first sound, the first gleam, of the steel was saluted with a devout rapture. The holy lance was drawn from its recess, wrapt in a veil of silk and gold, and exposed to the veneration of the crusaders; their anxious suspense burst forth in a general shout of joy and hope, and the desponding troops were again inflamed with the enthusiasm of valour. Whatever had been the arts, and whatever might be the sentiments of the chiefs, they skilfully improved this fortunate revolution by every aid that discipline and devotion could afford. The soldiers were dismissed to their quarters, with an injunction to fortify their minds and bodies for the approaching conflict, freely to bestow their last pittance on themselves and their horses, and to expect with the dawn of day the signal of victory. On the festival of St. Peter and St. Paul, the gates of Antioch were thrown open; a martial psalm, "Let the Lord arise, and let his enemies be scattered!" was chaunted by a procession of priests and monks; the battle array was marshalled in twelve divisions, in honour of the twelve apostles; and the holy lance, in the absence of Raymond, was entrusted to the hands of his chaplain. The influence of this relic or trophy was felt by the servants, and perhaps by the enemies, of Christ; [104] and its potent energy was heightened by an accident, a stratagem, or a rumour, of a miraculous complexion. Three knights, *Celestial warriors* in white garments and resplendent arms, either issued, or seemed to issue, from the hills: the voice of Adhemar, the pope's legate, proclaimed them as the martyrs St. George, St. Theodore, and St. Maurice; the tumult of battle allowed no time for doubt or scrutiny; and the welcome apparition dazzled the eyes or the imagination of a fanatic army. In the season of danger and triumph, the revelation of Bartholemy of Marseilles was unanimously asserted; but, as soon as the temporary service was accomplished, the personal dignity and liberal alms which the count of Toulouse derived from the custody of the holy lance provoked the envy, and awakened the reason, of his rivals. A

---

[104] The Mahometan Aboulmahasen (apud de Guignes, tom. ii. p. 95) is more correct in his account of the holy lance than the Christians, Anna Comnena and Abulpharagius: the Greek princess confounds it with a nail of the cross (l. xi. p. 326 [c. 6]); the Jacobite primate, with St. Peter's staff (p. 242).

Norman clerk presumed to sift, with a philosophic spirit, the truth of the legend, the circumstances of the discovery, and the character of the prophet; and the pious Bohemond ascribed their deliverance to the merits and intercession of Christ alone. For a while the Provincials defended their national palladium with clamours and arms; and new visions condemned to death and hell the profane sceptics who presumed to scrutinise the truth and merit of the discovery. The prevalence of incredulity compelled the author to submit his life and veracity to the judgment of God. A pile of faggots, four feet high and fourteen feet long, was erected in the midst of the camp; the flames burnt fiercely to the elevation of thirty cubits; and a narrow path of twelve inches was left for the perilous trial. The unfortunate priest of Marseilles traversed the fire with dexterity and speed: but his thighs and belly were scorched by the intense heat; he expired the next day, and the logic of believing minds will pay some regard to his dying protestations of innocence and truth. Some efforts were made by the Provincials to substitute a cross, a ring, or a tabernacle, in the place of the holy lance, which soon vanished in contempt and oblivion.[105] Yet the revelation of Antioch is gravely asserted by succeeding historians; and such is the progress of credulity that miracles, most doubtful on the spot and at the moment, will be received with implicit faith at a convenient distance of time and space.

*The state of the Turks or caliphs of Egypt*

The prudence or fortune of the Franks had delayed their invasion till the decline of the Turkish empire.[106] Under the manly government of the three first sultans, the kingdoms of Asia were united in peace and justice; and the innumerable armies which they led in person were equal in courage, and superior in discipline, to the barbarians of the West. But at the time of the crusade, the inheritance of Malek Shah was disputed by his four sons; their private ambition was insensible of the public danger; and, in the vicissitudes of their fortune, the royal vassals were ignorant, or regardless, of the true object of their allegiance. The twenty-eight emirs who marched with the standard of Kerboga were his rivals or enemies; their hasty levies were drawn from the towns and tents of Mesopotamia and

---

[105] The two antagonists who express the most intimate knowledge and the strongest conviction of the *miracle*, and of the *fraud*, are Raymond des Agiles and Radulphus Cadomensis, the one attached to the Count of Toulouse, the other to the Norman prince. Fulcherius Carnotensis presumes to say, Audite fraudem et non fraudem! and afterwards, Invenit lanceam, fallaciter occultatam forsitan. The rest of the herd are loud and strenuous.

[106] See M. de Guignes (tom. ii. p. ii. p. 223, &c.); and the articles of *Barkiarok, Mohammed, Sangiar*, in d'Herbelot

Syria; and the Turkish veterans were employed or consumed in the civil wars beyond the Tigris. The caliph of Egypt embraced this opportunity of weakness and discord to recover his ancient possessions; and his sultan Aphdal besieged Jerusalem and Tyre, expelled the children of Ortok, and restored in Palestine the civil and ecclesiastical authority of the Fatimites.[107] They heard with astonishment of the vast armies of Christians that had passed from Europe to Asia, and rejoiced in the sieges and battles which broke the power of the Turks, the adversaries of their sect and monarchy. But the same Christians were the enemies of the prophet; and from the overthrow of Nice and Antioch, the motive of their enterprise, which was gradually understood, would urge them forward to the banks of the Jordan, or perhaps of the Nile. An intercourse of epistles and embassies, which rose and fell with the events of war, was maintained between the throne of Cairo and the camp of the Latins; and their adverse pride was the result of ignorance and enthusiasm. The ministers of Egypt declared in an haughty, or insinuated in a milder, tone that their sovereign, the true and lawful commander of the faithful, had rescued Jerusalem from the Turkish yoke; and that the pilgrims, if they would divide their numbers and lay aside their arms, should find a safe and hospitable reception at the sepulchre of Jesus. In the belief of their lost condition, the caliph Mostali despised their arms and imprisoned their deputies: the conquest and victory of Antioch prompted him to solicit those formidable champions with gifts of horses and silk robes, of vases, and purses of gold and silver; and, in his estimate of their merit or power, the first place was assigned to Bohemond, and the second to Godfrey. In either fortune the answer of the crusaders was firm and uniform: they disdained to inquire into the private claims or possessions of the followers of Mahomet: whatsoever was his name or nation, the usurper of Jerusalem was their enemy; and, instead of prescribing the mode and terms of their pilgrimage, it was only by a timely surrender of the city and province, their sacred right, that he could deserve their alliance or deprecate their impending and irresistible attack.[108]

---

[107] The emir, or sultan [really vezīr; called sultān in Egypt under the Fātimids], Aphdal recovered Jerusalem and Tyre, A.H. 489 [1096] (Renaudot, Hist. Patriarch. Alexandrin. p. 478; De Guignes, tom. i. p. 249, from Abulfeda and Ben Schounah). Jerusalem ante adventum vestrum recuperavimus, Turcos ejecimus, say the Fatimite ambassadors.

[108] See the transactions between the caliphs of Egypt and the crusaders, in William of Tyre (l. iv. c. 24, l. vi. c. 19) and Albert Aquensis (l. iii. c. 59), who are more sensible of their importance than the contemporary writers.

Delay of the
Franks.  A.D.
1098, July—
A.D. 1099,
May
Yet this attack, when they were within the view and reach of
their glorious prize, was suspended above ten months after the
defeat of Kerboga.  The zeal and courage of the crusaders were
chilled in the moment of victory : and, instead of marching to
improve the consternation, they hastily dispersed to enjoy the
luxury, of Syria.  The causes of this strange delay may be found
in the want of strength and subordination.  In the painful and
various service of Antioch the cavalry was annihilated ; many
thousands of every rank had been lost by famine, sickness, and
desertion ; the same abuse of plenty had been productive of a
third famine ; and the alternative of intemperance and distress
had generated a pestilence, which swept away above fifty
thousand of the pilgrims.  Few were able to command and none
were willing to obey : the domestic feuds, which had been stifled
by common fear, were again renewed in acts, or at least in sentiments, of hostility ; the future of Baldwin and Bohemond excited the envy of their companions ; the bravest knights were
enlisted for the defence of their new principalities ; and count
Raymond exhausted his troops and treasures in an idle expedition into the heart of Syria.[109]  The winter was consumed in
discord and disorder ; a sense of honour and religion was rekindled in the spring ; and the private soldiers, less susceptible
of ambition and jealousy, awakened with angry clamours the
indolence of their chiefs.  In the month of May, the relics of
this mighty host proceeded from Antioch to Laodicea : about
forty thousand Latins, of whom no more than fifteen hundred
horse and twenty thousand foot were capable of immediate
service.  Their easy march was continued between Mount
Libanus and the sea-shore ; their wants were liberally supplied
by the coasting traders of Genoa and Pisa ; and they drew large
contributions from the emirs of Tripoli, Tyre, Sidon, Acre, and
Cæsarea, who granted a free passage and promised to follow the
example of Jerusalem.  From Cæsarea [110] they advanced into the
midland country ; their clerks recognised the sacred geography
of Lydda, Ramla, Emaus, and Bethlem ; and, as soon as they
descried the holy city, the crusaders forgot their toils, and
claimed their reward.[111]

Their march
to Jerusalem.
A.D. 1099,
May 13—
June 6

---

[109] [Raymond captured Albara, and one of his men captured [the village of]
Tell Mannas.  They also attacked Maarra, but did not take it at the first attempt.
Raymond and Bohemond captured it in December.]

[110] [Before they reached Caesarea they were delayed by a three months' siege of
Arka (a strong citadel under Mt. Lebanon, not far from Tripolis), which they left
untaken.]

[111] The greatest part of the march of the Franks is traced, and most accurately
traced, in Maundrell's Journey from Aleppo to Jerusalem (p. 11-67): un des

Jerusalem has derived some reputation from the number and importance of her memorable sieges. It was not till after a long and obstinate contest that Babylon and Rome could prevail against the obstinacy of the people, the craggy ground that might supersede the necessity of fortifications, and the walls and towers that would have fortified the most accessible plain.[112] These obstacles were diminished in the age of the crusades. The bulwarks had been completely destroyed, and imperfectly restored ; the Jews, their nation and worship, were for ever banished ; but nature is less changeable than man, and the site of Jerusalem, though somewhat softened and somewhat removed, was still strong against the assaults of an enemy. By the experience of a recent siege, and a three years' possession, the Saracens of Egypt had been taught to discern, and in some degree to remedy, the defects of a place which religion, as well as honour, forbade them to resign. Aladin, or Iftikhar, the caliph's lieutenant, was entrusted with the defence ; his policy strove to restrain the native Christians by the dread of their own ruin and that of the holy sepulchre ; to animate the Moslems by the assurance of temporal and eternal rewards. His garrison is said to have consisted of forty thousand Turks and Arabians ; and, if he could muster twenty thousand of the inhabitants, it must be confessed that the besieged were more numerous than the besieging army.[113] Had the diminished strength and numbers of the Latins allowed them to grasp the whole circumference of four thousand yards (about two English miles and a half),[114] to what useful purpose should they have descended into the valley of Ben Hinnom and torrent of

meilleurs morceaux, sans contredit, qu'on ait dans ce genre (d'Anville, Mémoire sur Jérusalem, p. 27).

[112] See the masterly description of Tacitus (Hist. v. 11, 12, 13), who supposes that the Jewish lawgivers had provided for a perpetual state of hostility against the rest of mankind.

[113] The lively scepticism of Voltaire is balanced with sense and erudition by the French author of the Esprit des Croisades (tom. iv. p. 386-388), who observes that, according to the Arabians, the inhabitants of Jerusalem must have exceeded 200,000 ; that in the siege of Titus, Josephus collects 1,300,000 Jews ; that they are stated by Tacitus himself at 600,000 ; and that the largest defalcation that his *accepimus* can justify will still leave them more numerous than the Roman army.

[114] Maundrell, who diligently perambulated the walls, found a circuit of 4630 paces, or 4167 English yards (p. 109, 110) ; from an authentic plan, d'Anville concludes a measure nearly similar, of 1960 French *toises* (p. 23-29), in his scarce and valuable tract. For the topography of Jerusalem, see Reland (Palestina, tom. ii. p. 832-860). [Cp. above, vol. 2, p. 454. Guy Le Strange, Palestine under the Muslims, p. 83-223.]

Kedron,[115] or approached the precipices of the south and east, from whence they had nothing either to hope or fear? Their siege was more reasonably directed against the northern and western sides of the city. Godfrey of Bouillon erected his standard on the first swell of Mount Calvary; to the left, as far as St. Stephen's gate, the line of attack was continued by Tancred and the two Roberts; and count Raymond established his quarters from the citadel to the foot of Mount Sion, which was no longer included within the precincts of the city. On the fifth day, the crusaders made a general assault, in the fanatic hope of battering down the walls without engines, and of scaling them without ladders. By the dint of brutal force they burst the first barrier, but they were driven back with shame and slaughter to the camp; the influence of vision and prophecy was deadened by the too frequent abuse of those pious stratagems; and time and labour were found to be the only means of victory. The time of the siege was indeed fulfilled in forty days, but they were forty days of calamity and anguish. A repetition of the old complaint of famine may be imputed in some degree to the voracious or disorderly appetite of the Franks; but the stony soil of Jerusalem is almost destitute of water; the scanty springs and hasty torrents were dry in the summer season; nor was the thirst of the besiegers relieved, as in the city, by the artificial supply of cisterns and aqueducts. The circumjacent country is equally destitute of trees for the uses of shade or building; but some large beams were discovered in a cave by the crusaders: a wood near Sichem, the enchanted grove of Tasso,[116] was cut down; the necessary timber was transported to the camp, by the vigour and dexterity of Tancred; and the engines were framed by some Genoese artists, who had fortunately landed in the harbour of Jaffa. Two moveable turrets were constructed at the expense, and in the stations, of the duke of Lorraine and the count of Toulouse, and rolled forwards with devout labour, not to the most accessible, but to the most neglected, parts of the fortification.

---

[115] Jerusalem was possessed only of the torrent of Kedron, dry in summer, and of the little spring or brook of Siloe (Reland, tom. i. p. 294, 300). Both strangers and natives complained of the want of water, which, in time of war, was studiously aggravated. Within the city, Tacitus mentions a perennial fountain, an aqueduct, and cisterns for rain-water. The aqueduct was conveyed from the rivulet Tekoe [Tekūa, 10 miles south of Jerusalem], or Etham, which is likewise mentioned by Bohadin (in Vit. Saladin. p. 238 [c. 157]).

[116] Gierusalemme Liberata, canto xiii. It is pleasant enough to observe how Tasso has copied and embellished the minutest details of the siege.

Raymond's tower was reduced to ashes by the fire of the besieged; but his colleague was more vigilant and successful;
the enemies were driven by his archers from the rampart; the
draw-bridge was let down; and on a Friday, at three in the [July 15]
afternoon, the day and hour of the Passion, Godfrey of Bouillon
stood victorious on the walls of Jerusalem.  His example was
followed on every side by the emulation of valour; and, about
four hundred and sixty years after the conquest of Omar, the
holy city was rescued from the Mahometan yoke.  In the pillage of public and private wealth, the adventurers had agreed
to respect the exclusive property of the first occupant; and the
spoils of the great mosque, seventy lamps and massy vases of
gold and silver, rewarded the diligence, and displayed the
generosity, of Tancred.  A bloody sacrifice was offered by his
mistaken votaries to the God of the Christians; resistance
might provoke, but neither age nor sex could mollify, their
implacable rage; they indulged themselves three days in a
promiscuous massacre; [117] and the infection of the dead bodies
produced an epidemic disease.  After seventy thousand Moslems had been put to the sword, and the harmless Jews had
been burnt in their synagogue, they could still reserve a multitude of captives whom interest or lassitude persuaded them to
spare.  Of these savage heroes of the cross, Tancred alone betrayed some sentiments of compassion; yet we may praise the
more selfish lenity of Raymond, who granted a capitulation and
safe-conduct to the garrison of the citadel. [118]  The holy sepulchre was now free; and the bloody victors prepared to accomplish their vow.  Bareheaded and barefoot, with contrite hearts,
and in an humble posture, they ascended the hill of Calvary,
amidst the loud anthems of the clergy; kissed the stone which
had covered the Saviour of the world; and bedewed with tears
of joy and penitence the monument of their redemption.  This
union of the fiercest and most tender passions has been variously
considered by two philosophers: by the one, [119] as easy and

[117] Besides the Latins, who are not ashamed of the massacre, see Elmacin
(Hist. Saracen. p. 363), Abulpharagius (Dynast. p. 243), and M. de Guignes (tom.
ii. p. ii. p. 99), from Aboulmahasen.

[118] The old tower Psephina, in the middle ages Neblosa, was named Castellum
Pisanum, from the patriarch Daimbert.  It is still the citadel, the residence of the
Turkish aga, and commands a prospect of the Dead Sea, Judea, and Arabia
(D'Anville, p. 19-23).   It was likewise called the Tower of David, πύργος παμμε-
γεθέστατος.  [The Phasael of Josephus, B. J. 5, 4, 3.]

[119] Hume, in his History of England, vol. i. p. 311, 312, octavo edition.

natural ; by the other,[120] as absurd and incredible. Perhaps it is too rigorously applied to the same persons and the same hour : the example of the virtuous Godfrey awakened the piety of his companions ; while they cleansed their bodies, they purified their minds ; nor shall I believe that the most ardent in slaughter and rapine were the foremost in the procession to the holy sepulchre.

Election and reign of Godfrey of Bouillon. A.D. 1099, July 23—A.D. 1100, July 18

Eight days after this memorable event, which Pope Urban did not live to hear, the Latin chiefs proceeded to the election of a king, to guard and govern their conquests in Palestine. Hugh the Great and Stephen of Chartres had retired with some loss of reputation, which they strove to regain by a second crusade and an honourable death. Baldwin was established at Edessa, and Bohemond at Antioch ; and the two Roberts, the duke of Normandy [121] and the count of Flanders, preferred their fair inheritance in the West to a doubtful competition or a barren sceptre. The jealousy and ambition of Raymond were condemned by his own followers, and the free, the just, the unanimous voice of the army proclaimed Godfrey of Bouillon the first and most worthy of the champions of Christendom. His magnanimity accepted a trust as full of danger as of glory ; but in a city where his Saviour had been crowned with thorns the devout pilgrim rejected the name and ensigns of royalty ; and the founder of the kingdom of Jerusalem contented himself with the modest title of Defender and Baron of the Holy Sepulchre. His government of a single year,[122] too short for the public happiness, was interrupted in the first fortnight by a summons to the field, by the approach of the vizir or sultan of Egypt, who had been too slow to prevent, but who was impatient to avenge, the loss of Jerusalem. His total overthrow in the battle of Ascalon sealed the establishment of the Latins in Syria, and signalised the valour of the French princes, who, in this action, bade a long farewell to the holy wars. Some glory might be derived from the prodigious inequality of numbers, though I shall not count the myriads of horse and foot on the

Battle of Ascalon. A.D. 1099, August 12

[120] Voltaire, in his Essai sur l'Histoire Générale, tom. ii. c. 54, p. 345, 346.

[121] The English ascribe to Robert of Normandy, and the Provincials to Raymond of Toulouse, the glory of refusing the crown ; but the honest voice of tradition has preserved the memory of the ambition and revenge (Villehardouin, No. 136) of the count of St. Giles. He died at the siege of Tripoli, which was possessed by his descendants.

[122] See the election, the battle of Ascalon, &c. in William of Tyre, l. ix. c. 1-12, and in the conclusion of the Latin historians of the first crusade.

side of the Fatimites ; but, except three thousand Ethiopians or Blacks, who were armed with flails or scourges of iron, the barbarians of the South fled on the first onset, and afforded a pleasing comparison between the active valour of the Turks and the sloth and effeminacy of the natives of Egypt. After suspending before the holy sepulchre the sword and standard of the sultan, the new king (he deserves the title) embraced his departing companions, and could retain only with the gallant Tancred three hundred knights and two thousand foot-soldiers for the defence of Palestine. His sovereignty was soon attacked by a new enemy, the only one against whom Godfrey was a coward. Adhemar, Bishop of Puy, who excelled both in council and action, had been swept away in the last plague of Antioch ; the remaining ecclesiastics preserved only the pride and avarice of their character ; and their seditious clamours had required that the choice of a bishop should precede that of a king. The revenue and jurisdiction of the lawful patriarch were usurped by the Latin clergy ; the exclusion of the Greeks and Syrians was justified by the reproach of heresy or schism ; [123] and, under the iron yoke of their deliverers, the Oriental Christians regretted the tolerating government of the Arabian caliphs. Daimbert, Archbishop of Pisa, had long been trained in the secret policy of Rome : he brought a fleet of his countrymen to the succour of the Holy Land, and was installed, without a competitor, the spiritual and temporal head of the church. The new patriarch [124] immediately grasped the sceptre which had been acquired by the toil and blood of the victorious pilgrims ; and both Godfrey and Bohemond submitted to receive at his hands the investiture of their feudal possessions. Nor was this sufficient ; Daimbert claimed the immediate property of Jerusalem and Jaffa : instead of a firm and generous refusal, the hero negotiated with the priest ; a quarter of either city was ceded to the church ; and the modest bishop was satisfied with an eventual reversion of the rest, on the death of Godfrey without children, or on the future acquisition of a new seat at Cairo or Damascus.

---

[123] Renaudot, Hist. Patriarch. Alex. p. 479.

[124] See the claims of the patriarch Daimbert, in William of Tyre (l. ix. c. 15-18, x. 4, 7, 9), who asserts with marvellous candour the independence of the conquerors and kings of Jerusalem. [Arnulf was first elected Patriarch, but was deposed and replaced by Daimbert. Cp. Guibertus, vii. c. 15. Albert of Aix says that Daimbert owed his election chiefly to money, collectione potens pecuniae quam electione novae ecclesiae (vii. c. 7).]

The kingdom
of Jerusalem.
A.D. 1099-1187
[6]
Without this indulgence, the conqueror would have almost been stripped of his infant kingdom, which consisted only of Jerusalem and Jaffa, with about twenty villages and towns of the adjacent country.[125]   Within this narrow verge, the Mahometans were still lodged in some impregnable castles ; and the husbandman, the trader, and the pilgrims were exposed to daily and domestic hostility.   By the arms of Godfrey himself, and of the two Baldwins, his brother and cousin, who succeeded to the throne, the Latins breathed with more ease and safety ; and at length they equalled, in the extent of their dominions, though not in the millions of their subjects, the ancient princes of Judah and Israel.[126]   After the reduction of the maritime cities of Laodicea, Tripoli, Tyre, and Ascalon,[127] which were powerfully assisted by the fleets of Venice, Genoa, and Pisa, and even of Flanders and Norway,[128] the range of sea-coast from Scanderoon to the borders of Egypt was possessed by the Christian pilgrims.   If the prince of Antioch [129] disclaimed his supremacy,

[125] Willerm. Tyr. l. x. 19.   The Historia Hierosolymitana of Jacobus a Vitriaco (l. i. c. 21-50) and the Secreta Fidelium Crucis of Marinus Sanutus (l. iii. p. 1) describe the state and conquests of the Latin kingdom of Jerusalem.   [The work of Marinus (edited in Bongarsius, ii. p. 1 *sqq*.) was written A.D. 1306-1321.   This Marinus Sanutus is distinguished as *senior* from his later namesake, author of the Chronicon Venetum.   The first Book of the work of James de Vitry is printed in Bongarsius, i. p. 1047 *sqq*., along with Bk. iii., which is by a different author.   Bk. ii. seems never to have been printed since the old edition of Moschus, 1597.   For the history of the kingdom of Jerusalem, cp. below, p. 322, note 1.]

[126] An actual muster, not including the tribes of Levi and Benjamin, gave David an army of 1,300,000, or 1,574,000 fighting men ; which, with the addition of women, children, and slaves, may imply a population of thirteen millions, in a country sixty leagues in length and thirty broad.   The honest and rational Le Clerc (Comment. on 2 Samuel, xxiv. and 1 Chronicles, xxi.) æstuat angusto in limite, and mutters his suspicion of a false transcript,—a dangerous suspicion !

[127] These sieges are related, each in its proper place, in the great history of William of Tyre, from the ixth to the xviiith book, and more briefly told by Bernardus Thesaurarius (de Acquisitione Terræ Sanctæ, c. 89-98, p. 732-740).   Some domestic facts are celebrated in the Chronicles of Pisa, Genoa, and Venice, in the vith, ixth, and xiith tomes of Muratori.   [Baldwin I. took Tripoli in 1109 and gave it to Bertram, son of Raymond of Toulouse.   Tyre surrendered in 1124.   The year 1143 may be taken as the central year after which the kingdom begins to decline and the Christians have to fight not for conquest but for defence.   Ascalon, however, was won ten years later (1153).   In 1152 the County of Edessa was surrendered to Manuel Comnenus.]

[128] Quidam populus de insulis occidentis egressus, et maxime de eâ parte quæ Norvegia dicitur.   William of Tyre (l. xi. c. 14, p. 804) marks their course per Britannicum mare et Calpen to the siege of Sidon.

[129] [For the history of the principality of Antioch, which deserves more attention than it has received, see E. Rey's Résumé chronologique de la histoire des princes d'Antioche, in the Revue de l'Orient Latin, iv. 321 *sqq*. (1896).   The *Bella Antiochena* of Gualterius Cancellarius was printed in Bongarsius (vol. i.), but an improved text is published in the Recueil, vol. v. p. 81 *sqq*. and there is a new ed. by Hagenmeyer (1896).]

the counts of Edessa and Tripoli owned themselves the vassals
of the king of Jerusalem : the Latins reigned beyond the
Euphrates ; and the four cities of Hems, Hamah, Damascus, and
Aleppo were the only relics of the Mahometan conquests in
Syria.[130]   The laws and language, the manners and titles, of the
French nation and Latin church, were introduced into these
transmarine colonies.   According to the feudal jurisprudence,
the principal states and subordinate baronies descended in the line
of male and female succession ;[131] but the children of the first
conquerors,[132] a motley and degenerate race, were dissolved by
luxury of the climate ; the arrival of new crusaders from Europe
was a doubtful hope and a casual event.   The service of the
feudal tenures[133] was performed by six hundred and sixty-six
knights, who might expect the aid of two hundred more under
the banner of the count of Tripoli ; and each knight was
attended to the field by four squires or archers on horseback.[134]
Five thousand and seventy-five *serjeants*, most probably foot-
soldiers, were supplied by the churches and the cities ; and the
whole legal militia of the kingdom could not exceed eleven
thousand men, a slender defence against the surrounding myriads
of Saracens and Turks.[135]   But the firmest bulwark of Jerusalem
was founded on the knights of the Hospital of St. John,[136] and of

---

[130] Benelathir, apud de Guignes, Hist. des Huns, tom. ii. part ii. p. 150, 151,
A.D. 1127.   He must speak of the inland country.

[131] Sanut very sensibly descants on the mischiefs of female succession in a land,
nostibus circumdata, ubi cuncta virilia et virtuosa esse deberent.   Yet, at the
summons, and with the approbation, of her feudal lord, a noble damsel was
obliged to choose a husband and champion (Assises de Jérusalem, c. 242, &c.).
See in M. de Guignes (tom. i. p. 441-471) the accurate and useful tables of these
dynasties, which are chiefly drawn from the *Lignages d'Outremer*.

[132] They were called by derision *Poullains*, *Pullani*, and their name is never
pronounced without contempt (Ducange, Gloss. Latin. tom. v. p. 535; and
Observations sur Joinville, p. 84, 85 ; Jacob. a Vitriaco, Hist. Hierosol. l. i. c. 67,
72 ; and Sanut, l. iii. p. viii. c. 2, p. 182).   Illustrium virorum qui ad Terræ
Sanctæ . . . liberationem in ipsâ manserunt degeneres filii . . . in deliciis
enutriti, molles et effœminati, &c.   [The word does not necessarily imply mixture
of blood ; it is "used loosely as we use the word Creole" (Bishop Stubbs in
Glossary to Itin. Regis Ricardi, p. 455).]

[133] This authentic detail is extracted from the Assises de Jérusalem (c. 324, 326-
331).   Sanut (l. iii. p. viii. c. i. p. 174) reckons only 518 knights and 5775
followers.

[134] The sum-total, and the division, ascertain the service of the three great
baronies at 100 knights each ; and the text of the Assises, which extends the
number to 500, can only be justified by this supposition.

[135] Yet on great emergencies (says Sanut) the barons brought a voluntary aid ;
decentem comitivam militum juxta statum suum.

[136] William of Tyre (l. xviii. c. 3, 4, 5) relates the ignoble origin and early insolence of the Hospitalers, who soon deserted their humble patron, St. John the

the temple of Solomon; [137] on the strange association of a monastic and military life, which fanaticism might suggest, but which
policy must approve. The flower of the nobility of Europe
aspired to wear the cross, and to profess the vows, of these
respectable orders; their spirit and discipline were immortal;
and the speedy donation of twenty-eight thousand farms, or
manors,[138] enabled them to support a regular force of cavalry
and infantry for the defence of Palestine. The austerity of the
convent soon evaporated in the exercise of arms; the world was
scandalized by the pride, avarice, and corruption of these Christian soldiers; their claims of immunity and jurisdiction disturbed
the harmony of the church and state; and the public peace
was endangered by their jealous emulation. But in their most
dissolute period, the knights of the Hospital and Temple
maintained their fearless and fanatic character; they neglected
to live, but they were prepared to die, in the service of Christ
and the spirit of chivalry, the parent and offspring of the
crusades, has been transplanted by this institution from the holy
sepulchre to the isle of Malta.[139]

Eleemosynary, for the more august character of St. John the Baptist. (See the
ineffectual struggles of Pagi, Critica, A.D. 1099, No. 14-18.) They assumed the
profession of arms about the year 1120; the Hospital was *mater*, the Temple *filia*
the Teutonic order was founded A.D. 1190, at the siege of Acre (Mosheim, Institut
p. 389, 390). [The order of the Temple was founded about 1118. The Hospital
was an older foundation, instituted by merchants of Amalfi for the relief of [sic]
pilgrims; but as a military order it was younger than the Temple; in fact it was
the foundation of the Templars which suggested the transformation of the Hospital
into a military order. The Templars were distinguished by a white cloak and
red cross, the Hospitallers by a white cross. Bishop Stubbs, dwelling on the
degeneration of the Franks in Palestine at the time of the Second or Third
Crusade, observes: "The only sound element in the country was the organiza
tion of the military orders. These procured a constant succession of fresh and
healthy blood from Europe, they were not liable to the evils of minorities, their
selfish interests were bound up with the strength of the kingdom. If one grand
master fell another took his place. . . . It may be safely said that if Palestine
could have been recovered and maintained by the Western powers it would have
been by the knights of the Temple and the Hospital. If their system had been
adopted, Palestine might have been still in Christian hands; or at least have con
tinued so as long as Cyprus" (Introduction to Itin. Regis Ricardi, p. cvi. cvii.).]

[137] See St. Bernard de Laude Novæ Militiæ Templi, composed A.D. 1132-1136
in Opp. tom. i. p. ii. p. 547-563, edit. Mabillon. Venet. 1750. Such an encomium
which is thrown away on the dead Templars, would be highly valued by the
historians of Malta.

[138] Matthew Paris, Hist. Major, p. 544. He assigns to the Hospitalers 19,000
to the Templars 9000 *maneria*, a word of much higher import (as Ducange has
rightly observed) in the English than in the French idiom. *Manor* is a lordship
*manoir* a dwelling.

[139] In the three first books of the Histoire des Chevaliers de Malthe, par l'Abbé
de Vertot, the reader may amuse himself with a fair, and sometimes flattering
picture of the order, while it was employed for the defence of Palestine. The sub
sequent books pursue their emigrations to Rhodes and Malta.

The spirit of freedom, which pervades the feudal institutions, was felt in its strongest energy by the volunteers of the cross, who elected for their chief the most deserving of his peers. Amidst the slaves of Asia, unconscious of the lesson or example, a model of political liberty was introduced ; and the laws of the French kingdom are derived from the purest source of equality and justice.   Of such laws, the first and indispensable condition is the assent of those whose obedience they require, and for whose benefit they are designed.   No sooner had Godfrey of Bouillon accepted the office of supreme magistrate than he solicited the public and private advice of the Latin pilgrims who were the best skilled in the statutes and customs of Europe.   From these materials, with the counsel and approbation of the patriarch and barons, of the clergy and laity, Godfrey composed the ASSISE OF JERUSALEM,[140] a precious monument of feudal jurisprudence.   The new code, attested by the seals of the king, the patriarch, and the viscount of Jerusalem, was deposited in the holy sepulchre, enriched with the improvements of succeeding times, and respectfully consulted as often as any doubtful question arose in the tribunals of Palestine. With the kingdom and city all was lost ; [141] the fragments of the written law were preserved by jealous tradition,[142] and variable practice, till the middle of the thirteenth century ; the code was restored by the pen of John d'Ibelin, count of Jaffa, one of the principal feudatories ; [143] and the final revision was accom-

[140] The Assises de Jérusalem, in old Law-French, were printed with Beaumanoir's Coutumes de Beauvoisis (Bourges and Paris, 1690, in folio), and illustrated by Gaspard Thaumas de la Thaumassière, with a comment and glossary.   An Italian version had been published in 1535, at Venice, for the use of the kingdom of Cyprus.   [The authoritative edition is that of the Comte de Beugnot : vol. i. Assises de la Haute Cour, 1841 ; vol. ii. Assises de la Cour des bourgeois, 1843.]

[141] A la terre perdue, tout fut perdu, is the vigorous expression of the Assise (c. 81 [see Beugnot, vol. i. c. 47 in the Livre de Philippe de Navarre, p. 522 ; la ttre fust perdue—et tout ce fust perdu quant Saladin prist Jerusalem]).   Yet erusalem capitulated with Saladin : the queen and the principal Christians eparted in peace ; and a code so precious and so portable could not provoke the varice of the conquerors.   I have sometimes suspected the existence of this riginal copy of the Holy Sepulchre, which might be invented to sanctify and authenticate the traditionary customs of the French in Palestine. [See Appendix 16.]

[142] A noble lawyer, Raoul de Tabarie, denied the prayer of King Amauri A.D. 1195-1205), that he would commit his knowledge to writing ; and frankly eclared, que de ce qu' il savoit ne feroit-il ja nul borjois son pareill, ne nul sage omme lettré (c. 281).

[143] The compiler of this work, Jean d'Ibelin, was Count of Jaffa and Ascalon, ord of Baruth (Berytus) and Rames, and died A.D. 1266 (Sanut, l. iii. p. xii. , 5, 8).   The family of Ibelin, which descended from a younger brother of a ount of Chartres in France, long flourished in Palestine and Cyprus (see the

plished in the year thirteen hundred and sixty-nine, for the use
of the Latin kingdom of Cyprus.[144]

The justice and freedom of the constitution were maintained
by two tribunals of unequal dignity, which were instituted by
Godfrey of Bouillon after the conquest of Jerusalem. The
king, in person, presided in the upper court, the court of the
barons. Of these the four most conspicuous were the prince of
Galilee, the lord of Sidon and Cæsarea, and the counts of Jaffa
and Tripoli, who, perhaps with the constable and marshal,[145]
were in a special manner the compeers and judges of each other.
But all the nobles, who held their lands immediately of the
crown, were entitled and bound to attend the king's court ; and
each baron exercised a similar jurisdiction in the subordinate
assemblies of his own feudatories. The connection of lord and
vassal was honourable and voluntary : reverence was due to the
benefactor, protection to the dependent ; but they mutually
pledged their faith to each other, and the obligation on either
side might be suspended by neglect or dissolved by injury. The
cognisance of marriages and testaments was blended with religion
and usurped by the clergy ; but the civil and criminal causes of
the nobles, the inheritance and tenure of their fiefs, formed the
proper occupation of the supreme court. Each member was the
judge and guardian both of public and private rights. It was
his duty to assert with his tongue and sword the lawful claims
of the lord ; but, if an unjust superior presumed to violate the
freedom or property of a vassal, the confederate peers stood
forth to maintain his quarrel by word and deed. They boldly
affirmed his innocence and his wrongs ; demanded the restitution

Lignages de de-ça Mer, or d'Outremer, c. 6, at the end of the Assises de Jérusalem, an original book, which records the pedigrees of the French adventurers).

[144] By sixteen commissioners chosen in the states of the island, the work was
finished the 3d of November, 1369, sealed with four seals, and deposited in the
cathedral of Nicosia (see the preface to the Assises).

[145] The cautious John d'Ibelin argues, rather than affirms, that Tripoli is the
fourth barony, and expresses some doubt concerning the right or pretension of the
constable and marshal (c. 323 [c. 269, cp. c. 271]). [Tripoli was the fourth fief of
the *kingdom* of Jerusalem, but it was not a barony of the *principality* of Jerusalem.
The four fiefs of the kingdom were : (1) the principality of Jerusalem ; (2) the
principality of Antioch ; (3) the county of Edessa ; (4) the county of Tripoli. The
four baronies of the principality were : (1) the principality of Galilee ; (2) the lordship of Sidon and Cæsarea (Cæsarea being held as a fief of Sidon); (3) the county of
Jaffa and Ascalon ; (4) the principality of Hebron or St. Abraham, to which was
afterwards joined the lordship of Kerak and Montreal beyond the Jordan (including all the south of Palestine except Ascalon). There is a good map of the Principality of Jerusalem in the Eng. tr. of Behā ad-din in the Palestine Pilgrims'
Text Society.]

of his liberty or his lands ; suspended, after a fruitless demand, their own service ; rescued their brother from prison ; and employed every weapon in his defence, without offering direct violence to the person of their lord, which was ever sacred in their eyes.[146] In their pleadings, replies, and rejoinders, the advocates of the court were subtile and copious ; but the use of argument and evidence was often superseded by judicial combat ; and the Assise of Jerusalem admits in many cases this barbarous institution, which has been slowly abolished by the laws and manners of Europe.

The trial by battle was established in all criminal cases which affected the life or limb or honour of any person ; and in all civil transactions of or above the value of one mark of silver. It appears that in criminal cases the combat was the privilege of the accuser, who, except in a charge of treason, avenged his personal injury or the death of those persons whom he had a right to represent; but, wherever, from the nature of the charge, testimony could be obtained, it was necessary for him to produce witnesses of the fact. In civil cases, the combat was not allowed as the means of establishing the claim of the demandant ; but he was obliged to produce witnesses who had, or assumed to have, knowledge of the fact. The combat was then the privilege of the defendant ; because he charged the witness with an attempt by perjury to take away his right. He came, therefore, to be in the same situation as the appellant in criminal cases. It was not, then, as a mode of proof that the combat was received, nor as making negative evidence (according to the supposition of Montesquieu) ; [147] but in every case the right to offer battle was founded on the right to pursue by arms the redress of an injury ; and the judicial combat was fought on the same principle, and with the same spirit, as a private duel. Champions were only allowed to women, and to men maimed or past the age of sixty. The consequence of a defeat was death to the person accused, or to the champion or witness, as well as to the accuser himself ;

*Law of judicial combats*

---

[146] Entre seignor et homme ne n'a que la foi ; . . . mais tant que l'homme doit son seignor reverence en toutes choses (c. 206). Tous les hommes dudit yaume sont par la dite Assise tenus les uns as autres . . . et en celle manière ue le seignor mette main ou face mettre au cors ou au fié d'aucun d'yaus sans gard et sans connoissance de court, que tous les autres doivent venir devant le ignor, &c. (212). The form of their remonstrances is conceived with the noble mplicity of freedom.

[147] See l'Esprit des Loix, l. xxviii. In the forty years since its publication, no ork has been more read and criticized ; and the spirit of inquiry which it has cited is not the least of our obligations to the author.

but in civil cases the demandant was punished with infamy and the loss of his suit, while his witness and champion suffered an ignominious death. In many cases, it was in the option of the judge to award or to refuse the combat ; but two are specified in which it was the inevitable result of the challenge : if a faithful vassal gave the lie to his compeer, who unjustly claimed any portion of their lord's demesnes ; or if an unsuccessful suitor presumed to impeach the judgment and veracity of the court. He might impeach them, but the terms were severe and perilous: in the same day he successively fought *all* the members of the tribunal, even those who had been absent ; a single defeat was followed by death and infamy ; and, where none could hope for victory, it is highly probable that none would adventure the trial. In the Assise of Jerusalem, the legal subtlety of the count of Jaffa is more laudably employed to elude, than to facilitate, the judicial combat, which he derives from a principle of honour rather than of superstition.[148]

Court of burgesses

Among the causes which enfranchised the plebeians from the yoke of feudal tyranny, the institution of cities and corporations is one of the most powerful ; and, if those of Palestine are coeval with the first crusade, they may be ranked with the most ancient of the Latin world. Many of the pilgrims had escaped from their lords under the banner of the cross ; and it was the policy of the French princes to tempt their stay by the assurance of the rights and privileges of freemen. It is expressly declared in the Assise of Jerusalem that, after instituting, for his knights and barons, the court of Peers, in which he presided himself, Godfrey of Bouillon established a second tribunal, in which his person was represented by his viscount. The jurisdiction of this inferior court extended over the burgesses of the kingdom ; and it was composed of a select number of the most discreet and worthy citizens, who were sworn to judge, according to the laws, of the actions and fortunes of their equals.[149] In the conquest and settlement of new cities, the example of Jerusalem was imitated by the kings and their great vassals ; and above

[148] For the intelligence of this obscure and obsolete jurisprudence (c. 80-111), I am deeply indebted to the friendship of a learned lord, who, with an accurate and discerning eye, has surveyed the philosophic history of law. By his studies, posterity might be enriched ; the merit of the orator and the judge can be *felt* only by his contemporaries. [The reference is to Lord Loughborough.]

[149] Louis le Gros, who is considered as the father of this institution in France, did not begin his reign till nine years (A. D. 1108) after Godfrey of Bouillon (Assises, c. 2, 324). For its origin and effects, see the judicious remarks of Dr. Robertson (History of Charles V. vol. i. p. 30-36, 251-265, quarto edition).

thirty similar corporations were founded before the loss of the Holy Land. Another class of subjects, the Syrians,[150] or Oriental Syrians Christians, were oppressed by the zeal of the clergy, and protected by the toleration of the state. Godfrey listened to their reasonable prayer that they might be judged by their own national laws. A third court was instituted for their use, of limited and domestic jurisdiction; the sworn members were Syrians, in blood, language, and religion; but the office of the president (in Arabic, of the *rais*) was sometimes exercised by the viscount of the city. At an immeasurable distance below the *nobles*, the *burgesses*, and the *strangers*, the Assise of Jerusalem condescends to mention the *villains* and *slaves*, the peasants Villains and of the land and the captives of war, who were almost equally slaves considered as the objects of property. The relief or protection of these unhappy men was not esteemed worthy of the care of the legislator; but he diligently provides for the recovery, though not indeed for the punishment, of the fugitives. Like hounds, or hawks, who had strayed from the lawful owner, they might be lost and claimed; the slave and falcon were of the same value; but three slaves, or twelve oxen, were accumulated to equal the price of the war-horse; and a sum of three hundred pieces of gold was fixed, in the age of chivalry, as the equivalent of the more noble animal.[151]

[150] Every reader conversant with the historians of the crusades, will understand, by the peuple des Suriens, the Oriental Christians, Melchites, Jacobites, or Nestorians, who had all adopted the use of the Arabic language (vol. v. p. 145).

[151] See the Assises de Jérusalem (310-312). These laws were enacted as late as the year 1358, in the kingdom of Cyprus. In the same century, in the reign of Edward I., I understand, from a late publication (of his Book of Account), that the price of a war-horse was not less exorbitant in England.

CHAPTER LIX

*Preservation of the Greek Empire—Numbers, Passage, and Event
of the Second and Third Crusades—St. Bernard—Reign of
Saladin in Egypt and Syria—His Conquest of Jerusalem—
Naval Crusades—Richard the First of England—Pope Innocent
the Third ; and the Fourth and Fifth Crusades—The Emperor
Frederic the Second—Louis the Ninth of France ; and the two
last Crusades—Expulsion of the Latins or Franks by the Mame-
lukes*

Success of
Alexius.
A.D. 1097-1118

IN a style less grave than that of history, I should perhaps compare the Emperor Alexius [1] to the jackal, who is said to follow
the steps, and to devour the leavings, of the lion. Whatever
had been his fears and toils in the passage of the first crusade,
they were amply recompensed by the subsequent benefits which
he derived from the exploits of the Franks. His dexterity and
vigilance secured their first conquest of Nice ; and from this
threatening station the Turks were compelled to evacuate the
neighbourhood of Constantinople. While the crusaders, with
blind valour, advanced into the midland countries of Asia, the
crafty Greek improved the favourable occasion when the emirs
of the sea-coast were recalled to the standard of the sultan. The
Turks were driven from the isles of Rhodes and Chios : the cities
of Ephesus and Smyrna, of Sardes, Philadelphia, and Laodicea,
were restored to the empire, which Alexius enlarged from the
Hellespont to the banks of the Mæander and the rocky shores
of Pamphylia. The churches resumed their splendour ; the
towns were rebuilt and fortified ; and the desert country was
peopled with colonies of Christians, who were gently removed
from the more distant and dangerous frontier. In these paternal

---

[1] Anna Comnena relates her father's conquests in Asia Minor, Alexiad, l. xi. p.
321-325 [c. 5, 6], l. xiv. p. 419 [c. 1] ; his Cilician war against Tancred and Bohemond, p. 328-342 [c. 7-12] ; the war of Epirus, with tedious prolixity, l. xii. xiii.
[c. 1-12], p. 345-406 ; the death of Bohemond, l. xiv. p. 419 [c. 1]. [The best complete history of the events described in this Chapter, from A.D. 1100 to 1291, is the
new work of Röhricht, Die Geschichte des Königreichs Jerusalem, 1898.]

cares, we may forgive Alexius, if he forgot the deliverance of the holy sepulchre; but, by the Latins, he was stigmatized with the foul reproach of treason and desertion. They had sworn fidelity and obedience to his throne; but *he* had promised to assist their enterprise in person, or, at least, with his troops and treasures; his base retreat dissolved their obligations; and the sword, which had been the instrument of their victory, was the pledge and title of their just independence. It does not appear that the emperor attempted to revive his obsolete claims over the kingdom of Jerusalem; [2] but the borders of Cilicia and Syria were more recent in his possession, and more accessible to his arms. The great army of the crusaders was annihilated or dispersed; the principality of Antioch was left without a head, by the surprise and captivity of Bohemond: his ransom had oppressed him with a heavy debt; and his Norman followers were insufficient to repel the hostilities of the Greeks and Turks. In this distress, Bohemond embraced a magnanimous resolution, of leaving the defence of Antioch to his kinsman, the faithful Tancred, of arming the West against the Byzantine empire, and of executing the design which he inherited from the lessons and example of his father Guiscard. His embarkation was clandestine; and, if we may credit a tale of the Princess Anne, he passed the hostile sea closely secreted in a coffin. [3] But his reception in France was dignified by the public applause and his marriage with the king's daughter; his return was glorious, since the bravest spirits of the age enlisted under his veteran command; and he repassed the Adriatic at the head of five thousand horse and forty thousand foot, assembled from the most remote climates of Europe. [4] The strength of Durazzo and prudence of Alexius, the progress of famine and approach of winter, eluded his ambitious hopes; and the venal confederates were seduced from his standard. A treaty of peace [5] suspended the fears of the Greeks; and they

---

[2] The kings of Jerusalem submitted, however, to a nominal dependence; and in the dates of their inscriptions (one is still legible in the church of Bethlem) they respectfully placed before their own the name of the reigning emperor (Ducange, Dissertations sur Joinville, xxvii. p. 319).

[3] Anna Comnena adds that, to complete the imitation, he was shut up with a dead cock; and condescends to wonder how the barbarian could endure the confinement and putrefaction. This absurd tale is unknown to the Latins.

[4] Ἀπὸ Θούλης [Anna, xii. c. 9, cp. ii. c. 9], in the Byzantine Geography, must mean England; yet we are more credibly informed that our Henry I. would not suffer him to levy any troops in his kingdom (Ducange, Not. ad Alexiad, p. 41).

[5] The copy of the treaty (Alexiad, l. xiii. p. 406-416 [c. 12]) is an original and curious piece, which would require, and might afford, a good map of the principality of Antioch.

were finally delivered by the death of an adversary whom neither
oaths could bind nor dangers could appal nor prosperity could
satiate. His children succeeded to the principality of Antioch ;
but the boundaries were strictly defined, the homage was clearly
stipulated, and the cities of Tarsus and Malmistra [6] were restored
to the Byzantine emperors. Of the coast of Anatolia, they
possessed the entire circuit from Trebizond to the Syrian gates.
The Seljukian dynasty of Roum [7] was separated on all sides from
the sea and their Musulman brethren ; the power of the sultans
was shaken by the victories, and even the defeats, of the Franks ;
and after the loss of Nice they removed their throne to Cogni
or Iconium, an obscure and inland town above three hundred
miles from Constantinople.[8] Instead of trembling for their
capital, the Comnenian princes waged an offensive war against
the Turks, and the first crusade prevented the fall of the declining empire.

Expeditions
by land : the
first crusade,
A.D. 1101 ;
the second of
Conrad III.
and Louis
VII. A.D.
1147 ; the
third of
Frederic I.
A.D. 1189
In the twelfth century, three great emigrations marched by
land from the West to the relief of Palestine. The soldiers
and pilgrims of Lombardy, France, and Germany were excited
by the example and success of the first crusade.[9] Forty-eight
years after the deliverance of the holy sepulchre, the emperor
and the French king, Conrad the Third and Louis the Seventh,
undertook the second crusade to support the falling fortunes of
the Latins.[10] A grand division of the third crusade was led

---

[6] [Mopsuestia, corrupted to Mampsista, Mansista, Mamista (Anna Comnena),
whence Mamistra, Malmistra. In Turkish the form has become ultimately
Missis ; in Arabic it is al-Massīsa.]

[7] See in the learned work of M. de Guignes (tom. ii. part ii.) the history of the
Seljukians of Iconium, Aleppo, and Damascus, as far as it may be collected from
the Greeks, Latins, and Arabians. The last are ignorant or regardless of the
affairs of *Roum*.

[8] Iconium is mentioned as a station by Xenophon, and by Strabo [xii. 6, section
1] with the ambiguous title of Κωμόπολις (Cellarius, tom. ii. p. 121). Yet St. Paul
found in that place a multitude (πλῆθος) of Jews and Gentiles. Under the corrupt
name of *Kunijah*, it is described as a great city, with a river and gardens, three
leagues from the mountains, and decorated (I know not why) with Plato's tomb
(Abulfeda, tabul. xvii. p. 303, vers. Reiske ; and the Index Geographicus of Schultens
from Ibn Said). [It is Soatra, not Iconium, that Strabo describes as Κωμόπολις in
the passage to which Cellarius refers.]

[9] For this supplement to the first crusade, see Anna Comnena (Alexias, l. xi. p.
331 [c. 8], &c.) and the viiith book of Albert Aquensis [and Ekkehard of Aura,
Hierosolymita, in Recueil, Hist. Occ. vol. v.].

[10] For the second crusade of Conrad III. and Louis VII. see William of Tyre
(l. xvi. c. 18-29), Otho of Frisingen (l. i. c. 34-45, 59, 60), Matthew Paris (Hist.
Major, p. 68), Struvius (Corpus Hist. Germanicæ, p. 372, 373), Scriptores Rerum
Francicarum a Duchesne, tom. iv. ; Nicetas, in Vit. Manuel. l. i. c. 4, 5, 6, p.
41-48 ; Cinnamus, l. ii. p. 41-49 [p. 73 sqq., ed. Bonn]. [Among the western

by the emperor Frederic Barbarossa,[11] who sympathized with
his brothers of France and England in the common loss of
Jerusalem.  These three expeditions may be compared in their
resemblance of the greatness of numbers, their passage through
the Greek empire, and the nature and event of their Turkish
warfare ; and a brief parallel may save the repetition of a tedious
narrative.  However splendid it may seem, a regular story of
the crusades would exhibit a perpetual return of the same
causes and effects ; and the frequent attempts for the defence
and recovery of the Holy Land would appear so many faint and
unsuccessful copies of the original.

I. Of the swarms that so closely trod in the footsteps of the _Their_
first pilgrims, the chiefs were equal in rank, though unequal in _number_
fame and merit, to Godfrey of Bouillon and his fellow-adven-
turers.  At their head were displayed the banners of the dukes
of Burgundy, Bavaria and Aquitain : the first a descendant of
Hugh Capet, the second a father of the Brunswick line ; the
archbishop of Milan, a temporal prince, transported, for the
benefit of the Turks, the treasures and ornaments of his church
and palace ; and the veteran crusaders, Hugh the Great and
Stephen of Chartres, returned to consummate their unfinished
vow.  The huge and disorderly bodies of their followers moved
forwards in two columns ; and, if the first consisted of two
hundred and sixty thousand persons, the second might possibly
amount to sixty thousand horse and one hundred thousand
foot.[12]  The armies of the second crusade might have claimed
the conquest of Asia : the nobles of France and Germany were
animated by the presence of their sovereigns ; and both the
rank and personal characters of Conrad and Louis gave a dignity to their cause and a discipline to their force, which might
be vainly expected from the feudatory chiefs.  The cavalry of

ources, Odo de Deogilo (Deuil), De Profectione Ludovici VII. regis Francorum in
orientem, is important : Migne, Patrol. Lat. vol. 185, p. 1205 _sqq_.  For a full
numeration of the sources, see Kugler, Studien zur Geschichte des zweiten
Kreuzzuges, 1866.]

[11] For the third crusade, of Frederic Barbarossa, see Nicetas in Isaac. Angel.
ii. c. 3-8, p. 257-266 ; Struv. (Corpus Hist. Germ. p. 414), and two historians,
who probably were spectators, Tagino (in Scriptor. Freher. tom. i. p. 406-416,
edit. Struv.) and the Anonymus de Expeditione Asiaticâ ; Fred. I. (in Canisii,
Antiq. Lection. tom. iii. p. ii. p. 498-526, edit. Basnage).  [A. Chroust, Tageno,
Ansbert und die Historia Peregrinorum, 1892.  Fischer, Geschichte des Kreuzzuges
Kaiser Friedrichs I., 1870.]

[12] Anne, who states these later swarms at 40,000 horse, and 100,000 foot, calls
them Normans, and places at their head two brothers of Flanders.  The Greeks
were strangely ignorant of the names, families, and possessions of the Latin
princes.

the emperor, and that of the king, was each composed of
seventy thousand knights and their immediate attendants in
the field,[13] and, if the light-armed troops, the peasant infantry,
the women and children, the priests and monks, be rigorously
excluded, the full account will scarcely be satisfied with four
hundred thousand souls.  The West, from Rome to Britain, was
called into action ; the kings of Poland and Bohemia obeyed
the summons of Conrad ; and it is affirmed by the Greeks and
Latins that, in the passage of a strait or river, the Byzantine
agents, after a tale of nine hundred thousand, desisted from the
endless and formidable computation.[14]  In the third crusade, as
the French and English preferred the navigation of the Mediterranean, the host of Frederic Barbarossa was less numerous.
Fifteen thousand knights, and as many squires, were the flower
of the German chivalry ; sixty thousand horse and one hundred
thousand foot were mustered by the emperor in the plains of
Hungary ; and after such repetitions we shall no longer be
startled at the six hundred thousand pilgrims which credulity
has ascribed to this last emigration.[15]  Such extravagant reckonings prove only the astonishment of contemporaries ; but their
astonishment most strongly bears testimony to the existence of
an enormous though indefinite multitude.  The Greeks might
applaud their superior knowledge of the arts and stratagems of
war, but they confessed the strength and courage of the French
cavalry and the infantry of the Germans ; [16] and the strangers

[13] William of Tyre, and Matthew Paris, reckon 70,000 loricati in each of the
armies.  [The same number is given by the Annals of Pöhlde (ad ann. 1147),
which were first published in Pertz's Mon. xvi. p. 48 sqq., in 1859.]

[14] The imperfect enumeration is mentioned by Cinnamus (ἐννενήκοντα μυριάδες)
[in connexion with the crossing of the Danube ; Nicetas (p. 87, ed. Bonn) speaks
of a numbering at the crossing of the Hellespont], and confirmed by Odo de Diogilo
apud Ducange ad Cinnamum, with the more precise sum of 900,556.  [The
Annals of Magdeburg give 650,000, and the Annals of Egmond 1,600,000.]  Why
must therefore the version and comment suppose the modest and insufficient
reckoning of 90,000 ?  Does not Godfrey of Viterbo (Pantheon, p. xix. in Muratori, tom. vii. p. 462) exclaim
———Numerum si poscere quæras—
Millia millena milites agmen erat ?

[15] This extravagant account is given by Albert of Stade (apud Struvium, p. 414
[Chronicon ; Pertz, Mon. xvi. p. 283 sqq.]) ; my calculation is borrowed from
Godfrey of Viterbo, Arnold of Lubeck [Chronica Slavorum, Pertz, Mon. xxi. p.
115 sqq.], apud eundem, and Bernard Thesaur. (c. 169, p. 804).  The original
writers are silent.  The Mahometans gave him 200,000 or 260,000 men (Bohadin,
in Vit. Saladin. p. 110).

[16] I must observe that, in the second and third crusades, the subjects of Conrad and Frederic are styled by the Greeks and Orientals Alamanni.  The Lech
and Tzechi of Cinnamus are the Poles and Bohemians ; and it is for the French
that he reserves the ancient appellation of Germans.  He likewise names the
Βρίττιοι, or Βριταννοί [Βρίττιοί τε καὶ Βρετανοί, ii. 12].

are described as an iron race, of gigantic stature, who darted fire from their eyes, and spilt blood like water on the ground. Under the banners of Conrad, a troop of females rode in the attitude and armour of men; and the chief of these Amazons, from their gilt spurs and buskins, obtained the epithet of the Golden-footed Dame.

II. The numbers and character of the strangers was an object of terror to the effeminate Greeks, and the sentiment of fear is nearly allied to that of hatred.    This aversion was suspended or softened by the apprehension of the Turkish power; and the invectives of the Latins will not bias our more candid belief that the Emperor Alexius dissembled their insolence, eluded their hostilities, counselled their rashness, and opened to their ardour the road of pilgrimage and conquest.   But, when the Turks had been driven from Nice and the sea-coast, when the Byzantine princes no longer dreaded the distant sultans of Cogni, they felt with purer indignation the free and frequent passage of the western barbarians, who violated the majesty, and endangered the safety, of the empire.    The second and third crusades were undertaken under the reign of Manuel Comnenus and Isaac Angelus.    Of the former, the passions were always impetuous and often malevolent; and the natural union of a cowardly and a mischievous temper was exemplified in the latter, who, without merit or mercy, could punish a tyrant and occupy his throne. It was secretly, and perhaps tacitly, resolved by the prince and people to destroy, or at least to discourage, the pilgrims by every species of injury and oppression; and their want of prudence and discipline continually afforded the pretence or the opportunity.    The Western monarchs had stipulated a safe passage and fair market in the country of their Christian brethren; the treaty had been ratified by oaths and hostages; and the poorest soldier of Frederic's army was furnished with three marks of silver to defray his expenses on the road.    But every engagement was violated by treachery and injustice; and the complaints of the Latins are attested by the honest confession of a Greek historian, who has dared to prefer truth to his country.[17]    Instead of an hospitable reception, the gates of the cities, both in Europe and Asia, were closely barred against the crusaders; and the scanty pittance of food was let down in baskets from the

*Passage through the Greek empire*

---

[17] Nicetas was a child at the second crusade, but in the third he commanded against the Franks the important post of Philippopolis. Cinnamus is infected with national prejudice and pride.

walls. Experience or foresight might excuse this timid jealousy ; but the common duties of humanity prohibited the mixture of chalk, or other poisonous ingredients, in the bread ; and, should Manuel be acquitted of any foul connivance, he is guilty of coining base money for the purpose of trading with the pilgrims. In every step of their march they were stopped or misled : the governors had private orders to fortify the passes, and break down the bridges against them : the stragglers were pillaged and murdered ; the soldiers and horses were pierced in the woods by arrows from an invisible hand ; the sick were burnt in their beds ; and the dead bodies were hung on gibbets along the highways. These injuries exasperated the champions of the cross, who were not endowed with evangelical patience ; and the Byzantine princes, who had provoked the unequal conflict, promoted the embarkation and march of these formidable guests. On the verge of the Turkish frontiers, Barbarossa spared the guilty Philadelphia,[18] rewarded the hospitable Laodicea, and deplored the hard necessity that had stained his sword with any drops of Christian blood. In their intercourse with the monarchs of Germany and France, the pride of the Greeks was exposed to an anxious trial. They might boast that on the first interview the seat of Louis was a low stool beside the throne of Manuel ; [19] but no sooner had the French king transported his army beyond the Bosphorus than he refused the offer of a second conference, unless his brother would meet him on equal terms, either on the sea or land. With Conrad and Frederic the ceremonial was still nicer and more difficult : like the successors of Constantine, they styled themselves Emperors of the Romans,[20] and firmly maintained the purity of their title and dignity. The first of these representatives of Charlemagne would only converse with Manuel on horseback in the open field ; the second, by passing the Hellespont rather than the Bosphorus, declined the view of Constantinople and its sovereign. An emperor who

[18] The conduct of the Philadelphians is blamed by Nicetas, while the anonymous German accuses the rudeness of his countrymen (culpâ nostrâ). History would be pleasant, if we were embarrassed only by *such* contradictions. It is likewise from Nicetas that we learn the pious and humane sorrow of Frederic.

[19] Χθαμαλὴ ἕδρα, which Cinnamus translates into Latin by the word Σελλίον. Ducange works very hard to save his king and country from such ignominy (sur Joinville, dissertat. xxvii. p. 317-320). Louis afterwards insisted on a meeting in mari ex æquo, not ex equo, according to the laughable readings of some Mss.

[20] Ego Romanorum imperator sum, ille Romaniorum (Anonym. Canis. p. 512). The public and historical style of the Greeks was 'Ρὴξ . . . *princeps*. Yet Cinnamus owns, that 'Ιμπεράτωρ is synonymous to Βασιλεύς.

had been crowned at Rome was reduced in the Greek epistles
to the humble appellation of *Rex*, or prince of the Alemanni ;
and the vain and feeble Angelus affected to be ignorant of the
name of one of the greatest men and monarchs of the age.
While they viewed with hatred and suspicion the Latin pilgrims,
the Greek emperors maintained a strict, though secret, alliance
with the Turks and Saracens.   Isaac Angelus complained that
by his friendship for the great Saladin he had incurred the
enmity of the Franks ; and a mosque was founded at Constantinople for the public exercise of the religion of Mahomet.[21]

III. The swarms that followed the first crusade were destroyed   Turkish
in Anatolia by famine, pestilence, and the Turkish arrows : and   warfare
the princes only escaped with some squadrons of horse to accomplish their lamentable pilgrimage.    A just opinion may be
formed of their knowledge and humanity : of their knowledge,
from the design of subduing Persia and Chorasan in their way to
Jerusalem ; of their humanity, from the massacre of the Christian people, a friendly city, who came out to meet them with
palms and crosses in their hands.   The arms of Conrad and
Louis were less cruel and imprudent ; but the event of the
second crusade was still more ruinous to Christendom ; and the
Greek Manuel is accused by his own subjects of giving seasonable intelligence to the sultan, and treacherous guides to the
Latin princes.   Instead of crushing the common foe, by a double
attack at the same time but on different sides, the Germans were
urged by emulation, and the French were retarded by jealousy.
Louis had scarcely passed the Bosphorus when he was met by the   [October,
returning emperor, who had lost the greatest part of his army in   A.D. 1147]
glorious, but unsuccessful, actions on the banks of the Mæander.[22]
The contrast of the pomp of his rival hastened the retreat of
Conrad : the desertion of his independent vassals reduced him
to his hereditary troops; and he borrowed some Greek vessels to
execute by sea the pilgrimage of Palestine.[23]   Without studying

---

[21] In the epistles of Innocent III. (xiii. p. 184), and the History of Bohadin (p.
129, 130), see the views of a pope and a cadhi on this *singular* toleration.

[22] [This is quite inaccurate.   At Nicæa, Conrad divided his army.   About
15,000 took the coast route under Bishop Otto of Freising, the king's brother.
Conrad himself proceeded to Dorylæum with the main army ; but after a march
of eleven days want of supplies forced him to turn back.   The enemy harassed
the retreat, and 30,000 Germans are said to have perished.   Conrad met the
French army at Nicæa.]

[23] [This, too, is an inaccurate account.   Louis proceeded westward to Lopadium,
where he waited for Conrad, and the two kings advanced together (by
Adramyttium, Pergamum, and Smyrna) to Ephesus, where they spent Christ-

the lessons of experience or the nature of war, the king of France advanced through the same country to a similar fate. The vanguard, which bore the royal banner and the oriflamme of St. Denys,[24] had doubled their march with rash and inconsiderate speed ; and the rear, which the king commanded in person, no longer found their companions in the evening camp. In darkness and disorder, they were encompassed, assaulted, and overwhelmed by the innumerable host of Turks, who, in the art of war, were superior to the Christians of the twelfth century. Louis, who climbed a tree in the general discomfiture, was saved by his own valour and the ignorance of his adversaries ; and with the dawn of day he escaped alive, but almost alone, to the camp of the vanguard. But, instead of pursuing his expedition by land, he was rejoiced to shelter the relics of his army in the friendly seaport of Satalia.[25] From thence he embarked for Antioch ; but so penurious was the supply of Greek vessels that they could only afford room for his knights and nobles ; and the plebeian crowd of infantry was left to perish at the foot of the Pamphylian hills. The emperor and the king embraced and wept at Jerusalem ; their martial trains, the remnant of mighty armies, were joined to the Christian powers of Syria, and a fruitless siege of Damascus was the final effort of the second crusade. Conrad and Louis embarked for Europe with the personal fame of piety and courage ; but the Orientals had braved these potent monarchs of the Franks, with whose names and military forces they had been so often threatened.[26] Perhaps they had still

[Near Laodicea]

[February 2, A.D. 1148]

mas, 1147, as we learn from Conrad's letter to the abbot Wibald of Corvei (an important source ; published in the collection of Wibald's letters, in Jaffé, Bib. rer. Germ. i. no. 78). Here Conrad fell ill, and returned to Constantinople on the Emperor's invitation. He set sail from Constantinople on March 10, 1148, and reached Acre in April. During their joint march Louis VII. appears to have shown every consideration to his fellow-sovereign. The other part of Conrad's army, led by Otto of Freising, was cut to pieces near Mount Cadmus, south of Laodicea. It is to this misfortune that Gibbon's " action on the banks of the Mæander " refers. The same region was also disastrous to the army of Louis VII.]

24 As counts of Vexin, the kings of France were the vassals and advocates of the monastery of St. Denys. The saint's peculiar banner, which they received from the abbot, was of a square form and a red or *flaming* colour. The *oriflamme* appeared at the head of the French armies from the xiith to the xvth century (Ducange sur Joinville, dissert. xviii. p. 244-253).

25 [The ancient Attalia.  ᾽ς ᾽Αττάλειαν.]

26 The original French histories of the second crusade are the Gesta Ludovici VII. published in the ivth volume of Duchesne's Collection. The same volume contains many original letters of the king, of Suger his minister, &c., the best documents of authentic history. [This work, the Gesta Ludovici VII., is a Latin translation from the Grandes Chroniques de France ; in which the history of the

more to fear from the veteran genius of Frederic the First, who in his youth had served in Asia under his uncle Conrad. Forty campaigns in Germany and Italy had taught Barbarossa to command ; and his soldiers, even the princes of the empire, were accustomed under his reign to obey. As soon as he lost sight of Philadelphia and Laodicea, the last cities of the Greek frontier, he plunged into the salt and barren desert, a land (says the historian) of horror and tribulation.[27] During twenty days, every step of his fainting and sickly march was besieged by the innumerable hordes of Turkmans,[28] whose numbers and fury seemed after each defeat to multiply and inflame. The emperor continued to struggle and to suffer ; and such was the measure of his calamities that, when he reached the gates of Iconium, no more than one thousand knights were able to serve on horseback. By a sudden and resolute assault, he defeated the guards, and stormed the capital, of the sultan,[29] who humbly sued for pardon and peace. The road was now open, and Frederic advanced in a career of triumph, till he was unfortunately drowned in a petty torrent of Cilicia.[30] The remainder of his Germans was consumed by sickness and desertion, and the emperor's son expired with the greatest part of his Swabian vassals at the siege of Acre. Among the Latin heroes, Godfrey of Bouillon and Frederic Barbarossa alone could achieve the passage of the Lesser Asia ; yet even their success was a warning, and in the last and most experienced ages of the crusades every nation preferred the sea to the toils and perils of an inland expedition.[31]

reign of Louis VII. is based on the Historia Ludovici, an extract from the Continuatio Sangermanensis of Aimoin (written c. 1170-80). This original has been edited recently by A. Molinier, Vie de Louis le Gros par Suger (caps. 1-7 are the work of the Abbot Suger), 1887.]

[27] Terram horroris et salsuginis, terram siccam, sterilem, inamaenam. Anonym. Canis. p. 517. The emphatic language of a sufferer.

[28] Gens innumera, sylvestris, indomita, praedones sine ductore. The sultan of Cogni might sincerely rejoice in their defeat. Anonym. Canis. p. 517, 518.

[29] See in the anonymous writer in the collection of Canisius, Tagino, and Bohadin (Vit. Saladin. p. 119, 120, c. 70 [leg. 69]), the ambiguous conduct of Kilidge Arslan, sultan of Cogni, who hated and feared both Saladin and Frederic.

[30] The desire of comparing two great men has tempted many writers to drown Frederic in the river Cydnus, in which Alexander so imprudently bathed (Q. Curt. l. iii. c. 4, 5). But, from the march of the emperor, I rather judge that his Saleph is the Calycadnus, a stream of less fame, but of a longer course. [This judgment is right. Frederick was drowned in the Geuk Su or Calycadnus on his march from Laranda to Seleucia.]

[31] Marinus Sanutus, A.D. 1321, lays it down as a precept, Quod stolus ecclesiae per terram nullatenus est ducenda. He resolves, by the divine aid, the objection, or rather exception, of the first crusade (Secreta Fidelium Crucis, l. ii. pars ii. c. i. p. 37).

Obstinacy of
the enthusi-
asm of the
crusades
The enthusiasm of the first crusade is a natural and simple
event, while hope was fresh, danger untried, and enterprise
congenial to the spirit of the times.  But the obstinate perseverance of Europe may indeed excite our pity and admiration ;
that no instruction should have been drawn from constant and
adverse experience ; that the same confidence should have
repeatedly grown from the same failures ; that six succeeding
generations should have rushed headlong down the precipice
that was open before them ; and that men of every condition
should have staked their public and private fortunes on the
desperate adventure of possessing or recovering a tomb-stone
two thousand miles from their country.  In a period of two
centuries after the council of Clermont, each spring and summer
produced a new emigration of pilgrim warriors for the defence
of the Holy Land ; but the seven great armaments or crusades
were excited by some impending or recent calamity : the nations
were moved by the authority of their pontiffs, and the example
of their kings : their zeal was kindled, and their reason was
silenced, by the voice of their holy orators ; and among these
Character and
mission of
St. Bernard.
A.D. 1091-1153 Bernard,[32] the monk or the saint, may claim the most honourable
place.  About eight years before the first conquest of Jerusalem,
he was born of a noble family in Burgundy ; at the age of
three-and-twenty, he buried himself in the monastery of Citeaux,
then in the primitive fervour of the institution ; at the end of
two years he led forth her third colony, or daughter, to the
valley of Clairvaux [33] in Champagne ; and was content, till the
hour of his death, with the humble station of abbot of his own
community.  A philosophic age has abolished, with too liberal
and indiscriminate disdain, the honours of these spiritual heroes.
The meanest amongst them are distinguished by some energies

---

[32] The most authentic information of St. Bernard must be drawn from his own
writings, published in a correct edition by Père Mabillon [2 vols. 1667], and
reprinted at Venice 1750, in six volumes in folio.  Whatever friendship could
recollect, or superstition could add, is contained in the two lives, by his disciples,
in the vith volume: whatever learning and criticism could ascertain, may be found
in the prefaces of the Benedictine editor.  [Mabillon's collection contains 444
letters ; in Migne's Patr. Lat. vol. 182 there are 495.  The life and works have been
translated into English by S. J. Eales, 1889.—Neander, Der heilige Bernhard und
sein Zeitalter (new ed. 1890) ; J. Cotter Morrison, The Life and Times of St. Bernhard of Clairvaux (new ed. 1884).  There are endless other monographs.]

[33] Clairvaux, surnamed the Valley of Absynth, is situate among the woods near
Bar-sur-Aube in Champagne.  St. Bernard would blush at the pomp of the church
and monastery ; he would ask for the library, and I know not whether he would be
much edified by a tun of 800 muids (914 1-7th hogsheads), which almost rivals
that of Heidelberg (Mélanges Tirés d'une Grande Bibliothèque, tom. xlvi. p.
15-20).

of the mind ; they were at least superior to their votaries and
disciples ; and in the race of superstition they attained the prize
for which such numbers contended. In speech, in writing, in
action, Bernard stood high above his rivals and contemporaries ;
his compositions are not devoid of wit and eloquence ; and he
seems to have preserved as much reason and humanity as may
be reconciled with the character of a saint. In a secular
life he would have shared the seventh part of a private
inheritance ; by a vow of poverty and penance, by closing
his eyes against the visible world,[34] by the refusal of all
ecclesiastical dignities, the abbot of Clairvaux became the oracle
of Europe and the founder of one hundred and sixty convents.
Princes and pontiffs trembled at the freedom of his apostolical
censure : France, England, and Milan consulted and obeyed
his judgment in a schism of the church ; the debt was repaid
by the gratitude of Innocent the Second ; and his successor
Eugenius the Third was the friend and disciple of the holy
Bernard. It was in the proclamation of the second crusade
that he shone as the missionary and prophet of God, who called
the nations to the defence of his holy sepulchre.[35] At the parliament of Vézelay he spoke before the king ; and Louis the [A.D. 1146]
Seventh, with his nobles, received their crosses from his hand.
The abbot of Clairvaux then marched to the less easy conquest
of the emperor Conrad : a phlegmatic people, ignorant of his [at Speyer]
language, was transported by the pathetic vehemence of his
tone and gestures ; and his progress from Constance to Cologne
was the triumph of eloquence and zeal. Bernard applauds his
own success in the depopulation of Europe ; affirms that cities
and castles were emptied of their inhabitants ; and computes
that only one man was left behind for the consolation of seven
widows.[36] The blind fanatics were desirous of electing him for

[34] The disciples of the saint (Vit. 1ma, l. iii. c. 2, p. 1232 ; Vit. 2da, c. 16, No.
45, p. 1383) record a marvellous example of his pious apathy. Juxta lacum etiam
Lausannensem totius diei itinere pergens, penitus non attendit, aut se videre non
vidit. Cum enim vespere facto de eodem lacu socii colloquerentur, interrogabat
eos ubi lacus ille esset ; et mirati sunt universi. To admire or despise St. Bernard
as he ought, the reader, like myself, should have before the windows of his library
the beauties of that incomparable landscape.

[35] Otho Frising. l. i. c. 4. Bernard. Epist. 363, ad Francos Orientales, Opp.
tom. i. p. 328. Vit. 1ma, l. iii. c. 4, tom. vi. p. 1235.

[36] Mandastis et obedivi . . . multiplicati sunt super numerum ; vacuantur urbes
et castella ; et *pene* jam non inveniunt quem apprehendant septem mulieres unum
virum ; adeo ubique viduæ vivis remanent viris. Bernard. Epist. p. 247 [*leg.* p.
246 ; *ep.* 247 ; p. 447 ap. Migne]. We must be careful not to construe *pene* as a
substantive.

their general ; but the example of the hermit Peter was before his eyes ; and, while he assured the crusaders of the divine favour, he prudently declined a military command, in which failure and victory would have been almost equally disgraceful to his character.[37] Yet, after the calamitous event, the abbot of Clairvaux was loudly accused as a false prophet, the author of the public and private mourning ; his enemies exulted, his friends blushed, and his apology was slow and unsatisfactory. He justifies his obedience to the commands of the pope ; expatiates on the mysterious ways of Providence ; imputes the misfortunes of the pilgrims to their own sins ; and modestly insinuates that his mission had been approved by signs and wonders.[38] Had the fact been certain, the argument would be decisive ; and his faithful disciples, who enumerate twenty or thirty miracles in a day, appeal to the public assemblies of France and Germany, in which they were performed.[39] At the present hour such prodigies will not obtain credit beyond the precincts of Clairvaux ; but in the preternatural cures of the blind, the lame, or the sick, who were presented to the man of God, it is impossible for us to ascertain the separate shares of accident, of fancy, of imposture, and of fiction.

Progress of the Mahometans

Omnipotence itself cannot escape the murmurs of its discordant votaries ; since the same dispensation which was applauded as a deliverance in Europe was deplored, and perhaps arraigned, as a calamity in Asia. After the loss in Jerusalem the Syrian fugitives diffused their consternation and sorrow : Bagdad mourned in the dust ; the Cadhi Zeineddin of Damascus tore his beard in the caliph's presence ; and the whole divan shed tears at his melancholy tale.[40] But the commanders of the faithful could only weep ; they were themselves captives in the hands of the Turks ; some temporal power was restored to the last age of the Abbassides ; but their humble ambition was con-

[37] Quis ego sum ut disponam [castrorum] acies, ut egrediar ante facies armatorum, aut quid tam remotum a professione meâ, [etiam] si vires [suppeterent etiam], si peritia [non deesset], &c. epist. 256, tom. i. p. 259 [leg. 258]. He speaks with contempt of the hermit Peter, vir quidam, epist. 363 [p. 586 ap. Migne].

[38] Sic [leg. sed] dicunt forsitan iste, unde scimus quod a Domino sermo egressus sit ? Quæ signa tu facis, ut credamus tibi ? Non est quod ad ista ipse respondeam ; parcendum verecundiæ meæ ; responde tu pro me, et pro te ipso, secundum quæ vidisti et audisti [leg. audisti et vidisti], et [leg. aut certe] secundum quod te [leg. tibi] inspiraverit Deus. Consolat. [De Consideratione ad Eugenium, iii. Papam] l. ii. c. 1 [p. 744 ap. Migne] ; Opp. tom. ii. p. 421-423.

[39] See the testimonies in Vita 1ma, l. iv. c. 5, 6. Opp. tom. vi. p. 1258-1261, l. vi. c. 1-17, p. 1287-1314.

[40] Abulmahasen apud de Guignes, Hist. des Huns, tom. ii. p. ii. p. 99.

fined to Bagdad and the adjacent province. Their tyrants, the Seljukian sultans, had followed the common law of the Asiatic dynasties, the unceasing round of valour, greatness, discord, degeneracy, and decay : their spirit and power were unequal to the defence of religion ; and, in his distant realm of Persia, the Christians were strangers to the name and the arms of Sangiar, the last hero of his race.[41] While the sultans were involved in the silken web of the harem, the pious task was undertaken by their slaves, the Atabeks,[42] a Turkish name, which, like the Byzantine patricians, may be translated by Father of the Prince. Ascansar, a valiant Turk, had been the favourite of Malek Shah, from whom he received the privilege of standing on the right hand of the throne ; but, in the civil wars that ensued on the monarch's death, he lost his head and the government of Aleppo. His domestic emirs persevered in their attachment to his son Zenghi, who proved his first arms against the Franks in the defeat of Antioch ; thirty campaigns in the service of the caliph and sultan established his military fame ; and he was invested with the command of Mosul, as the only champion that could avenge the cause of the prophet. The public hope was not disappointed : after a siege of twenty-five days, he stormed the city of Edessa, and recovered from the Franks their conquests beyond the Euphrates :[43] the martial tribes of Curdistan were subdued by the independent sovereign of Mosul and Aleppo : his soldiers were taught to behold the camp as their only country ; they trusted to his liberality for their rewards ; and their absent families were protected by the vigilance of Zenghi. At the head of these veterans, his son Noureddin gradually united the Mahometan powers ; added the kingdom of Damascus

*The Atabeks of Syria*

*[Guardians]*

*[Aksunkur]*

Zenghi.
A.D. 1127-1145
[1146]

Noureddin.
A.D. 1145
[1146]-1174

---

[41] See his *article* in the Bibliothèque Orientale of d'Herbelot, and de Guignes, tom. ii. p. i. p. 230-261. Such was his valour that he was styled the second Alexander ; and such the extravagant love of his subjects that they prayed for the sultan a year after his decease. Yet Sangiar might have been made prisoner by the Franks, as well as by the Uzes [Ghuzz]. He reigned near fifty years (A.D. 1103-1152), and was a munificent patron of Persian poetry. [Muizz ad-dīn Abū-l-Hārith Sinjar, A.D. 1117-1157 ; his power was practically confined to Khurāsān.]

[42] See the Chronology of the Atabeks of Irak and Syria, in de Guignes, tom. i. p. 254 ; and the reigns of Zenghi and Noureddin in the same writer (tom. ii. p. ii. p. 147-221), who uses the Arabic text of Benelathir, Ben Schouna, and Abulfeda ; the Bibliothèque Orientale, under the articles *Atabeks* and *Noureddin ;* and the Dynasties of Abulpharagius, p. 250-267, vers. Pocock. [For life of Zengī see Stanley Lane-Poole, Saladin, chaps. 3 and 4 ; for the genealogy of the Atabeks, the same writer's Mohammadan Dynasties.]

[43] William of Tyre (l. xvi. c. 4, 5, 7) describes the loss of Edessa, and the death of Zenghi. The corruption of his name into *Sanguin,* afforded the Latins a comfortable allusion to his *sanguinary* character and end, fit sanguine sanguinolentus.

to that of Aleppo, and waged a long and successful war against the Christians of Syria: he spread his ample reign from the Tigris to the Nile, and the Abbassides rewarded their faithful servant with all the titles and prerogatives of royalty. The Latins themselves were compelled to own the wisdom and courage, and even the justice and piety, of this implacable adversary.[44] In his life and government, the holy warrior revived the zeal and simplicity of the first caliphs. Gold and silk were banished from his palace; the use of wine from his dominions; the public revenue was scrupulously applied to the public service; and the frugal household of Noureddin was maintained from the legitimate share of the spoil, which he vested in the purchase of a private estate. His favourite Sultana sighed for some female object of expense: "Alas," replied the king, "I fear God, and am no more than the treasurer of the Moslems. Their property I cannot alienate; but I still possess three shops in the city of Hems: these you may take, and these alone can I bestow." His chamber of justice was the terror of the great and the refuge of the poor. Some years after the sultan's death, an oppressed subject called aloud in the streets of Damascus, "O Noureddin, Noureddin, where art thou now? Arise, arise, to pity and protect us!" A tumult was apprehended, and a living tyrant blushed and trembled at the name of a departed monarch.

Conquest of Egypt by the Turks. A.D. 1163-1169

By the arms of the Turks and Franks, the Fatimites had been deprived of Syria. In Egypt the decay of their character and influence was still more essential. Yet they were still revered as the descendants and successors of the prophet; they maintained their visible state in the palace of Cairo; and their person was seldom violated by the profane eyes of subjects or strangers. The Latin ambassadors[45] have described their own introduction through a series of gloomy passages, and glittering porticoes; the scene was enlivened by the warbling of birds and

[44] Noradinus [Nūr ad-dīn Mahmūd ibn Zangī] (says William of Tyre, l. xx. 33) maximus nominis et fidei Christianæ persecutor; princeps tamen justus, vafer, providus, et secundum gentis suæ traditiones religiosus. To this Catholic witness, we may add the primate of the Jacobites (Abulpharag. p. 267), quo non alter erat inter reges vitæ ratione magis laudabili, aut quæ pluribus justitiæ experimentis abundaret. The true praise of kings is after their death, and from the mouth of their enemies. [He won Damascus in 1154.]

[45] From the ambassador, William of Tyre (l. xix. c. 17, 18) describes the palace of Cairo. In the caliph's treasure were found, a pearl as large as a pigeon's egg, a ruby weighing seventeen Egyptian drams, an emerald a palm and a half in length, and many vases of crystal and porcelain of China (Renaudot, p. 536).

the murmur of fountains; it was enriched by a display of rich furniture and rare animals; of the Imperial treasures, something was shown, and much was supposed; and the long order of unfolding doors was guarded by black soldiers and domestic eunuchs. The sanctuary of the presence-chamber was veiled with a curtain; and the vizir, who conducted the ambassadors, laid aside his scymetar, and prostrated himself three times on the ground; the veil was then removed; and they beheld the commander of the faithful, who signified his pleasure to the first slave of the throne. But this slave was his master; the vizirs or sultans had usurped the supreme administration of Egypt; the claims of the rival candidates were decided by arms; and the name of the most worthy, of the strongest, was inserted in the royal patent of command. The factions of Dargham and Shawer [46] alternately expelled each other from the capital and country; and the weaker side implored the dangerous protection of the Sultan of Damascus, or the king of Jerusalem, the perpetual enemies of the sect and monarchy of the Fatimites. By his arms and religion the Turk was most formidable; but the Frank, in an easy direct march, could advance from Gaza to the Nile; while the intermediate situation of his realm compelled the troops of Noureddin to wheel round the skirts of Arabia, a long and painful circuit, which exposed them to thirst, fatigue, and the burning winds of the desert. The secret zeal and ambition of the Turkish prince [First expedition to Egypt] aspired to reign in Egypt under the name of the Abbassides; but the restoration of the suppliant Shawer was the ostensible motive of the first expedition; and the success was entrusted to the emir Shiracouh, [47] a valiant and veteran commander. Dargham was oppressed and slain; but the ingratitude, the [A.D. 1164] jealousy, the just apprehensions, of his more fortunate rival, soon provoked him to invite the king of Jerusalem to deliver Egypt from his insolent benefactors. To this union, the forces [Bilbeys besieged for 3 months] of Shiracouh were unequal; he relinquished the premature conquest; and the evacuation of Belbeis, or Pelusium, was the condition of his safe retreat. As the Turks defiled before the enemy, and their general closed the rear, with a vigilant eye, and a battle-axe in his hand, a Frank presumed to ask him if he were not afraid of an attack? "It is doubtless in your power to begin the attack," replied the intrepid emir, "but rest

[46] [Shāwar had been governor of Upper Egypt, Dirghām the chief of the guard; both became vezīrs.]

[47] [Asad ad-Dīn Abū l-Hārith Shīrkūh (= Lion of the Faith, Father of the Lion, Mountain Lion).]

assured that not one of my soldiers will go to paradise till he has sent an infidel to hell." His report of the riches of the land, the effeminacy of the natives, and the disorders of the government, revived the hopes of Noureddin; the caliph of Bagdad applauded the pious design; and Shiracouh descended into Egypt a second time with twelve thousand Turks and eleven thousand Arabs.[47a] Yet his forces were still inferior to the confederate armies of the Franks and Saracens; and I can discern an unusual degree of military art in his passage of the Nile, his retreat into Thebais, his masterly evolutions in the battle of Babain, the surprise of Alexandria, and his marches and counter-marches in the flats and valley of Egypt, from the tropic to the sea. His conduct was seconded by the courage of his troops, and on the eve of action a Mamaluke[48] exclaimed, " If we cannot wrest Egypt from the Christian dogs, why do we not renounce the honours and rewards of the sultan, and retire to labour with the peasants, or to spin with the females of the harem?" Yet after all his efforts in the field,[49] after the obstinate defence of Alexandria[50] by his nephew Saladin, an honourable capitulation and retreat concluded the second enterprise of Shiracouh; and Noureddin reserved his abilities for a third and more propitious occasion. It was soon offered by the ambition and avarice of Amalric, or Amaury, king of Jerusalem, who had imbibed the pernicious maxim that no faith should be kept with the enemies of God.[50a] A religious warrior, the great master of the hospital, encouraged him to proceed; the emperor of Constantinople either gave, or promised, a fleet to act with the armies of Syria; and the perfidious Christian, unsatisfied with spoil and subsidy, aspired to the conquest of Egypt. In this emergency the Moslems turned their eyes towards the sultan of Damascus; the vizir, whom danger encompassed on

[Second expedition to Egypt. A.D. 1167]

[Battle of al Babain]

[Amalric reigned, A.D. 1162-73]

[Third expedition to Egypt. A.D. 1168-9]

---

[47a] [So William of Tyre; but Ibn al Athīr gives the total number as 2000.]

[48] *Mamluc* [mamlūk], plur. *Mamalic* [mamālīk], is defined by Pocock (Prolegom. ad Abulpharag. p. 7), and d'Herbelot (p. 545), servum emptitium, seu qui pretio numerato in domini possessionem cedit. They frequently occur in the war of Saladin (Bohadin, p. 236, &c.); and it was only the *Bahartie* [Bahrī ; that is *of the river ;* they are opposed to the Burjī (*of the fort*) Mamlūks who succeeded them] Mamalukes that were first introduced into Egypt by his descendants [namely by the Sultān Al-Sālih (1240-1249), who organized Turkish slaves as a bodyguard]

[49] Jacobus a Vitriaco (p. 1116) gives the king of Jerusalem no more than 37 [*leg.* 370] knights. Both the Franks and the Moslems report the superior number of the enemy ; a difference which may be solved by counting or omitting the unwarlike Egyptians.

[50] It was the Alexandria of the Arabs, a middle term in extent and riches between the period of the Greeks and Romans, and that of the Turks (Savary, Lettres sur l'Egypte, tom. i. p. 25, 26).

[50a] [Acc. to William of Tyre, Amalric was personally unwilling to undertake the invasion.]

all sides, yielded to their unanimous wishes, and Noureddin seemed to be tempted by the fair offer of one third of the revenue of the kingdom.[50b] The Franks were already at the gates of Cairo; but the suburbs, the old city, were burnt on their approach; they were deceived by an insidious negotiation; and their vessels were unable to surmount the barriers of the Nile. They prudently declined a contest with the Turks in the midst of an hostile country;[50c] and Amaury retired into Palestine, with the shame and reproach that always adhere to unsuccessful injustice. After this deliverance, Shiracouh was invested with a robe of honour, which he soon stained with the blood of the unfortunate Shawer. For a while, the Turkish emirs condescended to hold the office of vizir; but this foreign conquest precipitated the fall of the Fatimites themselves; and the bloodless change was accomplished by a message and a word. The caliphs had been degraded by their own weakness and the tyranny of the vizirs: their subjects blushed, when the descendant and successor of the prophet presented his naked hand to the rude grip of a Latin ambassador; they wept when he sent the hair of his women, a sad emblem of their grief and terror, to excite the pity of the sultan of Damascus. By the command of Noureddin, and the sentence of the doctors, the holy names of Abubeker, Omar, and Othman were solemnly restored; the caliph Mosthadi, of Bagdad, was acknowledged in the public prayers as the true commander of the faithful; and the green livery of the sons of Ali was exchanged for the black colour of the Abbassides. The last of his race, the caliph Adhed,[51] who survived only ten days, expired in happy ignorance of his fate; his treasures secured the loyalty of the soldiers, and silenced the murmurs of the sectaries; and in all subsequent revolutions Egypt has never departed from the orthodox tradition of the Moslems.[52]

The hilly country beyond the Tigris is occupied by the pastoral tribes of the Curds;[53] a people hardy, strong, savage,

*(marginal notes)* [Fustat burned, Nov. 1168]

[End of the Fatimite caliphs. A.D. 1171]

[Sept. 13]

[Reign and character of Saladin. A.D. 1171-1193]

---

[50b] [This offer was made on the occasion of the *first* expedition.]

[50c] [They did not decline the contest, but the Turks evaded them.]

[51] [Al-Ādid Abū-Mohammad Abd-Allāh, A.D. 1160-71.]

[52] For this great revolution of Egypt, see William of Tyre (l. xix. 5-7, 12-31, xx. 5-12), Bohadin (in Vit. Saladin. p. 30-39), Abulfeda (in Excerpt. Schultens, p. 1-12), d'Herbelot (Bibliot. Orient. *Abhed, Fathemah,* but very incorrect), Renaudot (Hist. Patriarch. Alex. p. 522-525, 532-537), Vertot (Hist. des Chevaliers de Malthe, tom. i. p. 141-163, in 4to), and M. de Guignes (tom. ii. p. ii. p. 185-215).

[53] For the Curds, see de Guignes, tom. i. p. 416, 417, the Index Geographicus Schultens, and Tavernier, Voyages, p. i. p. 308, 309. The Ayoubites [the name Ayyūb corresponds to Job] descended from the tribe of the Rawadiæi [Rawadīya],

impatient of the yoke, addicted to rapine, and tenacious of the
government of their national chiefs.   The resemblance of name,
situation, and manners seem to identify them with the Carduchians of the Greeks;[54] and they still defend against the
Ottoman Porte the antique freedom which they asserted against
the successors of Cyrus.   Poverty and ambition prompted them
to embrace the profession of mercenary soldiers : the service of
his father and uncle prepared the reign of the great Saladin;[55]
and the son of Job or Ayub, a simple Curd, magnanimously
smiled at his pedigree, which flattery deduced from the Arabian

[before 3rd expedition]

caliphs.[56]   So unconscious was Noureddin of the impending
ruin of his house that he constrained the reluctant youth to
follow his uncle Shiracouh into Egypt; his military character

[2nd exped.]

was established by the defence of Alexandria ; and, if we may
believe the Latins, he solicited and obtained from the Christian
general the *profane* honours of knighthood.[57]   On the death of
Shiracouh, the office of grand vizir was bestowed on Saladin, as
the youngest and least powerful of the emirs ; but with the
advice of his father, whom he invited to Cairo, his genius obtained the ascendant over his equals, and attached the army
to his person and interest.   While Noureddin lived, these ambitious Curds were the most humble of his slaves ; and the indiscreet murmurs of the divan were silenced by the prudent
Ayub, who loudly protested that at the command of the sultan
he himself would lead his son in chains to the foot of the
throne.   "Such language," he added in private, " was prudent
and proper in an assembly of your rivals ; but we are now above

one of the noblest ; but, as *they* were infected with the heresy of the Metempsychosis,
the orthodox sultans insinuated that their descent was only on the mother's side,
and that their ancestor was a stranger who settled among the Curds.

[54] See the ivth book of the Anabasis of Xenophon.  The ten thousand suffered
more from the arrows of the free Carduchians than from the splendid weakness of
the Great King.

[55] We are indebted to the Professor Schultens (Lugd. Bat. 1755, 1732, in folio)
for the richest and most authentic materials, a life of Saladin [Salāh ad-Dīn], by his
friend and minister the cadhi Bohadin [Bahā ad-Dīn], and copious extracts from
the history of his kinsman, the Prince Abulfeda of Hamah.  To these we may add,
the article of *Salaheddin* in the Bibliothèque Orientale, and all that may be gleaned
from the dynasties of Abulpharagius.  [Also the articles in the Biographical dictionary of Ibn Khallikān, transl. by the Baron de Slane.  Marin's Histoire de
Saladin, publ. in 1758, is scholarly and well written.  A new life from the original
sources has just been written by Mr. Stanley Lane-Poole.]

[56] Since Abulfeda was himself an Ayoubite, he may share the praise, for imitat-
ing, at least tacitly, the modesty of the founder.

[57] Hist. Hierosol. in the Gesta Dei per Francos, p. 1152. [Itin. Reg. Ricard.,
i. c. 3 ; and cp. the romance L'ordene de chevalerie, in App. to Marin's Hist. de
Saladin.]   A similar example may be found in Joinville (p. 42, edition du
Louvre) ; but the pious St. Louis refused to dignify infidels with the order of
Christian knighthood (Ducange, Observations, p. 70).

# OF THE ROMAN EMPIRE 341

fear and obedience; and the threats of Noureddin shall not
extort the tribute of a sugar-cane." His seasonable death re- [A.D. 1174]
lieved them from the odious and doubtful conflict: his son, a
minor of eleven years of age, was left for a while to the emirs
of Damascus; and the new lord of Egypt was decorated by the
caliph with every title [58] that could sanctify his usurpation in [A.D. 1175]
the eyes of the people. Nor was Saladin long content with the
possession of Egypt; he despoiled the Christians of Jerusalem,
and the Atabeks of Damascus, Aleppo, and Diarbekir; Mecca [A.D. 1174-83]
and Medina acknowledged him for their temporal protector,
his brother subdued the distant regions of Yemen, or the Happy
Arabia; and at the hour of his death his empire was spread
from the African Tripoli to the Tigris, and from the Indian
ocean to the mountains of Armenia. In the judgment of his
character, the reproaches of treason and ingratitude strike
forcibly on *our* minds, impressed as they are with the principle
and experience of law and loyalty. But his ambition may in
some measure be excused by the revolutions of Asia,[59] which
had erased every notion of legitimate succession; by the recent
example of the Atabeks themselves; by his reverence to the
son of his benefactor; his humane and generous behaviour to
the collateral branches; by *their* incapacity and *his* merit; by
the approbation of the caliph, the sole source of all legitimate
power; and, above all, by the wishes and interest of the people,
whose happiness is the first object of government. In *his*
virtues, and in those of his patron, they admired the singular
union of the hero and the saint; for both Noureddin and Saladin
are ranked among the Mahometan saints; and the constant
meditation of the holy wars appears to have shed a serious and
sober colour over their lives and actions. The youth of the
latter [60] was addicted to wine and women; but his aspiring
spirit soon renounced the temptations of pleasure for the graver
follies of fame and dominion. The garment of Saladin was of
coarse woollen; water was his only drink; and, while he emu-

[58] In these Arabic titles, *religionis* [dīn] must always be understood; *Noureddin*, lumen r.; *Ezzodin*, decus; *Amadoddin*, columen; [*Bahā*,—lustre]: our
hero's proper name was Joseph, and he was styled *Salahoddin*, salus; *Al
Malichus Al Nasirus*, rex defensor; *Abu Medaffir* [Abū-l-Muzaffar], pater
victoriæ. Schultens, Præfat. [Saladin was not acknowledged by the Caliph
till A.D. 1175. He did not despoil Jerusalem nor the Atabegs of Damascus, who
did not exist apart from Aleppo.]
[59] Abulfeda, who descended from a brother of Saladin, observes, from many
examples, that the founders of dynasties took the guilt for themselves, and left the
reward to their innocent collaterals (Excerpt. p. 10).
[60] See his life and character in Renaudot, p. 537-548. [There is no evidence for
youthful dissipation on the part of Saladin, beyond his recorded resolve to renounce pleasure when he became vezīr of Egypt.]

lated the temperance, he surpassed the chastity, of his Arabian prophet. Both in faith and practice he was a rigid Musulman; he ever deplored that the defence of religion had not allowed him to accomplish the pilgrimage of Mecca; but at the stated hours, five times each day, the sultan devoutly prayed with his brethren; the involuntary omission of fasting was scrupulously repaid; and his perusal of the Koran on horseback, between the approaching armies, may be quoted as a proof, however ostentatious, of piety and courage.[61] The superstitious doctrine of the sect of Shafei was the only study that he deigned to encourage; the poets were safe in his contempt; but all profane science was the object of his aversion; and a philosopher, who had vented some speculative novelties, was seized and strangled by the command of the royal saint. The justice of his divan was accessible to the meanest suppliant against himself and his ministers; and it was only for a kingdom that Saladin would deviate from the rule of equity. While the descendants of Seljuk and Zenghi held his stirrup, and smoothed his garments, he was affable and patient with the meanest of his servants. So boundless was his liberality, that he distributed twelve thousand horses at the siege of Acre; and, at the time of his death, no more than forty-seven drams of silver, and one piece of gold coin, were found in the treasury; yet in a martial reign the tributes were diminished, and the wealthy citizens enjoyed without fear or danger, the fruits of their industry. Egypt Syria, and Arabia, were adorned by the royal foundations of hospitals, colleges, and mosques; and Cairo was fortified with a wall and citadel; but his works were consecrated to public use;[62] nor did the sultan indulge himself in a garden or palace of private luxury. In a fanatic age, himself a fanatic, the genuine virtues of Saladin commanded the esteem of the Christians the emperor of Germany gloried in his friendship;[63] the Greek emperor solicited his alliance;[64] and the conquest of Jerusalem diffused, and perhaps magnified, his fame both in the East and West.

His conquest of the kingdom. A.D. 1187, July 3 During its short existence, the kingdom of Jerusalem[65] was

[61] His civil and religious virtues are celebrated in the first chapter of Bohad: (p. 4-30), himself an eye-witness and an honest bigot.

[62] In many works, particularly Joseph's well in the castle of Cairo, the sulta and the patriarch have been confounded by the ignorance of natives and traveller

[63] Anonym. Canisii, tom. iii. p. ii. p. 504.

[64] Bohadin, p. 129, 130.

[65] For the Latin kingdom of Jerusalem, see William of Tyre, from the ixt to the xxiid book. Jacob. a Vitriaco, Hist. Hierosolym. l. i. and Sanutus, Secret Fidelium Crucis, l. iii. p. vi.-ix.

supported by the discord of the Turks and Saracens ; and both
the Fatimite caliphs and the sultans of Damascus were tempted
to sacrifice the cause of their religion to the meaner considerations of private and present advantage. But the powers of
Egypt, Syria, and Arabia were now united by an hero, whom
nature and fortune had armed against the Christians. All without now bore the most threatening aspect ; and all was feeble
and hollow in the internal state of Jerusalem.[66] After the two
first Baldwins, the brother and cousin of Godfrey of Bouillon, [Baldwin I.
the sceptre devolved by female succession to Melisenda, daughter A.D. 1100-18;
Baldwin II.
of the second Baldwin, and her husband Fulk, Count of Anjou, A.D. 1118-31]
[Fulk, 1131-43]
the father, by a former marriage, of our English Plantagenets.
Their two sons, Baldwin the Third and Amaury, waged a strenu- [Baldwin III.
ous and not unsuccessful war against the infidels ; but the son 1143-62;
Amalric,
of Amaury, Baldwin the Fourth, was deprived by the leprosy, a 1163-73]
[Baldwin IV.
gift of the crusades, of the faculties both of mind and body. His 1174-85;
Baldwin V.
sister, Sybilla, the mother of Baldwin the Fifth, was his natural 1185-6]
heiress. After the suspicious death of her child, she crowned
her second husband, Guy of Lusignan, a prince of a handsome [Guy, 1186-92]
person, but of such base renown that his brother Jeffrey was
heard to exclaim, " Since they have made *him* a king, surely
they would have made *me* a god ! " The choice was generally
blamed ; and the most powerful vassal, Raymond, count of Tripoli, who had been excluded from the succession and regency,
entertained an implacable hatred against the king, and exposed
his honour and conscience to the temptations of the sultan. Such

[66] [Some instructive observations have been made on the degeneracy of the race
of the western settlers in Palestine, as a cause of the decline of the kingdom, by
Bishop Stubbs (Itin. Regis. Ricardi, Introd. p. xcv. *sqq.*). "There were eleven
kings of Jerusalem in the twelfth century ; under the first four, who were all of
European birth, the state was acquired and strengthened ; under the second four,
who were born in Palestine, the effects of the climate and the infection of Oriental
habits were sadly apparent ; of these four three were minors at the time of their
accession, and one was a leper. The noble families which were not recruited, as
the royal family was, with fresh members from Europe, fell more early into weakness and corruption. . . . The moral degradation of the Franks need not have
entailed destruction from enemies not less degraded ; and their inferiority in numbers would have been more than compensated by the successions of pilgrims. . . .
But the shortness and precariousness of life was an evil without remedy and in its
effects irreparable. Of these the most noticeable was perhaps one which would
have arisen under any system, the difficulty of carrying on a fixed policy whilst the
administrators were perpetually changing ; but scarcely second to this was the
influence in successions which was thrown into the hands of women. The European
women were less exposed than the men to the injurious climate or to the fatigues
of military service ; and many of them having been born in Palestine were in a
measure acclimatized. The feudal rights and burdens of heiress-ship, marriage, and
dower, were strictly observed ; consequently most of the heiresses lived to have two
or three husbands and two or three families."]

were the guardians of the holy city : a leper, a child, a woman,
a coward, and a traitor ; yet its fate was delayed twelve years
by some supplies from Europe, by the valour of the military
orders, and by the distant or domestic avocations of their great
enemy.   At length, on every side the sinking state was encircled
and pressed by an hostile line ; and the truce was violated by
the Franks, whose existence it protected.   A soldier of fortune,
Reginald of Chatillon, had seized a fortress on the edge of the
desert, from whence he pillaged the caravans, insulted Mahomet, and threatened the cities of Mecca and Medina.   Saladin
condescended to complain ; rejoiced in the denial of justice ;
and, at the head of fourscore thousand horse and foot, invaded
the Holy Land.   The choice of Tiberias for his first siege was
suggested by the count of Tripoli, to whom it belonged ; and
the king of Jerusalem was persuaded to drain his garrisons, and
to arm his people, for the relief of that important place.[67]   By
the advice of the perfidious Raymond, the Christians were betrayed into a camp destitute of water ; he fled on the first onset,
with the curses of both nations ;[68] Lusignan was overthrown,
with the loss of thirty thousand men ; and the wood of the true
cross, a dire misfortune ! was left in the power of the infidels.
The royal captive was conducted to the tent of Saladin ; and,
as he fainted with thirst and terror, the generous victor presented him with a cup of sherbet cooled in snow, without
suffering his companion, Reginald of Chatillon, to partake of this
pledge of hospitality and pardon.   " The person and dignity of
a king," said the sultan, " are sacred ; but this impious robber
must instantly acknowledge the prophet, whom he has blas-
phemed, or meet the death which he has so often deserved."
On the proud or conscientious refusal of the Christian warrior,
Saladin struck him on the head with his scymetar, and Reginald
was dispatched by the guards.[69]   The trembling Lusignan was

[Violation of the Truce by attack on the Egyptian caravan. A.D. 1187] [Fortress of Karak]

[Battle of Hittin or Tiberias. A.D. 1187, July 4]

[67] Templarii ut apes bombabant et Hospitalarii ut venti stridebant, et barones
se exitio offerebant, et Turcopuli (the Christian light troops) semet ipsi in ignem
injiciebant (Ispahani de Expugnatione Kudsiticâ, p. 18, apud Schultens) : a specimen of Arabian eloquence, somewhat different from the style of Xenophon !   [80,000
as the number of Saladin's army must be an exaggeration.   He had 12,000 regular
levies.   Perhaps his force amounted to 25 or 30 thousand.   Mr. Oman (Art of
War, ii. p. 322) puts it at 60 or 70 thousand.   For a plan of the locality see *ib.* p. 326.]
[68] The Latins affirm, the Arabians insinuate, the treason of Raymond ; but, had
he really embraced their religion, he would have been a saint and a hero in the
eyes of the latter.   [The treachery of Raymond is not proved and is probably un-
true.   Cp. Ernoul, ed. Mas-Latrie, p. 169.]
[69] Reaud, Reginald, or Arnold de Châtillon, is celebrated by the Latins in his
life and death ; but the circumstances of the latter are more distinctly related by
Bohadin and Abulfeda ; and Joinville (Hist. de St. Louis, p. 70) alludes to the

sent to Damascus to an honourable prison, and speedy ransom ; but the victory was stained by the execution of two hundred and thirty knights of the hospital, the intrepid champions and [and the Temple] martyrs of their faith. The kingdom was left without a head ; and of the two grand masters of the military orders, the one was slain, and the other was made a prisoner. From all the cities, both of the sea-coast and the inland country, the garrisons had been drawn away for this fatal field. Tyre and Tripoli alone could escape the rapid inroad of Saladin ; and three months after the battle of Tiberias he appeared in arms before the gates of Jerusalem.[70]

He might expect that the siege of a city so venerable on and city of earth and in heaven, so interesting to Europe and Asia, would Jerusalem, A.D. 1187, rekindle the last sparks of enthusiasm ; and that, of sixty October 2 [3] thousand Christians, every man would be a soldier, and every soldier a candidate for martyrdom. But queen Sybilla trembled for herself and her captive husband ; and the barons and knights, who had escaped from the sword and the chains of the Turks, displayed the same factious and selfish spirit in the public ruin. The most numerous portion of the inhabitants were composed of the Greek and Oriental Christians, whom experience had taught to prefer the Mahometan before the Latin yoke ;[71] and the holy sepulchre attracted a base and needy crowd, without arms or courage, who subsisted only on the charity of the pilgrims. Some feeble and hasty efforts were made for the defence of Jerusalem ; but in the space of fourteen days a victorious army drove back the sallies of the besieged, planted their engines, opened the wall to the breadth of fifteen cubits, applied their scaling ladders, and erected on the breach twelve banners of the prophet and the sultan. It was in vain that a bare-foot procession of the queen, the women, and the monks implored the Son of God to save his tomb and his inheritance from impious violation. Their sole hope was in the mercy of the conqueror, and to their first suppliant deputation that mercy was sternly denied. "He had sworn to avenge the patience and long-suffering of the Moslems ; the hour of forgiveness was elapsed,

practice of Saladin, of never putting to death a prisoner who had tasted his bread and salt. Some of the companions of Arnold had been slaughtered, and almost sacrificed, in a valley of Mecca, ubi sacrificia mactantur (Abulfeda, p. 32). [Reginald had been prince of Antioch in 1154 (by marriage with Constance, the heiress. He had been a prisoner at Aleppo for sixteen years, and, after his release, married another heiress, Stephanie of Hebron. He took part in the battle of Ramlah in which Saladin was vanquished in 1177.]

[70] Vertot, who well describes the loss of the kingdom and city (Hist. des Chevaliers de Malthe, tom. i. l. ii. p. 226-278), inserts two original epistles of a knight-templar.

[71] Renaudot, Hist. Patriarch. Alex. p. 545.

and the moment was now arrived to expiate in blood, the innocent blood which had been spilt by Godfrey and the first crusaders." But a desperate and successful struggle of the Franks admonished the sultan that his triumph was not yet secure; he listened with reverence to a solemn adjuration in the name of the common Father of mankind; and a sentiment of human sympathy mollified the rigour of fanaticism and conquest. He consented to accept the city, and to spare the inhabitants. The Greek and Oriental Christians were permitted to live under his dominion; but it was stipulated, that in forty days all the Franks and Latins should evacuate Jerusalem, and be safely conducted to the sea-ports of Syria and Egypt; that ten pieces of gold should be paid for each man, five for each woman, and one for every child; and that those who were unable to purchase their freedom should be detained in perpetual slavery. Of some writers it is a favourite and invidious theme to compare the humanity of Saladin with the massacre of the first crusade. The difference would be merely personal; but we should not forget that the Christians had offered to capitulate, and that the Mahometans of Jerusalem sustained the last extremities of an assault and storm. Justice is indeed due to the fidelity with which the Turkish conqueror fulfilled the conditions of the treaty; and he may be deservedly praised for the glance of pity which he cast on the misery of the vanquished. Instead of a rigorous exaction of his debt, he accepted a sum of thirty thousand byzants, for the ransom of seven thousand poor; two or three thousand more were dismissed by his gratuitous clemency; and the number of slaves was reduced to eleven or fourteen thousand persons. In his interview with the queen, his words, and even his tears, suggested the kindest consolations; his liberal alms were distributed among those who had been made orphans or widows by the fortune of war; and, while the knights of the hospital were in arms against him, he allowed their more pious brethren to continue, during the term of a year, the care and service of the sick. In these acts of mercy, the virtue of Saladin deserves our admiration and love: he was above the necessity of dissimulation; and his stern fanaticism would have prompted him to dissemble, rather than to affect, this profane compassion for the enemies of the Koran. After Jerusalem had been delivered from the presence of the strangers, the sultan made his triumphant entry, his banners waving in the wind, and to the harmony of martial music. The great mosque of Omar, which had been converted into a church, was again consecrated to one God and his prophet Mahomet ; the walls and pavement were purified with rose-water ; and a pulpit, the labour of Noureddin, was erected in the sanctuary. But, when the golden cross that glittered on the dome was cast down, and dragged through the streets, the Christians of every sect uttered a lamentable groan, which was answered by the joyful shouts of the Moslems. In four ivory chests the patriarch had collected the crosses, the images, the vases, and the relics of the holy place : they were seized by the conqueror, who was desirous of presenting the caliph with the trophies of Christian idolatry. He was persuaded, however, to entrust them to the patriarch and prince of Antioch ; and the pious pledge was redeemed by Richard of England, at the expense of fifty-two thousand byzants of gold.[72]

The nations might fear and hope the immediate and final expulsion of the Latins from Syria ; which was yet delayed above a century after the death of Saladin.[73] In the career of victory, he was first checked by the resistance of Tyre ; the troops and garrisons, which had capitulated, were imprudently conducted to the same port : their numbers were adequate to the defence of the place ; and the arrival of Conrad of Montferrat inspired the disorderly crowd with confidence and union. His father, a venerable pilgrim, had been made prisoner in the battle of Tiberias ; but that disaster was unknown in Italy and Greece, when the son was urged by ambition and piety to visit the inheritance of his royal nephew, the infant Baldwin. The view of the Turkish banners warned him from the hostile coast of Jaffa ;[73a] and Conrad was unanimously hailed as the prince and champion of Tyre, which was already besieged by the conqueror of Jerusalem. The firmness of his zeal, and perhaps his knowledge of a generous foe, enabled him to brave the threats of the sultan, and to declare that, should his aged parent be exposed before the walls, he himself would discharge the first arrow, and glory in his descent from a Christian martyr.[74] The Egyptian

*The third crusade, by sea. A.D. 1188*

*[Tyre besieged. Nov. 9, A.D. 1187]*

[72] For the conquest of Jerusalem, Bohadin (p. 67-75) and Abulfeda (p. 40-43) are our Moslem witnesses. Of the Christian, Bernard Thesaurarius (c. 151-167) is the most copious and authentic ; see likewise Matthew Paris (p. 120-124). [See also Ibn al-Athīr ; Imād ad-Dīn ; Abū Shāma (in Goergens, Quellenbeiträge zur Geschichte der Kreuzzüge) ; De expugn. Terræ Sanctæ (cp. Appendix 1).]

[73] The sieges of Tyre and Acre are most copiously described by Bernard Thesaurarius (de Acquisitione Terræ Sanctæ, c. 167-179), the author of the Historia Hierosolymitana (p. 1150-1172, in Bongarsius), Abulfeda (p. 43-50), and Bohadin (p. 75-179).

[73a] [It was at Acre that Conrad called.]

[74] I have followed a moderate and probable representation of the fact ; by Vertot, who adopts without reluctance a romantic tale, the old marquis is actually exposed to the darts of the besieged.

fleet was allowed to enter the harbour of Tyre; but the chain was suddenly drawn, and five galleys were either sunk or taken; a thousand Turks were slain in a sally; and Saladin, after burning his engines, concluded a glorious campaign by a disgraceful retreat to Damascus. He was soon assailed by a more formidable tempest. The pathetic narratives, and even the pictures, that represented in lively colours the servitude and profanation of Jerusalem, awakened the torpid sensibility of Europe; the emperor, Frederic Barbarossa, and the kings of France and England assumed the cross; and the tardy magnitude of their armaments was anticipated by the maritime states of the Mediterranean and the Ocean. The skilful and provident Italians first embarked in the ships of Genoa, Pisa, and Venice. They were speedily followed by the most eager pilgrims of France, Normandy, and the Western Isles. The powerful succour of Flanders, Frise, and Denmark filled near an hundred vessels; and the northern warriors were distinguished in the field by a lofty stature and a ponderous battle-axe.[75] Their increasing multitudes could no longer be confined within the walls of Tyre, or remain obedient to the voice of Conrad. They pitied the misfortunes, and revered the dignity, of Lusignan, who was released from prison, perhaps to divide the army of the Franks. He proposed the recovery of Ptolemais, or Acre, thirty miles to the south of Tyre: and the place was first invested by two thousand horse and thirty thousand foot under his nominal command. I shall not expatiate on the story of this memorable siege, which lasted near two years, and consumed, in a narrow space, the forces of Europe and Asia. Never did the flame of enthusiasm burn with fiercer and more destructive rage; nor could the true believers, a common appellation, who consecrated their own martyrs, refuse some applause to the mistaken zeal and courage of their adversaries. At the sound of the holy trumpet, the Moslems of Egypt, Syria, Arabia, and the Oriental provinces assembled under the servant of the prophet:[76] his camp was pitched and removed within a few miles of Acre; and he laboured, night and day, for the relief of his brethren and

*[margin note: [Siege raised. Jan. 1, A.D. 1188]]*

*[margin note: Siege of Acre. A.D. 1189, July—A.D. 1191, July]*

---

[75] Northmanni et Gothi, et cæteri populi insularum quæ inter occidentem et septemtrionem sitæ sunt, gentes bellicosæ, corporis proceri, mortis intrepidæ, bipennibus armatæ, navibus rotundis quæ Ysnachiæ [= esnecca, νάκκα] dicuntur advectæ.

[76] The historian of Jerusalem (p. 1108) adds the nations of the East from the Tigris to India, and the swarthy tribes of Moors and Getulians, so that Asia and Africa fought against Europe.

the annoyance of the Franks. Nine battles, not unworthy of the name, were fought in the neighbourhood of Mount Carmel, with such vicissitude of fortune that in one attack the sultan forced his way into the city ; [76a] that in one sally the Christians penetrated to the royal tent. By the means of divers and pigeons a regular correspondence was maintained with the besieged ; and, as often as the sea was left open, the exhausted garrison was withdrawn, and a fresh supply was poured into the place. The Latin camp was thinned by famine, the sword, and the climate ; but the tents of the dead were replenished with new pilgrims, who exaggerated the strength and speed of their approaching countrymen. The vulgar was astonished by the report that the pope himself, with an innumerable crusade, was advanced as far as Constantinople. The march of the emperor filled the East with more serious alarms ; the obstacles which he encountered in Asia, and perhaps in Greece, were raised by the policy of Saladin ; his joy on the death of Barbarossa was measured by his esteem ; and the Christians were rather dismayed than encouraged at the sight of the duke of Swabia and his wayworn remnant of five thousand Germans. At length, in the spring of the second year, the royal fleets of France and England cast anchor in the bay of Acre, and the siege was more vigorously prosecuted by the youthful emulation of the two kings, Philip Augustus and Richard Plantagenet. After every resource had been tried, and every hope was exhausted, the defenders of Acre submitted to their fate ; a capitulation was granted, but their lives and liberties were taxed at the hard conditions of a ransom of two hundred thousand pieces of gold, the deliverance of one hundred nobles and fifteen hundred inferior captives, and the restoration of the wood of the holy cross. Some doubts in the agreement, and some delay in the execution, rekindled the fury of the Franks, and three thousand Moslems, almost in the sultan's view, were beheaded by the command of the sanguinary Richard.[77] By the conquest of Acre the Latin powers acquired a strong town and a convenient harbour ; but the advantage was most dearly purchased. The

---

[76a] [More than once.]

[77] Bohadin, p. 180 ; and this massacre is neither denied nor blamed by the Christian historians. Alacriter jussa complentes (the English soldiers), says Galfridus a Vinesauf (l. iv. c. iv. p. 346), who fixes at 2700 the number of victims ; who are multiplied to 5000 by Roger Hoveden (p. 697, 698). The humanity or avarice of Philip Augustus was persuaded to ransom his prisoners (Jacob. a Vitriaco, l. i. c. 98 [*leg.* 99], p. 1122).

minister and historian of Saladin computes, from the report of the enemy, that their numbers, at different periods, amounted to five or six hundred thousand; that more than one hundred thousand Christians were slain; that a far greater number was lost by disease or shipwreck; and that a small portion of this mighty host could return in safety to their native countries.[78]

Richard of England, in Palestine. A.D. 1191, 1192 Philip Augustus and Richard the First are the only kings of France and England who have fought under the same banners; but the holy service in which they were enlisted was incessantly disturbed by their national jealousy; and the two factions which they protected in Palestine were more averse to each other than to the common enemy. In the eyes of the Orientals the French monarch was superior in dignity and power; and, in the emperor's absence, the Latins revered him as their temporal chief.[79] His exploits were not adequate to his fame. Philip was brave, but the statesman predominated in his character; he was soon weary of sacrificing his health and interest on a [July, 1191] barren coast; the surrender of Acre became the signal of his departure: nor could he justify this unpopular desertion by leaving the duke of Burgundy, with five hundred knights and ten thousand foot, for the service of the Holy Land. The King of England, though inferior in dignity, surpassed his rival in wealth and military renown;[80] and, if heroism be confined to brutal and ferocious valour, Richard Plantagenet will stand high among the heroes of the age. The memory of *Cœur de Lion*, of the lion-hearted prince, was long dear and glorious to his English subjects; and, at the distance of sixty years, it was celebrated in proverbial sayings by the grandsons of the Turks and Saracens against whom he had fought: his tremendous name was employed by the Syrian mothers to silence their infants; and, if an horse suddenly started from the way, his rider was wont to exclaim, " Dost thou think King Richard is in that bush?"[81] His cruelty to the Mahometans was the

[78] Bohadin, p. 14. He quotes the judgment of Balianus and the prince of Sidon, and adds, Ex illo mundo quasi hominum paucissimi redierunt. Among the Christians who died before St. John d'Acre, I find the English names of De Ferrers, Earl of Derby (Dugdale, Baronage, p. i. p. 260), Mowbray (idem, p. 124), de Mandevil, de Fiennes, St. John, Scrope, Pigot, Talbot, &c.

[79] Magnus hic apud eos, interque reges eorum tum virtute, tum majestate eminens . . . summus rerum arbiter (Bohadin, p. 159). He does not seem to have known the names either of Philip or Richard.

[80] Rex Angliæ præstrenuus . . . rege Gallorum minor apud eos censebatur ratione regni atque dignitatis; sed tum divitiis florentior, tum bellicâ virtute multo erat celebrior (Bohadin, p. 161). A stranger might admire those riches; the national historians will tell with what lawless and wasteful oppression they were collected.

[81] Joinville, p. 17.   Cuides-tu que ce soit le roi Richart?

effect of temper and zeal; but I cannot believe that a soldier, so free and fearless in the use of his lance, would have descended to whet a dagger against his valiant brother, Conrad of Montferrat, who was slain at Tyre by some secret assassins.[82]   After [A.D. 1192] the surrender of Acre and the departure of Philip, the king of England led the crusaders to the recovery of the sea-coast; and the cities of Cæsarea and Jaffa were added to the fragments of the kingdom of Lusignan. A march of one hundred miles from Acre to Ascalon was a great and perpetual battle of [At Ascalon. Jan., A.D. eleven days.[83] In the disorder of his troops, Saladin remained 1192] on the field with seventeen guards, without lowering his stan- [Battle of dard or suspending the sound of his brazen kettle-drum: he [Arsuf. Sept. 7, A.D. 1191] again rallied and renewed the charge; and his preachers or heralds called aloud on the *Unitarians* manfully to stand up against the Christian idolaters. But the progress of these idolaters was irresistible; and it was only by demolishing the walls and buildings of Ascalon that the sultan could prevent them from occupying an important fortress on the confines of Egypt. During a severe winter the armies slept; but in the spring the Franks advanced within a day's march of Jerusalem, under the leading standard of the English king; and his active spirit intercepted a convoy, or caravan, of seven thousand camels. Saladin[84] had fixed his station in the holy city; but the city was struck with consternation and discord: he fasted; he prayed; [June, A.D. he preached; he offered to share the dangers of the siege; but [1192] his Mamalukes, who remembered the fate of their companions at Acre, pressed the sultan with loyal or seditious clamours to preserve *his* person and *their* courage for the future defence of the religion and empire.[85]   The Moslems were delivered by

[82] Yet he was guilty in the opinion of the Moslems, who attest the confession of the assassins that they were sent by the king of England (Bohadin, p. 225); and his only defence is an absurd and palpable forgery (Hist. de l'Académie des Inscriptions, tom. xvi. p. 155-163), a pretended letter from the prince of the assassins, the Sheich, or old man of the mountain, who justified Richard, by assuming to himself the guilt or merit of the murder. [For the forged letter see Röhricht, Regesta Regni Hierosol. 715. Cp. Itin. regis Ric. V. c. 26, where the old man of the mountain is called *Senior de Musse, i.e.,* of Masyâf, a fort of the Assassins in the Ansarîya Mts. See S. Guyard, Un grand-maître des Assassins.]

[83] [The march was 60 miles from Acre to Jaffa, where there was a long halt. Richard approached twice within sight of Jerusalem, Jan. and June, 1192.]

[84] See the distress and pious firmness of Saladin, as they are described by Bohadin (p. 7-9; 235-237), who himself harangued the defenders of Jerusalem. Their fears were not unknown to the enemy (Jacob. a Vitriaco, l. i. c. 100, p. 1123; Vinisauf, l. v. c. 50, p. 399).

[85] Yet, unless the sultan, or an Ayoubite prince, remained in Jerusalem, nec Curdi Turcis, nec Turci essent obtemperaturi Curdis (Bohadin, p. 236). He draws aside a corner of the political curtain.

the sudden or, as they deemed, the miraculous retreat of the
Christians;[86] and the laurels of Richard were blasted by the
prudence or envy of his companions. The hero, ascending an
hill, and veiling his face, exclaimed with an indignant voice,
"Those who are unwilling to rescue, are unworthy to view, the
sepulchre of Christ!" After his return to Acre, on the news
that Jaffa was surprised by the sultan, he sailed with some
merchant vessels, and leaped foremost on the beach; the castle
was relieved by his presence; and sixty thousand Turks and
Saracens fled before his arms. The discovery of his weakness
provoked them to return in the morning;[86a] and they found
him carelessly encamped before the gates with only seventeen
knights and three hundred archers. Without counting their
numbers, he sustained their charge; and we learn from the
evidence of his enemies, that the king of England, grasping his
lance, rode furiously along their front, from the right to the
left wing, without meeting an adversary who dared to encounter
his career.[87] Am I writing the history of Orlando or Amadis?

His treaty
and de-
parture. A.D.
1192, Sep-
tember

During these hostilities a languid and tedious negotiation[88]
between the Franks and the Moslems was started, and continued,
and broken, and again resumed, and again broken. Some acts
of royal courtesy, the gift of snow and fruit, the exchange of
Norway hawks and Arabian horses, softened the asperity of religious war: from the vicissitude of success the monarchs might
learn to suspect that Heaven was neutral in the quarrel; nor,
after the trial of each other, could either hope for a decisive
victory.[89] The health both of Richard and Saladin appeared to

[86] Bohadin (p. 237), and even Jeffrey de Vinisauf (l. vi. c. 1-8, p. 403-409)
ascribe the retreat to Richard himself; and Jacobus a Vitriaco observes that
in his impatience to depart, in alterum virum mutatus est (p. 1123). Yet Joinville,
a French knight, accuses the envy of Hugh, duke of Burgundy (p. 116), without
supposing, like Matthew Paris, that he was bribed by Saladin.

[86a] [Not exactly: four days later.]

[87] The expeditions to Ascalon, Jerusalem, and Jaffa are related by Bohadin
(p. 184-249) and Abulfeda (p. 51, 52). The author of the Itinerary, or the
monk of St. Albans, cannot exaggerate the Cadhi's account of the prowess
of Richard (Vinisauf, l. vi. c. 14-24, p. 412-421; [Matthew Paris], Hist. Major,
p. 137-143); and on the whole of this war there is a marvellous agreement between the Christian and Mahometan writers, who mutually praise the virtues of
their enemies. [For Jaffa cp. the Chron. Anglicanum of Ralph of Coggeshall
(Rolls Series), who was informed by Hugh Neville, an eye-witness.]

[88] See the progress of negotiation and hostility, in Bohadin (p. 207-260),
who was himself an actor in the treaty. Richard declared his intention of
returning with new armies to the conquest of the Holy Land; and Saladin
answered the menace with a civil compliment (Vinisauf, l. vi. c. 28, p. 423).

[89] The most copious and original account of this holy war is Galfridi a Vinisauf
Itinerarium Regis Anglorum Richardi et aliorum in Terram Hierosolymorum, in
six books, published in the iid volume of Gale's Scriptores Hist. Anglicanæ (p.

be in a declining state; and they respectively suffered the evils of distant and domestic warfare: Plantagenet was impatient to punish a perfidious rival who had invaded Normandy in his absence; and the indefatigable sultan was subdued by the cries of the people, who was the victim, and of the soldiers, who were the instruments, of his martial zeal. The first demands of the king of England were the restitution of Jerusalem, Palestine, and the true cross; and he firmly declared, that himself and his brother-pilgrims would end their lives in the pious labour, rather than return to Europe with ignominy and remorse. But the conscience of Saladin refused, without some weighty compensation, to restore the idols, or promote the idolatry, of the Christians: he asserted, with equal firmness, his religious and civil claim to the sovereignty of Palestine; descanted on the importance and sanctity of Jerusalem; and rejected all terms of the establishment, or partition, of the Latins. The marriage which Richard proposed, of his sister with the sultan's brother, was defeated [Joan] by the difference of faith; the princess abhorred the embraces of a Turk; and Adel, or Saphadin, would not easily renounce a plurality of wives. A personal interview was declined by Saladin, who alleged their mutual ignorance of each other's language; [89a] and the negotiation was managed with much art and delay by their interpreters and envoys. The final agreement was equally disapproved by the zealots of both parties, by the Roman pontiff, and the caliph of Bagdad. It was stipulated that Jerusalem and the holy sepulchre should be open, without tribute or vexation, to the pilgrimage of the Latin Christians; that after the demolition of Ascalon, they should inclusively possess the sea coast from Jaffa to Tyre; that the count of Tripoli and the prince of Antioch should be comprised in the truce; and that, during three years and three months, all hostilities should cease. The principal chiefs of the two armies swore to the observance of the treaty; but the monarchs were

247-429). [This work is still sometimes referred to under the name of Geoffrey Vinsauf, though Bishop Stubbs (who has edited it for the Rolls Series under the title Itinerarium Regis Ricardi, 1864) has demonstrated that it is not his work. It was written by an eye-witness of the capture of Jerusalem, and published between 1200 and 1220 (Stubbs, *op. cit.* Introduction, p. lxx.); and Bishop Stubbs advocates the authorship of a certain Richard, canon of the Holy Trinity in Aldgate (cp. App. 1).] Roger Hoveden [ed. Stubbs, 4 vols., 1868-71] and Matthew Paris [ed. Luard, 7 vols., 1872-83] afford likewise many valuable materials; and the former describes with accuracy the discipline and navigation of the English fleet. [Add Ralph of Coggeshall, Rolls Series; cp. Appendix 1.]

[89a] [Not the reason assigned. Saladin alleged unwillingness to fight with a king after a friendly interview.]

satisfied with giving their word and their right hand; and the
royal Majesty was excused from an oath, which always implies
some suspicion of falsehood and dishonour. Richard embarked
for Europe, to seek a long captivity and a premature grave
and the space of a few months concluded the life and glories

**Death of Saladin. A.D. 1193, March 4**

of Saladin. The Orientals describe his edifying death, which
happened at Damascus; but they seem ignorant of the equa
distribution of his alms among the three religions,[90] or of the
display of a shroud, instead of a standard, to admonish the Eas
of the instability of human greatness. The unity of empire wa
dissolved by his death; his sons were oppressed by the stronge
arm of their uncle Saphadin; the hostile interests of the Sultan
of Egypt, Damascus, and Aleppo [91] were again revived; and the
Franks or Latins stood, and breathed, and hoped, in their for
tresses along the Syrian coast.

**Innocent III. A.D. 1198-1216**

The noblest monument of a conqueror's fame, and of th
terror which he inspired, is the Saladine tenth, a general tax
which was imposed on the laity, and even the clergy, of th
Latin church, for the service of the holy war. The practice wa
too lucrative to expire with the occasion; and this tribute be
came the foundation of all the tithes and tenths on ecclesiastica
benefices which have been granted by the Roman pontiffs t
Catholic sovereigns, or reserved for the immediate use of th
apostolic see.[92] This pecuniary emolument must have tende
to increase the interest of the Popes in the recovery of Palestine
after the death of Saladin they preached the crusade by thei
epistles, their legates, and their missionaries; and the accom
plishment of the pious work might have been expected from
the zeal and talents of Innocent the Third.[93] Under that youn
and ambitious priest the successors of St. Peter attained th
full meridian of their greatness; and in a reign of eightee
years he exercised a despotic command over the emperors an
kings, whom he raised and deposed; over the nations, whom a
interdict of months or years deprived, for the offence of the
rulers, of the exercise of Christian worship. In the council

[90] Even Vertot (tom. i. p. 251) adopts the foolish notion of the indifference
Saladin, who professed the Koran with his last breath.
[91] See the succession of the Ayoubites, in Abulpharagius (Dynast. p. 227, &c
and the tables of M. de Guignes, l'Art de Vérifier les Dates, and the Bibliothèq
Orientale.
[92] Thomassin (Discipline de l'Eglise, tom. iii. p. 311-374) has copiously treat
of the origin, abuses, and restrictions of these *tenths*. A theory was started, b
not pursued, that they were rightfully due to the pope, a tenth of the Levites' ten
to the high-priest (Selden on Tithes. See his Works, vol. iii. p. ii. p. 1083).
[93] See the Gesta Innocentii III. [by a contemporary] in Muratori, Script. R
Ital. (tom. iii. p. 486-568) [Migne, P. L. 214, p. xvii *sqq.*].

the Lateran he acted as the ecclesiastical, almost as the temporal, sovereign of the East and West. It was at the feet of his legate that John of England surrendered his crown ; and Innocent may boast of the two most signal triumphs over sense and humanity, the establishment of transubstantiation and the origin of the inquisition. At his voice, two crusades, the fourth and the fifth, were undertaken ; but, except a king of Hungary, the princes of the second order were at the head of the pilgrims ; he forces were inadequate to the design ; nor did the effects correspond with the hopes and wishes of the pope and the people. The fourth crusade was diverted from Syria to Constantinople ; and the conquest of the Greek or Roman empire by the Latins will form the proper and important subject of the next chapter. In the fifth,[94] two hundred thousand Franks were landed at the eastern mouth of the Nile. They reasonably hoped that Palestine must be subdued in Egypt, the seat and torehouse of the sultan ; and, after a siege of sixteen months, he Moslems deplored the loss of Damietta. But the Christian rmy was ruined by the pride and insolence of the legate Pelagius, who, in the pope's name, assumed the character of general ; he sickly Franks were encompassed by the waters of the Nile and the Oriental forces ; and it was by the evacuation of Damietta that they obtained a safe retreat, some concessions for the pilgrims, and the tardy restitution of the doubtful relic of the true cross. The failure may in some measure be ascribed to the abuse and multiplication of the crusades, which were preached at the same time against the pagans of Livonia, the Moors of Spain, the Albigeois of France, and the kings of Sicily of the imperial family.[95] In these meritorious services the volunteers might acquire at home the same spiritual indulgence and a larger measure of temporal rewards ; and even the popes, in

*The fourth crusade.*
*A.D. 1203*

*The fifth.*
*A.D. 1218*

[94] See the vth crusade, and the siege of Damietta, in Jacobus a Vitriaco (l. iii. p. 25-1149, in the Gesta Dei of Bongarsius), an eye-witness, Bernard Thesaurarius Script. Muratori, tom. vii. p. 825-846, c. 190-207), a contemporary, and Sanutus Secreta Fidel. Crucis, l. iii. p. xi. c. 4-9), a diligent compiler ; and of the Arabians, Abulpharagius (Dynast. p. 294), and the Extracts at the end of Joinville (p. 533, 7, 540, 547, &c.). [Also the Gesta obsidionis Damiatae in Muratori, S. R. I. 8, p. 84 *sqq.* ; and Röhricht, Quinti belli sacri Script. min. p. 73 *sqq.* 1879. Holder-Egger has vindicated the authorship for John Cadagnellus (Neues Archiv, 16, 287 *f.* 1891).]

[95] To those who took the cross against Mainfroy, the pope (A.D. 1255) granted plenissimam peccatorum remissionem. Fideles mirabantur quod tantum eis protteret pro sanguine Christianorum effundendo quantum pro cruore infidelium quando (Matthew Paris, p. 785). A high flight for the reason of the xiiith century !

their zeal against a domestic enemy, were sometimes tempt
to forget the distress of their Syrian brethren. From the la
age of the crusades they derived the occasional command of
army and revenue ; and some deep reasoners have suspect
that the whole enterprise, from the first synod of Placentia, w
contrived and executed by the policy of Rome. The suspici
is not founded either in nature or in fact. The successors
St. Peter appear to have followed, rather than guided, the i
pulse of manners and prejudice ; without much foresight of t
seasons or cultivation of the soil, they gathered the ripe a
spontaneous fruits of the superstition of the times. They gather
these fruits without toil or personal danger : in the council
the Lateran, Innocent the Third declared an ambiguous reso
tion of animating the crusaders by his example ; but the pi
of the sacred vessel could not abandon the helm ; nor w
Palestine ever blessed with the presence of a Roman pontif

The emperor<br>Frederic II.<br>in Palestine.<br>A.D. 1228 The persons, the families, and estates of the pilgrims w
under the immediate protection of the popes ; and these spirit
patrons soon claimed the prerogative of directing their ope
tions, and enforcing, by commands and censures, the accompli
ment of their vow. Frederic the Second,[97] the grandson
Barbarossa, was successively the pupil, the enemy, and the vict
of the church. At the age of twenty-one years, and in obedie
to his guardian Innocent the Third, he assumed the cross ;
same promise was repeated at his royal and imperial coronatio
[Nov., A.D.<br>1225] and his marriage with the heiress of Jerusalem [98] for ever bo
him to defend the kingdom of his son Conrad. But, as Frede
advanced in age and authority, he repented of the rash enga
ments of his youth ; his liberal sense and knowledge taught l
to despise the phantoms of superstition and the crowns of A
he no longer entertained the same reverence for the success
of Innocent ; and his ambition was occupied by the restorat
of the Italian monarchy from Sicily to the Alps. But the succ

[96] This simple idea is agreeable to the good sense of Mosheim (Institut.
Eccles. p. 332) and the fine philosophy of Hume (Hist. of England, vol. i. p.

[97] The original materials for the crusade of Frederic II. may be drawn
Richard de St. Germano (in Muratori, Script. Rerum Ital. tom. vii. p. 1002-
[Chronica regni Siciliæ, a contemporary work preserved in two redactions :
Pertz, Mon. xix. p. 323 sqq. ; and Gaudenzi (in the Monumenti Storici, publi
by the Società Napolitana di storia patria), 1888]), and Matthew Paris (p. 286,
300, 302, 304). The most rational moderns are Fleury (Hist. Ecclés. tom.
Vertot (Chevaliers de Malthe, tom. i. l. iii.), Giannone (Istoria Civile di Na
tom. ii. l. xvi.), and Muratori (Annali d'Italia, tom. x.).

[98] [Yolande, daughter of John of Brienne.]

this project would have reduced the popes to their primitive simplicity; and, after the delays and excuses of twelve years, they urged the emperor, with entreaties and threats, to fix the time and place of his departure for Palestine. In the harbours of Sicily and Apulia, he prepared a fleet of one hundred galleys, and of one hundred vessels, that were framed to transport and land two thousand five hundred knights, with their horses and attendants; his vassals of Naples and Germany formed a powerful army; and the number of English crusaders was magnified to sixty thousand by the report of fame. But the inevitable or affected slowness of these mighty preparations consumed the strength and provisions of the more indigent pilgrims; the multitude was thinned by sickness and desertion, and the sultry summer of Calabria anticipated the mischiefs of a Syrian campaign. At length the emperor hoisted sail at Brundusium, with a fleet and army of forty thousand men; but [A.D. 1227] he kept the sea no more than three days; and his hasty retreat, which was ascribed by his friends to a grievous indisposition, was excused by his enemies as a voluntary and obstinate disobedience. For suspending his vow was Frederic excommunicated by Gregory the Ninth; for presuming, the next year, to accomplish his vow, he was again excommunicated by the same pope.[99] While he served under the banner of the cross, a crusade was preached against him in Italy; and after his return he was compelled to ask pardon for the injuries which he had suffered. The clergy and military orders of Palestine were previously instructed to renounce his communion and dispute his commands; and in his own kingdom the emperor was forced to consent that the orders of the camp should be issued in the name of God and of the Christian republic. Frederic entered Jerusalem [March 18, in triumph; and with his own hands (for no priest would perform the office) he took the crown from the altar of the holy sepulchre. But the patriarch cast an interdict on the church which his presence had profaned; and the knights of the hospital and temple informed the sultan [100] how easily he might be surprised and slain in his unguarded visit to the river Jordan. In such a state of fanaticism and faction, victory was hopeless and defence was difficult; but the conclusion of an advantageous peace may be imputed to the discord of the Mahometans, and their

[A.D. 1229]

---

[99] Poor Muratori knows what to think, but knows not what to say, "Chinò qui capo," &c. p. 322.

[100] [Al-Kāmil Moḥammad, 1218-1238.]

personal esteem for the character of Frederic. The enemy of
the church is accused of maintaining with the miscreants an intercourse of hospitality and friendship, unworthy of a Christian ;
of despising the barrenness of the land ; and of indulging a profane thought that, if Jehovah had seen the kingdom of Naples,
he never would have selected Palestine for the inheritance of
his chosen people. Yet Frederic obtained from the sultan the
restitution of Jerusalem, of Bethlem and Nazareth, of Tyre and
Sidon ; the Latins were allowed to inhabit and fortify the city ;
an equal code of civil and religious freedom was ratified for the
sectaries of Jesus, and those of Mahomet ; and, while the former
worshipped at the holy sepulchre, the latter might pray and
preach in the mosque of the temple,[101] from whence the prophet
undertook his nocturnal journey to heaven. The clergy deplored this scandalous toleration ; and the weaker Moslems
were gradually expelled ; but every rational object of the
crusades was accomplished without bloodshed ; the churches
were restored, the monasteries were replenished ; and, in the
space of fifteen years, the Latins of Jerusalem exceeded the
number of six thousand. This peace and prosperity, for which
they were ungrateful to their benefactor, was terminated by the

Invasion of
the Cariz-
mians.  A.D.
1243

irruption of the strange and savage hordes of Carizmians.[102]
Flying from the arms of the Moguls, those shepherds of the
Caspian rolled headlong on Syria ;[103] and the union of the Franks
with the sultans of Aleppo, Hems, and Damascus was insufficient to stem the violence of the torrent. Whatever stood
against them was cut off by the sword or dragged into captivity

[Battle of
Gaza.  A.D.
1244, Oct. 14]

the military orders were almost exterminated in a single battle
and in the pillage of the city, in the profanation of the holy
sepulchre, the Latins confess and regret the modesty and discipline of the Turks and Saracens.

St. Louis, and
the sixth
crusade.
A.D. 1248-1254

Of the seven crusades, the two last were undertaken by Louis
the Ninth, king of France, who lost his liberty in Egypt, and
his life on the coast of Africa. Twenty-eight years after his
death, he was canonized at Rome ; and sixty-five miracles were
readily found, and solemnly attested, to justify the claim of the

[101] The clergy artfully confounded the mosque, or church of the temple, with
the holy sepulchre ; and their wilful error has deceived both Vertot and Muratori.

[102] The irruption of the Carizmians, or Corasmins, is related by Matthew Paris
(p. 546, 547), and by Joinville, Nangis, and the Arabians (p. 111, 112, 191, 19
528, 530).

[103] [They were called in as allies by the Sultan of Egypt, As-Sālih Ayyūb.]

royal saint.[104] The voice of history renders a more honourable
testimony, that he united the virtues of a king, an hero, and a
man ; that his martial spirit was tempered by the love of private
and public justice ; and that Louis was the father of his people,
the friend of his neighbours, and the terror of the infidels.
Superstition alone, in all the extent of her baleful influence,[105]
corrupted his understanding and his heart ; his devotion stooped
to admire and imitate the begging friars of Francis and Dominic ;
he pursued with blind and cruel zeal the enemies of the faith ;
and the best of kings twice descended from his throne to seek
the adventures of a spiritual knight-errant. A monkish historian would have been content to applaud the most despicable
part of his character ; but the noble and gallant Joinville,[106]
who shared the friendship and captivity of Louis, has traced
with the pencil of nature the free portrait of his virtues, as well
as of his failings. From this intimate knowledge we may learn
to suspect the political views of depressing their great vassals,
which are so often imputed to the royal authors of the crusades.
Above all the princes of the middle age, Louis the Ninth successfully laboured to restore the prerogatives of the crown, but
it was at home, and not in the East, that he acquired for himself and his posterity ; his vow was the result of enthusiasm and
sickness ; and, if he were the promoter, he was likewise the
victim, of this holy madness. For the invasion of Egypt, France
was exhausted of her troops and treasures ; he covered the
sea of Cyprus with eighteen hundred sails ; the most modest
enumeration amounts to fifty thousand men ; and, if we might
trust his own confession, as it is reported by Oriental vanity,
he disembarked nine thousand five hundred horse, and one

[104] Read, if you can, the life and miracles of St. Louis, by the confessor of
Queen Margaret (p. 291-523. Joinville, du Louvre).

[105] He believed all that Mother-church taught (Joinville, p. 10), but he cautioned
Joinville against disputing with infidels. " L'omme lay," said he in his old
language, " quand il ot medire de la loy Chrestienne, ne doit pas deffendre la loy
Chrestienne ne mais que de l'espée, de quoi il doit donner parmi le ventre dedens,
ant comme elle y peut entrer " (p. 12 [c. 10]).

[106] I have two editions of Joinville : the one (Paris, 1688) most valuable for the
Observations of Ducange ; the other (Paris, au Louvre, 1761) most precious for
the pure and authentic text, a Ms. of which has been recently discovered. The
last editor proves that the history of St. Louis was finished A.D. 1309, without ex-
plaining, or even admiring, the age of the author, which must have exceeded
ninety years (Preface, p. xi., Observations de Ducange, p. 17). [Joinville's Histoire de Saint Louys IX. may be now most conveniently consulted in one of the
editions of Natalis de Wailly (1867, 1874, &c.). The fine Paris edition of 1761
was edited by Mellot, Sallier, and Capperonnier, and included the Annals of
William des Nangis.]

hundred and thirty thousand foot, who performed their pilgrimage under the shadow of his power.[107]

He takes
Damietta.
A.D. 1249
[May]

In complete armour, the oriflamme waving before him, Louis leaped foremost on the beach; and the strong city of Damietta, which had cost his predecessors a siege of sixteen months, was abandoned on the first assault by the trembling Moslems. But Damietta was the first and last of his conquests; and in the fifth and sixth crusades the same causes, almost on the same ground, were productive of similar calamities.[108] After a ruinous delay, which introduced into the camp the seeds of an epidemical disease, the Franks advanced from the sea-coast towards the capital of Egypt, and strove to surmount the unseasonable inundation of the Nile, which opposed their progress. Under the eye of their intrepid monarch, the barons and knights of France displayed their invincible contempt of danger and discipline: his brother, the count of Artois, stormed with inconsiderate valour the town of Massoura; and the carrier-pigeons announced to the inhabitants of Cairo, that all was lost. But a soldier, who

[A.D. 1250,
March]

afterwards usurped the sceptre, rallied the flying troops; the main body of the Christians was far behind their vanguard; and Artois was overpowered and slain. A shower of Greek fire was incessantly poured on the invaders; the Nile was commanded by the Egyptian galleys, the open country by the Arabs; all provisions were intercepted; each day aggravated the sickness and famine; and about the same time a retreat was found to be necessary and impracticable. The Oriental writers confess that Louis might have escaped, if he would have deserted his subjects: he was made prisoner, with the greatest part of his nobles; all who could not redeem their lives by service or

His captivity
in Egypt.
A.D. 1250,
April 5—
May 6

ransom were inhumanly massacred; and the walls of Cairo were decorated with a circle of Christian heads.[109] The king of France was loaded with chains; but the generous victor, a great-

[107] Joinville, p. 32; Arabic Extracts, p. 549.

[108] The last editors have enriched their Joinville with large and curious extracts from the Arabic historians, Macrizi, Abulfeda, &c. See likewise Abulpharagius (Dynast. p. 322-325), who calls him by the corrupt name of *Redefrans*. Matthew Paris (p. 683, 684) has described the rival folly of the French and English who fought and fell at Massoura. [Makrizi's important work is now accessible in Quatremère's French translation. See Appendix 1. The crusade has been recently narrated by Mr. E. J. Davis in a work entitled Invasion of Egypt in A.D. 1249 by Louis IX. of France and a History of the Contemporary Sultans of Egypt (1897).]

[109] Savary, in his agreeable Lettres sur l'Egypt, has given a description of Damietta (tom. i. lettre xxiii. p. 274-290) and a narrative of the expedition of St. Louis (xxv. p. 306). [In his Art of War, ii. p. 338-50, Mr. Oman gives a full account of the battle of Mansurah. He shows that the battle was lost because the reckless charge of Robert of Artois led to the separation of the cavalry and infantry; and it was only by a combination of cavalry and infantry that it was possible to deal with the horse-archers of the East.]

grandson of the brother of Saladin, sent a robe of honour to his royal captive; and his deliverance, with that of his soldiers, was obtained by the restitution of Damietta [110] and the payment of four hundred thousand pieces of gold. In a soft and luxurious climate, the degenerate children of the companions of Noureddin and Saladin were incapable of resisting the flower of European chivalry; they triumphed by the arms of their slaves or Mamalukes, the hardy natives of Tartary, who at a tender age had been purchased of the Syrian merchants, and were educated in the camp and palace of the sultan. But Egypt soon afforded a new example of the danger of prætorian bands; and the rage of these ferocious animals, who had been let loose on the strangers, was provoked to devour their benefactor. In the pride of conquest, Touran Shah,[111] the last of his race, was murdered by his Mamalukes; and the most daring of the assassins entered the chamber of the captive king, with drawn scymetars, and their hands imbrued in the blood of their sultan. The firmness of Louis commanded their respect;[112] their avarice prevailed over cruelty and zeal; the treaty was accomplished; and the king of France, with the relics of his army, was permitted to embark for Palestine. He wasted four years within the walls of Acre, unable to visit Jerusalem, and unwilling to return without glory to his native country.

[A.D. 1250, May 4]

[Return to France. A.D. 1254]

The memory of his defeat excited Louis, after sixteen years of wisdom and repose, to undertake the seventh and last of the crusades. His finances were restored, his kingdom was enlarged; a new generation of warriors had arisen, and he embarked with fresh confidence at the head of six thousand horse and thirty

---

[110] For the ransom of St. Louis, a million of byzants was asked and granted; but the sultan's generosity reduced that sum to 800,000 byzants, which are valued by Joinville at 400,000 French livres of his own time, and expressed by Matthew Paris by 100,000 marks of silver (Ducange, Dissertation xx. sur Joinville).

[111] [Al-Muazzam Tūrān Shāh, A.D. 1249-50.]

[112] The idea of the emirs to choose Louis for their sultan is seriously attested by Joinville (p. 77, 78), and does not appear to me so absurd as to M. de Voltaire (Hist. Générale, tom. ii. p. 386, 387). The Mamalukes themselves were strangers, rebels, and equals; they had felt his valour, they hoped his conversion: and such a motion, which was not seconded, might be made perhaps by a secret Christian in their tumultuous assembly. [An interesting monument of Mamlūk history at this time is a coin of the Mamlūk queen, Shajar ad-Durr, the Tree of Pearls, who had risen from the condition of a slave. When the French landed in 1249, she concealed the death of her husband Sālih. After the battle of Mansurah, the heir died, and she was proclaimed queen, and reigned alone 2½ months. Then she married one Aibak; slew him; and was herself beaten to death by the slaves of a divorced wife of Aibak. The coin was struck at the moment of the discomfiture of St. Louis. See Stanley Lane-Poole, Coins and Medals, p. 158-161.]

thousand foot. The loss of Antioch had provoked the enterprise ; a wild hope of baptizing the King of Tunis tempted him to steer for the African coast ; and the report of an immense treasure reconciled his troops to the delay of their voyage to the Holy Land. Instead of a proselyte he found a siege ; the French

His death before Tunis, in the seventh crusade. A.D. 1270, Aug. 25

panted and died on the burning sands ; St. Louis expired in his tent ; and no sooner had he closed his eyes than his son and successor gave the signal of the retreat.[113] " It is thus," says a lively writer, " that a Christian king died near the ruins of Carthage, waging war against the sectaries of Mahomet, in a land to which Dido had introduced the deities of Syria." [114]

The Mamalukes of Egypt. A.D. 1250-1517

A more unjust and absurd constitution cannot be devised than that which condemns the natives of a country to perpetual servitude, under the arbitrary dominion of strangers and slaves. Yet such has been the state of Egypt above five hundred years. The most illustrious sultans of the Baharite and Borgite dynasties [115] were themselves promoted from the Tartar and Circassian bands ; and the four-and-twenty beys, or military chiefs, have ever been succeeded not by their sons but by their servants. They produce the great charter of their liberties, the treaty of

[Conquered by Salim I. A.D. 1517]

Selim the First with the republic ; [116] and the Othman emperor still accepts from Egypt a slight acknowledgment of tribute and subjection.[117] With some breathing intervals of peace and order, the two dynasties are marked as a period of rapine and bloodshed ; [118] but their throne, however shaken, reposed on the

[113] See the expedition in the Annals of St. Louis, by William de Nangis, p. 270-287, and the Arabic Extracts, p. 545, 555 of the Louvre edition of Joinville. [R. Steinfeld, Ludwigs des Heiligen Kreuzzug nach Tunis, 1270, und die Politik Karls I. von Sizilien (1896).]

[114] Voltaire, Hist. Générale, tom. ii. p. 391.

[115] The chronology of the two dynasties of Mamalukes, the Baharites, Turks or Tartars of Kipzak, and the Borgites, Circassians, is given by Pocock (Prolegom. ad Abulpharag. p. 6-31), and de Guignes (tom. i. p. 264-270) [see S. Lane-Poole, Mohammadan Dynasties, p. 80-83] ; their history from Abulfeda, Macrizi, &c., to the beginning of the 15th century, by the same M. de Guignes (tom. iv. p. 110-328). [Weil's Gesch. der Chalifen, vols. 4 and 5.]

[116] Savary, Lettres sur l'Egypt, tom. ii. lettre xv. p. 189-208. I much question the authenticity of this copy ; yet it is true that Sultan Selim concluded a treaty with the Circassians or Mamalukes of Egypt, and left them in possession of arms, riches, and power. See a new Abrégé de l'Histoire Ottomane, composed in Egypt, and translated by M. Digeon (tom. i. p. 55-58, Paris, 1781), a curious, authentic, and national history.

[117] [And Egypt was governed by a Turkish Pasha, whose power was limited by the council of beys.]

[118] Si totum quo regnum occupârunt tempus respicias, presertim quod fini propius, reperies illud bellis, pugnis, injuriis, ac rapinis refertum (Al Jannabi, apud Pocock, p. 31). The reign of Mohammed (A.D. 1311-1341) affords an happy exception (de Guignes, tom. iv. p. 208-210).

two pillars of discipline and valour; their sway extended over
Egypt, Nubia, Arabia, and Syria; their Mamalukes were multiplied from eight hundred to twenty-five thousand horse; and
their numbers were increased by a provincial militia of one
hundred and seven thousand foot, and the occasional aid of
sixty-six thousand Arabs.[119]    Princes of such power and spirit
could not long endure on their coast an hostile and independent nation; and, if the ruin of the Franks was postponed about
forty years, they were indebted to the cares of an unsettled
reign, to the invasion of the Mogols, and to the occasional aid of
some warlike pilgrims.    Among these, the English reader will
observe the name of our first Edward, who assumed the cross in
the lifetime of his father Henry.    At the head of a thousand
soldiers, the future conqueror of Wales and Scotland delivered
Acre from a siege; marched as far as Nazareth with an army of
nine thousand men; emulated the fame of his uncle Richard;
extorted, by his valour, a ten years' truce; and escaped, with a
dangerous wound, from the dagger of a fanatic *assassin*.[120]    Anti-
och,[121] whose situation had been less exposed to the calamities Loss of<br>Antioch.<br>A.D. 1268,<br>June 12
of the holy war, was finally occupied and ruined by Bondocdar,
or Bibars,[122] sultan of Egypt and Syria; the Latin principality was
extinguished; and the first seat of the Christian name was dis-
peopled by the slaughter of seventeen, and the captivity of one
hundred thousand, of her inhabitants.    The maritime towns of
Laodicea, Gabala, Tripoli, Berytus, Sidon, Tyre, and Jaffa, and
the stronger castles of the Hospitalers and Templars, successively fell; and the whole existence of the Franks was confined
to the city and colony of St. John of Acre, which is sometimes
described by the more classic title of Ptolemais.

After the loss of Jerusalem, Acre,[123] which is distant about
seventy miles, became the metropolis of the Latin Christians,

[119] They are now reduced to 8500; but the expense of each Mamaluke may be
rated at 100 louis, and Egypt groans under the avarice and insolence of these
strangers (Voyages de Volney, tom. i. p. 89-187).
[120] See Carte's History of England, vol. ii. p. 165-175, and his original authors,
Thomas Wikes [Wykes; ed. by Luard, Annales Monastici, iv. 1869] and Walter
Hemingford [Walterus Gisburniensis; ed. by H. C. Hamilton for the English
Historical Society, 1848] (l. iii. c. 34, 35) in Gale's Collections (tom. ii. p. 97, 589-
592).    They are both ignorant of the Princess Eleanor's piety in sucking the
poisoned wound, and saving her husband at the risk of her own life.
[121] Sanutus, Secret. Fidelium Crucis, l. iii. p. xii. c. 9, and de Guignes, Hist. des
Huns, tom. iv. p. 143, from the Arabic historians.
[122] [Baybars al-Bundukdārī = the arbalestier.]
[123] The state of Acre is represented in all the chronicles of the times, and most
accurately in John Villani, l. vii. c. 144, in Muratori, Scriptores Rerum Italicarum,
tom. xiii. p. 337, 338.

and was adorned with strong and stately buildings, with aqueducts, an artificial port, and a double wall.   The population was
increased by the incessant streams of pilgrims and fugitives ;  in
the pauses of hostility the trade of the East and West was
attracted to this convenient station ; and the market could offer
the produce of every clime and the interpreters of every tongue.
But in this conflux of nations every vice was propagated and
practised ; of all the disciples of Jesus and Mahomet, the male
and female inhabitants of Acre were esteemed the most corrupt ;
nor could the abuse of religion be corrected by the discipline of
law.   The city had many sovereigns, and no government.   The
kings of Jerusalem and Cyprus, of the house of Lusignan, the
princes of Antioch, the counts of Tripoli and Sidon, the great
masters of the Hospital, the Temple, and the Teutonic order,
the republics of Venice, Genoa, and Pisa, the pope's legate, the
kings of France and England, assumed an independent command ; seventeen tribunals exercised the power of life and death ;
every criminal was protected in the adjacent quarter ; and the
perpetual jealousy of the nations often burst forth in acts of
violence and blood.   Some adventurers, who disgraced the en-
sign of the cross, compensated their want of pay by the plunder
of the Mahometan villages ; nineteen Syrian merchants, who
traded under the public faith, were despoiled and hanged by
the Christians ; and the denial of satisfaction justified the arms
of the sultan Khalil.   He marched against Acre, at the head of
sixty thousand horse and one hundred and forty thousand foot ;
his train of artillery (if I may use the word) was numerous and
weighty ; the separate timbers of a single engine were transported in one hundred waggons ; and the royal historian, Abulfeda, who served with the troops of Hamah, was himself a
spectator of the holy war.   Whatever might be the vices of the
Franks, their courage was rekindled by enthusiasm and despair ;
but they were torn by the discord of seventeen chiefs, and overwhelmed on all sides by the power of the sultan.   After a siege
of thirty-three days, the double wall was forced by the Moslems ;
the principal tower yielded to their engines ; the Mamalukes
made a general assault ; the city was stormed ; and death or
slavery was the lot of sixty thousand Christians.   The convent,
or rather fortress, of the Templars resisted three days longer ;
but the great master was pierced with an arrow ; and, of five
hundred knights, only ten were left alive, less happy than the
victims of the sword, if they lived to suffer on a scaffold in the
unjust and cruel proscription of the whole order.   The king of

The loss of
Acre and the
Holy Land.
A.D. 1291,
May 18

Jerusalem, the patriarch and the great master of the Hospital effected their retreat to the shore; but the sea was rough, the vessels were insufficient; and great numbers of the fugitives were drowned before they could reach the isle of Cyprus, which might comfort Lusignan for the loss of Palestine. By the command of the sultan, the churches and fortifications of the Latin cities were demolished; a motive of avarice or fear still opened the holy sepulchre to some devout and defenceless pilgrims; and a mournful and solitary silence prevailed along the coast which had so long resounded with the WORLD'S DEBATE.[124]

[124] See the final expulsion of the Franks, in Sanutus, l. iii. p. xii. c. 11-22. Abulfeda, Macrizi, &c., in de Guignes, tom. iv. p. 162, 164, and Vertot, tom. i. l. iii. p. 407-428. [An important source for the siege of Acre is the anonymous *De Excidio urbis Acconis* (falsely ascribed to Adenulf of Anagnia) published in Martene and Durand, Ampliss. Collectio, vol. 5, p. 757 *sqq.*]

CHAPTER LX

*Schism of the Greeks and Latins—State of Constantinople—Revolt of the Bulgarians—Isaac Angelus dethroned by his brother Alexius—Origin of the Fourth Crusade—Alliance of the French and Venetians with the son of Isaac—Their naval expedition to Constantinople—The two Sieges, and final Conquest of the City by the Latins*

Schism of the Greeks

THE restoration of the Western empire by Charlemagne was speedily followed by the separation of the Greek and Latin churches.[1]   A religious and national animosity still divides the two largest communions of the Christian world ; and the schism of Constantinople, by alienating her most useful allies and provoking her most dangerous enemies, has precipitated the decline and fall of the Roman empire in the East.

Their aversion to the Latins

In the course of the present history the aversion of the Greeks for the Latins has been often visible and conspicuous. It was originally derived from the disdain of servitude, inflamed, after the time of Constantine, by the pride of equality or dominion, and finally exasperated by the preference which their rebellious subjects had given to the alliance of the Franks.   In every age the Greeks were proud of their superiority in profane and religious knowledge ; they had first received the light of Christianity ; they had pronounced the decrees of the seven general councils ; they alone possessed the language of Scripture and philosophy ; nor should the barbarians, immersed in the darkness of the West,[2] presume to argue on the high and

[1] In the successive centuries, from the ixth to the xviiith, Mosheim traces the schism of the Greeks, with learning, clearness, and impartiality : the *filioque* (Institut. Hist. Eccles. p. 277); Leo III. p. 303 ; Photius, p. 307, 308 ; Michael Cerularius, p. 370, 371, &c. [The relation between the eastern and western churches is traced by M. Duchesne in his essay L'église grecque et le schisme grec, in Eglises séparées, p. 163 *sqq.*]

[2] Ἄνδρες δυσσεβεῖς καὶ ἀποτροπαῖοι, ἄνδρες ἐκ σκότους ἀναδύντες, τῆς γὰρ Ἑσπερίου μοίρας ὑπῆρχον γεννήματα (Phot. Epist. p. 47, edit. Montacut).   The Oriental patriarch continues to apply the images of thunder, earthquake, hail, wild-boar, præcursors of Antichrist, &c. &c.

mysterious questions of theological science.   These barbarians despised, in their turn, the restless and subtle levity of the Orientals, the authors of every heresy ; and blessed their own simplicity, which was content to hold the tradition of the apostolic church.   Yet, in the seventh century, the synods of Spain, and afterwards of France, improved or corrupted the Nicene creed, on the mysterious subject of the third person of the Trinity.[3]   In the long controversies of the East, the nature and generation of the Christ had been scrupulously defined ; and the well-known relation of Father and Son seemed to convey a faint image to the human mind.   The idea of birth was less analogous to the Holy Spirit, who, instead of a divine gift or attribute, was considered by the Catholics as a substance, a person, a God ; he was not begotten, but, in the orthodox style, he *proceeded*. Did he proceed from the Father alone, perhaps *by* the Son ? or from the Father *and* the Son ?   The first of these opinions was asserted by the Greeks, the second by the Latins ; and the addition to the Nicene creed of the word *filioque* kindled the flame of discord between the Oriental and the Gallic churches. In the origin of the dispute the Roman pontiffs affected a character of neutrality and moderation ;[4] they condemned the innovation, but they acquiesced in the sentiment of their Transalpine brethren ; they seemed desirous of casting a veil of silence and charity over the superfluous research ; and, in the correspondence of Charlemagne and Leo the Third, the Pope assumes the liberality of a statesman, and the prince descends to the passions and prejudices of a priest.[5]   But the orthodoxy of Rome spontaneously obeyed the impulse of her temporal policy ; and the *filioque*, which Leo wished to erase, was transcribed in the symbol, and chaunted in the liturgy, of the

*Procession of the Holy Ghost*

[3] The mysterious subject of the procession of the Holy Ghost is discussed in the historical, theological, and controversial sense, or nonsense, by the Jesuit Petavius (Dogmata Theologica, tom. ii. l. vii. p. 362-440).   [Technically, the Greeks were right.   The *filioque* was an innovation on the symbolum recognized by the first four Councils.]

[4] Before the shrine of St. Peter he placed two shields of the weight of 94½ pounds of pure silver, on which he inscribed the text of both creeds (utroque symbolo), pro amore et *cautelâ* orthodoxæ fidei (Anastas. in Leon. III. in Muratori, tom. iii. pars i. p. 208).   His language most clearly proves that neither the filioque nor the Athanasian creed were received at Rome about the year 830.

[5] The Missi of Charlemagne pressed him to declare that all who rejected the *filioque*, at least the doctrine, must be damned.   All, replies the Pope, are not capable of reaching the altiora mysteria ; qui potuerit, et non voluerit, salvus esse non potest (Collect. Concil. tom. ix. p. 277-286).   The *potuerit* would leave a large loop-hole of salvation !

Vatican. The Nicene and Athanasian creeds are held as the Catholic faith, without which none can be saved; and both Papists and Protestants must now sustain and return the anathemas of the Greeks, who deny the procession of the Holy Ghost from the Son, as well as from the Father. Such articles of faith are not susceptible of treaty; but the rules of discipline will vary in remote and independent churches; and the reason, even of divines, might allow that the difference is inevitable and harmless. The craft or superstition of Rome has imposed on her priests and deacons the rigid obligation of celibacy; among the Greeks, it is confined to the bishops; the loss is compensated by dignity or annihilated by age; and the parochial clergy, the papas, enjoy the conjugal society of the wives whom they have married before their entrance into holy orders. A question concerning the *Azyms* was fiercely debated in the eleventh century, and the essence of the Eucharist was supposed, in the East and West, to depend on the use of leavened or unleavened bread. Shall I mention in a serious history the furious reproaches that were urged against the Latins, who, for a long while, remained on the defensive? They neglected to abstain, according to the apostolical decree, from things strangled and from blood; they fasted, a Jewish observance! on the Saturday of each week; during the first week of Lent they permitted the use of milk and cheese;[6] their infirm monks were indulged in the taste of flesh; and animal grease was substituted for the want of vegetable oil; the holy chrism or unction in baptism was reserved to the episcopal order; the bishops, as the bridegrooms of their churches, were decorated with rings; their priests shaved their faces, and baptized by a single immersion. Such were the crimes which provoked the zeal of the patriarchs of Constantinople; and which were justified with equal zeal by the doctors of the Latin church.[7]

Bigotry and national aversion are powerful magnifiers of every object of dispute; but the immediate cause of the schism of the

*Variety of ecclesiastical discipline*

*Ambitious quarrels of Photius, patriarch of Constantinople, with the Popes. A.D. 857-886*

[6] In France, after some harsher laws, the ecclesiastical discipline is now relaxed milk, cheese and butter are become a perpetual, and eggs an annual, indulgence in Lent (Vie privée des François, tom. ii. p. 27-38).

[7] The original monuments of the schism, of the charges of the Greeks against the Latins, are deposited in the Epistles of Photius (Epist. Encyclica, ii. p. 47-61 [Ep. 4 in the ed. of Valettas, p. 165 *sqq.*] and of Michael Cerularius (Canis. Antiq. Lectiones, tom. iii. p. i. p. 281-324, edit. Basnage, with the prolix answe of Cardinal Humbert [in C. Will, Acta et scripta quae de controversiis ecclesia graecae et latinae seculo xi. composita extant, p. 172 *sqq.*; and in Migne, P. G vol. 120, 752 *sqq.*]).

Greeks may be traced in the emulation of the leading prelates, who maintained the supremacy of the old metropolis superior to all, and of the reigning capital inferior to none, in the Christian world. About the middle of the ninth century, Photius,[8] an ambitious layman, the captain of the guards and principal secretary, was promoted by merit and favour to the more desirable office of patriarch of Constantinople.[9] In science, even ecclesi- [25 Dec., 858] astical science, he surpassed the clergy of the age;[10] and the purity of his morals has never been impeached; but his ordination was hasty, his rise was irregular; and Ignatius, his abdicated predecessor, was yet supported by the public compassion and the obstinacy of his adherents. They appealed to the tribunal of Nicholas the First, one of the proudest and most aspiring of the Roman pontiffs, who embraced the welcome opportunity of judging and condemning his rival of the East. Their quarrel was embittered by a conflict of jurisdiction over the king and nation of the Bulgarians; nor was their recent conversion to Christianity of much avail to either prelate, unless he could number the proselytes among the subjects of his power. With the aid of his court, the Greek patriarch was victorious; but in the furious contest he deposed, in his turn, the successor of St. Peter, and involved the Latin Church in the reproach of heresy and schism. Photius sacrificed the peace of the world to a short and precarious reign; he fell with his patron, the Cæsar Bardas; and Basil the Macedonian performed an act of [A.D. 867] justice in the restoration of Ignatius, whose age and dignity had not been sufficiently respected. From his monastery, or prison, Photius solicited the favour of the emperor by pathetic complaints and artful flattery; and the eyes of his rival were scarcely closed when he was again restored to the throne of [A.D. 877] Constantinople. After the death of Basil, he experienced the vicissitudes of courts and the ingratitude of a royal pupil; the [A.D. 886] patriarch was again deposed, and in his last solitary hours he might regret the freedom of a secular and studious life. In [Photius died each revolution, the breath, the nod, of the sovereign had been c. 891] accepted by a submissive clergy; and a synod of three hundred

---

[8] The xth volume of the Venice edition of the Councils contains all the acts of the synods, and history of Photius; they are abridged with a faint tinge of prejudice or prudence, by Dupin and Fleury. [The fullest modern history of Photius is Hergenröther's Biography, cp. Appendix 1.]

[9] [As successor of Ignatius, who was deposed because he excommunicated the Cæsar Bardas for incest with his stepdaughter.]

[10] [Cp. Appendix 1.]

bishops was always prepared to hail the triumph, or to stigma-
tize the fall, of the holy or the execrable Photius.[11]   By a
delusive promise of succour or reward, the popes were tempted
to countenance these various proceedings, and the synods of
Constantinople were ratified by their epistles or legates.   But
the court and the people, Ignatius and Photius, were equally
adverse to their claims ; their ministers were insulted or imprisoned ; the procession of the Holy Ghost was forgotten ;
Bulgaria was for ever annexed to the Byzantine throne ; and
the schism was prolonged by the rigid censure of all the multiplied ordinations of an irregular patriarch.   The darkness and
corruption of the tenth century suspended the intercourse, without reconciling the minds, of the two nations.   But, when the
Norman sword restored the churches of Apulia to the jurisdiction of Rome, the departing flock was warned, by a petulant
epistle of the Grecian patriarch, to avoid and abhor the errors
of the Latins.   The rising majesty of Rome could no longer

The popes
excommuni-
cate the
patriarch of
Constantino-
ple and the
Greeks.
A.D. 1054,
July 16

brook the insolence of a rebel ; and Michael Cerularius was
excommunicated in the heart of Constantinople by the pope's
legates.   Shaking the dust from their feet, they deposited on
the altar of St. Sophia a direful anathema,[12] which enumerates
the seven mortal heresies of the Greeks, and devotes the guilty
teachers, and their unhappy sectaries, to the eternal society of
the devil and his angels.   According to the emergencies of the
church and state a friendly correspondence was sometimes resumed ; the language of charity and concord was sometimes affected ; but the Greeks have never recanted their errors ; the
popes have never repealed their sentence ; and from this
thunderbolt we may date the consummation of the schism.
It was enlarged by each ambitious step of the Roman pontiffs ;
the emperors blushed and trembled at the ignominious fate
of their royal brethren of Germany ; and the people was scandalized by the temporal power and military life of the Latin
clergy.[13]

[11] The synod of Constantinople, held in the year 869, is the viiith of the general
councils, the last assembly of the East which is recognised by the Roman church.
She rejects the synods of Constantinople of the years 867 and 879, which were,
however, equally numerous and noisy ; but they were favourable to Photius.

[12] See this anathema in the Councils, tom. xi. p. 1457-1460.   [See Hergenröther,
Photius, vol. iii. p. 730 sqq. for the conflict under Cerularius.   Cp. Gfrörer,
Byzantinische Geschichten, vol. iii. cap. 23, p. 514 sqq.]

[13] Anna Comnena (Alexiad, l. i. p. 31-33 [c. 13]) represents the abhorrence, not
only of the church, but of the palace, for Gregory VII., the popes, and the Latin
communion.   The style of Cinnamus and Nicetas is still more vehement.   Yet
how calm is the voice of history compared with that of polemics !

The aversion of the Greeks and Latins [14] was nourished and manifested in the three first expeditions to the Holy Land. Alexius Comnenus contrived the absence at least of the formidable pilgrims ; his successors, Manuel and Isaac Angelus, conspired with the Moslems for the ruin of the greatest princes of the Franks ; and their crooked and malignant policy was seconded by the active and voluntary obedience of every order of their subjects. Of this hostile temper a large portion may doubtless be ascribed to the difference of language, dress, and manners, which severs and alienates the nations of the globe. The pride, as well as the prudence, of the sovereign was deeply wounded by the intrusion of foreign armies, that claimed a right of traversing his dominions and passing under the walls of his capital ; his subjects were insulted and plundered by the rude strangers of the West ; and the hatred of the pusillanimous Greeks was sharpened by secret envy of the bold and pious enterprises of the Franks. But these profane causes of national enmity were fortified and inflamed by the venom of religious zeal. Instead of a kind embrace, an hospitable reception from their Christian brethren of the East, every tongue was taught to repeat the names of schismatic and heretic, more odious to an orthodox ear than those of pagan and infidel ; instead of being loved for the general conformity of faith and worship, they were abhorred for some rules of discipline, some questions of theology, in which themselves or their teachers might differ from the Oriental church. In the crusade of Louis the Seventh, the Greek clergy washed and purified the altars which had been defiled by the sacrifice of a French priest. The companions of Frederic Barbarossa deplore the injuries which they endured, both in word and deed, from the peculiar rancour of the bishops and monks. Their prayers and sermons excited the people against the impious barbarians ; and the patriarch is accused of declaring that the faithful might obtain the redemption of all their sins by the extirpation of the schismatics.[15] An enthusiast,

Enmity of the Greeks and Latins. A.D. 1100-1200

[14] [The disputes over trivial points of theology and ceremony were the expression the national enmity of the Greeks and Latins ; and this aversion was the true use of the schism ; the questions of controversy were a pretext.]

[15] His anonymous historian (de Expedit. Asiat. Fred. I. in Canisii Lection. Ant. tom. iii. pars ii. p. 511, edit. Basnage) mentions the sermons of the Greek triarch, quomodo Græcis injunxerat in remissionem peccatorum peregrinos occidere et delere de terrâ. Tagino observes (in Scriptores Freher. tom. i. p. 409, it. Struv.), Græci hæreticos nos appellant ; clerici et monachi dictis et factis perquuntur. We may add the declaration of the emperor Baldwin fifteen years afterwards : Hæc est (gens) quæ Latinos omnes non hominum nomine, sed canum

named Dorotheus, alarmed the fears, and restored the confidence, of the emperor, by a prophetic assurance that the German heretic, after assaulting the gate of Blachernes, would be made a signal example of the divine vengeance. The passage of these mighty armies were rare and perilous events ; but the crusades introduced a frequent and familiar intercourse between the two nations, which enlarged their knowledge without abating their prejudices. The wealth and luxury of Constantinople demanded the productions of every climate ; these imports were balanced by the art and labour of her numerous inhabitants ; her situation invites the commerce of the world ; and, in every period of her existence, that commerce has been in the hands of foreigners. After the decline of Amalphi, the Venetians, Pisans, and Genoese introduced their factories and settlements into the capital of the empire ; their services were rewarded with honours and immunities ; they acquired the possession of lands and houses ; their families were multiplied by marriages with the natives ; and, after the toleration of a Mahometan mosque, it was impossible to interdict the churches of the Roman rite.[16]   The two wives of Manuel Comnenus [17] were of the race of the Franks : the first, a sister-in-law of the Emperor Conrad ; the second, a daughter of the prince of Antioch; he obtained for his son Alexius, a daughter of Philip Augustus, king of France ; and he bestowed his own daughter on a Marquis of Montferrat, who was educated and dignified in the palace of Constantinople. The Greek encountered the arms, and aspired to the empire, of the West ; he esteemed the valour, and trusted the fidelity, of the Franks ; [18] their military talents were unfitly recompensed by the lucrative offices of judges and treasurers ; the policy of Manuel had solicited the alliance of the pope ; and the popular voice accused him of a partial bias

The Latins at Constantinople

dignabatur ; quorum sanguinem effundere pene inter merita reputabant (Gesta Innocent. III. c. 92, in Muratori, Script. Rerum Italicarum, tom. iii. pars i. p. 536).   There may be some exaggeration, but it was as effectual for the action and re-action of hatred.

[16] See Anna Comnena (Alexiad, l. vi. p. 161, 162 [c. 5]), and a remarkable passage of Nicetas (in Manuel, l. v. c. 9), who observes of the Venetians, κατὰ σμήνη καὶ φρατρίας τὴν Κωνσταντινούπολιν τῆς οἰκείας ἠλλάξαντο, &c.

[17] Ducange, Fam. Byzant. p. 186, 187.

[18] Nicetas in Manuel, l. vii. c. 2.   Regnante enim (Manuele) . . . apud eum tantam Latinus populus repererat gratiam ut neglectis Græculis suis tanquam viris mollibus et effœminatis, . . . solis Latinis grandia committeret negotia . . . erga eos profusâ liberalitate abundabat . . . ex omni orbe ad eum tanquam ad benefactorem nobiles et ignobiles concurrebant.   Willerm. Tyr. xxii. c. 10.

to the nation and religion of the Latins.[19]   During his reign, and that of his successor Alexius, they were exposed at Constantinople to the reproach of foreigners, heretics, and favourites ; and this triple guilt was severely expiated in the tumult which announced the return and elevation of Andronicus.[20] The people rose in arms ; from the Asiatic shore the tyrant dispatched his troops and galleys to assist the national revenge ; and the hopeless resistance of the strangers served only to justify the rage, and sharpen the daggers, of the assassins.   Neither age nor sex nor the ties of friendship or kindred could save the victims of national hatred and avarice and religious zeal ; the Latins were slaughtered in their houses and in the streets ; their quarter was reduced to ashes ; the clergy were burnt in their churches, and the sick in their hospitals ; and some estimate may be formed of the slain from the clemency which sold above four thousand Christians in perpetual slavery to the Turks. The priests and monks were the loudest and most active in the destruction of the schismatics ; and they chaunted a thanksgiving to the Lord, when the head of a Roman cardinal, the pope's legate, was severed from his body, fastened to the tail of a dog, and dragged with savage mockery through the city. The more diligent of the strangers had retreated, on the first alarm, to their vessels, and escaped through the Hellespont from the scene of blood.   In their flight they burned and ravaged two hundred miles of the sea-coast ;  inflicted a severe revenge on the guiltless subjects of the empire ; marked the priests and monks as their peculiar enemies ; and compensated, by the accumulation of plunder, the loss of their property and friends.   On their return, they exposed to Italy and Europe the wealth and weakness, the perfidy and malice of the Greeks, whose vices were painted as the genuine characters of heresy and schism.   The scruples of the first crusaders had neglected the fairest opportunities of securing, by the possession of Constantinople, the way to the Holy Land ; a domestic revolution invited and almost compelled the French and Venetians to achieve the conquest of the Roman empire of the East.

their massacre.   A.D. 1183

[19] The suspicions of the Greeks would have been confirmed, if they had seen the political epistles of Manuel to pope Alexander III., the enemy of his enemy Frederic I., in which the emperor declares his wish of uniting the Greeks and Latins as one flock under one shepherd, &c. (see Fleury, Hist. Ecclés. tom. xv. p. 187, 213, 243).

[20] See the Greek and Latin Narratives in Nicetas (in Alexio Comneno, c. 10), and William of Tyre (l. xxii. c. 10-13) : the first, soft and concise ; the second, loud, copious, and tragical.

Reign and character of IsaacAngelus. A.D. 1185-1195. Sept. 12

In the series of the Byzantine princes, I have exhibited the hypocrisy and ambition, the tyranny and fall of Andronicus, the last male of the Comnenian family who reigned at Constantinople. The revolution, which cast him headlong from the throne, saved and exalted Isaac Angelus,[21] who descended by the females from the same Imperial dynasty. The successor of a second Nero might have found it an easy task to deserve the esteem and affection of his subjects; they sometimes had reason to regret the administration of Andronicus. The sound and vigorous mind of the tyrant was capable of discerning the connection between his own and the public interest; and, while he was feared by all who could inspire him with fear, the unsuspected people and the remote provinces might bless the inexorable justice of their master. But his successor was vain and jealous of the supreme power which he wanted courage and abilities to exercise; his vices were pernicious, his virtues (if he possessed any virtues) were useless, to mankind; and the Greeks, who imputed their calamities to his negligence, denied him the merit of any transient or accidental benefits of the times. Isaac slept on the throne, and was awakened only by the sound of pleasure; his vacant hours were amused by comedians and buffoons, and even to these buffoons the emperor was an object of contempt; his feasts and buildings exceeded the examples of royal luxury; the number of his eunuchs and domestics amounted to twenty thousand; and a daily sum of four thousand pounds of silver would swell to four millions sterling the annual expense of his household and table. His poverty was relieved by oppression; and the public discontent was inflamed by equal abuses in the collection and the application of the revenue. While the Greeks numbered the days of their servitude, a flattering prophet, whom he rewarded with the dignity of patriarch, assured him of a long and victorious reign of thirty-two years; during which he should extend his sway to mount Libanus, and his conquests beyond the Euphrates. But his only step towards the accomplishment of the prediction was a splendid and scandalous embassy to Saladin,[22] to demand

---

[21] The history of the reign of Isaac Angelus is composed, in three books, by the senator Nicetas (p. 288-290); and his offices of logothete, or principal secretary and judge of the veil, or palace, could not bribe the impartiality of the historian. He wrote, it is true, after the fall and death of his benefactor. [Cp. above, vol. p. 507.]

[22] See Bohadin, Vit. Saladin. p. 129-131, 226, vers. Schultens. The ambassador of Isaac was equally versed in the Greek, French, and Arabic languages: a rare instance in those times. His embassies were received with honour, dismissed without effect, and reported with scandal in the West.

the restitution of the holy sepulchre, and to propose an offensive
and defensive league with the enemy of the Christian name.  In
these unworthy hands, of Isaac and his brother, the remains of
the Greek empire crumbled into dust.  The island of Cyprus,
whose name excites the ideas of elegance and pleasure, was
usurped by his namesake, a Comnenian prince ; and, by a strange
concatenation of events, the sword of our English Richard bestowed that kingdom on the house of Lusignan, a rich compensation for the loss of Jerusalem.[23]

The honour of the monarchy and the safety of the capital were
deeply wounded by the revolt of the Bulgarians and Wallachians.
Since the victory of the second Basil, they had supported, above
an hundred and seventy years, the loose dominion of the Byzantine princes ; but no effectual measures had been adopted to impose the yoke of laws and manners on these savage tribes.[24]  By
the command of Isaac, their sole means of subsistence, their flocks
and herds, were driven away, to contribute towards the pomp of
the royal nuptials ; and their fierce warriors were exasperated
by the denial of equal rank and pay in the military service.
Peter and Asan, two powerful chiefs, of the race of the ancient
kings,[25] asserted their own rights and the national freedom; their
demoniac impostors proclaimed to the crowd that their glorious
patron, St. Demetrius, had for ever deserted the cause of the
Greeks ; and the conflagration spread from the banks of the

[23] [For Cyprus under the Lusignans, the chief work is L. de Mas-Latrie's Histoire
de l'île de Chypre dans le règne des princes de la maison de Lusignan, 3 vols.
1855-61.]

[24] [For the Bulgarians and Wallachians in the 11th century, we have some interesting notices in the Strategicon of Cecaumenos (see vol. 5, Appendix, p. 505) ;
especially the account of the revolt of the Wallachians of Thessaly (Great Vlachia)
in A.D. 1066, c. 171 *sqq.*]

[25] Ducange, Familiæ Dalmaticæ, p. 318-320.  The original correspondence of
the Bulgarian king and the Roman pontiff is inscribed in the Gesta Innocent. III.
c. 66-82, p. 513-525.  [For the foundation of the Second Bulgarian (or Vlacho-
Bulgarian) kingdom, see Jireček, Geschichte der Bulgaren, c. 14 ; Xénopol, Histoire
des Roumains, p. 172 *sqq.*, and L'empire valacho-bulgare in the Revue Historique,
47 (1897), p. 278 *sqq.*  There is a Russian monograph, by T. Uspenski (1879).  The
two Asēns claimed to be descended from the old tsars ; but we cannot pay much regard
to such a claim.  The question is whether they were Bulgarians or Vlachs.  The
Roumanians would gladly believe that they were Vlachs ; and they appeal to an incident recorded by Nicetas (in Alex. Is. fil. i. c. 5, p. 617, ed. Bonn).  A priest was
taken prisoner, and he besought Asēn in Vlach, " which was also his language "
(δεῖται τοῦ Ἀσὰν ἀφεθῆναι, δι' ὁ μο φ ω ν ί α ς ὡς ἴδρις τῆς τῶν Βλάχων φωνῆς).  The natural
inference from this piece of evidence is confirmed by the fact that (1) Pope Innocent
III. in his correspondence with John Asēn II. (Calo-John) speaks to him as a Vlach
or Roman (see next note) ; and (2) western historians assert that he was a Vlach
(*e.g.*, Villehardouin, Conquête de Constantinople, xliii. sect. 202, ce Johannis était
un Blaque).]

Danube to the hills of Macedonia and Thrace.   After some faint efforts, Isaac Angelus and his brother acquiesced in their independence ; and the imperial troops were soon discouraged by the bones of their fellow-soldiers, that were scattered along the passes of mount Hæmus.   By the arms and policy of John or Joannices, the second kingdom of Bulgaria was firmly established. The subtle barbarian sent an embassy to Innocent the Third, to acknowledge himself a genuine son of Rome in descent and religion,[26] and humbly received from the pope the licence of coining money, the royal title, and a Latin archbishop or patriarch. The Vatican exulted in the spiritual conquest of Bulgaria, the first object of the schism ; and, if the Greeks could have preserved the prerogatives of the church, they would gladly have resigned the rights of the monarchy.

The Bulgarians were malicious enough to pray for the long life of Isaac Angelus, the surest pledge of their freedom and prosperity.   Yet their chiefs could involve in the same indiscriminate contempt the family and nation of the emperor.   " In all the Greeks," said Asan to his troops, " the same climate and character and education will be productive of the same fruits.   Behold my lance," continued the warrior, " and the long streamers that float in the wind.   They differ only in colour ; they are formed of the same silk, and fashioned by the same workman ; nor has the stripe that is stained in purple any superior price or value above its fellows." [27]   Several of these candidates for the purple successively rose and fell under the empire of Isaac : a general who had repelled the fleets of Sicily was driven to revolt and ruin by the ingratitude of the prince ; and his luxurious repose was disturbed by secret conspiracies and popular insurrections.   The emperor was saved by accident, or the merit of his servants : he was at length oppressed by an ambitious brother, who, for the hope of a precarious diadem, forgot the obligations of nature, of loyalty, and of friend-

[John II. A.D. 1197-1207]

Usurpation and character of Alexius Angelus. A.D. 1195—1203, April 8

---

[26] The pope acknowledges his pedigree, a nobili urbis Romæ prosapiâ genitores tui originem traxerunt.   This tradition, and the strong resemblance of the Latin and Wallachian idioms, is explained by M. d'Anville (États de l'Europe, p. 258-262).   The Italian colonies of the Dacia of Trajan were swept away by the tide of emigration from the Danube to the Volga, and brought back by another wave from the Volga to the Danube.   Possible, but strange !   [Compare Appendix 11.]

[27] This parable is in the best savage style ; but I wish the Wallach had not introduced the classic name of Mysians, the experiment of the magnet or loadstone, and the passage of an old comic poet (Nicetas, in Alex. Comneno, l. i. p. 299, 300).

ship.[28] While Isaac in the Thracian valleys pursued the idle and solitary pleasures of the chase, his brother, Alexius Angelus, was invested with the purple by the unanimous suffrage of the camp; the capital and the clergy subscribed to their choice; and the vanity of the new sovereign rejected the name of his fathers for the lofty and royal appellation of the Comnenian race. On the despicable character of Isaac I have exhausted the language of contempt; and can only add that in a reign of eight years the baser Alexius [29] was supported by the masculine vices of his wife Euphrosyne. The first intelligence of his fall was conveyed to the late emperor by the hostile aspect and pursuit of the guards, no longer his own; he fled before them above fifty miles, as far as Stagyra in Macedonia; but the fugitive, without [Stagira] an object or a follower, was arrested, brought back to Constantinople, deprived of his eyes, and confined in a lonesome tower, on a scanty allowance of bread and water. At the moment of the revolution, his son Alexius, whom he educated in the hope of empire, was twelve years of age.[30] He was spared by the usurper, and reduced to attend his triumph both in peace and war; but, as the army was encamped on the sea-shore, an Italian vessel facilitated the escape of the royal youth; and, in the disguise of a common sailor, he eluded the search of his enemies, passed the Hellespont, and found a secure refuge in the isle of Sicily. After saluting the threshold of the apostles, and imploring the protection of Pope Innocent the Third, Alexius accepted the kind invitation of his sister Irene, the wife of Philip of Swabia, king of the Romans. But in his passage through Italy he heard that the flower of Western chivalry was assembled at Venice for the deliverance of the Holy Land; and a ray of hope was kindled in his bosom, that their invincible swords might be employed in his father's restoration.

About ten or twelve years after the loss of Jerusalem, the nobles of France were again summoned to the holy war by the voice of a third prophet, less extravagant, perhaps, than Peter [The fourth crusade, A.D. 1198]

---

[28] The Latins aggravate the ingratitude of Alexius, by supposing that he had been released by his brother Isaac from Turkish captivity. This pathetic tale had doubtless been repeated at Venice and Zara; but I do not readily discover its grounds in the Greek historians.

[29] See the reign of Alexius Angelus, or Comnenus, in the three books of Nicetas, p. 291-352.

[30] [Alexius is generally said to be the son of Margaret of Hungary, Isaac's second wife. But this is doubtful. Cp. Pears, Fall of Constantinople, p. 268, note 2.]

the hermit, but far below St. Bernard in the merit of an orato
and a statesman. An illiterate priest of the neighbourhood o
Paris, Fulk of Neuilly,[31] forsook his parochial duty, to assum
the more flattering character of a popular and itinerant mission
ary. The fame of his sanctity and miracles was spread ove
the land; he declaimed with severity and vehemence agains
the vices of the age; and his sermons, which he preached i
the streets of Paris, converted the robbers, the usurpers, th
prostitutes, and even the doctors and scholars of the university
No sooner did Innocent the Third ascend the chair of St. Pete
than he proclaimed, in Italy, Germany, and France, the obliga
tion of a new crusade.[32] The eloquent pontiff described th
ruin of Jerusalem, the triumph of the Pagans, and the sham
of Christendom; his liberality proposed the redemption of sins
a plenary indulgence to all who should serve in Palestine, eithe
a year in person or two years by a substitute;[33] and, among hi
legates and orators who blew the sacred trumpet, Fulk o
Neuilly was the loudest and most successful. The situation o
the principal monarchs was averse to the pious summons. Th
emperor Frederic the Second was a child; and his kingdor
of Germany was disputed by the rival houses of Brunswick an
Swabia, the memorable factions of the Guelphs and Ghibeline
Philip Augustus of France had performed, and could not b
persuaded to renew, the perilous vow; but, as he was not le
ambitious of praise than of power, he cheerfully instituted
perpetual fund for the defence of the Holy Land. Richar
of England was satiated with the glory and misfortunes of h
first adventure, and he presumed to deride the exhortations
Fulk of Neuilly, who was not abashed in the presence of king
"You advise me," said Plantagenet, "to dismiss my thre
daughters, pride, avarice, and incontinence: I bequeath the
to the most deserving; my pride to the knights-templars, m
avarice to the monks of Cisteaux, and my incontinence to th

[31] See Fleury, Hist. Ecclés. tom. xvi. p. 26, &c., and Villehardouin, No.
with the observations of Ducange, which I always mean to quote with the origin
text.

[32] The contemporary life of Pope Innocent III., published by Baluze and Mur
tori (Scriptores Rerum Italicarum, tom. iii. pars i. p. 486-568), is most valuab
for the important and original documents which are inserted in the text. T
bull of the crusade may be read, c. 84, 85.

[33] Por ce que cil pardon fut issi gran, si s'en esmeurent mult li cuers des gen
et mult s'en croisierent, porce que li pardons ere si gran. Villehardouin, No.
Our philosophers may refine on the cause of the crusades, but such were t
genuine feelings of a French knight.

prelates." But the preacher was heard and obeyed by the great vassals, the princes of the second order; and Theobald, or Thibaut, count of Champagne, was the foremost in the holy race. The valiant youth, at the age of twenty-two years, was encouraged by the domestic examples of his father, who marched in the second crusade, and of his elder brother, who had ended his days in Palestine with the title of King of Jerusalem: two thousand two hundred knights owed service and homage to his peerage; [34] the nobles of Champagne excelled in all the exercises of war; [35] and, by his marriage with the heiress of Navarre, Thibaut could draw a band of hardy Gascons from either side of the Pyrenæan mountains. His companion in arms was Louis, count of Blois and Chartres; like himself of regal lineage, for both the princes were nephews, at the same time, of the kings of France and England. In a crowd of prelates and barons, who imitated their zeal, I distinguish the birth and merit of Matthew of Montmorency; the famous Simon of Montfort, the scourge of the Albigeois; and a valiant noble, Jeffrey of Villehardouin, [36] marshal of Champagne, [37] who has condescended, in the rude idiom of his age and country, [38] to write or dictate [39] an original narrative of the councils and actions in which he bore a memorable part. At the same time, Baldwin, count of Flanders, who had married the sister of Thibaut, assumed the cross at Bruges, with his brother Henry and the

*embraced by the Barons of France*

[34] This number of fiefs (of which 1800 owed liege homage) was enrolled in the church of St. Stephen at Troyes, and attested, A.D. 1213, by the marshal and butler of Champagne (Ducange, Observ. p. 254).

[35] Campania . . . militiæ privilegio singularius excellit . . . in tyrociniis . . . prolusione armorum, &c. Ducange, p. 249, from the old Chronicle of Jerusalem, A.D. 1177-1199.

[36] The name of Villehardouin was taken from a village and castle in the diocese of Troyes, near the river Aube, between Bar and Arcis. The family was ancient and noble; the elder branch of our historian existed after the year 1400; the younger, which acquired the principality of Achaia, merged in the house of Savoy (Ducange, p. 235-245).

[37] This office was held by his father and his descendants, but Ducange has not hunted it with his usual sagacity. I find that, in the year 1356, it was in the family of Conflans; but these provincials have been long since eclipsed by the national marshals of France.

[38] This language, of which I shall produce some specimens, is explained by Vigenere and Ducange, in a version and glossary. The President des Brosses (Méchanisme des Langues, tom. ii. p. 83) gives it as the example of a language which has ceased to be French, and is understood only by grammarians.

[39] His age, and his own expression, moi que ceste oeuvre *dicta* (No. 62, &c.), may justify the suspicion (more probable than Mr. Wood's on Homer) that he could neither read nor write. Yet Champagne may boast of the two first historians, the noble authors of French prose, Villehardouin and Joinville.

principal knights and citizens of that rich and industrious province.[40]  The vow which the chiefs had pronounced in churches, they ratified in tournaments; the operations of war were debated in full and frequent assemblies; and it was resolved to seek the deliverance of Palestine in Egypt, a country, since Saladin's death, which was almost ruined by famine and civil war.  But the fate of so many royal armies displayed the toils and perils of a land expedition ; and, if the Flemings dwelt along the ocean, the French barons were destitute of ships and ignorant of navigation.  They embraced the wise resolution of choosing six deputies or representatives, of whom Villehardouin was one, with a discretionary trust to direct the motions, and to pledge the faith, of the whole confederacy.  The maritime states of Italy were alone possessed of the means of transporting the holy warriors with their arms and horses; and the six deputies proceeded to Venice, to solicit, on motives of piety or interest, the aid of that powerful republic.

State of the Venetians. A.D. 697-1200     In the invasion of Italy by Attila, I have mentioned [41] the flight of the Venetians from the fallen cities of the continent, and their obscure shelter in the chain of islands that line the extremity of the Adriatic gulf.  In the midst of the waters, free, indigent, laborious, and inaccessible, they gradually coalesced into a republic ; the first foundations of Venice were laid in the island of Rialto ; and the annual election of the twelve tribunes was superseded by the permanent office of a duke or doge.  On the verge of the two empires, the Venetians exult in the belief of primitive and perpetual independence.[42]  Against the Latins, their antique freedom has been asserted by the sword, and may be justified by the pen.  Charlemagne himself resigned all claim of sovereignty to the islands of the Adriatic gulf ; his son Pepin was repulsed in the attacks of the *lagunas*, or canals, too deep for the cavalry, and too shallow for the vessels ; and in every age, under the German Cæsars, the lands of the republic have been clearly distinguished from the kingdom of Italy.  But the in-

[40] The crusade and reigns of the counts of Flanders, Baldwin and his brother Henry, are the subject of a particular history by the Jesuit Doutremens (Constantinopolis Belgica, Turnaci, 1638, in 4to), which I have only seen with the eyes of Ducange.

[41] History, &c. vol. iii. p. 469-471.

[42] The foundation and independence of Venice, and Pepin's invasion, are discussed by Pagi (Critica, tom. iii. A.D. 810, No. 4, &c.) and Beretti (Dissert. Chorograph. Italiæ medii Ævi, in Muratori, Script. tom. x. p. 153).  The two critics have a slight bias, the Frenchman adverse, the Italian favourable, to the republic.

habitants of Venice were considered by themselves, by strangers, and by their sovereigns, as an inalienable portion of the Greek empire; [43] in the ninth and tenth centuries, the proofs of their subjection are numerous and unquestionable; and the vain titles, the servile honours, of the Byzantine court, so ambitiously solicited by their dukes, would have degraded the magistrates of a free people. But the bands of this dependence, which was never absolute or rigid, were imperceptibly relaxed by the ambition of Venice and the weakness of Constantinople. Obedience was softened into respect, privilege ripened into prerogative, and the freedom of domestic government was fortified by the independence of foreign dominion. The maritime cities of Istria and Dalmatia bowed to the sovereigns of the Adriatic; and, when they armed against the Normans in the cause of Alexius, the emperor applied, not to the duty of his subjects, but to the gratitude and generosity of his faithful allies. The sea was their patrimony; [44] the western parts of the Mediterranean, from Tus-

[43] When the son of Charlemagne asserted his right of sovereignty, he was answered by the loyal Venetians, ὅτι ἡμεῖς δοῦλοι θέλομεν εἶναι τοῦ ῾Ρωμαίων βασιλέως (Constantin. Porphyrogenit. de Administrat. Imperii, pars ii. c. 28, p. 85); and the report of the ixth establishes the fact of the xth century, which is confirmed by the embassy of Liutprand of Cremona. The annual tribute, which the emperor allows them to pay to the king of Italy, alleviates, by doubling, their servitude; but the hateful word δοῦλοι must be translated, as in the charter of 827 (Laugier, Hist. de Venise, tom. i. p. 67, &c.), by the softer appellation of *subditi*, or *fideles*. [The relation of Venice to the Empire has been most recently investigated by E. Lentz. He establishes the actual, not merely formal, dependence of Venice on Constantinople up to about the years 836-40 (Das Verhältniss Venedigs zu Byzanz; Th. i., Venedig als byzantinische Provinz, 1891). About that time the weakness of the Eastern Empire enabled Venice gradually to work her way to a position of independence. By military expeditions, undertaken on her own account, against the Slavonic pirates of the Adriatic and the Saracens who carried their depredations to Dalmatia and the northern part of the Eastern Riviera, and by entering into independent compacts with the neighbouring cities of Italy, Venice changed her condition from that of a province to that of a responsible power, and, when the Eastern Empire regained strength under Basil, it was impracticable to recall her to her former subordinate position, and the Emperors were perforce content with a nominal subjection. The man whose policy achieved this result was the Doge Peter Tradonicus. (Lentz, Der allmähliche Uebergang Venedigs von faktischer zu nomineller Abhängigkeit von Byzanz, in Byz. Zeitsch. iii. p. 64 *sqq.* 1894.) The earliest independent treaty made by Venice was the Pactum Lotharii of 840: a treaty not with the Emperor Lothar, but with a number of Italian cities under the auspices of Lothar (see A. Fanta, Die Verträge der Kaiser mit Venedig bis zum Jahre, 983: in Suppl. I. to the Mittheilungen des Inst. für österr. Geschichtsforschung, 1881; and for the text Romanin, Storia documentata di Venezia, i. 356). For the later relations of Venice with the Eastern Empire, especially in the 12th century, see, C. Neumann in Byz. Zeitsch. i. p. 366 *sqq.* ; and for the development of Venetian commerce, and the bearings thereon of the Golden Bulls granted by the Emperors, Heyd, Histoire du commerce du Levant au moyen âge, 1885.]

[44] See the xxvth and xxxth dissertations of the Antiquitates Medii Ævi of Muratori. From Anderson's History of Commerce, I understand that the Venetians did not

cany to Gibraltar, were indeed abandoned to their rivals of Pisa and Genoa; but the Venetians acquired an early and lucrative share of the commerce of Greece and Egypt. Their riches increased with the increasing demand of Europe; their manufactures of silk and glass, perhaps the institution of their bank, are of high antiquity; and they enjoyed the fruits of their industry in the magnificence of public and private life. To assert her flag, to avenge her injuries, to protect the freedom of navigation, the republic could launch and man a fleet of an hundred galleys; and the Greeks, the Saracens, and the Normans were encountered by her naval arms. The Franks of Syria were assisted by the Venetians in the reduction of the sea-coast; but their zeal was neither blind nor disinterested; and, in the conquest of Tyre, they shared the sovereignty of a city, the first seat of the commerce of the world. The policy of Venice was marked by the avarice of a trading, and the insolence of a maritime power; yet her ambition was prudent; nor did she often forget that, if armed galleys were the effect and safeguard, merchant-vessels were the cause and supply, of her greatness. In her religion she avoided the schism of the Greeks, without yielding a servile obedience to the Roman pontiff; and a free intercourse with the infidels of every clime appears to have allayed betimes the fever of superstition. Her primitive government was a loose mixture of democracy and monarchy; the doge was elected by the votes of the general assembly: as long as he was popular and successful, he reigned with the pomp and authority of a prince; but in the frequent revolutions of the state he was deposed, or banished, or slain, by the justice or injustice of the multitude. The twelfth century produced the first rudiments of the wise and jealous aristocracy, which has reduced the doge to a pageant, and the people to a cypher.[45]

trade to England before the year 1323. The most flourishing state of their wealth and commerce in the beginning of the xvth century is agreeably described by the Abbé Dubos (Hist. de la Ligue de Cambray, tom. ii. p. 443-480).

[45] The Venetians have been slow in writing and publishing their history. Their most ancient monuments are, 1. The rude Chronicle (perhaps) of John Sagorninus (Venezia, 1765, in 8vo), which represents the state and manners of Venice in the year 1008. [Johannes was chaplain of the Doge Peter II., at the beginning of the 11th century. The name Sagorninus is due to an error as to the authorship. The chronicle has been edited by Montricolo in the Fonti per la storia d'Italia. Cronache Veneziane antich. i. p. 59 sqq. 1890.] 2. The larger history of the doge (1342-1354), Andrew Dandolo, published for the first time in the xiith tom. of Muratori, A.D. 1738. [H. Simonsfeld, Andreas Dandolo und seine Geschichtswerke, 1876.] The History of Venice, by the Abbé Laugier (Paris, 1728), is a work of some merit, which I have chiefly used for the constitutional part. [Daru's Histoire de Venise is most convenient for general reference. Romanin's Storia documentata di Venezia is very highly spoken of.]

When the six ambassadors of the French pilgrims arrived at Alliance of<br>the French<br>and Venetians Venice, they were hospitably entertained in the palace of St. Mark by the reigning duke : his name was Henry Dandolo ; [46] and he shone in the last period of human life as one of the most illustrious characters of the time.  Under the weight of years, and after the loss of his eyes,[47] Dandolo retained a sound understanding and a manly courage ; the spirit of an hero, ambitious to signalise his reign by some memorable exploits ; and the wisdom of a patriot, anxious to build his fame on the glory and advantage of his country.  He praised the bold enthusiasm and liberal confidence of the barons and their deputies : in such a cause, and with such associates, he should aspire, were he a private man, to terminate his life ; but he was the servant of the republic, and some delay was requisite to consult, on this arduous business, the judgment of his colleagues.  The proposal of the French was first debated by the six *sages* who had been recently appointed to control the administration of the doge ; it was next disclosed to the forty members of the council of state ; and finally communicated to the legislative assembly of four hundred and fifty representatives, who were annually chosen in the six quarters of the city.  In peace and war, the doge was still the chief of the republic ; his legal authority was supported by the personal reputation of Dandolo ; his arguments of public interest were balanced and approved ; and he was authorised to inform the ambassadors of the following conditions of the treaty.[48]  It was proposed that the crusaders should assemble at Venice, on the feast of St. John of the ensuing year ; that flat-bottomed vessels should be prepared for four thousand five hundred horses, and

[46] Henry Dandolo was eighty-four at his election (A.D. 1192), and ninety-seven at his death (A.D. 1205) [probably not quite so old].  See the Observations of Ducange sur Villehardouin, No. 204.  But this *extraordinary* longevity is not observed by the original writers ; nor does there exist another example of an hero near an hundred years of age.  Theophrastus might afford an instance of a writer of ninety-nine ; but instead of ἐννενήκοντα (Procem. ad Character.), I am much inclined to read ὀγδομήκοντα, with his last editor Fischer, and the first thoughts of Casaubon.  It is scarcely possible that the powers of the mind and body should support themselves till such a period of life.

[47] The modern Venetians (Laugier, tom. ii. p. 119) accuse the emperor Manuel ; but the calumny is refuted by Villehardouin and the old writers, who suppose that Dandolo lost his eyes by a wound (No. 34, and Ducange).

[48] See the original treaty in the Chronicle of Andrew Dandolo, p. 323-326.  [It was agreed that Egypt should be the object of attack (see above, p. 380).  A special reason for this decision is said by Gunther (in Riant's Exuviae Sacrae, i. 71) to have been the distress then prevailing in Egypt owing to the fact that the Nile had not risen for five years.]

nine thousand squires, with a number of ships sufficient for the
embarkation of four thousand five hundred knights and twenty
thousand foot ; that during a term of nine months they should
be supplied with provisions, and transported to whatsoever coast
the service of God and Christendom should require ; and that
the republic should join the armament with a squadron of fifty
galleys. It was required that the pilgrims should pay, before
their departure, a sum of eighty-five thousand marks of silver ;
and that all conquests, by sea and land, should be equally divided
among the confederates. The terms were hard ; but the emergency was pressing, and the French barons were not less profuse
of money than of blood. A general assembly was convened to
ratify the treaty ; the stately chapel and palace of St. Mark
were filled with ten thousand citizens ; and the noble deputies
were taught a new lesson of humbling themselves before the
majesty of the people. " Illustrious Venetians," said the marshal
of Champagne, " we are sent by the greatest and most powerful
barons of France, to implore the aid of the masters of the sea
for the deliverance of Jerusalem. They have enjoined us to fall
prostrate at your feet ; nor will we rise from the ground till you
have promised to avenge with us the injuries of Christ." The
eloquence of their words and tears,[49] their martial aspect and
suppliant attitude, were applauded by an universal shout ; as it
were, says Jeffrey, by the sound of an earthquake. The venerable doge ascended the pulpit, to urge their request by those
motives of honour and virtue which alone can be offered to a
[March, A.D. 1201] popular assembly ; the treaty was transcribed on parchment, attested with oaths and seals, mutually accepted by the weeping
and joyful representatives of France and Venice, and dispatched
to Rome for the approbation of Pope Innocent the Third.[50] Two
thousand marks were borrowed of the merchants for the first
expenses of the armament. Of the six deputies, two repassed
the Alps to announce their success, while their four companions
made a fruitless trial of the zeal and emulation of the republics
of Genoa and Pisa.

[49] A reader of Villehardouin must observe the frequent tears of the marshal and
his brother knights. Sachiez que la ot mainte lerme plorée de pitié (No. 17) ;
mult plorant (ibid.) ; mainte lerme plorée (No. 34) ; si orent mult pitié et plore-
rent mult durement (No. 60) ; i ot mainte lerme plorée de pitié (No. 202). They
weep on every occasion of grief, joy, or devotion.

[50] [Innocent approved with reserve (for he distrusted Venice, with good reason),
making a special condition that no Christian town should be attacked. Cp. Gesta
Innocentii, 84.]

The execution of the treaty was still opposed by unforeseen difficulties and delays.[51] The marshal, on his return to Troyes, was embraced and approved by Thibaut, count of Champagne, who had been unanimously chosen general of the confederates. But the health of that valiant youth already declined, and soon became hopeless; and he deplored the untimely fate which condemned him to expire, not in a field of battle, but on a bed of sickness. To his brave and numerous vassals the dying prince distributed his treasures; they swore in his presence to accomplish his vow and their own; but some there were, says the marshal, who accepted his gifts and forfeited their word. The more resolute champions of the cross held a parliament at Soissons for the election of a new general; but such was the incapacity, or jealousy, or reluctance, of the princes of France that none could be found both able and willing to assume the conduct of the enterprise. They acquiesced in the choice of a stranger, of Boniface, marquis [August, A.D. 1201] of Montferrat, descended of a race of heroes, and himself of conspicuous fame in the wars and negotiations of the times;[52] nor could the piety or ambition of the Italian chief decline this honourable invitation. After visiting the French court, where he was received as a friend and kinsman, the marquis, in the church of Soissons, was invested with the cross of a pilgrim and the staff of a general; and immediately repassed the Alps, to prepare for the distant expedition of the East.[53] About the festival of the Pentecost, he displayed his banner, and marched towards Venice at the head of the Italians: he was preceded or

[51] [In the meantime Venice had played the Crusaders false. It had been agreed that the object of the expedition was to be Egypt. During the months which elapsed between the treaty with the Crusaders (March, 1201) and the date they were to assemble at Venice (June 24, 1202), the Republic negotiated with the Sultan of Egypt; her envoys concluded a treaty with him on May 13, 1202, and it was ratified at Venice in July. By this treaty, Venice undertook that the Crusade should not attack Egypt, and received in return important concessions: a quarter in Alexandria, and the privilege that all pilgrims who visited the Holy Sepulchre under her protection should be safe (a privilege of great pecuniary value). It is clear that this treaty, carefully concealed, proves that the diversion of the Fourth Crusade was a deliberate plan and not an accident. The treaty was first exposed by Hopf (Ersch und Gruber, Enzyklopädie, vol. 85, p. 188). It is mentioned by Ernoul (William of Tyre's Continuator), Recueil, vol. 2, p. 250.]

[52] By a victory (A.D. 1191) over the citizens of Asti, by a crusade to Palestine, and by an embassy from the pope to the German princes (Muratori, Annali d'Italia, tom. x. p. 163, 202).

[53] [Boniface of Montferrat went in October, 1201, to the court of Philip of Swabia, who was son-in-law of Isaac Angelus; and he remained there till the first months of 1202, when he departed with an embassy to Pope Innocent to plead at Rome the cause of young Alexius. (See Gesta Innocentii, 84.) At Philip's court a plot was hatched. See below, note 63.]

followed by the counts of Flanders and Blois, and the most respectable barons of France ; and their numbers were swelled by
the pilgrims of Germany,[54] whose object and motives were similar
to their own.  The Venetians had fulfilled, and even surpassed,
their engagements; stables were constructed for the horses, and
barracks for the troops; the magazines were abundantly replenished with forage and provisions ; and the fleet of transports, ships,
and galleys was ready to hoist sail, as soon as the republic had received the price of the freight and armament.[55]  But that price far
exceeded the wealth of the crusaders who were assembled at
Venice.  The Flemings, whose obedience to their court was voluntary and precarious, had embarked in their vessels for the long navigation of the ocean and Mediterranean ; and many of the French
and Italians had preferred a cheaper and more convenient passage
from Marseilles and Apulia to the Holy Land.  Each pilgrim
might complain that, after he had furnished his own contribution,
he was made responsible for the deficiency of his absent brethren :
the gold and silver plate of the chiefs, which they freely delivered
to the treasury of St. Mark, was a generous but inadequate sacrifice ; and, after all their efforts, thirty-four thousand marks were
still wanting to complete the stipulated sum.  The obstacle was
removed by the policy and patriotism of the doge,[56] who proposed to the barons that, if they would join their arms in reducing some revolted cities of Dalmatia, he would expose his person
in the holy war, and obtain from the republic a long indulgence,
till some wealthy conquest should afford the means of satisfying
the debt.  After much scruple and hesitation, they chose rather
to accept the offer than to relinquish the enterprise ; and the first

[54] See the crusade of the Germans in the Historia C. P. of Gunther (Canisii
Antiq. Lect. tom. iv. p. v. viii.), who celebrates the pilgrimage of his abbot Martin,
one of the preaching rivals of Fulk of Neuilly.  His monastery, of the Cistercian
order, was situate in the diocese of Basil.  [Gunther was prior of Päris in Elsass.
The work has been separately edited by the Count de Riant, 1875.]

[55] [The price was 4 marks a horse and 2 a man ; which, reckoning the mark at
52 francs, amounts to £180,000.  Pears, Fall of Constantinople, p. 234.]

[56] [According to Robert de Clari, the Venetians kept the Crusaders imprisoned
in the island of S. Niccolò di Lido, and applied the screw of starvation.  Two
proposals were then made ; the first was, that the expedition should start for the
East, and that the spoil of the first city d'outremer which they attacked should be
appropriated to pay the debt to Venice ; the second was that Zara should be attacked, but this was confided only to the chiefs and concealed from the mass of
the host, until they reached the doomed city.  The account in the text, which represents the enterprise against Zara as started for the purpose of accommodating the
difficulty, and the Venetians as honestly prepared at this stage to transport the
Crusaders to the East, provided they were paid, is the account which Villehardouin
successfully imposed upon the world.]

hostilities of the fleet and army were directed against Zara,[57] a Siege of Zara.<br>Nov. 10 strong city of the Sclavonian coast, which had renounced its allegiance to Venice and implored the protection of the king of Hungary.[58] The crusaders burst the chain or boom of the harbour ; landed their horses, troops, and military engines ; and compelled the inhabitants, after a defence of five days, to surrender at discretion ; their lives were spared, but the revolt was punished [Nov. 24] by the pillage of their houses and the demolition of their walls. The season was far advanced ; the French and Venetians resolved to pass the winter in a secure harbour and plentiful country ; but their repose was disturbed by national and tumultuous quarrels of the soldiers and mariners. The conquest of Zara had scattered the seeds of discord and scandal ; the arms of the allies had been stained in their outset with the blood, not of infidels, but of Christians ; the king of Hungary and his new subjects were themselves enlisted under the banner of the cross, and the scruples of the devout were magnified by the fear or lassitude of the reluctant pilgrims. The pope had excommunicated the false crusaders, who had pillaged and massacred their brethren ; [59] and only the marquis Boniface and Simon of Montfort escaped these spiritual thunders ; the one by his absence from the siege, the other by his final departure from the camp. Innocent might absolve the simple and submissive penitents of France ; but he was provoked by the stubborn reason of the Venetians, who refused to confess their guilt, to accept their pardon, or to allow, in their temporal concerns, the interposition of a priest.

The assembly of such formidable powers by sea and land had Alliance of<br>the crusaders<br>with the<br>Greek prince,<br>the young<br>Alexius revived the hopes of young [60] Alexius ; and, both at Venice and Zara, he solicited the arms of the crusaders for his own restora-

---

[57] Jadera, now Zara, was a Roman colony, which acknowledged Augustus for its parent. It is now only two miles round, and contains five or six thousand inhabitants ; but the fortifications are strong, and it is joined to the mainland by a bridge. See the travels of the two companions, Spon and Wheler (Voyage de Dalmatie, de Grèce, &c. tom. i. p. 64-70 ; Journey into Greece, p. 8-14) ; the last of whom, by mistaking *Sestertia* for *Sestertii*, values an arch with statues and columns at twelve pounds. If in his time there were no trees near Zara, the cherry-rees were not yet planted which produce our incomparable *marasquin*.

[58] Katona (Hist. Critica Reg. Hungariæ, Stirpis Arpad. tom. iv. p. 536-558) collects all the facts and testimonies most adverse to the conquerors of Zara.

[59] See the whole transaction, and the sentiments of the pope, in the Epistles of Innocent III. Gesta, c. 86-88.

[60] A modern reader is surprised to hear of the valet de Constantinople, as applied to young Alexius on account of his youth, like the *infants* of Spain, and the *nobilissimus puer* of the Romans. The pages and *valets* of the knights were as noble as themselves (Villehardouin and Ducange, No. 36).

tion and his father's [61] deliverance. The royal youth was recommended by Philip, king of Germany ; [62] his prayers and presence excited the compassion of the camp; and his cause was embraced and pleaded by the marquis of Montferrat [63] and the doge of Venice. A double alliance and the dignity of Cæsar had connected with the Imperial family the two elder brothers of Boniface ; [64] he expected to derive a kingdom from the important service ; and the more generous ambition of Dandolo was eager to secure the inestimable benefits of trade and dominion that might accrue to his country.[65] Their influence procured a favourable audience for the ambassadors of Alexius ; and, if the magnitude of his offers excited some suspicion, the motives and rewards which he displayed might justify the delay and diversion of those forces which had been consecrated to the deliverance of Jerusalem. He promised, in his own and his father's name, that, as soon as they should be seated on the throne of Constantinople, they would terminate the long schism of the Greeks, and submit themselves and their people to the lawful supremacy of the Roman church. He engaged to recompense the labours and merits of the crusaders by the immediate payment of two hundred thousand marks of silver ; to accompany them in person to Egypt ; or, if it should be judged more advantageous, to maintain, during a year, ten thousand

[61] The Emperor Isaac is styled by Villehardouin, *Sursac* (No. 35, &c.), which may be derived from the French *Sire*, or the Greek Κύρ (κύριος) melted into his proper name [from *Sire;* for Κύρ could not become *Sur*] ; the farther corruptions of Tursac and Conserac will instruct us what licence may have been used in the old dynasties of Assyria and Egypt.

[62] [Whose court he visited A.D. 1201.]

[63] [The conduct of the Marquis of Montferrat was not more ingenuous than that of Dandolo. He was, no more than Dandolo, a genuine crusader ; he used the crusaders for his own purpose, and that purpose was, from the beginning, to restore Alexius. The plan was arranged during the winter at the court of Philip of Swabia to which Alexius had betaken himself after his escape from Constantinople ; Boniface, as we have seen, was there too (above, p. 385, note 53) ; and there can be no doubt that there was a complete understanding between them. Cp. Gesta Innocentii, 83. Philip nursed the dream of a union of the eastern and the western empires. Thus Boniface and Dandolo (for different reasons) agreed on the policy of diverting their expedition to Constantinople long before it started ; they hoodwinked the mass of the crusaders ; and the difficulties about payment were pressed only for the purpose of accomplishing the ultimate object.]

[64] Reinier and Conrad : the former married Maria, daughter of the Emperor Manuel Comnenus ; the latter was the husband of Theodora Angela, sister of the Emperors Isaac and Alexius. Conrad abandoned the Greek court and princess for the glory of defending Tyre against Saladin (Ducange, Fam. Byzant. p. 187, 203)

[65] Nicetas (in Alexio Comneno, l. iii. c. 9) accuses the doge and Venetians as the first authors of the war against Constantinople, and considers only as a κῦμα ὑπὲ [*leg.* ἐπὶ] κύματι the arrival and shameful offers of the royal exile.

men, and, during his life, five hundred knights, for the service
of the Holy Land. These tempting conditions were accepted
by the republic of Venice; and the eloquence of the doge and
marquis persuaded the counts of Flanders, Blois, and St.
Pol, with eight barons of France, to join in the glorious enterprise.
A treaty of offensive and defensive alliance was confirmed by
their oaths and seals; and each individual, according to his
situation and character, was swayed by the hope of public or
private advantage; by the honour of restoring an exiled monarch;
or by the sincere and probable opinion that their efforts in Palestine would be fruitless and unavailing, and that the acquisition
of Constantinople must precede and prepare the recovery of
Jerusalem. But they were the chiefs or equals of a valiant
band of freemen and volunteers, who thought and acted for
themselves; the soldiers and clergy were divided; and, if a
large majority subscribed to the alliance, the numbers and
arguments of the dissidents were strong and respectable.[66] The
boldest hearts were appalled by the report of the naval
power and impregnable strength of Constantinople; and their
apprehensions were disguised to the world, and perhaps to
themselves, by the more decent objections of religion and
duty. They alleged the sanctity of a vow, which had drawn
them from their families and homes to rescue the holy sepulchre;
nor should the dark and crooked counsels of human policy divert
them from a pursuit, the event of which was in the hands of
the Almighty. Their first offence, the attack of Zara, had been
severely punished by the reproach of their conscience and the
censures of the pope; nor would they again imbrue their hands
in the blood of their fellow-Christians. The apostle of Rome
had pronounced; nor would they usurp the right of avenging
with the sword the schism of the Greeks and the doubtful
usurpation of the Byzantine monarch. On these principles or
pretences, many pilgrims, the most distinguished for their valour
and piety, withdrew from the camp; and their retreat was less
pernicious than the open or secret opposition of a discontented
party, that laboured, on every occasion, to separate the army
and disappoint the enterprise.

Notwithstanding this defection, the departure of the fleet and
army was vigorously pressed by the Venetians, whose zeal for

Voyage from
Zara to Con-
stantinople.
A.D. 1203,
April 7—June
24

[66] Villehardouin and Gunther represent the sentiments of the two parties. The
abbot Martin left the army at Zara, proceeded to Palestine, was sent ambassador
to Constantinople, and became a reluctant witness of the second siege.

the service of the royal youth concealed a just resentment to his nation and family. They were mortified by the recent preference which had been given to Pisa, the rival of their trade ; they had a long arrear of debt and injury to liquidate with the Byzantine court ; and Dandolo might not discourage the popular tale that he had been deprived of his eyes by the emperor Manuel, who perfidiously violated the sanctity of an ambassador. A similar armament, for ages, had not rode the Adriatic ; it was composed of one hundred and twenty flat-bottomed vessels or *palanders* for the horses ; two hundred and forty transports filled with men and arms ; seventy store-ships laden with provisions ; and fifty stout galleys, well prepared for the encounter of an enemy.[67] While the wind was favourable, the sky serene, and the water smooth, every eye was fixed with wonder and delight on the scene of military and naval pomp which overspread the sea. The shields of the knights and squires, at once an ornament and a defence, were arranged on either side of the ships ; the banners of the nations and families were displayed from the stern ; our modern artillery was supplied by three hundred engines for casting stones and darts ; the fatigues of the way were cheered with the sound of music ; and the spirits of the adventurers were raised by the mutual assurance that forty thousand Christian heroes were equal to the conquest of the world.[68]  In the navigation [69] from Venice and Zara, the fleet was successfully steered by the skill and experience of the Venetian pilots ; at Durazzo the confederates first landed on the territory of the Greek empire ; the isle of

[67] The birth and dignity of Andrew Dandolo gave him the motive and the means of searching in the archives of Venice the memorable story of his ancestor. His brevity seems to accuse the copious and more recent narratives of Sanudo (in Muratori, Script. Rerum Italicarum, tom. xx.), Blondus, Sabellicus, and Rhamnusius.

[68] Villehardouin, No. 62.  His feelings and expressions are original ; he often weeps, but he rejoices in the glories and perils of war with a spirit unknown to a sedentary writer.

[69] In this voyage, almost all the geographical names are corrupted by the Latins. The modern appellation of Chalcis, and all Euboea, is derived from its *Euripus*, *Evripo*, *Negri-po*, *Negropont*, which dishonours our maps (d'Anville, Géographie Ancienne, tom. i. p. 263).  [Negroponte is a corruption of ʹστὸν Εὔριπον (divided στὸ Νεύριπον) with an attempt to make sense in the spirit of popular etymology : negroponte, " black bridge," being suggested to Italians by the bridge of Chalcis connecting the island with the mainland.   But we also find the intermediate form *Egripons* (e.g., in the letters of Pope Innocent).   It is remarkable that in the 10th century the town of Chalcis (or the whole island ?) is called Χρῆπος (see Const. Porphyr. de Caer. ii., c. 44, p. 657, ὁ ἄρχων Χρήπου), apparently from Εὔριπος.]

Corfu afforded a station and repose; [70] they doubled, without
accident, the perilous cape of Malea, the southern point of
Peloponnesus, or the Morea; made a descent in the islands of
Negropont and Andros; and cast anchor at Abydus, on the
Asiatic side of the Hellespont. These preludes of conquest
were easy and bloodless; the Greeks of the provinces, without
patriotism or courage, were crushed by an irresistible force; the
presence of the lawful heir might justify their obedience; and
it was rewarded by the modesty and discipline of the Latins.
As they penetrated through the Hellespont, the magnitude of
their navy was compressed in a narrow channel; and the face
of the waters was darkened with innumerable sails. They again
expanded in the bason of the Propontis, and traversed that
placid sea, till they approached the European shore, at the
abbey of St. Stephen, three leagues to the west of Constantinople. The prudent doge dissuaded them from dispersing
themselves in a populous and hostile land; and, as their stock
of provisions was reduced, it was resolved, in the season of harvest, to replenish their store-ships in the fertile islands of the
Propontis. With this resolution they directed their course; but
a strong gale and their own impatience drove them to the
eastward; and so near did they run to the shore and city that
some volleys of stones and darts were exchanged between the
ships and the rampart. As they passed along, they gazed with
admiration on the capital of the East, or, as it should seem, of
the earth, rising from her seven hills, and towering over the
continents of Europe and Asia. The swelling domes and lofty
spires of five hundred palaces and churches were gilded by the
sun and reflected in the waters; the walls were crowded with
soldiers and spectators, whose numbers they beheld, of whose
temper they were ignorant; and each heart was chilled by the
reflection that, since the beginning of the world, such an enterprise had never been undertaken by such an handful of warriors.
But the momentary apprehension was dispelled by hope and
valour; and every man, says the marshal of Champagne, glanced
his eye on the sword or lance which he must speedily use in the
glorious conflict.[71] The Latins cast anchor before Chalcedon;

[70] [At Corfù, Alexius joined the army as a *protégé* of Boniface; and here the
matter was first clearly brought before the Crusaders and hotly debated in an
assembly. See Robert de Clari, § 32, 33.]

[71] Et sachiez que il ne ot si hardi cui le cuer ne fremist (c. 67). . . . Chascuns
regardoit ses armes . . . que par tems en aront mestier (c. 68). Such is the
honesty of courage!

the mariners only were left in the vessels; the soldiers, horses, and arms were safely landed; and, in the luxury of an Imperial palace, the barons tasted the first-fruits of their success. On the third day, the fleet and army moved towards Scutari, the Asiatic suburb of Constantinople; a detachment of Greek horse was surprised and defeated by fourscore French knights; and, in a halt of nine days, the camp was plentifully supplied with forage and provisions.

Fruitless negotiation of the emperor    In relating the invasion of a great empire, it may seem strange that I have not described the obstacles which should have checked the progress of the strangers. The Greeks, in truth, were an unwarlike people; but they were rich, industrious, and subject to the will of a single man, had that man been capable of fear when his enemies were at a distance, or of courage when they approached his person. The first rumour of his nephew's alliance with the French and Venetians was despised by the usurper Alexius; his flatterers persuaded him that in his contempt he was bold and sincere; and each evening, in the close of the banquet, he thrice discomfited the barbarians of the West. These barbarians had been justly terrified by the report of his naval power; and the sixteen hundred fishing-boats of Constantinople [72] could have manned a fleet to sink them in the Adriatic, or stop their entrance in the mouth of the Hellespont. But all force may be annihilated by the negligence of the prince and the venality of his ministers. The great duke, or admiral, made a scandalous, almost a public auction of the sails, the masts, and the rigging; the royal forests were reserved for the more important purpose of the chase; and the trees, says Nicetas, were guarded by the eunuchs like the groves of religious worship. [73] From this dream of pride Alexius was awakened by the siege of Zara and the rapid advances of the Latins: as soon as he saw the danger was real, he thought it inevitable, and his vain presumption was lost in abject despondency and despair. He suffered these contemptible barbarians to pitch their camp in the sight of the palace; and his apprehensions were thinly disguised by the pomp and menace of a suppliant embassy. The sovereign of the Romans was astonished (his

---

[72] Eandem urbem plus in solis navibus piscatorem abundare, quam illos in toto navigio. Habebat enim mille et sexcentas piscatorias naves . . . Bellicas autem sive mercatorias habebant infinitæ multitudinis et portum tutissimum. Gunther, Hist. C. P. c. 8, p. 10.

[73] Καθάπερ ἱερῶν ἀλσέων, εἰπεῖν δὲ καὶ θεοφυτεύτων παραδείσων ἐφέιδοντο τουτωνί. Nicetas in Alex. Comneno, l. iii. c. 9, p. 348.

ambassadors were instructed to say) at the hostile appearance of the strangers. If these pilgrims were sincere in their vow for the deliverance of Jerusalem, his voice must applaud, and his treasures should assist, their pious design ; but, should they dare to invade the sanctuary of empire, their numbers, were they ten times more considerable, should not protect them from his just resentment. The answer of the doge and barons was simple and magnanimous : " In the cause of honour and justice," they said, " we despise the usurper of Greece, his threats, and his offers. *Our* friendship and *his* allegiance are due to the lawful heir, to the young prince who is seated among us, and to his father, the emperor Isaac, who has been deprived of his sceptre, his freedom, and his eyes, by the crime of an ungrateful brother. Let that brother confess his guilt and implore forgiveness, and we ourselves will intercede that he may be permitted to live in affluence and security. But let him not insult us by a second message ; our reply will be made in arms, in the palace of Constantinople."

On the tenth day of their encampment at Scutari, the crusaders prepared themselves, as soldiers and as Catholics, for the passage of the Bosphorus. Perilous indeed was the adventure ; the stream was broad and rapid ; in a calm the current of the Euxine might drive down the liquid and unextinguishable fires of the Greeks ; and the opposite shores of Europe were defended by seventy thousand horse and foot in formidable array. On this memorable day, which happened to be bright and pleasant, the Latins were distributed in six battles, or divisions ; the first, or vanguard, was led by the count of Flanders, one of the most powerful of the Christian princes in the skill and number of his cross-bows. The four successive battles of the French were commanded by his brother Henry, the counts of St. Pol and Blois, and Matthew of Montmorency, the last of whom was honoured by the voluntary service of the marshal and nobles of Champagne. The sixth division, the rear-guard and reserve of the army, was conducted by the marquis of Montferrat, at the head of the Germans and Lombards. The chargers, saddled, with their long caparisons dragging on the ground, were embarked in the flat *palanders ;* [74] and the knights stood by the

Passage of the Bosphorus. July 6

[74] From the version of Vigenère I adopt the well-sounding word *palander*, which is still used, I believe, in the Mediterranean. But had I written in French, I should have preferred the original and expressive denomination of *vessiers*, or *huissiers*, from the *huis*, or door, which was let down as a drawbridge ; but which, at sea, was closed into the side of the ship (see Ducange au Villehardouin, No. 14, and Joinville, p. 27, 28, édit. du Louvre).

sides of their horses, in complete armour, their helmets laced,
and their lances in their hands. Their numerous train of *serjeants* [75] and archers occupied the transports ; and each transport
was towed by the strength and swiftness of a galley. The six
divisions traversed the Bosphorus, without encountering an
enemy or an obstacle ; to land the foremost was the wish, to
conquer or die was the resolution, of every division and of every
soldier. Jealous of the pre-eminence of danger, the knights in
their heavy armour leaped into the sea, when it rose as high as
their girdle ; the serjeants and archers were animated by their
valour ; and the squires, letting down the drawbridges of the
palanders, led the horses to the shore. Before the squadrons
could mount, and form, and couch their lances, the seventy
thousand Greeks had vanished from their sight ; the timid
Alexius gave the example to his troops ; and it was only by the
plunder of his rich pavilions that the Latins were informed that
they had fought against an emperor. In the first consternation
of the flying enemy, they resolved, by a double attack, to open
the entrance of the harbour. The tower of Galata,[76] in the suburb of Pera, was attacked and stormed by the French, while
the Venetians assumed the more difficult task of forcing the
boom or chain that was stretched from that tower to the Byzantine shore. After some fruitless attempts, their intrepid perseverance prevailed ; twenty ships of war, the relics of the
Grecian navy, were either sunk or taken ; the enormous and
massy links of iron were cut asunder by the shears, or broken
by the weight of the galleys ; [77] and the Venetian fleet, safe and
triumphant, rode at anchor in the port of Constantinople. By

[75] To avoid the vague expressions of followers, &c., I use, after Villehardouin,
the word *serjeants* for all horsemen who were not knights. There were serjeants
at arms, and serjeants at law ; and, if we visit the parade and Westminster-hall,
we may observe the strange result of the distinction (Ducange, Glossar. Latin,
*Servientes*, &c. tom. vi. p. 226-231).

[76] It is needless to observe that on the subject of Galata, the chain, &c., Ducange
is accurate and full. Consult likewise the proper chapters of the C. P. Christiana
of the same author. The inhabitants of Galata were so vain and ignorant that
they applied to themselves St. Paul's Epistle to the Galatians. [The chain was
fixed, on the city side, close to the gate of St. Eugenius. Part of the chain is still
preserved in the court of the church of St. Irene. Cp. Mordtmann, Esquisse topo-
graphique de Constantinople, p. 49.]

[77] The vessel that broke the chain was named the Eagle, *Aquila* (Dandol.
Chronicon. p. 322), which Blondus (de Gestis Venet.) has changed into *Aquilo*,
the north wind. Ducange, Observations, No. 83, maintains the latter reading
but he had not seen the respectable text of Dandolo ; nor did he enough consider
the topography of the harbour. The south-east would have been a more effectual
wind.

these daring achievements, a remnant of twenty thousand Latins solicited the licence of besieging a capital which contained above four hundred thousand inhabitants,[78] able, though not willing, to bear arms in the defence of their country. Such an account would indeed suppose a population of near two millions ; but, whatever abatement may be required in the numbers of the Greeks, the *belief* of those numbers will equally exalt the fearless spirit of their assailants.

In the choice of the attack, the French and Venetians were divided by their habits of life and warfare. The former affirmed with truth that Constantinople was most accessible on the side of the sea and the harbour. The latter might assert with honour that they had long enough trusted their lives and fortunes to a frail bark and a precarious element, and loudly demanded a trial of knighthood, a firm ground, and a close onset, either on foot or horseback. After a prudent compromise, of employing the two nations by sea and land in the service best suited to their character, the fleet covering the army, they both proceeded from the entrance to the extremity of the harbour ; the stone-bridge of the river was hastily repaired ; and the six battles of the French formed their encampment against the front of the capital, the basis of the triangle which runs about four miles from the port to the Propontis.[79] On the edge of a broad ditch, at the foot of a lofty rampart, they had leisure to contemplate the difficulties of their enterprise. The gates to the right and left of their narrow camp poured forth frequent sallies of cavalry and light infantry, which cut off their stragglers, swept the country of provisions, sounded the alarm five or six times in the course of each day, and compelled them to plant a palisade, and sink an entrenchment, for their immediate safety. In the supplies and convoys the Venetians had been too sparing, or the Franks too voracious ; the usual complaints of hunger and scarcity were heard, and perhaps felt ; their stock of flour would be exhausted in three

First siege and conquest of Constantinople by the Latins. July 7-18

---

[78] Quatre cens mil homes ou plus (Villehardouin, No. 134) must be understood of *men* of a military age. Le Beau (Hist. du Bas Empire, tom. xx. p. 417) allows Constantinople a million of inhabitants, of whom 60,000 horse, and an infinite number of foot-soldiers. In its present decay the capital of the Ottoman empire may contain 400,000 souls (Bell's Travels, vol. ii. p. 401, 402) ; but, as the Turks keep no registers, and as circumstances are fallacious, it is impossible to ascertain (Niebuhr, Voyage en Arabie, tom. i. p. 18, 19) the real populousness of their cities.

[79] On the most correct plans of Constantinople, I know not how to measure more than 4000 paces. Yet Villehardouin computes the space at three leagues (No. 86). If his eye were not deceived, he must reckon by the old Gallic league of 1500 paces, which might still be used in Champagne.

weeks ; and their disgust of salt meat tempted them to taste the
flesh of their horses.  The trembling usurper was supported by
Theodore Lascaris, his son-in-law, a valiant youth, who aspired
to save and to rule his country ; the Greeks, regardless of that
country, were awakened to the defence of their religion ; but
their firmest hope was in the strength and spirit of the Varangian
guards, of the Danes and English, as they are named in the writers of the times.[80]    After ten days' incessant labour the ground
was levelled, the ditch filled, the approaches of the besiegers
were regularly made, and two hundred and fifty engines of
assault exercised their various powers to clear the rampart, to
batter the walls, and to sap the foundations.  On the first appearance of a breach the scaling-ladders were applied ; the numbers that defended the vantage-ground repulsed and oppressed
the adventurous Latins ; but they admired the resolution of
fifteen knights and serjeants, who had gained the ascent, and
maintained their perilous station till they were precipitated or
[July 17]   made prisoners by the Imperial guards.  On the side of the
harbour, the naval attack was more successfully conducted by the
Venetians ; and that industrious people employed every resource
that was known and practised before the invention of gun-powder.
A double line, three bow-shots in front, was formed by the galleys
and ships ; and the swift motion of the former was supported by
the weight and loftiness of the latter, whose decks and poops
and turret were the platforms of military engines, that discharged
their shot over the heads of the first line.  The soldiers, who
leapt from the galleys on shore, immediately planted and ascended their scaling-ladders, while the large ships, advancing
more slowly into the intervals, and lowering a drawbridge, opened
a way through the air from their masts to the rampart.  In the
midst of the conflict, the doge, a venerable and conspicuous form,
stood aloft, in complete armour, on the prow of his galley.  The
great standard of St. Mark was displayed before him ; his threats,
promises, and exhortations urged the diligence of the rowers ;
his vessel was the first that struck ; and Dandolo was the first
warrior on the shore.  The nations admired the magnanimity of
the blind old man, without reflecting that his age and infirmities
diminished the price of life and enhanced the value of immortal
glory.  On a sudden, by an invisible hand (for the standard-

---

[80] The guards, the Varangi, are styled by Villehardouin (No. 89, 95, &c.) Englois
et Danois avec leurs haches.  Whatever had been their origin, a French pilgrim
could not be mistaken in the nations of which they were at that time composed.

bearer was probably slain), the banner of the republic was fixed on the rampart; twenty-five towers were rapidly occupied; and, by the cruel expedient of fire, the Greeks were driven from the adjacent quarter. The doge had dispatched the intelligence of his success, when he was checked by the danger of his confederates. Nobly declaring that he would rather die with the pilgrims than gain a victory by their destruction, Dandolo relinquished his advantage, recalled his troops, and hastened to the scene of action. He found the six weary diminutive *battles* of the French encompassed by sixty squadrons of the Greek cavalry, the least of which was more numerous than the largest of their divisions. Shame and despair had provoked Alexius to the last effort of a general sally; but he was awed by the firm order and manly aspect of the Latins; and, after skirmishing at a distance, withdrew his troops in the close of the evening. The silence or tumult of the night exasperated his fears; and the timid usurper, collecting a treasure of ten thousand pounds of gold, basely deserted his wife, his people, and his fortune; threw himself into a bark, stole through the Bosphorus, and landed in shameful safety in an obscure harbour of Thrace. As soon as they were apprised of his flight, the Greek nobles sought pardon and peace in the dungeon where the blind Isaac expected each hour the visit of the executioner. Again saved and exalted by the vicissitudes of fortune, the captive in his Imperial robes was replaced on the throne, and surrounded with prostrate slaves, whose real terror and affected joy he was incapable of discerning. At the dawn of day hostilities were suspended; and the Latin chiefs were surprised by a message from the lawful and reigning emperor, who was impatient to embrace his son and to reward his generous deliverers.[81]

But these generous deliverers were unwilling to release their hostage, till they had obtained from his father the payment, or at least the promise, of their recompense. They chose four ambassadors, Matthew of Montmorency, our historian the marshal of Champagne, and two Venetians, to congratulate the emperor. The gates were thrown open on their approach, the streets on both sides were lined with the battle-axes of the Danish and

*Restoration of the Emperor Isaac Angelus, and his son Alexius. July 19*

---

[81] For the first siege and conquest of Constantinople, we may read the original letter of the crusaders to Innocent III. Gesta, c. 91, p. 533, 534; Villehardouin, No. 75-99; Nicetas in Alexio Comneno, l. iii. c. 10, p. 349-352; Dandolo, in Chron. p. 322. Gunther and his abbot Martin were not yet returned from their obstinate pilgrimage to Jerusalem, or St. John d'Acre, where the greatest part of the company had died of the plague.

English guard : the presence chamber glittered with gold and
jewels, the false substitutes of virtue and power ; by the side of
the blind Isaac his wife was seated, the sister of the king of
Hungary ; and by her appearance the noble matrons of Greece
were drawn from their domestic retirement and mingled witht h :
circle of senators and soldiers.  The Latins, by the mouth of the
marshal, spoke like men conscious of their merits, but who respected the work of their own hands ; and the emperor clearly
understood that his son's engagement with Venice and the pilgrims must be ratified without hesitation or delay.  Withdrawing
into a private chamber with the empress, a chamberlain, an interpreter, and the four ambassadors, the father of young Alexius
inquired with some anxiety into the nature of his stipulations : the
submission of the Eastern empire to the pope, the succour of the
Holy Land, and a present contribution of two hundred thousand
marks of silver.—"These conditions are weighty," was his prudent
reply ; " they are hard to accept and difficult to perform.  But no
conditions can exceed the measure of your services and deserts."
After this satisfactory assurance, the barons mounted on horseback, and introduced the heir of Constantinople to the city and
palace : his youth and marvellous adventures engaged every heart
[Aug. 1] in his favour, and Alexius was solemnly crowned with his father
in the dome of St. Sophia.  In the first days of his reign, the
people, already blessed with the restoration of plenty and peace,
was delighted by the joyful catastrophe of the tragedy ; and the
discontent of the nobles, their regret, and their fears, were covered
by the polished surface of pleasure and loyalty.  The mixture of
two discordant nations in the same capital might have been pregnant with mischief and danger ; and the suburb of Galata, or
Pera, was assigned for the quarters of the French and Venetians.
But the liberty of trade and familiar intercourse was allowed between the friendly nations ; and each day the pilgrims were
tempted by devotion or curiosity to visit the churches and palaces
of Constantinople.  Their rude minds, insensible perhaps of the
finer arts, were astonished by the magnificent scenery ; and the
poverty of their native towns enhanced the populousness and
riches of the first metropolis of Christendom.[82]  Descending from
his state, young Alexius was prompted by interest and gratitude
to repeat his frequent and familiar visits to his  Latin allies ; and

----

[82] Compare, in the rude energy of Villehardouin (No. 66, 100), the inside and
outside views of Constantinople, and their impression on the minds of the pilgrims :
Cette ville (says he) que de totes les autres ére souveraine.  See the parallel passages
of Fulcherius Carnotensis, Hist. Hierosol. l. i. c. 4, and Will. Tyr. ii. 3, xx. 26.

in the freedom of the table, the gay petulance of the French sometimes forgot the emperor of the East.[83] In their more serious conferences, it was agreed that the re-union of the two churches must be the result of patience and time ; but avarice was less tractable than zeal ; and a large sum was instantly disbursed to appease the wants, and silence the importunity, of the crusaders.[84] Alexius was alarmed by the approaching hour of their departure ; their absence might have relieved him from the engagement which he was yet incapable of performing ; but his friends would have left him, naked and alone, to the caprice and prejudice of a perfidious nation. He wished to bribe their stay, the delay of a year, by undertaking to defray their expense and to satisfy, in their name, the freight of the Venetian vessels. The offer was agitated in the council of the barons ; and, after a repetition of their debates and scruples, a majority of votes again acquiesced in the advice of the doge and the prayer of the young emperor. At the price of sixteen hundred pounds of gold, he prevailed on the marquis of Montferrat to lead him with an army round the provinces of Europe ; to establish his authority, and pursue his uncle, while Constantinople was awed by the presence of Baldwin and his confederates of France and Flanders. The expedition was successful : the blind emperor exulted in the success of his arms, and listened to the predictions of his flatterers, that the same Providence which had raised him from the dungeon to the throne would heal his gout, restore his sight, and watch over the long prosperity of his reign. Yet the mind of the suspicious old man was tormented by the rising glories of his son ; nor could his pride conceal from his envy that, while his own name was pronounced in faint and reluctant acclamations, the royal youth was the theme of spontaneous and universal praise.[85]

By the recent invasion the Greeks were awakened from a dream of nine centuries ; from the vain presumption that the

Quarrel of the Greeks and Latins

[83] As they played at dice, the Latins took off his diadem, and clapped on his head a woollen or hairy cap, τὸ μεγαλοπρεπὲς καὶ παγκλέϊστον κατερρύπαινεν ὄνομα (Nicetas, p. 358). If these merry companions were Venetians, it was the insolence of trade and a commonwealth.

[84] Villehardouin, No. 101. Dandolo, p. 322. The Doge affirms that the Venetians were paid more slowly than the French ; but he owns that the histories of the two nations differed on that subject. Had he read Villehardouin ? The Greeks complained, however, quod totius Graeciæ opes transtulisset (Gunther, Hist. C. P. c. 13). See the lamentations and invectives of Nicetas (p. 355 [in Isaac. et Alex. c. 1]).

[85] The reign of Alexius Comnenus occupies three books in Nicetas, p. 291-352. The short restoration of Isaac and his son is dispatched in five [four] chapters, p. 352-362.

capital of the Roman empire was impregnable to foreign arms. The strangers of the West had violated the city, and bestowed the sceptre, of Constantine : their Imperial clients soon became as unpopular as themselves: the well-known vices of Isaac were rendered still more contemptible by his infirmities ; and the young Alexius was hated as an apostate, who had renounced the manners and religion of his country.   His secret covenant with the Latins was divulged or suspected; the people, and especially the clergy, were devoutly attached to their faith and superstition ; and every convent and every shop resounded with the danger of the church and the tyranny of the pope.[86]   An empty treasury could ill supply the demands of regal luxury and foreign extortion ; the Greeks refused to avert, by a general tax, the impending evils of servitude and pillage ; the oppression of the rich excited a more dangerous and personal resentment ; and, if the emperor melted the plate, and despoiled the images, of the sanctuary, he seemed to justify the complaints of heresy and sacrilege. During the absence of marquis Boniface and his Imperial pupil, Constantinople was visited with a calamity which might be justly imputed to the zeal and indiscretion of the Flemish pilgrims.[87] In one of their visits to the city they were scandalized by the aspect of a mosque or synagogue, in which one God was worshipped, without a partner or a son.[88]   Their effectual mode of controversy was to attack the infidels with the sword, and their habitation with fire ; but the infidels, and some Christian neighbours, presumed to defend their lives and properties ; and the flames which bigotry had kindled consumed the most orthodox and innocent structures.   During eight days and nights the conflagration spread above a league in front, from the harbour to the Propontis, over the thickest and most populous regions of the city.   It is not easy to count the stately churches and palaces that were reduced to a smoking ruin, to value the merchandise that perished in the trading streets, or to number the families that were involved in the common destruction.   By this outrage,

---

[86] When Nicetas reproaches Alexius for his impious league, he bestows the harshest names on the pope's new religion, μεῖζον καὶ ἀτοπώτατον . . . παρεκτροπὴν πίστεως . . . τῶν τοῦ Πάπα προνομίων καινισμόν . . . μετάθεσίν τε καὶ μεταποίησιν τῶι παλαιῶν Ῥωμαίοις ἐθῶν (p. 348 [in Alex. iii. c. 9]).   Such was the sincere language of every Greek to the last gasp of the empire.

[87] Nicetas (p. 355 [c. 2]) is positive in the charge, and specifies the Fleming: (Φλαμίονες), though he is wrong in supposing it an ancient name.   Villehardouir (No. 107) exculpates the barons, and is ignorant (perhaps affectedly ignorant) o the names of the guilty.

[88] [The mosque of the Musulman merchants.]

which the doge and the barons in vain affected to disclaim, the name of the Latins became still more unpopular ; and the colony of that nation, above fifteen thousand persons, consulted their safety in a hasty retreat from the city to the protection of their standard in the suburb of Pera. The emperor returned in triumph ; but the firmest and most dexterous policy would have been insufficient to steer him through the tempest which overwhelmed the person and government of that unhappy youth. His own inclination and his father's advice attached him to his benefactors ; but Alexius hesitated between gratitude and patriotism, between the fear of his subjects and of his allies.[89] By his feeble and fluctuating conduct he lost the esteem and confidence of both ; and, while he invited the marquis of Montferrat to occupy the palace, he suffered the nobles to conspire, and the people to arm, for the deliverance of their country. Regardless of his painful situation, the Latin chiefs repeated their demands, resented his delays, suspected his intentions, and exacted a decisive answer of peace or war. The haughty summons was delivered by three French knights and three Venetian deputies, who girded their swords, mounted their horses, pierced through the angry multitude, and entered with a fearless countenance the palace and presence of the Greek emperor. In a peremptory tone they recapitulated their services and his engagements ; and boldly declared that, unless their just claims were fully and immediately satisfied, they should no longer hold him either as a sovereign or a friend. After this defiance, the first that had ever wounded an Imperial car, they departed without betraying any symptoms of fear ; but their escape from a servile palace and a furious city astonished the ambassadors themselves ; and their return to the camp was the signal of mutual hostility.

Among the Greeks, all authority and wisdom were overborne by the impetuous multitude, who mistook their rage for valour, their numbers for strength, and their fanaticism for the support and inspiration of Heaven. In the eyes of both nations, Alexius was false and contemptible ; the base and spurious race of the Angeli was rejected with clamorous disdain ; and the people of Constantinople encompassed the senate, to demand at their hands a more worthy emperor. To every senator, conspicuous by his birth or dignity, they successively presented the purple ; by each

*The war renewed. A.D. 1204*

---

[89] Compare the suspicions and complaints of Nicetas (p. 359-362 [c. 3, 4]) with the blunt charges of Baldwin of Flanders (Gesta Innocent. III. c. 92, p. 534), cum patriarchâ et mole nobilium, nobis promissis perjurus et mendax.

senator the deadly garment was repulsed ; the contest lasted three days ; and we may learn from the historian Nicetas, one of the members of the assembly, that fear and weakness were the guardians of their loyalty. A phantom, who vanished in oblivion, was forcibly proclaimed by the crowd;[90] but the author of the tumult, and the leader of the war, was a prince of the house of Ducas ; and his common appellation of Alexius must be discriminated by the epithet of Mourzoufle,[91] which in the vulgar idiom expressed the close junction of his black and shaggy eye-brows. At once a patriot and a courtier, the perfidious Mourzoufle, who was not destitute of cunning and courage, opposed the Latins both in speech and action, inflamed the passions and prejudices of the Greeks, and insinuated himself into the favour and confidence of Alexius, who trusted him with the office of Great Chamberlain and tinged his buskins with the colours of royalty. At the dead of night he rushed into the bed-chamber with an affrighted aspect, exclaiming that the palace was attacked by the people and betrayed by the guards. Starting from his couch, the unsuspecting prince threw himself into the arms of his enemy, who had contrived his escape by a private staircase. But that staircase terminated in a prison ; Alexius was seized, stripped, and loaded with chains ; and, after tasting some days the bitterness of death, he was poisoned, or strangled, or beaten with clubs, at the command, and in the presence, of the tyrant. The emperor Isaac Angelus soon followed his son to the grave, and Mourzoufle, perhaps, might spare the superfluous crime of hastening the extinction of impotence and blindness.

Alexius and his father deposed by Mourzoufle. Feb. 8

Second siege. January-April

The death of the emperors, and the usurpation of Mourzoufle, had changed the nature of the quarrel. It was no longer the disagreement of allies who over-valued their services or neglected their obligations : the French and Venetians forgot their complaints against Alexius, dropt a tear on the untimely fate of their companion, and swore revenge against the perfidious nation who had crowned his assassin. Yet the prudent doge was still inclined to negotiate ;[92] he asked as a debt, a subsidy, or a fine,

---

[90] His name was Nicholas Canabus : he deserved the praise of Nicetas, and the vengeance of Mourzoufle (p. 362 [c. 4]).

[91] Villehardouin (No. 116) speaks of him as a favourite, without knowing that he was a prince of the blood, *Angelus* and *Ducas*. Ducange, who pries into every corner, believes him to be the son of Isaac Ducas Sebastocrator, and second cousin of young Alexius.

[92] [From this time, Boniface, having lost his *protégé* Alexius, was no longer in cordial co-operation with the Doge. Dandolo carried out the rest of his plan himself. Cp. Pears, Fall of Constantinople, p. 334.]

fifty thousand pounds of gold, about two millions sterling ; nor would the conference have been abruptly broken, if the zeal or policy of Mourzoufle had not refused to sacrifice the Greek church to the safety of the state.[93] Amidst the invectives of his foreign and domestic enemies, we may discern that he was not unworthy of the character which he had assumed, of the public champion : the second siege of Constantinople was far more laborious than the first ; the treasury was replenished, the discipline was restored, by a severe inquisition into the abuses of the former reign ; and Mourzoufle, an iron mace in his hand, visiting the posts and affecting the port and aspect of a warrior, was an object of terror to his soldiers, at least, and to his kinsmen. Before and after the death of Alexius, the Greeks made two vigorous and well-conducted attempts to burn the navy in the harbour ; but the skill and courage of the Venetians repulsed the fire-ships ; and the vagrant flames wasted themselves without injury in the sea.[94] In a nocturnal sally the Greek emperor was vanquished by Henry, brother of the count of Flanders ; the advantages of number and surprise aggravated the shame of his defeat ; his buckler was found on the field of battle ; and the Imperial standard,[95] a divine image of the Virgin, was presented, as a trophy and a relic, to the Cistercian monks, the disciples of St. Bernard. Near three months, without excepting the holy season of Lent, were consumed in skirmishes and preparations, before the Latins were ready or resolved for a general assault. The land-fortifications had been found impregnable ; and the Venetian pilots represented that, on the shore of the Propontis, the anchorage was unsafe, and the ships must be driven by the current far away to the straits of the Hellespont : a prospect not unpleasing to the reluctant pilgrims, who sought every opportunity of breaking the army. From the harbour, therefore, the assault was determined by the assailants and expected by the besieged ; and the emperor had placed his scarlet pavilions on a neighbouring height, to direct and animate the efforts of his troops. A fearless spectator, whose mind could entertain the ideas of pomp and pleasure,

---

[93] This negotiation, probable in itself, and attested by Nicetas (p. 365 [in Murz. c. 2]), is omitted as scandalous by the delicacy of Dandolo and Villehardouin.

[94] Baldwin mentions both attempts to fire the fleet (Gest. c. 92, p. 534, 535) ; Villehardouin (No. 113-115) only describes the first. It is remarkable that neither of these warriors observe any peculiar properties in the Greek fire.

[95] Ducange (No. 119) pours forth a torrent of learning on the *Gonfanon Imperial*. This banner of the Virgin is shown at Venice as a trophy and relic ; if it be genuine, the pious doge must have cheated the monks of Citeaux.

might have admired the long array of two embattled armies,
which extended above half a league, the one on the ships and
galleys, the other on the walls and towers, raised above the ordi-
[April 9] nary level by several stages of wooden turrets. Their first fury
was spent in the discharge of darts, stones, and fire, from the
engines ; but the water was deep ; the French were bold ; the
Venetians were skilful: they approached the walls ; and a desperate conflict of swords, spears, and battle-axes was fought on the
trembling bridges that grappled the floating to the stable bat-
teries. In more than an hundred places the assault was urged
and the defence was sustained ; till the superiority of ground and
numbers finally prevailed, and the Latin trumpets sounded a
[April 12] retreat. On the ensuing days the attack was renewed with
equal vigour and a similar event ; and in the night the doge and
the barons held a council, apprehensive only for the public
danger ; not a voice pronounced the words of escape or treaty ;
and each warrior, according to his temper, embraced the hope
of victory or the assurance of a glorious death.[96] By the experience of the former siege, the Greeks were instructed, but
the Latins were animated ; and the knowledge that Constantinople *might* be taken was of more avail than the local precautions which that knowledge had inspired for its defence. In the
third assault two ships were linked together to double their
strength ; a strong north wind drove them on the shore ; the
bishops of Troyes and Soissons led the van ; and the auspicious
names of the *Pilgrim* and the *Paradise* resounded along the
line.[97] The episcopal banners were displayed on the walls ; an
hundred marks of silver had been promised to the first adventurers ; and, if their reward was intercepted by death, their
names have been immortalised by fame. Four towers were
scaled ; three gates were burst open ; and the French knights,
who might tremble on the waves, felt themselves invincible on
horseback on the solid ground. Shall I relate that the thousands
who guarded the emperor's person fled on the approach, and
before the lance, of a single warrior ? Their ignominious flight
is attested by their countryman Nicetas ; an army of phantoms
marched with the French hero, and he was magnified to a giant

---

[96] Villehardouin (No. 126) confesses that mult ere grant peril: and Guntherus
(Hist. C. P. c. 13) affirms that nulla spes victoriæ arridere poterat. Yet the knight
despises those who thought of flight, and the monk praises his countrymen who
were resolved on death.

[97] Baldwin and all the writers honour the names of these two galleys, felici
auspicio.

in the eyes of the Greeks.[98] While the fugitives deserted their posts and cast away their arms, the Latins entered the city under the banners of their leaders ; the streets and gates opened for their passage ; and either design or accident kindled a third conflagration, which consumed in a few hours the measure of three of the largest cities of France.[99] In the close of the evening, the barons checked their troops and fortified their stations ; they were awed by the extent and populousness of the capital, which might yet require the labour of a month, if the churches and palaces were conscious of their internal strength. But in the morning a suppliant procession, with crosses and images, announced the submission of the Greeks and deprecated the wrath of the conquerors: the usurper escaped through the golden gate ; the palaces of Blachernæ and Boucoleon were occupied by the count of Flanders and the marquis of Montferrat ; and the empire, which still bore the name of Constantine and the title of Roman, was subverted by the arms of the Latin pilgrims.[100]

Constantinople had been taken by storm ; and no restraints, except those of religion and humanity, were imposed on the conquerors by the laws of war. Boniface, marquis of Montferrat, still acted as their general ; and the Greeks, who revered his name as their future sovereign, were heard to exclaim in a lamentable tone, " Holy marquis-king, have mercy upon us ! " His prudence or compassion opened the gates of the city to the fugitives ; and he exhorted the soldiers of the cross to spare the lives of their fellow-Christians. The streams of blood that flow down the pages of Nicetas may be reduced to the slaughter of two thousand of his unresisting countrymen ;[101] and the greater

*Pillage of Constantinople.*
*[April, 12, 13]*

---

[98] With an allusion to Homer, Nicetas calls him ἐννέα ὀργυίας [ἐννεόργυιος], nine orgyæ, or eighteen yards high, a stature which would indeed have excused the terror of the Greek. [In Murz. c. 2, p. 754, ed. B.] On this occasion, the historian seems fonder of the marvellous than of his country, or perhaps of truth. Baldwin exclaims in the words of the psalmist, Persequitur unus ex nobis centum alienos.

[99] Villehardouin (No. 130) is again ignorant of the authors of *this* more legitimate fire, which is ascribed by Gunther to a quidam comes Teutonicus (c. 14). They seem ashamed, the incendiaries !

[100] For the second siege and conquest of Constantinople, see Villehardouin (No. 113-132), Baldwin's iid Epistle to Innocent III. (Gesta, c. 92, p. 534-537), with the whole reign of Mourzoufle in Nicetas (p. 363-375); and borrow some hints from Dandolo (Chron. Venet. p. 323-330) and Gunther (Hist. C. P. c. 14-18), who add the decorations of prophecy and vision. The former produces an oracle of the Erythræan sybil, of a great armament on the Adriatic, under a blind chief, against Byzantium, &c. Curious enough, were the prediction anterior to the fact.

[101] Ceciderunt tamen eâ die civium quasi duo millia, &c. (Gunther, c. 18). Arithmetic is an excellent touchstone to try the amplifications of passion and rhetoric.

part was massacred, not by the strangers, but by the Latins who had been driven from the city, and who exercised the revenge of a triumphant faction. Yet of these exiles, some were less mindful of injuries than of benefits ; and Nicetas himself was indebted for his safety to the generosity of a Venetian merchant. Pope Innocent the Third accuses the pilgrims of respecting, in their lust, neither age nor sex nor religious profession ; and bitterly laments that the deeds of darkness, fornication, adultery, and incest were perpetrated in open day ; and that noble matrons and holy nuns were polluted by the grooms and peasants of the Catholic camp.[102] It is indeed probable that the licence of victory prompted and covered a multitude of sins ; but it is certain that the capital of the East contained a stock of venal or willing beauty, sufficient to satiate the desires of twenty thousand pilgrims ; and female prisoners were no longer subject to the right or abuse of domestic slavery. The marquis of Montferrat was the patron of discipline and decency ; the count of Flanders was the mirror of chastity : they had forbidden, under pain of death, the rape of married women, or virgins, or nuns ; and the proclamation was sometimes invoked by the vanquished [103] and respected by the victors. Their cruelty and lust were moderated by the authority of the chiefs and feelings of the soldiers ; for we are no longer describing an irruption of the northern savages ; and, however ferocious they might still appear, time, policy, and religion had civilised the manners of the French, and still more of the Italians. But a free scope was allowed to their avarice, which was glutted, even in the holy week, by the pillage of Constantinople. The right of victory, unshackled by any promise or treaty, had confiscated the public and private wealth of the Greeks ; and every hand, according to its size and strength, might lawfully execute the sentence, and seize the forfeiture. A portable and universal standard of exchange was found in the coined and uncoined metals of gold and silver, which each captor at home or abroad might convert into the possessions

---

[102] Quidam (says Innocent III. Gesta, c. 94, p. 538) nec religioni, nec ætati, nec sexui pepercerunt ; sed fornicationes, adulteria, et incestus in occulis omnium exercentes, non solum maritatas et viduas, sed et matronas et virgines Deoque dicatas, exposuerunt spurcitiis garcionum. Villehardouin takes no notice of these common incidents.

[103] Nicetas saved, and afterwards married, a noble virgin (p. 380 [in Urb. Capt., c. 3]), whom a soldier, ἐπὶ μάρτυσι πολλοῖς ὀνηδὸν ἐπιβρωμώμενος, had almost violated in spite of the ἐντολαί, ἐντάλματα εὖ γεγονότων.

most suitable to his temper and situation. Of the treasures which trade and luxury had accumulated, the silks, velvets, furs, the gems, spices and rich moveables, were the most precious, as they could not be procured for money in the ruder countries of Europe. An order of rapine was instituted ; nor was the share of each individual abandoned to industry or chance. Under the tremendous penalties of perjury, excommunication and death, the Latins were bound to deliver their plunder into the common stock : three churches were selected for the deposit and distribution of the spoil ; a single share was allowed to a foot soldier ; two for a serjeant on horseback ; four to a knight ; and larger proportions according to the rank and merit of the barons and princes. For violating this sacred engagement, a knight, belonging to the count of St. Paul, was hanged, with his shield and coat of arms round his neck : his example might render similar offenders more artful and discreet ; but avarice was more powerful than fear ; and it is generally believed that the secret far exceeded the acknowledged plunder. Yet the magnitude of the prize surpassed the largest scale of experience or expectation.[104]    After the whole had been equally divided between the French and Venetians, fifty thousand marks were deducted to satisfy the debts of the former, and the demands of the latter. The residue of the French amounted to four hundred thousand marks of silver,[105] about eight hundred thousand pounds sterling ; nor can I better appreciate the value of that sum in the public and private transactions of the age than by defining it at seven times the annual revenue of the kingdom of England.[106]

In this great revolution, we enjoy the singular felicity of comparing the narratives of Villehardouin and Nicetas, the opposite feelings of the marshal of Champagne and the Byzantine

*Division of the spoil*

*Misery of the Greeks*

[104] Of the general mass of wealth, Gunther observes, ut de pauperibus et advenis cives ditissimi redderentur (Hist. C. P. c. 18) ; Villehardouin (No. 132 [250]), that since the creation, ne fu tant gaaignié dans [*leg.* en] une ville ; Baldwin (Gesta, c. 92), ut tantum tota non videatur possidere Latinitas.

[105] Villehardouin, No. 133-135.    Instead of 400,000, there is a various reading of 500,000.    The Venetians had offered to take the whole booty, and to give 400 marks to each knight, 200 to each priest and horseman, and 100 to each foot-soldier : they would have been great losers (Le Beau, Hist. du Bas-Empire, tom. xx. p. 506 :—I know not from whence).

[106] At the council of Lyons (A.D. 1245) the English ambassadors stated the revenue of the crown as below that of the foreign clergy, which amounted to 60,000 marks a year (Matthew Paris, p. 451 ; Hume's History of England, vol. ii. p. 170).

senator.[107]    At the first view, it should seem that the wealth of
Constantinople was only transferred from one nation to another,
and that the loss and sorrow of the Greeks is exactly balanced
by the joy and advantage of the Latins.    But in the miserable
account of war the gain is never equivalent to the loss, the
pleasure to the pain ; the smiles of the Latins were transient
and fallacious ; the Greeks for ever wept over the ruins of their
country ; and their real calamities were aggravated by sacrilege
and mockery.    What benefits accrued to the conquerors from
the three fires which annihilated so vast a portion of the buildings and riches of the city ?    What a stock of such things as
could neither be used or transported was maliciously or wantonly
destroyed !    How much treasure was idly wasted in gaming,
debauchery, and riot !    And what precious objects were bartered
for a vile price by the impatience or ignorance of the soldiers,
whose reward was stolen by the base industry of the last of the
Greeks !    These alone who had nothing to lose might derive
some profit from the revolution ; but the misery of the upper
ranks of society is strongly painted in the personal adventures
of Nicetas himself.    His stately palace had been reduced to
ashes in the second conflagration ; and the senator, with his
family and friends, found an obscure shelter in another house
which he possessed near the church of St. Sophia.    It was
the door of this mean habitation that his friend, the Venetian
merchant, guarded, in the disguise of a soldier, till Nicetas could
save, by a precipitate flight, the relics of his fortune and the
chastity of his daughter.    In a cold wintry season these fugitives, nursed in the lap of prosperity, departed on foot ; his wife
was with child ; the desertion of their slaves compelled them to
carry their baggage on their own shoulders ; and their women,
whom they placed in the centre, were exhorted to conceal their
beauty with dirt, instead of adorning it with paint and jewels.
Every step was exposed to insult and danger ; the threats of
the strangers were less painful than the taunts of the plebeians,
with whom they were now levelled ; nor did the exiles breathe
in safety till their mournful pilgrimage was concluded at Selymbria, above forty miles from the capital.    On the way they
overtook the patriarch, without attendance, and almost without
apparel, riding on an ass, and reduced to a state of apostolical

---

[107] The disorders of the sack of Constantinople, and his own adventures, are
feelingly described by Nicetas, p. 367-369, and in the Status Urb. C. P. p. 375-384.
His complaints even of sacrilege are justified by Innocent III. (Gesta, c. 92) ; but
Villehardouin does not betray a symptom of pity or remorse.

poverty, which, had it been voluntary, might perhaps have been meritorious. In the meanwhile his desolate churches were profaned by the licentiousness and party-zeal of the Latins. After stripping the gems and pearls, they converted the chalices into drinking-cups; their tables, on which they gamed and feasted, were covered with the pictures of Christ and the saints; and they trampled under foot the most venerable objects of the Christian worship. In the cathedral of St. Sophia the ample veil of the sanctuary was rent asunder for the sake of the golden fringe; and the altar, a monument of art and riches, was broken in pieces and shared among the captors.[108] Their mules and horses were laden with the wrought silver and gilt carvings, which they tore down from the doors and pulpit; and, if the beasts stumbled under the burden, they were stabbed by their impatient drivers, and the holy pavement streamed with their impure blood. A prostitute was seated on the throne of the patriarch; and that daughter of Belial, as she is styled, sung and danced in the church, to ridicule the hymns and processions of the Orientals. Nor were the repositories of the royal dead secure from violation; in the church of the Apostles the tombs of the emperors were rifled; and it is said that after six centuries the corpse of Justinian was found without any signs of decay or putrefaction. In the streets the French and Flemings clothed themselves and their horses in painted robes and flowing head-dresses of linen; and the coarse intemperance of their feasts[109] insulted the splendid sobriety of the East. To expose the arms of a people of scribes and scholars, they affected to display a pen, an ink-horn, and a sheet of paper, without discerning that the instruments of science and valour were *alike* feeble and useless in the hands of the modern Greeks.

Their reputation and their language encouraged them, however, to despise the ignorance, and to overlook the progress, of the Latins.[110] In the love of the arts the national difference was still more obvious and real; the Greeks preserved with

*Sacrilege and mockery*

*Destruction of the statues*

---

[108] [For the plunder of the church, see the Chronicle of Novgorod, in Hopf's Chroniques Gréco-Romanes.]

[109] If I rightly apprehend the Greek of Nicetas's receipts, their favourite dishes were boiled buttocks of beef, salt pork and pease, and soup made of garlic and sharp or sour herbs (p. 382).

[110] Nicetas uses very harsh expressions, παρ' ἀγραμμάτοις βαρβάροις, καὶ τέλεον ἀναλφαβήτοις (Fragment. apud Fabric. Bibliot. Græc. tom. vi. p. 414). This reproach, it is true, applies most strongly to their ignorance of Greek, and of Homer. In their own language, the Latins of the xiith and xiiith centuries were not destitute of literature. See Harris's Philological Inquiries, p. iii. c. 9, 10, 11.

reverence the works of their ancestors, which they could not imitate ; and, in the destruction of the statues of Constantinople, we are provoked to join in the complaints and invectives of the Byzantine historian.[111]  We have seen how the rising city was adorned by the vanity and despotism of the Imperial founder ; in the ruins of paganism some gods and heroes were saved from the axe of superstition ; and the forum and hippodrome were dignified with the relics of a better age.  Several of these are described by Nicetas,[112] in a florid and affected style ; and from his descriptions I shall select some interesting particulars.  1. The victorious charioteers were cast in bronze, at their own or the public charge, and fitly placed in the hippodrome ; they stood aloft in their chariots, wheeling round the goal ; the spectators could admire their attitude, and judge of the resemblance ; and of these figures the most perfect might have been transported from the Olympic stadium.  2. The sphynx, river-horse, and crocodile denote the climate and manufacture of Egypt and the spoils of that ancient province.  3. The she-wolf suckling Romulus and Remus : a subject alike pleasing to the *old* and the *new* Romans, but which could rarely be treated before the decline of the Greek sculpture.  4. An eagle holding and tearing a serpent in his talons : a domestic monument of the Byzantines, which they ascribed, not to a human artist, but to the magic power of the philosopher Apollonius, who, by his talisman, delivered the city from such venomous reptiles.  5. An ass and his driver, which were erected by Augustus in his colony of Nicopolis, to commemorate a verbal omen of the victory of Actium. 6. An equestrian statue, which passed, in the vulgar opinion, for Joshua, the Jewish conqueror, stretching out his hand to stop the course of the descending sun.  A more classical tradition recognised the figures of Bellerophon and Pegasus ; and the free attitude of the steed seemed to mark that he trode on air rather than on the earth.  7. A square and lofty obelisk of brass : the sides were embossed with a variety of picturesque and rural

[111] Nicetas was of Chonæ in Phrygia ([near] the old Colossæ of St. Paul) ; he raised himself to the honours of senator, judge of the veil, and great logothete beheld the fall of the empire, retired to Nice, and composed an elaborate history from the death of Alexius Comnenus to the reign of Henry. [See above, vol. 5, Appendix, p. 507.]

[112] A manuscript of Nicetas, in the Bodleian library, contains this curious fragment on the statues of Constantinople, which fraud, or shame, or rather carelessness, has dropt in the common editions.  It is published by Fabricius (Bibliot Græc. tom. vi. p. 405-416), and immoderately praised by the late ingenious Mr Harris of Salisbury (Philological Inquiries, p. iii. c. 5, p. 301-312).

scenes : birds singing ; rustics labouring or playing on their pipes ;
sheep bleating ; lambs skipping ; the sea, and a scene of fish and
fishing ; little naked Cupids laughing, playing, and pelting each
other with apples ; and, on the summit, a female figure turning
with the slightest breath, and thence denominated *the wind's at-* [Anemo-
*tendant.*  8. The Phrygian shepherd presenting to Venus the ᵈᵘˡˡᵒⁿ]
prize of beauty, the apple of discord.  9. The incomparable
statue of Helen, which is delineated by Nicetas in the words of
admiration and love : her well-turned feet, snowy arms, rosy lips,
bewitching smiles, swimming eyes, arched eye-brows, the harmony
of her shape, the lightness of her drapery, and her flowing locks
that waved in the wind : a beauty that might have moved her
barbarian destroyers to pity and remorse.  10. The manly or
divine form of Hercules,[113] as he was restored to life by the
master-hand of Lysippus, of such magnitude that his thumb
was equal to the waist, his leg to the stature, of a common
man ;[114] his chest ample, his shoulders broad, his limbs strong
and muscular, his hair curled, his aspect commanding.  Without his bow, or quiver, or club, his lion's skin thrown carelessly
over him, he was seated on an osier basket, his right leg
and arm stretched to the utmost, his left knee bent, and sup-
porting his elbow, his head reclining on his left hand, his
countenance indignant and pensive.  11. A colossal statue of
Juno, which had once adorned her temple of Samos ; the enormous head by four yoke of oxen was laboriously drawn to the
palace.  12. Another colossus, of Pallas or Minerva, thirty feet
in height, and representing, with admirable spirit, the attributes
and character of the martial maid.  Before we accuse the Latins,
it is just to remark that this Pallas was destroyed after the first
siege by the fear and superstition of the Greeks themselves.[115]
The other statues of brass which I have enumerated were broken
and melted by the unfeeling avarice of the crusaders ; the cost
and labour were consumed in a moment ; the soul of genius
evaporated in smoke ; and the remnant of base metal was coined
into money for the payment of the troops.  Bronze is not the

[113] To illustrate the statue of Hercules, Mr. Harris quotes a Greek epigram, and
engraves a beautiful gem, which does not however copy the attitude of the statue.
In the latter, Hercules had not his club, and his right leg and arm were extended.

[114] I transcribe these proportions, which appear to me inconsistent with each
other, and may possibly show that the boasted taste of Nicetas was no more than
affectation and vanity.

[115] Nicetas, in Isaaco Angelo et Alexio, c. 3, p. 359.  The Latin editor very
properly observes that the historian, in his bombast style, produces ex pulice ele-
phantem.

most durable of monuments : from the marble form of Phidias
and Praxiteles the Latins might turn aside with stupid contempt; [116] but, unless they were crushed by some accidental injury,
those useless stones stood secure on their pedestals. [117]   The most
enlightened of the strangers, above the gross and sensual pursuits
of their countrymen, more piously exercised the right of conquest
in the search and seizure of the relics of the saints. [118]   Immense
was the supply of heads and bones, crosses and images, that were
scattered by this revolution over the churches of Europe ; and
such was the increase of pilgrimage and oblation that no branch,
perhaps, of more lucrative plunder was imported from the East. [119]
Of the writings of antiquity many that still existed in the twelfth
century are now lost.   But the pilgrims were not solicitous to
save or transport the volumes of an unknown tongue ; the perish-
able substance of paper or parchment can only be preserved by
the multiplicity of copies ; the literature of the Greeks had almost
centred in the metropolis ; and, without computing the extent
of our loss, we may drop a tear over the libraries that have
perished in the triple fire of Constantinople. [120]

[116] In two passages of Nicetas (edit. Paris, p. 360.   Fabric. p. 408), the Latins
are branded with the lively reproach of οἱ τοῦ καλοῦ ἀνέραστοι βάρβαροι, and their
avarice of brass is clearly expressed.   Yet the Venetians had the merit of removing
four bronze horses from Constantinople to the place of St. Mark (Sanuto, Vite de'
Dogi, in Muratori, Script. Rerum Italicarum, tom. xxii. p. 534).

[117] Winckelman, Hist. de l'Art, tom. iii. p. 269, 270.

[118] See the pious robbery of the abbot Martin, who transferred a rich cargo to
his monastery of Paris, diocese of Basil (Gunther, Hist. C. P. c. 19, 23, 24).   Yet
in secreting this booty the saint incurred an excommunication, and perhaps broke
his oath.

[119] Fleury, Hist. Ecclés. tom. xvi. p. 139-145.

[120] I shall conclude this chapter with the notice of a modern history, which
illustrates the taking of Constantinople by the Latins ; but which has fallen somewhat late into my hands.   Paolo Ramusio, the son of the compiler of Voyages, was
directed by the senate of Venice to write the history of the conquest ; and this order,
which he received in his youth, he executed in a mature age, by an elegant Latin
work, de Bello Constantinopolitano et Imperatoribus Comnenis per Gallos et
Venetos restitutis [Libri vi. ; older edition, 1604] (Venet. 1635, in folio).   Ramusio
[Rannusio], or Rhamnusus, transcribes and translates, sequitur ad unguem, a Ms.
of Villehardouin, which he possessed ; but he enriches his narrative with Greek and
Latin materials, and we are indebted to him for a correct state of the fleet, the
names of the fifty Venetian nobles who commanded the galleys of the republic,
and the patriot opposition of Pantaleon Barbus to the choice of the doge for
emperor.

## CHAPTER LXI

*Partition of the Empire by the French and Venetians—Five Latin Emperors of the Houses of Flanders and Courtenay—Their Wars against the Bulgarians and Greeks—Weakness and Poverty of the Latin Empire—Recovery of Constantinople by the Greeks—General Consequences of the Crusades*

AFTER the death of the lawful princes, the French and Venetians, confident of justice and victory, agreed to divide and regulate their future possessions.[1] It was stipulated by treaty, that twelve electors, six of either nation, should be nominated; that a majority should choose the emperor of the East; and that, if the votes were equal, the decision of chance should ascertain the successful candidate. To him, with all the titles and prerogatives of the Byzantine throne, they assigned the two palaces of Boucoleon and Blachernæ, with a fourth part of the Greek monarchy. It was defined that the three remaining portions should be equally shared between the republic of Venice and the barons of France; that each feudatory, with an honourable exception for the doge, should acknowledge and perform the duties of homage and military service to the supreme head of the empire; that the nation which gave an emperor should resign to their brethren the choice of a patriarch; and that the pilgrims, whatever might be their impatience to visit the Holy Land, should devote another year to the conquest and defence of the Greek provinces. After the conquest of Constantinople by the Latins, the treaty was confirmed and executed; and the first and most important step was the creation of an emperor. The six electors of the French nation were

*Election of the emperor Baldwin I. A.D. 1204, May 9-16 [Partition treaty]*

*[from March 31, 1204]*

---

[1] See the original treaty of partition, in the Venetian Chronicle of Andrew Dandolo, p. 326-330 [Tafel und Thomas, Urkunden zur ältern Handels- und Staatsgeschichte der Republik Venedig, i. 454. The treaty was concluded and drawn up before the city was taken], and the subsequent election in Villehardouin, No. 136-140, with Ducange in his Observations, and the 1st book of his Histoire de Constantinople sous l'Empire des François.

all ecclesiastics, the abbot of Loces, the archbishop elect of Acre
in Palestine, and the bishops of Troyes, Soissons, Halberstadt,
and Bethlehem, the last of whom exercised in the camp the
office of pope's legate ; their profession and knowledge were
respectable ; and, as *they* could not be the objects, they were
best qualified to be authors, of the choice.  The six Venetians
were the principal servants of the state, and in this list the
noble families of Querini and Contarini are still proud to discover their ancestors.  The twelve assembled in the chapel of
the palace ; and, after the solemn invocation of the Holy Ghost,
they proceeded to deliberate and vote.  A just impulse of respect and gratitude prompted them to crown the virtues of the
doge ; his wisdom had inspired their enterprise ; and the most
youthful knights might envy and applaud the exploits of blindness and age.  But the patriot Dandolo was devoid of all personal ambition, and fully satisfied that he had been judged
worthy to reign.  His nomination was overruled by the Venetians themselves ; his countrymen, and perhaps his friends,[2] represented, with the eloquence of truth, the mischiefs that might
arise to national freedom and the common cause from the union
of two incompatible characters, of the first magistrate of a republic and the emperor of the East.  The exclusion of the doge
left room for the more equal merits of Boniface and Baldwin ;
and at their names all meaner candidates respectfully withdrew.
The marquis of Montferrat was recommended by his mature age
and fair reputation, by the choice of the adventurers and the
wishes of the Greeks ; nor can I believe that Venice, the mis-
tress of the sea, could be seriously apprehensive of a petty lord
at the foot of the Alps.[3]  But the count of Flanders was the
chief of a wealthy and warlike people ; he was valiant, pious,
and chaste ; in the prime of life, since he was only thirty-two
years of age ; a descendant of Charlemagne, a cousin of the
king of France, and a compeer of the prelates and barons who
had yielded with reluctance to the command of a foreigner.
Without the chapel, these barons, with the doge and marquis at
their head, expected the decision of the twelve electors.  It was

    [2] After mentioning the nomination of the doge by a French elector, his kins-
man Andrew Dandolo approves his exclusion, quidam Venetorum fidelis et nobilis
senex, usus oratione satis probabili, &c., which has been embroidered by modern
writers from Blondus to Le Beau.

    [3] Nicetas (p. 384), with the vain ignorance of a Greek, describes the marquis of
Montferrat as a *maritime* power. Λαμπαρδίαν δὲ οἰκεῖσθαι παράλιον·  Was he de-
ceived by the Byzantine theme of Lombardy, which extended along the coast of
Calabria ?

announced by the bishop of Soissons, in the name of his colleagues : " Ye have sworn to obey the prince whom we should
choose : by our unanimous suffrage, Baldwin, count of Flanders
and Hainault, is now your sovereign, and the emperor of the
East ". He was saluted with loud applause, and the proclamation was re-echoed throughout the city by the joy of the Latins
and the trembling adulation of the Greeks. Boniface was the
first to kiss the hand of his rival, and to raise him on the buckler ; and Baldwin was transported to the cathedral and solemnly
invested with the purple buskins. At the end of three weeks
he was crowned by the legate, in the vacancy of a patriarch ; but
the Venetian clergy soon filled the chapter of St. Sophia, seated
Thomas Morosini on the ecclesiastical throne, and employed
every art to perpetuate, in their own nation, the honours and
benefices of the Greek church.[4] Without delay, the successor
of Constantine instructed Palestine, France, and Rome of this
memorable revolution. To Palestine he sent, as a trophy, the
gates of Constantinople and the chain of the harbour ;[5] and
adopted from the Assise of Jerusalem the laws or customs best
adapted to a French colony and conquest in the East.[6] In his
epistles, the natives of France are encouraged to swell that
colony and to secure that conquest, to people a magnificent city
and a fertile land, which will reward the labours both of the
priest and the soldier. He congratulates the Roman pontiff on
the restoration of his authority in the East ; invites him to extinguish the Greek schism by his presence in a general council ;
and implores his blessing and forgiveness for the disobedient
pilgrims. Prudence and dignity are blended in the answer
of Innocent.[7] In the subversion of the Byzantine empire, he
arraigns the vices of man and adores the providence of God ;
the conquerors will be absolved or condemned by their future

---

[4] They exacted an oath from Thomas Morosini to appoint no canons of St.
Sophia, the lawful electors, except Venetians who had lived ten years at Venice,
&c. But the foreign clergy were envious, the pope disapproved this national
monopoly, and of the six Latin patriarchs of Constantinople only the first and
last were Venetians.

[5] Nicetas, p. 383.

[6] [The Assises of Jerusalem, at least the Assise of the Haute Cour, was probably
not codified so early as 1204. But it had been introduced into the Peloponnesus
before 1275.]

[7] The Epistles of Innocent III. are a rich fund for the ecclesiastical and civil institution of the Latin empire of Constantinople ; and the most important of these
epistles (of which the collection in 2 vols. in folio, is published by Stephen Baluze)
are inserted in his Gesta, in Muratori, Script. Rerum Italicarum, tom. iii. p. 1, c.
94-105. [Migne, Patrol. Lat., vols. 214, 215, 216.]

conduct ; the validity of their treaty depends on the judgment of St. Peter ; but he inculcates their most sacred duty of establishing a just subordination of obedience and tribute, from the Greeks to the Latins, from the magistrate to the clergy, and from the clergy to the pope.

Division of the Greek empire

In the division of the Greek provinces,[8] the share of the Venetians was more ample than that of the Latin emperor. No more than one fourth was appropriated to his domain ; a clear moiety of the remainder was reserved for Venice ; and the other moiety was distributed among the adventurers of France and Lombardy. The venerable Dandolo was proclaimed despot of Romania, and invested, after the Greek fashion, with the purple buskins. He ended, at Constantinople, his long and glorious life ; and, if the prerogative was personal, the title was used by his successors till the middle of the fourteenth century, with the singular though true addition of lords of one fourth and a half of the Roman empire.[9] The doge, a slave of the state, was seldom permitted to depart from the helm of the republic ; but his place was supplied by the *bail*, or regent, who exercised a supreme jurisdiction over the colony of Venetians ; they possessed three of the eight quarters of the city ; and his independent tribunal was composed of six judges, four counsellors, two chamberlains, two fiscal advocates, and a constable. Their long experience of the Eastern trade enabled them to select their portion with discernment ; they had rashly accepted the dominion and defence of Hadrianople ; but it was the more reasonable aim of their policy to form a chain of factories and cities and islands along the maritime coast, from the neighbourhood of Ragusa to the Hellespont and the Bosphorus. The labour and cost of such extensive conquests exhausted their treasury ; they abandoned their maxims of government, adopted a feudal system, and contented themselves with the homage of their nobles,[10] for the possessions which these private vassals

[8] In the treaty of partition, most of the names are corrupted by the scribes ; they might be restored, and a good map, suited to the last age of the Byzantine empire, would be an improvement of geography ; but, alas ! d'Anville is no more ! [The act of partition annexed to the treaty with geographical notes was edited by Tafel in his Symbolæ criticæ geographiam Byzantinam Spectantes, part 2.]

[9] Their style was Dominus quartæ partis et dimidiæ imperii Romani, till Giovanni Dolfino, who was elected Doge in the year 1356 (Sanuto, p. 530, 641). For the government of Constantinople, see Ducange, Histoire de C. P. p. 37.

[10] Ducange (Hist. de C. P. ii. 6) has marked the conquests made by the state or nobles of Venice of the islands of Candia, Corfu, Cephalonia, Zante, Naxos, Paros, Melos, Andros, Myconè, Scyro, Cea, and Lemnos. [See Appendix 18.]

undertook to reduce and maintain. And thus it was that the family of Sanut acquired the duchy of Naxos, which involved the greatest part of the Archipelago. For the price of ten thousand marks the republic purchased of the marquis of Montferrat the fertile island of Crete, or Candia, with the ruins of an hundred cities ; [11] but its improvement was stinted by the proud and narrow spirit of an aristocracy ; [12] and the wisest senators would confess that the sea, not the land, was the treasury of St. Mark. In the moiety of the adventurers, the marquis Boniface might claim the most liberal reward ; and, besides the isle of Crete, his exclusion from the throne was compensated by the royal title and the provinces beyond the Hellespont. But he prudently exchanged that distant and difficult conquest for the kingdom of Thessalonica, or Macedonia, twelve days' journey from the capital, where he might be supported by the neighbouring powers of his brother-in-law the king of Hungary.[13] His progress was hailed by the voluntary or reluctant acclamations of the natives ; and Greece, the proper and ancient Greece, again received a Latin conqueror,[14] who trod with indifference that classic ground. He viewed with a careless eye the beauties of the valley of Tempe ; traversed with a cautious step the

[11] Boniface sold the isle of Candia, Aug. 12, A.D. 1204. See the acts in Sanuto, p. 533 ; but I cannot understand how it could be his mother's portion, or how she could be the daughter of an emperor Alexius. [Boniface's *Refutatio Cretis* is printed in Tafel u. Thomas, Urkunden, 512, and in Buchon, Recherches et Matériaux, i. 10. Crete had been formally promised him by the young Alexius. He seems to have claimed Thessalonica on the ground that his brother had been created king of Thessalonica by Manuel, see above, p. 372. The erection of the kingdom of Thessalonica was by no means agreeable to Baldwin ; it threatened, weakened, and perhaps ruined the Empire of Romania. It was nearly coming to war between Baldwin and Boniface, but the Doge persuaded Baldwin to yield.]

[12] In the year 1212, the doge Peter Zani sent a colony to Candia, drawn from every quarter of Venice. But, in their savage manners and frequent rebellions, the Candiots may be compared to the Corsicans under the yoke of Genoa ; and, when I compare the accounts of Belon and Tournefort, I cannot discern much difference between the Venetian and the Turkish island.

[13] [He married Margaret, widow of Isaac Angelus.]

[14] Villehardouin (No. 159, 160, 173-177) and Nicetas (p. 387-394) describe the expedition into Greece of the marquis Boniface. The Choniate might derive his information from his brother Michael, archbishop of Athens, whom he paints as an orator, a statesman, and a saint. His encomium of Athens, and the description of Tempe, should be published from the Bodleian Ms. of Nicetas (Fabric. Bibliot. Græc. tom. vi. p. 405), and would have deserved Mr. Harris's inquiries. [The works of Michael Akominatos have been published in a full edition by S. Lampros (1879-80, 2 vols.). The dirge on Athens had been already published by Boissonade in Anecdota Græca, 5, p. 373 *sqq.* (1833). Gregorovius in his Gesch. der Stadt Athen im Mittelalter (where he draws a most interesting sketch of Akominatos in caps. 7 and 8) gives specimens of a German translation of the dirge, p. 243-4.]

straits of Thermopylæ; occupied the unknown cities of Thebes, Athens, and Argos;[15] and assaulted the fortifications of Corinth and Napoli,[16] which resisted his arms. The lots of the Latin pilgrims were regulated by chance, or choice, or subsequent exchange; and they abused, with intemperate joy, the triumph over the lives and fortunes of a great people. After a minute survey of the provinces, they weighed in the scales of avarice the revenue of each district, the advantage of the situation, and the ample or scanty supplies for the maintenance of soldiers and horses. Their presumption claimed and divided the long-lost dependencies of the Roman sceptre; the Nile and Euphrates rolled through their imaginary realms; and happy was the warrior who drew for his prize the palace of the Turkish sultan of Iconium.[17] I shall not descend to the pedigree of families and the rent-rolls of estates, but I wish to specify that the counts of Blois and St. Pol were invested with the duchy of Nice and the lordship of Demotica;[18] the principal fiefs were held by the service of constable, chamberlain, cup-bearer, butler, and chief cook; and our historian, Jeffrey of Villehardouin, obtained a fair establishment on the banks of the Hebrus, and united the double office of marshal of Champagne and Romania. At the head of his knights and archers each baron mounted on horseback to secure the possession of his share, and their first efforts were generally successful. But the public force was weakened by their dispersion; and a thousand quarrels must arise under

[15] [Leo Sguros of Nauplia made himself master of Nauplia, Argos, Corinth, and Thebes. He besieged Athens (see below, p. 484, note 72); and the Acropolis, defended by the archbishop Akominatos, defied him. From Thebes he went to Thessaly, and meeting the Emperor Alexius at Larissa married his daughter and received from him the title of *Sebastohypertatos*. When Boniface and his knights approached, father-in-law and son-in-law retreated to Thermopylæ, but did not await the approach of the enemy. Bodonitza close to the pass was granted by Boniface as a fief to Guy Pallavicini. Before he proceeded against Thebes, Amphissa, which about this time assumes the name Salona (or Sula), was taken, and given with the neighbouring districts including Delphi and the port of Galaxidi to Thomas of Stromoncourt. For Thebes and Athens see below, p. 484.]

[16] Napoli di Romania, or Nauplia, the ancient sea-port of Argos, is still a place of strength and consideration, situate on a rocky peninsula, with a good harbour (Chandler's Travels into Greece, p. 227). [It narrowly escaped becoming the capital of the modern kingdom of Greece.]

[17] I have softened the expression of Nicetas, who strives to expose the presumption of the Franks. See de Rebus post C. P. expugnatam, p. 375-384.

[18] A city surrounded by the river Hebrus, and six leagues to the south of Hadrianople, received from its double wall the Greek name of Didymoteichos, insensibly corrupted into Demotica and Dimot. I have preferred the more convenient and modern appellation of Demotica. This place was the last Turkish residence of Charles XII.

a law, and among men, whose sole umpire was the sword. Within three months after the conquest of Constantinople, the emperor and the king of Thessalonica drew their hostile followers into the field ; they were reconciled by the authority of the doge, the advice of the marshal, and the firm freedom of their peers.[19]

Two fugitives, who had reigned at Constantinople, still asserted the title of emperor ; and the subjects of their fallen throne might be moved to pity by the misfortunes of the elder Alexius, or excited to revenge by the spirit of Mourzoufle. A domestic alliance, a common interest, a similar guilt, and a merit of extinguishing his enemies, a brother and a nephew, induced the more recent usurper to unite with the former the relics of his power. Mourzoufle was received with smiles and honours in the camp of his father Alexius ; but the wicked can never love, and should rarely trust, their fellow-criminals : he was seized in the bath, deprived of his eyes, stripped of his troops and treasures, and turned out to wander an object of horror and contempt to those who with more propriety could hate, and with more justice could punish, the assassin of the emperor Isaac and his son. As the tyrant, pursued by fear or remorse, was stealing over to Asia, he was seized by the Latins of Constantinople, and condemned, after an open trial, to an ignominious death. His judges debated the mode of his execution, the axe, the wheel, or the stake ; and it was resolved that Mourzoufle[20] should ascend the Theodosian column, a pillar of white marble of one hundred and forty-seven feet in height.[21] From the summit he was cast down headlong, and dashed in pieces on the pavement, in the presence of innumerable spectators, who filled the forum of Taurus, and admired the accomplishment of an old prediction, which was explained by this singular event.[22] The fate of Alexius

Revolt of the Greeks. A.D. 1204, &c.

---

[19] Their quarrel is told by Villehardouin (No. 146-158) with the spirit of freedom. The merit and reputation of the marshal are acknowledged by the Greek historian (p. 387), μέγα παρὰ τοῖς Λατίνων δυναμένου στρατεύμασι : unlike some modern heroes, whose exploits are only visible in their own memoirs.

[20] See the fate of Mourzoufle, in Nicetas (p. 393), Villehardouin (No. 141-145, 163), and Guntherus (c. 20, 21). Neither the marshal nor the monk afford a grain of pity for a tyrant or rebel, whose punishment, however, was more unexampled than his crime.

[21] The column of Arcadius, which represents in basso-relievo his victories, or those of his father Theodosius, is still extant at Constantinople. It is described and measured, Gyllius (Topograph. iv. 7), Banduri (ad l. i. Antiquit. C. P. p. 507, &c.), and Tournefort (Voyage du Levant, tom. ii. lettre xii. p. 231). [Nothing of the column remains now except its base.]

[22] The nonsense of Gunther and the modern Greeks concerning this *columna fatidica* is unworthy of notice ; but it is singular enough that, fifty years before the

is less tragical : he was sent by the marquis a captive to Italy, and a gift to the king of the Romans; but he had not much to applaud his fortune, if the sentence of imprisonment and exile were changed from a fortress in the Alps to a monastery in Asia. But his daughter, before the national calamity, had been given in marriage to a young hero, who continued the succession, and restored the throne, of the Greek princes.[23] The valour of Theodore Lascaris was signalised in the two sieges of Constantinople. After the flight of Mourzoufle, when the Latins were already in the city, he offered himself as their emperor to the soldiers and people ; and his ambition, which might be virtuous, was undoubtedly brave. Could he have infused a soul into the multitude, they might have crushed the strangers under their feet ; their abject despair refused his aid; and Theodore retired to breathe the air of freedom in Anatolia, beyond the immediate view and pursuit of the conquerors. Under the title, at first of despot, and afterwards of emperor, he drew to his standard the bolder spirits, who were fortified against slavery by the contempt of life ; and, as every means was lawful for the public safety, implored without scruple the alliance of the Turkish sultan. Nice, where Theodore established his residence, Prusa and Philadelphia, Smyrna and Ephesus, opened their gates to their deliverer; he derived strength and reputation from his victories, and even from his defeats ; and the successor of Constantine preserved a fragment of the empire from the banks of the Mæander to the suburbs of Nicomedia, and at length of Constantinople. Another portion, distant and obscure, was possessed by the lineal heir of the Comneni, a son of the virtuous Manuel, a grandson of the tyrant Andronicus. His name was Alexius ; and the epithet of *great* was applied perhaps to his stature, rather than to his exploits. By the indulgence of the Angeli,[24] he was appointed governor

*Theodore Lascaris, Emperor of Nice. A.D. 1204-1222*

*The dukes and emperors of Trebizond*

Latin conquest, the poet Tzetzes (Chiliad, ix. 277) relates the dream of a matron, who saw an army in the forum, and a man sitting on the column, clapping his hands and uttering a loud exclamation.

[23] The dynasties of Nice, Trebizond, and Epirus (of which Nicetas saw the origin without much pleasure or hope) are learnedly explored, and clearly represented, in the Familiæ Byzantinæ of Ducange.

[24] [Rather, by the help of his aunt queen Thamar of Iberia. On the death of Andronicus in 1185 his two grandsons, Alexius and David, escaped to Iberia. Their aunt helped Alexius to found the independent state of Trapezus in 1204 ; and there he assumed the title of Grand-Komnenos. His brother David seized Paphlagonia. The Comneni never made common cause with the Emperors of Nicæa against the common enemies, either Turks or Latins. On the contrary, Theodore Lascaris defeated David and wrested his kingdom from him, leaving him only a small region about Sinope (1212), and in 1214 the Turks captured Sinope and

or duke of Trebizond : [25] his birth gave him ambition, the revolution independence; and, without changing his title, he reigned
in peace from Sinope to the Phasis, along the coast of the Black
Sea. His nameless son and successor [26] is described as the vassal
of the sultan, whom he served with two hundred lances ; that
Comnenian prince was no more than duke of Trebizond, and the
title of emperor was first assumed by the pride and envy of the
grandson of Alexius. In the West, a third fragment was saved The despots
from the common shipwreck by Michael, a bastard of the house of Epirus
of Angeli,[27] who, before the revolution, had been known as an
hostage, a soldier, and a rebel. His flight from the camp of the
marquis Boniface secured his freedom ; by his marriage with the
governor's daughter he commanded the important place of
Durazzo, assumed the title of despot, and founded a strong and
conspicuous principality in Epirus, Ætolia, and Thessaly, which
have ever been peopled by a warlike race. The Greeks, who
had offered their service to their new sovereigns, were excluded
by the haughty Latins [28] from all civil and military honours, as a

David fell fighting. On the other hand Alexius maintained himself at Trebizond,
and the Empire of Trebizond survived the Turkish conquest of Constantinople by
eight years.]

[25] Except some facts in Pachymer and Nicephorus Gregoras, which will hereafter
be used, the Byzantine writers disdain to speak of the empire of Trebizond, or
principality of the *Lazi ;* and among the Latins, it is conspicuous only in the
romances of the xivth or xvth centuries. Yet the indefatigable Ducange has dug
out (Fam. Byz. p. 192) two authentic passages in Vincent of Beauvais (l. xxxi. c.
144), and the protonotary Ogerius (apud Wading, A.D. 1279, No. 4). [The short
history of the Emperors of Trebizond from 1204-1426, by Michael Panaretos of
Trebizond (lived in first half of 15th century) was published by Tafel at the end of
his edition of Eustathius (p. 362 *sqq.*), 1833. It is translated in St. Martin's ed.
of Lebeau's Hist. du bas-empire, vol. xx. p. 482 *sqq.* The first, who went
thoroughly into the history of Trebizond, was Fallmerayer, and he published more
material. See the Abhandlungen of the Bavarian Academy, 3 cl., vol. 3, 1843 ;
and Geschichte des Kaiserthums von Trapezunt, 1827. The story is told at length
by Finlay in History of Greece, vol. iv. p. 307 *sqq.* But there is much more
material, and A. Papadopulos-Kerameus has recently (1897) issued vol. i. of Fontes
Historiæ Imperii Trapezuntini. And a new history of Trapezus, from the earliest
times to the present day, has appeared in modern Greek : Ἱστορία τῆς Τραπεζοῦντος
(Odessa), 1898, by T. E. Evangelides.]

[26] [His stepson Andronicus Gidos succeeded him in 1222, and was succeeded in
1235 by John, the eldest son of Alexius, who reigned only three years. Then came
Manuel ; and then John, who assumed the title " Emperor of the East, Iberia and
Peratea," avoiding the title of Roman Emperor, in order to keep the peace with
the Palaeologi of Constantinople. Peratea was a part of the Crimea which acknowledged his sway.]

[27] [Michael was natural son of Constantine Angelus, uncle of the Emperors Isaac
and Alexius III. He and his successors assumed the name *Comnenus Angelus
Ducas.* Michael was murdered in 1214 and succeeded by his brother Theodore.]

[28] The portrait of the French Latins is drawn in Nicetas by the hand of prejudice
and resentment : οὐδὲν τῶν ἄλλων ἐθνῶν εἰς Ἄρεος ἔργα παρασυμβεβλῆσθαι ἠνείχοντο, ἀλλ᾿
οὐδέ τις τῶν χαρίτων ἢ τῶν μουσῶν παρὰ τοῖς βαρβάροις τούτοις ἐπεξενίζετο, καὶ παρὰ τοῦτο
οἶμαι τὴν φύσιν ἦσαν ἀνήμεροι, καὶ τὸν χόλον εἶχον τοῦ λόγου προτρέχοντα.

nation born to tremble and obey. Their resentment prompted
them to show that they might have been useful friends, since
they could be dangerous enemies; their nerves were braced by
adversity; whatever was learned or holy, whatever was noble or
valiant, rolled away into the independent states of Trebizond,
Epirus, and Nice; and a single patrician is marked by the ambiguous praise of attachment and loyalty to the Franks. The vulgar herd of the cities and the country would have gladly submitted
to a mild and regular servitude; and the transient disorders
of war would have been obliterated by some years of industry
and peace. But peace was banished, and industry was crushed,
in the disorders of the feudal system. The *Roman* emperors
of Constantinople, if they were endowed with abilities, were
armed with power for the protection of their subjects; their laws
were wise and their administration was simple. The Latin throne
was filled by a titular prince, the chief, and often the servant, of
his licentious confederates: the fiefs of the empire, from a kingdom to a castle, were held and ruled by the sword of the barons;
and their discord, poverty, and ignorance extended their ramifi-
cations of tyranny to the most sequestered villages. The Greeks
were oppressed by the double weight of the priest, who was invested with temporal power, and of the soldier, who was inflamed
by fanatic hatred: and the insuperable bar of religion and language for ever separated the stranger and the native. As long
as the crusaders were united at Constantinople, the memory of
their conquest and the terror of their arms imposed silence on
the captive land; their dispersion betrayed the smallness of their
numbers and the defects of their discipline; and some failures and
mischances revealed the secret that they were not invincible.
As the fear of the Greeks abated, their hatred increased. They
murmured; they conspired; and, before a year of slavery had
elapsed, they implored or accepted the succour of a barbarian,
whose power they had felt, and whose gratitude they trusted.[29]

The Bulgarian war. A.D. 1205    The Latin conquerors had been saluted with a solemn and
early embassy from John, or Joannice, or Calo-John, the re-
volted chief of the Bulgarians and Walachians. He deemed
himself their brother, as the votary of the Roman pontiff, from
whom he had received the regal title and an holy banner; and
in the subversion of the Greek monarchy he might aspire to

[29] I here begin to use, with freedom and confidence, the eight books of the
Histoire de C. P. sous l'Empire des François, which Ducange has given as a
supplement to Villehardouin; and which, in a barbarous style, deserves the praise
of an original and classic work.

the name of their friend and accomplice. But Calo-John was astonished to find that the count of Flanders had assumed the pomp and pride of the successors of Constantine; and his ambassadors were dismissed with an haughty message, that the rebel must deserve a pardon by touching with his forehead the footstool of the Imperial throne. His resentment [30] would have exhaled in acts of violence and blood; his cooler policy watched the rising discontent of the Greeks; affected a tender concern for their sufferings; and promised that their first struggles for freedom should be supported by his person and kingdom. The conspiracy was propagated by national hatred, the firmest band of association and secrecy: the Greeks were impatient to sheathe their daggers in the breasts of the victorious strangers; but the execution was prudently delayed, till Henry, the emperor's brother, had transported the flower of his troops beyond the Hellespont. Most of the towns and villages of Thrace were true to the moment and the signal: and the Latins, without arms or suspicion, were slaughtered by the vile and merciless revenge of their slaves. From Demotica, the first scene of the massacre, the surviving vassals of the count of St. Pol escaped to Hadrianople; but the French and Venetians who occupied that city were slain or expelled by the furious multitude; the garrisons that could effect their retreat fell back on each other towards the metropolis; and the fortresses that separately stood against the rebels were ignorant of each other's and of their sovereign's fate. The voice of fame and fear announced the revolt of the Greeks and the rapid approach of their Bulgarian ally; and Calo-John, not depending on the forces of his own kingdom, had drawn from the Scythian wilderness a body of fourteen thousand Comans, who drank, as it was said, the blood of their captives, and sacrificed the Christians on the altars of their gods.[31]

Alarmed by this sudden and growing danger, the emperor dispatched a swift messenger to recall count Henry and his troops; and, had Baldwin expected the return of his gallant

---

[30] In Calo-John's answer to the Pope, we may find his claims and complaints (Gesta Innocent. III. c. 108, 109); he was cherished at Rome as the prodigal son. [The name *Kalo*-John was also used of John Vatatzes, and of the young John Lascaris, son of Theodore ii.; see Mêliarakês, Ἱστορία τοῦ βασ. τῆς Νικαίας, p. 541, note.]

[31] The Comans were a Tartar or Turkman horde, which encamped in the xiith and xiiith centuries on the verge of Moldavia. The greater part were Pagans, but some were Mahometans, and the whole horde was converted to Christianity (A.D. 1370) by Lewis, king of Hungary. [See above, p. 147, n. 52, and p. 238, n. 36.]

brother, with a supply of twenty thousand Armenians, he might have encountered the invader with equal numbers and a decisive

March

superiority of arms and discipline. But the spirit of chivalry could seldom discriminate caution from cowardice; and the Emperor took the field with an hundred and forty knights, and their train of archers and serjeants. The marshal, who dissuaded and obeyed, led the vanguard in their march to Hadrianople; the main body was commanded by the count of Blois; the aged doge of Venice followed with the rear; and their scanty numbers were increased on all sides by the fugitive Latins. They undertook to besiege the rebels of Hadrianople; and such was the pious tendency of the crusades that they employed the holy week in pillaging the country for their subsistence, and in framing engines for the destruction of their fellow-Christians. But the Latins were soon interrupted and alarmed by the light cavalry of the Comans, who boldly skirmished to the edge of their imperfect lines; and a proclamation was issued by the marshal of Romania, that on the trumpet's sound the cavalry should mount and form, but that none, under pain of death, should abandon themselves to a desultory and dangerous pursuit. This wise injunction was first disobeyed by the count of Blois, who involved the emperor in his rashness and ruin. The Comans, of the Parthian or Tartar school, fled before their first charge; but, after a career of two leagues, when the knights and their horses were almost breathless, they suddenly turned, rallied, and encompassed the heavy

Defeat and captivity of Baldwin. A.D. 1205, April 15

squadrons of the Franks. The count was slain on the field; the emperor was made prisoner; and, if the one disdained to fly, if the other refused to yield, their personal bravery made a poor atonement for their ignorance or neglect of the duties of a general.[32]

Proud of his victory and his royal prize, the Bulgarian advanced to relieve Hadrianople and achieve the destruction of the Latins. They must inevitably have been destroyed, if the marshal of Romania had not displayed a cool courage and consummate skill, uncommon in all ages, but most uncommon in those times, when war was a passion rather than a science.

Retreat of the Latins

His grief and fears were poured into the firm and faithful bosom of the doge; but in the camp he diffused an assurance of safety,

---

[32] Nicetas, from ignorance or malice, imputes the defeat to the cowardice of Dandolo (p. 383); but Villehardouin shares his own glory with his venerable friend, qui viels home ére et gote ne veoit, mais mult ére sages et preus et vigueros (No. 193).

which could only be realised by the general belief. All day he maintained his perilous station between the city and the barbarians : Villehardouin decamped in silence at the dead of night ; and his masterly retreat of three days would have deserved the praise of Xenophon and the ten thousand. In the rear the Marshal supported the weight of the pursuit ; in the front he moderated the impatience of the fugitives ; and, wherever the Comans approached, they were repelled by a line of impenetrable spears. On the third day, the weary troops beheld the sea, the solitary town of Rodosto,[33] and their friends, who had landed from the Asiatic shore. They embraced, they wept ; but they united their arms and counsels ; and, in his brother's absence, count Henry assumed the regency of the empire, at once in a state of childhood and caducity.[34] If the Comans withdrew from the summer-heats, seven thousand Latins, in the hour of danger, deserted Constantinople, their brethren, and their vows. Some partial success was overbalanced by the loss of one hundred and twenty knights in the field of Rusium ; and of the Imperial domain no more was left than the capital, with two or three adjacent fortresses on the shores of Europe and Asia. The king of Bulgaria was resistless and inexorable ; and Calo-John respectfully eluded the demands of the pope, who conjured his new proselyte to restore peace and the emperor to the afflicted Latins. The deliverance of Baldwin was no longer, he said, in the power of man : that prince had died in prison ; and the manner of his death is variously related by ignorance and credulity. The lovers of a tragic legend will be pleased to hear that the royal captive was tempted by the amorous queen of the Bulgarians ; that his chaste refusal exposed him to the falsehood of a woman and the jealousy of a savage ; that his hands and feet were severed from his body ; that his bleeding trunk was cast among the carcases of dogs and horses ; and that he breathed three days before he was devoured by the birds of prey.[35] About twenty years afterwards, in a wood of the Nether-

*Death of the Emperor*

---

[33] The truth of geography and the original text of Villehardouin (No. 194 [366]) place Rodosto [Rhædestus] three days' journey (trois jornées) from Hadrianople ; but Vigenère, in his version, has most absurdly substituted *trois heures ;* and this error, which is not corrected by Ducange, has entrapped several moderns, whose names I shall spare.

[34] The reign and end of Baldwin are related by Villehardouin and Nicetas (p. 386-416) ; and their omissions are supplied by Ducange, in his Observations, and to the end of his first book.

[35] After brushing away all doubtful and improbable circumstances, we may prove the death of Baldwin : 1. By the firm belief of the French barons (Villehar-

lands, an hermit announced himself as the true Baldwin, the emperor of Constantinople, and the lawful sovereign of Flanders. He related the wonders of his escape, his adventures, and his penance, among a people prone to believe and to rebel : and, in the first transport, Flanders acknowledged her long-lost sovereign. A short examination before the French court detected the impostor, who was punished with an ignominious death ; but the Flemings still adhered to the pleasing error ; and the countess Jane is accused by the gravest historians of sacrificing to her ambition the life of an unfortunate father.[36]

Reign and character of Henry. A.D. 1206, Aug. 20—A.D. 1216, June 11 In all civilised hostility a treaty is established for the exchange or ransom of prisoners ; and, if their captivity be prolonged, their condition is known, and they are treated according to their rank with humanity or honour. But the savage Bulgarian was a stranger to the laws of war ; his prisons were involved in darkness and silence ; and above a year elapsed before the Latins could be assured of the death of Baldwin, before his brother, the regent Henry, would consent to assume the title of emperor. His moderation was applauded by the Greeks as an act of rare and inimitable virtue. Their light and perfidious ambition was eager to seize or anticipate the moment of a vacancy, while a law of succession, the guardian both of the prince and people, was gradually defined and confirmed in the hereditary monarchies of Europe. In the support of the Eastern empire Henry was gradually left without an associate, as the heroes of the crusade retired from the world or from the war. The doge of Venice, [June 1] the venerable Dandolo, in the fulness of years and glory, sunk into the grave. The marquis of Montferrat was slowly recalled from the Peloponnesian war to the revenge of Baldwin and the defence of Thessalonica. Some nice disputes of feudal homage and service were reconciled in a personal interview between the emperor and the king ; they were firmly united by mutual esteem and the common danger ; and their alliance was sealed by the [Agnes] nuptial of Henry with the daughter of the Italian prince. He soon deplored the loss of his friend and father. At the persuasion of some faithful Greeks, Boniface made a bold and successful inroad among the hills of Rhodope : the Bulgarians fled on his

douin, No. 230). 2. By the declaration of Calo-John himself, who excuses his not releasing the captive emperor, quia debitum carnis exsolverat cum carcere teneretur (Gesta Innocent. III., c. 109).

[36] See the story of this impostor from the French and Flemish writers in Ducange, Hist. de C. P. iii. 9 ; and the ridiculous fables that were believed by the monks of St. Alban's in Matthew Paris, Hist. Major, p. 271, 272.

approach; they assembled to harass his retreat. On the intelligence that his rear was attacked, without waiting for any defensive armour, he leaped on horseback, couched his lance, and drove the enemies before him; but in the rash pursuit he was pierced with a mortal wound; and the head of the king of [near Mosynopolis] Thessalonica was presented to Calo-John, who enjoyed the honours, without the merit, of victory. It is here, at this melancholy event, that the pen or the voice of Jeffrey of Villehardouin seems to drop or to expire;[37] and, if he still exercised his military office of marshal of Romania, his subsequent exploits are buried in oblivion.[38] The character of Henry was not unequal to his arduous situation: in the siege of Constantinople, and beyond the Hellespont, he had deserved the fame of a valiant knight and a skilful commander; and his courage was tempered with a degree of prudence and mildness unknown to his impetuous brother. In the double war against the Greeks of Asia and the Bulgarians of Europe, he was ever the foremost on shipboard or on horseback; and, though he cautiously provided for the success of his arms, the drooping Latins were often roused by his example to save and to second their fearless emperor. But such efforts, and some supplies of men and money from France, were of less avail than the errors, the cruelty, and the death of their most formidable adversary. When the despair of the Greek subjects invited Calo-John as their deliverer, they hoped that he would protect their liberty and adopt their laws; they were soon taught to compare the degrees of national ferocity, and to execrate the savage conqueror, who no longer dissembled his intention of dispeopling Thrace, of demolishing the cities, and of transplanting the inhabitants beyond the Danube. Many towns and villages of Thrace were already evacuated; an heap of ruins marked the place of Philippopolis, and a similar calamity was expected at Demotica and Hadrianople by the first authors of the revolt. They raised a cry of grief and repentance to the throne of Henry; the emperor alone had the magnanimity to forgive and

---

[37] Villehardouin, No. 257. I quote, with regret, this lamentable conclusion, where we lose at once the original history, and the rich illustrations of Ducange. The last pages may derive some light from Henry's two epistles to Innocent III. (Gesta, c. 106, 107). [Villehardouin's story is poorly continued by Henry of Valenciennes, whose chronicle is printed along with Villehardouin in Wailly's edition (ed. 3, 1882).]

[38] The marshal was alive in 1212, but he probably died soon afterwards, without returning to France (Ducange, Observations sur Villehardouin, p. 238). His fief of Messinople, the gift of Boniface, was the ancient Maximianopolis, which flourished in the time of Ammianus Marcellinus, among the cities of Thrace (No. 141). [Messinopolis is the Mosynopolis of Greek historians.]

trust them. No more than four hundred knights, with their serjeants and archers, could be assembled under his banner; and with this slender force he fought and repulsed the Bulgarian, who, besides his infantry, was at the head of forty thousand horse. In this expedition, Henry felt the difference between an hostile and a friendly country; the remaining cities were preserved by his arms; and the savage, with shame and loss, was compelled to relinquish his prey. The siege of Thessalonica was the last of the evils which Calo-John inflicted or suffered; he was stabbed in the night in his tent; and the general, perhaps the assassin, who found him weltering in his blood, ascribed the blow, with general applause, to the lance of St. Demetrius.[39] After several victories the prudence of Henry concluded an honourable peace with the successor of the tyrant, and with the Greek princes of Nice and Epirus. If he ceded some doubtful limits, an ample kingdom was reserved for himself and his feudatories; and his reign, which lasted only ten years, afforded a short interval of prosperity and peace. Far above the narrow policy of Baldwin and Boniface, he freely entrusted to the Greeks the most important offices of the state and army; and this liberality of sentiment and practice was the more seasonable, as the princes of Nice and Epirus had already learned to seduce and employ the mercenary valour of the Latins. It was the aim of Henry to unite and reward his deserving subjects of every nation and language; but he appeared less solicitous to accomplish the impracticable union of the two churches. Pelagius, the pope's legate, who acted as the sovereign of Constantinople, had interdicted the worship of the Greeks, and sternly imposed the payment of tithes, the double procession of the Holy Ghost, and a blind obedience to the Roman pontiff. As the weaker party, they pleaded the duties of conscience, and implored the rights of toleration : "Our bodies," they said, "are Cæsar's, but our souls belong only to God". The persecution was checked by the firmness of the emperor;[40] and, if we can believe that the same prince was poisoned by the Greeks themselves, we must entertain a contemptible idea of the sense and gratitude of mankind. His valour was a vulgar attribute which he shared with ten thousand knights; but Henry possessed the superior courage to oppose,

[39] The church of this patron of Thessalonica was served by the canons of the holy sepulchre, and contained a divine ointment which distilled daily and stupendous miracles (Ducange, Hist. de C. P. ii. 4).

[40] Acropolita (c. 17) observes the persecution of the legate, and the toleration of Henry ('Ερη, ['Ερρη gen. ; 'Ερρης nom.] as he calls him) κλυδῶνα κατεστόρεσε.

in a superstitious age, the pride and avarice of the clergy. In the cathedral of St. Sophia, he presumed to place his throne on the right hand of the patriarch; and this presumption excited the sharpest censure of pope Innocent the Third.[41] By a salutary edict, one of the first examples of the laws of mortmain, he prohibited the alienation of fiefs; many of the Latins, desirous of returning to Europe, resigned their estates to the church for a spiritual or temporal reward; these holy lands were immediately discharged from military service; and a colony of soldiers would have been gradually transformed into a college of priests.[42]

The virtuous Henry died at Thessalonica, in the defence of that kingdom, and of an infant, the son of his friend Boniface. In the two first emperors of Constantinople, the male line of the counts of Flanders was extinct. But their sister Yolande was the wife of a French prince, the mother of a numerous progeny; and one of her daughters had married Andrew, king of Hungary, a brave and pious champion of the cross. By seating him on the Byzantine throne, the barons of Romania would have acquired the forces of a neighbouring and warlike kingdom; but the prudent Andrew revered the laws of succession; and the princess Yolande, with her husband, Peter of Courtenay, count of Auxerre, was invited by the Latins to assume the empire of the East. The royal birth of his father, the noble origin of his mother, recommended to the barons of France the first-cousin of their king. His reputation was fair, his possessions were ample, and in the bloody crusade against the Albigeois the soldiers and the priests had been abundantly satisfied of his zeal and valour. Vanity might applaud the elevation of a French emperor of Constantinople; but prudence must pity, rather than envy, his treacherous and imaginary greatness. To assert and adorn his title, he was reduced to sell or mortgage the best of his patrimony. By these expedients, the liberality of his royal kinsman, Philip Augustus, and the national spirit of chivalry, he was enabled to pass the Alps at the head of one hundred and forty knights and five thousand five hundred serjeants and archers. After some hesitation, pope Honorius the Third was persuaded to crown the successor of Constantine; but he performed the ceremony in a

*Peter of Courtenay emperor of Constantinople. A.D. 1217, April 9*

[41] [The dispute with Innocent was compromised at a parliament which Henry held at Ravennika in northern Greece (near Zeituni?) on May 2, 1210.]

[42] See the reign of HENRY, in Ducange (Hist. de C. P. l. i. c. 35-41, l. ii. c. 1-22), who is much indebted to the Epistles of the Popes. Le Beau (Hist. du Bas Empire, tom. xxi. p. 120-122) has found, perhaps in Doutreman, some laws of Henry, which determined the service of fiefs and the prerogatives of the emperor.

church without the walls, lest he should seem to imply, or to bestow, any right of sovereignty over the ancient capital of the empire.    The Venetians had engaged to transport Peter and his forces beyond the Adriatic, and the empress, with her four children, to the Byzantine palace ; but they required, as the price of their service, that he should recover Durazzo from the despot of Epirus.    Michael Angelus, or Comnenus, the first of his dynasty, had bequeathed the succession of his power and ambition to Theodore, his legitimate brother, who already threatened and invaded the establishments of the Latins.    After discharging his debt by a fruitless assault, the emperor raised the siege to prosecute a long and perilous journey over land from Durazzo to Thessalonica.    He was soon lost in the mountains of Epirus ; the passes were fortified ; his provisions exhausted ; he was delayed and deceived by a treacherous negotiation ; and, after Peter of Courtenay and the Roman legate had been arrested in a banquet, the French troops, without leaders or hopes, were eager to exchange their arms for the delusive promise of mercy and bread. The Vatican thundered ; and the impious Theodore was threatened with the vengeance of earth and heaven ; but the captive emperor and his soldiers were forgotten, and the reproaches of the pope are confined to the imprisonment of his legate.    No sooner was he satisfied by the deliverance of the priest and a promise of spiritual obedience, than he pardoned and protected the despot of Epirus.    His peremptory commands suspended the ardour of the Venetians and the king of Hungary ; and it was only by a natural or untimely death [43] that Peter of Courtenay was released from his hopeless captivity.[44]

The long ignorance of his fate, and the presence of the lawful sovereign, of Yolande, his wife or widow, delayed the proclamation of a new emperor.    Before her death, and in the midst of her grief, she was delivered of a son, who was named Baldwin, the last and most unfortunate of the Latin princes of Constantinople.    His birth endeared him to the barons of Romania ; but his childhood would have prolonged the troubles of a minority, and his claims were superseded by the elder claims of his breth-

[A.D. 1214]

His captivity
and death.
A.D. 1217-1219

Robert, Emperor of Constantinople.
A.D. 1221-1228

[43] Acropolita (c. 14) affirms that Peter of Courtenay died by the sword (ἔργον μαχαίρας γενέσθαι) ; but from his dark expressions, I should conclude a previous capacity, ὡς πάντας ἄρδην δεσμώτας ποιῆσαι σὺν πᾶσι σκεύεσι.    The Chronicle of Auxerre delays the emperor's death till the year 1219 ; and Auxerre is in the neighbourhood of Courtenay.

[44] See the reign and death of Peter of Courtenay in Ducange (Hist. de C. P. l. ii. c. 22-28), who feebly strives to excuse the neglect of the emperor by Honorius III.

ren. The first of these, Philip of Courtenay, who derived from his mother the inheritance of Namur, had the wisdom to prefer the substance of a marquisate to the shadow of an empire ; and on his refusal, Robert, the second of the sons of Peter and Yolande, was called to the throne of Constantinople. Warned by his father's mischance, he pursued his slow and secure journey through Germany and along the Danube ; a passage was opened by his sister's marriage with the king of Hungary ; and the emperor Robert was crowned by the patriarch in the cathedral of St. Sophia. But his reign was an æra of calamity and disgrace; and the colony, as it was styled, of New France yielded on all sides to the Greeks of Nice and Epirus. After a victory, which he owed to his perfidy rather than his courage, Theodore Angelus entered the kingdom of Thessalonica, expelled the feeble [A.D. 1222] Demetrius, the son of the marquis Boniface, erected his standard on the walls of Hadrianople, and added, by his vanity, a third or fourth name to the list of rival emperors. The relics of the Asiatic province were swept away by John Vataces, the son-in-law and successor of Theodore Lascaris, and who, in a triumphant reign of thirty-three years, displayed the virtues both of peace and war. Under his discipline, the swords of the French mer- [A.D. 1222-54] cenaries were the most effectual instrument of his conquests, and their desertion from the service of their country was at once a symptom and a cause of the rising ascendant of the Greeks. By the construction of a fleet he obtained the command of the Hellespont, reduced the islands of Lesbos and Rhodes,[45] attacked the Venetians of Candia, and intercepted the rare and parsimonious succours of the West. Once, and once only, the Latin emperor sent an army against Vataces ; and, in the defeat of that army, the veteran knights, the last of the original conquerors, [Battle of Poimanenos. were left on the field of battle. But the success of a foreign A.D. 1224] enemy was less painful to the pusillanimous Robert than the insolence of his Latin subjects, who confounded the weakness of the emperor and of the empire. His personal misfortunes will prove the anarchy of the government and the ferociousness of the times. The amorous youth had neglected his Greek bride, the daughter of Vataces, to introduce into the palace a beautiful maid, of a private, though noble, family of Artois ; and her mother had been tempted by the lustre of the purple to forfeit

---

[45] [When the empire was overthrown by the crusaders, Leo Gabalas made himself master of Rhodes. In 1233 John Vatatzes compelled him to acknowledge his supremacy, but left him in possession. The island was conquered by the knights of St. John in 1310.]

her engagements with a gentleman of Burgundy. His love was converted into rage; he assembled his friends, forced the palace gates, threw the mother into the sea, and inhumanly cut off the nose and lips of the wife or concubine of the emperor. Instead of punishing the offender, the barons avowed and applauded the savage deed,[46] which, as a prince and as a man, it was impossible that Robert should forgive. He escaped from the guilty city to implore the justice or compassion of the pope; the emperor was coolly exhorted to return to his station; before he could obey, he sunk under the weight of grief, shame, and impotent resentment.[47]

Baldwin II. and John of Brienne, Emperors of Constantinople. A.D. 1228-1237

It was only in the age of chivalry that valour could ascend from a private station to the thrones of Jerusalem and Constantinople. The titular kingdom of Jerusalem had devolved to Mary, the daughter of Isabella, and Conrad of Montferrat, and the grand-daughter of Almeric or Amaury. She was given to John of Brienne, of a noble family in Champagne, by the public voice, and the judgment of Philip Augustus, who named him as the most worthy champion of the Holy Land.[48] In the fifth crusade, he led an hundred thousand Latins to the conquest of Egypt; by him the siege of Damietta was achieved; and the subsequent failure was justly ascribed to the pride and avarice of the legate. After the marriage of his daughter with Frederic the Second,[49] he was provoked by the emperor's ingratitude to accept the command of the army of the church; and, though advanced in life, and despoiled of royalty, the sword and spirit of John of Brienne were still ready for the service of Christendom. In the seven years of his brother's reign Baldwin of Courtenay had not emerged from a state of childhood, and the barons of Romania felt the strong necessity of placing the sceptre in the hands of a man and a hero. The veteran king of Jerusalem might have

[46] Marinus Sanutus (Secreta Fidelium Crucis, l. ii. p. 4, c. 18, p. 73) is so much delighted with this bloody deed that he has transcribed it in his margin as a bonum exemplum. Yet he acknowledges the damsel for the awful wife of Robert.

[47] See the reign of Robert in Ducange (Hist. de C. P. l. iii. c. 1-12). [Finlay thinks that Robert should have "seized the culprit immediately, and hung him in his armour before the palace gates, with his shield round his neck" (iv. p. 114).]

[48] Rex igitur Franciæ, deliberatione habitâ, respondit nuntiis, se daturum hominem Syriæ partibus aptum, in armis probum (*preux*), in bellis securum, in agendis providum, Johannem comitem Brennensem. Sanut. Secret. Fidelium, l. iii. p. xi. c. 4, p. 205. Matthew Paris, p. 159.

[49] Giannone (Istoria Civile, tom. ii. l. xvi. p. 380-385) discusses the marriage of Frederic II. with the daughter of John of Brienne, and the double union of the crowns of Naples and Jerusalem.

disdained the name and office of regent ; they agreed to invest [A.D. 1229] him for his life with the title and prerogatives of emperor, on the sole condition that Baldwin should marry his second daughter [Mary] and succeed at a mature age to the throne of Constantinople.[50] The expectation, both of the Greeks and Latins, was kindled by the renown, the choice, and the presence of John of Brienne ; and they admired his martial aspect, his green and vigorous age of more than fourscore years, and his size and stature, which surpassed the common measure of mankind.[51]  But avarice and the love of ease appear to have chilled the ardour of enterprise ; his troops were disbanded, and two years rolled away without action or honour, till he was awakened [52] by the dangerous alliance of Vataces, emperor of Nice, and of Azan, king of Bulgaria.[53]  They besieged Constantinople by sea and land, [A.D. 1235] with an army of one hundred thousand men, and a fleet of three hundred ships of war ; while the entire force of the Latin emperor was reduced to one hundred and sixty knights and a small addition of serjeants and archers.  I tremble to relate that, instead of defending the city, the hero made a sally at the head of his cavalry ; and that, of forty-eight squadrons of the enemy, no more than three escaped from the edge of his invincible sword.  Fired by his example, the infantry and citizens boarded the vessels that anchored close to the walls ; and twenty-five were dragged in triumph into the harbour of Constantinople.

[50] [For the act see Buchon, Recherches et Matériaux, p. 21-23.]

[51] Acropolita, c. 27.  The historian was at that time a boy, and educated at Constantinople.  In 1233, when he was eleven years old, his father broke the Latin chain, left a splendid fortune, and escaped to the Greek court of Nice, where his son was raised to the highest honours.

[52] [He did not arrive at Constantinople till 1231.]

[53] [For this able and humane prince, see Jireček, Geschichte der Bulgaren, chap. xvi.  He defeated the forces of Thessalonica and Epirus in the battle of Klokotnitza (near the Strymon), 1230, and extended his power over the greater part of Thrace, Macedonia and Albania.  His empire touched three seas and included the cities of Belgrade and Hadrianople.  An inscription in the cathedral of Trnovo, which he built, records his deeds as follows : "In the year 6738 [= 1230] Indiction 3, I, Joannes Asēn, the Tsar, faithful servant of God in Christ, sovereign of the Bulgarians, son of the old Asēn, have built this magnificent church and adorned it with paintings, in honour of the Forty Martyrs, with whose help, in the 12th year of my reign, when the church was painted, I made an expedition to Romania and defeated the Greek army and took the Tsar, Kyr Thodor Komnin, prisoner, with all his bolyars.  I conquered all the countries from Odrin [Hadrianople] to Dratz [Durazzo],—Greek, Albanian and Servian.  The Franks have only retained the towns about Tzarigrad [Constantinople] and that city itself ; but even they submitted to my empire when they had no other Emperor but me, and I permitted them to continue, as God so willed.  For without him neither work nor word is accomplished.  Glory to him for ever, Amen." (Jireček, p. 251-2.)]

[A.D. 1236]
At the summons of the emperor, the vassals and allies armed
in her defence ; broke through every obstacle that opposed their
passage ; and, in the succeeding year, obtained a second victory
over the same enemies.  By the rude poets of the age, John of
Brienne is compared to Hector, Roland, and Judas Maccabæus ; [54]
but their credit and his glory receives some abatement from the
silence of the Greeks.[55]  The empire was soon deprived of the
[A.D. 1237]
last of her champions ; and the dying monarch was ambitious to
enter paradise in the habit of a Franciscan friar.[56]

Baldwin II.
A.D. 1237,
March 23–
A.D. 1261,
July 25
In the double victory of John of Brienne, I cannot discover
the name or exploits of his pupil Baldwin, who had attained the
age of military service, and who succeeded to the Imperial
dignity on the decease of his adopted father.[57]  The royal
youth was employed on a commission more suitable to his
temper ; he was sent to visit the Western courts, of the pope
more especially, and of the king of France ; to excite their
pity by the view of his innocence and distress ; and to obtain
some supplies of men or money for the relief of the sinking
empire.  He thrice repeated these mendicant visits, in which
he seemed to prolong his stay and postpone his return ; of the
five-and-twenty years of his reign, a greater number were spent
abroad than at home ; and in no place did the emperor deem
himself less free and secure than in his native country and his
capital.  On some public occasions, his vanity might be soothed
by the title of Augustus and by the honours of the purple ; and

[54] Philip Mouskes, bishop of Tournay (A.D. 1274-1282), has composed a poem,
or rather a string of verses, in bad old Flemish French, on the Latin emperors of
Constantinople, which Ducange has published at the end of Villehardouin.  [What
Ducange published was an extract from the Chronique rimée of Mouskès, which
began with the Trojan war.  The whole work was first published by De Reiffenberg
in 1836.  Gibbon identifies Mouskès with Philip of Ghent, who became bishop of
Tournay in 1274.  This is an error.  Mouskès was a native of Tournay and died in
1244.]  See p. 224, for the prowess of John of Brienne.

> N'Aie, Ector, Roll' ne Ogiers
> Ne Judas Machabeus li fiers
> Tant ne fit d'armes en estors
> Com fist li Rois Jehans cel jors,
> Et il defors et il dedans
> La paru sa force et ses sens
> Et li hardiment qu'il avoit.

[55] [John Asēn, threatened by the approach of Zenghis Khan (see below, chap.
lxiv.), gave up the war and made a separate peace and alliance with the Eastern
Emperors.  But the alliance was soon abandoned, and Asēn returned to his friendship with Nicæa.]

[56] See the reign of John de Brienne, in Ducange, Hist. de C. P. l. iii. c. 13-26.

[57] See the reign of Baldwin II. till his expulsion from Constantinople, in Ducange (Hist. de C. P. l. iv. c. 1-34, the end l. v. c. 1-33).

at the general council of Lyons, when Frederic the Second was excommunicated and deposed, his Oriental colleague was enthroned on the right hand of the pope. But how often was the exile, the vagrant, the Imperial beggar humbled with scorn, insulted with pity, and degraded in his own eyes and those of the nations! In his first visit to England he was stopt at Dover by a severe reprimand that he should presume, without leave, to enter an independent kingdom. After some delay, Baldwin, however, was permitted to pursue his journey, was entertained with cold civility, and thankfully departed with a present of seven hundred marks.[58] From the avarice of Rome he could only obtain the proclamation of a crusade, and a treasure of indulgences : a coin whose currency was depreciated by too frequent and indiscriminate abuse. His birth and misfortunes recommended him to the generosity of his cousin, Lewis the Ninth ; but the martial zeal of the saint was diverted from Constantinople to Egypt and Palestine ; and the public and private poverty of Baldwin was alleviated, for a moment, by the alienation of the marquisate of Namur and the lordship of Courtenay, the last remains of his inheritance.[59] By such shameful or ruinous expedients he once more returned to Romania, with an army of thirty thousand soldiers, whose numbers [A.D. 1239] were doubled in the apprehension of the Greeks. His first dispatches to France and England announced his victories and his hopes ; he had reduced the country round the capital to the distance of three days' journey ; and, if he succeeded against an important though nameless city (most probably Chiorli),[60] [A.D. 1240] the frontier would be safe and the passage accessible. But these expectations (if Baldwin was sincere) quickly vanished like a dream ; the troops and treasures of France melted away in his unskilful hands ; and the throne of the Latin emperor was protected by a dishonourable alliance with the Turks and Comans. To secure the former, he consented to bestow his niece on the unbelieving sultan of Cogni ; to please the latter,

[58] Matthew Paris relates the two visits of Baldwin II. to the English court, p. 396, 637 ; his return to Greece armatâ manu, p. 407, his letters of his nomen formidabile, &c., p. 481 (a passage which had escaped Ducange), his expulsion, p. 850.

[59] Louis IX. disapproved and stopped the alienation of Courtenay (Ducange, l. iv. c. 23). It is now annexed to the royal demesne, but granted for a term (*engage*) to the family of Boulanvilliers. Courtenay, in the election of Nemours in the Isle de France, is a town of 900 inhabitants, with the remains of a castle (Mélanges tirés d'une grande Bibliothèque, tom. xiv. p. 74-77).

[60] [Tzurulos.]

he complied with their Pagan rites : a dog was sacrificed between the two armies ; and the contracting parties tasted each
other's blood, as a pledge of their fidelity.[61]  In the palace or
prison of Constantinople, the successor of Augustus demolished
the vacant houses for winter-fuel, and stripped the lead from
the churches for the daily expenses of his family.  Some
usurious loans were dealt with a scanty hand by the merchants
of Italy ; and Philip, his son and heir, was pawned at Venice
as the security for a debt.[62]  Thirst, hunger, and nakedness
are positive evils ; but wealth is relative ; and a prince, who
would be rich in a private station, may be exposed by the increase of his wants to all the anxiety and bitterness of poverty.

The holy
crown of
thorns

But in this abject distress the emperor and empire were still
possessed of an ideal treasure, which drew its fantastic value
from the superstition of the Christian world.  The merit of
the true cross was somewhat impaired by its frequent division ;
and a long captivity among the infidels might shed some suspicion on the fragments that were produced in the East and
West.  But another relic of the Passion was preserved in the
Imperial chapel of Constantinople ; and the crown of thorns,
which had been placed on the head of Christ, was equally
precious and authentic.  It had formerly been the practice of
the Egyptian debtors to deposit, as a security, the mummies of
their parents ; and both their honour and religion were bound
for the redemption of the pledge.  In the same manner, and
in the absence of the emperor, the barons of Romania borrowed
the sum of thirteen thousand one hundred and thirty-four pieces
of gold,[63] on the credit of the holy crown ; they failed in the
performance of their contract ; and a rich Venetian, Nicholas
Querini, undertook to satisfy their impatient creditors, on condition that the relic should be lodged at Venice, to become his
absolute property if it were not redeemed within a short and
definite term.  The barons apprised their sovereign of the hard
treaty and impending loss ; and, as the empire could not afford a ransom of seven thousand pounds sterling, Baldwin was

[61] Joinville, p. 104, édit. du Louvre.  A Coman prince, who died without
baptism, was buried at the gates of Constantinople with a live retinue of slaves and
horses.

[62] Sanut. Secret. Fidel. Crucis, l. ii. p. iv. c. 18, p. 73.

[63] Under the words *Perparus, Perpera, Hyperperum,* Ducange is short and vague :
Monetæ genus.  From a corrupt passage of Guntherus (Hist. C. P. c. 8, p. 10),
I guess that the Perpera was the nummus aureus, the fourth part of a mark of
silver, or about ten shillings sterling in value.  In lead it would be too contemptible.

anxious to snatch the prize from the Venetians, and to vest it
with more honour and emolument in the hands of the most
Christian king.[64]  Yet the negotiation was attended with some
delicacy.  In the purchase of relics, the saint would have started
at the guilt of simony ; but, if the mode of expression were
changed, he might lawfully repay the debt, accept the gift, and
acknowledge the obligation.  His ambassadors, two Domini-
cans, were dispatched to Venice, to redeem and receive the holy
crown, which had escaped the dangers of the sea and the galleys
of Vataces.  On opening a wooden box, they recognised the
seals of the doge and barons, which were applied on a shrine of
silver ; and within this shrine the monument of the Passion
was inclosed in a golden vase.  The reluctant Venetians yielded
to justice and power ; the emperor Frederic granted a free
and honourable passage ; the court of France advanced as far
as Troyes in Champagne, to meet with devotion this inestimable
relic ; it was borne in triumph through Paris by the king himself, barefoot, and in his shirt ; and a free gift of ten thousand
marks of silver reconciled Baldwin to his loss.  The success
of this transaction tempted the Latin emperor to offer with
the same generosity the remaining furniture of his chapel ; [65] a
large and authentic portion of the true cross ; the baby-linen
of the Son of God ; the lance, the spunge, and the chain, of his
Passion ; the rod of Moses ; and part of the scull of St. John the
Baptist.  For the reception of these spiritual treasures, twenty
thousand marks were expended by St. Louis on a stately foundation, the holy chapel of Paris, on which the muse of Boileau
has bestowed a comic immortality.  The truth of such remote
and ancient relics, which cannot be proved by any human
testimony, must be admitted by those who believe in the
miracles which they have performed.  About the middle of the
last age, an inveterate ulcer was touched and cured by an holy
prickle of the holy crown : [66] the prodigy is attested by the

[64] For the translation of the holy crown, &c. from Constantinople to Paris, see
Ducange (Hist. de C. P. l. iv. c. 11-14, 24, 35), and Fleury (Hist. Ecclés. tom.
xvii. p. 201-204).

[65] Mélanges tirés d'une grande Bibliothèque, tom. xliii. p. 201-205.  The
Lutrin of Boileau exhibits the inside, the soul and manners of the *Sainte Chapelle ;*
and many facts relative to the institution are collected and explained by his com-
mentators, Brossette and de St. Marc.

[66] It was performed A.D. 1656, March 24, on the niece of Pascal ; and that
superior genius, with Arnauld, Nicole, &c. were on the spot to believe and attest
a miracle which confounded the Jesuits, and saved Port Royal (Oeuvres de Racine, tom. vi. p. 176-187, in his eloquent History of Port Royal).

most pious and enlightened Christians of France; nor will the fact be easily disproved, except by those who are armed with a general antidote against religious credulity.[67]

Progress of the Greeks. A.D. 1237-1261

The Latins of Constantinople [68] were on all sides encompassed and pressed : their sole hope, the last delay of their ruin, was in the division of their Greek and Bulgarian enemies; and of this hope they were deprived by the superior arms and policy of Vataces, emperor of Nice. From the Propontis to the rocky coast of Pamphylia, Asia was peaceful and prosperous under his reign ; and the events of every campaign extended his influence in Europe. The strong cities of the hills of Macedonia and Thrace were rescued from the Bulgarians ; and their kingdom was circumscribed by its present and proper limits, along the southern banks of the Danube. The sole emperor of the Romans could no longer brook that a lord of Epirus, a Comnenian prince of the West, should presume to dispute or share the honours of

[A.D. 1243]

the purple ; and the humble Demetrius changed the colour of his buskins, and accepted with gratitude the appellation of despot. His own subjects were exasperated by his baseness and incapacity : they implored the protection of their supreme lord. After some resistance, the kingdom of Thessalonica was united to the empire of Nice ; [69] and Vataces reigned without a competitor from the Turkish borders to the Adriatic gulf. The princes of Europe revered his merit and power ; and, had he subscribed

---

[67] Voltaire (Siècle de Louis XIV. c. 37 ; Oeuvres, tom. ix. p. 178, 179) strives to invalidate the fact ; but Hume (Essays, vol. ii. p. 483, 484), with more skill and success, seizes the battery, and turns the cannon against his enemies.

[68] The gradual losses of the Latins may be traced in the third, fourth, and fifth books of the compilation of Ducange; but of the Greek conquests he has dropped many circumstances, which may be recovered from the large history of George Acropolita, and the three first books of Nicephorus Gregoras, two writers of the Byzantine series, who have had the good fortune to meet with learned editors, Leo Allatius at Rome, and John Boivin in the Academy of Inscriptions of Paris.

[69] [The conquest of Thessalonica, from the young Demetrius, son of Boniface, by Theodore Angelus, despot of Epirus, and Theodore's assumption of the Imperial title A.D. 1222, have been briefly mentioned above, p. 431. His brother Manuel, and then his son John, succeeded to the Empire of Salonica. It was a matter of political importance for Vatatzes to bring this rival Empire into subjection ; he marched against Thessalonica, but raised the siege (A.D. 1243) on condition that John should lay down the title of Emperor and assume that of despot. John died in the following year and was succeeded by his brother Demetrius ; but in 1246 Demetrius was removed by Vatatzes, and Thessalonica became definitely part of the empire of Nicæa. Thus the Thessalonian empire lasted 1222-1243. Meanwhile Epirus had split off from the empire of Salonica, in 1236-7, under Michael II. (a bastard son of Michael I.), whose Despotate survived that Empire. See below, note 71.]

# OF THE ROMAN EMPIRE 439

an orthodox creed, it should seem that the pope would have abandoned without reluctance the Latin throne of Constantinople. But the death of Vataces, the short and busy reign of Theodore his son, and the helpless infancy of his grandson John, suspended the restoration of the Greeks. In the next chapter I shall explain their domestic revolutions; in this place it will be sufficient to observe that the young prince was oppressed by the ambition of his guardian and colleague, Michael Palæologus, who displayed the virtues and vices that belong to the founder of a new dynasty. The emperor Baldwin had flattered himself that he might recover some provinces or cities by an impotent negotiation. His ambassadors were dismissed from Nice with mockery and contempt. At every place which they named, Palæologus alleged some special reason which rendered it dear and valuable in his eyes: in the one he was born; in another he had been first promoted to military command; and in a third he had enjoyed, and hoped long to enjoy, the pleasures of the chase. "And what, then, do you propose to give us?" said the astonished deputies. "Nothing," replied the Greek, "not a foot of land. If your master be desirous of peace, let him pay me, as an annual tribute, the sum which he receives from the trade and customs of Constantinople. On these terms I may allow him to reign. If he refuses, it is war. I am not ignorant of the art of war, and I trust the event to God and my sword." [70] An expedition against the despot of Epirus was the first prelude of his arms. If a victory was followed by a defeat; if the race of the Comneni or Angeli survived in those mountains his efforts and his reign; the captivity of Villehardouin, prince of Achaia, deprived the Latins of the most active and powerful vassal of their expiring monarchy.[71] The republics of Venice and Genoa disputed, in the first of their naval wars, the command of the sea and the commerce of the East. Pride and interest attached the Venetians to the defence of Constantinople: their rivals were tempted to promote the designs of her enemies, and the alliance of the Genoese with the

[Theodore II.<br>A.D. 1254-8]<br><br>
Michael<br>Palæologus,<br>the Greek Emperor. A.D.<br>1259, Dec. 1<br>[Jan. 1260]<br><br>
[Michael II.]<br>[Battle of<br>Pelagonia.<br>Autumn,<br>A.D. 1259]

[70] George Acropolita, c. lxxviii. p. 89, 90, edit. Paris.

[71] [This victory was won by John Palæologus, brother of Michael, in the plain of Pelagonia near Kastoria, in Macedonia. The despot of Epirus, Michael II. (bastard of Michael I.), had extended his sway to the Vardar, and threatened Salonica. He was supported by Manfred, king of Sicily, who sent four hundred knights to his aid, as well as William Villehardouin, prince of Achaia. Finlay places the coronation of Michael Palæologus in Jan. 1259—*before* the battle of Pelagonia (iii. 339); but it seems to have been subsequent, in Jan. 1260; see Méliarakês, Ἱστορία τοῦ βασιλείου τῆς Νικαίας κ.τ.λ. (1898), p. 536-543.]

Constanti-
nople re-
covered by
the Greeks,
A.D. 1261,
June [July] 25

schismatic conqueror provoked the indignation of the Latin church.[72]

Intent on his great object, the emperor Michael visited in person and strengthened the troops and fortifications of Thrace. The remains of the Latins were driven from their last possessions ; he assaulted without success the suburbs of Galata ;[73] and corresponded with a perfidious baron,[74] who proved unwilling, or unable, to open the gates of the metropolis. The next spring,[75] his favourite general, Alexius Strategopulus, whom he had decorated with the title of Cæsar, passed the Hellespont with eight hundred horse and some infantry,[76] on a secret expedition. His instructions enjoined him to approach, to listen, to watch, but not to risk any doubtful or dangerous enterprise against the city. The adjacent territory between the Propontis and the Black Sea was cultivated by an hardy race of peasants and outlaws, exercised in arms, uncertain in their allegiance, but inclined by language, religion, and present advantage, to the party of the Greeks. They were styled the *volunteers*,[77] and by their free service the army of Alexius, with the regulars of Thrace and the Coman auxiliaries,[78] was augmented to the number of five and twenty thousand men. By the ardour of the volunteers,

[72] The Greeks, ashamed of any foreign aid, disguise the alliance and succour of the Genoese ; but the fact is proved by the testimony of J. Villani (Chron. l. vi. c. 71, in Muratori, Script. Rerum Italicarum, tom. xiii. p. 202, 203) and William de Nangis (Annales de St. Louis, p. 248, in the Louvre Joinville), two impartial foreigners ; and Urban IV. threatened to deprive Genoa of her archbishop. [For the treaty of Michael with Genoa in March, 1261, see Buchon, Recherches et matériaux, p. 462 *sqq.* (in French), or Zacharia v. Lingenthal, Jus. Græco-Rom., iii. p. 574 *sqq.* (in Latin). The Genoese undertook to furnish a fleet ; but when these ships arrived Michael was already in possession of the city.]

[73] [Spring, 1260.]

[74] [Anseau de Cayeux (if that is the name), who was married to a sister-in-law of John Vatatzes. Cp. Méliarakès, *op. cit.* p. 551-2.]

[75] [Michael himself this spring passed and repassed repeatedly from Asia to Europe. He first took Selymbria, which was a valuable basis for further operations (Pachymeres, p. 110). Ecclesiastical business then recalled him to Asia ; and having settled this he recrossed the Hellespont and for the second time besieged Galata (Pachymeres, p. 118 *sqq.*). He raised the siege and returned to Nymphæum, where he concluded the treaty with the Genoese.]

[76] Some precautions must be used in reconciling the discordant numbers ; the 800 soldiers of Nicetas ; the 25,000 of Spandugino (apud Ducange, l. v. c. 24) ; the Greeks and Scythians of Acropolita ; and the numerous army of Michael, in the Epistles of pope Urban IV. (i. 129).

[77] Θεληματάριοι. They are described and named by Pachymer (l. ii. c. 14). [The chief of these, who was very active in the capture of the city, was named Kutritzakês.]

[78] It is needless to seek these Comans in the deserts of Tartary, or even of Moldavia. A part of the horde had submitted to John Vataces and was probably settled as a nursery of soldiers on some waste lands of Thrace (Cantacuzen. l. i. c. 2).

and by his own ambition, the Cæsar was stimulated to disobey the precise orders of his master, in the just confidence that success would plead his pardon and reward. The weakness of Constantinople, and the distress and terror of the Latins, were familiar to the observation of the volunteers; and they represented the present moment as the most propitious to surprise and conquest. A rash youth, the new governor of the Venetian colony, had sailed away with thirty galleys and the best of the French knights, on a wild expedition to Daphnusia, a town on the Black Sea, at a distance of forty leagues ; [79] and the remaining Latins were without strength or suspicion. They were informed that Alexius had passed the Hellespont; but their apprehensions were lulled by the smallness of his original numbers, and their imprudence had not watched the subsequent increase of his army. If he left his main body to second and support his operations, he might advance unperceived in the night with a chosen detachment. While some applied scaling ladders to the lowest part of the walls, they were secure of an old Greek, who would introduce their companions through a subterranean passage into his house ; [80] they could soon on the inside break an entrance through the golden gate, which had been long obstructed ; and the conqueror would be in the heart of the city, before the Latins were conscious of their danger. After some debate, the Cæsar resigned himself to the faith of the volunteers ; they were trusty, bold, and successful ; and in describing the plan I have already related the execution and success.[81] But no sooner had Alexius passed the threshold of the golden gate than he trembled at his own rashness ; he paused, he deliberated, till the desperate volunteers urged him forwards by the assurance that in retreat lay the greatest and most inevitable danger. Whilst the Cæsar kept his regulars in firm array, the Comans dispersed themselves on all sides ; an alarm was sounded, and the threats of fire and pillage compelled the citizens to a decisive resolution. The Greeks of Constan-

[Marco Gradenigo]

---

[79] [Daphnusia, a town on a little island (now desert and named Kefken Adassi) off the coast of Bithynia, about 70 miles east of the mouth of the Bosphorus. *Thynias* was another name. Cp. Ramsay, Hist. Geography of Asia Minor, p. 182.]

[80] [Near the Gate of Selymbria or Pegæ (see above, vol. ii., plan opp. p. 149) ; and it was through this gate that the entrance was to be broken.]

[81] The loss of Constantinople is briefly told by the Latins ; the conquest is described with more satisfaction by the Greeks : by Acropolita (c. 85), Pachymer (l. ii. c. 26, 27), Nicephorus Gregoras (l. iv. c. 1, 2). See Ducange, Hist. de C. P. l. v. c. 19-27. [It is also described by Phrantzes, p. 17-20, ed. Bonn ; and in an anonymous poem on the Loss (1204) and Recovery (1261) of Constantinople, composed in A.D. 1392 (published by Buchon, Recherches historiques 2, p. 335 *sqq.*, 1845).]

tinople remembered their native sovereigns; the Genoese merchants, their recent alliance and Venetian foes; every quarter was in arms; and the air resounded with a general acclamation of "Long life and victory to Michael and John, the august emperors of the Romans!" Their rival Baldwin was awakened by the sound; but the most pressing danger could not prompt him to draw his sword in the defence of a city which he deserted, perhaps, with more pleasure than regret: he fled from the palace to the sea-shore, where he descried the welcome sails of the fleet returning from the vain and fruitless attempt on Daphnusia. Constantinople was irrecoverably lost; but the Latin emperor and the principal families embarked on board the Venetian galleys, and steered for the isle of Euboea, and afterwards for Italy, where the royal fugitive was entertained by the pope and Sicilian king with a mixture of contempt and pity. From [A.D. 1272] the loss of Constantinople to his death, he consumed thirteen years, soliciting the Catholic powers to join in his restoration: the lesson had been familiar to his youth; nor was his last exile more indigent or shameful than his three former pilgrimages to the courts of Europe. His son Philip was the heir of an ideal empire; and the pretensions of *his* daughter Catherine [A.D. 1267] were transported by her marriage to Charles of Valois, the brother of Philip the Fair, king of France. The house of Courtenay was represented in the female line by successive alliances, till the title of emperor of Constantinople, too bulky and sonorous for a private name, modestly expired in silence and oblivion.[82]

General consequences of the crusades    After this narrative of the expeditions of the Latins to Palestine and Constantinople, I cannot dismiss the subject without revolving the general consequences on the countries that were the scene, and on the nations that were the actors, of these memorable crusades.[83] As soon as the arms of the Franks were withdrawn, the impression, though not the memory, was erased in the Mahometan realms of Egypt and Syria. The faithful

[82] See the three last books (l. v.-viii.), and the genealogical tables of Ducange. In the year 1382, the titular emperor of Constantinople was James de Baux [titular Emperor, 1373-1383], duke of Andria in the kingdom of Naples, the son of Margaret, daughter of Catherine de Valois [married to Philip of Tarentum], daughter of Catherine [married to Charles of Valois], daughter of Philip, son of Baldwin II. (Ducange, l. viii. c. 37, 38). It is uncertain whether he left any posterity.

[83] Abulfeda, who saw the conclusion of the crusades, speaks of the kingdom of the Franks, and those of the negroes, as equally unknown (Prolegom. ad Geograph.). Had he not disdained the Latin language, how easily might the Syrian prince have found books and interpreters!

disciples of the prophet were never tempted by a profane desire
to study the laws or language of the idolaters ; nor did the simplicity of their primitive manners receive the slightest alteration
from their intercourse in peace and war with the unknown
strangers of the West. The Greeks, who thought themselves
proud, but who were only vain, shewed a disposition somewhat
less inflexible. In the efforts for the recovery of their empire
they emulated the valour, discipline, and tactics of their antagonists. The modern literature of the West they might justly
despise ; but its free spirit would instruct them in the rights of
man ; and some institutions of public and private life were
adopted from the French. The correspondence of Constantinople and Italy diffused the knowledge of the Latin tongue ; and
several of the fathers and classics were at length honoured with
a Greek version.[84] But the national and religious prejudices of
the Orientals were inflamed by persecution ; and the reign of
the Latins confirmed the separation of the two churches.

If we compare, at the æra of the crusades, the Latins of
Europe with the Greeks and Arabians, their respective degrees
of knowledge, industry and art, our rude ancestors must be
content with the third rank in the scale of nations. Their successive improvement and present superiority may be ascribed to
a peculiar energy of character, to an active and imitative spirit,
unknown to their more polished rivals, who at that time were
in a stationary or retrograde state. With such a disposition, the
Latins should have derived the most early and essential benefits
from a series of events which opened to their eyes the prospect
of the world, and introduced them to a long and frequent intercourse with the more cultivated regions of the East. The first
and most obvious progress was in trade and manufactures, in the
arts which are strongly prompted by the thirst of wealth, the
calls of necessity, and the gratification of the sense or vanity.
Among the crowd of unthinking fanatics, a captive or a pilgrim
might sometimes observe the superior refinements of Cairo and

[84] A short and superficial account of these versions from Latin into Greek is
given by Huet (de Interpretatione et de claris Interpretibus, p. 131-135). Maximus
Planudes, a monk of Constantinople (A.D. 1327-1353 [born c. 1260, died 1310]),
has translated Cæsar's Commentaries, the Somnium Scipionis, the Metamorphoses
and Heroides of Ovid, [the proverbial philosophy of the elder Cato, Boethius' De
Consolatione], &c. (Fabric. Bib. Græc. tom. x. p. 533 [ed. Harl. xi. 682 *sqq.* ;
Krumbacher, Gesch. der byz. Litt. 543 *sqq.* The Letters of Planudes have been
edited by M. Treu (1890), who has established the chronology of his life (Zur Gesch.
der Ueberlieferung von Plutarchs Moralia, 1877)].)

Constantinople : the first importer of windmills [85] was the benefactor of nations ; and, if such blessings are enjoyed without any
grateful remembrance, history has condescended to notice the
more apparent luxuries of silk and sugar, which were transported
into Italy from Greece and Egypt. But the intellectual wants
of the Latins were more slowly felt and supplied ; the ardour of
studious curiosity was awakened in Europe by different causes
and more recent events ; and, in the age of the crusades, they
viewed with careless indifference the literature of the Greeks
and Arabians. Some rudiments of mathematical and medicinal
knowledge might be imparted in practice and in figures ; necessity might produce some interpreters for the grosser business of
merchants and soldiers ; but the commerce of the Orientals had
not diffused the study and knowledge of their languages in the
schools of Europe.[86] If a similar principle of religion repulsed
the idiom of the Koran, it should have excited their patience
and curiosity to understand the original text of the gospel ; and
the same grammar would have unfolded the sense of Plato and
the beauties of Homer. Yet in a reign of sixty years, the
Latins of Constantinople disdained the speech and learning of
their subjects ; and the manuscripts were the only treasures
which the natives might enjoy without rapine or envy. Aristotle was indeed the oracle of the Western universities ; but it
was a barbarous Aristotle ; and, instead of ascending to the
fountain-head, his Latin votaries humbly accepted a corrupt and
remote version from the Jews and Moors of Andalusia. The
principle of the crusades was a savage fanaticism ; and the most
important effects were analogous to the cause. Each pilgrim
was ambitious to return with his sacred spoils, the relics of
Greece and Palestine ; [87] and each relic was preceded and followed by a train of miracles and visions. The belief of the
Catholics was corrupted by new legends, their practice by new
superstitions ; and the establishment of the inquisition, the
mendicant orders of monks and friars, the last abuse of indul-

[85] Windmills, first invented in the dry country of Asia Minor, were used in Normandy as early as the year 1105 (Vie privée des François, tom. i. p. 42, 43 ; Ducange, Gloss. Latin. tom. iv. p. 474).

[86] See the complaints of Roger Bacon (Biographia Britannica, vol. i. p. 418,
Kippis's edition). If Bacon himself, or Gerbert, understood *some* Greek, they were
prodigies, and owed nothing to the commerce of the East.

[87] Such was the opinion of the great Leibnitz (Oeuvres de Fontenelle, tom. v. p.
458), a master of the history of the middle ages. I shall only instance the pedigree
of the Carmelites, and the flight of the house of Loretto, which were both derived
from Palestine.

gences, and the final progress of idolatry, flowed from the baleful fountain of the holy war. The active spirit of the Latins preyed on the vitals of their reason and religion ; and, if the ninth and tenth centuries were the times of darkness, the thirteenth and fourteenth were the age of absurdity and fable.

In the profession of Christianity, in the cultivation of a fertile land, the northern conquerors of the Roman empire insensibly mingled with the provincials and rekindled the embers of the arts of antiquity. Their settlements about the age of Charlemagne had acquired some degree of order and stability, when they were overwhelmed by new swarms of invaders, the Normans, Saracens,[88] and Hungarians, who replunged the western countries of Europe into their former state of anarchy and barbarism. About the eleventh century, the second tempest had subsided by the expulsion or conversion of the enemies of Christendom : the tide of civilisation, which had so long ebbed, began to flow with a steady and accelerated course ; and a fairer prospect was opened to the hopes and efforts of the rising generations. Great was the success, and rapid the progress, during the two hundred years of the crusades ; and some philosophers have applauded the propitious influence of these holy wars, which appear to me to have checked, rather than forwarded, the maturity of Europe.[89] The lives and labours of millions, which were buried in the East, would have been more profitably employed in the improvement of their native country : the accumulated stock of industry and wealth would have overflowed in navigation and trade ; and the Latins would have been enriched and enlightened by a pure and friendly correspondence with the climates of the East. In one respect I can indeed perceive the accidental operation of the crusades, not so much in producing a benefit, as in removing an evil. The larger portion of the inhabitants of Europe was chained to the soil, without freedom, or property, or knowledge ; and the two orders of ecclesiastics and nobles, whose numbers were comparatively small, alone deserved the name of citizens and men. This oppressive system was supported by the arts of the clergy and

[88] If I rank the Saracens with the barbarians, it is only relative to their wars, or rather inroads, in Italy and France, where their sole purpose was to plunder and destroy.

[89] On this interesting subject, the progress of society in Europe, a strong ray of philosophic light has broke from Scotland in our own times ; and it is with private as well as public regard that I repeat the names of Hume, Robertson, and Adam Smith.

the swords of the barons. The authority of the priests operated
in the darker ages as a salutary antidote : they prevented the
total extinction of letters, mitigated the fierceness of the times,
sheltered the poor and defenceless, and preserved or revived
the peace and order of civil society. But the independence,
rapine, and discord of the feudal lords were unmixed with any
semblance of good ; and every hope of industry and improvement was crushed by the iron weight of the martial aristocracy.
Among the causes that undermined the Gothic edifice, a conspicuous place must be allowed to the crusades. The estates
of the barons were dissipated, and their race was often extinguished, in these costly and perilous expeditions. Their poverty
extorted from their pride those charters of freedom which unlocked the fetters of the slave, secured the farm of the peasant
and the shop of the artificer, and gradually restored a substance
and a soul to the most numerous and useful part of the community. The conflagration which destroyed the tall and barren
trees of the forest gave air and scope to the vegetation of the
smaller and nutritive plants of the soil.

---

## DIGRESSION ON THE FAMILY OF COURTENAY.

The purple of three emperors who have reigned at Constantinople will authorise or excuse a digression on the origin and
singular fortunes of the house of COURTENAY,[90] in the three principal branches : I. Of Edessa ; II. Of France ; and III. Of England ; of which the last only has survived the revolutions of
eight hundred years.

Origin of the
family of
Courtenay.
A.D. 1020

I. Before the introduction of trade, which scatters riches, and
of knowledge, which dispels prejudice, the prerogative of birth
is most strongly felt and most humbly acknowledged. In every
age the laws and manners of the Germans have discriminated
the ranks of society : the dukes and counts, who shared the
empire of Charlemagne, converted their office to an inheritance ;
and to his children each feudal lord bequeathed his honour and

---

[90] I have applied, but not confined, myself to *A Genealogical History of the Noble
and Illustrious Family of Courtenay, by Ezra Cleaveland, Tutor to Sir William
Courtenay, and Rector of Honiton ; Exon.* 1735, *in folio.* The first part is extracted from William of Tyre ; the second from Bouchet's French history ; and the
third from various memorials, public, provincial, and private, of the Courtenays of
Devonshire. The rector of Honiton has more gratitude than industry, and more
industry than criticism.

his sword. The proudest families are content to lose, in the darkness of the middle ages, the tree of their pedigree, which, however deep and lofty, must ultimately rise from a plebeian root ; and their historians must descend ten centuries below the Christian æra, before they can ascertain any lineal succession by the evidence of surnames, of arms, and of authentic records. With the first rays of light [91] we discern the nobility and opulence of Atho, a French knight : his nobility, in the rank and title of a nameless father ; his opulence, in the foundation of the castle of Courtenay, in the district of Gatinois, about fifty-six miles to the south of Paris. From the reign of Robert, the son of Hugh Capet, the barons of Courtenay are conspicuous among the immediate vassals of the crown ; and Joscelin, the grandson of Atho and a noble dame, is enrolled among the heroes of the first crusade. A domestic alliance (their mothers were sisters) attached him to the standard of Baldwin of Bruges, the second count of Edessa : a princely fief, which he was worthy to receive, and able to maintain, announces the number of his martial followers ; and, after the departure of his cousin, Joscelin himself was invested with the county of Edessa on both sides of the Euphrates. By economy in peace his territories were replenished with Latin and Syrian subjects : his magazines with corn, wine, and oil ; his castles with gold and silver, with arms and horses. In a holy warfare of thirty years he was alternately a conqueror and a captive ; but he died like a soldier, in an horse-litter at the head of his troops ; and his last glance beheld the flight of the Turkish invaders who had presumed on his age and infirmities. His son and successor, of the same name, was less deficient in valour than in vigilance ; but he sometimes forgot that dominion is acquired and maintained by the same arts. He challenged the hostility of the Turks, without securing the friendship of the prince of Antioch ; and, amidst the peaceful luxury of Turbessel, in Syria,[92] Joscelin neglected the defence of the Christian frontier beyond the Euphrates. In his absence, Zenghi, the first of the Atabeks, besieged and stormed his capital, Edessa, which was feebly defended by a timorous and disloyal

I. The counts of Edessa. A.D. 1101-1152

---

[91] The primitive record of the family is a passage of the Continuator of Aimoin, a monk of Fleury, who wrote in the xiith century. See his Chronicle, in the Historians of France (tom. xi. p. 176).

[92] Turbessel, or as it is now styled Telbesher, is fixed by d'Anville four and twenty miles from the great passage over the Euphrates at Zeugma. [Tell Bāsher, now Saleri Kaleh, "a large mound with ruins near the village of Tulbashar," two days' journey north of Aleppo (Sir C. Wilson, note to Bahā ad-Dīn, p. 58).]

crowd of Orientals ; the Franks were oppressed in a bold attempt
for its recovery, and Courtenay ended his days in the prison of
Aleppo. He still left a fair and ample patrimony. But the
victorious Turks oppressed on all sides the weakness of a widow
and orphan ; and, for the equivalent of an annual pension, they
resigned to the Greek emperor the charge of defending, and the
shame of losing, the last relics of the Latin conquest. The
countess-dowager of Edessa retired to Jerusalem with her two
children : the daughter, Agnes, became the wife and mother of
a king ; the son, Joscelin the Third, accepted the office of seneschal, the first of the kingdom, and held his new estates in Palestine by the service of fifty knights. His name appears with
honour in all the transactions of peace and war ; but he finally
vanishes in the fall of Jerusalem ; and the name of Courtenay,
in this branch of Edessa, was lost by the marriage of his two
daughters with a French and a German baron.[93]

II. The Courte-
nays of France
II. While Joscelin reigned beyond the Euphrates, his elder
brother, Milo, the son of Joscelin, the son of Atho, continued,
near the Seine, to possess the castle of their fathers, which was
at length inherited by Rainaud, or Reginald, the youngest of his
three sons. Examples of genius or virtue must be rare in the
annals of the oldest families ; and, in a remote age, their pride
will embrace a deed of rapine and violence ; such, however, as
could not be perpetrated without some superiority of courage, or
at least of power. A descendant of Reginald of Courtenay may
blush for the public robber who stripped and imprisoned several
merchants, after they had satisfied the king's duties at Sens and
Orleans. He will glory in the offence, since the bold offender
could not be compelled to obedience and restitution, till the
regent and the count of Champagne prepared to march against
him at the head of an army.[94] Reginald bestowed his estates
Their alliance
with the royal
family. A.D.
1150
on his eldest daughter, and his daughter on the seventh son of
king Louis the Fat ; and their marriage was crowned with a
numerous offspring. We might expect that a private should
have merged in a royal name ; and that the descendants of Peter
of France and Elizabeth of Courtenay would have enjoyed the

[93] His possessions are distinguished in the Assises of Jerusalem (c. 326) among
the feudal tenures of the kingdom, which must therefore have been collected between
the years 1153 and 1187. His pedigree may be found in the Lignages d'Outremer,
c. 16.

[94] The rapine and satisfaction of Reginald de Courtenay are preposterously
arranged in the epistles of the abbot and regent Suger (cxiv. cxvi.), the best
memorials of the age (Duchesne, Scriptores Hist. Franc. tom. iv. p. 530).

title and honours of princes of the blood.   But this legitimate
claim was long neglected and finally denied ; and the causes of
their disgrace will represent the story of this second branch.
1. Of all the families now extant, the most ancient, doubtless,
and the most illustrious is the house of France, which has occupied the same throne above eight hundred years, and descends,
in a clear and lineal series of males, from the middle of the ninth
century.[95]   In the age of the crusades it was already revered
both in the East and West.   But from Hugh Capet to the marriage of Peter no more than five reigns or generations had
elapsed ; and so precarious was their title that the eldest sons,
as a necessary precaution, were previously crowned during the
lifetime of their fathers.   The peers of France have long maintained their precedency before the younger branches of the
royal line ; nor had the princes of the blood, in the twelfth
century, acquired that hereditary lustre which is now diffused
over the most remote candidates for the succession.   2. The
barons of Courtenay must have stood high in their own estima-
tion, and in that of the world, since they could impose on the
son of a king the obligation of adopting for himself and all his
descendants the name and arms of their daughter and his wife.
In the marriage of an heiress with her inferior or her equal, such
exchange was often required and allowed ; but, as they continued
to diverge from the regal stem, the sons of Louis the Fat were
insensibly confounded with their maternal ancestors ; and the
new Courtenays might deserve to forfeit the honours of their
birth, which a motive of interest had tempted them to renounce.
3. The shame was far more permanent than the reward, and a
momentary blaze was followed by a long darkness.   The eldest
son of these nuptials, Peter of Courtenay, had married, as I have
already mentioned, the sister of the counts of Flanders, the two
first emperors of Constantinople ; he rashly accepted the invita-

[95] In the beginning of the xith century, after naming the father and grandfather
of Hugh Capet, the monk Glaber is obliged to add, cujus genus valde in-ante re-
peritur obscurum.   Yet we are assured that the great-grandfather of Hugh Capet
was Robert the Strong, count of Anjou (A.D. 863-873), a noble Frank of Neustria,
Neustricus . . . generosæ stirpis, who was slain in the defence of his country
against the Normans, dum patriæ fines tuebatur.   Beyond Robert, all is conjecture
or fable.   It is a probable conjecture that the third race descended from the second
by Childebrand, the brother of Charles Martel.   It is an absurd fable that the
second was allied to the first by the marriage of Ansbert, a Roman senator and
the ancestor of St. Arnoul, with Blitilde, a daughter of Clotaire I.   The Saxon
origin of the house of France is an ancient but incredible opinion.   See a judicious
memoir of M. de Foncemagne (Mémoires de l'Académie des Inscriptions, tom. xx.
p. 548-579).   He had promised to declare his own opinion in a second memoir,
which has never appeared.

tion of the barons of Romania ; his two sons, Robert and Baldwin, successively held and lost the remains of the Latin empire in the East, and the grand-daughter of Baldwin the Second again mingled her blood with the blood of France and of Valois.    To support the expenses of a troubled and transitory reign, their patrimonial estates were mortgaged or sold ; and the last emperors of Constantinople depended on the annual charity of Rome and Naples.

While the elder brothers dissipated their wealth in romantic adventures, and the castle of Courtenay was profaned by a plebeian owner, the younger branches of that adopted name were propagated and multiplied.    But their splendour was clouded by poverty and time : after the decease of Robert, great butler of France, they descended from princes to barons ; the next generations were confounded with the simple gentry ; the descendants of Hugh Capet could no longer be visible in the rural lords of Tanlay and of Champignelles.    The more adventurous embraced, without dishonour, the profession of a soldier ; the least active and opulent might sink, like their cousins of the branch of Dreux, into the condition of peasants.    Their royal descent, in a dark period of four hundred years, became each day more obsolete and ambiguous ; and their pedigree, instead of being enrolled in the annals of the kingdom, must be painfully searched by the minute diligence of heralds and genealogists.    It was not till the end of the sixteenth century, on the accession of a family almost as remote as their own, that the princely spirit of the Courtenays again revived ; and the question of the nobility provoked them to assert the royalty of their blood.    They appealed to the justice and compassion of Henry the Fourth ; obtained a favourable opinion from twenty lawyers of Italy and Germany, and modestly compared themselves to the descendants of king David, whose prerogatives were not impaired by the lapse of ages, or the trade of a carpenter.[96]    But every ear was deaf, and every circumstance was adverse, to their lawful claims.    The Bourbon kings were justified by the neglect of the Valois ; the princes of the blood, more recent and lofty, disdained the alliance

[96] Of the various petitions, apologies, &c., published by the *princes* of Courtenay, I have seen the three following all in octavo : 1. De Stirpe et Origine Domus de Courtenay : addita sunt Responsa celeberrimorum Europæ Jurisconsultorum, Paris, 1607.    2. Représentation du Procédé tenu a l'instance faicte devant le Roi, par Messieurs de Courtenay, pour la conversation de l'Honneur et Dignité de leur Maison, Branch de la Royalle Maison de France, a Paris, 1613.    3. Représentation du subject qui a porté Messieurs de Salles et de Fraville, de la Maison de Courtenays, à se retirer hors du Royaume, 1614.    It was an homicide, for which the Courtenays expected to be pardoned, or tried, as princes of the blood.

of this humble kindred ; the parliament, without denying their
proofs, eluded a dangerous precedent by an arbitrary distinction
and established St. Louis as the first father of the royal line.[97] A
repetition of complaints and protests was repeatedly disregarded:
and the hopeless pursuit was terminated in the present century
by the death of the last male of the family.[98] Their painful
and anxious situation was alleviated by the pride of conscious
virtue ; they sternly rejected the temptations of fortune and
favour ; and a dying Courtenay would have sacrificed his son, if
the youth could have renounced, for any temporal interest, the
right and title of a legitimate prince of the blood of France.[99]

III. According to the old register of Ford Abbey, the Courtenays of Devonshire are descended from Prince *Florus*, the second
son of Peter, and the grandson of Louis the Fat.[100] This fable
of the grateful or venal monks was too respectfully entertained by
our antiquaries, Camden [101] and Dugdale ; [102] but it is so clearly
repugnant to truth and time, that the rational pride of the family
now refuses to accept this imaginary founder. Their most faithful historians believe that, after giving his daughter to the king's
son, Reginald of Courtenay abandoned his possessions in France,
and obtained from the English monarch a second wife and a new
inheritance. It is certain, at least, that Henry the Second distinguished in his camps and councils *a* Reginald, of the name,
arms, and, as it may be fairly presumed, of the genuine race of

III. The
Courtenays of
England

---

[97] The sense of the parliaments is thus expressed by Thuanus : Principis nomen
nusquam in Galliâ tributum, nisi iis qui per matres e regibus nostris originem re-
petunt : qui nunc tantum a Ludovico Nono beatæ memoriæ numerantur : nam
*Cortinaei* et Drocenses, a Ludovico crasso genus ducentes, hodie inter eos minime
recensentur :—a distinction of expediency rather than justice. The sanctity of
Louis IX. could not invest him with any special prerogative, and all the descendants
of Hugh Capet must be included in his original compact with the French nation.

[98] The last male of the Courtenays was Charles Roger, who died in the year
1730, without leaving any sons. The last female was Helen de Courtenay, who
married Louis de Beaufremont. Her title of Princesse du Sang Royal de France
was suppressed (February 7, 1737) by an *arrêt* of the parliament of Paris.

[99] The singular anecdote to which I allude, is related in the Recueil des Pièces
intéressantes et peu connues (Maestricht, 1786, in four vols. 12mo) ; and the unknown editor [M. de la Place, of Calais] quotes his author, who had received it
from Helen de Courtenay, Marquise de Beaufremont.

[100] Dugdale, Monasticon Anglicanum, vol. i. p. 786. Yet this fable must have
been invented before the reign of Edward III. The profuse devotion of the three
first generations to Ford Abbey was followed by oppression on one side and ingratitude on the other ; and in the sixth generation the monks ceased to register
the births, actions, and deaths of their patrons.

[101] In his Britannia, in the list of the earls of Devonshire. His expression, e
regio sanguine ortos credunt, betrays, however, some doubt or suspicion.

[102] In his Baronage, p. i. p. 634, he refers to his own Monasticon. Should he
not have corrected the register of Ford Abbey, and annihilated the phantom Florus,
by the unquestionable evidence of the French historians?

the Courtenays of France. The right of wardship enabled a feudal lord to reward his vassal with the marriage and estate of a noble heiress; and Reginald of Courtenay acquired a fair establishment in Devonshire, where his posterity has been seated above six hundred years.[103] From a Norman baron, Baldwin de Brioniis, who had been invested by the Conqueror, Hawise, the wife of Reginald, derived the honour of Okehampton, which was held by the service of ninety-three knights; and a female might claim the manly offices of hereditary viscount or sheriff, and of captain of the royal castle of Exeter. Their son Robert married the sister of the earl of Devon; at the end of a century, on the failure of the family of Rivers,[104] his great-grandson, Hugh the Second, succeeded to a title which was still considered as a territorial dignity; and twelve earls of Devonshire, of the name of Courtenay, have flourished in a period of two hundred and twenty years. They were ranked among the chief of the barons of the realm; nor was it till after a strenuous dispute that they yielded to the fief of Arundel the first place in the parliament of England; their alliances were contracted with the noblest families, the Veres, Despensers, St. Johns, Talbots, Bohuns, and even the Plantagenets themselves; and in a contest with John of Lancaster, a Courtenay, bishop of London, and afterwards archbishop of Canterbury, might be accused of profane confidence in the strength and number of his kindred. In peace, the earls of Devon resided in their numerous castles and manors of the west; their ample revenue was appropriated to devotion and hospitality; and the epitaph of Edward, surnamed, from his misfortunes, the *blind*, from his virtues, the *good*, Earl, inculcates with much ingenuity a moral sentence, which may, however, be abused by thoughtless generosity. After a grateful commemoration of the fifty-five years of union and happiness, which he enjoyed with Mabel his wife, the good Earl thus speaks from the tomb:

> What we gave, we have;
> What we spent, we had;
> What we left, we lost.[105]

*The Earls of Devonshire* (margin note)

---

[103] Besides the third and most valuable book of Cleaveland's History, I have consulted Dugdale, the father of our genealogical science (Baronage, p. i. p. 634-643).

[104] This great family, de Ripuariis, de Redvers, de Rivers, ended, in Edward the First's time, in Isabella de Fortibus, a famous and potent dowager, who long survived her brother and husband (Dugdale, Baronage, p. i. p. 254-257).

[105] Cleaveland, p. 142. By some it is assigned to a Rivers, earl of Devon; but the English denotes the xvth rather than the xiiith century.

But their *losses*, in this sense, were far superior to their gifts and expenses; and their heirs, not less than the poor, were the objects of their paternal care. The sums which they paid for livery and seisin attest the greatness of their possessions; and several estates have remained in their family since the thirteenth and fourteenth centuries. In war, the Courtenays of England fulfilled the duties, and deserved the honours, of chivalry. They were often entrusted to levy and command the militia of Devonshire and Cornwall; they often attended their supreme lord to the borders of Scotland; and in foreign service, for a stipulated price, they sometimes maintained fourscore men at arms and as many archers. By sea and land they fought under the standard of the Edwards and Henries; their names are conspicuous in battles, in tournaments, and in the original list of the order of the Garter; three brothers shared the Spanish victory of the Black Prince; and in the lapse of six generations the English Courtenays had learned to despise the nation and country from which they derived their origin. In the quarrel of the two Roses, the earls of Devon adhered to the house of Lancaster, and three brothers successively died either in the field or on the scaffold. Their honours and estates were restored by Henry the Seventh; a daughter of Edward the Fourth was not disgraced by the nuptials of a Courtenay; their son, who was created marquis of Exeter, enjoyed the favour of his cousin, Henry the Eighth; and in the camp of Cloth of Gold he broke a lance against the French monarch. But the favour of Henry was the prelude of disgrace; his disgrace was the signal of death; and of the victims of the jealous tyrant, the marquis of Exeter is one of the most noble and guiltless. His son Edward lived a prisoner in the Tower, and died an exile at Padua; and the secret love of Queen Mary, whom he slighted, perhaps for the princess Elizabeth, has shed a romantic colour on the story of this beautiful youth. The relics of his patrimony were conveyed into strange families by the marriages of his four aunts; and his personal honours, as if they had been legally extinct, were revived by the patents of succeeding princes. But there still survived a lineal descendant of Hugh, the first earl of Devon, a younger branch of the Courtenays, who have been seated at Powderham Castle above four hundred years, from the reign of Edward the Third to the present hour. Their estates have been increased by the grant and improvement of lands in Ireland, and they have been recently restored to the honours of the peerage. Yet the Courtenays still retain the plaintive motto, which asserts the innocence, and deplores the fall, of their ancient house.[106] While they sigh for past greatness, they are doubtless sensible of present blessings ; in the long series of the Courtenay annals, the most splendid æra is likewise the most unfortunate ; nor can an opulent peer of Britain be inclined to envy the emperors of Constantinople, who wandered over Europe to solicit alms for the support of their dignity and the defence of their capital.

[106] *Ubi lapsus ! Quid feci ?* a motto which was probably adopted by the Powderham branch, after the loss of the earldom of Devonshire, &c. The primitive arms of the Courtenays were, *or, three torteaux, gules*, which seem to denote their affinity with Godfrey of Bouillon and the ancient counts of Boulogne.

[Some further information on the family of the Courtenays will be found in a short note in the Gentleman's Magazine for July, 1839, p. 39. Cp. Smith's note in his ed. of Gibbon, vol. vii. p. 354.]

## CHAPTER LXII

*The Greek Emperors of Nice and Constantinople—Elevation and Reign of Michael Palæologus—His false Union with the Pope and the Latin Church—Hostile Designs of Charles of Anjou— Revolt of Sicily—War of the Catalans in Asia and Greece— Revolutions and Present State of Athens*

THE loss of Constantinople restored a momentary vigour to the Greeks. From their palaces the princes and nobles were driven into the field ; and the fragments of the falling monarchy were grasped by the hands of the most vigorous or the most skilful candidates. In the long and barren pages of the Byzantine annals,[1] it would not be an easy task to equal the two characters of Theodore Lascaris and John Ducas Vataces,[2] who re-planted and upheld the Roman standard at Nice in Bithynia. The difference of their virtues was happily suited to the diversity of their situation. In his first efforts the fugitive Lascaris commanded only three cities and two thousand soldiers ; his reign was the season of generous and active despair ; in every military operation he staked his life and crown ; and his enemies, of the Hellespont and the Mæander, were surprised by his celerity and subdued by his boldness. A victorious reign

*Restoration of the Greek empire*

*Theodore Lascaris. A.D. 1004 ????*

---

[1] For the reigns of the Nicene emperors, more especially of John Vataces and his son, their minister, George Acropolita, is the only genuine contemporary ; but George Pachymer returned to Constantinople with the Greeks, at the age of nineteen (Hanckius, de Script. Byzant. c. 33, 34, p. 564-578 ; Fabric. Bibliot. Græc. tom. vi. p. 448-460). Yet the history of Nicephorus Gregoras, though of the xivth century, is a valuable narrative from the taking of Constantinople by the Latins. [We have subsidiary contemporary sources, such as the autobiography of Nicephorus Blemmydes (recently edited by A. Heisenberg, 1896), who was an important person at the courts of Vatatzes and Theodore II. See Appendix 1. The Empire of Nicæa and Despotate of Epirus have been treated in the histories of Finlay and Hopf, but more fully in a recently published special work in modern Greek by Antonios Mêliarakês : 'Ἱστορία τοῦ βασιλείου τῆς Νικαίας καὶ τοῦ δεσποτάτου τῆς Ἠπείρου, 1898.]

[2] Nicephorus Gregoras (l. ii. c. 1) distinguishes between the ὀξεῖα ὁρμή of Lascaris, and the εὐστάθεια of Vataces. The two portraits are in a very good style.

John Ducas
Vataces. A.D.
1222-1255
[1254], Oct. 30

of eighteen years expanded the principality of Nice to the magnitude of an empire. The throne of his successor and son-in-law, Vataces, was founded on a more solid basis, a larger scope, and more plentiful resources ; and it was the temper as well as the interest of Vataces to calculate the risk, to expect the moment, and to ensure the success of his ambitious designs. In the decline of the Latins I have briefly exposed the progress of the Greeks : the prudent and gradual advances of a conqueror, who, in a reign of thirty-three years, rescued the provinces from national and foreign usurpers, till he pressed on all sides the Imperial city, a leafless and sapless trunk, which must fall at the first stroke of the axe. But his interior and peaceful administration is still more deserving of notice and praise.[3] The calamities of the times had wasted the numbers and the substance of the Greeks ; the motives and the means of agriculture were extirpated ; and the most fertile lands were left without cultivation or inhabitants. A portion of this vacant property was occupied and improved by the command, and for the benefit, of the emperor ; a powerful hand and a vigilant eye supplied and surpassed, by a skilful management, the minute diligence of a private farmer ; the royal domain became the garden and granary of Asia ; and without impoverishing the people the sovereign acquired a fund of innocent and productive wealth. According to the nature of the soil, his lands were sown with corn or planted with vines ; the pastures were filled with horses and oxen, with sheep and hogs ; and, when Vataces presented to the empress a crown of diamonds and pearls, he informed her with a smile that this precious ornament arose from the sale of the eggs of his innumerable poultry. The produce of his domain was applied to the maintenance of his palace and hospitals, the calls of dignity and benevolence ; the lesson was still more useful than the revenue ; the plough was restored to its ancient security and honour ; and the nobles were taught to seek a sure and independent revenue from their estates, instead of adorning their splendid beggary by the oppression of the people, or (what is almost the same) by the favours of the court. The superfluous stock of corn and cattle was eagerly purchased by the Turks, with whom Vataces preserved a strict and sincere alliance ; but he discouraged the importation of foreign manufactures, the costly silks of the East and the curious labours of

---

[3] Pachymer, l. i. c. 23, 24 ; Nic. Greg. l. ii. c. 6. The reader of the Byzantines must observe how rarely we are indulged with such precious details.

the Italian looms. " The demands of nature and necessity,
was he accustomed to say, " are indispensable ; but the influence
of passion may rise and sink at the breath of a monarch" ; and
both his precept and example recommended simplicity of manners and the use of domestic industry. The education of youth
and the revival of learning were the most serious objects of his
care ; and, without deciding the precedency, he pronounced
with truth that a prince and a philosopher [4] are the two most
eminent characters of human society. His first wife was Irene,
the daughter of Theodore Lascaris, a woman more illustrious
by her personal merit, the milder virtues of her sex, than by
the blood of the Angeli and Comneni, that flowed in her
veins and transmitted the inheritance of the empire. After
her death, he was contracted to Anne, or Constance, a natural [A.D. 1244]
daughter of the emperor Frederic the Second ; [5] but, as the
bride had not attained the years of puberty, Vataces placed
in his solitary bed an Italian damsel of her train ; [6] and his amorous weakness bestowed on the concubine the honours, though
not the title, of lawful empress. His frailty was censured as
a flagitious and damnable sin by the monks ; and their rude
invectives exercised and displayed the patience of the royal
lover. A philosophic age may excuse a single vice, which was
redeemed by a crowd of virtues ; and, in the review of his
faults, and the more intemperate passions of Lascaris, the judgment of their contemporaries was softened by gratitude to the
second founders of the empire.[7] The slaves of the Latins, without law or peace, applauded the happiness of their brethren who
had resumed their national freedom ; and Vataces employed

[4] Μόνοι γὰρ ἁπάντων ἀνθρώπων ὀνομαστότατοι βασιλεὺς καὶ φιλόσοφος (Georg. Acro-
pol. c. 32). The emperor, in a familiar conversation, examined and encouraged
the studies of his future logothete.

[5] [Her mother was Bianca Lancia of Piedmont. Frederick seems to have
married her ultimately (towards the close of his life) and legitimised her children
(Matthew Paris, ed. Lond., vol. 7, p. 216). The lady's true name was Constance
(as western writers called her) ; only Greek writers name her Anna, so that she
was probably baptized under this name into the Greek church.]

[6] [The Greek writers call her the Μαρκεζίνα—Marchioness. Her *liaison* with the
Emperor caused an incident which produced a quarrel between him and Nicephorus
Blemmydes. She entered the Monastery of St. Gregory in grand costume.
Blemmydes, when he observed her presence, ordered the communion service to be
discontinued. Vatatzes refused to punish a just man, as the Marchioness demanded, but showed his resentment by breaking off all relations with him. Besides Nicephorus Gregoras, i. p. 45, 46, we have a description of the incident
from the pen of Blemmydes himself in his autobiography, c. 41 (ed. Heisenberg).]

[7] Compare Acropolita (c. 18, 52) and the two first books of Nicephorus Gregoras.

the laudable policy of convincing the Greeks of every dominion that it was their interest to be enrolled in the number of his subjects.

Theodore Las-
caris II. A.D.
1255, October
30—A.D. 1259
[1258], August
A strong shade of degeneracy is visible between John Vataces and his son Theodore ; between the founder who sustained the weight, and the heir who enjoyed the splendour, of the Imperial crown.[8]   Yet the character of Theodore was not devoid of energy ; he had been educated in the school of his father, in the exercise of war and hunting: Constantinople was yet spared; but in the three years of a short reign he thrice led [A.D. 1256,
1257] his armies into the heart of Bulgaria.[9]   His virtues were sullied by a choleric and suspicious temper : the first of these may be ascribed to the ignorance of control ; and the second might naturally arise from a dark and imperfect view of the corrup- [1257] tion of mankind.   On a march in Bulgaria he consulted on a question of policy his principal ministers ; and the Greek logothete, George Acropolita, presumed to offend him by the declaration of a free and honest opinion.   The emperor half unsheathed his scymetar ; but his more deliberate rage reserved Acropolita for a baser punishment.   One of the first officers of the empire was ordered to dismount, stripped of his robes, and extended on the ground in the presence of the prince and army. In this posture he was chastised with so many and such heavy blows from the clubs of two guards or executioners that, when Theodore commanded them to cease, the great logothete was scarcely able to rise and crawl away to his tent.   After a seclusion of some days, he was recalled by a peremptory mandate to his seat in council ; and so dead were the Greeks to the sense of honour and shame that it is from the narrative of the sufferer himself that we acquire the knowledge of his disgrace.[10]

---

[8] A Persian saying, that Cyrus was the *father*, and Darius the *master*, of his subjects, was applied to Vataces and his son.   But Pachymer (l. i. c. 23) has mistaken the mild Darius for the cruel Cambyses, despot or tyrant of his people.   By the institution of taxes, Darius had incurred the less odious, but more contemptible name of Κάπηλος, *merchant* or *broker* (Herodotus, iii. 89).

[9] [Theodore led two expeditions in person against the Bulgarians, in 1256 and 1257.   At the end of the second expedition he had a meeting with Theodora Petraleipha, the wife of Michael II., Despot of Epirus, at Thessalonica, where a marriage was both arranged and celebrated between his daughter Maria and her son Nicephorus.   The third expedition, to which Gibbon refers, was that of 1259 against Michael II., which however was conducted not by Theodore but by Michael Palæologus, the future emperor.]

[10] Acropolita (c. 63) seems to admire his own firmness in sustaining a beating and not returning to council till he was called.   He relates the exploits of Theodore, and his own services, from c. 53 to c. 74 of his History.   See the third book of Nicephorus Gregoras.   [Among some unpublished works of this remarkable

The cruelty of the emperor was exasperated by the pangs of sickness, the approach of a premature end, and the suspicion of poison and magic.[11] The lives and fortunes, the eyes and limbs, of his kinsmen and nobles were sacrificed to each sally of passion ; and, before he died, the son of Vataces might deserve from the people, or at least from the Court, the appellation of tyrant. A matron of the family of the Palæologi [12] had provoked his anger by refusing to bestow her beauteous daughter on the vile plebeian who was recommended by his caprice. Without regard to her birth or age, her body, as high as the neck, was inclosed in a sack with several cats, who were pricked with pins to irritate their fury against their unfortunate fellow-captive. In his last hours the emperor testified a wish to forgive and be forgiven, a just anxiety for the fate of John, his son and successor, who, at the age of eight years, was condemned to the dangers of a long minority. His last choice entrusted the office of guardian to the sanctity of the patriarch Arsenius, and to the courage of George Muzalon, the great domestic, who was equally distinguished by the royal favour and the public hatred. Since their connection with the Latins, the names and privileges of hereditary rank had insinuated themselves into the Greek monarchy ; and the noble families [13] were provoked by the elevation of a worthless favourite, to whose influence they imputed the errors and calamities of the late reign. In the first council after the emperor's death, Muzalon, from a lofty throne, pronounced a laboured apology of his conduct and intentions : his modesty was subdued by an unanimous assurance of esteem and fidelity ; and his most inveterate enemies were the loudest to salute him as the guardian and saviour

*Minority of John Lascaris. A.D. 1259 [1258], August*

monarch, Theodore Lascaris, is an encomium on George Acropolites. There is also a rhetorical estimate of his contemporary Frederick II., a work which ought to have been published long ago. George Acropolites made a collection of his letters ; some of these are extant but not yet printed. Professor Krumbacher designates Theodore II. " as statesman, writer, and man, one of the most interesting figures of Byzantium, a sort of oriental parallel to his great contemporary Frederick II. ; a degenerate, no doubt; intellectually highly gifted, bodily weak, without moral force, with a nervous system fatally preponderant " (*op. cit.* p. 478). On his theological productions cp. J. Dräseke, Byz. Zeitschrift, iii. p. 498 *sqq.*] [Since this note was written, an edition of the Correspondence of Theodore Lasceris was published by N. Festa.]

11 [He seems to have suffered from a cerebral disease, and to have been subject to fits of epilepsy. Cp. Mêliarakês, *op. cit.* p. 479.]

12 [A sister of Michael Palæologus.]

13 Pachymer (l. i. c. 21) names and discriminates fifteen or twenty Greek families, καὶ ὅσοι ἄλλοι, οἷς ἡ μεγαλογενὴς σειρὰ καὶ χρυσῆ συγκεκρότητο. Does he mean, by this decoration, a figurative or a real golden chain ? Perhaps both.

of the Romans. Eight days were sufficient to prepare the execution of the conspiracy. On the ninth,[14] the obsequies of the deceased monarch were solemnised in the cathedral of Magnesia,[15] an Asiatic city, where he expired, on the banks of the Hermus and at the foot of Mount Sipylus. The holy rites were interrupted by a sedition of the guards : Muzalon, his brothers, and his adherents were massacred at the foot of the altar ; and the absent patriarch was associated with a new colleague, with Michael Palæologus, the most illustrious, in birth and merit, of the Greek nobles.[16]

Family and character of Michael Palæologus

Of those who are proud of their ancestors, the far greater part must be content with local or domestic renown : and few there are who dare trust the memorials of their family to the public annals of their country. As early as the middle of the eleventh century, the noble race of the Palæologi [17] stands high and conspicuous in the Byzantine history : it was the valiant George Palæologus who placed the father of the Comneni on the throne ; and his kinsmen or descendants continue, in each generation, to lead the armies and councils of the state. The purple was not dishonoured by their alliance ; and, had the law of succession, and female succession, been strictly observed, the wife of Theodore Lascaris must have yielded to her elder sister, the mother of Michael Palæologus, who afterwards raised his family to the throne. In his person, the splendour of birth was dignified by the merit of the soldier and statesman : in his early youth he was promoted to the office of *Constable* or commander of the French mercenaries ; the private expense of a day never exceeded three pieces of gold ; but his ambition was rapacious and profuse ; and his gifts were doubled by the graces of his conversation and manners. The love of the soldiers and people excited the jealousy of the court ; and Michael thrice escaped

[κοντό σταυλος]

[14] [So Pachymeres, Gregoras, and Phrantzes ; but Acropolita says the *third*, p. 165, ed. Bonn.]

[15] The old geographers, with Cellarius and d'Anville, and our travellers, particularly Pocock and Chandler, will teach us to distinguish the two Magnesias of Asia Minor, of the Mæander and of Sipylus. The latter, our present object, is still flourishing for a Turkish city, and lies eight hours, or leagues, to the north-east of Smyrna (Tournefort, Voyage du Levant, tom. iii. lettre xxiii. p. 365-370. Chandler's Travels into Asia Minor, p. 267).

[16] See Acropolita (c. 75, 76, &c.), who lived too near the times ; Pachymer (l. i. c. 13-25) ; Gregoras (l. iii. c. 3-5).

[17] The pedigree of Palæologus is explained by Ducange (Famil. Byzant. p. 230, &c.) ; the events of his private life are related by Pachymer (l. i. c. 7-12), and Gregoras (l. ii. 8, l. iii. c. 2, 4, l. iv. 1), with visible favour to the father of the reigning dynasty.

from the dangers in which he was involved by his own imprudence or that of his friends. I. Under the reign of Justice and Vataces, a dispute arose [18] between two officers, one of whom accused the other of maintaining the hereditary right of the Palæologi. The cause was decided, according to the new jurisprudence of the Latins, by single combat : the defendant was overthrown ; but he persisted in declaring that himself alone was guilty ; and that he had uttered these rash or treasonable speeches without the approbation or knowledge of his patron. Yet a cloud of suspicion hung over the innocence of the constable ; he was still pursued by the whispers of malevolence ; and a subtile courtier, the archbishop of Philadelphia, urged him to accept the judgment of God in the fiery proof of the ordeal.[19] Three days before the trial, the patient's arm was inclosed in a bag and secured by the royal signet ; and it was incumbent on him to bear a red-hot ball of iron three times from the altar to the rails of the sanctuary, without artifice and without injury. Palæologus eluded the dangerous experiment with sense and pleasantry. " I am a soldier," said he, " and will boldly enter the lists with my accusers ; but a layman, a sinner like myself, is not endowed with the gift of miracles. Your piety, most holy prelate, may deserve the interposition of Heaven, and from your hands I will receive the fiery globe, the pledge of my innocence." The archbishop started ; the emperor smiled ; and the absolution or pardon of Michael was approved by new rewards and new services. II. In the succeeding reign, as he held the government of Nice, he was secretly informed that the mind of the absent prince was poisoned with jealousy ; and that death or blindness would be his final reward. Instead of awaiting the return and sentence of [A.D. 1257] Theodore, the constable, with some followers, escaped from the city and the empire ; and, though he was plundered by the Turkmans of the desert, he found an hospitable refuge in the court of the sultan. In the ambiguous state of an exile, Michael reconciled the duties of gratitude and loyalty ; drawing his sword against the Tartars ; admonishing the garrisons of the

[18] Acropolita (c. 50) relates the circumstances of this curious adventure, which seems to have escaped the more recent writers.

[19] Pachymer (l. i. c. 12), who speaks with proper contempt of this barbarous trial, affirms that he had seen in his youth many persons who had sustained, without injury, the fiery ordeal. As a Greek, he is credulous ; but the ingenuity of the Greeks might furnish some remedies of art or fraud against their own superstition or that of their tyrant.

Roman limit ; and promoting, by his influence, the restoration of peace, in which his pardon and recall were honourably included. III. While he guarded the West against the despot of Epirus, Michael was again suspected and condemned in the palace ; and such was his loyalty or weakness that he submitted to be led in chains above six hundred miles from Durazzo to Nice. The civility of the messenger alleviated his disgrace ; the emperor's sickness dispelled his danger ; and the last breath of Theodore, which recommended his infant son, at once acknowledged the innocence and the power of Palæologus.

His elevation to the throne

But his innocence had been too unworthily treated, and his power was too strongly felt, to curb an aspiring subject in the fair field that was offered to his ambition.[20]   In the council after the death of Theodore, he was the first to pronounce, and the first to violate, the oath of allegiance to Muzalon ; and so dexterous was his conduct that he reaped the benefit, without incurring the guilt, or at least the reproach, of the subsequent massacre. In the choice of a regent, he balanced the interests and passions of the candidates ; turned their envy and hatred from himse.f against each other, and forced every competitor to own that, after his own claims, those of Palæologus were best entitled to the preference.   Under the title of Great Duke, he accepted or assumed, during a long minority, the active powers of government ; the patriarch was a venerable name ; and the factious nobles were seduced, or oppressed, by the ascendant of his genius. The fruits of the economy of Vataces were deposited in a strong castle on the banks of the Hermus,[21] in the custody of the faithful Varangians ; the constable retained his command or influence over the foreign troops ; he employed the guards to possess the treasure, and the treasure to corrupt the guards ; and, whatsoever might be the abuse of the public money, his character was above the suspicion of private avarice.   By himself, or by his emissaries, he strove to persuade every rank of subjects that their own prosperity would rise in just proportion to the establishment of his authority.   The weight of taxes was suspended, the perpetual theme of popular complaint ; and he prohibited the trials by the ordeal and judicial combat.   These barbaric institutions were

---

[20] Without comparing Pachymer to Thucydides or Tacitus, I will praise his narrative (l. i. c. 13-32, l. iii. c. 1-9), which pursues the ascent of Palæologus with eloquence, perspicuity, and tolerable freedom.   Acropolita is more cautious, and Gregoras more concise.

[21] [In Astytzion on the Scamander.   The treasures here were deposited by Theodore II.]

already abolished or undermined in France [22] and England ; [23] and the appeal to the sword offended the sense of a civilised,[24] and the temper of an unwarlike, people. For the future maintenance of their wives and children the veterans were grateful ; the priest and the philosopher applauded his ardent zeal for the advancement of religion and learning ; and his vague promise of rewarding merit was applied by every candidate to his own hopes. Conscious of the influence of the clergy, Michael successfully laboured to secure the suffrage of that powerful order. Their expensive journey from Nice to Magnesia afforded a decent and ample pretence ; the leading prelates were tempted by the liberality of his nocturnal visits ; and the incorruptible patriarch was flattered by the homage of his new colleague, who led his mule by the bridle into the town, and removed to a respectful distance the importunity of the crowd. Without renouncing his title by royal descent, Palæologus encouraged a free discussion into the advantages of elective monarchy ; and his adherents asked, with the insolence of triumph, What patient would trust his health, or what merchant would abandon his vessel, to the *hereditary* skill of a physician or a pilot ? The youth of the emperor and the impending dangers of a minority required the support of a mature and experienced guardian ; of an associate raised above the envy of his equals, and invested with the name and prerogatives of royalty. For the interest of the prince and people, without any views for himself or his family, the Great Duke consented to guard and instruct the son of Theodore ; but he sighed for the happy moment when he might restore to his firmer hands the administration of his patrimony, and enjoy the blessings of a private station. He was first invested with the title and prerogatives of *despot*, which bestowed the purple orna-

---

[22] The judicial combat was abolished by St. Louis in his own territories ; and his example and authority were at length prevalent in France (Esprit des Loix, l. xxviii. c. 29).

[23] In civil cases, Henry II. gave an option to the defendant ; Glanville prefers the proof by evidence, and that by judicial combat is reprobated in the Fleta. Yet the trial by battle has never been abrogated in the English law, and it was ordered by the judges as late as the beginning of the last century.

[24] Yet an ingenious friend has urged to me, in mitigation of this practice, 1. *That*, in nations emerging from barbarism, it moderates the licence of private war and arbitrary revenge. 2. *That* it is less absurd than the trials by the ordeal, or boiling water, or the cross, which it has contributed to abolish. 3. *That* it served at least as a test of personal courage : a quality so seldom united with a base disposition that the danger of the trial might be some check to a malicious prosecutor, and an useful barrier against injustice supported by power. The gallant and unfortunate earl of Surrey might probably have escaped his unmerited fate, had not his demand of the combat against his accuser been over-ruled.

ments, and the second place in the Roman monarchy. It was afterwards agreed that John and Michael should be proclaimed as joint emperors, and raised on the buckler, but that the pre-eminence should be reserved for the birth-right of the former. A mutual league of amity was pledged between the royal part-ners ; and, in case of a rupture, the subjects were bound, by their oath of allegiance, to declare themselves against the aggressor : an ambiguous name, the seed of discord and civil war. Palæolo-gus was content; but on the day of his coronation, and in the cathedral of Nice, his zealous adherents most vehemently urged the just priority of his age and merit. The unseasonable dispute was eluded by postponing to a more convenient opportunity the coronation of John Lascaris; and he walked with a slight diadem in the train of his guardian, who alone received the Imperial crown from the hands of the patriarch. It was not without ex-treme reluctance that Arsenius abandoned the cause of his pupil; but the Varangians brandished their battle-axes ; a sign of assent was extorted from the trembling youth ; and some voices were heard, that the life of a child should no longer impede the settle-ment of the nation. A full harvest of honours and employments was distributed among his friends by the grateful Palæologus. In his own family he created a despot and two sebastocrators ; Alexius Strategopulus was decorated with the title of Cæsar ; and that veteran commander soon repaid the obligation, by re-storing Constantinople to the Greek emperor.

[Jan., A.D. 1260]

Michael Palæologus Emperor. A.D. 1260, Jan. 1

Recovery of Constanti-nople. A.D. 1261, July 25

It was in the second year of his reign, while he resided in the palace and gardens of Nymphæum,[25] near Smyrna, that the first messenger arrived at the dead of night ; and the stupendous intelligence was imparted to Michael, after he had been gently waked by the tender precaution of his sister Eulogia. The man was unknown or obscure ; he produced no letters from the vic-torious Cæsar ; nor could it easily be credited, after the defeat of Vataces and the recent failure of Palæologus himself, that the capital had been surprised by a detachment of eight hundred

[25] The site of Nymphæum is not clearly defined in ancient or modern geography. [Turkish Nif ; it lay on the road from Smyrna to Sardis. Cp. Ramsay, Asia Minor, p. 108.] But from the last hours of Vataces (Acropolita, c. 52) it is evident the palace and gardens of his favourite residence were in the neighbourhood of Smyrna. Nymphæum might be loosely placed in Lydia (Gregoras, l. vi. 6). [Pachymeres says that Michael was at Nymphæum when he received the glad tidings ; but Gregoras says Nicaea, and Acropolites says Meteorion. As Acro-polites was with Michael at the time, we must follow him (so Méliarakès, p. 509). Meteorion " must have been in the Hermos valley, and may possibly be the purely Byzantine fortress Gurduk Kalesi, a few miles north of Thyateira, near the site of Attaleia " (Ramsay, op. cit. p. 131).]

soldiers.  As an hostage, the doubtful author was confined, with
the assurance of death or an ample recompense ; and the court
was left some hours in the anxiety of hope and fear, till the messengers of Alexius arrived with the authentic intelligence, and
displayed the trophies of the conquest, the sword and sceptre,[26]
the buskins and bonnet,[27] of the usurper Baldwin, which he had
dropt in his precipitate flight.  A general assembly of the bishops,
senators, and nobles was immediately convened, and never perhaps was an event received with more heartfelt and universal
joy.  In a studied oration, the new sovereign of Constantinople
congratulated his own and the public fortune.  " There was a
time," said he, " a far distant time, when the Roman empire extended to the Adriatic, the Tigris, and the confines of Ethiopia.
After the loss of the provinces, our capital itself, in these last
and calamitous days, has been wrested from our hands by the
barbarians of the West.  From the lowest ebb, the tide of prosperity has again returned in our favour ; but our prosperity was
that of fugitives and exiles ; and, when we were asked, Which
was the country of the Romans ? we indicated with a blush the
climate of the globe and the quarter of the heavens.  The Divine
Providence has now restored to our arms the city of Constantine,
the sacred seat of religion and empire ; and it will depend on
our valour and conduct to render this important acquisition the
pledge and omen of future victories."  So eager was the im-   Return of the
patience of the prince and people that Michael made his trium-   Greek Em-
phal entry into Constantinople only twenty days after the ex-   peror. A.D.
pulsion of the Latins.  The golden gate was thrown open at his   1261, Aug. 14
approach ; the devout conqueror dismounted from his horse ;
and a miraculous image of Mary, the Conductress, was borne
before him, that the divine Virgin in person might appear to
conduct him to the temple of her Son, the cathedral of St.
Sophia.  But, after the first transport of devotion and pride, he
sighed at the dreary prospect of solitude and ruin.  The palace
was defiled with smoke and dirt, and the gross intemperance of
the Franks ; whole streets had been consumed by fire, or were
decayed by the injuries of time ; the sacred and profane edifices

[26] This sceptre, the emblem of justice and power, was a long staff, such as was
used by the heroes in Homer.  By the latter Greeks it was named *Dicanice*, and
the Imperial sceptre was distinguished as usual by the red or purple colour.

[27] Acropolita affirms (c. 87) that this bonnet was after the French fashion ; but
from the ruby at the point or summit Ducange (Hist. de C. P. l. v. c. 28, 29)
believes that it was the high-crowned hat of the Greeks.  Could Acropolita mistake
the dress of his own court?

were stripped of their ornaments; and, as if they were conscious of their approaching exile, the industry of the Latins had been confined to the work of pillage and destruction. Trade had expired under the pressure of anarchy and distress; and the number of inhabitants had decreased with the opulence of the city. It was the first care of the Greek monarch to reinstate the nobles in the palaces of their fathers; and the houses or the ground which they occupied were restored to the families that could exhibit a legal right of inheritance. But the far greater part was extinct or lost; the vacant property had devolved to the lord; he repeopled Constantinople by a liberal invitation to the provinces; and the brave *volunteers* were seated in the capital which had been recovered by their arms. The French barons and the principal families had retired with their emperor; but the patient and humble crowd of Latins was attached to the country, and indifferent to the change of masters. Instead of banishing the factories of the Pisans, Venetians, and Genoese, the prudent conqueror accepted their oaths of allegiance, encouraged their industry, confirmed their privileges, and allowed them to live under the jurisdiction of their proper magistrates. Of these nations, the Pisans and Venetians preserved their respective quarters in the city; but the services and powers of the Genoese deserved at the same time the gratitude[28] and the jealousy of the Greeks. Their independent colony was first planted at the sea-port town of Heraclea in Thrace. They were speedily recalled, and settled in the exclusive possession of the suburb of Galata, an advantageous post, in which they revived the commerce, and insulted the majesty, of the Byzantine empire.[29]

Palæologus blinds and banishes the young Emperor, A.D. 1261, Dec. 25

The recovery of Constantinople was celebrated as the æra of a new empire: the conqueror, alone, and by the right of the sword, renewed his coronation in the church of St. Sophia; and the name and honours of John Lascaris, his pupil and lawful sovereign, were insensibly abolished. But his claims still lived in the minds of the people; and the royal youth must speedily attain the years of manhood and ambition. By fear or conscience, Palæologus was restrained from dipping his hands in innocent and royal blood; but the anxiety of an usurper and a parent

[28] [The Genoese had sent ships, in accordance with the treaty of Nymphæum; but these had not arrived in time to be of actual service.]

[29] See Pachymer (l. 2, c. 28-33), Acropolita (c. 88), Nicephorus Gregoras (l. iv. 7), and for the treatment of the subject Latins, Ducange (l. v. c. 30, 31).

urged him to secure his throne by one of those imperfect crimes so familiar to the modern Greeks. The loss of sight incapacitated the young prince for the active business of the world : instead of the brutal violence of tearing out his eyes, the visual nerve was destroyed by the intense glare of a red-hot bason,[30] and John Lascaris was removed to a distant castle, where he spent many years in privacy and oblivion. Such cool and deliberate guilt may seem incompatible with remorse ; but, if Michael could trust the mercy of Heaven, he was not inaccessible to the reproaches and vengeance of mankind, which he had provoked by cruelty and treason. His cruelty imposed on a servile court the duties of applause or silence ; but the clergy had a right to speak in the name of their invisible master; and their holy legions were led by a prelate, whose character was above the temptations of hope or fear. After a short abdication of his dignity, Arsenius [31] had consented to ascend the ecclesiastical throne of Constantinople, and to preside in the restoration of the church. His pious simplicity was long deceived by the arts of Palæologus ; and his patience and submission might soothe the usurper, and protect the safety of the young prince. On the news of his inhuman treatment, the patriarch unsheathed the spiritual sword ; and superstition, on this occasion, was enlisted in the cause of humanity and justice. In a synod of bishops, who were stimulated by the example of his zeal, the patriarch pronounced a sentence of excommunication ; though his prudence still repeated the name of Michael in the public prayers. The eastern prelates had not adopted the dangerous maxims of ancient Rome ; nor did they presume to enforce their censures, by deposing princes, or absolving nations from their oaths of allegiance. But the Christian who had been separated from God and the church became an object of horror ; and, in a turbulent and fanatic capital that horror might arm the hand of an assassin or inflame a sedition of the people.

*is excommunicated by the Patriarch Arsenius. A.D. 1262-1268*

---

[30] This milder invention for extinguishing the sight was tried by the philosopher Democritus on himself, when he sought to withdraw his mind from the visible world : a foolish story ! The word *abacinare*, in Latin and Italian, has furnished Ducange (Gloss. Latin.) with an opportunity to review the various modes of blinding ; the more violent were, scooping, burning with an iron or hot vinegar, and binding the head with a strong cord till the eyes burst from their sockets. Ingenious tyrants !

[31] See the first retreat and restoration of Arsenius, in Pachymer (l. ii. c. 15, l. iii. c. 1, 2), and Nicephorus Gregoras (l. iii. c. 1, l. iv. c. 1). Posterity justly accused the ἀφέλεια and ῥᾳθυμία of Arsenius, the virtues of an hermit, the vices of a minister (l. xii. c. 2).

Palæologus felt his danger, confessed his guilt, and deprecated his judge : the act was irretrievable ; the prize was obtained ; and the most rigorous penance, which he solicited, would have raised the sinner to the reputation of a saint. The unrelenting patriarch refused to announce any means of atonement or any hopes of mercy ; and condescended only to pronounce that, for so great a crime, great indeed must be the satisfaction. " Do you require," said Michael, " that I should abdicate the empire ? " And at these words he offered, or seemed to offer, the sword of state. Arsenius eagerly grasped this pledge of sovereignty ; but, when he perceived that the emperor was unwilling to purchase absolution at so dear a rate, he indignantly escaped to his cell, and left the royal sinner kneeling and weeping before the door.[32]

Schism of the Arsenites. A.D. 1266-1312    The danger and scandal of this excommunication subsisted above three years, till the popular clamour was assuaged by time and repentance ; till the brethren of Arsenius condemned his inflexible spirit, so repugnant to the unbounded forgiveness of the gospel. The emperor had artfully insinuated that, if he were still rejected at home, he might seek, in the Roman pontiff, a more indulgent judge ; but it was far more easy and effectual to find or to place that judge at the head of the Byzantine church. Arsenius was involved in a vague rumour of conspiracy and disaffection ; some irregular steps in his ordination and government were liable to censure ; a synod deposed him from the episcopal office ; and he was transported under a guard of soldiers to a small island of the Propontis. Before his exile, he sullenly requested that a strict account might be taken of the treasures of the church ; boasted that his whole riches, three pieces of gold, had been earned by transcribing the Psalms ; continued to assert the freedom of his mind ; and denied, with his last breath, the pardon which was implored by the royal sinner.[33] After some delay, Gregory, bishop of Hadrianople, was translated to the Byzantine throne ; but his authority was found insufficient to support the absolution of the emperor ; and Joseph, a reverend monk, was substituted to that important function. This edifying scene was represented

[32] The crime and excommunication of Michael are fairly told by Pachymer (l. iii. c. 10, 14, 19, &c.), and Gregoras (l. iv. c. 4). His confession and penance restored their freedom.

[33] Pachymer relates the exile of Arsenius (l. v. c. 1-16); he was one of the commissaries who visited him in the desert island. The last testament of the unforgiving patriarch is still extant (Dupin, Bibliothèque Ecclésiastique. tom. x. p. 95).

in the presence of the senate and people; at the end of six years, the humble penitent was restored to the communion of the faithful; and humanity will rejoice that a milder treatment of the captive Lascaris was stipulated as a proof of his remorse. But the spirit of Arsenius still survived in a powerful faction of the monks and clergy, who persevered above forty-eight years in an obstinate schism. Their scruples were treated with tenderness and respect by Michael and his son; and the reconciliation of the Arsenites was the serious labour of the church and state. In the confidence of fanaticism, they had proposed to try their cause by a miracle; and, when the two papers that contained their own and the adverse cause were cast into a fiery brazier, they expected that the Catholic verity would be respected by the flames. Alas! the two papers were indiscriminately consumed, and this unforeseen accident produced the union of a day, and renewed the quarrel of an age.[34] The final treaty displayed the victory of the Arsenites; the clergy abstained during forty days from all ecclesiastical functions; a slight penance was imposed on the laity; the body of Arsenius was deposited in the sanctuary; and in the name of the departed saint the prince and people were released from the sins of their fathers.[35]

The establishment of his family was the motive, or at least the pretence, of the crime of Palæologus; and he was impatient to confirm the succession, by sharing with his eldest son the honours of the purple. Andronicus, afterwards surnamed the Elder, was proclaimed and crowned emperor of the Romans, in the fifteenth year of his age; and, from the first æra of a prolix and inglorious reign, he held that august title nine years as the colleague, and fifty as the successor, of his father. Michael himself, had he died in a private station, would have been thought more worthy of the empire; and the assaults of his temporal and spiritual enemies left him few moments to labour for his own fame or the happiness of his subjects. He wrested from the Franks several of the noblest islands of the

*[margin note:]* Reign of Michael Palæologus. A.D. 1259, Dec. 1—A.D. 1282, Dec. 11  Reign of Andronicus the Elder. A.D. 1273, Nov. 8—A.D. 1332, Feb. 13

---

[34] Pachymer (l. vii. c. 22) relates this miraculous trial like a philosopher, and treats with similar contempt a plot of the Arsenites, to hide a revelation in the coffin of some old saint (l. vii. c. 13). He compensates this incredulity by an image that weeps, another that bleeds (l. vii. c. 30), and the miraculous cures of a deaf and a mute patient (l. xi. c. 32).

[35] The story of the Arsenites is spread through the thirteen books of Pachymer. Their union and triumph are reserved for Nicephorus Gregoras (l. vii. c. 9), who neither loves nor esteems these sectaries.

Archipelago, Lesbos, Chios, and Rhodes;[36] his brother Constantine was sent to command in Malvasia and Sparta; and the eastern side of the Morea, from Argos and Napoli to Cape Tænarus, was repossessed by the Greeks.[37] This effusion of Christian blood was loudly condemned by the patriarch; and the insolent priest presumed to interpose his fears and scruples between the arms of princes. But, in the prosecution of these Western conquests, the countries beyond the Hellespont were left naked to the Turks; and their depredations verified the prophecy of a dying senator, that the recovery of Constantinople would be the ruin of Asia. The victories of Michael were achieved by his lieutenants; his sword rusted in the palace; and, in the transactions of the emperor with the popes and the king of Naples, his political arts were stained with cruelty and fraud.[38]

His union with the Latin church. A.D. 1274-1277    I. The Vatican was the most natural refuge of a Latin emperor, who had been driven from his throne; and pope Urban the Fourth appeared to pity the misfortunes, and vindicate the cause, of the fugitive Baldwin. A crusade, with plenary indulgence, was preached by his command against the schismatic Greeks; he excommunicated their allies and adherents; solicited Louis the Ninth in favour of his kinsman; and demanded a tenth of the ecclesiastic revenues of France and England for the service of the holy war.[39] The subtile Greek, who watched the rising tempest of the West, attempted to suspend or soothe the hostility of the pope, by suppliant embassies and respectful letters; but he insinuated that the establishment of peace must prepare the reconciliation and obedience of the Eastern church. The Roman court could not be deceived by so gross an artifice; and Michael was admonished that the repentance of the son should precede the forgiveness of the father; and that *faith* (an ambiguous word) was the only basis of friendship and alliance.

[36] [These islands were subject to Michael, but not conquered by him; see Appendix 18.]

[37] [Michael released William Villehardouin, prince of Achaia, who had been taken prisoner at the battle of Pelagonia (see above, p. 439). For his liberty William undertook to become a vassal of the Empire, and to hand over to Michael the fortresses of Misithra, Maina and Monemvasia. See (besides Pachymeres, Gibbon's source) the Chronicle of Morea (in Buchon, Chroniques Etrangères. Cp. App. 1).]

[38] Of the xiii books of Pachymer, the first six (as the ivth and vth of Nicephorus Gregoras) contain the reign of Michael, at the time of whose death he was forty years of age. Instead of breaking, like his editor the Père Poussin, his history into two parts, I follow Ducange and Cousin, who number the xiii books in one series.

[39] Ducange, Hist. de C. P. l. v. c. 33, &c. from the Epistles of Urban IV.

After a long and affected delay, the approach of danger and the importunity of Gregory the Tenth compelled him to enter on a more serious negotiation ; he alleged the example of the great Vataces ; and the Greek clergy, who understood the intentions of their prince, were not alarmed by the first steps of reconciliation and respect. But, when he pressed the conclusion of the treaty, they strenuously declared that the Latins, though not in name, were heretics in fact, and that they despised those strangers as the vilest and most despicable portion of the human race.[40]   It was the task of the emperor to persuade, to corrupt, to intimidate, the most popular ecclesiastics, to gain the vote of each individual, and alternately to urge the arguments of Christian charity and the public welfare. The texts of the fathers and the arms of the Franks were balanced in the theological and political scale ; and, without approving the addition to the Nicene creed, the most moderate were taught to confess that the two hostile propositions of proceeding from the Father BY the Son, and of proceeding from the Father AND the Son, might be reduced to a safe and catholic sense.[41]   The supremacy of the pope was a doctrine more easy to conceive, but more painful to acknowledge ; yet Michael represented to his monks and prelates that they might submit to name the Roman bishop as the first of the patriarchs, and that their distance and discretion would guard the liberties of the Eastern church from the mischievous consequences of the right of appeal.   He protested that he would sacrifice his life and empire rather than yield the smallest point of orthodox faith or national independence ; and this declaration was sealed and ratified by a golden bull.   The patriarch Joseph withdrew to a monastery, to resign or resume his throne, according to the event of the treaty ; the letters of union and obedience were subscribed by the emperor, his son Andronicus, and thirty-five archbishops and metropolitans, with their respective synods ; and the episcopal list was multiplied by many dioceses which were annihilated under the yoke of the infidels. An embassy was composed of some trusty ministers and pre-

---

[40] From their mercantile intercourse with the Venetians and Genoese, they branded the Latins as κάπηλοι and βάναυσοι (Pachymer, l. v. c. 10).   " Some are heretics in name ; others, like the Latins, in fact," said the learned Veccus (l. v. c. 12), who soon afterwards became a convert (c. 15, 16), and a patriarch (c. 24).

[41] In this class we may place Pachymer himself, whose copious and candid narrative occupies the vth and vith books of his history.   Yet the Greek is silent on the council of Lyons, and seems to believe that the popes always resided in Rome and Italy.

[A.D. 1274]

lates; they embarked for Italy, with rich ornaments and rare perfumes for the altar of St. Peter; and their secret orders authorised and recommended a boundless compliance. They were received in the general council of Lyons, by pope Gregory the Tenth, at the head of five hundred bishops.[42] He embraced with tears his long-lost and repentant children; accepted the oath of the ambassadors, who abjured the schism in the name of the two emperors; adorned the prelates with the ring and mitre; chaunted in Greek and Latin the Nicene creed, with the addition of *filioque;* and rejoiced in the union of the East and West, which had been reserved for his reign. To consummate this pious work, the Byzantine deputies were speedily followed by the pope's nuncios; and their instruction discloses the policy of the Vatican, which could not be satisfied with the vain title of supremacy. After viewing the temper of the prince and people, they were enjoined to absolve the schismatic clergy who should subscribe and swear their abjuration and obedience; to establish in all the churches the use of the perfect creed; to prepare the entrance of a cardinal legate, with the full powers and dignity of his office; and to instruct the emperor in the advantages which he might derive from the temporal protection of the Roman pontiff.[43]

His persecution of the Greeks. A.D. 1277-1282    But they found a country without a friend, a nation in which the names of Rome and Union were pronounced with abhorrence. The patriarch Joseph was indeed removed; his place was filled by Veccus,[44] an ecclesiastic of learning and moderation; and the emperor was still urged by the same motives, to persevere in the same professions. But, in his private language, Palæologus affected to deplore the pride, and to blame the innovations, of the Latins; and, while he debased his character by this double hypocrisy, he justified and punished the opposition of his subjects. By the joint suffrage of the new and the ancient Rome, a sentence

---

[42] See the Acts of the Council of Lyons in the year 1274. Fleury, Hist. Ecclésiastique, tom. xviii. p. 181-199. Dupin, Bibliot. Eccles. tom. x. p. 135. [George Acropolites was the chief ambassador of Michael.]

[43] This curious instruction, which has been drawn with more or less honesty by Wading and Leo Allatius from the archives of the Vatican, is given in an abstract or version by Fleury (tom. xviii. p. 252-258).

[44] [Johannes Veccus (Patriarch 1275) was the chief theologian who supported the Union. His work, On the Union and Peace of the Churches of Old and New Rome, and others on the same subject, were published in the Græcia Orthodoxa of Leo Allatius (vol. i., 1652) and will be found in Migne, P. G. vol. 141. His most formidable controversial opponent, Gregory of Cyprus (for whose works see Migne, vol. 142), became Patriarch in 1283.]

of excommunication was pronounced against the obstinate schismatics; the censures of the church were executed by the sword
of Michael; on the failure of persuasion, he tried the arguments
of prison and exile, of whipping and mutilation: those touch-
stones, says an historian, of cowards and the brave. Two Greeks
still reigned in Ætolia, Epirus, and Thessaly, with the appellation of despots; they had yielded to the sovereign of Constantinople; but they rejected the chains of the Roman pontiff, and
supported their refusal by successful arms. Under their protection, the fugitive monks and bishops assembled in hostile
synods, and retorted the name of heretic with the galling addition of apostate: the prince of Trebizond was tempted to
assume the forfeit title of emperor; and even the Latins of
Negropont, Thebes, Athens, and the Morea forgot the merits
of the convert, to join, with open or clandestine aid, the enemies
of Palæologus. His favourite generals, of his own blood and
family, successively deserted or betrayed the sacrilegious trust.
His sister Eulogia, a niece, and two female cousins, conspired
against him; another niece, Mary queen of Bulgaria, negotiated
his ruin with the sultan of Egypt; and in the public eye their
treason was consecrated as the most sublime virtue.[45] To the
pope's nuncios, who urged the consummation of the work,
Palæologus exposed a naked recital of all that he had done and
suffered for their sake. They were assured that the guilty
sectaries, of both sexes and every rank, had been deprived
of their honours, their fortunes, and their liberty; a spreading list of confiscation and punishment, which involved many
persons, the dearest to the emperor, or the best deserving of
his favour. They were conducted to the prison, to behold
four princes of the royal blood chained in the four corners, and
shaking their fetters in an agony of grief and rage. Two of
these captives were afterwards released, the one by submission,
the other by death; but the obstinacy of their two companions
was chastised by the loss of their eyes; and the Greeks, the
least adverse to the union, deplore that cruel and inauspicious
tragedy.[46] Persecutors must expect the hatred of those whom

[45] This frank and authentic confession of Michael's distress is exhibited in barbarous Latin by Ogerius, who signs himself Protonotarius Interpretum, and transcribed by Wading from the Mss. of the Vatican (A.D. 1278, No. 3). His Annals
of the Franciscan order, the Fratres Minores, in xvii volumes in folio (Rome, 1741),
I have now accidentally seen among the waste paper of a bookseller.

[46] See the vith book of Pachymer, particularly the chapters i, 11, 16, 18, 24-27.
He is the more credible, as he speaks of this persecution with less anger than
sorrow.

they oppress; but they commonly find some consolation in the testimony of their conscience, the applause of their party, and, perhaps, the success of their undertaking. But the hypocrisy of Michael, which was prompted only by political motives, must have forced him to hate himself, to despise his followers, and to esteem and envy the rebel champions, by whom he was detested and despised.[47] While his violence was abhorred at Constantinople, at Rome his slowness was arraigned and his sincerity suspected; till at length pope Martin the Fourth excluded the Greek emperor from the pale of a church into which he was striving to reduce a schismatic people. No sooner had the tyrant expired than the union was dissolved and abjured by unanimous consent; the churches were purified; the penitents were reconciled; and his son Andronicus, after weeping the sins and errors of his youth, most piously denied his father the burial of a prince and a Christian.[48]

[A.D. 1280]

The union dissolved, A.D. 1283

II. In the distress of the Latins, the walls and towers of Constantinople had fallen to decay; they were restored and fortified by the policy of Michael, who deposited a plenteous store of corn and salt provisions, to sustain the siege which he might hourly expect from the resentment of the Western powers. Of these, the sovereign of the Two Sicilies was the most formidable neighbour; but, as long as they were possessed by Mainfroy, the bastard of Frederic the Second, his monarchy was the bulwark rather than the annoyance of the Eastern empire. The usurper, though a brave and active prince, was sufficiently employed in the defence of his throne; his proscription by successive popes had separated Mainfroy from the common cause of the Latins; and the forces that might have besieged Constantinople were detained in a crusade against the domestic enemy of Rome. The prize of her avenger, the crown of the Two Sicilies, was won and worn by the brother of St. Louis, by Charles, count of Anjou and Provence, who led the

Charles of Anjou subdues Naples and Sicily, A.D. 1266, Feb. 26

[Manfred]

47 [Finlay shows no mercy to Michael.] " He was a type of the empire he re-established and transmitted to his descendants. He was selfish, hypocritical, able and accomplished, an inborn liar, vain, meddling, ambitious, cruel and rapacious. He has gained renown in history as the restorer of the Eastern Empire; he ought to be execrated as the corrupter of the Greek race, for his reign affords a signal example of the extent to which a nation may be degraded by the misconduct of its sovereign when he is entrusted with despotic power" (vol. 3, p. 372).]

48 Pachymer, l. vii. c. 1-11, 17. The speech of Andronicus the Elder (lib. xii. c. 2) is a curious record, which proves that, if the Greeks were the slaves of the emperor, the emperor was not less the slave of superstition and the clergy.

chivalry of France on this holy expedition.[49] The disaffection of his Christian subjects compelled Mainfroy to enlist a colony of Saracens, whom his father had planted in Apulia; and this odious succour will explain the défiance of the Catholic hero, who rejected all terms of accommodation : " Bear this message," said Charles, " to the sultan of Nocera, that God and the sword are umpire between us ; and that he shall either send me to paradise, or I will send him to the pit of hell ". The armies met, and, though I am ignorant of Mainfroy's doom in the other world, in this he lost his friends, his kingdom, and his life, in the bloody battle of Benevento. Naples and Sicily were immediately peopled with a warlike race of French nobles ; and their aspiring leader embraced the future conquest of Africa, Greece, and Palestine. The most specious reasons might point his first arms against the Byzantine empire ; and Palæologus, diffident of his own strength, repeatedly appealed from the ambition of Charles to the humanity of St. Louis, who still preserved a just ascendant over the mind of his ferocious brother. For a while the attention of that brother was confined at home by the invasion of Conradin, the last heir of the imperial house of Swabia ; but the hapless boy sunk in the unequal conflict; and his execution on a public scaffold taught the rivals of Charles to tremble for their heads as well as their dominions. A second respite was obtained by the last crusade of St. Louis to the African coast ; and the double motive of interest and duty urged the king of Naples to assist, with his powers and his presence, the holy enterprise. The death of St. Louis released him from the importunity of a virtuous censor ; the king of Tunis confessed himself the tributary and vassal of the crown of Sicily ; and the boldest of the French knights were free to enlist under his banner against the Greek empire. A treaty and a marriage united his interest with the house of Courtenay; his daughter, Beatrice, was promised to Philip, son and heir of the emperor Baldwin ; a pension of six hundred ounces of gold was allowed for his maintenance ; and his generous father dis-

*Threatens the Greek empire, A.D. 1270, &c.*

49 The best accounts, the nearest the time, the most full and entertaining, of the conquest of Naples by Charles of Anjou, may be found in the Florentine Chronicles of Ricordano Malespina (*leg.* Malespini] (c. 175-193) and Giovanni Villani (l. vii. 1-10, 25-30), which are published by Muratori in the viiith and xiiith volumes of the historians of Italy. In his Annals (tom. xi. p. 56-72), he has abridged these great events, which are likewise described in the Istoria Civile of Giannone (tom. l. xix. ; tom. iii. l. xx.). [The chronicle attributed to Malespini has been proved not to be the original but to depend on Villani. See Scheffer-Boichorst, in Sybels Historische Zeitschrift, 24, p. 274 *sqq.* (1870).]

tributed among his allies the kingdoms and provinces of the East, reserving only Constantinople, and one day's journey round the city, for the Imperial domain.[50] In this perilous moment, Palaeologus was the most eager to subscribe the creed, and implore the protection, of the Roman pontiff, who assumed, with propriety and weight, the character of an angel of peace, the common father of the Christians. By his voice the sword of Charles was chained in the scabbard; and the Greek ambassadors beheld him, in the pope's antichamber, biting his ivory sceptre in a transport of fury, and deeply resenting the refusal to enfranchise and consecrate his arms. He appears to have respected the disinterested mediation of Gregory the Tenth; but Charles was insensibly disgusted by the pride and partiality of Nicholas the Third; and his attachment to his kindred, the Ursini family, alienated the most strenuous champion from the service of the church. The hostile league against the Greeks of Philip the Latin emperor, the king of the Two Sicilies, and the republic of Venice, was ripened into execution; and the election of Martin the Fourth, a French pope, gave a sanction to the cause. Of the allies, Philip supplied his name, Martin a bull of excommunication, the Venetians, a squadron of forty galleys; and the formidable powers of Charles consisted of forty counts, ten thousand men at arms, a numerous body of infantry, and a fleet of more than three hundred ships and transports. A distant day was appointed for assembling this mighty force in the harbour of Brindisi; and a previous attempt was risked with a detachment of three hundred knights, who invaded Albania and besieged the fortress of Belgrade. Their defeat might amuse with a triumph the vanity of Constantinople; but the more sagacious Michael, despairing of his arms, depended on the effects of a conspiracy; on the secret workings of a rat who gnawed the bow-string[51] of the Sicilian tyrant.

[A.D. 1280]

Palaeologus instigates the revolt of Sicily. A.D. 1280

Among the proscribed adherents of the house of Swabia John of Procida forfeited a small island of that name in the bay of Naples. His birth was noble, but his education was learned; and, in the poverty of exile, he was relieved by the practice of physic, which he had studied in the school of Salerno. Fortune had left him nothing to lose except life; and

50 Ducange, Hist. de C. P. l. v. c. 49-56, l. vi. c. 1-13. See Pachymer, l. iv. c. 29, l. v. c. 7-10, 25, l. vi. c. 30, 32, 33, and Nicephorus Gregoras, l. iv. 5, l. v. v. 1, 6

51 The reader of Herodotus will recollect how miraculously the Assyrian host of Sennacherib was disarmed and destroyed (l. ii. c. 141).

o despise life is the first qualification of a rebel. Procida was
endowed with the art of negotiation, to enforce his reasons and
disguise his motives ; and, in his various transactions with na-
ions and men, he could persuade each party that he laboured
olely for *their* interest. The new kingdoms of Charles were
afflicted by every species of fiscal and military oppression ; [52] and
he lives and fortunes of his Italian subjects were sacrificed to
the greatness of their master and the licentiousness of his fol-
owers. The hatred of Naples was repressed by his presence ;
but the looser government of his vicegerents excited the con-
empt, as well as the aversion, of the Sicilians ; the island was
oused to a sense of freedom by the eloquence of Procida ; and
he displayed to every baron his private interest in the common
ause. In the confidence of foreign aid, he successively visited
the courts of the Greek emperor and of Peter, king of Arra- [Peter III.]
on,[53] who possessed the maritime countries of Valentia and
Catalonia. To the ambitious Peter a crown was presented,
which he might justly claim by his marriage with the sister of [*leg.* daughter]
Mainfroy, and by the dying voice of Conradin, who from the
scaffold had cast a ring to his heir and avenger. Palæologus
was easily persuaded to divert his enemy from a foreign war by
rebellion at home ; and a Greek subsidy of twenty-five thou-
and ounces of gold was most profitably applied to arm a Cata-
an fleet, which sailed under an holy banner to the specious
attack of the Saracens of Africa. In the disguise of a monk or
beggar, the indefatigable missionary of revolt flew from Constantinople to Rome, and from Sicily to Saragossa ; the treaty
was sealed with the signet of pope Nicholas himself, the enemy
of Charles ; and his deed of gift transferred the fiefs of St.
Peter from the house of Anjou to that of Arragon. So widely
diffused and so freely circulated, the secret was preserved above
two years with impenetrable discretion ; and each of the conspirators imbibed the maxim of Peter, who declared that he
would cut off his left hand, if it were conscious of the intentions
of his right. The mine was prepared with deep and dangerous

---

[52] According to Sabas Malaspina (Hist. Sicula, l. iii. c. 16, in Muratori, tom.
ii. p. 832), a zealous Guelph, the subjects of Charles, who had reviled Mainfroy
as a wolf, began to regret him as a lamb ; and he justifies their discontent by the
oppressions of the French government (l. vi. c. 2, 7). See the Sicilian manifesto
of Nicholas Specialis (l. i. c. 11, in Muratori, tom. x. p. 930).

[53] See the character and counsels of Peter of Arragon, in Mariana (Hist. Hispan.
xiv. c. 6, tom. ii. p. 133). The reader forgives the Jesuit's defects, in favour
always of his style, and often of his sense.

artifice ; but it may be questioned whether the instant explosion of Palermo were the effect of accident or design.

On the vigil of Easter, a procession of the disarmed citizens visited a church without the walls ; and a noble damsel was rudely insulted by a French soldier.[54] The ravisher was instantly punished with death ; and, if the people was at first scattered by a military force, their numbers and fury prevailed :

The Sicilian<br>Vespers. A.D.<br>1282, March 30 the conspirators seized the opportunity ; the flame spread over the island ; and eight thousand French were exterminated in a promiscuous massacre, which has obtained the name of the SICILIAN VESPERS.[55] From every city the banners of freedom and the church were displayed ; the revolt was inspired by the presence or the soul of Procida ; and Peter of Arragon, who sailed from the African coast to Palermo, was saluted as the king and saviour of the isle. By the rebellion of a people on whom he had so long trampled with impunity, Charles was astonished and confounded ; and in the first agony of grief and devotion he was heard to exclaim, " O God ! if thou hast decreed to humble me, grant me at least a gentle and gradual descent from the pinnacle of greatness ". His fleet and army, which already filled the sea-ports of Italy, were hastily recalled from the service of the Grecian war ; and the situation of Messina exposed that town to the first storm of his revenge. Feeble in themselves, and yet hopeless of foreign succour, the citizens would have repented and submitted, on the assurance of full pardon and their ancient privileges. But the pride of the monarch was already rekindled ; and the most fervent intreaties of the legate could extort no more than a promise, that he would forgive the remainder, after a chosen list of eight hundred rebels had been yielded to his discretion. The despair of the Messinese renewed their courage ; Peter of Arragon approached to their relief ; [56] and his rival was driven

---

[54] After enumerating the sufferings of his country, Nicholas Specialis adds in the true spirit of Italian jealousy, Quæ omnia et graviora quidem, ut arbitror, patienti animo Siculi tolerassent, nisi (quod primum cunctis dominantibus cavendum est) alienas fæminas invasissent (l. i. c. 2, p. 924).

[55] The French were long taught to remember this bloody lesson : " If I am provoked," said Henry the Fourth, " I will breakfast at Milan, and dine at Naples ". " Your Majesty," replied the Spanish ambassador, " may perhaps arrive in Sicily for vespers."

[56] This revolt, with the subsequent victory, are related by two national writers, Bartholemy a Neocastro (in Muratori, tom. xiii. [and in Del Re, Cronisti e scrittori, vol. 2]) and Nicholas Specialis (in Muratori, tom. x.), the one a contemporary, the other of the next century. The patriot Specialis disclaims the name

back by the failure of provision, and the terrors of the equinox, to the Calabrian shore. At the same moment, the Catalan admiral, the famous Roger de Loria, swept the channel with an invincible squadron : the French fleet, more numerous in transports than in galleys, was either burnt or destroyed ; and the same blow assured the independence of Sicily and the safety of the Greek empire. A few days before his death, the emperor Michael rejoiced in the fall of an enemy whom he hated and esteemed ; and perhaps he might be content with the popular judgment that, had they not been matched with each other, Constantinople and Italy must speedily have obeyed the same master.[57] From this disastrous moment, the life of Charles was a series of misfortunes ; his capital was insulted, his son was made prisoner, and he sunk into the grave without recovering the isle of Sicily, which, after a war of twenty years, was finally severed from the throne of Naples, and transferred, as an independent kingdom, to a younger branch of the house of Arragon.[58]

Defeat of Charles. Oct. 2

I shall not, I trust, be accused of superstition ; but I must remark that, even in this world, the natural order of events will sometimes afford the strong appearances of moral retribution. The first Palæologus had saved his empire by involving the kingdoms of the West in rebellion and blood ; and from these seeds of discord uprose a generation of iron men, who assaulted and endangered the empire of his son. In modern times our debts and taxes are the secret poison, which still corrodes the bosom of peace ; but in the weak and disorderly government of the middle ages it was agitated by the present evil of the disbanded armies. Too idle to work, too proud to beg, the mercenaries were accustomed to a life of rapine : they could rob with more dignity and effect under a banner and a chief ; and the sovereign, to whom their service was useless

The service and war of the Catalans in the Greek empire. A.D. 1303-1307

of rebellion and all previous correspondence with Peter of Arragon (nullo communicato consilio), who *happened* to be with a fleet and army on the African coast (l. i. c. 4, 9). [For the Sicilian vespers and the sequel, see also the contemporary chronicle of Bernard d'Esclot (an obscure figure), which is published by Buchon in his Chroniques Etrangères (1860), c. 81 *sqq.* ; and also an anonymous contemporary relation of the conspiracy of John Prochyta, in the Sicilian idiom ; of which Buchon (*ib.* p. 736 *sqq.*) has given a French translation.]

[57] Nicephorus Gregoras (l. v. c. 6) admires the wisdom of Providence in this equal balance of states and princes. For the honour of Palæologus, I had rather this balance had been observed by an Italian writer.

[58] See the Chronicle of Villani, the xith volume of the Annali d'Italia of Muratori, and the xxth and xxist books of the Istoria Civile of Giannone.

and their presence importunate, endeavoured to discharge the
torrent on some neighbouring countries. After the peace of
Sicily, many thousands of Genoese, *Catalans*,[59] &c., who had
fought, by sea and land, under the standard of Anjou or
Arragon, were blended into one nation by the resemblance of
their manners and interest. They heard that the Greek provinces of Asia were invaded by the Turks : they resolved to
share the harvest of pay and plunder ; and Frederic, king of
Sicily, most liberally contributed the means of their departure.
In a warfare of twenty years, a ship, or a camp, was become
their country ; arms were their sole profession and property ;
valour was the only virtue which they knew ; their women had
imbibed the fearless temper of their lovers and husbands ; it
was reported that, with a stroke of their broad sword, the
Catalans could cleave a horseman and an horse ; and the report
itself was a powerful weapon. Roger de Flor was the most
popular of their chiefs ; and his personal merit overshadowed
the dignity of his prouder rivals of Arragon. The offspring of
a marriage between a German gentleman [60] of the court of
Frederic the Second and a damsel of Brindisi, Roger was successively a templar, an apostate, a pirate, and at length the
richest and most powerful admiral of the Mediterranean. He
sailed from Messina to Constantinople, with eighteen galleys,
four great ships, and eight thousand adventurers ; and his previous treaty was faithfully accomplished by Andronicus the
Elder, who accepted with joy and terror this formidable succour.[61] A palace was allotted for his reception, and a niece of
the emperor was given in marriage to the valiant stranger,
who was immediately created Great Duke or Admiral of Romania. After a decent repose, he transported his troops over
the Propontis, and boldly led them against the Turks ; in two
bloody battles thirty thousand of the Moslems were slain ;

[Sept. 1303]

[Megaduc]

[59] In this motley multitude, the Catalans and Spaniards, the bravest of the
soldiery, were styled by themselves and the Greeks *Amogavares* [Al-mugavari=
scouts]. Moncada derives their origin from the Goths, and Pachymer (l. xi. c.
22) from the Arabs ; and, in spite of national and religious pride, I am afraid the
latter is in the right.

[60] [A falconer (Ramon Muntaner, c. 194). His name was Richard Blum. It
was translated by an Italian equivalent. See Buchon's note.]

[61] [Before he went himself, Roger sent envoys to make the terms. The Emperor's niece, whom he married, was daughter of the Bulgarian Tsar, John Asēn
IV. (whom Muntaner calls the emperador Lantzaura, c. 199). As to the numbers
of the expedition Muntaner says (c. 201) that there were about 36 sail ; 1500 horsemen ; 4000 almogavars ; 1000 foot-soldiers ; as well as the oarsmen and sailors.]

[A.D. 1304

he raised the siege of Philadelphia, and deserved the name of the deliverer of Asia. But, after a short season of prosperity, the cloud of slavery and ruin again burst on that unhappy province. The inhabitants escaped (says a Greek historian) from the smoke into the flames ; and the hostility of the Turks was less pernicious than the friendship of the Catalans. The lives and fortunes which they had rescued, they considered as their own ; the willing or reluctant maid was saved from the race of circumcision for the embraces of a Christian soldier ; the exaction of fines and supplies was enforced by licentious rapine and arbitrary executions ; and, on the resistance of Magnesia, the Great Duke besieged a city of the Roman empire.[62] These disorders he excused by the wrongs and passions of a victorious army ; nor would his own authority or person have been safe, had he dared to punish his faithful followers, who were defrauded of the just and covenanted price of their services. The threats and complaints of Andronicus disclosed the nakedness of the empire. His golden bull had invited no more than five hundred horse and a thousand foot soldiers ; yet the crowd of volunteers, who migrated to the East, had been enlisted and fed by his spontaneous bounty. While his bravest allies were content with three byzants, or pieces of gold, for their monthly pay, an ounce or even two ounces of gold were assigned to the Catalans, whose annual pension would thus amount to near an hundred pounds sterling ; one of their chiefs had modestly rated at three hundred thousand crowns the value of his *future* merits ; and above a million had been issued from the treasury for the maintenance of these costly mercenaries. A cruel tax had been imposed on the corn of the husbandman : one third was retrenched from the salaries of the public officers ; and the standard of the coin was so shamefully debased that of the four-and-twenty parts only five were of pure gold.[63] At the summons of the emperor, Roger evacuated a

---

[62] Some idea may be formed of the population of these cities, from the 36,000 inhabitants of Tralles, which, in the preceding reign, was rebuilt by the emperor, and ruined by the Turks (Pachymer, l. vi. c. 20, 21).

[63] I have collected these pecuniary circumstances from Pachymer (l. xi. c. 21 : l. xii. c. 4, 5, 8, 14, 19), who describes the progressive degradation of the gold coin. Even in the prosperous times of John Ducas Vataces, the byzants were composed in equal proportions of the pure and the baser metal. The poverty of Michael Palæologus compelled him to strike a new coin, with nine parts, or carats, of gold, and fifteen of copper alloy. After his death the standard rose to ten carats, till in the public distress it was reduced to the moiety. The Prince was relieved for a moment, while credit and commerce were for ever blasted. In France, the gold coin is of twenty-two carats (one-twelfth alloy), and the standard of England and Holland is still higher.

province which no longer supplied the materials of rapine ; but he refused to disperse his troops ; and, while his style was respectful, his conduct was independent and hostile. He protested that, if the emperor should march against him, he would advance forty paces to kiss the ground before him ; but, in rising from this prostrate attitude, Roger had a life and sword at the service of his friends. The Great Duke of Romania condescended to accept the title and ornaments of Cæsar ; but he rejected the new proposal of the government of Asia, with a subsidy of corn and money, on condition that he should reduce his troops to the harmless number of three thousand men. Assassination is the last resource of cowards. The Cæsar was tempted to visit the royal residence of Hadrianople : in the apart-[March 28, A.D. 1305] ment, and before the eyes, of the empress, he was stabbed by the Alani [63a] guards ; [64] and, though the deed was imputed to their private revenge, his countrymen, who dwelt at Constantinople in the security of peace, were involved in the same proscription by the prince or people. The loss of their leader intimidated the crowd of adventurers, who hoisted the sails of flight, and were soon scattered round the coasts of the Mediterranean. But a veteran band of fifteen hundred Catalans or French stood firm in the strong fortress of Gallipoli o the Hellespont, displayed the banners of Arragon, and offered to revenge and justify their chief by an equal combat of ten or an hundred warriors. Instead of accepting this bold defiance, the emperor Michael, the son and colleague of Andronicus, resolved to oppress them with the weight of multitudes : every nerve was strained to form an army of thirteen thousand horse and thirty thousand foot ; and the Propontis was covered with the ships of the Greeks and Genoese. In two battles by sea and land, these mighty forces were encountered and overthrown by the despair and discipline of the Catalans ; the young emperor fled to the palace ; and an insufficient guard of light horse was left for the protection of the open country. Victory renewed the hopes and numbers of the adventurers : every nation was blended under the name and standard of the *great company ;* and three thousand Turkish proselytes deserted from the Imperial service to join this mili-

---

[63a] [Is this a misprint for Alanic or Alan ?]

[64] [Roger had crossed to Europe to help the Emperor Andronicus against the Bulgarians. Before returning he wished to take leave of the young Emperor " Kyr Michael " who was at Hadrianople, though it was known that Michael bore him a grudge. Roger's wife and others tried to dissuade him, in vain (Muntaner, c. 213, 215).]

tary association.  In the possession of Gallipoli,[65] the Catalans
intercepted the trade of Constantinople and the Black Sea,
while they spread their devastations on either side of the Hellespont over the confines of Europe and Asia.  To prevent their
approach, the greatest part of the Byzantine territory was laid
waste by the Greeks themselves : the peasants and their cattle
retired into the city ; and myriads of sheep and oxen, for which
neither place nor food could be procured, were unprofitably
slaughtered on the same day.  Four times the emperor Andronicus sued for peace, and four times he was inflexibly repulsed,
till the want of provisions, and the discord of the chiefs, compelled the Catalans to evacuate the banks of the Hellespont and
the neighbourhood of the capital.  After their separation from
the Turks, the remains of the great company pursued their march
through Macedonia and Thessaly, to seek a new establishment
in the heart of Greece.[66]

After some ages of oblivion, Greece was awakened to new
misfortunes by the arms of the Latins.  In the two hundred and
fifty years between the first and the last conquest of Constantinople, that venerable land was disputed by a multitude of petty
tyrants; without the comforts of freedom and genius, her ancient
cities were again plunged in foreign and intestine war ; and, if
servitude be preferable to anarchy, they might repose with joy
under the Turkish yoke.  I shall not pursue the obscure and
various dynasties that rose and fell on the continent or in the
isles , [67] but our silence on the fate of ATHENS [68] would argue a
strange ingratitude to the first and purest school of liberal science
and amusement.  In the partition of the empire, the principality

Revolution of
Athens.  A.D.
1204-1456

---

[65] [Ramon Muntaner, the historian of the expedition, was for a long time captain of Gallipoli, and he describes (c. 225) the good time he had.]

[66] The Catalan war is most copiously related by Pachymer, in the xith, xiith,
and xiiith books, till he breaks off in the year 1308.  Nicephorus Gregoras (l. vii.
3-6) is more concise and complete.  Ducange, who adopts these adventurers as
French, has hunted their footsteps with his usual diligence (Hist. de C. P. l. vi. c.
22-46).  He quotes an Arragonese history, which I have read with pleasure, and
which the Spaniards extol as a model of style and composition (Expedicion de los
Catalanes y Arragoneses contra Turcos y Griegos ; Barcelona, 1623, in quarto ;
Madrid, 1777, in octavo).  Don Francisco de Moncada, Conde de Osona, may
imitate Cæsar or Sallust ; he may transcribe the Greek or Italian contemporaries ;
but he never quotes his authorities, and I cannot discern any national records of
the exploits of his countrymen.  [See Appendix 1.]

[67] [For a summary of the island dynasties see Appendix 18.]

[68] See the laborious history of Ducange, whose accurate table of the French
dynasties recapitulates the thirty-five passages in which he mentions the dukes of
Athens.  [Gregorovius, Geschichte der Stadt Athen im Mittelalter.]

[A.D. 1205-1225] of Athens and Thebes was assigned to Otho de la Roche, a noble warrior of Burgundy,[69] with the title of Great Duke,[70] which the Latins understood in their own sense, and the Greeks more foolishly derived from the age of Constantine.[71] Otho followed the standard of the marquis of Montferrat ; the ample state, which he acquired by a miracle of conduct or fortune,[72] was peaceably inherited by his son and two grandsons,[73] till the family, though not the nation, was changed, by the marriage of an heiress, into the elder branch of the house of Brienne. The [A.D. 1308] son of that marriage, Walter de Brienne, succeeded to the duchy of Athens ; and, with the aid of some Catalan mercenaries, whom he invested with fiefs, reduced above thirty castles of the vassal or neighbouring lords. But, when he was informed of the approach and ambition of the great company, he collected a force [Battle of the Cephisus or Orchomenos. A.D. 1310, March] of seven hundred knights, six thousand four hundred horse, and eight thousand foot, and boldly met them on the banks of the river Cephisus in Bœotia.[74] The Catalans amounted to no more than three thousand five hundred horse and four thousand foot; but the deficiency of numbers was compensated by stratagem and order. They formed round their camp an artificial inun-

---

[69] He is twice mentioned by Villehardouin with honour (No. 151, 235) ; and under the first passage Ducange observes all that can be known of his person and family.

[70] From these Latin princes of the xivth century, Boccace, Chaucer, and Shake-speare have borrowed their Theseus *Duke* of Athens. [And Dante, Inferno, 12, 17.] An ignorant age transfers its own language and manners to the most distant times. [Otto de la Roche had not the ducal title. He called himself *sire* (not *grand sire*) or dominus Athenarum. The title is μέγας κύρ in the Chronicle of Morea. The ducal title was first assumed by Guy I. in 1260 with permission of Louis IX. of France. Megara went along with Athens as a *pertinence* (cum pertinentia Megaron, in the Act of Partition).]

[71] The same Constantine gave to Sicily a king, to Russia the *magnus dapifer* of the empire, to Thebes the *primicerius :* and these absurd fables are properly lashed by Ducange (ad Nicephor. Greg. l. vii. c. 5). By the Latins, the lord of Thebes was styled, by corruption, the Megas Kurios, or Grand Sire ! [See last note. He took his title from Athens, not from Thebes.]

[72] *Quodam miraculo*, says Alberic. He was probably received by Michael Choniates, the archbishop who had defended Athens against the tyrant Leo Sgurus [A.D. 1204] (Nicetas in Baldwino [p. 805, ed. Bonn]). Michael was the brother of the historian Nicetas ; and his encomium of Athens is still extant in Ms. in the Bodleian Library (Fabric. Bibliot. Græc. tom. vi. p. 405). [See above, p. 418, note 15. It is supposed that Archbishop Akominatos made conditions of surrender with Boniface. The Western soldiers sacrilegiously pillaged the Parthenon church. Akominatos left Athens after its occupation by De la Roche.]

[73] [This should be : nephew, two grand-nephews, and a great-grand-nephew, Guy II. A.D. 1287-1308. Guy II.'s aunt Isabella had married Hugh de Brienne ; Walter de Brienne was their son.]

[74] [See Ramon Muntaner, chap. 240.]

dation : the duke and his knights advanced without fear or precaution on the verdant meadow; their horses plunged into the bog ; and he was cut in pieces, with the greatest part of the French cavalry.  His family and nation were expelled ; and his son, Walter de Brienne, the titular duke of Athens, the tyrant of Florence, and the constable of France, lost his life in the field of Poitiers.  Attica and Bœotia were the rewards of the victorious Catalans; they married the widows and daughters of the slain ; and during fourteen years the great company was the terror of the Grecian states.  Their factions drove them to acknowledge the sovereignty of the house of Arragon ; [75] and, during the remainder of the fourteenth century, Athens, as a government or an appanage, was successively bestowed by the kings of Sicily.  After the French and Catalans, the third dynasty was that of the Accaioli, a family, plebeian at Florence, potent at Naples, and sovereign in Greece.  Athens, which they embellished with new buildings, became the capital of a state that extended over Thebes, Argos, Corinth, Delphi, and a part of Thessaly ; and their reign was finally determined by Mahomet the Second, who strangled the last duke, and educated his sons in the discipline and religion of the seraglio.[76] [A.D. 1311-1326] [A.D. 1386] [A.D. 1456]

Athens,[77] though no more than the shadow of her former self, still contains about eight or ten thousand inhabitants : of these, three-fourths are Greeks in religion and language ; and the Turks, who compose the remainder, have relaxed, in their intercourse with the citizens, somewhat of the pride and gravity of their national character.  The olive-tree, the gift of Minerva, flourishes in Attica ; nor has the honey of Mount Hymettus lost any part of its exquisite flavour ; [78] but the languid trade is monopolized by strangers; and the agriculture of a barren *Present state of Athens*

ruins of antiquity ; and such is the debasement of their char-

[75] [They also held Neopatras in Thessaly ; their title was Duke of Athens and Neopatras ; and the kings of Spain retained the title.]

[76] [For the Acciajoli see Appendix 17.]

[77] The modern account of Athens, and the Athenians, is extracted from Spon (Voyage en Grèce, tom. ii. p. 79-199) and Wheler (Travels into Greece, p. 337-414), Stuart (Antiquities of Athens, *passim*), and Chandler (Travels into Greece, p. 23-172).    The first of these travellers visited Greece in the year 1676, the last 1765 ; and ninety years had not produced much difference in the tranquil scene.   [At the end of the 12th century Michael Akominatos deplores the decline of Athens (for his dirge see above, p. 417, note 14).    He says that he has become a barbarian by living so long in Athens (ed. Lampros, vol. 2, p. 44).]

[78] The ancients, or at least the Athenians, believed that all the bees in the world had been propagated from Mount Hymettus.    They taught that health might be preserved, and life prolonged, by the external use of oil and the internal use of honey (Geoponica, l. xv. c. 7, p. 1089-1094, edit. Niclas).

land is abandoned to the vagrant Walachians. The Athenians are still distinguished by the subtlety and acuteness of their understandings; but these qualities, unless ennobled by freedom and enlightened by study, will degenerate into a low and selfish cunning; and it is a proverbial saying of the country, " From the Jews of Thessalonica, the Turks of Negropont, and the Greeks of Athens, good Lord, deliver us!" This artful people has eluded the tyranny of the Turkish bashaws by an expedient which alleviates their servitude and aggravates their shame. About the middle of the last century, the Athenians chose for their protector the Kislar Aga, or chief black eunuch of the seraglio. This Æthiopian slave, who possesses the Sultan's ear, condescends to accept the tribute of thirty thousand crowns; his lieutenant, the Waywode, whom he annually confirms, may reserve for his own about five or six thousand more; and such is the policy of the citizens that they seldom fail to remove and punish an oppressive governor. Their private differences are decided by the archbishop, one of the richest prelates of the Greek church, since he possesses a revenue of one thousand pounds sterling; and by a tribunal of the eight *geronti* or elders, chosen in the eight quarters of the city. The noble families cannot trace their pedigree above three hundred years; but their principal members are distinguished by a grave demeanour, a fur cap, and the lofty appellation of *archon*. By some, who delight in the contrast, the modern language of Athens is represented as the most corrupt and barbarous of the seventy dialects of the vulgar Greek; [79] this picture is too darkly coloured; but it would not be easy, in the country of Plato and Demosthenes, to find a reader, or a copy, of their works. The Athenians walk with supine indifference among the glorious ruins of antiquity; and such is the debasement of their character that they are incapable of admiring the genius of their predecessors. [80]

[79] Ducange, Glossar. Græc. Præfat. p. 8, who quotes for his author Theodosius Zygomalas, a modern grammarian [of the 16th cent.]. Yet Spon (tom. ii. p. 194), and Wheler (p. 355), no incompetent judges, entertain a more favourable opinion of the Attic dialect.

[80] Yet we must not accuse them of corrupting the name of Athens, which they still call Athini. From the εἰς τὴν Ἀθήνην we have formed our own barbarism of *Setines*. [*Setines* comes from (στὰ)ς Ἀθήνας.]

## CHAPTER LXIII

*Civil Wars, and Ruin of the Greek Empire—Reigns of Andronicus, the Elder and Younger, and John Palæologus—Regency, Revolt, Reign, and Abdication, of John Cantacuzene—Establishment of a Genoese Colony at Pera or Galata—Their Wars with the Empire and City of Constantinople*

THE long reign of Andronicus[1] the Elder is chiefly memorable by the disputes of the Greek church, the invasion of the Catalans, and the rise of the Ottoman power. He is celebrated as the most learned and virtuous prince of the age; but such virtue and such learning contributed neither to the perfection of the individual nor to the happiness of society. A slave of the most abject superstition, he was surrounded on all sides by visible and invisible enemies; nor were the flames of hell less dreadful to his fancy than those of a Catalan or Turkish war. Under the reign of the Palæologi, the choice of the patriarch was the most important business of the state; the heads of the Greek church were ambitious and fanatic monks; and their vices or virtues, their learning or ignorance, were equally mischievous or contemptible. By his intemperate discipline, the patriarch Athanasius[2] excited the hatred of the clergy and people: he was heard to declare that the sinner should swallow the last dregs of the cup of penance; and the foolish tale was propagated of his punishing a sacrilegious ass that had tasted the lettuce of a convent-garden. Driven from the throne by [A.D. 1294] the universal clamour, Athanasius composed, before his retreat, two papers of a very opposite cast. His public testament was

*Superstition of Andronicus and the times. A.D. 1282-1320*

---

[1] Andronicus himself will justify our freedom in the invective (Nicephorus Gregoras, l. i. c. 1) which he pronounced against historic falsehood. It is true that his censure is more pointedly urged against calumny than against adulation.

[2] For the anathema in the pigeon's nest, see Pachymer (l. ix. c. 24), who relates the general history of Athanasius (l. viii. c. 13-16, 20-24; l. x. c. 27-29, 31-36; l. xi. c. 1-3, 5, 6; l. xiii. c. 8, 10, 23, 35), and is followed by Nicephorus Gregoras (l. vi. c. 5, 7; l. vii. c. 1, 9), who includes the second retreat of this second Chrysostom.

in the tone of charity and resignation; the private codicil breathed the direst anathemas against the authors of his disgrace, whom he excluded for ever from the communion of the Holy Trinity, the angels, and the saints. This last paper he enclosed in an earthen pot, which was placed, by his order, on the top of one of the pillars in the dome of St. Sophia, in the distant hope of discovery and revenge. At the end of four years, some youths, climbing by a ladder in search of pigeons' nests, detected the fatal secret; and, as Andronicus felt himself touched and bound by the excommunication, he trembled on the brink of the abyss which had been so treacherously dug under his feet. A synod of bishops was instantly convened to debate this important question; the rashness of these clandestine anathemas was generally condemned; but, as the knot could be untied only by the same hand, as that hand was now deprived of the crosier, it appeared that this posthumous decree was irrevocable by any earthly power. Some faint testimonies of repentance and pardon were extorted from the author of the mischief; but the conscience of the emperor was still wounded, and he desired, with no less ardour than Athanasius himself, the restoration of a patriarch by whom alone he could be healed. At the dead of night a monk rudely knocked at the door of the royal bed-chamber, announcing a revelation of plague and famine, of inundations and earthquakes. Andronicus started from his bed, and spent the night in prayer, till he felt, or thought that he felt, a slight motion of the earth. The emperor, on foot, led the bishops and monks to the cell of Athanasius; and, after a proper resistance, the saint, from whom this message had been sent, consented to absolve the prince and [A.D. 1303] govern the church of Constantinople. Untamed by disgrace and hardened by solitude, the shepherd was again odious to the flock; and his enemies contrived a singular and, as it proved, a successful mode of revenge. In the night they stole away the foot-stool or foot-cloth of his throne, which they secretly replaced with the decoration of a satirical picture. The emperor was painted with a bridle in his mouth, and Athanasius leading the tractable beast to the feet of Christ. The authors of the libel were detected and punished; but, as their lives had [A.D. 1311] been spared, the Christian priest in sullen indignation retired to his cell; and the eyes of Andronicus, which had been opened for a moment, were again closed by his successor.

If this transaction be one of the most curious and important of a reign of fifty years, I cannot at least accuse the brevity of

my materials, since I reduce into some few pages the enormous
folios of Pachymer,[3] Cantacuzene,[4] and Nicephorus Gregoras,[5]
who have composed the prolix and languid story of the times.
The name and situation of the emperor John Cantacuzene
might inspire the most lively curiosity. His memorials of forty
years extend from the revolt of the younger Andronicus to his
own abdication of the empire; and it is observed that, like
Moses and Cæsar, he was the principal actor in the scenes
which he describes. But in this eloquent work we should
vainly seek the sincerity of an hero or a penitent. Retired in
a cloister from the vices and passions of the world, he presents
not a confession, but an apology, of the life of an ambitious
statesman. Instead of unfolding the true counsels and characters of men, he displays the smooth and specious surface of
events, highly varnished with his own praises and those of his
friends. Their motives are always pure ; their ends always
legitimate ; they conspire and rebel without any views of interest ; and the violence which they inflict or suffer is celebrated as the spontaneous effect of reason and virtue.

After the example of the first of the Palæologi, the elder
Andronicus associated his son Michael to the honours of the
purple ; and, from the age of eighteen to his premature death,
that prince was acknowledged, above twenty-five years, as the
second emperor of the Greeks.[6] At the head of an army, he
excited neither the fears of the enemy nor the jealousy of the
court ; his modesty and patience were never tempted to compute the years of his father ; nor was that father compelled
to repent of his liberality either by the virtues or vices of his

*First disputes between the elder and younger Andronicus. A.D. 1320*

---

[3] Pachymer, in seven books, 377 folio pages, describes the first twenty-six years
of Andronicus the Elder ; and marks the date of his composition by the current
news or lie of the day (A.D. 1308). Either death or disgust prevented him from
resuming the pen.

[4] After an interval of twelve years from the conclusion of Pachymer, Cantacuzenus takes up the pen ; and his first book (c. 1-59, p. 9-150) relates the civil
war and the eight last years of the elder Andronicus. The ingenious comparison
of Moses and Cæsar is fancied by his French translator, the president Cousin.

[5] Nicephorus Gregoras more briefly includes the entire life and reign of Andronicus the Elder (l. vi. c. i. ; l. x. c. 1, p. 96-291). This is the part of which
Cantacuzene complains as a false and malicious representation of his conduct.

[6] He was crowned May 21, 1295, and died October 12, 1320 (Ducange, Fam.
Byz. p. 239). His brother, Theodore, by a second marriage, inherited the marquisate of Montferrat, apostatized to the religion and manners of the Latins (ὅτι
καὶ γνώμῃ καὶ πίστει καὶ σχήματι, καὶ γενείων κουρᾷ καὶ πᾶσιν ἔθεσιν Λατῖνος ἦν ἀκραιφνής,
Nic. Greg. l. ix. c. 1), and founded a dynasty of Italian princes, which was extinguished A.D. 1533 (Ducange, Fam. Byz. p. 249-253).

son. The son of Michael was named Andronicus from his grandfather, to whose early favour he was introduced by that nominal
resemblance. The blossoms of wit and beauty increased the
fondness of the elder Andronicus ; and, with the common vanity
of the age, he expected to realise in the second, the hope which
had been disappointed in the first, generation. The boy was
educated in the palace as an heir and a favourite ; and, in the
oaths and acclamations of the people, the *august triad* was
formed by the names of the father, the son, and the grandson.
But the younger Andronicus was speedily corrupted by his
infant greatness, while he beheld, with puerile impatience, the
double obstacle that hung, and might long hang, over his rising
ambition. It was not to acquire fame, or to diffuse happiness,
that he so eagerly aspired; wealth and impunity were in his
eyes the most precious attributes of a monarch ; and his first
indiscreet demand was the sovereignty of some rich and fertile
island, where he might lead a life of independence and pleasure.
The emperor was offended by the loud and frequent intemperance which disturbed his capital ; the sums which his parsi-
mony denied were supplied by the Genoese usurers of Pera ;
and the oppressive debt, which consolidated the interest of a
faction, could be discharged only by a revolution. A beautiful
female, a matron in rank, a prostitute in manners, had instructed the younger Andronicus in the rudiments of love ; but
he had reason to suspect the nocturnal visits of a rival ; and a
stranger passing through the street was pierced by the arrows
of his guards, who were placed in ambush at her door. That
stranger was his brother, prince Manuel, who languished and
died of his wound ; and the emperor Michael, their common
father, whose health was in a declining state, expired on the
[A.D. 1320] eighth day, lamenting the loss of both his children.[7] However
guiltless in his intention, the younger Andronicus might impute
a brother's and a father's death to the consequence of his own
vices ; and deep was the sigh of thinking and feeling men,
when they perceived, instead of sorrow and repentance, his ill-
dissembled joy on the removal of two odious competitors. By
these melancholy events, and the increase of his disorders, the
mind of the elder emperor was gradually alienated ; and, after

[7] We are indebted to Nicephorus Gregoras (l. viii. c. 1) for the knowledge of
this tragic adventure ; while Cantacuzene more discreetly conceals the vices of
Andronicus the Younger, of which he was the witness and perhaps the associate
(l. i. c. 1, &c.).

many fruitless reproofs, he transferred on another grandson [8] his hopes and affection.  The change was announced by the new oath of allegiance to the reigning sovereign and the *person* whom he should appoint for his successor ; and the acknowledged heir, after a repetition of insults and complaints, was exposed to the indignity of a public trial.  Before the sentence, which would probably have condemned him to a dungeon or a cell, the emperor was informed that the palace courts were filled with the armed followers of his grandson ; the judgment was softened to a treaty of reconciliation ; and the triumphant escape of the prince encouraged the ardour of the younger faction.

Yet the capital, the clergy, and the senate adhered to the person, or at least to the government, of the old emperor ; and it was only in the provinces, by flight, and revolt, and foreign succour, that the malcontents could hope to vindicate their cause and subvert his throne.  The soul of the enterprise was the great domestic, John Cantacuzene ; the sally from Constantinople is the first date of his actions and memorials ; and, if his own pen be most descriptive of his patriotism, an unfriendly historian has not refused to celebrate the zeal and ability which he displayed in the service of the young emperor. That prince escaped from the capital under the pretence of hunting ; erected his standard at Hadrianople ; and, in a few days, assembled fifty thousand horse and foot, whom neither honour nor duty could have armed against the barbarians. Such a force might have saved or commanded the empire ; but their counsels were discordant, their motions were slow and doubtful, and their progress was checked by intrigue and negotiation.  The quarrel of the two Andronici was protracted, and suspended, and renewed, during a ruinous period of seven years.  In the first treaty the relics of the Greek empire were divided : Constantinople, Thessalonica, and the islands, were left to the elder, while the younger acquired the sovereignty of the greatest part of Thrace, from Philippi to the Byzantine limit.  By the second treaty he stipulated the payment of his troops, his immediate coronation, and an adequate share of the power and revenue of the state.  The third civil war was terminated by the surprise of Constantinople, the final retreat of the old emperor, and the sole reign of his victorious grandson.

*Three civil wars between the two emperors. A.D. 1321, April 20 —A.D. 1328, May 23*

*Coronation of the younger Andronicus. A.D. 1325, Feb. 2*

---

[8] His destined heir was Michael Catharus, the bastard of Constantine his second son.  In this project of excluding his grandson Andronicus, Nicephorus Gregoras (l. viii. c. 3 [p. 295-6, ed. Bonn]) agrees with Cantacuzene (l. i. c. 1, 2).

The reasons of this delay may be found in the characters of the men and of the times. When the heir of the monarchy first pleaded his wrongs and his apprehensions, he was heard with pity and applause ; and his adherents repeated on all sides the inconsistent promise that he would increase the pay of the soldiers and alleviate the burdens of the people. The griev- ances of forty years were mingled in his revolt ; and the rising generation was fatigued by the endless prospect of a reign whose favourites and maxims were of other times. The youth of Andronicus had been without spirit, his age was without rever- ence ; his taxes produced an annual revenue of five hundred thousand pounds ; yet the richest of the sovereigns of Christen- dom was incapable of maintaining three thousand horse and twenty galleys, to resist the destructive progress of the Turks.[9] " How different," said the younger Andronicus, " is my situa- tion from that of the son of Philip ! Alexander might com- plain that his father would leave him nothing to conquer ; alas ! my grandsire will leave me nothing to lose." But the Greeks were soon admonished that the public disorders could not be healed by a civil war ; and their young favourite was not destined to be the saviour of a falling empire. On the first repulse, his party was broken by his own levity, their intestine discord, and the intrigues of the ancient court, which tempted each malcontent to desert or betray the cause of rebellion. An- dronicus the Younger was touched with remorse, or fatigued with business, or deceived by negotiation ; pleasure rather than power was his aim ; and the licence of maintaining a thousand hounds, a thousand hawks, and a thousand huntsmen, was suffi- cient to sully his fame and disarm his ambition.

The elder An- dronicus abdi- cates the government. A.D. 1328, May 24

Let us now survey the catastrophe of this busy plot and the final situation of the principal actors.[10] The age of Andronicus was consumed in civil discord ; and, amidst the events of war and treaty, his power and reputation continually decayed, till the fatal night in which the gates of the city and palace were opened without resistance to his grandson. His principal com- mander scorned the repeated warnings of danger ; and retiring

[9] See Nicephorus Gregoras, l. viii. c. 6. The younger Andronicus complained that in four years and four months a sum of 350,000 byzants of gold was due to him for the expenses of his household (Cantacuzen. l. i. c. 48). Yet he would have remitted the debt, if he might have been allowed to squeeze the farmers of the revenue.

[10] I follow the chronology of Nicephorus Gregoras, who is remarkably exact. It is proved that Cantacuzene has mistaken the dates of his own actions, or rather that his text has been corrupted by ignorant transcribers.

to rest in the vain security of ignorance, abandoned the feeble monarch, with some priests and pages, to the terrors of a sleepless night. These terrors were quickly realised by the hostile shouts which proclaimed the titles and victory of Andronicus the Younger; and the aged emperor, falling prostrate before an image of the Virgin, dispatched a suppliant message to resign the sceptre and to obtain his life at the hands of the conqueror. The answer of his grandson was decent and pious; at the prayer of his friends, the younger Andronicus assumed the sole administration; but the elder still enjoyed the name and pre-eminence of the first emperor, the use of the great palace, and a pension of twenty-four thousand pieces of gold, one half of which was assigned on the royal treasure, and the other on the fishery of Constantinople. But his impotence was soon exposed to contempt and oblivion; the vast silence of the palace was disturbed only by the cattle and poultry of the neighbourhood, which roved with impunity through the solitary courts; and a reduced allowance of ten thousand pieces of gold [11] was all that he could ask and more than he could hope. His calamities were embittered by the gradual extinction of sight: his confinement was rendered each day more rigorous; and during the absence and sickness of his grandson, his inhuman keepers, by the threats of instant death, compelled him to exchange the purple for the monastic habit and profession. The [A.D. 1330] monk *Antony* had renounced the pomp of the world: yet he had occasion for a coarse fur in the winter-season; and, as wine was forbidden by his confessor, and water by his physician, the sherbet of Egypt was his common drink. It was not without difficulty that the late emperor could procure three or four pieces to satisfy these simple wants; and, if he bestowed the gold to relieve the more painful distress of a friend, the sacrifice is of some weight in the scale of humanity and religion. Four years after his abdication, Andronicus, or Antony, expired in a cell, in the seventy-fourth year of his age; and the last strain of adulation could only promise a more splendid crown of glory in heaven than he had enjoyed upon earth. [12]

*His death. A.D. 1332, Feb. 13*

---

[11] I have endeavoured to reconcile the 24,000 [*leg.* 12,000] pieces of Cantacuzene (l. ii. c. i. [vol. i. p. 311, ed. Bonn]) with the 10,000 of Nicephorus Gregoras (l. ix. c. 2); the one of whom wished to soften, the other to magnify, the hardships of the old emperor.

[12] See Nicephorus Gregoras (l. ix. 6-8, 10, 14; l. x. c. 1). The historian had tasted of the prosperity, and shared the retreat, of his benefactor; and that friendship, which "waits or to the scaffold or the cell," should not lightly be accused as "a hireling, a prostitute to praise".

Nor was the reign of the younger, more glorious or fortunate than that of the elder, Andronicus.[13] He gathered the fruits of ambition: but the taste was transient and bitter; in the supreme station he lost the remains of his early popularity; and the defects of his character became still more conspicuous to the world. The public reproach urged him to march in person against the Turks; nor did his courage fail in the hour of trial; but a defeat and wound were the only trophies of his expedition in Asia, which confirmed the establishment of the Ottoman monarchy. The abuses of the civil government attained their full maturity and perfection; his neglect of forms, and the confusion of national dresses, are deplored by the Greeks as the fatal symptoms of the decay of the empire. Andronicus was old before his time; the intemperance of youth had accelerated the infirmities of age; and, after being rescued from a dangerous malady by nature, or physic, or the Virgin, he was snatched

away before he had accomplished his forty-fifth year. He was twice married; and, as the progress of the Latins in arms and arts had softened the prejudices of the Byzantine court, his two wives were chosen in the princely houses of Germany and Italy. The first, Agnes at home, Irene in Greece, was daughter of the duke of Brunswick. Her father[14] was a petty lord[15] in the poor and savage regions of the north of Germany;[16] yet he

---

[13] The sole reign of Andronicus the younger is described by Cantacuzene (l. ii. c. 1-40, p. 191-339) and Nicephorus Gregoras (l. ix. c. 7—l. xi. c. 11, p. 262-361).

[14] Agnes, or Irene, was the daughter of duke Henry the Wonderful, the chief of the house of Brunswick, and the fourth in descent from the famous Henry the Lion, duke of Saxony and Bavaria, and conqueror of the Salvi on the Baltic coast. Her brother Henry was surnamed the *Greek*, from his two journeys into the East; but these journeys were subsequent to his sister's marriage; and I am ignorant *how* Agnes was discovered in the heart of Germany, and recommended to the Byzantine court (Rimius, Memoirs of the House of Brunswick, p. 126-137).

[15] Henry the Wonderful was the founder of the branch of Grubenhagen, extinct in the year 1596 (Rimius, p. 287). He resided in the castle of Wolfenbüttel, and possessed no more than a sixth part of the allodial estates of Brunswick and Luneburg, which the Guelph family had saved from the confiscation of their great fiefs. The frequent partitions among brothers had almost ruined the princely houses of Germany, till that just but pernicious law was slowly superseded by the right of primogeniture. The principality of Grubenhagen, one of the last remains of the Hercynian forest, is a woody, mountainous, and barren tract (Busching's Geography, vol. vi. p. 270-286; English translation).

[16] The royal author of the Memoirs of Brandenburg will teach us how justly, in a much later period, the north of Germany deserved the epithets of poor and barbarous (Essai sur les Mœurs, &c.). In the year 1306, in the woods of Luneburg, some wild people, of the Vened race, were allowed to bury alive their infirm and useless parents (Rimius, p. 136).

derived some revenue from his silver mines ;[17] and his family is celebrated by the Greeks as the most ancient and noble of the Teutonic name.[18] After the death of this childless princess, Andronicus sought in marriage, Jane, the sister of the count of Savoy ;[19] and his suit was preferred to that of the French king.[20] The count respected in his sister the superior majesty of a Roman empress ; her retinue was composed of knights and ladies ; she was regenerated and crowned in St. Sophia, under the more orthodox appellation of Anne ; and, at the nuptial feast, the Greeks and Italians vied with each other in the martial exercises of tilts and tournaments.

The empress Anne of Savoy survived her husband. Their son, John Palæologus, was left an orphan and an emperor, in the ninth year of his age ; and his weakness was protected by the first and most deserving of the Greeks. The long and cordial friendship of his father for John Cantacuzene is alike honourable to the prince and the subject. It had been formed amidst the pleasures of their youth ; their families were almost equally noble ;[21] and the recent lustre of the purple was amply compensated by the energy of a private education. We have seen that the young emperor was saved by Cantacuzene from the power of his grandfather ; and, after six years of civil war, the same favourite brought him back in triumph to the

Reign of John Palæologus.<br>A.D. 1341, June 15—A.D. 1391

Fortune of John Cantacu-zenus

---

[17] The assertion of Tacitus that Germany was destitute of the precious metals must be taken, even in his own time, with some limitation (Germania, c. 5, Annal. xi. 20). According to Spener (Hist. Germaniæ Pragmatica, tom. i. p. 351), *Argentifodinae* in Hercyniis montibus, imperante Othone magno (A.D. 968), primum apertæ, largam etiam opes augendi dederunt copiam ; but Rimius (p. 258, 259) defers till the year 1016 discovery of the silver mines of Grubenhagen, or the Upper Hartz, which were productive in the beginning of the xivth century, and which still yield a considerable revenue to the house of Brunswick.

[18] Cantacuzene has given a most honourable testimony, ἦν δ' ἐκ Γερμανῶν αὕτη θυγατὴρ δουκὸς ντὶ μπρουζούικ (the modern Greeks employ the ντ for the δ, and the μπ for the β, and the whole will read, in the Italian idiom, di Brunzuic), τοῦ παρ' αὐτοῖς ἐπιφανεστάτου, καὶ λαμπρότητι πάντας τοὺς ὁμοφύλους ὑπερβάλλοντος τοῦ γένους. The praise is just in itself, and pleasing to an English ear.

[19] Anne, or Jane, was one of the four daughters of Amédée the Great, by a second marriage, and half-sister of his successor, Edward count of Savoy (Anderson's Tables, p. 650). See Cantacuzene (l. i. c. 40-42).

[20] That king, if the fact be true, must have been Charles the Fair, who, in five years (1321-1326), was married to three wives (Anderson, p. 628). Anne of Savoy arrived at Constantinople in February, 1326.

[21] The noble race of the Cantacuzeni (illustrious from the xith century in the Byzantine annals) was drawn from the Paladins of France, the heroes of those romances which, in the xiiith century, were translated and read by the Greeks (Ducange, Fam. Byzant. p. 258). [Monograph on Cantacuzene : V. Parisot, Cantacuzène, Homme d'état et historien, 1845.]

palace of Constantinople.  Under the reign of Andronicus the
Younger, the great domestic ruled the emperor and the empire ; and it was by his valour and conduct that the isle of
Lesbos and the principality of Ætolia were restored to their
ancient allegiance.  His enemies confess that, among the public
robbers, Cantacuzene alone was moderate and abstemious ; and
the free and voluntary account which he produces of his own
wealth [22] may sustain the presumption that it was devolved by
inheritance, and not accumulated by rapine.  He does not indeed specify the value of his money, plate, and jewels ; yet,
after a voluntary gift of two hundred vases of silver, after much
had been secreted by his friends and plundered by his foes,
his forfeit treasures were sufficient for the equipment of a fleet
of seventy galleys.  He does not measure the size and number
of his estates ; but his granaries were heaped with an incredible
store of wheat and barley ; and the labour of a thousand yoke
of oxen might cultivate, according to the practice of antiquity,
about sixty-two thousand five hundred acres of arable land.[23]
His pastures were stocked with two thousand five hundred brood
mares, two hundred camels, three hundred mules, five hundred
asses, five thousand horned cattle, fifty thousand hogs, and
seventy thousand sheep : [24] a precious record of rural opulence,
in the last period of the empire, and in a land, most probably
in Thrace, so repeatedly wasted by foreign and domestic hostility.  The favour of Cantacuzene was above his fortune.  In
the moments of familiarity, in the hour of sickness, the emperor
was desirous to level the distance between them, and pressed
his friend to accept the diadem and purple.  The virtue of the
great domestic, which is attested by his own pen, resisted the
dangerous proposal ; but the last testament of Andronicus the
Younger named him the guardian of his son and the regent of
the empire.

He is left
regent of the
empire

His regency is
attacked,
A.D. 1341

Had the regent found a suitable return of obedience and

[22] See Cantacuzene (l. iii. c. 24, 30, 36).

[23] Saserna, in Gaul, and Columella, in Italy or Spain, allow two yoke of oxen,
two drivers, and six labourers, for two hundred jugera (125 English acres) of arable
land ; and three more men must be added if there be much underwood (Columella
de Re Rusticâ, l. ii. c. 13, p. 441, edit. Gesner).

[24] In this enumeration (l. iii. c. 30), the French translation of the President
Cousin is blotted with three palpable and essential errors.  1. He omits the 1000
yoke of working oxen.  2. He interprets the πεντακόσιαι πρὸς δισχιλίαις, by the
number of fifteen hundred.  [The mistake has not been corrected in the Bonn
edition, vol. ii. p. 185.]  3. He confounds myriads with chiliads, and gives Cantacuzene no more than 5000 hogs.  Put not your trust in translations !

gratitude, perhaps he would have acted with pure and zealous
fidelity in the service of his pupil.[25] A guard of five hundred
soldiers watched over his person and the palace; the funeral
of the late emperor was decently performed; the capital was
silent and submissive; and five hundred letters, which Cantacuzene dispatched in the first month, informed the provinces of
their loss and their duty. The prospect of a tranquil minority by Apo-
was blasted by the Great Duke or Admiral Apocaucus; and, to caucus
exaggerate *his* perfidy, the Imperial historian is pleased to magnify his own imprudence in raising him to that office against
the advice of his more sagacious sovereign. Bold and subtle,
rapacious and profuse, the avarice and ambition of Apocaucus
were by turns subservient to each other; and his talents were
applied to the ruin of his country. His arrogance was heightened by the command of a naval force and an impregnable
castle, and, under the mask of oaths and flattery, he secretly
conspired against his benefactor. The female court of the empress was bribed and directed; he encouraged Anne of Savoy
to assert, by the law of nature, the tutelage of her son; the by the em-
love of power was disguised by the anxiety of maternal ten- press Anne of
derness; and the founder of the Palæologi had instructed his Savoy
posterity to dread the example of a perfidious guardian. The
patriarch John of Apri was a proud and feeble old man, encom- by the
passed by a numerous and hungry kindred. He produced an patriarch
obsolete epistle of Andronicus, which bequeathed the prince
and people to his pious care: the fate of his predecessor Arsenius prompted him to prevent, rather than punish, the crimes
of an usurper; and Apocaucus smiled at the success of his own
flattery, when he beheld the Byzantine priest assuming the
state and temporal claims of the Roman pontiff.[26] Between
three persons so different in their situation and character, a
private league was concluded: a shadow of authority was restored to the senate; and the people was tempted by the name
of freedom. By this powerful confederacy, the great domestic
was assaulted at first with clandestine, at length with open, arms.
His prerogatives were disputed; his opinions slighted; his friends

[25] See the regency and reign of John Cantacuzenus, and the whole progress of
the civil war, in his own history (l. iii. c. 1-100, p. 348-700), and in that of Nice
phorus Gregoras (l. xii. c. 1—l. xv. c. 9, p. 353-492).

[26] He assumed the royal privilege of red shoes or buskins; placed on his head
a mitre of silk and gold; subscribed his epistles with hyacinth or green ink; and
claimed for the new, whatever Constantine had given to the ancient, Rome (Cantacuzen. l. iii. c. 36; Nic. Gregoras, l. xiv. c. 3).

persecuted ; and his safety was threatened both in the camp and city. In his absence on the public service, he was accused of treason ; proscribed as an enemy of the church and state ; and delivered, with all his adherents, to the sword of justice, the vengeance of the people, and the power of the devil : his fortunes were confiscated ; his aged mother was cast into prison ; all his past services were buried in oblivion ; and he was driven by injustice to perpetrate the crime of which he was accused.[27] From the review of his preceding conduct, Cantacuzene appears to have been guiltless of any treasonable designs ; and the only suspicion of his innocence must arise from the vehemence of his protestations, and the sublime purity which he ascribes to his own virtue. While the empress and the patriarch still affected the appearance of harmony, he repeatedly solicited the permission of retiring to a private, and even a monastic, life. After he had been declared a public enemy, it was his fervent wish to throw himself at the feet of the young emperor, and to receive without a murmur the stroke of the executioner : it was not without reluctance that he listened to the voice of reason, which inculcated the sacred duty of saving his family and friends, and proved that he could only save them by drawing the sword and assuming the Imperial title.

Cantacuzene assumes the purple. A.D. 1341, Oct. 26   In the strong city of Demotica, his peculiar domain, the emperor John Cantacuzenus was invested with the purple buskins ; his right leg was clothed by his noble kinsmen, the left by the Latin chiefs, on whom he conferred the order of knighthood. But even in this act of revolt he was still studious of loyalty ; and the titles of John Palæologus and Anne of Savoy were proclaimed before his own name and that of his wife Irene. Such vain ceremony is a thin disguise of rebellion, nor are there perhaps any *personal* wrongs that can authorise a subject to take arms against his sovereign ; but the want of preparation and success may confirm the assurance of the usurper that this decisive step was the effect of necessity rather than of choice. Constantinople adhered to the young emperor ; the king of Bulgaria was invited to the relief of Hadrianople ; the principal cities of Thrace and Macedonia, after some hesitation, renounced their obedience to the great domestic ; and the leaders of the troops and provinces were induced, by their private interest, to prefer the loose do-

---

[27] Nic. Gregoras (l. xii. c. 5) confesses the innocence and virtues of Cantacuzenus, the guilt and flagitious vices of Apocaucus ; nor does he dissemble the motive of his personal and religious enmity to the former ; νῦν δὲ διὰ κακίαν ἄλλων αἴτιος ὁ πραότατος τῆς τῶν ὅλων ἔδοξεν εἶναι φθορᾶς.

minion of a woman and a priest.[28]   The army of Cantacuzene, in
sixteen divisions, was stationed on the banks of the Melas, to
tempt or intimidate the capital; it was dispersed by treachery
or fear ; and the officers, more especially the mercenary Latins,
accepted the bribes, and embraced the service, of the Byzantine
court.   After this loss, the rebel emperor (he fluctuated between the two characters) took the road of Thessalonica with
a chosen remnant; but he failed in his enterprise on that important place; and he was closely pursued by the Great Duke,
his enemy Apocaucus, at the head of a superior power by sea
and land.   Driven from the coast, in his march, or rather flight,
into the mountains of Servia, Cantacuzene assembled his troops
to scrutinise those who were worthy and willing to accompany
his broken fortunes.   A base majority bowed and retired ; and
his trusty band was diminished to two thousand, and at last
to five hundred, volunteers.   The *cral*,[29] or despot of the Ser- [Stephen Dushan]
vians, received him with generous hospitality ; but the ally was
insensibly degraded to a suppliant, an hostage, a captive ; and,
in this miserable dependence, he waited at the door of the barbarian, who could dispose of the life and liberty of a Roman
emperor.   The most tempting offers could not persuade the
cral to violate his trust; but he soon inclined to the stronger
side; and his friend was dismissed without injury to a new vicissitude of hopes and perils.   Near six years the flame of discord
burnt with various success and unabated rage : the cities were The civil war.
distracted by the faction of the nobles and the plebeians—the A.D. 1341-1347
Cantacuzeni and Palæologi ; and the Bulgarians, the Servians,
and the Turks were invoked on both sides as the instruments
of private ambition and the common ruin.   The regent deplored
the calamities of which he was the author and victim : and his
own experience might dictate a just and lively remark on the

[28] [The people seem to have clung to the legitimate heir ; the officials to have
supported Cantacuzene.]

[29] The princes of Servia (Ducange, Famil. Dalmaticæ, &c., c. 2-4, 9) were styled
Despots in Greek, and Cral in their native idiom (Ducange, Gloss. Græc. p. 751).
That title, the equivalent of king, appears to be of Sclavonic origin, from whence
it has been borrowed by the Hungarians, the modern Greeks, and even by the
Turks (Leunclavius, Pandect. Turc. p. 422), who reserve the name of Padishah for
the Emperor.   To obtain the latter instead of the former is the ambition of the
French at Constantinople (Avertissement á l'Histoire de Timur Bec, p. 39).   [The
Servian and Bulgarian *Kral*, "king," from which the Hungarian *Király*, "king," is
borrowed, seems to be derived from *Karl* the Great ; just as the German and
Slavonic word for Emperor is from the name of Cæsar.   We find Κράλ in a Greek
diploma of King (and saint) Stephen of Hungary : ἐγὼ Στέφανος Χριστιανὸς ὁ καὶ κράλ
πάσης Οὐγγρίας.   It is cited in Hunfalvy's Magyarország Ethnographiája, p. 322.]

different nature of foreign and civil war. "The former," said
he, "is the external warmth of summer, always tolerable, and
often beneficial; the latter is the deadly heat of a fever, which
consumes without a remedy the vitals of the constitution." [30]

**Victory of Cantacuzene**

The introduction of barbarians and savages into the contests of civilised nations is a measure pregnant with shame and
mischief; which the interest of the moment may compel, but
which is reprobated by the best principles of humanity and
reason. It is the practice of both sides to accuse their enemies
of the guilt of the first alliances; and those who fail in their
negotiations are loudest in their censure of the example which
they envy and would gladly imitate. The Turks of Asia were
less barbarous, perhaps, than the shepherds of Bulgaria and
Servia; [31] but their religion rendered them the implacable foes
of Rome and Christianity. To acquire the friendship of their
emirs, the two factions vied with each other in baseness and
profusion; the dexterity of Cantacuzene obtained the preference;

[30] Nic. Gregoras, l. xii. c. 14. It is surprising that Cantacuzene has not inserted
this just and lively image in his own writings.

[31] [The author does not seem to realise, he certainly has not brought out, the
dominant position of Servia at this time under its king Stephen Dushan, a name
which deserves a place in the history of the Fall of the Roman Empire. Servia
was the strongest power in the peninsula under Stephen (1331-1355), and its
boundaries extended from the Danube to the gulf of Arta. "He was a man of
great ambition and was celebrated for his gigantic stature and personal courage.
His subjects boasted of his liberality and success in war; his enemies reproached
him with faithlessness and cruelty. He had driven his father Stephen VII. [Urosh
III.] from the throne, and the old man had been murdered in prison by the rebellious
nobles of Servia, who feared lest a reconciliation should take place with his son.
Stephen Dushan passed seven years of his youth at Constantinople, where he
became acquainted with all the defects of the Byzantine government and with all the
vices of Greek society. The circumstances in which the rival Emperors were placed
during the year 1345 were extremely favourable to his ambitious projects, and he
seized the opportunity to extend his conquests in every direction. To the east he
rendered himself master of the whole valley of the Strymon, took the large and
flourishing city of Serres and garrisoned all the fortresses as far as the wall that
defended the pass of Christopolis. He extended his dominions along the shores of
the Adriatic, and to the south he carried his arms to the gulf of Ambracia. He
subdued the Vallachians of Thessaly, and placed strong garrisons in Achrida,
Kastoria and Joannina. Flushed with victory he at last formed the ambitious
scheme of depriving the Greeks of their political and ecclesiastical supremacy in
the Eastern Empire and transferring them to the Servians" (Finlay, iv. p. 441-2).
In 1346 he was crowned at Skopia as "Tsar of the Serbs and Greeks," and gave
his son the title of Kral; and he raised his archbishop to the rank of Patriarch.
The prosperity of his reign is better shown by the growth of trade in the Servian
towns than by the increase of Servian territory. Moreover Stephen did for Servia
what Yaroslav did for Russia; he drew up a code of laws, which might be quoted
to modify Gibbon's contemptuous references to the Servians as barbarians. This
Zakonik has been repeatedly edited by Shafarik, Miklosich, Novakovich and
Zigel.]

but the succour and victory were dearly purchased by the marriage of his daughter with an infidel, the captivity of many thousand Christians, and the passage of the Ottomans into Europe, the last and fatal stroke in the fall of the Roman empire. The inclining scale was decided in his favour by the death of [A.D. 1345, June 11] Apocaucus, the just, though singular, retribution of his crimes. A crowd of nobles or plebeians, whom he feared or hated, had been seized by his orders in the capital and the provinces ; and the old palace of Constantine was assigned for the place of their confinement. Some alterations in raising the walls and narrowing the cells had been ingeniously contrived to prevent their escape and aggravate their misery ; and the work was incessantly pressed by the daily visits of the tyrant. His guards watched at the gate, and, as he stood in the inner court to overlook the architects, without fear or suspicion, he was assaulted and laid breathless on the ground, by two resolute prisoners of the Palæologian race,[32] who were armed with sticks and animated by despair. On the rumour of revenge and liberty, the captive multitude broke their fetters, fortified their prison, and exposed from the battlements the tyrant's head, presuming on the favour of the people and the clemency of the empress. Anne of Savoy might rejoice in the fall of an haughty and ambitious minister ; but, while she delayed to resolve or to act, the populace, more especially the mariners, were excited by the widow of the Great Duke to a sedition, an assault, and a massacre. The prisoners (of whom the far greater part were guiltless or inglorious of the deed) escaped to a neighbouring church ; they were slaughtered at the foot of the altar ; and in his death the monster was not less bloody and venomous than in his life. Yet his talents alone upheld the cause of the young emperor ; and his surviving associates, suspicious of each other, abandoned the conduct of the war, and rejected the fairest terms of accommodation. In the beginning of the dispute, the empress felt and complained that she was deceived by the enemies of Cantacuzene ; the patriarch was employed to preach against the forgiveness of injuries ; and her promise of immortal hatred was sealed by an oath under the penalty of excommunication.[33]

[32] The two avengers were both Palæologi, who might resent, with royal indignation, the shame of their chains. The tragedy of Apocaucus may deserve a peculiar reference to Cantacuzene (l. iii. c. 86 [*leg*. 87-8]) and Nic. Gregoras (l. xiv. c. 10).

[33] Cantacuzene accuses the patriarch, and spares the empress, the mother of his sovereign (l. iii. 33, 34), against whom Nic. Gregoras expresses a particular animosity (l. xiv. 10, 11 ; xv. 5). It is true that they do not speak exactly of the same time.

But Anne soon learned to hate without a teacher : she beheld the misfortunes of the empire with the indifference of a stranger : her jealousy was exasperated by the competition of a rival empress ; and, on the first symptoms of a more yielding temper, she threatened the patriarch to convene a synod and degrade him from his office. Their incapacity and discord would have afforded the most decisive advantage ; but the civil war was protracted by the weakness of both parties ; and the moderation of Cantacuzene has not escaped the reproach of timidity and indolence. He successively recovered the provinces and cities ; [34] and the realm of his pupil was measured by the walls of Constantinople ; but the metropolis alone counterbalanced the rest of the empire ; nor could he attempt that important conquest, till he had secured in his favour the public voice and a private correspondence. An Italian, of the name of Facciolati,[35] had succeeded to the office of Great Duke : the ships, the guards, and the golden gate were subject to his command ; but his

He re-enters Constantinople. A.D. 1347, January [February] 8

[34] [" The Greek Empire consisted of several detached provinces when Cantacuzenos seated himself on the throne ; and the inhabitants of these different parts could only communicate freely by sea. The direct intercourse by land, even between Constantinople and Thessalonica, by the Egnatian Way, was interrupted, for the Servian Emperor possessed Amphipolis, and all the country about the mouth of the Strymon from Philippi to the lake Bolbe. The nucleus of the imperial power consisted of the city of Constantinople and the greater part of Thrace. On the Asiatic side of the Bosphorus, the Greek possessions were confined to the suburb of Skutari, a few forts and a narrow strip of coast extending from Chalcedon to the Black Sea. In Thrace the frontier extended from Sozopolis along the mountains to the south-west, passing about a day's journey to the north of Adrianople, and descending to the Aegean Sea at the pass and fortress of Christopolis. It included the districts of Morrah and the Thracian Chalkidike [of which Gratianopolis was the chief town]. The second portion of the Empire in importance consisted of the rich and populous city of Thessalonica, with the western part of the Macedonian Chalkidike and its three peninsulas of Cassandra, Longos and Agionoros [Ἅγιον Ὄρος]. By land it was entirely enclosed in the Servian empire. The third detached portion of the empire consisted of a part of Vallachian Thessaly and of Albanian Epirus, which formed a small imperial province interposed between the Servian empire and the Catalan duchy of Athens and Neopatras. The fourth consisted of the Greek province in the Peloponnesus, which obtained the name of the Despotat of Misithra, and embraced about one third of the peninsula. Cantacuzenos conferred the government on his second son, Manuel, who preserved his place by force of arms after his father was driven from the throne. The remaining fragments of the empire consisted of a few islands in the Aegean Sea which had escaped the domination of the Venetians, the Genoese, and the Knights of St. John ; and of the cities of Philadelphia and Phocaea, which still recognised the suzerainty of Constantinople, though surrounded by the territories of the emirs of Aidin and Saroukhan. Such were the relics of the Byzantine empire." Finlay, iv. p. 447-8.]

[35] The traitor and treason are revealed by Nic. Gregoras (l. xv. c. 8), but the name is more discreetly suppressed by his great accomplice (Cantacuzen. l. iii. c. 99).

humble ambition was bribed to become the instrument of treachery ; and the revolution was accomplished without danger or bloodshed. Destitute of the powers of resistance or the hope of relief, the inflexible Anne would have still defended the palace, and have smiled to behold the capital in flames, rather than in the possession of a rival. She yielded to the prayers of her friends and enemies ; and the treaty was dictated by the conqueror, who professed a loyal and zealous attachment to the son of his benefactor. The marriage of his daughter with John Palæologus was at length consummated : the hereditary right of the pupil was acknowledged ; but the sole administration during ten years was vested in the guardian. Two emperors and three empresses were seated on the Byzantine throne ; and a general amnesty quieted the apprehensions, and confirmed the property, of the most guilty subjects. The festival of the coronation and nuptials was celebrated with the appearance of concord and magnificence, and both were equally fallacious. During the late troubles, the treasures of the state, and even the palace, had been alienated or embezzled : the royal banquet was served in pewter or earthenware ; and such was the proud poverty of the times that the absence of gold and jewels was supplied by the paltry artifices of glass and gilt leather.[36]

I hasten to conclude the personal history of John Cantacu- zene.[37] He triumphed and reigned ; but his reign and triumph were clouded by the discontent of his own and the adverse faction. His followers might style the general amnesty an act of pardon for his enemies and of oblivion for his friends : [38] in his cause their estates had been forfeited or plundered ; and, as they wandered naked and hungry through the streets, they cursed the selfish generosity of a leader who, on the throne of the empire, might relinquish without merit his private inherit- ance. The adherents of the empress blushed to hold their lives and fortunes by the precarious favour of an usurper ; and the

Reign of John Cantacuzene. A.D. 1347, Jan. 8—A.D. 1355, January

---

[36] Nic. Greg. l. xv. 11. There were, however, some pearls, but very thinly sprinkled. The rest of the stones had only παντοδαπὴν χροιὰν πρὸς τὸ διαυγές.

[37] From his return to Constantinople, Cantacuzene continues his history, and that of the empire, one year beyond the abdication of his son Matthew, A.D. 1357 (l. iv. c. 1-50, p. 705-911). Nicephorus Gregoras ends with the synod of Constanti- nople, in the year 1351 (l. xxii. c. 3, p. 660, the rest, to the conclusion of the xxivth book, p. 717, is all controversy) ; and his fourteen last books are still Mss. in the king of France's library. [See Appendix 1.]

[38] The emperor (Cantacuzen. l. iv. c. 1) represents his own virtues, and Nic. Gregoras (l. xv. c. 11) the complaints of his friends, who suffered by its effects. I have lent them the words of our poor cavaliers after the Restoration.

thirst of revenge was concealed by a tender concern for the succession, and even the safety, of her son. They were justly alarmed by a petition of the friends of Cantacuzene, that they might be released from their oath of allegiance to the Palæologi and entrusted with the defence of some cautionary towns : a measure supported with argument and eloquence ; and which was rejected (says the Imperial historian) "by *my* sublime and almost incredible virtue ". His repose was disturbed by the sound of plots and seditions ; and he trembled lest the lawful prince should be stolen away by some foreign or domestic enemy, who would inscribe his name and his wrongs in the banners of rebellion. As the son of Andronicus advanced in the years of manhood, he began to feel and to act for himself ; and his rising ambition was rather stimulated than checked by the imitation of his father's vices. If we may trust his own professions, Cantacuzene laboured with honest industry to correct these sordid and sensual appetites, and to raise the mind of the young prince to a level with his fortune. In the Servian expedition [39] the two emperors showed themselves in cordial harmony to the troops and provinces ; and the younger colleague was initiated by the elder in the mysteries of war and government. After the conclusion of the peace, Palæologus was left at Thessalonica, a royal residence and a frontier station, to secure by his absence the peace of Constantinople, and to withdraw his youth from the temptations of a luxurious capital. But the distance weakened the powers of control, and the son of Andronicus was surrounded with artful or unthinking companions, who taught him to hate his guardian, to deplore his exile, and to vindicate his rights. A private treaty with the cral or despot of Servia was soon followed by an open revolt ; and Cantacuzene, on the throne of the elder Andronicus, defended the cause of age and prerogative, which in his youth he had so vigorously attacked. At his request, the empress-mother undertook the voyage of Thessalonica, and the office of mediation : she returned without success ; and

[39] [One important consequence of the Servian conquests, and the wars connected therewith, may be noticed here,—the Albanian invasion of Greece. The highlanders of northern Epirus, descendants of the ancient Illyrians, and speaking an idiom which represents the old Illyrian language, descended into Thessaly, laid it waste, and were a terror to the Catalan adventurers themselves. They settled in the Thessalian mountains and spread over Greece, where they formed a new element in the population. The Albanian settlers speak their own language, amid the surrounding Greeks, to the present day, therein differing remarkably from the Slavonic settlers, who adopted the Greek tongue. For the Albanians, see Hahn, Albanesische Studien.]

unless Anne of Savoy was instructed by adversity, we may doubt
the sincerity, or at least the fervour, of her zeal. While the
regent grasped the sceptre with a firm and vigorous hand, she
had been instructed to declare that the ten years of his legal
administration would soon elapse ; and that, after a full trial of
the vanity of the world, the emperor Cantacuzene sighed for the
repose of a cloister, and was ambitious only of an heavenly crown.
Had these sentiments been genuine, his voluntary abdication
would have restored the peace of the empire, and his conscience
would have been relieved by an act of justice. Palæologus alone *John Palæolo-*
was responsible for his future government ; and, whatever might *gus takes up arms against*
be his vices, they were surely less formidable than the calamities *him. A.D. 1353*
of a civil war, in which the barbarians and infidels were again
invited to assist the Greeks in their mutual destruction. By the
arms of the Turks, who now struck a deep and everlasting root
in Europe, Cantacuzene prevailed in the third conquest in which
he had been involved ; and the young emperor, driven from the
sea and land, was compelled to take shelter among the Latins of
the isle of Tenedos. His insolence and obstinacy provoked the
victor to a step which must render the quarrel irreconcileable ;
and the association of his son Matthew, whom he invested with
the purple, established the succession in the family of the Cantacuzeni. But Constantinople was still attached to the blood of
her ancient princes ; and this last injury accelerated the restoration of the rightful heir. A noble Genoese espoused the cause
of Palæologus, obtained a promise of his sister, and achieved the
revolution with two galleys and two thousand five hundred
auxiliaries. Under the pretence of distress they were admitted
into the lesser port ; a gate was opened, and the Latin shout of
" Long life and victory to the emperor John Palæologus ! " was
answered by a general rising in his favour. A numerous and
loyal party yet adhered to the standard of Cantacuzene ; but he
asserts in his history (does he hope for belief ?) that his tender
conscience rejected the assurance of conquest : that, in free
obedience to the voice of religion and philosophy, he descended
from the throne and embraced with pleasure the monastic habit
and profession.[40] So soon as he ceased to be a prince, his suc- *Abdication of*
cessor was not unwilling that he should be a saint ; the remainder *Cantacuzene. A.D. 1355,*
of his life was devoted to piety and learning ; in the cells of *January*

[40] The awkward apology of Cantacuzene (l. iv. c. 39-42), who relates, with
visible confusion, his own downfall, may be supplied by the less accurate but more
honest narratives of Matthew Villani (l. iv. c. 46, in the Script. Rerum Ital. tom.
xiv. p. 268) and Ducas (c. 10, 11).

Constantinople and mount Athos, the monk Joasaph was respected as the temporal and spiritual father of the emperor ; and, if he issued from his retreat, it was as the minister of peace, to subdue the obstinacy, and solicit the pardon, of his rebellious son.[41]

Dispute concerning the light of mount Thabor. A.D. 1341-1351

Yet in the cloister, the mind of Cantacuzene was still exercised by theological war. He sharpened a controversial pen against the Jews and Mahometans ; [42] and in every state he defended with equal zeal the divine light of mount Thabor, a memorable question which consummates the religious follies of the Greeks. The fakirs of India [43] and the monks of the Oriental church were alike persuaded that in total abstraction of the faculties of the mind and body the purer spirit may ascend to the enjoyment and vision of the Deity. The opinion and practice of the monasteries of mount Athos [44] will be best represented in the words of an abbot who flourished in the eleventh century. "When thou art alone in thy cell," says the ascetic teacher, " shut thy door, and seat thyself in a corner ; raise thy mind above all things vain and transitory ; recline thy beard and chin on thy breast ; turn thy eyes and thy thoughts towards the middle of thy belly, the region of the navel ; and search the place of the heart, the seat of the soul. At first, all will be dark and comfortless ; but, if you persevere day and night, you will feel an ineffable joy ; and no sooner has the soul discovered the place of the heart than it is involved in a mystic and etherial light." This light, the production of a distempered fancy, the creature of an empty stomach and an empty brain, was adored by the Quietists as the pure and perfect essence of God himself ; and, as long as the folly was confined to mount Athos,

['Ησυχά-στaι]

[41] Cantacuzene, in the year 1375, was honoured with a letter from the pope (Fleury, Hist. Ecclés. tom. xx. p. 250). His death is placed, by a respectable authority, on the 20th of November, 1411 (Ducange, Fam. Byzant. p. 260). But, if he were of the age of his companion Andronicus the Younger, he must have lived 116 years : a rare instance of longevity, which in so illustrious a person would have attracted universal notice. [Date of death : A.D. 1383.]

[42] His four discourses, or books, were printed at Basil, 1543 (Fabric. Bibliot. Græc. tom. vi. p. 473) [reprinted in Migne, Patr. Gr. vol. 154, p. 372 *sqq.*]. He composed them to satisfy a proselyte who was assaulted with letters from his friends of Ispahan. Cantacuzene had read the Koran ; but I understand from Maracci that he adopts the vulgar prejudices and fables against Mahomet and his religion.

[43] See the Voyages de Bernier, tom. i. p. 127.

[44] Mosheim, Institut. Hist. Eccles. p. 522, 523. Fleury, Hist. Ecclés. tom. xx. p. 22, 24, 107-114, &c. The former unfolds the causes with the judgment of a philosopher, the latter transcribes and translates with the prejudices of a Catholic priest.

the simple solitaries were not inquisitive how the divine essence could be a *material* substance, or how an *immaterial* substance could be perceived by the eyes of the body. But in the reign of the younger Andronicus these monasteries were visited by Barlaam,[45] a Calabrian monk, who was equally skilled in philosophy and theology ; who possessed the languages of the Greeks and Latins ; and whose versatile genius could maintain their opposite creeds, according to the interest of the moment. The indiscretion of an ascetic revealed to the curious traveller the secrets of mental prayer ; and Barlaam embraced the opportunity of ridiculing the Quietists, who placed the soul in the navel ; of accusing the monks of mount Athos of heresy and blasphemy. His attack compelled the more learned to renounce or dissemble the simple devotion of their brethren ; and Gregory Palamas introduced a scholastic distinction between the essence and operation of God.[46] His inaccessible essence dwells in the midst of an uncreated and eternal light ; and this beatific vision of the saints had been manifested to the disciples on mount Thabor, in the transfiguration of Christ. Yet this distinction could not escape the reproach of polytheism ; the eternity of the light of Thabor was fiercely denied ; and Barlaam still charged the Palamites with holding two eternal substances, a visible and an invisible God. From the rage of the monks of mount Athos, who threatened his life, the Calabrian retired to Constantinople, where his smooth and specious manners introduced him to the favour of the great domestic and the emperor. The court and the city were involved in this theological dispute, [Barlaam condemned . which flamed amidst the civil war ; but the doctrine of Bar-Synod of 1341] laam was disgraced by his flight and apostacy ; the Palamites triumphed ; and their adversary, the patriarch John of Apri, was deposed by the consent of the adverse factions of the state. In the character of emperor and theologian, Cantacuzene presided

---

[45] Basnage (in Canisii Antiq. Lectiones, tom. iv. p. 363-368) has investigated the character and story of Barlaam. The duplicity of his opinions had inspired some doubts of the identity of his person. See likewise Fabricius (Bibliot. Græc. tom. x. p. 427-432). [G. Mandolori, Fra Barlaamo Calabrese, maestro del Petrarca, 1888.]

[46] [The chief upholders of Barlaam were Gregory Akindynos (for whose works see Migne, P. G. vol. 151) and Nicephorus Gregoras, whose Φλωρέντιος ἢ περὶ σοφίας (in Jahns Archiv, 10, p. 485 *sqq.*, 1844) is founded on a dispute with Barlaam. The chief opponent was Gregory Palamas, who had lived at Athos, and came forward as defender of the Hesychasts, to whose doctrine he gave a dogmatic basis (cp. Ehrhard, ap. Krumbacher, p. 103). Some of his works are printed in Migne, P. G. vols. 150, 151 ; a large number are happily buried in Mss.]

in the synod of the Greek church, which established, as an article of faith, the uncreated light of mount Thabor ; and, after so many insults, the reason of mankind was slightly wounded by the addition of a single absurdity. Many rolls of paper or parchment have been blotted ; and the impenitent sectaries, who refused to subscribe the orthodox creed, were deprived of the honours of Christian burial ; but in the next age the question was forgotten ; nor can I learn that the axe or the faggot were employed for the extirpation of the Barlaamite heresy.[47]

Establishment of the Genoese at Pera or Galata. A.D. 1261-1347

For the conclusion of this chapter I have reserved the Genoese war, which shook the throne of Cantacuzene and betrayed the debility of the Greek empire. The Genoese, who, after the recovery of Constantinople, were seated in the suburb of Pera or Galata, received that honourable fief from the bounty of the emperor. They were indulged in the use of their laws and magistrates ; but they submitted to the duties of vassals and subjects : the forcible word of *liegemen* [48] was borrowed from the Latin jurisprudence ; and their *podestà*, or chief, before he entered on his office, saluted the Emperor with loyal acclamations and vows of fidelity. Genoa sealed a firm alliance with the Greeks ; and, in case of a defensive war, a supply of fifty empty galleys, and a succour of fifty galleys completely armed and manned, was promised by the republic to the empire. In the revival of a naval force it was the aim of Michael Palæologus to deliver himself from a foreign aid ; and his vigorous government contained the Genoese of Galata within those limits which the insolence of wealth and freedom provoked them to exceed. A sailor threatened that they should soon be masters of Constantinople, and slew the Greek who resented this national affront ; and an armed vessel, after refusing to salute the palace, was guilty of some acts of piracy in the Black Sea. Their countrymen threatened to support their cause ; but the long and open village of Galata was instantly surrounded by the Imperial troops ; till, in the moment of the assault, the pros-

---

[47] See Cantacuzene (l. ii. c. 39, 40 ; l. iv. c. 3, 23-25) and Nic. Gregoras (l. xi. c. 10 ; l. xv. 3, 7, &c.), whose last books, from the 19th to the 24th, are almost confined to a subject so interesting to the authors. Boivin (in Vit. Nic. Gregoræ), from the unpublished books, and Fabricius (Bibliot. Græc. tom. x. p. 462-473), or rather Montfaucon, from the Mss. of the Coislin Library, have added some facts and documents. [Sauli, Colonia dei Genovesi in Galata.]

[48] Pachymer (l. v. c. 10) very properly explains λιζίους (*ligios*) by ἰδίους. The use of these words in the Greek and Latin of the feudal times, may be amply understood from the Glossaries of Ducange (Græc. p. 811, 812, Latin. tom. iv. p. 109-111).

trate Genoese implored the clemency of their sovereign. The defenceless situation which secured their obedience exposed them to the attack of their Venetian rivals, who, in the reign of the elder Andronicus, presumed to violate the majesty of the throne. On the approach of their fleets, the Genoese, with their families and effects, retired into the city; their empty habitations were reduced to ashes; and the feeble prince, who had viewed the destruction of his suburb, expressed his resentment, not by arms, but by ambassadors. This misfortune, however, was advantageous to the Genoese, who obtained, and imperceptibly abused, the dangerous licence of surrounding Galata with a strong wall; of introducing into the ditch the waters of the sea; of erecting lofty turrets; and of mounting a train of military engines on the rampart. The narrow bounds in which they had been circumscribed were insufficient for the growing colony; each day they acquired some addition of landed property; and the adjacent hills were covered with their villas and castles, which they joined and protected by new fortifications.[49] The navigation and trade of the Euxine was the patrimony of the Greek emperors, who commanded the narrow entrance, the gates, as it were, of that inland sea. In the reign of Michael Palæologus, their prerogative was acknowledged by the sultan of Egypt, who solicited and obtained the liberty of sending an annual ship for the purchase of slaves in Circassia and the Lesser Tartary: a liberty pregnant with mischief to the Christian cause, since these youths were transformed by education and discipline into the formidable Mamalukes.[50] From the colony of Pera the Genoese engaged with superior advantage in the lucrative trade of the Black Sea; and their industry supplied the Greeks with fish and corn, two articles of food almost equally important to a superstitious people. The spontaneous bounty of nature appears to have bestowed the harvests of the Ukraine, the produce of a rude and savage

*Their trade and insolence*

---

[49] The establishment and progress of the Genoese at Pera, or Galata, is described by Ducange (C. P. Christiana, l. i. p. 68, 69), from the Byzantine historians, Pachymer (l. ii. c. 35, l. v. 10, 30, l. ix. 15, l. xii. 6, 9), Nicephorus Gregoras (l. v. c. 4, l. vi. c. 11, l. ix. c. 5, l. xi. c. 1, l. xv. c. 1, 6), and Cantacuzene (l. i. c. 12, l. ii. c. 29, &c.). [The golden Bulls of Michael VIII. (A.D. 1261) and Andronicus the Elder (A.D. 1304) granting privileges to the Genoese will be found in Zachariä, Jus Græco-Romanum, iii. p. 574 *sqq.*, p. 623 *sqq.*]

[50] Both Pachymer (l. iii. c. 3-5) and Nic. Gregoras (l. iv. c. 7) understand and deplore the effects of this dangerous indulgence. Bibars, sultan of Egypt, himself a Tartar, but a devout Musulman, obtained from the children of Zingis the permission to build a stately mosque in the capital of Crimea (De Guignes, Hist. des Huns, tom. iii. p. 343).

husbandry; and the endless exportation of salt fish and caviar
is annually renewed by the enormous sturgeons that are caught
at the mouth of the Don, or Tanais, in their last station of
the rich mud and shallow water of the Mæotis.[51]   The waters
of the Oxus, the Caspian, the Volga, and the Don opened
a rare and laborious passage for the gems and spices of India;
and, after three months' march, the caravans of Carizme met
the Italian vessels in the harbours of Crimea.[52]   These various
branches of trade were monopolized by the diligence and the
power of the Genoese.   Their rivals of Venice and Pisa were
forcibly expelled; the natives were awed by the castles and
cities, which arose on the foundations of their humble factories;
and their principal establishment of Caffa[53] was besieged without effect by the Tartar powers.   Destitute of a navy, the
Greeks were oppressed by these haughty merchants, who fed
or famished Constantinople, according to their interest.   They
proceeded to usurp the customs, the fishery, and even the toll,
of the Bosphorus; and, while they derived from these objects
a revenue of two hundred thousand pieces of gold, a remnant
of thirty thousand was reluctantly allowed to the emperor.[54]
The colony of Pera or Galata acted, in peace and war, as an
independent state; and, as it will happen in distant settlements, the Genoese podestà too often forgot that he was the
servant of his own masters.

Their war
with the em-
peror Canta-
cuzene.  A.D.
1348

These usurpations were encouraged by the weakness of the
elder Andronicus, and by the civil wars that afflicted his age
and the minority of his grandson.   The talents of Cantacuzene
were employed to the ruin, rather than the restoration, of the
empire; and after his domestic victory he was condemned to
an ignominious trial, whether the Greeks or the Genoese should
reign in Constantinople.   The merchants of Pera were offended
by his refusal of some contiguous lands, some commanding

[51] Chardin (Voyages en Perse, tom. i. p. 48) was assured at Caffa that these
fishes were sometimes twenty-four or twenty-six feet long, weighed eight or nine
hundred pounds, and yielded three or four quintals of caviar.   The corn of the
Bosphorus had supplied the Athenians in [and long before] the time of Demosthenes.

[52] De Guignes, Hist. des Huns, tom. iii. p. 343, 344.   Viaggi di Ramusio, tom.
i. fol. 400.   But this land or water carriage could only be practicable when Tartary was united under a wise and powerful monarch.

[53] Nic. Gregoras (l. xiii. c. 12) is judicious and well-informed on the trade and
colonies of the Black Sea.   Chardin describes the present ruins of Caffa, where,
in forty days, he saw above 400 sail employed in the corn and fish trade (Voyages
en Perse, tom. i. p. 46-48).

[54] See Nic. Gregoras, l. xvii. c. 1.

heights, which they proposed to cover with new fortifications; and in the absence of the emperor, who was detained at De- motica by sickness, they ventured to brave the debility of a female reign. A Byzantine vessel, which had presumed to fish at the mouth of the harbour, was sunk by these audacious strangers; the fishermen were murdered. Instead of suing for pardon, the Genoese demanded satisfaction; required, in an haughty strain, that the Greeks should renounce the exercise of navigation; and encountered, with regular arms, the first sallies of the popular indignation. They instantly occupied the debateable land; and by the labour of a whole people, of either sex and of every age, the wall was raised, and the ditch was sunk, with incredible speed. At the same time they attacked and burnt two Byzantine galleys; while the three others, the remainder of the Imperial navy, escaped from their hand; the habitations without the gates, or along the shore, were pillaged and destroyed; and the care of the regent, of the empress Irene, was confined to the preservation of the city. The return of Cantacuzene dispelled the public consternation: the em- peror inclined to peaceful counsels; but he yielded to the obstinacy of his enemies, who rejected all reasonable terms, and to the ardour of his subjects, who threatened, in the style of scripture, to break them in pieces like a potter's vessel. Yet they reluctantly paid the taxes that he imposed for the con- struction of ships and the expenses of the war; and, as the two nations were masters, the one of the land, the other of the sea, Constantinople and Pera were pressed by the evils of a mutual siege. The merchants of the colony, who had believed that a few days would terminate the war, already murmured at their losses; the succours from their mother-country were delayed by the factions of Genoa; and the most cautious em- braced the opportunity of a Rhodian vessel to remove their families and effects from the scene of hostility. In the spring, the Byzantine fleet, seven galleys and a train of smaller vessels, issued from the mouth of the harbour and steered in a single line along the shore of Pera; unskilfully presenting their sides to the beaks of the adverse squadron. The crews were com- posed of peasants and mechanics; nor was their ignorance compensated by the native courage of barbarians. The wind was strong, the waves were rough; and no sooner did the Greeks perceive a distant and inactive enemy, than they leaped headlong into the sea, from a doubtful to an inevitable peril. The troops that marched to the attack of the lines of Pera were

Destruction of his fleet. A.D. 1349

struck at the same moment with a similar panic; and the
Genoese were astonished, and almost ashamed, at their double
victory. Their triumphant vessels, crowned with flowers, and
dragging after them the captive galleys, repeatedly passed and
repassed before the palace. The only virtue of the emperor
was patience, and the hope of revenge his sole consolation.
Yet the distress of both parties interposed a temporary agreement; and the shame of the empire was disguised by a thin
veil of dignity and power. Summoning the chiefs of the colony,
Cantacuzene affected to despise the trivial object of the debate;
and, after a mild reproof, most liberally granted the lands, which
had been previously resigned to the seeming custody of his
officers.[55]

Victory of the
Genoese over
the Venetians
and Greeks.
A.D. 1352, Feb.
13

But the emperor was soon solicited to violate the treaty, and
to join his arms with the Venetians, the perpetual enemies of
Genoa and her colonies. While he compared the reasons of
peace and war, his moderation was provoked by a wanton insult
of the inhabitants of Pera, who discharged from their rampart a
large stone that fell in the midst of Constantinople. On his just
complaint, they coldly blamed the imprudence of their engineer;
but the next day the insult was repeated, and they exulted in a
second proof that the royal city was not beyond the reach of
their artillery. Cantacuzene instantly signed his treaty with the
Venetians; but the weight of the Roman empire was scarcely
felt in the balance of these opulent and powerful republics.[56]
From the straits of Gibraltar to the mouth of the Tanais, their
fleets encountered each other with various success; and a memorable battle was fought in the narrow sea, under the walls of
Constantinople. It would not be an easy task to reconcile the
accounts of the Greeks, the Venetians, and the Genoese;[57] and,
while I depend on the narrative of an impartial historian,[58] I shall

[55] The events of this war are related by Cantacuzene (l. iv. c. 11) with obscurity
and confusion, and by Nic. Gregoras (l. xvii. c. 1-7) in a clear and honest narrative.
The priest was less responsible than the prince for the defeat of the fleet.

[56] The second war is darkly told by Cantacuzene (l. iv. c 18, p. 24, 25, 28-32),
who wishes to disguise what he dares not deny. I regret this part of Nic. Gregoras,
which is still in Ms. at Paris. [It has since been edited, see Appendix 1.]

[57] Muratori (Annali d'Italia, tom. xii. p. 144) refers to the most ancient Chronicles
of Venice (Caresinus [Raffaino Carasini; ob. 1390], the continuator of Andrew
Dandolus, tom. xii. p. 421, 422), and Genoa (George Stella [ob. 1420], Annales
Genuenses, tom. xvii. p. 1091, 1092); both which I have diligently consulted in his
great Collection of the Historians of Italy.

[58] See the Chronicle of Matteo Villani of Florence, l. ii. c. 59, 60, p. 145-147, c.
74, 75, p. 156, 157, in Muratori's Collection, tom. xiv.

borrow from each nation the facts that redound to their own disgrace and the honour of their foes. The Venetians, with their allies, the Catalans, had the advantage of number; and their fleet, with the poor addition of eight Byzantine galleys, amounted to seventy-five sail; the Genoese did not exceed sixty-four; but in those times their ships of war were distinguished by the superiority of their size and strength. The names and families of their naval commanders, Pisani and Doria, are illustrious in the annals of their country; but the personal merit of the former was eclipsed by the fame and abilities of his rival. They engaged in tempestuous weather; and the tumultuary conflict was continued from the dawn to the extinction of light. The enemies of the Genoese applaud their prowess; the friends of the Venetians are dissatisfied with their behaviour; but all parties agree in praising the skill and boldness of the Catalans, who, with many wounds, sustained the brunt of the action. On the separation of the fleets, the event might appear doubtful; but the thirteen Genoese galleys, that had been sunk or taken, were compensated by a double loss of the allies: of fourteen Venetians, ten Catalans, and two Greeks; and even the grief of the conquerors expressed the assurance and habit of more decisive victories. Pisani confessed his defeat by retiring into a fortified harbour, from whence, under the pretext of the orders of the senate, he steered with a broken and flying squadron for the isle of Candia, and abandoned to his rivals the sovereignty of the sea. In a public epistle,[59] addressed to the doge and senate, Petrarch employs his eloquence to reconcile the maritime powers, the two luminaries of Italy. The orator celebrates the valour and victory of the Genoese, the first of men in the exercise of naval war; he drops a tear on the misfortunes of their Venetian brethren; but he exhorts them to pursue with fire and sword the base and perfidious Greeks; to purge the metropolis of the East from the heresy with which it was infected. Deserted by their friends, the Greeks were incapable of resistance; and, three months after the battle, the emperor Cantacuzene solicited and subscribed a treaty, which for ever banished the Venetians and Catalans, and granted to the Genoese a monopoly of trade and

*[Battle of Brachophagos or Prote]*

*Their treaty with the empire. May 6*

---

[59] The Abbé de Sade (Mémoires sur la Vie de Pétrarque, tom. iii. p. 257-263) translates this letter, which he had copied from a Ms. in the king of France's library. Though a servant of the Duke of Milan, Petrarch pours forth his astonishment and grief at the defeat and despair of the Genoese in the following year (p. 323-332).

almost a right of dominion.[60]  The Roman empire (I smile in transcribing the name) might soon have sunk into a province of Genoa, if the ambition of the republic had not been checked by the ruin of her freedom and naval power.  A long contest of one hundred and thirty years was determined by the triumph of Venice ; and the factions of the Genoese compelled them to seek for domestic peace under the protection of a foreign lord, the duke of Milan, or the French king.  Yet the spirit of commerce survived that of conquest ; and the colony of Pera still awed the capital, and navigated the Euxine, till it was involved by the Turks in the final servitude of Constantinople itself.

[60] [Text (the Latin copy) in Sauli, Colonia dei Genovesi in Galata, ii. 216 ; and in Zachariä, Jus Graeco-Romanum, iii. 706. ]

# APPENDIX

## 1. AUTHORITIES

### GREEK SOURCES

PHOTIUS was born at Constantinople about A.D. 820. He was related by blood to the Patriarch Tarasius, and by marriage to the Empress Theodora (wife of Theophilus). He had enjoyed an excellent training in grammar and philology, and devoted his early years to teaching, a congenial employment which he did not abandon after he had been promoted to the Patriarchate (A.D. 858). "His house was still a salon of culture, the resort of the curious who desired instruction. Books were read aloud and the master of the house criticized their style and their matter."[1] He was an indefatigable collector of books, and his learning probably surpassed that of any of the mediæval Greeks (not excepting Psellus). For his historical importance and public career see above, p. 369-70.

Of his profane works the most famous—which Gibbon singles out—was his *Myriobiblon* or *Bibliotheca*, written (before A.D. 858) for his brother Tarasius, who had been absent in the East and desired information about the books which had been read and discussed in the circle of Photius while he was away. It contains most valuable extracts from historians whose works are no longer extant, and the criticisms of Photius are marked by acuteness and independence. The *Lexicon*, compiled doubtless by a secretary or pupil, is a later work.[2] There are about 260 extant letters (in Migne, P. G. vol. 102; and edition by Valettas, 1864).

A recent critic has said that the importance of Photius as a theologian has been often exaggerated.[3] Of his theological writings only those pertaining to the controversy of the day need be mentioned here. In the treatise On the Mystagogia of the Holy Ghost he has put together all the evidence from scripture and the Fathers in favour of the Greek doctrine, but assigns more weight to theological argument than to authority. This is characteristic of the man. It is also to be observed (as Ehrhard remarks) that he does not attack the Roman church directly; but he appeals to previous Popes as supporters of the true view, in opposition to Jerome, Augustine, &c.

Two of the homilies of Photius have historical importance as sources for the Russian invasion of A.D. 860. They were edited by P. Uspenski in 1864, and with improved text by A. Nauck in Lexicon Vindobonense, p. 201-232 (1867); reprinted in Müller's Frag. Hist. Gr. 5, p. 162 *sqq*.

The works of Photius (except the Lexicon) are collected in Migne's Patr. Gr. vols. 101-104. The chief work on Photius is that of J. Hergenröther, in 3 volumes: Photius, Patriarch von Konstantinopel, sein Leben, seine Schriften, und das griechische Schisma (1867-9), a learned, thorough, and impartial work.

The *Tactica* of the Emperor LEO VI. contains a great deal that is merely a re-edition of the Strategicon ascribed to the Emperor Maurice. The general

---

[1] Krumbacher, Gesch. der Byz. Litt. p. 516.  [2] Ed. S. A. Naber, 1864-5.
[3] Ehrhard, in Krumbacher's Byz. Litt. p 74.

organisation, the drill, the rules for marching and camping, the arms, are still the same as in the 6th century. But there is a great deal that is new. A good account and criticism of the work will be found in Mr. Oman's History of the Art of War, vol. 2, p. 184 *sqq*. "The reader is distinctly prepossessed in favour of Leo by the frank and handsome acknowledgment which he makes of the merits and services of his general, Nicephorus Phocas, whose successful tactics and new military devices are cited again and again with admiration. The best parts of his book are the chapters on organisation, recruiting. the services of transport and supply, and the methods required for dealing with the various barbarian neighbours of the empire. . . . The weakest point, on the other hand,—as is perhaps natural,—is that which deals with strategy. . . . Characteristic, too, of the author's want of aggressive energy, and of the defensive system which he made his policy. is the lack of directions for campaigns of invasion in an enemy's country. Leo contemplates raids on hostile soil, but not permanent conquests. . . . Another weak point is his neglect to support precept by example ; his directions would be much the clearer if he would supplement them by definite historical cases in which they had led to success" (*ib.*, p. 184-5).

Zachariä von Lingenthal propounded [4] the theory that the Leo to whom the title of the Tactics ascribes the authorship was not Leo VI. but Leo III., and that consequently the work belongs to the first half of the eighth century. But internal evidence is inconsistent with this theory.[5] Besides the references to Nicephorus Phocas mentioned above, the author speaks of "our father the Emperor Basil,' and describes his dealings with the Slavs, 18, § 101 ; the Bulgarians who were still heathen in the reign of Leo the Iconoclast appear as Christians in this treatise, 18, § 42, 44, and 61 ; the capture of Theodosiopolis from the Saracens (under Leo VI., cp. Const. Porph., de Adm. Imp. c. 45, p. 199-200, ed. Bonn) is mentioned.

The most interesting chapters of the work are c. 18, which contains an account of the military customs of the nations with which the empire was brought into hostile contact (Saracens, Bulgarians, Hungarians, Slavs, Franks), and c. 19, on naval warfare (see below, Appendix 5). [The edition of Meursius used by Gibbon is reprinted in Migne's Patr Gr. 107, p. 671 *sqq*.]

Only a part of the two Books De Cerimoniis aulae Byzantinae which pass under the name of CONSTANTINE PORPHYROGENNETOS is really due to that Emperor.

The first 83 chapters of Bk. I. represent the treatise on the *Court Ceremonies* which he compiled by putting together existing documents which prescribed the order of the various ceremonies. The work is arranged as follows : Chaps. 1-37, religious ceremonies (thus chap. 1 gives the order of processions to the Great Church —St. Sophia ; chap. 2, the ceremonies on Christmas Day ; chap. 3, those on the Epiphany, &c., in the order of the calendar) ; chaps. 38-44, the ceremonies on great secular occasions, such as the coronation of the Emperor and the Empress ; chaps. 45-59, ceremonies on the promotions of ministers and palace functionaries ; chaps. 60-64, an Emperor's funeral, and other solemnities ; chaps. 65-83, palace banquets, public games, and other ceremonies.[6]

The remaining chapters of Bk. I. are an excrescence and were added at a later date. Chaps. 84-95 are an extract from the work of Peter the Patrician who wrote under Justinian I. (cp. headings to chaps. 84 and 95). Chap. 96 contains an account of the inauguration of Nicephorus Phocas, and chap. 97 perhaps dates from the reign of Tzimisces.

There are two Appendices to Bk. I. concerning the proceedings to be adopted when an Emperor goes forth on a military expedition. Both date from the reign of Constantine VII. ; and the second (p. 455 *sqq*. ed. Bonn) is from the pen of Constantine himself.

---

[4] In Byz. Zeitschrift. ii. 606 *sqq*.; iii. 437 *sqq*.
[5] Which is accepted by K. Schenk, Byz. Zeitschrift, v. 298-9.
[6] C. 83 contains the famous Γοτθικον or Gothic Weihnachtspiel which has given rise to much discussion, German antiquarians vainly trying to find in the acclamations old German words.

The second Book is a much later compilation (perhaps put together in the early part of the eleventh century) in which some documents drawn up in the time of Constantine VII. have been incorporated. It professes (in the Preface, p. 516) to contain matters which had never been committed to writing. It contains the descriptions of many ceremonies ; but written documents have been interpolated, contrary to the intention of the writer of the Preface. Thus chaps. 44 and 45 contain the returns of the expenses, &c., of naval armaments ; chap. 50 contains a list of themes which belongs to the reign of Leo VI. ; chap. 52, a separate treatise on the order of precedence at Imperial banquets composed by Philotheus protospatharius in A.D. 900 ; chap. 54 is a list of patriarchs and metropolitans drawn up by Epiphanius of Cyprus.

The Ceremonies are included in the Bonn ed. of the Byzantine writers (1829), with Reiske's notes in a separate volume. On the composition of the work see A. Rambaud, L'empire grec au xme siècle, p. 128 sqq., also Krumbacher, Byz. Litt. p. 254-5 ; for the elucidation of the ceremonies, &c., D. Bieliaiev, Byzantina, vol. 2 (1893).

The work on the *Themes* (in 2 Books, see above, p. 66 sqq.) was composed while Romanus I. was still alive, and after, probably not very long after, A.D. 934 (see Rambaud, L'empire grec au dixième siècle, p. 165). For an Armenian general Melias is mentioned, who was alive in 934, as recently dead ; and the theme of Seleucia is noticed, which seems to have been formed after 934. For the contents of the book cp. below, Appendix 3.

The treatise on the *Administration of the Empire* is dealt with in a separate note below, Appendix 4.

George Codinus (probably 15th century) is merely a name, associated with three works : a short, worthless chronicle (ed. Bonn, 1843) ; an account of the offices of the Imperial Court and of St. Sophia, generally quoted as *De Officiis* (ed. Bonn, 1839) ; the Πατρια of Constantinople (ed. Bonn, 1843). But it is only with the third of these works that Codinus, whoever he was, can have any connexion. The Chronicle is anonymous in the Mss., and there is no reason for ascribing it to Codinus. The *De Officiis* is likewise anonymous, and the attribution of it to Codinus was due to the blunder of an editor ; it is a composition of the end of the 14th and beginning of the 15th century. As for the Πάτρια Κωνσταντινοπόλεως, Codinus may have been connected with it in the capacity of a copyist. Later Mss. give the work under his name. But he was no more than a copyist. The other Mss. do not know him, and the original anonymous work belongs to the end of the tenth century [7]—to the reign of Basil II.

The compilation, entitled the Πάτρια, consists of five distinct works : (1) on the founding of Constantinople and the origin of its various parts ; (2) the topography of the city ; (3) its works of art ; (4) its buildings (churches, palaces, hospitals, &c.) ; (5) the building of St. Sophia. In the reign of Alexius Comnenus the compilation was arranged in sections on a topographical plan ; and the famous "Anonymus," edited by Banduri (in the Imperium Orientale, vol. i.), is simply a copy of this Comnenian edition. The chief sources of the Patria are : (a) the Patria of Hesychius of Miletus ; (b) Παραστάσεις σύντομοι χρονικαί, an anonymous work composed between the reigns of Leo III. and Theophilus ; it has been edited recently (Munich, 1898) by Th. Preger, who is preparing an edition of the Patria ; (c) an anonymous narrative concerning St. Sophia (source of the last part of the treatise) ; (d) a lost chronicle.

EUSTATHIUS, educated at Constantinople, became Archbishop of Thessalonica in 1175 ; he died c. 1193. Besides his famous commentaries on Homer, his commentary on Pindar, and his paraphrase of the geographical poem of Dionysius, he composed an account of the Norman siege of Thessalonica in A.D. 1185. This

---

[7] The date A.D. 995 is furnished by a notice on p. 114, ed. B. The later Mss. contain some additions, which do not appear in the older.

original work was published by L. F. Tafel in A.D. 1832 (Eustathii Opuscula, i. p. 267-307) and reprinted by Bekker at the end of the Bonn ed. of Leo Grammaticus. There are also extant various speeches (*e.g.* a funeral oration by the Emperor Manuel) which have been published by Tafel either in his edition of the lesser works of Eustathius or in his treatise De Thessalonica ejusque agro (1839). A collection of letters (some not by Eustathius but by Psellus) is also published by Tafel (Eustathii Op. p. 507 *sqq.*) and some others by Regel, Font. rer. Byz. i. (1892).

GEORGE ACROPOLITES, born in 1217 at Constantinople, migrated to Nicæa at the age of eighteen, and studied there under the learned Nicephorus Blemmydes. He was appointed (1244) to the office of Grand Logothete, and instructed the young prince Theodore Lascaris who afterwards became Emperor. Unsuccessful as a general in the war with the Despot of Epirus (1257), he was made prisoner, and after his release he was employed by Michael Palæologus as a diplomatist. He represented the Greek Emperor at the Council of Lyons, for the purpose of bringing about a reunion of the Greek and Latin Churches. He died in 1282. His history embraces the period from 1203 to the recovery of Constantinople in 1261, and is thus a continuation of Nicetas. For the second half of the period treated it is not only a contemporary work, but the work of one who was in a good position for observing political events. [The Χρονικὴ συγγραφή in its original form was published by Leo Allatius 1651, and is reprinted in the Venice and Bonn collections. An abridgment was published by Dousa in 1614. There is also, in a Ms. at Milan, a copy of the work with interpolations (designated as such) by a contemporary of Acropolites (see Krumbacher, Gesch, der byz. Litt., p. 287 ; A. Heisenberg, Studien zur Textgeschichte des Georgios Akropolites, 1894).]

GEORGE PACHYMERES (A.D. 1242-1310) carries us on from the point where Acropolites deserts us. He is the chief literary figure of the first fifty years of the restored Empire. His work in 13 Books begins at A.D. 1255 and comes down to 1308. His chief interest was in the theological controversies of the day, and there is far too much theology and disputation about dogma in his history ; but this was what absorbed the attention of the men of his time. "Pachymeres, by his culture and literary activity, overtops his contemporaries, and may be designated as the greatest Byzantine Polyhistor of the 13th century. We see in him the lights and shadows of the age of the Palæologi. He is not wanting in learning, originality, and wit. But he does not achieve the independence of view and expression, which distinguishes a Photius or a Psellus." Other works of Pachymeres are extant, but only his autobiography in hexameter verses need be mentioned here (it was suggested by Gregory Nazianzen's περὶ ἑαυτοῦ). It is worthy of note—as a symptom of the approaching renaissance—that Pachymeres adopted the *Attic*, instead of the Roman, *names* of the months. [The edition of Possinus, used by Gibbon, was reprinted in the Bonn collection, 1835.]

NICEPHORUS GREGORAS (1295-c. 1359) of Heraclea in Pontus was educated at Constantinople, and enjoyed the teaching of Theodore Metochites, who was distinguished not only as a trusted councillor of the Emperor Andronicus, but as a man of encyclopædic learning.[8] Nicephorus won the favour of Andronicus, but on that Emperor's deposition in 1328 his property was confiscated and he had to live in retirement. He came forth from his retreat to do theological battle with the pugnacious Barlaam of Calabria, who was forming a sort of school in Constantinople (see above, c. lxiii. p. 507) ; and his victory in this controversy was rewarded by reinstatement in his property and offices.

---

[8] His chief literary remains are a collection of Miscellaneous Essays, which has been edited by C. G. Müller and T. Kiessling, 1821 : and a large number of rhetorical exercises and astronomical and scientific treatises. His occasional poems have not yet been completely published.

Subsequently he played a prominent part in the renewed attempts at reuniting the eastern and western churches. He fell into disfavour with Cantacuzenus and was banished to a monastery. His Roman History in 37 Books begins with the Latin capture of Constantinople in 1204, and reaches to 1359. But the greater part of this period, 1204-1320, is treated briefly in the first 7 Books, which may be regarded as an introduction to the main subject of his work, namely his own times (1320-1359). This history, like that of Pachymeres, is disproportionately occupied with theological disputation, and is, as Krumbacher says, "eine memoirenhafte Parteischrift im vollsten Sinne des Wortes". In style, Gregoras essays to imitate Plato; for such base uses has Platonic prose been exploited. [Only Books 1-24 were accessible to Gibbon, as he complains (ed. Boivin, 1702). The remaining Books 25-37 (numbered 23-36) were first edited by Bekker in the Bonn ed. vol. 3, 1855. Among other works of Gregoras may be mentioned his funeral oration on Theodore Metochites, ed. by Meursius, 1618 (Th. Metochitae hist. Rom., liber singularis).]

For the Emperor Cantacuzenus and his history see above, cap. lxiii. and cp. p. 495, n. 21. [In the Bonn series, ed. by Schopen in 3 vols., 1828-32 ]

Nicephorus Blemmydes was, beside George Acropolites, the most important literary figure at the court of the Emperor of Nicaea. He was born at Constantinople (c. 1198), and soon after the Latin Conquest migrated to Asia; and in Prusa, Nicaea, Smyrna, and Scamander he received a liberal education under the best masters of the day. He became proficient in logic, rhetoric and mathematics, and studied medicine. He finally embraced a clerical career; he took an active part in the controversies with the Latins in the reign of John Vatatzes, and was a teacher of the young prince Theodore Lascaris. The extant (not yet published) correspondence of Theodore and Blemmydes testifies their friendly intimacy. But Blemmydes was an opinionated man; he was constantly offending and taking offence; and he finally became a monk and retired to a monastery at Ephesus which he built himself. He had the refusal of the Patriarchate in 1255, and he died c. 1272. His autobiography and his letters (monuments of pedantry and conceit) have importance for the history of his time. Besides theological, scientific, and other works, he composed an icon basilike (βασιλικός ανδριάς) for his royal pupil.[9] [The autobiography (in two parts) has been edited by A. Heisenberg, 1896. An edition of the Letters is a desideratum.]

In the first quarter of the 14th century, a native of the Morea, certainly half a Frank, and possibly half a Greek, by birth, composed a versified chronicle of the Latin conquest of the Peloponnesus and its history during the 13th century. This work is generally known as the Chronicle of Morea.[10] The author is thoroughly Grecized, so far as language is concerned; he writes the vulgar tongue as a native; but feels towards the Greeks the dislike and contempt of a ruling stranger for the conquered population. He may have been a Gasmul (Γασμοῦλος, supposed to be derived from gas (garçon) and mulus), as the offspring of a Frank father by a Greek mother was called. It is a thoroughly prosaic work, thrown into the form of wooden political verses; and what it loses in literary interest through its author's lack of talent, it gains in historical objectivity. A long prologue relates the events of the first and the fourth crusades; the main part of the work embraces the history of the Principality of Achaea from 1205 to 1292. The book appealed to the Franks, not to the Greeks, of the Peloponnesus; and shows how Greek had become the language of the conquerors. It was treely translated into French soon after its composition; and this version (with a continuation down to 1304), which was made before the year 1341, is preserved (under the title "The Book of the Conquest of Constantinople and the Empire of Roumania

---

[9] It will be found in Migne, P. G., vol. 142, p. 611 sqq.
[10] It is sometimes referred to as Βιβλίον τῆς κουγκεστας, a title which the first editor Buchon gave it without authority.

and the country of the Principality of Morea"). J. A. Buchon was the first to edit both the Greek and the French ; but he sought to show that the French was the original and the Greek the version. The true relation of the two texts has been established by the researches of Dr. John Schmitt (Die Chronik von Morea, 1889), who is now the chief authority on the work.

As an example of the style of this famous work, I quote a few lines from the description of the investiture of Geoffrey (Ντζεφρές) Villehardouin with Morea.

Μὲ δακτυλίδιον χρυσὸν εὐθὺς τὸν ρεβεστίζει (invests),
κ' ἀφοῦ τὸν ἐπαράδωσε κ' ἐποῖκε του τὸ ὁμάντζιο (homage),
τότε τὸν μετελάλησε καὶ λέγει πρὸς ἐκεῖνον·
" Μισὲρ Ντζεφρὲ, ἀπὸ τοῦ νῦν ἄνθρωπος μ' εἶσαι λίζιος (liege),
ἀφοῦ τὸν τόπον σου κρατεῖς ἀπὸ τὴν αὐθεντειάν μου·
κ' ἁρμόζει νὰ εἶσαι εἰς ἐμὲ ἀληθινὸς εἰς πάντα
κ' ἐγὼ πάλιν ν' ἀποθαρρῶ τὰ πάντα μου 's ἐσένα·
ἐπεὶ ὀφείλω νὰ διαβῶ ἐκεῖσ' εἰς τὴν Φραγκίαν,
παρακαλῶ καὶ ὁρίζω σε διὰ τὴν ἐμὴν ἀγάπην,
τὸν τόπον, τὸν ἐκέρδισα ἐδῶ εἰς τὸν Μωρέαν,
παράλαβε καὶ κράτειε τον, δι' ἐμένα τὸν φυλάττης
εἰς τέτοιον τρόπον κ' ἀφορμὴν δίκαιός μου νᾶσαι μπάϊλος (bailiff)
τοῦ νὰ κρατῆς τὴν αὐθεντειάν ὥσπερ ἐγὼ αὐτός μου κ.τ.λ."

κ' ὅσον ταῖς ἐκατεστησε ταῖς συμφωνιαῖς ἐκείναις
ὁ Καμπανέσης ὥρθωσεν, ἐδιάβηκεν ἐκεῖθεν·
οὐδὲν ἠθέλησε ποσῶς μετ' αὐτὸν νὰ ἐπάρῃ
μόνον δύο καβαλλαρίους καὶ δώδεκα σεργέντ̓αις.
μὲ κάτεργον (galley) ἐπέρασεν, ὑπάει[11] τῆς Βενετίας,
κ' ἐδιάβη ὁλόρθα 's τὴν Φραγκιὰν ἐκεῖσε 's τὴν Τζαμπάνια
κ' ἔμεινεν ὁ μισὲρ Ντζεφρὲς αὐθέντης εἰς τὸν τόπον.

[Of the Greek original there are two widely different redactions, of which one, preserved in a Paris Ms., was published by Buchon in his Chroniques étrangères relatives aux expeditions françaises pendant le xiii. siècle, in 1840 ; the other, preserved in a Copenhagen Ms., was published in the second volume of his Recherches historiques sur la principauté française de Morée et ses hautes baronies (1845), while in the first vol. of this latter work he edited the French text. A final edition, with the Paris and Copenhagen texts on opposite pages, by Dr. John Schmitt, is in preparation.][12]

## SLAVONIC SOURCES

The old Russian chronicle, which goes by the name of NESTOR and comprises the history of Russia and the neighbouring countries from the middle of the ninth century to the year 1110, has come down in two redactions : (1) the Laurentian Ms., written by Laurence of Souzdal in 1377, and (2) the Hypatian, written in the monastery of St. Hypatius at Kostroma in the 15th century. All other Mss. can be traced back to either of these two. In neither of them does the old chronicle stand alone ; it is augmented by continuations which are independent.

The work was compiled apparently in the year 1114-1115,[13] and it can be divided into two parts.[14] (1) Caps. 1-12, without chronological arrangement. It is to this part alone that the title refers : " History of old times by the monk of the monastery of Theodosius Peshtcherski, of the making of Russia, and who reigned first at Kiev (cp. c. 6), and of the origin of the Russian land ". (2) The rest of the

[11] ὑπάγει, " goes ".      [12] There are also versions in Aragonese and in Italian.
[13] Sreznevski, Drevnije pamjatniky russk. pisima i jazyka, p. 47.
[14] Cp. Bestiuzhev-Riumin, O sostavie russkich Lietopisei (in the Lietopisi zaniatii archeogr. Kommissii, 1865-6), p. 19-35.

works, chaps. 13-89, is arranged in the form of annals. It falls into three parts, indicated by the compiler in cap. 13. (a) Caps. 14-36, from the year 852 to death of Sviatoslav, 972; (b) caps. 37-58, to the death of Jaroslav, 1054; (c) caps. 59-89, to the death of Sviatopolk, 1114.[15]

Sources of the chronicle:[16] (1) George the monk, in an old Bulgarian translation of 10th century (cp. chap. 11; see also chaps. 24, 65). (2) A work ascribed to Methodius of Patara (3rd cent.): "On the things which happened from the creation and the things which will happen in the future"—also doubtless through a Slavonic translation.[17] (3) Lives of the apostles of the Slavs, Cyril and Methodius. (4) The Bible. (5) The Palaia (collection of Bible-stories), in Slavonic form. (6) The Symbolum Fidei of Michael Syncellus in Slavonic version (c. 42). (7) Oral information indicated by the chronicler; communications of (a) the monk Jeremiah who was old enough to remember the conversion of the Russians, c. 68; (b) Gurata Rogovich of Novgorod, c. 80; (c) John, an old man of ninety, from whose mouth the chronicler received many notices. (8) A relation of the murder of Boris and Gleb by their brother Sviatopolk; an account which does not agree with the biography of these saints by the monk Nestor, but does agree with the relation of the monk Jacob.[18] (9) A Paschal calendar in which there were a few notices entered opposite to some of the years. (10) Written and dated notices preserved at Kiev, beginning with A.D. 882, the year in which the centre of the Russian realm was transferred from Novgorod to Kiev. Srkulj conjectures that these notices were drawn up in the Norse language by a Norman who had learned to write in England or Gaul, and perhaps in Runic characters. (11) Local chronicles, cp. a chronicle of Novgorod, of the existence of which we are otherwise certified. (12) Possibly a relation of the story of Vasilko, c. 82.

The traditional view that the monk Nestor, who wrote the biography of Boris and (Hleb, and a life of Theodosius of Peshtcherski (see above, p. 166), was the author of the chronicle is generally rejected. Nestor lived in the latter part of the 11th century, and, as we do not know the date of his death, so far as chronology is concerned, he *might* have compiled the chronicle in 1115. But not only does the account of Boris and Gleb (as noticed above) not agree with Nestor's biography of those sainted princes, but there are striking discrepancies between the chronicler's and Nestor's accounts of Theodosius. And, while the chronicler expressly says that he was an eye-witness, Nestor expressly says that he derived his information from others. It is very hard to get over this. There are two other candidates for the authorship: (1) Sylvester, abbot of St. Michael, who states, at the end of the Chronicle in the Laurentian Ms., that he "wrote these books of annals" in A.D. 1116; as long as Nestor was regarded as the author, the word for *wrote* was interpreted as *copied* (though a different compound is usually employed in that sense), but Golubinski and Kostomarov have proposed to regard the abbot as the author and not a mere copyist; (2) the monk Basil who is mentioned in the story of Vasilko (c. 82), and speaks there in the first person: "I went to find Vasilko". But this may be explained by supposing that the compiler of the chronicle has mechanically copied, without making the necessary change of person, a relation of the episode of Vasilko written by this Basil. The authorship of the chronicle is not solved; we can only say that the compiler was a monk of the Peshtcherski monastery of Kiev.

[For a minute study of Nestor the editions of the Laurentian (1846 and 1872) and the Hypatian (1846 and 1871) Mss. published by the Archæographical Commis-

---

[15] There is a question as to the end of the chronicle. M. Leger thinks it reached down to 1113; but in the Laurentian Ms it stops in 1110

[16] See a good Summary in Stjepan Srkulj, Die Entstehung der ältesten russischen sogenannten Nestorchronik (1896), p. 7 sqq.; Leger, Introduction to his translation, p. xiv.-xvii.; Pogodin, Nestor, eine hist.-crit. Untersuchung, tr. Loewe (1844); Bestuzhev-Riumin, op cit.

[17] Suhomlinov ascribes the work to the Patriarch Methodius of the 9th century See Srkulj, op. cit. p. 10

[18] Sreznevski. Skazanie o sv. Borisie i Gliebie, 1860. Some think that Jacob used the account in the Chronicle, c. 47.

sion must be used. For ordinary purposes the text of Miklosich (1860) is still convenient. Excellent French translation by L. Leger, Chronique dite de Nestor, 1884, with an index [19] which is half a commentary.]

## LATIN AND OTHER WESTERN SOURCES

AMATUS of Salerno, monk of Monte Cassino and bishop of an unknown see, wrote about A.D. 1080 a history of the Norman conquest of southern Italy, taking as a model the Historia Langobardorum of Paul the Deacon. We do not possess the work in its original shape, but only in a faulty French translation, made perhaps c. 1300 A.D., which has survived in a single Ms. It was edited for the first time, and not well, by Champollion-Figeac in 1835 (L'Ystoire de li Normant et la Chronique de Robert Viscart, par Aimé, moine de Mont-Cassin), but has been recently edited by O. Delarc, 1892. The work is divided into 8 Books, and embraces the history of the Normans from their first appearance in Italy to A.D. 1078. "It is," says Giesebrecht, "no dry monosyllabic annalistic account, but a full narrative of the conquest with most attractive details, told with charming *naïveté*. Yet Amatus does not overlook the significance of the events which he relates, in their ecumenical context. His view grasps the contemporary Norman conquest of England, the valiant feats of the French knights against the Saracens of Spain, and the influence of Norman mercenaries in the Byzantine empire. In beginning his work (which he dedicates to the Abbot Desiderius, Robert Guiscard's intimate friend) he is conscious that a red thread runs through all these undertakings of the knight-errants and that God has some special purpose in His dealings with this victorious race." [For criticism of the work, the most important study is that of F. Hirsch in Forschungen zur deutschen Geschichte, 8, p. 205 *sqq.* (1868).]

Amatus was unknown to Gibbon, but he was a source of the most important works which Gibbon used. He was one of the sources of the poem of WILLIAM OF APULIA (begun c. A.D. 1099, finished by A.D. 1111), who also utilised the Annals of Bari. Now that we have Amatus (as well as the Annals of Bari) the value of William lies in the circumstance that he used also a lost biography of Robert Guiscard. [New ed. by Wilmans, in Pertz, Mon. ix p. 239 *sqq.*]

Amatus was also a source of GEOFFREY MALATERRA, who wrote the history of the Normans in Sicily (up to 1099) at the instance of Count Roger (see above, Gibbon's notes in chap. lvi.). [For the relation of this to the Anonymi Vaticani Historia Sicula, see A. Heskel, Die Hist. Sic. des Anon. Vat. und des Gaufredus Malaterra, 1891.]

LEO, monk and librarian of Monte Cassino, afterwards Cardinal-bishop of Ostia (died 1115), wrote a chronicle of his monastery, which he carried down to A.D. 1075. It is a laudable work, for which ample material (discreetly used by Leo) lay in the library of the monastery. [Ed. by Wattenbach in Pertz, Mon. vii. p. 574 *sqq.* Cp. Balzani, Le cronache Italiane nel medio evo, p. 150 *sqq.* (1884).] The work was continued (c. 1140) by the Deacon PETER, who belonged to the family of the Counts of Tusculum, as far as the year 1137. [Ed. Wattenbach, *ib.* p. 727 *sqq.*]

Other sources (Annales Barenses, Chron. breve Nortmannicum, &c.) are mentioned in the notes of chap. lvi. It should be observed that there is no good authority for the name "Lupus protospatharius," under which name one of the Bari chronicles is always cited. Contemporary Beneventane annals are preserved in (1) Annales Beneventani, in Pertz, Mon. iii. p. 173 *sqq.* and (2) the incomplete Chronicon of the Beneventane Falco (in Del Re's Cronisti, vol. i. p. 161 *sqq.*); both of which up to 1112 have a common origin. Cp. Giesebrecht, Gesch. der deutschen Kaiserzeit, iii. 1069.

The credibility of the history of HUGO FALCANDUS has been exhibited in some detail by F. Hillger (Das Verhältniss des Hugo Falcandus zu Romuald von

---

[19] There are unfortunately many mistakes in the references to the numbers of the chapters.

Salerno, 1878), and Gibbon s high estimate seems to be justified. Gibbon is also right in rejecting the guess of Clément the Benedictine that the historian is to be identified with Hugo Foucault, Abbot of St Denis (from 1186-1197). In the first place Foucault would never be Latinised as Falcandus. In the second place, the only plausible evidence for the identification does not bear examination. It is a letter of Peter of Blois to an abbot H. of St. Denys (Opera. ed. Giles, ep. 116, i. p. 178), in which Peter asks his correspondent to send him a *tractatus quem de statu aut potius de casu vestro in Sicilia descripsistis.* But this description does not apply to the Historia Sicula of Falcandus . and it has been shown by Schröter that the correspondent of Peter is probably not Hugo Foucault, but his successor in the abbacy, Hugo of Mediolanum. Schröter has fully refuted this particular identification, and has also refuted the view (held by Amari, Freeman, and others) that Falcandus was a Norman or Frank. On the contrary Falcandus was probably born in Sicily, which he knew well, especially Palermo, and when he wrote his history, he was living not north of the Alps (for he speaks of the Franks, &c., as *transalpini, transmontani*) but in southern Italy. He wrote his Historia Sicula, which reaches from 1154 to 1169, later than 1169, probably (in part at least) after 1181, for he speaks (p. 272, ed. Muratori) of Alexander III. as *qui tunc Romanae praesidebat ecclesiae,* and Alexander died in 1181 (F. Schröter, Uber die Heimath des Hugo Falcandus, 1880). The letter to Peter of Palermo which is prefixed to the History as a sort of dedication seems to have been a perfectly independent composition, written immediately after the death of William the Good in November, 1189 and before the election of Tancred two months later. [Opera cit. of Schröter and Hillger ; Freeman, Historical Essays, 3rd ser. ; and cp. Holzach. *op. cit.* above, p. 219, note 145 ; Del Re, preface to his edition (cp. above, p. 219, note 145).]

Compared with Falcandus, ROMUALD, Archbishop of Salerno, is by no means so ingenuous. Although he does not directly falsify facts, his deliberate omissions have the effect of falsifying history ; and these omissions were due to the desire of placing the Sicilian court in a favourable light. He is in fact a court historian, and his Annals clearly betray it. The tendency is shown in his cautious reserve touching the deeds and policy of the cruel and ambitious Chancellor Majo. Romuald was related to the royal family and was often entrusted with confidential and important missions. He was a strong supporter of the papacy, but it has been remarked that he entertained "national" ideas—Italy for the Italians, not for the trans-Alpines. He was a learned man and skilled in medicine. [Cp. above, p. 207, n. 111 ; p. 208, n. 116.]

The name of the author of the GESTA FRANCORUM was unknown even to those contemporary writers who made use of the work. Whatever his name was, he seems to have been a native of Southern Italy ; he accompanied the Norman crusaders who were led by Boemund, across the Illyric peninsula, and shared their fortunes till the end of 1098, when he separated from them at Antioch and attached himself to the Provençals, with whom he went on to Jerusalem. He was not an ecclesiastic like most authors of the age, but a knight. He wrote his history from time to time, during the crusade, according as he had leisure. It falls into eight divisions, each concluded by *Amen ;* and these divisions seem to mark the various stages of the composition ; they do not correspond to any artistic or logical distribution of the work. Having finished his book at Jerusalem, the author deposited it there—perhaps in the Church of the Holy Sepulchre—where it could be, and was, consulted or copied by pilgrims of an inquiring turn of mind. The author was a pious and enthusiastic crusader, genuinely interested in the religious object of the enterprise ; he entirely sinks his own individuality, and identifies himself with the whole company of his fellows. Up to the autumn of 1098 he is devoted to his own leader Boemund ; but after c. 29 it has been noticed that the laudatory epithets which have hitherto attended Boemund's name disappear, and, although no criticism is passed, the author thus, almost unintentionally shows his dissatisfaction with the selfish quarrels between Boemund and Raymond, and has clearly ceased to regard Boemund as a disinterested leader. No written sources were used by the author of the *Gesta* except the Bible and Sibylline Oracles. [See the edition by H. Hagenmeyer. 1889, with full introduction and exegetical notes.]

TUDEBOD of Sivrai, who himself took part in the First Crusade, incorporated (before A.D. 1111) almost the whole of the Gesta in his Historia de Hierosolymitano itinere ; and it used to be thought that the Gesta was merely an abridged copy of his work. The true relation of the two works was shown by H. von Sybel.

The HISTORIA BELLI SACRI an anonymous work, was compiled after A.D. 1131, from the Gesta and Tudebod. The works of Raymond of Ágiles and Radulf of Caen were also used. [Ed. in the Recueil, iii. p. 169 *sqq.*] The EXPEDITIO CONTRA TURCOS, c. 1094, is also for the most part an excerpt from the Gesta.

RAYMOND of Agiles, in his Historia Francorum qui ceperunt Jerusalem, gives the history of the First Crusade from the Provençal side. It has been shown by Hagenmeyer (Gesta Francorum, p. 50 *sqq.*) that he made use of the Gesta ; and Sybel, who held that the two works were entirely independent, remarks on the harmony of the narratives. Raymond is impulsive and gushing, he is super-stitious in the most vulgar sense ; but his good faith is undoubted, and he repro-duces truly his impressions of events. In details he seems to be very accurate. (See the criticism of Sybel, Gesch. des ersten Kreuzzuges, ed. 2, p. 15 *sqq.*, C. Klein, Raimund von Aguilers, 1892.)

FULCHER of Chartres accompanied the host of Robert of Normandy and Stephen of Blois through Apulia and Bulgaria to Nicaea. At Marash he went off with Baldwin against Edessa, and for events in Edessa he is the only eye-witness among the western historians ; but from the moment when he begins to be of unique value for Edessa, he becomes of minor importance for the general course of the Crusade. After Godfrey's death he accompanied Baldwin, the new king, to Jerusalem, and remained at his court. His work, which seems to have been written down as a sort of diary, from day to day or month to month, is of the highest importance for the kingdom of Jerusalem from the accession of Baldwin down to 1127 where it ends. Fulcher consulted the Gesta for the events of the First Crusade, of which he was not an eye-witness. (Cp. Sybel, *op. cit.* p. 46 *sqq.* Hagenmeyer, *op. cit.* p. 58 *sqq.*)

GUIBERT (born A.D. 1153), of good family, became abbot of Nogent in 1104. In his Historia quae dicitur Gesta per Francos, he has thrown the Gesta Francorum into a literary form and added a good deal from other sources. The history of the First Crusade ceases with Bk. 6, and in Bk. 7 he has cast together a variety of notices connected with the kingdom of Jerusalem up to 1104. He had been present at the Council of Clermont, he was personally acquainted with Count Robert of Flanders, from whom he derived some pieces of information, and he had various connexions throughout France which were useful to him in the composition of his book. He is conscious of his own importance, and proud of his literary style ; he writes with the air of a well-read dignitary of the Church. (Cp. Sybel, *op. cit.* p. 33-4.)

BALDRIC, who became Archbishop of Dol in 1107, was of a very different character and temper from Guibert. and has been taken under the special pro-tection of Sybel, who is pleased "to meet such a pure, peaceful, and cheerful nature in times so stern and warlike ". Baldric was opposed to the fashionable asceticism ; he lived in literary retirement, enjoying his books and garden, taking as little a part as he could in the ecclesiastical strife which raged around, and exercising as mildly as possible his archiepiscopal powers. He died in 1130. His Historia Jerusalem, composed in 1108, is entirely founded on the Gesta,— the work, as he says, of *nescio quis compilator* (in the Prologue). See Sybel, *op. cit.* p. 35 *sqq.*

Of little value is the compilation of ROBERT the Monk of Reims, who (sometime in the first two decades of the 12th century) undertook the task of translating the Gesta into a better Latin style and adding a notice on the Council of Clermont. It has been shown by Sybel that there is no foundation for the opinion that Robert took part in the Crusade or visited the Holy Land; had he done so, he would certainly have stated the circumstance in his Prologue. (Sybel, *op. cit.* p. 44-6.)

Of FULCO, who wrote an account in hexameters of the events of the First Crusade up to the siege of Nicaea, we know nothing more than that he was a contemporary and was acquainted with Gilo who continued the work. His account has no historical value; he used the Gesta, but did not rifle that source in such a wholesale manner as GILO of Toucy, his collaborator, who took up the subject at the siege of Nicaea. Gilo, who calls himself :

o nomine Parisiensis

incola Tuciaci non inficiandus alumnus,

was appointed in 1121 bishop of Tusculum, and composed his Libellus de via Hierosolymitana between 1118 and 1121. For the first four Books he used Robert the Monk and Albert of Aachen as well as the Gesta; for Bks. 5 and 6 he simply paraphrased the Gesta. (Cp. Hagenmeyer, *op. cit.* p. 74-6.) [Complete ed. in Migne, P. L. vol. 155.]

RADULF of Caen took no part in the Crusade, but he went to Palestine soon afterwards and stood in intimate relations with Tancred. After Tancred's death he determined to write an account of that leader's exploits, Gesta Tancredi in expeditione Hierosolymitana, which he dedicated to Arnulf, Patriarch of Jerusalem. For all that concerns Tancred personally his statements are of great value, but otherwise he has the position merely of a second-hand writer in regard to the general history of the First Crusade. The importance of his information about the capture of Antioch has been pointed out by Sybel. Hagenmeyer has made it probable that he used the Gesta. [Ed. in Muratori, Scr. rer. It., vol. 5, p. 285 *sqq.*; Recueil, iii. p. 603 *sqq.*]

The chronicle of ALBERT of Aachen contains one of the most remarkable of the narratives of the First Crusade. From this book, says Sybel, we hear the voice not of a single person, but of regiments speaking with a thousand tongues; we get a picture of western Europe as it was shaken and affected by that ecumenical event. The story is told vividly, uninterrupted by any reflections on the part of the author; who is profoundly impressed by the marvellous character of the tale which he has to tell; has no scruple in reporting inconsistent statements; and does not trouble himself much about chronology and topography. But the canon of Aachen, who compiled the work as we have it, in the third decade of the 12th century, is not responsible for the swing of the story. He was little more than the copyist of the history of an unknown writer, who belonged to the Lotharingian crusaders and settled in the kingdom of Jerusalem after the First Crusade. Thus we have, in Albert of Aachen, the history of the Crusade from the Lotharingian side. The unknown author probably composed his history some time after the events; Hagenmeyer has shown that he has made use of the Gesta. [The most important contribution to the criticism of Albert is the monograph of Kugler, Albert von Aachen, 1885, which is to be supplemented by Kühn's article in the Neues Archiv, 12, p. 545 *sqq.*, 1887.]

The Hierosolymita (or Libellus de expugnatione Hierosolymitana) of EKKE-HARD, of the Benedictine abbey of Aura near Kissingen, was published in the Amplissima Collectio of Martene and Durand (vol. 5, p. 511 *sqq.*), where it might have been consulted by Gibbon, but he does not seem to have known of it. Ekkehard went overland to Constantinople with a company of German pilgrims in 1101, sailed from the Imperial city to Joppa, remained six weeks in Palestine, and started on his return journey before the year was out. He became abbot of his monastery and died in 1125. His Chronicon Universale is a famous work, and is the chief authority for German history from A.D. 1080 to the year of the author's death. The Hierosolymita has the value of a contemporary work by one who had himself seen the Holy Land and the Greek Empire. [Edited in Pertz, Mon. vi. p. 265 *sqq.*; and by Riant in the Recueil, vol. 5, p. 1 *sqq.*; but most convenient is the separate edition of Hagenmeyer, 1877.]

Another contemporary writer on the First Crusade, who had himself visited Palestine, is CAFARO di Caschifelone, of Genoa. He went out with the Genoese squadron which sailed to the help of the Crusaders in 1100. He was at Jerusalem at Easter 1101 and took part in the sieges of Arsuf and Caesarea in the same year. He became afterwards a great person in his native city, was five times consul, composed Annales Genuenses, and died in 1166. His work De Liberatione civitatum Orientis was not accessible to Gibbon; for it was first published in 1859 by L. Ansaldo (Cronaca della prima Crociata, in vol. i. of the Acts of the Società Ligure di storia patria). It was then edited by Pertz, Mon. xviii. p. 40 *sqq.*; and in vol v. of the Recueil des historiens des croisades. Contents: chaps. 1-10 give the events of the First Crusade before the author's arrival on the scene; c. 11 relates the arrival of the Genoese fleet at Laodicea, and the defeat of the Lombard Expedition in Asia Minor in 1101; chaps. 12-18 (in the edition of the Recueil) are an extract from the Annales Genuenses, inserted in this place by the editor Riant, and describing the events of the year, 1100-1101; chaps. 19-27 enumerate the towns of Syria and their distances from one another; describe the capture of Margat in 1140 by the Crusaders; a naval battle between the Genoese and Greeks; and the capture of Tortosa, Tripolis, and other places. The work seems never to have been completed.

For the authorship of the Itinerarium Peregrinorum et Gesta regis Ricardi, see above, p. 352-3, note 89. It remains to be added that in its Latin form the work is not an original composition, but is a very free elaboration of a French poem written by a Norman named AMBROSE, in rhyming verses of seven syllables. In the prologue to the Latin work (p. 4, ed. Stubbs) the writer says *nos in castris fuisse cum scripsimus;* but we should expect him to mention the fact that he had first written his account in Franco-Gallic. Nicholas Trivet (at the beginning of the 14th cent.) distinctly ascribes the Itinerarium to Richard of London, Canon of the Holy Trinity (qui itinerarium regis prosa et metro scripsit); [20] but the contemporary Chronicon Terrae Sanctae (see below) states that the Prior of the Holy Trinity of London caused it to be translated from French into Latin (ex Gallica lingua in Latinum transferri fecit). [21] The natural inference is that Richard the Canon transformed the rhymed French of Ambrose into a Latin prose dress; but it is not evident why the name of Ambrose is suppressed. Nor is it quite clear whether Trivet, when he says *prosa et metro*, meant the French verse and the Latin prose, or whether *metro* refers to the Latin rhymes which are occasionally introduced (chiefly in Bk. I.) in the Itinerarium. [Extracts from the Carmen Ambrosii are edited by F. Liebermann (1885) in Pertz, Mon. 27, 532 *sqq.* See Wattenbach, Deutschlands Geschichtsquellen, ed. 6, ii. p. 316.]

For the crusade of Richard I. RALPH OF COGGESHALL's Chronicon Anglicanum (A.D. 1066-1223) is an important authority, and it was the source of the account in Matthew Paris. Ralph, who was abbot of the Cistercian Monastery of Coggeshall, in Essex, died about 1228, was not in the Holy Land himself, but he obtained his information from eye-witnesses (*e.g.*, from Hugh de Neville, who described for him the episode of Joppa in Aug., 1192, and from Anselm, the king's chaplain). [Edited in the Rolls series by J. Stevenson, 1875.]

Another contemporary account of the Third Crusade is contained in the CHRONICON TERRAE SANCTAE, ascribed without any reason to Ralph of Coggeshall, and printed along with his Chronicle in Martene and Durand, Ampl. Coll. vol. 5, and in the Rolls series (p. 209 *sqq.*). An independent narrative, derived apparently

[20] Stubbs, Introduction, p xli.　　　　　　　　　　[21] *Ib.*, p. xlii.

# APPENDIX 527

from a crusader's journal,[22] is incorporated in the Gesta Henrici II. et Ricardi I., which goes under the name of Benedict of Peterborough (who, though he did not compose the work, caused it to be compiled). [Edited by Stubbs in the Rolls series, 1867.] Material for Richard's Crusade will also be found in other contemporary English historians, such as Ralph de Diceto, William of Newburgh, &c.

WILLIAM OF TYRE is the greatest of the historians of the Crusades and one of the greatest historians of the Middle Ages. He was born in Palestine in 1127 and became archbishop of Tyre in 1174. A learned man, who had studied ancient Latin authors (whom he often cites), he had the advantage of being acquainted with Arabic, and he used Arabic books to compose a history of the Saracens from the time of Mohammad (see his Prologue to the History of the Crusades). He was always in close contact with the public affairs of the kingdom of Jerusalem, political as well as ecclesiastical. He was the tutor of Baldwin IV., and was made Chancellor of the kingdom by that king. His great work (Historia rerum in partibus transmarinis gestarum) falls into two parts : (1) Books 1-15, to A.D. 1144 : so far his narrative depends on "the relation of others" (Bk. 16, c. 1), and he has used (though he does not say so) the works of earlier writers (such as Fulcher of Chartres, and Albert of Aachen), as well as the memories of older men with whom he was acquainted ; but his judgment is throughout entirely independent. (2) Books 16-23, to A.D. 1184 : here he writes as a contemporary eye-witness, but he is careful and conscientious in informing himself, from every possible source, concerning the events which he relates ; and he is remarkably cautious in his statements of facts. The miraculous seldom plays a part in his story ; he is unfeignedly pious, but he seeks an earthly explanation of every earthly event.[23] His history, along with the Book of the Assises, is the chief material for forming a picture of the Latin colonies in Palestine. Chronology, Sybel remarks, is the weak side of his work ; and we may add that it is often spoiled by too much rhetoric. It was translated into French in the second quarter of the 13th century. [Included in the Recueil, Hist. Occ. vol. i. (1844).]

The work of William of Tyre was continued in French by ERNOUL (squire of Balian, lord of Ibelin ; he had taken part in the battle of Hittin and the siege of Jerusalem) down to 1229 ; and by BERNARD (the Treasurer of St. Peter at Corbie) down to 1231. These continuations were continued by anonymous writers down to 1277 ; and the French translation of William along with the continuations was current as a single work under the title of the Chronique d'Outremer, or L'Estoire de Éracles.[24] [The Continuations were first critically examined and analysed by M. de Mas Latrie,[25] who edited the works of Ernoul and Bernard (1871). Edition of Guillaume de Tyr et ses Continuateurs, by P. Paris, 2 vols., 1879-80.]

It may be added here that the charters and letters pertaining to the Kingdom of Jerusalem have been edited under the title Regesta Regni Hierosolymitani, by Röhricht, 1893. The numismatic material has been collected and studied by M. G. Schlumberger : Numismatique de l'Orient Latin, 1878.

Marshal VILLEHARDOUIN's Conquest of Constantinople is, along with Nicetas, the main guide of Gibbon in his account of the Fourth Crusade. Gibbon thought, and it has been generally thought till late years, that this famous book, composed by one of the wisest and most moderate of the Crusaders, was a perfectly naïve and candid narrative, partial indeed to the conduct of the conquerors, but still—when allowance has been made for the point of view—a faithful relation of facts without an *arrière pensée*. But, though there are some, like his editor M. de Wailly, who still maintain the unblemished candour of Villehardouin as an author, recent criticism in the light of new evidence leaves hardly room for reasonable doubt

22 Cp Stubbs, Introd. to Itinerarium, p. xxxviii.
23 Sybel, Gesch. des ersten Kreuzzuges, ed. 2, p. 120.
24 An absurd title taken from the opening sentence of William of Tyre.
25 Essai de classification, &c., in Bibl. de l'école des chartes, Sér. V. t. i. 38 *sqq.*, 140 *sqq.* (1860) ; and in his ed. of Ernoul and Bernard, p. 473 *sqq.*

that Villehardouin's work was deliberately intended to deceive the European public as to the actual facts of the Fourth Crusade. There can be no question that Villehardouin was behind the scenes; he represents the expedition against Constantinople as an accidental diversion, which was never intended when the Crusade was organized; and therefore his candour can be rescued only by proving that the episode of Constantinople was really nothing more than a diversion. But the facts do not admit of such an interpretation. During the year which elapsed between the consent of the Venetian Republic to transport the Crusaders and the time when the Crusaders assembled at Venice (A.D. 1201-2), the two most important forces concerned in the enterprise—Venice and Boniface of Montferrat—had determined to divert the Crusade from its proper and original purpose. Venice had determined that, wherever the knights sailed, they should *not* sail to the place whither she had undertaken to transport them, namely to the shores of Egypt. For in the course of that eventful year she made a treaty with the Sultan of Egypt, pledging herself that Egypt should not be invaded. And on his part, Boniface of Montferrat had arranged with the Emperor Philip and Alexius that the swords of the Crusaders should be employed at Constantinople. (For all this see above, p. 385, n. 51 and 53, and p. 388, n. 63.) On these facts, which were of the first importance, Villehardouin says not a word; and one cannot hesitate to conclude that his silence is deliberate. In fact, his book is, as has been said, an "official" version of the disgraceful episode. The Fourth Crusade shocked public opinion in Europe; men asked how such a thing had befallen, how the men who had gone forth to do battle against the infidels had been drawn aside from their pious purpose to attack Christian states. The story of Villehardouin, a studied suppression of the truth, was the answer. [Mm. Mas-Latrie and Riant take practically this point of view, which has been presented well and moderately by Mr. Pears in his Fall of Constantinople (an excellent work). M. J. Tessier, La diversion sur Zara et Constantinople (1884), defends Villehardouin. Cp. also L. Streit's Venedig und die Wendung des vierten Kreuzzuges gegen Constantinopel.—Editions: by N. de Wailly, 3rd ed., 1882; E. Bouchet, 2 vols., 1891.]

Besides Gunther's work, which Gibbon used (see p. 386, note 54), some new sources on the Fourth Crusade have been made accessible. The most important of these is the work of ROBERT DE CLARY, Li estoires de chiaus qui conquisent Constantinoble; which, being "non-official," supplies us with the check on Villehardouin. [Printed by Riant in 1868 and again in 1871, but in so few copies that neither issue could be properly called an edition. Edited (1873) by Hopf in his Chroniques Gréco-romaines, p. 1 *sqq.*]

Another contemporary account is preserved, the DEVASTATIO CONSTANTINOPOLI-TANA, by an anonymous Frank, and is an official diary of the Crusade. [Pertz, Mon. xvi. p. 9 *sqq.*; Hopf, Chron. Gréco-romaines, p. 86 *sqq.*]

The work of Moncada, which Ducange and Gibbon used for the history of the Catalan expedition, is merely a loose compilation of the original Chronicle of RAMON MUNTANER, who was not only a contemporary but one of the most prominent members of the Catalan Grand Company. A Catalonian of good family, born at Peralada, in 1255, he went to reside at Valencia in 1276, witnessed the French invasion of Philip the Bold in 1285, and in 1300 set sail for Sicily and attached himself to the fortunes of Roger de Flor, whom he accompanied to the east. He returned to the west in 1308; died and was buried at Valencia about 1336. The account of the doings of the Catalans in the east is of course written from their point of view; and the adventurer passes lightly over their pillage and oppression. It is one of the most interesting books of the period. [Most recent edition of the original Catalan, by J. Corolen, 1886; conveniently consulted in Buchon's French version, in Chroniques étrangères (1860). Monographs: A. Rubió y Lluch, La expedicion y dominacion de los Catalanes en oriente juzgedas por los Griegos, 1883. and Los Navarros en Grecia y el ducado Catalan de Atenas en la época de su invasion, 1886 (this deals with a later period).]

[To works on the Fourth Crusade may now be added W. Norden's Der vierte Kreuzzug im Rahmen der Beziehungen des Abendlandes zu Byzanz, 1898.]

[Extracts from the writers mentioned below, and others, will be found in vol. iv. of Michaud's Bibliothèque des Croisades (1829), translated and arranged by M. Reinaud.]

IMĀD AD-DĪN al-Kātib al-Ispahāni was born at Ispahan in A.D. 1125, and studied at Baghdad. He obtained civil service appointments, but fell into disfavour and was imprisoned ; after which he went to Damascus, where Nūr ad-Dīn was ruling. He became the friend of prince Saladin, and was soon appointed secretary of state under Nūr ad-Dīn, but after this potentate's death his position was precarious, and he set out to return to Baghdad. But hearing of Saladin's successes in Egypt he went back to Damascus and attached himself to his old friend. After Saladin's death (A.D. 1193) he withdrew into private life. He wrote a history of the Crusades with the affected title : Historia Cossica [Coss was a contemporary of Mohammad] de expugnatione Codsica [that is, Hierosolymitana], of which extracts were published by Schultens ; he also wrote a History of the Seljüks. See Wüstenfeld, Arabische Geschichtschreiber, no. 284.

BAHĀ AD-DĪN (the name is often corrupted to Bohadin) was born in 1145 at Mōsil, and became professor there in 1174 in the college founded by Kamāl ad-Dīn. In 1188 he made the pilgrimage to Mecca, and on his way back visited Damascus, where Saladin sent for him and offered him a professorship at Cairo. This he declined, but he afterwards took service under Saladin and was appointed judge of the army and to a high official post at Jerusalem. After Saladin's death he was made judge of Aleppo, where he founded a college and mosque, and a school for teaching the traditions of the Prophet. He died in 1234. His biography of Saladin is one of the most important sources for the Third Crusade, and the most important source for the life of Saladin. [Edited with French translation in vol. iii. of the Recueil des historiens des Croisades, Hist. Or. (Here too will be found a notice of the author's life by Ibn Khallikān.) Translation (unscholarly) published by the Palestine Exploration Fund, 1897.]

Abū l-Hasan Alī IBN AL-ATHĪR was born A.D. 1160. He studied at Mōsil and was there when Saladin besieged it in 1186. He was in Syria about 1189, so that he saw something of the Third Crusade. But he was a man of letters and took little part in public affairs. He wrote (1) a history of the Atābegs of Mōsil and (2) a universal history from the creation of the world to A.D. 1231. The part of this second work bearing on the Crusades, from A.D. 1098 to 1190, will be found in the Recueil, Hist. Or. vol. i. p. 189 sqq. ; and on the author's life see ib. p. 752 sqq. The history of the Atābegs is published in the 2nd part of vol. ii.

KAMĀL AD-DĪN ibn al-Adīm, born c. A.D. 1192, belonged to the family of the cadhis of Aleppo. Having studied at Baghdad and visited Damascus, Jerusalem, &c., he became judge of Aleppo himself, and afterwards vizier. When the Tartars destroyed the place in A.D. 1260, he fled to Egypt. He wrote a History of his native city, and part of this is the Récit de la première croisade et des quatorze années suivantes, published in Defrémery, Mémoires d'histoire orientale, 1854. [Recueil des hist. des Croisades, Hist. Or. vol. iii. p. 577 sqq.]

Abū-l-Kāsim ABD AR-RAHMĀN (called Abū Shāma, " father of moles ") was born in Damascus A.D. 1202 and assassinated A.D. 1266. He wrote Liber duorum hortorum de historia duorum regnorum, a history of the reigns of Nūr ad-Dīn and Saladin, which is edited by Quatremère in vol. ii. of the Recueil des hist. des Croisades, Hist. Or.

JALĀL AD-DĪN (A.D. 1207-1298) was born at Hamāh in Syria and afterwards went to Egypt, where he was a witness of the invasion of Louis IX. He visited Italy

(1260) as the ambassador of the Sultan Baybars to King Manfred. He was a teacher of Abū-l-Fidā, who lauds his wide knowledge. He wrote a history of the Ayyūbid lords of Egypt. The work which Reinaud used for Michaud's Bibliothèque des Croisades is either part of this history or a separate work.

Abū-l-Fidā, born at Damascus A.D. 1273, belonged to the family of the lords of Hamāh (a side branch of the Ayyūbids). He was present at the conquest of Tripolis in A.D. 1289 and at the siege of Acre (which fell A.D. 1291); and he joined in the military expeditions of his cousin Mahmūd II. of Hamāh. He took part also in the expeditions of the Egyptian Sultan, to whom he was always loyal. In A.D. 1310 he received himself the title of sultan, as lord of Hamāh. But in this new dignity, which he was reluctant to accept, he used to go every year to Cairo to present gifts to his liege lord. He died in A.D. 1332, having ruled Hamāh for eleven years. His great work, Compendium historiae generis humani, came down to A.D. 1329. (The first or pre-Mohammadan part has been edited with Lat. tr. by Fleischer in 1831 ; the second, or Life of Mohammad—ed. by Gagnier, 1723—was translated into French by M. des Vergers, 1837.) The post-Mohammadan part of this work was edited by Reiske in 5 vols. under the title Annales Moslemici, with Lat. transl. (1789-1794) ; Gibbon had access to extracts in the Auctarium to the Vita Saladini of Schultens (1732). A résumé of Abū-l-Fidā's account of the Crusades will be found in vol. i. of the Recueil, Hist. Or. [F. Wilken, Commentatio de bellorum cura ex Abulf. hist. 1798.]

A large number of extracts from Armenian writers, bearing on the Crusades, are published with French translation by Dulaurier in the Recueil des historiens des Croisades, Doc. Arm. tome i. Among these is the Chronological Table (A.D. 1076-1307) of HAITUM (p. 469 sqq.), who belonged to the family of the princes of Lampron, and became Count of Courcy (Gorigos). He became a monk of the Praemonstratensian order in 1305 and went to Cyprus. He visited Clement V. at Avignon, and Gibbon refers to the History of the Tartars, which he dictated, at the Pope's request, in French to Nicolas Falconi, who immediately translated it into Latin. This work of "Haythonus" is extant in both forms. Among the other sources included in this collection of Dulaurier may be mentioned : a rhymed chronicle on the kings of Little Armenia, by Vahram of Edessa, of the 13th cent. (p. 493 sqq.) ; works of St. Narses of Lampron (born 1153) ; extracts from Cyriac (Guiragos) of Gantzac (born 1201-2), who wrote ʒ history of Armenia [26] from the time of Gregory Illuminator to 1269-70. There ɑre also extracts from the chronicle of SAMUEL of Ani, which reached from the beginning of the world to 1177-8 (p. 447 sqq.), and from its continuation up to 1339-40 : this chronicle was published in a Latin translation by Mai and Zohrab, 1818, which is reprinted in Migne's Patr. Gr. 19, p. 599 sqq. But the best known of these Armenian authors is MATTHEW of Edessa, whose chronicle covers a century and three quarters (A.D. 963-1136). We know nothing of the author's life, except that he flourished in the first quarter of the 12th century. His work is interesting as well as valuable ; his style simple, without elegance and art ; for he was a man without much culture and had probably read little. He depended much on oral information (derived from "old men") ; but he has preserved a couple of original documents (one of them is a letter of the Emperor Tzimisces to an Armenian king, c. 16). He is an ardent Armenian patriot ; he hates the Greeks as well as the Turks, and he is, not without good cause, bitter against the Frank conquerors. [French translation by Dulaurier (along with the Continuation by the priest Gregory to A.D. 1164), 1858, in the Bibliothèque hist. Arménienne. Extracts in the Recueil, p. 1 sqq.]

MODERN WORKS. Finlay, History of Greece, vols. ii.-iv. ; Hopf, Griechische Geschichte (in Ersch und Gruber, Enzyklopädie, sub Griechenland) ; Gregoro-

---

[26] This has been translated (along with a tenth century historian, Uchtanes of Edessa) by Brosset, 1870-1.

vius, Geschichte der Stadt Athen im Mittelalter, 1897 ; Ranke, Weltgeschichte vol. 8. For military history, C. Oman, History of the Art of War, vol. 2 books iv. and v.

For the Normans : G. de Blasiis, La insurrezione pugliese e la conquista Normanna nel secolo xi., 1864 ; J. W. Barlow, The Normans in Southern Italy, 1886 ; O. Delarc, Les Normands en Italie, 1883 ; L. von Heinemann, Geschichte der Normannen in Unter-Italien und Sizilien, vol. i., 1893.

For the Crusades : F. Wilken, Geschichte der Kreuzzüge, 1807-32 ; Michaud, Histoire des Croisades (in 6 vols.), 1825 (Eng. tr. in 3 vols., by W. Robson, 1852) ; H. von Sybel, Geschichte des ersten Kreuzzuges, 1881 (ed. 2) ; B. von Kugler, Geschichte der Kreuzzüge, 1880, and Studien zur Gesch. des 2ten Kreuzzuges, 1866 ; Röhricht, Geschichte des Königreichs Jerusalem, 1898 ; H. Prutz, Kultur-geschichte der Kreuzzüge, 1883 ; Archer and Kingsford, The Crusades ; G. Le Strange, Palestine under the Muslims, 1390. For the institutions and organisa-tion of the Kingdom : G. Dodu, Hist. des institutions monarchiques dans le royaume latin de Jér., 1894.

## 2. SARACEN COINAGE—(P. 5)

The following account of the introduction of a separate coinage by the Omay-yads is taken from Mr. Stanley Lane-Poole's Coins and Medals, p. 164 *sqq*.

" It took the Arabs half a century to discover the need of a separate coinage of their own. At first they were content to borrow their gold and copper currency from the Byzantine Empire, which they had driven out of Syria, and their silver coins from the Sassanian kings of Persia, whom they had overthrown at the battles of Kadisia and Nehavend. The Byzantine gold served them till the seventy-sixth year of the Flight, when a new, but theologically unsound and con-sequently evanescent, type was invented, bearing the effigy of the reigning Khalif instead of that of Heraclius, and Arabic instead of Greek inscriptions. So, too, the Sassanian silver pieces were left unaltered, save for the addition of a gover-nor's name in Pehlvi letters. The Khalif 'Aly or one of his lieutenants seems to have attempted to inaugurate a purely Muslim coinage, exactly resembling that which was afterwards adopted ; but only one example of this issue is known to exist, in the Paris collection, together with three other silver coins struck at Damascus and Mery between A.H. 60 and 70, of a precisely similar type. These four coins are clearly early and ephemeral attempts at the introduction of a dis-tinctive Mohammadan coinage, and their recent discovery in no way upsets the received Muslim tradition that it was the Khalif 'Abd-El-Melik who, in the year of the Flight 76 (or, on the evidence of the coins themselves, 77), inaugurated the regular Muslim coinage which was thenceforward issued from all the mints of the empire, so long as the dynasty endured, and which gave its general character to the whole currency of the kingdoms of Islam. The copper coinage founded on the Byzantine passed through more and earlier phases than the gold and silver, but it always held [an] insignificant place in the Muslim currency. . . ."

The gold and silver coins of 'Abd-El-Melik "both bear the same formulæ of faith : on the obverse, in the area, 'There is no god but God alone, He hath no partner' ; around which is arranged a marginal inscription, 'Mohammad is the apostle of God, who sent him with the guidance and religion of truth, that he might make it triumph over all other religions in spite of the idolaters,' the gold stopping at ' other religions '. This inscription occurs on the reverse of the silver instead of the obverse, while the date inscription, which is found on the reverse of the gold, appears on the obverse of the silver. The reverse area declares that ' God is One, God is the Eternal: He begetteth not, nor is begotten' ; here the gold ends, but the silver continues, 'and there is none like unto Him'. The margin of the gold runs, 'In the name of God: the Dînâr was struck in the year seven and seventy' ; the silver substituting 'Dirhem' for 'Dînâr,' and in-serting the place of issue immediately after the word Dirhem, *e.g.*, 'El-Andalus (*i.e.* Andalusia) in the year 116'. The mint is not given on the early gold coins, probably because they were usually struck at the Khalif's capital, Damascus.

"These original dînârs (a name formed from the Roman denarius) and dirhems (drachma) of the Khalif of Damascus formed the model of all Muslim coinages for many centuries ; and their respective weights—65 and 43 grains—served as the standard of all subsequent issues up to comparatively recent times. The fineness was about ·979 gold in the dînârs, and ·960 to ·970 silver in the dirhem. The Mohammadan coinage was generally very pure. . . . At first ten dirhems went to the dînâr, but the relation varied from age to age."

Thus the dînâr of the Omayyad Caliphs, weighing on the average 65·3 grains of almost pure gold, was worth about 11s. 6d. In later times there were double dînârs, and under the Omayyads there were thirds of a dînâr, which weighed less than half a dirhem.

As to a coin which Gibbon supposes (p. 5, note 9) to be preserved in the Bodleian Library, Mr. S. Lane-Poole kindly informs me that no such coin exists there. "The Wâsit coins there preserved were acquired long after Gibbon's time and none has the date 88 A.H. There is a dirhem of that year in the British Museum weighing 44·6 grains. [S. Lane-Poole, Catalogue of Mohammadan Coins in the Bodleian Library, 1888 ; Catalogue of Oriental Coins in the British Museum, vol. i. no. 174 (1875).]"

## 3. THE THEMES OF THE ROMAN EMPIRE—(P. 62, 66 *sqq.*)

In the tenth century we find the Empire divided into a number of *themes*, each of which is governed by a *stratêgos*. Not only the title of the governor, but the word theme (θέμα, a regiment) shows their military origin. These themes existed in the eighth and ninth centuries ; they originated in the seventh. In the latter part of the seventh century we find the empire consisting of a number of large military provinces, not yet called themes, but probably known as στρατηγίαι. We have no official list of them ; but from literary notices we can reconstruct an approximate list of the provinces c. 700 A.D.:—[1]

| | |
|---|---|
| 1. The Armeniacs. | 6. The Helladics. |
| 2. The Anatolics. | 7. Italy. |
| 3. The Opsikion. | 8. Sicily. |
| 4. The Marines. | 9. Africa. |
| 5. Thrace. | |

We have to consider first how this system originated, and secondly how it developed into the system of themes which we find two centuries later.

The identification of the stratêgoi of the seventh century with the magistri militum of the sixth century gives the clue to the origin of the thematic system. (This was pointed out in Bury's Later Roman Empire, ii. 346-8.) The stratêgos of the Armeniacs is the magister militum of Armenia, instituted by Justinian ; the stratêgos of the Anatolics is the magister militum per Orientem ; the " count " of the Opsikians corresponds to the mag. mil. praesentalis ;[2] the stratêgos of Thrace is the mag. mil. per Thraciam ; the stratêgos of the Helladics is probably the representative of the mag. mil. per Illyricum. The magistri militum of Africa and Italy remain under the title of exarchs. The maritime provinces arose probably, as M. Diehl attractively suggests, from the province of Caria, Cyprus, Rhodes, the Cyclades and Scythia, instituted by Justinian, and placed by him under a quaestor Justinianus.

Thus, what happened was this. In the seventh century the old system of dioceses and provinces was swept away. Its place was taken by the already exist

---

[1] Diehl, L'origine des Thèmes, p. 9; Bury, Later Roman Empire, ii. p. 345.
[2] Diehl, *ib.* p. 15. M. Diehl has developed this explanation more fully.

ing division of the Empire into military provinces—the spheres of the magistri militum; and a new Greek nomenclature was introduced. The cause of the change was the extreme peril of the Empire from the Saracens. The needs of defence suggested a military organization; when the frontier was reduced and every province was exposed to the attacks of the enemy, there was a natural tendency to unite civil and military power. In the west, the exarch of Africa and the exarch of Italy are the magistri militum who have got into their hands the power of the Praetorian prefects of Africa and Italy respectively; and in the same way in the east, the stratêgoi of Thrace, the Anatolics, the Armeniacs and the Opsikians, have each a parcel of the prerogatives of the Praetorian Prefect of the East.

During the eighth and ninth centuries the provinces came to be generally called themes, and the list was modified in several ways. (1) It was reduced by losses of territory; thus Africa was lost. (2) Some of the large provinces were broken up into a number of smaller. (3) Some small frontier districts, which were called *clisurarchies* (κλεισοῖρα, a mountain pass), and had been dependent on one of the large districts, were raised to the dignity of independent themes. Thus the Bucellarian theme was formed in the north of Asia Minor between the Opsikian and the Armeniac themes. Then Paphlagonia was cut out as a separate province. The Thracesian theme was cut off the Anatolic. The Marine theme ultimately became three: the Cibyrrhaeot,[3] the theme of Samos, and the Aegean Sea. The Helladic province was divided into three (at least): Hellas, Nicopolis, and the Peloponnesus. The Dalmatian towns were constituted into a separate district; a separate theme seems to have been formed out of Calabria and the Ionian islands; but these islands were subsequently detached and constituted as the theme of Cephallenia. In the east of Asia Minor: Colonea, Lycandos, Sebastea, &c. The Armenine and Anatolic provinces were abridged by the creation of the themes of Charsianon and Cappadocia.

We can trace in the chronicles some changes of this kind which were carried out between the seventh and the tenth centuries. But it is not till the beginning of the tenth century that we get any official list to give us a general view of the divisions of the Empire. The treatise on the themes by the Emperor Constantine (see above, p. 66 *sqq.*), composed about A.D. 934, is generally taken as the basis of investigation, and, when historians feel themselves called upon to give a list of the Byzantine themes, they always quote his. In my opinion this is a mistake. We possess better lists than Constantine's, of a somewhat earlier date. Emperor though Constantine was, his list is not official; it is a concoction, in which actual facts are blended with unmethodical antiquarian research. His treatise is valuable indeed; but it should be criticised in the light of the *official* lists which we possess.

(1) The earliest list is one included in the Cletorologion of Philotheus (see above, p. 517): Const. Porph. De Cer. Bk. ii. c. 52, p. 713 14 and 727-8. The stratêgoi of the themes are enumerated with other officials in their order of precedence. The list used by Philotheus must date from the first years of the tenth century; it does not mention the themes of Langobardia and Sebastea, which existed before the death of Leo VI., but Cephallenia, which he created, appears in the enumeration.[4]

(2) The second list is a table of the salaries of the governors of themes and clisurae, in the reign of Leo VI., and is included in c. 50 of the Second Book of the De Cerimoniis. But its editor lived in the reign of Romanus I. For he speaks of the governors of Sebastea, Lycandos, Seleucia, Leontocomis, as having been *at that time*, that is in Leo's reign, clisurarchs (ὡς ὧν τότε κλεισουράρχης). In other words, a list was used in which these four districts appeared as clisurarchies. Subsequently they were made themes (strategiai) and the editor brought them

---

[3] The Cibyrrhaeot Theme was not promoted to thematic dignity till the latter part of the eighth century. This is proved by the seal of " Theophilus, Imperial spathar and turmarch of the Cibyrrhaeots," see Schlumberger, Sigillographie byzantine, p. 261.

[4] Rambaud, L'empire grec, p. 176.

| List I. (Leo VI.). | List II. (Leo VI. and Romanus I.). | Ibn Khordadbeh. | Constantine (Themes). | Constantine (De Adm.). |
|---|---|---|---|---|
| Anatolic | 1. Anatolic | Anatholos | 1. Anatolic | Anatolic |
| Armeniac | 2. Armeniac | El-Arsak | 2. Armeniac | Armeniac |
| Thracesian | 3. Thracesian | El-efesis | 3. Thracesian | Thracesian |
| Opsician | 4. Opsician | Elasik | 4. Opsician | Opsician |
| Bucellarian | 5. Bucellarian | Kalath (Galatia) | 5. Bucellarian | Bucellarian |
| Cappadocia | 6. Cappadocia | Kapadak | (Cappadocia) | Cappadocia |
| Charsianon | 7. Charsianon | Khorsoun | (Charsianon) | Charsianon |
| Colonia | 12. Coloneia | — | 10. Colonea | Colonea |
| Paphlagonia | 8. Paphlagonia | Afladjounyah | 7. Paphlagonia | Paphlagonia |
| Thrace | 9. Thrace | Thalaka | I. Thrace | Thrace [5] |
| Macedonia [6] | 10. Macedonia | Macedonia | II. Macedonia | Macedonia [5] |
| CHALDIA | 11. Chaldia | Kelkyeh | 8. Chaldia | Chaldia |
| Peloponnesus [7] | 21. Peloponnesus | — | VI. Peloponnesus | Peloponnesus [8] |
| Nicopolis | 22. Nicopolis | — | VII. Nicopolis | Nicopolis |
| Cibyrrhaeots | 18. Cibyrrhaeots | — | 14. Cibyrrhaeots | Cibyrrhaeots |
| Hellas | 23. Hellas | — | V. Hellas | Hellas [8] |
| Sicily | 24. Sicily | — | X. Sicily | Sicily |
| Strymon | 26. Strymon | — | III. Strymon. | Strymon [9] |
| Cephalenia | 27. Cephalenia | — | VII. Cephalenia | Cephallenia [10] |
| Thessalonica | 28. Thessalonica | — | IV. Thessalonica | Thessalonica |
| Dyrrhachium | 29. Dyrrhachium | Thorakia | IX. Dyrrhachium | Dyrrhachium |
| Samos | 19. Samos | — | 16. Samos | Samos |
| Aegean Sea [11] | 20. Aegean Sea | — | 17. Aegean Sea | Aegean Sea |
| Dalmatia [12] | 30. Dalmatia | — | — | Dalmatia |
| Cherson | 31. Cherson | — | XII. Cherson | Cherson |
| — | 13. Mesopotamia | — | 9. Mesopotamia | Mesopotamia |
| — | 14. Sebastea | — | 11. Sebastea | Sebastea |
| — | 15. Licandos | — | 12. Licandos | Lycandos |
| — | 16. Seleucea | Seleucia | 13. Seleucea | Seleucia |
| — | 17. Leontokomis | — | — | — |
| — | 25. Lagobardia [13] | — | XI. Longibardia | Longibardia |
| — | — | — | — | Calabria |
| — | — | Antamathie | [6. Optimaton] [14] | [Optimaton] |
| — | — | — | [15. Cyprus] | — |
| — | — | — | — | Theodosiopolis |

[5] The themes of Thrace and Macedonia were united in the eleventh and twelfth centuries. Cp. seals in Schlumberger, Sigillographie byzantine, p. 162-3.

[6] There is no evidence for the theme of Macedonia before the ninth century. For seals of ninth century see Schlumberger, Sig. byz. p. 111.

[7] For the Peloponnesus as an independent theme before the end of the eighth century cp. Schlumberger, Sig. byz. p. 179, n. 5.

[8] Hellas and Peloponnesus were united in the eleventh century. See seals in Schlumberger, Sig. byz. p. 188.

[9] The theme of Strymon (which probably did not touch the coast) was formed perhaps in the first half of the ninth century at latest. Cp. the seal of Theophilus (in Schlumberger Sig. byz. p. 108), which belongs to the iconoclastic period.

[10] Seals of Cephallenian theme are very rare. They begin to appear in the ninth century Schlumberger, ib. p. 207 sqq.

[11] No seal of the Aegean Sea is known earlier than the ninth century. Schlumberger ib. p. 193 sqq. The seal (No. 12, p. 195) which has "kommerkia of the islands of the Aegean Sea," and belongs to the seventh century, does not prove a theme of that name. But it might have been a designation of the big maritime theme before it was divided.

[12] There are seals of Bryennius, stratègos of Dalmatia, date ninth century; and another of a protomandator of Dalmatia (same period). Schlumberger, Sig. byz. p. 205.

[13] The official spelling (on seals) is Λαγουβαρδία or Λαγυβαρδία.

[14] The proper title of the chief of the Optimaton was Domestic. But we also find on seals a stratègos Optimaton and a catepano. See Schlumberger, Sig. byz. p. 244

up to date. But the list on which he worked seems to be later than the list used by Philotheus, for it includes the theme of Langobardia.

(3) Incomplete enumerations of the themes, in the reign of Romanus I., are given by some Arabic writers, especially by Ibn Khordadbeh (see M. Rambaud, L'empire grec, p. 182).

(4) The Treatise on the Themes. We must criticise Constantine for including Sicily and Cyprus, which did not belong to the Empire, and at the same time omitting Dalmatia, where there was the semblance of a province. Constantine raises the Optimaton to the dignity of a theme, but apologizes for doing so ; it is only a quasi-theme. In this he was justified ; for, though the Optimaton was not governed by a stratêgos but by a domesticus, and was not in a line with the other themes, it was a geographical province.

But the most serious matter that calls for criticism is Constantine's inconsistency in stating definitely that Charsianon and Cappadocia are themes, and yet not enumerating them in his list. He discusses them under the heading of the Armeniac theme, but they should have headings of their own. This unaccountable procedure has led to the supposition that these two themes were temporarily merged in the Armeniac, out of which they had originally been evolved.

(5) A number of notices in the treatise de Administratione supply material for reconstructing a list of the themes c. A.D. 950-2.

(6) To these sources must be added, the seals of the various military and civil officers of the themes. M. Gustave Schlumberger's important work, Sigillographie byzantine (1884), illustrates the lists.

Sardinia passed away from the empire in the 9th century, but it seems to have never formed a regular theme. We have however traces of its East-Roman governors in the 9th cent. A seal of Theodotus, who was "hypatos and dux of Sardinia," has been preserved ; and also seals of archons of Cagliari, with the curious style ΑΡΧΟΝΤΙ ΜΕΡΕΙΑΣ ΚΑΛΑΡΕΟΣ.

[Rambaud, L'empire grec au dixième siècle, p. 175 sqq. ; Bury, Later Roman Empire, vol. ii. p. 339 sqq. ; Diehl, L'origine du régime des thèmes dans l'empire byzantin (in Etudes d'histoire du moyen âge, dédiées à Gabriel Monod, 1896) ; Schlumberger, Sigillographie byzantine, passim (1884).]

### 4. CONSTANTINE PORPHYROGENNETOS ON THE ADMINISTRATION OF THE EMPIRE—(P. 62-91)

The treatise of Constantine Porphyrogennetos on the Administration of the Roman Empire is one of the most interesting books of the Middle Ages, and one of the most precious for the early mediæval history of south-eastern Europe. The author wrote it as a handbook for the guidance of his son Romanus. Internal evidence allows us to infer the exact date of its composition. Chaps. 1-29 were composed between A.D. 948 and 950 ; chap. 45 was composed in 952. The work was probably published in 953.

In his preface[1] Constantine promises his son instruction on four subjects. He will explain (1) which of the neighbouring nations may be a source of danger to the Empire, and what nations may be played off against those formidable neighbours ; (2) how the unreasonable demands of neighbouring peoples may be eluded. (3) He will give a geographical and ethnographical description of the various nations and an account of their relations with the Empire ; and (4) enumerate recent changes and innovations in the condition and administration of the Empire. This programme is followed. A summary of the contents of the book will probably interest readers of Gibbon, and it may be divided under these four heads.

[1] P. 66 ed. Bonn

## I. (Chaps. 1-12)

## II. (c. 13) [2]

## III. (c. 14-46

[2] The first two paragraphs of c. 13, with the title of the chapter (p. 81, ed. B.), really belong to part i., and should be separated from the rest of c. 13 (which ought to be entitled περὶ τῶν ἀκαίρων αἰτήσεων τῶν ἐθνῶν).

[3] P. 113, l. 6 to end ; this piece ought to be a separate chapter.

---

[4] See Finlay, ii. 354 *sqq.*, and R. Garnett, the Story of Gycia in the Eng. Hist. Review, vol. xii. p. 100 *sqq.* (1897), where it is made probable that this episode belongs not to the Byzantine, but to an earlier period of the history of Cherson, probably to 36-16 B.C.

## 5. THE BYZANTINE NAVY—(P. 91 *sqq.*)

The history of the Byzantine sea-power has still to be written. The chief sources (up to the tenth century) are Leo's *Tactics*, c. 19 (περὶ ναυμαχίας); the official returns of two expeditions to Crete in the tenth century, included in "Constantine's" *de Cerimoniis*, ii. c. 44 and 45; and (on naval commands under Basil I. and Leo VI.) Constantine, *De Adm. Imp.* c. 51. The chief modern studies that treat the subject are: Gfrörer, Das byzantinische Seewesen (c. 22 in his Byzantinische Geschichten, Bd. ii. p. 401 *sqq.*); C. de la Roncière, Charlemagne et la civilisation maritime au ixᵉ siècle (in Moyen Age, 2ᵉ sér. t. i. p. 201 *sqq.*, 1897); C. Neumann, Die byzantinische Marine; Ihre Verfassung und ihr Verfall. Studien zur Geschichte des 10 bis 12 Jahrhunderts (in Hist. Zeitschrift, B. 45, p. 1 *sqq.* 1898). Add G. Schlumberger, Nicéphore Phocas, p. 52-66.

In the 6th century, after the fall of the Vandal kingdom, the Empire had no sea-foes to fear, and there was therefore no reason to maintain a powerful navy. The Mediterranean, though all its coasts were not part of the Empire, was practically once more an Imperial lake. This circumstance is a sufficient defence against the indictment which Gfrörer[1] brought against Justinian for neglecting the navy. The scene changed in the second half of the seventh century, when the Saracens took to the sea. The Emperors had to defend their coasts and islands against a hostile maritime power. Consequently a new naval organization was planned and carried out ; and we must impute the merit of this achievement to the successors of Heraclius. We have indeed no notices, in any of our authorities, of the creation of the Imperial navies, but it is clear that the new system had been established before the days of Anastasius III. and Leo III. Under Basil I. and his son the naval organization was remodelled and improved ; the settlement of the Saracens in Crete, and their incursions in the Aegean, were facts which urgently forced the Emperors to look to their ships. From this time till the latter part of the eleventh century, the fleets of the Empire were the strongest in the Mediterranean.

There were two fleets, the Imperial and the Provincial (Thematic). Until the time of Basil, the Imperial fleet seems not to have been organized as a standing force. A system seems to have been established whereby, in case Constantinople itself were threatened, a squadron of vessels could be got together for its defence without much delay. This was managed by an arrangement with the shipowners of the capital ; but as to the nature of this arrangement (it seems to have been a sort of "indenture" system) we have only some obscure hints.[2] On the other hand, the several contingents of the provincial fleet, supplied by the themes of the Cibyrrhaeots, Samos, and the Aegean,[3] were always ready for action, like the thematic armies. A standing Imperial fleet seems to have been created by Basil, and to him we may probably ascribe the institution of the Imperial Admiral (δρουγγάριος τῶν πλοΐμων).[4] This admiral, the great Drungarios, was strictly commander of the Imperial fleet, but on occasions when the Imperial and Provincial fleets acted together he would naturally be the commander in chief. The admirals of the three divisions of the Provincial fleet had the title of drungarios, when they were first instituted.[5] But they were promoted to the title of *stratêgos*, which they continued to hold, after Basil had raised the name drungarios to new honour by conferring it upon the commander of the Imperial fleet. There can be little doubt, it seems to me, that τὰ πλόϊμα in this connexion means the Imperial fleet, and not (as Gfrörer maintained) both the Imperial and Provincial fleets.[6]

---

[1] *Op. cit.* p. 402-4.  [2] Theophanes, *sub* A.M. 6302, p. 487, ed. de Boor.

[3] Hellas also supplied naval contingents sometimes (as in the Cretan expedition, A.D. 902), but was not one of the fleet themes proper.

[4] Cp. Cedrenus, ii. p. 219, p. 227; Gfrörer, *op. cit.* p. 433.

[5] Cp. Leo, Tactics, 19, § 23, 24.

[6] Gfrörer (p. 415) has misunderstood the passage in Leo's Tactics referred to in the preceding note.

The Imperial fleet in the tenth century was larger than the Provincial. Thus in the Cretan expedition of A.D. 902—for which Gibbon gives the total figures (p. 93)—the contingents of the fleets were as follows :—

| | | | |
|---|---|---|---|
| Imperial Fleet | | { | 60 dromonds. |
| | | { | 40 pamphylians. |
| Provincial Fleet | Cibyrrh. Theme | { | 15 dromonds. |
| | | { | 16 pamphylians. |
| | Samos ,, | { | 10 dromonds. |
| | | { | 12 pamphylians. |
| | Aegean ,, | { | 10 dromonds. |
| | | { | 7 pamphylians. |
| | Total | { | 35 dromonds. |
| | | { | 35 pamphylians. |

(Helladic Theme, 10 dromonds.)

But, though the provincial squadrons formed a smaller armament, they had the advantage of being always prepared for war.

The causes of the decay of the Byzantine navy in the eleventh century have been studied by C. Neumann, in the essay cited above. He shows that the antimilitary policy of the emperors in the third quarter of that century affected the navy as well as the army (cp. above, vol. 5, p. 222, n. 67). But the main cause was the Seljūk conquest. It completely disorganized the themes which furnished the contingents of the Provincial fleet. In the 12th century the Emperors depended on the navy of Venice, which they paid by commercial privileges.

The dromonds or biremes were of different sizes and builds. Thus the largest size might be manned by a crew of 300 or 290. Those of a medium size might hold, like the old Greek triremes, about 200 men. There were still smaller ones, which, besides a hundred oarsmen who propelled them, contained only a few officers, steersmen, &c. (perhaps twenty in all). Then there were a special kind of biremes, distinguished by build, not by size, called Pamphylians, and probably remarkable for their swiftness. The Emperor Leo in his Tactics directs that the admiral's ship should be very large and swift and of Pamphylian build.[V] The pamphylians in the Cretan expedition of A.D. 902 were of two sizes : the larger manned by 160 men, the smaller by 130. The importance of these Pamphylian vessels ought, I think, to be taken in connexion with the importance of the Cibyrrhaeot theme (see above, App. 3), which received its name from Pamphylian Cibyra. We may suspect that Cibyra was a centre of shipbuilding.

Besides the biremes, ships with single banks of oars were used, especially for scouting purposes. They were called galleys.[8] The name dromond or "runner" was a general name for a warship and could be applied to the galleys[9] as well as to the biremes ; but in common use it was probably restricted to biremes, and even to those biremes which were not of Pamphylian build.

Gibbon describes the ξυλόκαστρον, an erection which was built above the middle deck of the largest warships, to protect the soldiers who cast stones and darts against the enemy. There was another wooden erection at the prow, which was also manned by soldiers, but it served the special purpose of protecting the fire-tube which was placed at the prow.

The combustible substances on which the Byzantines relied so much, and apparently with good reason, in their naval warfare, were of various kinds and were

[7] 19, § 37, τὸ δὴ λεγόμενον πάμφυλον. Gfrörer attempted to prove that the pamphylians were manned by chosen crews, and derived their name from πάμφυλος ("belonging to all nations"), not from the country. But the passage in the Tactics does not support this view. The admiral's ship is to be manned by ἐξ ἅπαντος τοῦ στρατοῦ ἐπιλέκτους ; but this proves nothing for other pamphylians. But the large number of pamphylians in both the Imperial and the Provincial fleet (cp. the numbers in the Cretan expedition, given above) disproves Gfrörer's hypothesis.

[8] Tactics, 19, § 10, γαλαίας ἢ μονήρεις. [9] Ibid.

used in various ways; and the confusion of them under the common name of Greek or marine fire has led to some misapprehensions. The simplest fire weapon was probably the "hand tube" ($\chi\epsilon\iota\rho\sigma\sigma\iota\phi\omega\nu$),[10] a tube full of combustibles, which was flung by the hand like a "squib" and exploded on board the enemy's vessel. The marines who cast these weapons were the "grenadiers" of the Middle Ages.[11] "Artificial fire"—probably in a liquid state—was also kept in pots ($\chi\upsilon\tau\rho\alpha\iota$), which may have been cast upon the hostile ships by engines. Such pots are represented in pictures of warships in an old Arabic Ms. preserved in the Bibliothèque Nationale, and reproduced by M. Schlumberger in his work on Nicephorus Phocas.[12] But there was another, and more interesting, method of hurling "artificial fire". This method anticipated the principle of later firearms: gunpowder was used to propel the missiles of destruction through a tube ($\sigma\iota\phi\omega\nu$). This is the only reasonable inference from the two certain facts that gunpowder was one of the artificial explosives used by the Byzantines in their naval warfare (see above, p. 11, note 22), and that combustibles which exploded when they reached the enemy's ships were propelled through tubes, which were managed by a gunner (siphonator). Thus the Byzantines just fell short of revolutionising warfare, by failing to apply their propelling powder to leaden missiles.

## 6. THE PAULICIAN HERESY—(C. LIV.)

In Gibbon's day the material for the origin, early history, and tenets of the Paulicians consisted of Bk. i. of the work of Photius on the Manichaeans, and the History of the Manichaeans by Petros Sikeliotes. The work of Photius was edited by J. C. Wolf in his Anecdota Graeca, i., ii. (1722); [1] but Gibbon did not consult it (above, chap. liv. note 1). There was further the account of the Bogomils in the *Panoplia* of Euthymius Zigabenus, a monk who lived under Alexius Comnenus and is celebrated in the Alexiad of Anna. A Latin translation was published by P. F. Zinos in 1555; the Greek text edited by a Greek monk (Metrophanes) in 1710. It may be read in Migne, P. G. vol. 130. The section on the Bogomils was edited separately by Gieseler in 1841-2.

The documents which have come to light since are closely connected with the accounts of Photius and Peter; they bring few new facts or fictions, but they bring material for criticizing the facts and fictions already known. (1) In 1849 Gieseler published a tract [2] of a certain Abbot Peter, containing an account of the Paulicians similar to that of Photius and Peter Sikeliotes (with whom Gieseler identified the author). (2) The publication of the chronicle of George Monachus by Muralt in 1859 showed that this chronicle had incorporated a similar account in his work.

We have then four documents, which presume one original account whereon all depend, directly or indirectly, if indeed one of them is not itself the original source. The problem of determining their relations to one another and the common original is complicated by (1) the nature of Photius, Bk. i., and (2) the variations in the Mss. of George Monachus.

The "First Book" of Photius falls into two parts: I. chaps. 1-15, which contains (*a*) a history of the Paulicians, chaps. 1-10; and (*b*) an account of earlier Manichaean movements, chaps. 11-14; II. chaps. 15-27, a history of the Paulicians, going over the same ground, but differently, and adding a brief notice of the revolt of Chrysocheir. Part I. (*a*) corresponds closely to the accounts of Abbot Peter, Peter Sik.,[3] and George Mon.; and its Photian authorship seems assured by the testimony of Euthymius Zigabenus. Part II. was a distinct composition originally, and was tacked on to the Photian work. Thus "Photius" resolves itself into two documents, one Photian, the other Pseudo-Photian.

[10] Tactics, 19, § 57.
[11] Some Arab grenades (first explained by de Saulcy) still exist. Cp. illustration in Schlumberger, Nicéphore Phocas, p. 59.
[12] P. 55, 57. [1] Reprinted in Migne, P. G. vol. 102.
[2] Title: Πέτρου ἐλαχίστου μοναχοῦ Ἡγουμένου περὶ Παυλικιανῶν τῶν καὶ Μανιχαίων.
[3] Peter Sik. reverses the order of (*a*) and (*b*).

The credit of having made this clear belongs to Karapet Ter-Mkrttschian, who published in 1893 a treatise entitled "Die Paulikianer in byzantinischen Kaiser-reiche und verwandte ketzerische Erscheinungen in Armenien". This investiga-tion, although it is ill arranged and leads to no satisfactory conclusion, has yet been of great use in opening up the whole question, as well as by publishing out-of-the-way evidence on various obscure Armenian sects. While Gieseler held that the treatise of the "Abbot Peter" was simply an extract from the work of Peter Sikeliotes, Ter-Mkrttschian tries to prove that the Abbot Peter is the oldest of our existing sources—the source of George Monachus, and Photius (Bk. 1 (a)). [The Armenian scholar further propounded (p. 122 sqq.) the impossible theory that Peter Sikeliotes wrote in the time of Alexius Comnenus—when the Paulician and Bogomil question was engaging the attention of the court and the public. It is impossible, because the date of the Vatican Ms. of the treatise of Peter is earlier. As to the Pseudo-Photian account, Ter-Mkrttschian holds that its autho-utilised the work of Euthymius Zigabenus (p. 8-9).]

After Ter-Mkrttschian came J. Friedrich (Der ursprüngliche bei Georgios Monachos nur theilweise erhaltene Bericht über die Paulikianer, published in the Sitzungsberichte of the Bavarian Academy, 1896, p. 67 sqq.). Friedrich denied that the Abbot Peter's tract was the source used by George Monachus; and he published (p. 70-81), as the original source of all the extant accounts, the passage of George Monachus as it appears in the Madrid Ms. of the chronicle. In this Ms. the passage is more than twice as long as in other Mss., the additional matter consisting chiefly of directions to Christians how they were to refute a Paulician heretic when they met one. According to Friedrich, the work of the Abbot Peter is an extract from this treatise, preserved in the Madrid Ms.; and the accounts in the other Mss. of George Monachus are likewise extracts.

But the view of Friedrich has been upset conclusively by C. de Boor, the only scholar who is thoroughly master of the facts about the Mss. of George Monachus. In a short paper in the Byzantinische Zeitschrift, vii. p. 40 sqq. (1898), de Boor has shown that the additional matter in the Madrid Ms. comes from an inter-polator. George seems to have made a second version of his chronicle, and in revising it he consulted his sources, or some of them, again. This seems to be the only hypothesis on which the peculiarities of one Ms., Coislin. 305, can be explained. In the case of the Paulician passage, de Boor points out that in the first form of his work (reproduced by Coislin. 305) he used an original source; from which he again drew at more length on a second revision (represented by the other Mss.). It is therefore the second revision which we must compare with the work of the Abbot Peter in order to determine whether the Abbot Peter is the original source. De Boor does not decide this; but calls attention to two passages which might seem to show that the Abbot used the second revision of George the Monk, and one passage which rather points to the independence of the Abbot. On the whole, the second alternative seems more probable.

The present state of the question may be summed up as follows: The (1) original sketch of the Paulician heresy, its origin and history—whereon all our extant accounts ultimately depend—is lost. This original work was used by (2) George the Monk (in the 9th century) for his chronicle; (a) in Coislin. 305 we have a shorter extract, (b) in the other Mss. (and Muralt's text) we have a fuller extract. (3) The tract of the Abbot Peter was either taken from the second edi-tion of George the Monk, or was independently extracted from the original work; but it was not the original work itself. (4) It is not quite certain whether the treatise of Photius was derived from the derivative work of the Abbot Peter (so Ter-Mkrttschian; and this is also the opinion of Ehrhard, ap. Krumbacher's Byz. Litt. p. 76; but Friedrich argues against this view, op. cit. p. 85-6); perhaps it is more likely that Photius also used the original work. (5) The position of Peter Sikeliotes is quite uncertain (see below). (6) The interpolation in the Madrid Ms. of George the Monk (see above) was added not later than the 10th century, in which period the Ms. was written. Then come (7) Euthymius Zigabenus in the Panoplia, c. 1100 A.D., and (8) Pseudo-Photius.

The unsolved problem touching Peter Sikeliotes would have no historical importance, except for his statements about his own mission to Tephrice, and the intention of the Paulicians of the east to send missionaries to Bulgaria, and the dedication of his work to an Archbishop of Bulgaria. He says that he himself was sent to Tephrice by Michael III. for the ransom of captives. But the title of the treatise is curious : Πέτρου Σικελιώτου ἱστορία . . . προσωποποιηθεῖσα ὡς πρὸς τὸν ᾿Αρχιεπίσκοπον Βουλγαρίας. The word προσωποποιηθεῖσα suggests that the historical setting of the treatise is fictitious. In denying the historical value of this evidence as to the propagation of Paulicianism in Bulgaria at such an early date, Ter-Mkrttschian (p. 13 sqq.) and Friedrich (p. 101-2) are agreed. According to the life of St. Clement of Bulgaria (ed. Miklorich, p. 34) the heresy did not enter the country till after Clement's death in A.D. 916 (Friedrich, ib.).

Ter-Mkrttschian endeavours to prove that the Paulicians were simply Marcionites. Friedrich argues against this view, on the ground of some statements in the text which he published from the Madrid Ms., where the creator of the visible world is identified with the devil. But these statements may have been interpolated in the tenth century from a Bogomil source.

On the Armenian Paulicians and cognate sects, see Döllinger's Beiträge zur Sektengeschichte des Mittelalters ; Ter-Mkrttschian's work, already cited ; and Conybeare's Key of Truth (see below). The basis of Döllinger's study was the treatise "Against the Paulicians" of the Armenian Patriarch John Ozniensis (published in his works, 1834, ed. Archer). Cp. Conybeare, op. cit. App. iv. Ter-Mkrttschian has rendered new evidence accessible.

In his History of the Bulgarians,[4] Jireček gives the result of the investigations of Rački and other Slavonic scholars into the original doctrines of the Bogomils. (1) They rejected the Old Testament, the Fathers, and ecclesiastical tradition. They accepted the New Testament, and laid weight on a number of old apocryphal works. (2) They held two principles, equal in age and power : one good (a triune being = God) ; the other bad (= Satan) ; who created the visible world, caused the Fall, governed the world during the period of the Old Testament. (3) The body of Christ the Redeemer was only an apparent, not a real body (for everything corporeal is the work of Satan) ; Mary was an angel. The sacraments are corporeal, and therefore Satanic, symbols. (4) They rejected the use of crucifixes and icons, and regarded churches as the abodes of evil spirits. (5) Only adults were received into their church ; the ceremony consisted of fasting and prayer—not baptism, for water is created by Satan. (6) They had no hierarchy ; but an executive, consisting of a senior or bishop, and two grades of Apostles. (7) Besides the ordinary Christians there was a special order of the Perfect or the Good, who renounced all earthly possessions, marriage, and the use of animal food. These chosen few dressed in black, lived like hermits, and were not allowed to speak to an unbeliever except for the purpose of converting him. (8) No Bogomil was allowed to drink wine. (9) The Bulgarian Bogomils prayed four times every day and four times every night ; the Greek seven times every day, five times every night. They prayed whenever they crossed a bridge or entered a village. They had no holy days. (10) They had a death-bed ceremony (called in the west la convenensa). Whoever died without the advantage of this ceremony went to hell, the ultimate abode of all unbelievers. They did not believe in a purgatory.

We cannot, however, feel certain that this is a fair presentation of the Bogomil doctrines. It is unfortunate that none of their books of ritual, &c., are known to exist.

As early as the tenth century a schism arose in the Bogomil church. A view was promulgated that Satan was not coeval with God, but only a later creation, a fallen angel. This view prevailed in the Bulgarian church, but the Dragoviči clung to the old dualism. The modified doctrine was adopted for the most part

[4] Geschichte der Bulgaren, p. 176 sqq.

by the Bogomils of the west (Albigenses, &c.) except at Toulouse and Albano on Lake Garda (Jireček, *op. cit.* p. 213).

The kinship of the Bogomil doctrines to the Paulician is obvious. But it has not been proved that they are historically derived from the Paulician ; though there are historical reasons for supposing Paulician influence.

Since the above was written, Mr. Conybeare published (1898) the Armenian text and an English translation of the book of the Paulicians of Thonrak in Armenia. This book is entitled the Key of Truth and seems to have been drawn up by the beginning of the ninth century. This liturgy considerably modifies our views touching the nature of Paulicianism, which appears to have had nothing to do with Marcionism, but to have been a revival of the old doctrine of Adoptionism according to which Jesus was a man and nothing more until in his thirtieth year he was baptized by John and the Spirit of God came down and entered into him ; then and thereby he became the Son of God. Of this Adoptionist view we have two ancient monuments, the *Shepherd of Hermas* and the *Acts of Archelaus.* The doctrine survived in Spain until the 8th and 9th centuries ; and this fact suggests the conjecture that it also lingered on in southern France, so that the heresy of the Cathars and Albigenses would not have been a mere imported Bogomilism, but an ancient local survival. Mr. Conybeare thinks that it lived on from early times in the Balkan peninsula " where it was probably the basis of Bogomilism ".

There can be no doubt that Mr. Conybeare's discovery brings us nearer to the true nature of Paulicianism. In this book the Paulicians speak for themselves, and free themselves from the charges of Manichaeism and dualism which have been always brought against them. Mr. Conybeare thinks that *Paulician,* the Armenian form of *Paulian,* is derived from Paul of Samosata, whose followers were known to the Greeks of the 4th century as Pauliani. Gregory Magistros [5] (who in the 11th century was commissioned by the Emperor Constantine IX. to drive the Paulicians or Thonraki out of Imperial Armenia) states that the Paulicians " got their poison from Paul of Samosata," the last great representative of the Adoptionist doctrine. Mr. Conybeare suggests that, the aim of the Imperial government having been to drive the Adoptionist Church outside the Empire, the Paulians " took refuge in Mesopotamia and later in the Mohammedan dominions generally, where they were tolerated and where their own type of belief, as we see from the *Acts of Archelaus*, had never ceased to be accounted orthodox. They were thus lost sight of almost for centuries by the Greek theologians of Constantinople and other great centres. When at last they again made themselves felt as the extreme left wing of the iconoclasts—the great party of revolt against the revived Greek paganism of the eighth century—it was the orthodox or Grecised Armenians that, as it were, introduced them afresh to the notice of the Greeks " (Introduction, p. cvi.).

## 7. THE SLAVS IN THE PELOPONNESUS—(P. 69)

All unprejudiced investigators now admit the cogency of the evidence which shows that by the middle of the eighth century there was a very large Slavonic element in the population of the Peloponnesus.[1] The Slavonic settlements began in the latter half of the sixth century, and in the middle of the eighth century the depopulation caused by the great plague invited the intrusion of large masses. The general complexion of the peninsula was so Slavonic that it was called

---

[5] Mr. Conybeare publishes a translation of letters of Gregory which bear on Paulicianism, in Appendix iii.

[1] The thesis of Fallmerayer, who denied that there were any descendants of the ancient Hellenes in Greece, was refuted by Hopf (and Hertzberg and others) ; but all Hopf's arguments are not convincing. Fallmerayer's brilliant book stimulated the investigation of the subject (Geschichte der Halbinsel Morea im Mittelalter, 2 vols., 1830-6).

Sclavonia. The only question to be determined is, how were these strangers distributed, and what parts of the Peloponnesus were Slavized? For answering these questions, the names of places are our chief evidence. Here, as in the Slavonic districts which became part of Germany, the Slavs ultimately gave up their own language and exerted hardly any sensible influence on the language which they adopted; but they introduced new local names which survived. It was just the reverse, as has been well remarked by Philippson, in the case of the Albanese settlers, who in the fourteenth century brought a new ethnical element into the Peloponnesus. The Albanians preserved their own language, but the old local names were not altered.

Now we find Slavonic names scattered about in all parts of the Peloponnesus; but they are comparatively few on the Eastern side, in Argolis and Eastern Laconia. They are numerous in Arcadia and Achaia, in Elis, Messenia and Western Laconia. But the existence of Slavonic settlements does not prove that the old Hellenic inhabitants were abolished in these districts. In fact we can only say that a large part of Elis, the slopes of Taygetus, and a district in the south of Laconia, were exclusively given over to the Slavs. Between Megalopolis and Sparta there was an important town, which has completely disappeared, called Veligosti; and this region was probably a centre of Slavonic settlers.

See the impartial investigation of Dr. A. Philippson, Zur Ethnographie des Peloponnes in Petermann's Mittheilungen, vol. 36, p. 1 sqq. and 33 sqq., 1890.

The conversion and Hellenization of the Slavs went on together from the ninth century, and, with the exception of the settlements in Taygetus and the Arcadian mountains, were completed by the twelfth century. At the time of the conquest of the Peloponnesus by Villehardouin, four ethnical elements are distinguished by Philippson : (1) Remains of the old Hellenes, mixed with Slavs, in Maina and Tzakonia, (2) Byzantine Greeks (i.e., Byzantinized Hellenes, and settlers from other parts of the Empire) in the towns. (3) Greek-speaking Slavo-Greeks (sprung from unions of Slavs and Greeks). (4) Almost pure Slavs in Arcadia and Taygetus. The 2nd and 3rd classes tend to coalesce and ultimately become indistinguishable (except in physiognomy).

The old Greek element lived on purest perhaps in the district between Mt. Parnon and the Sea—eastern Laconia. The inhabitants came to be called Tzakones and the district Tzakonia; and they developed a remarkable dialect of their own. They were long supposed to be Slavs. See A. Thumb, Die ethno-graphische Stellung der Zakonen (Indogerm, Forschungen, iv. 195 sqq., 1894).

Fallmerayer, in harmony with his Slavonic theory, proposed to derive the name Morea from the Slavonic more, sea. This etymology defied the linguistic laws of Slavonic word-formation. Other unacceptable derivations have been suggested, but we have at last got back to the old mulberry, but in a new sense. ὁ Μορέας is formed from μορέα, "mulberry tree," with the meaning "planta-tion or region of mulberry trees" (= μορεών). We find the name first applied to Elis, whence it spread to the whole Peloponnesus; and it is a memorial of the extensive cultivation of mulberries for the manufacture of silk. This explanation is due to the learned and scientific Greek philologist, M. G. N. Hatzidakês (Byz. Zeitsch. vol. 2, p. 283 sqq. and vol. 5, p. 341, sqq.).

## 8. EARLY HISTORY OF THE BULGARIANS—(P. 130 sqq.)

Bulgaria and Russia are Slavonic countries, Bulgarian and Russian are Slavonic languages; but it is an important historical fact that the true Bulgarians and the true Russians, who created these Slavonic states, were not Slavs them-selves and did not speak Slavonic tongues. The Russian invader was a Teuton; he belonged, at all events, to the same Indo-European family as the Slavs whom he conquered. But the Bulgarian invader was a Tartar, of wholly differ-ent ethnic affinities from the people whom he subdued. In both cases the conqueror was assimilated, gradually forgot his own tongue, and learned the language of his subjects; in both cases he gave the name of his own race to the state which he founded. And both cases point to the same truth touching the Slavs: their strong power of assimilation, and their lack of the political instinct and force which are necessary for creating and organizing a political union. Both Bulgaria and Russia were made by strangers.

(1) We first met Bulgarians in the fifth century, after the break-up of the Empire of Attila. We then saw them settled somewhere north of the Danube—it is best to say roughly between the Danube and the Dnieper—and sometimes appearing south of the Danube. (2) We saw them next, a century later, as subjects of the Avar empire. We saw also (above, vol. 4, App. 15) that they were closely connected with the tribes of the Uturgurs and Kotrigurs. (3) The next important event in the history of the Bulgarians is the break-up of the Avar empire. In this break-up they themselves assisted. In the reign of Heraclius, the Bulgarian king Kurt revolts against the chagan of the Avars and makes an alliance with Heraclius, towards the close of that emperor's reign (c. 635-6).[1] At this time the Bulgarians and their fellows the Utigurs seem to have been united under a common king; Kurt is designated as lord of the Utigurs. (4) The next movement seems to have been a westward migration of part of the Bulgarians. Crossing the Danube, some of the emigrants settled in Pannonia, in the now reduced realm of the Avars; and others went farther afield and found their final abodes in Italy on the shores of the Adriatic (see above, p. 130, note 5). (5) Kurt died in the reign of Constans II. His successor Bezmêr reigned only three years, and was succeeded by Isperich, who crossed the Danube and established the Bulgarian kingdom in Moesia in the reign of Constantine IV. (c. A.D. 679).

The Bulgarians on the Danube had kinsfolk far to the east, who in the tenth century lived between the Volga and the Kama. They are generally known as the Bulgarians of the Volga; their country was distinguished as Black Bulgaria[2] from White Bulgaria on the Danube. The city of the eastern Bulgarians was destroyed by Timour, but their name is still preserved in the village of Bolgary in the province of Kasan. They must have migrated northwards to these regions from the shores of the Lake of Azov, between the Dnieper and Don. For in the 8th century they were certainly in the neighbourhood of the Lake of Azov,[3] and were on the west side of the Don, while the kindred tribe of the Kotrags or Kotrigurs were over against them on the east bank. Towards the end of the ninth century the Mohammedan religion began to take root among the Bulgarians of the Volga, and the conversion was completed in the year A.D. 922. We have a good account of their country and their customs from the Arabic traveller Ibn Foslan.[4]

Thus, about the end of the seventh century, there were five settlements of the Bulgarians and their kinspeople in Europe. (1) The Bulgarians between the Don and Dnieper. (2) The Kotrags or Kotrigurs, their neighbours on the other side of the Don. (3) The Bulgarian kingdom of the Danube, in which the Utigurs had been merged. (4) The Bulgarian settlement in Pannonia. (5) The Bulgarian settlements in Italy.

The existence of these five lots of Bulgarians was accounted for by a legend which must have arisen soon after the foundation of the Bulgarian kingdom in Moesia. According to this legend King Kuvrat (Kurt) had five sons. When his

---

[1] Nicephorus, p. 24, ed. de Boor, Nicephorus calls him Kuvrat "lord of the Unogundurs" (i.e., the Utigurs, cp. above, vol. 4, App. 15); but he is clearly the same as Kuvrat (or Κοβρᾶτος) lord of the "Huns and Bulgarians" mentioned below, p. 36; the Krovat of Theophanes and the Kurt of the old Bulgarian list (see next Appendix). Theophanes identifies the Bulgarians and Unogundurs.

[2] Constantine Porph., De Adm. Imp. c. 12, ἡ μαύρη Βουλγαρία. Cp. Βελοχρωβατία (white Croatia), Μαυροβλαχία, &c.

[3] This appears from the account in Theophanes and Nicephorus.

[4] See C. M. Frähn, Aelteste Nachrichten über die Wolga-Bulgharen, in Memoirs of the Academy of St. Petersburg (series vi.), i. p. 550 (1832). Cp. Roesler, Romanische Studien, p. 242 sqq.

death approached he enjoined upon them not to separate. But they did not obey his command. The first, Batbaian, remained in his native land, according to his father's will; the second, Kotrag, crossed the Don and dwelled over against his brother; the third, Isperich, settled in Bessarabia; [5] the fourth migrated to Pannonia; the fifth to Italy. This story had been written down in some Greek book in the course of the eighth century; for Theophanes and Nicephorus derived it independently from the same written source.[6]

It is easy to separate the fact from the fiction. Both Kurt and Isperich are historical; Isperich may well have been Kurt's son (for only one short reign intervened between them); and their chronological relation corresponds to fact. Moreover the westward migration to Pannonia and Italy probably happened after Kurt's death, about the middle of the 7th century. The legendary parts of the tale are: (1) the five sons of Kurt and his deathbed commands; (2) the representation of the eponymous Kotragos as a son of Kurt, and the belief that the people of Kotragos branched off from the Bulgarians in the 7th century; (3) the chronological error of making the Bulgarians first come to the regions between the Dniester and the Danube under Isperich in the 7th century; and thus representing Kurt as a king reigning over Bulgarians east of the Dnieper.

Roesler, Hunfalvy and others have sustained that the Bulgarians were not of Turkish, but of Finnish race. But they have not proved their case.[7]

For the customs of the Danubian Bulgarians, which point to their Tartar origin, see the Responses of Pope Nicholas (in the ninth century) to the matters on which they consulted him.[8]

## 9. LIST OF ANCIENT BULGARIAN PRINCES—(P. 133)

A curious fragment of an old list of Bulgarian princes from the earliest times up to A.D. 765, was edited by A. Popov in 1866 (Obzor Chronographov russkoi redaktsii). It is reproduced by Jireček (Geschichte der Bulgaren, p. 127). The list is drawn up in the language of the Slavs of Bulgaria, but contains non-Slavonic words, belonging to the tongue of the Bulgarian conquerors. It may be translated as follows, with the exception of the Bulgarian words:—

[A.D. 124-424.] "Avitochol lived 300 years; he belonged to the race of Dulo; and his years were *dilom tvirem*.

[A.D. 424-574.] "Irnik lived 100 years and 50; he belonged to the race of Dulo; and his years were *dilom tvirem*.

[A.D. 574-576.] "Gostun ruled as viceroy for 2 years; he belonged to the race of Jermi; and his years were *dochs tvirem*.

[A.D. 576-636.] "Kur't reigned for 60 years; he was of the race of Dulo; but his years were *šegor véčem*.

[A.D. 636-639.] "Bezmêr 3 years; he was of the race of Dulo; but his years were *šegor véčem*.

"These 5 princes (k'nęz) held the principality on the other side of the Danube for 515 years, with shorn heads.

[A.D. 679.] "And then Isperich, prince, came to (this) side of the Danube, where (they are) till this day.

[A.D. 639-700.] 'Esperich, prince, 61 years; he was of the race of Dulo; his years were *verenialem*. ['Ασπαρουχ.]

[A.D. 700-720.] "Tervel 21 years; he was of the race of Dulo; his years were *tekučtem tvirem*. [Τερβέλης.]

[A.D. 720-748.] " . . .[1] 28 years; he was of the race of Dulo; his years were *dvanšechtem*.

---

[5] Onglos or Oglos (in Theophanes and Nicephorus), the corner between the Danube and the Dniester.

[6] Theoph. ad ann. 6171; Nicephorus, p. 33-4.

[7] For the Turkish side see Vámbéry, A magyarok eredete, cap. iv. p. 48 *sqq.*

[8] They will be found in any collection of Acta Conciliorum, *e.g.*, in Mansi, vol. xv.

[1] Possibly the preceding *tvirem* conceals the name of the successor of Tervel

[A.D. 748-753.]   "Sevar 5 years; he was of the race of Dulo; his years were
                  *tochal tom.*
[A.D. 753-760.]   "Kormisoš 17 years; [2] he was of the race of Vokil; his years
                  were *šegor tvirim.* [Κορμέσιος.]
                  'This prince changed the race of Dulo—that is to say Vich-
                  tun (?).
[?]               "Vinech [?] 7 years; he was of the race of Ukil; his name
                  was *šegoralem* (?).
[A.D. 760-763.]   "Telec 3 years; he was of the race of Ugain; and his years were
                  *somor altem.* He too was of another race, [Τελέτζης.]
[A.D. 764?]       "Umor 40 days; he was of the race of Ugil; his (years were)
                  *dilom tutom.*" [Οὔμαρος.]

Various attempts have been made to explain the Bulgarian words (which ought
to be numerals,[3] but which clearly do not correspond in all cases to the Slavonic
numbers) from Turkish dialects, or even from the Hungarian language, by Hilferding, Kunik and Radlov; [4] but none of these attempts are convincing.[5]

The last three reigns cause a difficulty, when we compare them with the notices
of Nicephorus (p. 69 and p. 70, ed. de Boor) and Theophanes (A.M. 6254 and
6256). There seems to be no room for a reign of 7 years between Kormisoš and
Telec; it is indeed considered uncertain whether *vinech* represents the name of a
prince or belongs closely to the preceding *vichtun*. The murder of Telec happened, according to Nicephorus and Theophanes, in A.D. 762 (after his defeat by
Constantine V. in June of that year); but Theophanes relates the elevation of
Telec under the same year. Then, according to the Greek historians, Sabinos,
son-in-law of Kormisoš, is elected prince; he makes peace with Constantine, but
is presently deposed and flies to Constantinople, Paganos (= Baian) being elevated in his place. We then find Umar set up by Sabinos, as a rival of Baian
apparently, and deposed by the Bulgarians, who set up in his stead Toktu, brother
of Baian, in A.D. 764—Baian being apparently dead; this is the account of Nicephorus. But Theophanes says nothing of Umar; but brings Baian (Paganos) to
Constantinople, where Constantine and Sabinos receive him. Both the Greek
writers agree that Constantine invaded Bulgaria in this year, but Nicephorus implies that it was in the interests of Sabinos and Umar. Now in the Bulgarian
list Sabinos and Baian do not appear.

The Greek historians are far more likely to have made a mistake in regard to
these events than the Bulgarian list. The confusion probably arises from the
simultaneous reigns of rival princes. If Vinech was the natural successor of
Kormisoš, his reign, lasting seven years from the death of Kormisoš, was mainly
titular; and the three years of Telec were synchronous with part of the seven
years of Vinech, and also with the reign of Baian, an usurper whom the list
entirely omits.

It would then turn out that *Sabinos* of the Greek historians corresponds to
*Vinech* of the list. As Sabinos raised up Umar (of his own Ukil family) to take
his place as prince in A.D. 764, the seven years of Sabinos would come to an end
in that year and we should place the death of Kormisoš in 758. As the years of
the Bulgarian list need not all be full years, and as Tervel may have died in 719
(he was still alive in 718-19, see Theophanes, *sub ann.*), there is no difficulty in
this supposition. We thus get:—

Kormisoš, c. A.D. 751-758.
Vinech (Savinos), A.D. 758-764.
Telec, A.D. 759-760 to 762.
[Baian, A.D. 762 to 764.]
Umar, A.D. 764.
Toktu, A.D. 764.

[2] Mistake for 7 (Jireček, p. 140 note).
[3] Certainly *večem, altem, dochs* suggest the Turkish numerals *üč, alti, dokuz.*
[4] Tomaschek suggested that they might be *epitheta ornantia.*
[5] The various suggestions are put together by Jireček apud Kuun, Relationum Hungarorum Hist. Antiquiss. ii. p. 12 *sqq.*

## 10. OMORTAG'S INSCRIPTION—(P. 134)

Readers of Gibbon may be interested in seeing the text of the remarkable inscription of a Greek architect employed by prince Omortag ; it was engraved on a pillar of red marble found at Trnovo. I take it from Jireček, Gesch. der Bulgaren (p. 148).

Γιωμ Ομορταγ ις τον παλεον υκον αυτου μενον επυησεν υπερθυμον υκον ις τον Δανουβην, κ'ανα μεσα τον δυο υκο τον πανθυμον . Καταμετρησας ις τον μεσον επυησα τουμβαν. Κε απο την αυτην μεσην της τουμβας εος την αυλιν μου την αρχεαν ισιν οργηε(ς) μυριαδες : β : κ'επι τον Δανουβιν ισην οργϊες μυριαδες : β : το δε αυτο τουβι εστιν πανθυμον. μετριστε 'ς τιν γιν. επυις' τα γραματα ταυτα ο ανθροπος κκ αλαζον αποθνισκι κε αλος γενατε κε ινα ο εσχατον γηνομενος. ταυτα θεορον υπομνησκετε τον πυισαντα αυτο. το δε ονομα του αρχοντος εστην Ωμορταγ καν . να συ βιβη ο θs ανοσϊ αυτον . ζισσετ . η : ρ.

This document states that Giom Omortag built a new palace on the Danube, and also a tomb, exactly halfway between this new palace and his old palace. Observe that he is called by the Bulgarian title khan, not by the Slavonic knez.

There are several difficulties in the interpretation of the inscription. This is not the place to discuss them, but in one point I may correct the interpretation and punctuation of Jireček. The second clause (κ'ανα μεσα, &c.) he translates freely "und in der Mitte beider ein (drittes) Haus, das grossartigste. Nach einer Vermessung errichtete ich in der Mitte ein Grabmal (jenes dritte Haus ?)." This will not do. Obviously the punctuation before καταμετρήσας should be removed, and the sentence is quite simple (equal to καὶ ἀνὰ μέσα τῶν δύο οἴκω(ν) τῶν πανθύμων καταμετρήσας εἰς την μέσην ἐποίησα τύμβον), "and between those two magnificent houses, having measured the ground, I made a tomb in the middle (halfway)".

## 11. THE NORTHERN LIMITS OF THE FIRST BULGARIAN KINGDOM —(P. 131)

There is evidence to show that the kingdom over which Isperich and Crum ruled was not confined to the Lower Moesia, the country between the Danube and the Balkan range. There is no doubt that their sway extended over the lands which form the modern kingdom of Roumania ; and it is possible that the sway of Crum extended over Siebenbürgen or Transylvania.

The extension of Bulgaria north of the Danube in the time of Crum is proved by a passage in the Anonymous writer of the ninth century, of whose work a fragment on the reign of Leo V. is preserved (see above, vol. 5, Appendix, p. 502). There we find "Bulgaria beyond the Danube" (ἐκεῖθεν τοῦ Ἴστρου ποταμοῦ, in the Bonn ed. of Leo Grammaticus, p. 345) ; Crum transported a multitude of prisoners thither. This is borne out by the Bavarian geographer of the ninth century, who mentions the country of the Bulgarians as one of the countries *north* of the Danube.[1]

The chief evidence cited for Bulgarian dominion over Transylvania in the ninth century is the enumeration of a number of Dacian towns as belonging to the regions occupied by the Bulgarians, in the Ravennate Geographer ;[2] and the circumstance that the Bulgarians used to sell salt to the Moravians[3] (there being salt mines in Transylvania, and none in Bulgaria south of the Danube).

[1] Ad septentrionalem plagam Danubii. . . . Vulgarii, regio est immensa et populus multus habens civitates V. The others mentioned are Bohemia and Moravia ; and the three countries are described as regions "que terminant in finibus nostris ". See Schafarik, Slawische Altertümer, ed. Wuttke, ii. p. 673.

[2] Ed. Pinder and Parthey, p. 185.

[3] Annals of Fulda in Pertz Mon. i. 408. Cp. Xénopol, Histoire des Roumains, i. p. 134. He cites other passages, which suggest, though they do not seem to me to prove, that the Bulgarians were common neighbours of Moravia and Francia.

To an unbiassed inquirer the evidence certainly renders it probable that during the 8th century when the Avar monarchy was weak and soon about to yield to the arms of Charles the Great, the Bulgarians extended their power over the Slavs and Vlachs of Siebenbürgen. This was certainly what under the circumstances was likely to happen; and the scanty evidence seems to point to the conclusion that it did happen. There is no reason to suppose that a part of the Bulgarian people settled in Siebenbürgen; only that Siebenbürgen was subject to the princes of Bulgaria during the ninth century until the Magyar invasion. Unfortunately, this question is mixed up with the burning Roumanian question; and the Hungarians firmly reject the idea of a Bulgarian period in Siebenbürgen. The first active promulgator of the view seems to have been Engel,[4] and Hunfalvy devotes several pages to the task of demolishing the "képzelt tiszai Bolgárság," as he calls it, "the imaginary Bulgaria on the Theiss".[5] The Roumanians welcome the notion of a northern Bulgaria, because it would explain the existence of the Bulgarian rite in the Roumanian church, and deprive the Hungarians of an argument for their doctrine, that the Roumanians are late intruders in Transylvania and carried the Bulgarian rite with them from the country south of the Danube.

But, apart from the Transylvanian question, there can be no doubt that Bulgaria included Walachia and extended to the Dniester under the early kings. There is no reason to suppose that when Isperich passed south of the Danube he gave up his dominion in Bessarabia. That Bessarabia was Bulgarian in the 8th century seems a permissible inference from the statement in the legend of the five sons of Kuvrat (see last note). And the fact that there was no other rival power to hold these regions seems to me to be almost conclusive. I am ready even to hazard the hypothesis that the influence of the Bulgarian kings in the 8th century extended as far as the Dnieper. Until the Hungarians came and took possession of Atelkuzu (see note [13], p. 551), there was no other great power nearer than the Khazars. On the Dnieper, during the first half of the 8th century, the Bulgarians would have been in contact with their own kinsfolk.

## 12. THE CONVERSION OF THE SLAVS

It is remarkable that Gibbon has given no account of the Apostles of the Slavs, the brothers Constantine and Methodius; whose work was far more important for the conversion of the Slavonic world to the Christian faith than that of Ulfilas for the conversion of the Germans. Little enough is known of the lives of these men, and their names were soon surrounded with discrepant traditions and legends in various countries—in Moravia and Bohemia, Pannonia and Bulgaria.

There seems no reason to doubt that they were born in Thessalonica, and the date of the birth of Constantine, at least, the elder of the two, probably falls between A.D. 820 and 830. In Thessalonica they were in the midst of Slavonic districts and had opportunities of becoming acquainted with the Slavonic language in their youth. Perhaps they both became monks when they were still young.[1] Constantine went to Constantinople and became a priest. His learning won him the title of Philosopher and the friendship of Photius;[2] but, when Photius started the doctrine of two souls in man, Constantine opposed him. It was probably soon after the elevation of Photius to the Patriarchate (A.D. 857) that Constantine, who had a gift for languages, was sent as a missionary to the Chazars (perhaps A.D. 860-1), who had begged the Emperor to send them a learned instructor. While he was at Cherson, learning the Chazaric language, he "discovered" the remains of the martyr Pope Clement I., which he after-

---

[4] In his Geschichte des alten Pannomiens und der Bulgarei (1767).

[5] Magyarország Ethnographiája, p. 167 sqq.

[1] Cp. Translatio Gauderici, c. 11. But according to the Pannonian legend, Vita Methodii, c. 2 (and the notice is accepted by Jireček, Gesch. der Bulgaren, p. 152) Methodius was appointed to the civil administration of a Slavonic district.

[2] Cp. the Preface of Anastasius to the Council of A.D. 869; Mansi, Conc. 16, 6

wards brought to Rome.[3]  On his return from Chazaria (A.D. 862) he received a new call.  Christianity had already made some way among the Slavs of Moravia, through the missionary activity of the bishops of Passau.  Thus Moravia seemed annexed to the Latin Church.  But the Moravian king Rastislav quarrelled with his German and Bulgarian neighbours, and, seeking the political support of the Eastern Emperor, he determined to bring Moravia into spiritual connexion with Constantinople.  He sent ambassadors to Michael III., asking for a man who would be able to teach his flock the Christian faith in their own tongue.  Constantine, by his knowledge of Slavonic and his missionary experience, was marked out as the suitable apostle ; and he went to Moravia, taking with him his brother Methodius (A.D. 863).  They worked among the Moravians for four and a half years, having apparently obtained the reluctant recognition of the bishop of Passau.  But prince Rastislav was fully resolved that the church of his country should not remain a dependency on the German see of Passau.  A new bishopric should be founded and Constantine should be the first bishop.  If Ignatius had been still Patriarch, Constantine would probably have sought episcopal ordination at his hands.  But the heretic Photius was in the Patriarchal chair ; there was schism between Rome and Constantinople ; and so it came about that Rastislav and Constantine had recourse to the Bishop of Rome.  Pope Nicholas invited the two brothers (A.D. 867), but died before their arrival ; and his successor Hadrian II. ordained them bishops (A.D. 868).  On this occasion Constantine changed his name to *Cyril*, by which he has become generally known.  But a premature death carried him away at Rome (Feb. 14, A.D. 869).  Methodius then went to Blatno on the Platten See in Pannonia (where Kocel, prince of the Slavs of those regions, held his court) as bishop of Pannonia—an ancient see which was now reconstituted. Here he exercised missionary influence upon neighbouring Croatia.  But presently he returned to Moravia, where Svatopluk had become king.  He died in A.D. 885.

The great achievement of Constantine or Cyril was the invention of a Slavonic alphabet.  His immediate missionary work was in Moravia ; but by framing an alphabet and translating the gospels into Slavonic he affected, as no other single man has ever done, every Slavonic people.  He did what Ulfilas did for the Goths, what Mesrob did for the Armenians, but his work was destined to have incomparably greater ecumenical importance than that of either.  The alphabet which he invented (doubtless in A.D. 863) is known as the *glagolitic ;* and we have a good many early documents written in this character in various parts of the Slavonic world.  But ultimately the use of it became confined to Istria and the Croatian coast ; for it was superseded by another alphabet, clearer and more practical, which was perhaps invented about half a century later by bishop Clement of Drenoviza.[4]  This later alphabet is known as the *cyrillic ;* and has been supposed —and is still supposed—by many to be the alphabet which Cyril invented.  But a study of the two characters makes it quite clear that the cyrillic is the later and was formed upon the glagolitic.  It was the framer of the glagolitic who possessed the creative genius ; and it was not unfair that, when the second form of the alphabet, with all its improvements, superseded the older, the name of the original inventor should be attached to the improved script.

Directly neither Cyril nor Methodius had anything to do with the conversion of Bulgaria.  But the conversion of Bulgaria took place in their days ; the invention of the alphabet facilitated the conversion ; and the application of the Moravian monarch to Constantinople probably induced the Bulgarian prince, Boris, to resolve, from political considerations, to abandon heathendom.  Making peace with the emperor, with whom he had been at war, he was baptized at the place where the peace was concluded, and the Emperor himself was his sponsor (probably A.D. 864).  He then introduced Christianity forcibly among his people, executing fifty-two persons who resisted.  But it was not long before he turned away from Constantinople and sought to connect the Bulgarian Church with Rome.  He sent envoys (A.D. 866) to Pope Nicholas I., with 106 questions, and

---

[3] This is the subject of the Translatio S. Clementis (in Acta Sanctorum, March 9), probably composed by the contemporary Gauderic, bishop of Velletri.  It is a valuable source for the lives of the Apostles.
[4] This is the view of Shafarik.

the answers of the Pope,[5] which are preserved, throw some interesting light on Bulgarian customs. If the successor of Nicholas had shown tact and discretion, Bulgaria might have been won for the Latin Church; but Hadrian II. tried the patience of Boris, and in A.D. 870 Bulgaria received an archbishop from Constantinople and ten bishoprics were founded. Boris sent his son Simeon to be educated at New Rome. It was not long before Slavonic books and the Slavonic liturgy were introduced into Bulgaria.

[Only a few works out of the enormous literature on the apostles of the Slavs can be quoted. J. A. Ginzel, Geschichte der Slawenapostel Cyrill und Method, und der Slawischen Liturgie (1857). L. Leger, Cyrille et Méthode (1868). Bonwetsch, Kyrillus und Methodius (1885). V. Jagić, article in the Zapiski of the Imperial Acad. of St. Petersburg, vol. li. (1886). L. K. Goetz, Gesch. der Slavenapostel Konstantinus und Methodius (1897). Cp. also the accounts in Golubinski's Hist. of the Bulgarian, Servian and Romanian Church, and in Bretholz's Geschichte Mährens.]

## 13. THE HUNGARIANS—(P. 137 sqq.)

The chief sources for the history of the Hungarians, before they took up their abode in Hungary, are (1) Leo, Tactics, c. 18, § 45 sqq. ; and Constantine Porphyrogennetos, De Adm. Imp., c. 38, 39, 40 ; (2) the account of Ibn Rusta, an Arabic writer who wrote A.D. 912-13 ; (3) some notices in western chronicles of the ninth century ; (4) traditions in the native chronicles of Hungary. It has been proved that the chronicle of the Anonymous Scribe of King Béla,[1] which used to be regarded as a trustworthy source for early Hungarian history, is a "Machwerk" of the 13th century ; [2] but the author as well as Simon de Kéza (for his Chronicon Hungaricum) had some old sources, from which they derived some genuine traditions, which criticism can detect and may use with discretion.

The main questions in dispute with regard to the Hungarians and their early antiquity are two : concerning their ethnical affinity, and concerning the course of their wanderings from the most primitive habitation, to which they can be traced, up to their appearance between the Dnieper and the Danube. It may be said, I think, that we have not sufficient data to justify dogmatism in regard to either of these questions.

As to their ethnical position, are the Hungarians Turkish or Finnic ? Their language shows both elements ; and the two rival theories appeal to it. Those who maintain that the Hungarians are Turkish explain the Finnic part of the vocabulary by a long sojourn in the neighbourhood of the Voguls and Ostjaks ; while those who hold that they were brethren of the Voguls, Ostjaks, and Finns, explain the Turkish element by borrowings in the course of their subsequent wanderings. For the latter theory it must be said that the most elementary portion of the Hungarian vocabulary is undoubtedly related to the Vogul, Ostjak, and their kindred languages. This comes out clearly in the numerals, and in a large number of common words.[3] If we set side by side

---

[5] Included in Collections of Acta Conciliorum.  [1] Best ed. by C. Fejérpataky (1892).
[2] R. Roesler, Romanische Studien, p. 147 sqq. On the Hungarian sources, see H Marczali, Ungarns Geschichtsquellen, 1882.
[3] As a specimen, for comparison of the Hungarian language with the Vogulic which is the most closely connected, I subjoin the names of the first seven numerals (the original numerical system seems to have been heptadic) :—

1 : H. egy, V. äk, äkve.
2 : H. két, kettö, V. kit, kiti.
3 : H. harm, V. korm.
4 : H. négy, V. neljä.
5 : H. öt, V. ät.
6 : H. hat, V. kat.
7 : H. hét, V. sat.

(The Turkish words for these numbers are totally different.)
The word for 100 is the same in both languages : H. száz, V. sat (Finnish sata). But 10 is quite different : H. tíz, V. lau (and Finnish kymmen differs from both); 20 coincides : H. húsz, V. kus ; and in the first part of the compound which signifies 8 (probably 10 − 2) the same element occurs : H. *nyol*-cz, V. *n'ala*-lu ; so for 80 : H. nyolcz-van, V. n'ol-sat (?- 100 − 20).

lists of Hungarian words which are clearly Turkish or clearly Finnic, leaving out all the unconvincing etymologies which the rival theorists serve up, it is difficult to avoid concluding that the primitive element is the Finnic. But the conclusion is far from certain ; and the wanderings of the Hungarians may suggest rather a people like the Patzinaks and Kumans, than like the Voguls and Finns.[4]

It seems most probable that the Magyars at one time dwelled in Jugria, in the regions of the Irtish, where they were neighbours of the Voguls. They migrated southward and in the beginning of the 9th century they had taken up their abode within the empire of the Chazars, and they amalgamated with themselves a Chazaric tribe called the Kabars (Const. Porph. c. 39), who became part of the Hungarian nation. These Kabars, according to Constantine, taught the Hungarians the tongue of the Chazars. Hence the upholders of the Finnic origin of the Turks can explain the Turkish element in Hungaria by a known cause, the coalition of the Kabars.

According to Constantine, the Hungarians abode only three years in " *Lebedia* near Chazaria ". This land of Lebedia was probably between the Don and the Dnieper ; and it is supposed that the date of their sojourn there was between A.D. 830 and 840. For it is in the reign of Theophilus, c. 837-39, that they first appear upon the horizon of the Eastern Empire (cp. George Mon. p. 818, ed. Bonn, where they are called Οὔγγροι, Οὔννοι, and Τοῦρκοι) ; and crossed the Danube. It cannot be determined whether the Hungarians when they made this expedition were living beyond the Dnieper in Lebedia, or had already left Lebedia and found a new home in the land between the Dnieper and Dniester. But it must have been about this time, a little before, or a little later, that the Patzinaks drove the Hungarians out of Lebedia and the Hungarians established themselves in Atelkuzu, as they called the land between Dnieper and Danube, where they abode about half a century. Here they came under Slavonic influence ; and it was here, doubtless, that they adopted the Slavonic title *voevod* (βοέβοδος, cp. above, p. 138) for their chieftains.

The same enemies, who had driven the Hungarians out of Lebedia, drove them again out of Atelkuzu. The Patzinaks were themselves subdued by a combined attack of the Khazars and the Uzes ; they crossed the Dnieper, dislodged the Hungarians, who were thus driven farther west ; and this was the cause of their settlement in the modern Hungary. The event happened fifty-five years before Constantine wrote c. 37 of his De Administratione ; *i.e.*, probably in A.D. 896 or 897 (cp. Appendix 4). The notice in Regino's Chronicle under the year 889 anticipates subsequent events.[5]

It is to the Hungarians as they were when they lived in Atelkuzu, and not to the contemporary Hungarians who were already settled in their final home, that the description of Ibn Rusta (taken from some earlier writer) applies. He describes their land as between the Patzinaks and the Esegel tribe of the Bulgarians (clearly a tribe north of the Danube, in Walachia or Bessarabia). Ibn Rusta further mentions two rivers in the land of the Hungarians, one of them greater than the Oxus. Probably the Dnieper and the Bug are meant.[6] He says that *Kende* is the title of their king, but there is another dignitary whom all obey in matters connected with attack or defence, and he is entitled *jila*. The *kende* clearly corresponds to the prince or ἄρχων of Constantine Porphyrogennetos (c. 40) ; Arpad, for example, was a kende. The *jila* is also mentioned by Constantine, as

---

[4] For the Finnic origin, P. Hunfalvy, Magyarország Ethnographiája, 1876, and Die Ungern oder Magyaren, 1881. For the Turkish, A Vámbéry, A Magyarok eredete, 1882. For the " Ugrian " or Finnic or " Ugro-Finnic " languages, see Budenz in the 4th vol. of Bezzenberger's Beiträge zur kunde der Indogermanischen Sprachen (Die Verzweigung der Ugrischen Sprachen).

[5] On the chronology see E. Dümmler, Geschichte des Ostfränkischen Reichs (ed. 2), iii. 438 *sqq.*—Count Géza Kuun in his Relationum Hungarorum—Hist. Antiquissima, vol. i. (1893) p. 136, departs entirely from the data of Constantine, and tries to establish, instead of a three years' sojourn in Lebedia and a long (fifty years') sojourn in Atelkuzu, a long sojourn in Lebedia (up to A.D. 889) and a short (seven or eight years') sojourn in Atelkuzu.

[6] Cp. Kuun, *op. cit.* vol. i. p. 184.

γυλᾶς ; to whom, however, he ascribes the function of a judge.[7] It seems that the title kende was adopted by the Hungarians from the Chazars ; for the title of the Chazar viceroy was *kenderchagan.*

Ibn Rusta says that the Hungarians rule over the Slavs, whom they oppress with heavy burdens ; that they worship fire ; that they trade in the slaves whom they capture, with Greek merchants at Kertsch.[8]

The reconstruction of Hungarian history between Jugria and Lebedia has been attempted, most recently and with great ingenuity, by Count Kuun. But, as there is not material sufficient to enable us to decide between various possibilities, it seems unnecessary to discuss here these hypotheses which are entirely in the air.[9]

A word may be said about the name Magyar. It was doubtless the name of a single tribe before it became the name of the whole people ; and the third of the 8 tribes enumerated by Constantine (c. 40 *ad init.*) was that of Megerê (τοῦ Μεγέρη). In another place (c. 37) Constantine mentions the Μάζαροι as dwelling in the 9th century near the river Ural, where they were neighbours of the Patzinaks ; but without any suggestion that they are identical with the Hungarians, whom he always calls *Turks.* Hungarian scholars find other traces of the Magyar name between the Black Sea and the Caspian : thus there are two villages called Mäjär in the neighbourhood of Derbend ;[10] and K. Szabo wished to detect the word in Muager (Μουαγέρην), whom Theophanes mentions as the brother of Gordas, king of the Huns near the Cimmerian Bosporus. It has also been proposed to connect the name of a fortress, τὸ Ματζάρων (mentioned by Theophylactus Simocatta, ii. 18, 7). It was on the confines of the Roman and Persian dominions, but its exact position is unknown. Without committing oneself to these last combinations, there seems to be some evidence, such as it is, associating the Magyar name with the regions between the Caspian and the Euxine. In that case, we might infer that the original Magyars were, like the Kabars, a Turkish tribe (akin to Patzinaks and Uzes) which coalesced with the (Finnic) Ugrians or Hungarians. This inference would be quite in accordance with the apparent probability that the Hungarians are "Mischvolk," a blend of two elements, Finnic and Turkish.

## 14. ORIGIN OF RUSSIA—(P. 147 *sqq.*)

No competent critic now doubts that the Russians, who founded states at Novgorod and Kiev, subdued the Slavonic tribes and organized them into a political power,—who, in short, made Russia—were of Scandinavian or Norse origin. It is therefore unnecessary to treat this matter any longer as a disputed question, though there are still "anti-Normans" in Russia ; it will be enough to state briefly the most important evidence. The evidence is indeed insuperable, except to insuperable prejudice.

(1) The early writers, who mention the Russians, attest their identity with the Scandinavians or Normans. The first notice is in the Annales Bertiniani *ad ann.* 839 (Pertz, Mon. i. 484), Rhos vocari dicebant . . . comperit eos gentis esse Sueonum. Liutprand (Antapodosis, v. 15) says that they were Normans (nos vero a positione loci nominamus Nordmannos). The chronicle of "Nestor" identifies them with the Varangians, or regards them as belonging to the Varangian stock ; and for the Scandinavian origin of the Varangians see above, p. 148, note 58. The Continuation of George the Monk (Symeon Magister) states more generally and less accurately their German origin (= Theoph. Contin. p. 423, ed. B., ἐκ Φράγγων γένους).[1]

---

[7] Constantine mentions a third dignitary, inferior to the γυλᾶς, and entitled *karchas.*

[8] The notice of Ibn Rusta will be found in some shape in all recent works on the early Hungarians, most recently in Kuun's work cited above, vol. i. p. 165-6, translated from the recent Arabic text of M. de Goeje. Ibn Rusta used to be called Ibn Dasta.

[9] In the foregoing paragraphs I have adopted Constantine's statements about Lebedia, as the only positive statement we have ; but there is much to be said still by way of criticism on these chapters of Constantine.

[10] Kuun, *op. cit.* p, 93.

[1] Yakūbi, writing before the end of the 9th cent., calls the heathen who attacked Seville in 844 *Rūs.*

(2) The Russians spoke Norse, not Slavonic. This is proved by the 9th chapter of Constantine's de Administratione, where the Russian and Slavonic languages are distinguished ('Ρωσιστί and Σκλαβινιστί), and the Russian names of the waterfalls are unmistakably Scandinavian. See below, Appendix 15.

(3) The names of the first Russian princes and the names of the signatories of the first Russian treaties are Norse. *Riurik* is the old Norse Hraerikr ; *Oleg* is Helgi ; *Olga*, Helga ; *Igor* ('Ιγγωρ ; Inger in Liutprand) is Ingvarr. The boyars who are named in the treaty of A.D. 912 (Nestor, c. 22) are Kary (Swedish, Kari), Ingeld (O. Norse, Ingialdr), Farlof (Swedish), Vermud (O. Norse, Vermunde), Rulaf (O. Norse, Hrodleifr), Ruald (O. Norse, Hroaldr), Goud (cp. Runic Kudi), Karn (Scandinavian), Frelaf (O. N., Fridleifr), Rouar (O. N., Hroarr), Trouan (O. N., Droandr), Lidoul (O. N., Lidufr ?), Fost (Swedish). There remain two uncertain names, Aktevou and Stemid. Similarly the large proportion of the names in the treaty of 945 (c. 27) are Scandinavian.

(4) The Finnish name for Sweden is *Ruotsi*, the Esthonian is *Rôts ;* and we can hardly hesitate to identify this with the name of Russia ; Old Slavonic Rous', Greek 'Ρώς.[2] This name (neither Finnish nor Slavonic) is derived by Thomsen from the Scandinavian *rods* (rods-menn = rowers, oarsmen) ; the difficulty is the dropping out of the dental in Rous, 'Ρώς.

Thus the current opinion which prevailed when the Russians first appeared on the stage of history ; the evidence of their language ; the evidence of their names ; and the survival of the ancient meaning of the Russian name in Finnic, concur in establishing the Scandinavian origin of the Russians.

For a development of these arguments and other minor evidence see Prof. V. Thomsen's work, The Relations between Ancient Russia and Scandinavia, and the Origin of the Russian State (Ilchester Lectures), 1877 ; E. Kunik, Die Berufung der Schwedischen Rodsen durch die Finnen und Slaven, 1844 ; and see Mémoires of the Imperial Academy of Russia, vii. sér. 22, p. 279 *sqq.* and 409 *sqq.* ; Bestuzhev-Riumin, Russkaia Istoriia (vol. i.), 1872 ; Pogodin, O proischoždenii Rusi, 1825, Drevniaia Russkaia Istoriia, 1871, and other works. The two most eminent opposition advocates are : Ilovaiski, Razyskaniia O nachalie Rusi, 1876, and Istoriia Rossii (Part 1, Kiev period), 1876 ; and Gedeonov, Izsliedovaniia o variazhskom voprosie, 1862, Variagi i Rus', 1876.

## 15. THE WATERFALLS OF THE DNIEPER—(P. 152, 153)

In the 9th chapter of his Treatise on the Administration of the Empire, Constantine Porphyrogennetos gives a most interesting description of the route of Russian merchants from Novgorod (Νεμογαρδάς) to Constantinople, by way of Kiev and the Dnieper, and enumerates the rapids of this river, giving in each case both its Russian and its Slavonic name. This passage is of high importance, for it shows that the language which Constantine meant by Russian ('Ρωσιστί) was Scandinavian and not Slavonic. Dr. Vilhelm Thomsen of Copenhagen in his Ilchester lectures on "Relations between Ancient Russia and Scandinavia, and the Origin of the Russian State" (1877) has supplied an excellent commentary.

1st waterfall is called Essupê ('Εσσουπῆ) in both languages, with the meaning *sleepless* (μὴ κοιμᾶσθαι). It follows that the two names sounded nearly alike to Constantine. The Slavonic for "do not sleep" would be *ne spi* (and perhaps 'Εσσουπῆ is an error for Νεσσουπῆ) ; and Professor Thomsen says that the corresponding phrase in Old Norse would be *sofeigi* or *sofattu*. This is not quite satisfactory.

2nd waterfall is (*a*) in Russian, Ulvorsi (Οὐλβορσί), and (*b*) in Slavonic, Ostrovuniprach ('Οστροβουνίπραχ), with the meaning the islet of the fall ; (*a*) = holm-fors ; (*b*) = ostrov'nii prag (islet-fall).

[2] 'Ρώς is the exact equivalent of Nestor's Rous', which is a collective tribe name = " the Russians ". 'Ρωσία, Russia, was formed from 'Ρώς, and the Russian name Rossiia was a later formation on Greek analogy.

3rd waterfall is called Gelandri (Γελανδρί), which in Slavonic means noise of the fall. Only one name is given, and it is said to be Slavonic. But it obviously represents the Norse participle *gellandi*, "the echoing"; so that the Slavonic name (probably nearly the same as the modern name *zvonets* with the same meaning) is omitted. Constantine's usual formula is Ῥωσιστί μὲν . . . Σκλαβανιστὶ δέ; but in this place he changes it : τὸν λεγόμενον Γελανδρί, ὃ ἑρμηνεύεται Σκλαβινιστὶ ἦχος φραγμοῦ. I would suggest that ζβινιτς or σβινιτς or something of the kind fell out after Σκλαβινιστί.

4th waterfall is Aeifor (Ἀειφόρ, so in Paris Ms. 2009) in Russian, and Neasit (Νεασήτ) in Slavonic,—so called, Constantine says, because pelicans make their nests in the stones. The Old Slavonic for pelican closely resembles Νεασήτ, but the fall cannot have been called pelican ; this must have been a misinterpretation. Thomsen very ingeniously suggests that the true name corresponded to the modern *Nenasytets* and meant insatiable (a name appropriate to the nature of this rapid) ; while Aeifor (ei-forr) meant everforward, ever-precipitate.

5th waterfall is Varuforos (βαρουφόρος) in Russian, Vulne prach (βουλνηπράχ) in Slavonic ; "because it forms a great lake," or, if we read δίνην for λίμνην, "because it forms a great vortex". Both words can be recognised at once as meaning "wave-fall".

6th waterfall is Leanti (Λεάντι) in Russian, Verutze (Βερούτζη) in Slavonic, meaning "the seething of water" (βράσμα νεροῦ). Verutze is obviously from *v'rieti*, to boil. Thomsen explains Leanti as the participle *hlaejandi*, laughing. In this case the meaning of the two names is not identical.

7th waterfall is Strukun (Στρούκουν, so in Paris Ms. 2009) in Russian, Napreze (Ναπρεζή) in Slavonic, meaning a small waterfall. Thomsen identifies Strukun with Norse *strok*, Swedish *struk*, a rapid current (especially where narrow—as in the case of this rapid) ; and suggests that the Slavonic name might be connected with *brz*, quick. I suspect that (Να-) πρεζή represents a diminutive of *porog, prag* (waterfall).

## 16. THE ASSISES OF JERUSALEM—(P. 317)

It is agreed by most competent critics of the present century that Godfrey of Bouillon neither drew up the Assises of Jerusalem as they have come down to us nor put into writing any code of law whatever. This is the opinion of such special students of the Crusades as Wilken, Sybel, Stubbs, Kugler, and Prutz ; and recently it has been very forcibly put by M. Gaston Dodu in his Histoire des Institutions monarchiques dans le royaume Latin de Jérusalem 1099-1291 (1894). In the first place, we find no mention of such a code in contemporary sources ; the earliest authorities who mention it are Ibelin and Philip of Novara in the 13th century. Then, supposing such a code had been compiled, it is hard to understand why it should have been placed in the Holy Sepulchre and why the presence of nine persons should have been necessary to consult it. For the purpose of a code is that it should be referred to without difficulty. Thirdly, the remark of William of Tyre as to the experience of Baldwin III. in judicial matters makes distinctly against the existence of a code. He says : juris consuetudinarii, quo regnum regebatur Orientale, plenam habens experientiam : ita ut in rebus dubiis etiam seniores regni principes eius consulerent experientiam et consulti pectoris eruditionem mirarentur (xvi. 2, cp. on Amalric i. xix. 2). The expression "the customary law by which the kingdom was governed" suggests that no code existed.

Fourthly, if the code existed, what became of it? Ibelin and Philip of Novara say that it was lost when Jerusalem was taken by Saladin in 1187. But the circumstances of that capture are inconsistent with the probability of such a loss. There were no military excesses and Saladin allowed the inhabitants a delay of forty days to sell or save their property before he entered the city (Ernoul, c. 18 ; cp. Dodu, p. 45). It is highly unlikely that the Christians would have failed to rescue a possession so valuable and portable as their Code. The Patriarch could not have overlooked it when he carried forth the treasures of the churches (as Ibn al-Athir mentions). And, if it were unaccountably forgotten, we should have to suppose that Saladin caused it to be destroyed afterwards when it was found. And had he done so, it is highly unlikely that the act would not have been mentioned by some of the Frank chroniclers.

The conclusion is that the kings of Jerusalem in the twelfth century did not give decisions according to a code drawn up at the time of the foundation of the kingdom, but themselves helped to build up a structure of Customary Law, which in the following century was collected and compiled in the book of the Assises by John Ibelin, A.D. 1255.

This book of Ibelin has not come down to us in its original form. There were two redactions: (1) at Nicosia in Cyprus in 1368 under the direction of an assembly of Cypriote lords, and (2) in the same place in 1531, by a commission appointed by the Venetian government. Both these rehandlings introduced a number of corrections into the *Assise de la haute cour*.

The *Assises de la cour des bourgeois* stand on a different footing. This work seems to have existed perhaps from the end of the twelfth century. It was not *supposed* to have been destroyed in 1187; it was not, so far as we know, edited by Ibelin; nor was it revised at Nicosia in 1368. (Cp. Dodu, p. 54, 55.)

The study of the Assises of Jerusalem may now be supplemented by the Assises of Antioch, preserved in an Armenian version, which has been translated into French (published by the Mekhitarist Society, Venice, 1876).

How far is the policy of Godfrey of Bouillon represented in the Assises? In answer to this question, the observations of Bishop Stubbs may be quoted:—[1]

"We trace his hand in the prescribing constant military service (not definite or merely for a certain period of each year), in the non-recognition of representation in inheritance, in the rules designed to prevent the accumulation of fiefs in a single hand, in the stringent regulations for the marriages of widows and heiresses. These features all belonged to an earlier age, to a time when every knight represented a knight's fee, and when no fee could be suffered to neglect its duty; when the maintenance of the conquered country was deemed more important than the inheritances of minors or the will of widows and heiresses. That these provisions were wise is proved by the fact that it was in these very points that the hazard of the Frank kingdom lay. . . . Other portions of the Assizes are to be ascribed to the necessities of the state of things that followed the recovery of Palestine by the Saracens; such, for instance, as the decision how far deforcement by the Turks defeats seisin; and were of importance only in the event of a reconquest."

## 17. THE ACCIAJOLI—(P. 485)

If Gibbon had been more fully acquainted with the history of the family of the Acciajoli, he would have probably devoted some pages to the rise of their fortunes. They rose to such power and influence in Greece in the 14th century that the subjoined account, taken from Finlay (vol. iv. p. 157 *sqq.*)—with a few additions in square brackets—will not be out of place.

"Several members of the family of Acciajoli, which formed a distinguished commercial company at Florence in the thirteenth century, settled in the Peloponnesus about the middle of the fourteenth, under the protection of Robert, king of Naples. Nicholas Acciajoli was invested, in the year 334, with the administration of the lands which the company had acquired in payment or in security of the loans it had made to the royal House of Anjou; and he acquired additional possessions in the principality of Achaia, both by purchase and grant, from Catherine of Valois, titular empress of Romania and regent of Achaia for her son prince Robert. [It is disputed whether he was her lover.] The encroachments of the mercantile spirit on the feudal system are displayed in the

[1] Itinerarium Regis Ricardi (Rolls series), Introduction, p. xc., xci.

concessions obtained by Nicholas Acciajoli in the grants he received from Catherine of Valois. He was invested with the power of mortgaging, exchanging, and selling his fiefs, without any previous authorisation from his suzerain. Nicholas acted as principal minister of Catherine during a residence of three years in the Morea; and he made use of his position, like a prudent banker, to obtain considerable grants of territory. He returned to Italy in 1341 and never again visited Greece; but his estates in Achaia were administered by his relations and other members of the banking house at Florence, many of whom obtained considerable fiefs for themselves through his influence.

"Nicholas Acciajoli was appointed hereditary grand seneschal of the kingdom of Naples by queen Jeanne, whom he accompanied in her flight to Provence when she was driven from her kingdom by Louis of Hungary. On her return he received the rich country of Amalfi, as a reward for his fidelity, and subsequently Malta was added to his possessions. He was an able statesman and a keen political intriguer; and he was almost the first example of the superior position the purse of the moneyed citizen was destined to assume over the sword of the feudal baron and the learning of the politic churchman. Nicholas Acciajoli was the first of that banking aristocracy which has since held an important position in European history. He was the type of a class destined at times to decide the fate of kingdoms and at times to arrest the progress of armies. He certainly deserved to have his life written by a man of genius, but his superciliousness and assumption of princely state, even in his intercourse with the friends of his youth, disgusted Boccaccio, who alone of Florentine contemporaries could have left a vivid sketch of the career which raised him from the partner of a banking-house to the rank of a great feudal baron and to live in the companionship of kings. Boccaccio, offended by his insolence, seems not to have appreciated his true importance as the type of a coming age and a new state of society; and the indignant and satirical record he has left of the pride and presumption of the mercantile noble is by no means a correct portrait of the Neapolitan minister. Yet even Boccaccio records in his usual truthful manner that Nicholas had dispersed powerful armies, though he unjustly depreciates the merit of the success, because the victory was gained by combinations effected by gold, and not by the headlong charge of a line of lances. [Boccaccio dedicated his *Donne illustri* to Niccolo's sister Andrea, the countess of Monte Oderisio.]

"Nicholas Acciajoli obtained a grant of the barony and hereditary governorship of the fortress of Corinth in the year 1358. He was already in possession of the castles of Vulcano [at Ithome], Piadha near Epidauros, and large estates in other parts of the Peloponnesus. He died in 1365; [1] and his sons Angelo and Robert succeeded in turn to the barony and government of Corinth. Angelo mortgaged Corinth to his relative [second cousin], Nerio Acciajoli, who already possessed fiefs in Achaia, and who took up his residence at Corinth on account of the political and military importance of the fortress as well as to enable him to administer the revenues of the barony in the most profitable manner.

"Nerio Acciajoli, though he held the governorship of Corinth only as the deputy of his relation, and the barony only in security of a debt, was nevertheless, from his ability, enterprising character, great wealth, and extensive connexions, one of the most influential barons of Achaia; and, from the disorderly state of the principality he was enabled to act as an independent prince.

"The Catalans were the constant rivals of the Franks of Achaia, and Nerio Acciajoli, as governor of Corinth, was the guardian of the principality against their hostile projects. The marriage of the young countess of Salona [whose father Count Lewis died 1382] involved the two parties in war. The mother of the bride was a Greek lady; she betrothed her daughter to Simeon [Stephen Ducas], son of the prince of Vallachian Thessaly; and the Catalans, with the two

---

[1] [There is a great memorial of Niccolo at Florence, the Gothic Certosa San Lorenzo. Gregorovius calls it "the first monument of historical relations between Florence and Greece"; for just as Pisa used her revenue from Constantinople to build her cathedral, Niccolo devoted moneys from Greece to build San Lorenzo. His tomb is to be seen in a subterranean chapel.]

Laurias at their head, supported this arrangement. But the barons of Achaia, headed by Nerio Acciajoli, pretended that the Prince of Achaia as feudal suzerain of Athens was entitled to dispose of the hand of the countess. Nerio was determined to bestow the young countess, with all her immense possessions, on a relative of the Acciajoli family, named Peter Sarrasin.[2] The war concerning the countess of Salona and her heritage appears to have commenced about the year 1386 [1385]. The Catalans were defeated ; and Nerio gained possession of Athens, Thebes, and Livadea."

"About the commencement of the year 1394 Ladislas, king of Naples, conferred on him by patent the title of Duke of Athens—Athens forming, as the king pretended, part of the principality of Achaia."

Nerio died in 1394. His illegitimate son Antonio inherited Thebes and Livadia, and wrested to himself the government of Athens, which Nerio's will had placed under the protection of Venice on behalf of his daughter (the wife of Count Tocco of Cephalonia). Under Antonio "Athens enjoyed uninterrupted tranquillity for forty years. The republic of Florence deemed it an object worthy of its especial attention to obtain a commercial treaty with the duchy, for the purpose of securing to the citizens of the republic all the privileges enjoyed by the Venetians, Catalans, and Genoese." The conclusion of this treaty is almost the only event recorded concerning the external relations of Athens during the long reign of Antonio. The Athenians appear to have lived happily under his government ; and he himself seems to have spent his time in a joyous manner, inviting his Florentine relations to Greece, and entertaining them with festivals and hunting parties. Yet he was neither a spendthrift nor a tyrant ; for Chalcocondylas, whose father lived at his court, records that, while he accumulated great wealth with prudent economy, he at the same time adorned the city of Athens with many new buildings. He died in 1435, and was succeeded by Nerio II., grandson of Donato, the brother of Nerio I.

[Buchon, Nouvelles Recherches, vols. i. and ii. ; L. Tanfani, Niccolo Acciajoli, 1863 ; Hopf, Hist. Duc. Att. Fontes ; Gregorovius, Geschichte der Stadt Athen im Mittelalter, vol. ii.]

## 18. THE ISLAND DYNASTIES AFTER THE LATIN CONQUEST—
### (P. 483)

The facts about the history of the Greek islands during the 13th, 14th and 15th centuries were enveloped in obscurity, and fictions and false hypotheses were current, until the industry of Professor C. Hopf drew the material from the archives of Vienna and Venice. His publications rendered the work of Buchon and Finlay obsolete so far as the islands are concerned. He won the right of referring with contempt to Buchon's schönrednerische Fabeleien und Finlays geistreich-unkritischer Hypothesenwust. The following list of the island-lordships is taken from his Urkunden und Zusätze zur Geschichte der Insel Andros und ihrer Beherrscher in dem Zeitraume von 1207 to 1566, published in the Sitzungsberichte of the Vienna Academy, 1856, vol. 21, p. 221 sqq.

| | |
|---|---|
| Corfu. | Venetian 1207-c. 1214 ; to Despotate of Epirus c. 1214-1259 ; King Manfred and Filippo Chinardo 1259-1267 ; Neapolitan 1267-1386 ; Venetian 1386-1797. |
| Cefalonia, Zante, Ithaca. | Despotate of Epirus 1205-1337 ; Greek Empire 1337-1357 ; the Tocchi 1357-1482. |
| Santa Maura. | Despotate of Epirus 1205-1331 ; Giorgi 1331-1362 ; the Tocchi 1362-1482. |
| Paxo. | With Cefalonia 1205-1357 ; St. Ippolyto 1357-1484 ; Ugoth (Gotti) 1484-1527. With Cerigotto 1527-1797. |
| Cerigo (Cythera). | The Venieri 1207-1269 ; the Monojanni 1267-1309 ; the Venieri 1309-1797. |

[2] [His own brother-in-law ; for he was married to Agnes Saraceno.]

Cerigotto.
The Viari 1207-1655; the Foscarini and Giustiniani 1655-1797.

Salamis.
With Athens.

Aegina.
With Carystos 1205-1317; Aragonese 1317-c. 1400; Cavopena c. 1400-1451; Venetian 1451-1537.

Delos, Gyaros, Cythnos, (Patmos).
With Naxos. [Sanudo allowed Patmos, the apostle's island, to preserve its independence.]

Tinos and Miconos.
The Ghisi 1207-1390; Venetian 1390-1718. (Held in fief by Venetian counts belonging to the houses of Bembo, Quirini, and Fabieri 1407-1429.)

Andros.
The Dandoli 1207-1233; the Ghisi 1233-c. 1250; the Sanudi c. 1250-1384; the Zeni 1384-1437; the Sommaripa 1437-1566.

Syra.
With Naxos.

Zia (Ceos).[1]
$\frac{1}{4}$: The Giustiniani 1207-1366; the da Coronia 1366-1464; the Gozzadini 1464-1537.
$\frac{1}{4}$: The Michieli 1207-1355; the Premarini 1355 forward.
$\frac{1}{2}$: The Ghisi 1207-1328; the Premarini 1328-1375.
$\frac{9}{16}$: The Premarini 1375-1537.
$\frac{7}{16}$: The Sanudi 1375-1405; the Gozzadini 1405-1537

Serfene (Seriphos).[1]
$\frac{1}{4}$: the Michieli 1207-1537;
$\frac{1}{4}$: the Giustiniani 1207-c. 1412; the Adoldi 1412 forward.
$\frac{1}{2}$: the Ghisi 1207-1334; the Bragadini 1334-1354; the Minotti 1354-1373; the Adoldi 1373-1432; the Michieli 1432-1537.

Thermia (Cythnos).
The Sanudi 1207-c. 1320; the Castelli c. 1322-1331; the Gozzadini 1331-1537.

Sifanto (Siphnos), Sikino, Polycandro (Pholegandros).
The Sanudi 1207-1269 (titular, 1341; the Grimani titular 1341-1537); Greek Empire 1269-1307; the da Coronia 1307-1464; the Gozzadini 1464-1617.

Milos and Cimolos.
The Sanudi 1207-1376; the Crispi 1376-1566.

Santorin (Thera) and Therasia.
The Barozzi 1207-1335; with Naxos 1335-1477; the Pisani 1477-1487; with Naxos 1487-1537.

Namfio (Anaphe).
The Foscoli 1207-1269; Greek Empire 1269-1307; the Gozzadini 1307-1420; the Crispi 1420-1469; the Barbari 1469-1528; the Pisani 1528-1537.

Nio (Anaea).
The Sanudi 1207-1269; Greek Empire 1269-1292; the Schiavi 1292-c. 1320; with Naxos c. 1320-1420; collateral branch of the Crispi 1420-1508; the Pisani 1508-1537.

Paros and Nausa.
With Naxos 1207-1389; the Sommaripa 1389-1516; the Venieri 1516-1531; the Sagredi 1531-1537.

Antiparos.
With Paros 1207-1439; the Loredani 1439-c. 1490; the Pisani 1490-1537.

Naxos.
The Sanudi 1207-1362; the Dalle Carceri 1362-1383; the Crispi 1383-1566.

[1] Ceos and Seriphos were under the Greek Empire from 1269 to 1296.

| | |
|---|---|
| Scyros, Sciathos, Chelidromi. Scopelos. | The Ghisi 1207-1269; Greek Empire 1269 1455; Venetian 1455-1537. |
| | The Ghisi 1207-1262; the Tiepoli 1262-1310; the Greek Empire 1310-1454; Venetian 1454-1538. |
| Negroponte. | $\frac{1}{3}$: the dalle Carceri 1205-1254; the Da Verona 1254-1383; the Sommaripa 1383-1470. |
| | $\frac{1}{3}$: the Peccorari 1205-1214; the dalle Carceri 1214-c. 1300; the Ghisi c. 1300-1390; Venetian 1390-1470. |
| | $\frac{1}{3}$: The da Verona 1205-1383; the da Noyer 1383-1470. |
| Carystos (in Negroponte). | The dalle Carceri 1205-c. 1254; the Cicons c. 1254-1292; the da Verona, 1292-1317; Aragonese 1317-1365; Venetian 1365-1386; the Giustiniani 1386-1404; Venetian 1404-1406; the Giorgi 1406-1470. |
| Lemnos. | The Navigajosi (with these, subsequently, the Gradenighi and Foscari) 1207-1269; Greek Empire 1269-1453; the Gattilusj 1453-1462. |
| Lesbos. | The Greek Empire 1205-1355; the Gattilusj 1355-1462. |
| Chios, Samos. | With Constantinople (Empire of Romania) 1205-1247; with Lesbos 1247-1303; the Zaccaria 1303-1333; Greek Empire 1333-1346; the joint stock company of the Giustiniani, in 14 and more branches, 1346-1566. |
| Nikaria (Icaria). | The Beazzani 1205-1333; with Chios 1333-1481; the knights of St. John 1309-1521. |
| Stampali (Astypalaea). | The Quirini 1207-1269; Greek Empire 1269-1310; the Quirini and Grimani 1310-1537. |
| Amorgos. | The Ghisi 1207-1269; Greek Empire 1269-1296 [? 1303]; the Ghisi 1296-1368; |
| | $\frac{1}{2}$: the Quirini 1368-1537; |
| | $\frac{1}{2}$: the Grimani 1368-1446; the Quirini 1446-1537. |
| Nisyros, Piscopia, Calchi. | With Rhodes 1205-1306; the Assanti 1306-1385; with Rhodes 1385-1521. |
| Rhodes. | Gavalas 1204-1246; Greek Empire 1246-1283; the Aidonoghlii 1283-1309; the Knights of St. John 1309-1521. |
| Scarpanto (Carpathos). | With Rhodes 1204-1306; the Moreschi 1306-1309; the Cornari 1309-1522. |
| Candia. | Montferrat 1203-1204; Venetian 1204-1669. |

[See further Hopf's Griechische Geschichte (cited above, App. 1, *ad fin.*); on Carystos, his art. in the Sitzungsber. of the Vienna Acad., 11, p. 555 *sqq.* (1853); on Andros, *ib.*, 16, p. 23 *sqq.* (1855); on Chios, his article on the Giustiniani in Ersch and Gruber's Enzyklopädie, vol. 68, p. 290 *sqq.*, 1859 (and see T. Bent, The Lords of Chios, Eng. Hist. Rev. 4, p. 467 *sqq.*, 1889); on the Archipelago his Veneto-byzantinische Analekten, 1860, and his article on the Ghisi in Ersch and Gruber, vol. 64, p. 336 *sqq.*, 1857; on Negroponte, see J. B. Bury, The Lombards and Venetians in Euboea, in Journal of Hellenic Studies, 7, p. 309 *sqq.*, 8, p. 194 *sqq.*, 9, p. 91 *sqq.* (1886-8); and L. de Mas Latrie in the Rev. de l' Orient Latin, 1, p. 413 *sqq.* (1893).]

THE ABERDEEN UNIVERSITY PRESS LIMITED